Adventuring in the California Desert

The Sierra Club Adventure Travel Guides

Adventuring Along the Gulf of Mexico, The Sierra Club Travel Guide to the Gulf Coast of the United States and Mexico from the Florida Keys to Yucatán, by Donald G. Schueler

Adventuring in Alaska, The Ultimate Travel Guide to the Great Land, Completely revised and updated, by Peggy Wayburn

Adventuring in the Alps, The Sierra Club Travel Guide to the Alpine Regions of France, Switzerland, Germany, Austria, Liechtenstein, Italy, and Yugoslavia, by William E. Reifsnyder and Marylou Reifsnyder

Adventuring in the Andes, The Sierra Club Travel Guide to Ecuador, Peru, Bolivia, the Amazon Basin, and the Galapagos Islands, by Charles Frazier with Donald Secreast

Adventuring in the California Desert, The Sierra Club Travel Guide to the Great Basin, Mojave, and Colorado Desert Regions of California, by Lynne Foster

Adventuring in the Pacific, The Sierra Club Travel Guide to the Islands of Polynesia, Melanesia, and Micronesia, by Susanna Margolis

Adventuring in the Rockies, The Sierra Club Travel Guide to the Rocky Mountain Regions of the United States and Canada, by Jeremy Schmidt

Adventuring in the San Francisco Bay Area, The Sierra Club Travel Guide to San Francisco, Marin, Sonoma, Napa, Solano, Contra Costa, Alameda, Santa Clara, San Mateo Counties and the Bay Islands, by Peggy Wayburn

Trekking in Nepal, West Tibet, and Bhutan, by Hugh Swift

Trekking in Pakistan and India, by Hugh Swift

Walking Europe from Top to Bottom, The Sierra Club Travel Guide to the Grande Randonnée Cinq (GR-5) through Holland, Belgium, Luxembourg, Switzerland and France, by Susanna Margolis and Ginger Harmon

Lynne Foster

Adventuring in the California Desert

*The Sierra Club Travel Guide
to the Great Basin, Mojave, and
Colorado Desert Regions of California*

Sierra Club Books   *San Francisco*

For U.S. Senator Alan Cranston, whose years of service to the people of California are exemplified by his efforts to protect the beauties and natural character of the California desert.

The Sierra Club, founded in 1892 by John Muir, has devoted itself to the study and protection of the earth's scenic and ecological resources—mountains, wetlands, woodlands, wild shores and rivers, deserts and plains. The publishing program of the Sierra Club offers books to the public as a nonprofit educational service in the hope that they may enlarge the public's understanding of the Club's basic concerns. The point of view expressed in each book, however, does not necessarily represent that of the Club. The Sierra Club has some sixty chapters coast to coast, in Canada, Hawaii, and Alaska. For information about how you may participate in its programs to preserve wilderness and the quality of life, please address inquiries to Sierra Club, 730 Polk Street, San Francisco, CA 94109.

Copyright © 1987 by Lynne Foster

Library of Congress Cataloging-in-Publication Data

Foster, Lynne, 1937–
   Adventuring in the California desert.

   Bibliography: p.
   Includes index.
     1. Deserts—California—Guide-books.
2. California—Description and travel—1981–
Guide-books. 3. Automobiles—Road guides—
California. 4. Hiking—California—Guide-books.
I. Sierra Club. II. Title.
F859.3.F67 1987   917.94′0453′09154   87–4720
ISBN 0–87156–721–0

Production Manager: Eileen Max
Cover design by Bonnie Smetts
Book design by Abigail Johnston
Maps by Pat Benn
Botanical drawings by Diane Purkey
Printed in the United States of America
10 9 8 7 6 5 4 3 2

Contents

11 The Western Mojave   237
     Tehachapi Mountains–Antelope Valley   237
     Cajon Pass–Victorville   249
     Rainbow Basin   258

12 The Historic Eastern Mojave   263
     Barstow–Baker South   267
     Kelso   270
     Providence Mountains   273
     New York Mountains–Lanfair Valley   277
     Cima Dome–Clark Mountain   283

13 Around Joshua Tree   288
     Joshua Tree National Monument   288
     Whitewater River–Yucca Valley   296
     Lucerne Valley–Ludlow   300
     Amboy–Desert Center   304

14 The Southeastern Mojave   309
     Palen Mountains–Colorado River   309
     Needles–Colorado River South   313
     Cadiz Valley–Old Woman Mountains   318
     Turtle Mountains–Mopah Range   324

15 Yuha Desert and Salton Sea   330
     McCain and Davies Valleys   330
     Yuha Basin   336
     Salton Sea   340
     Mecca Hills–Orocopia Mountains   348
     Palm Springs–Indio   356
     Anza-Borrego Desert State Park   361

16 The Colorado Desert   379
     Chuckwalla Mountains   379
     Blythe–Winterhaven   388
     Algodones Dunes–Cargo Muchacho Mountains   393

Appendices
     Plant List   403
     Food and Lodging   407

Acknowledgments

As with so many guidebooks, this one would not have been possible save for the help of many willing informants. Chief of these are Lyle Gaston and Jim Dodson.

To be perfectly truthful, the book was not my idea at all, but Jim Dodson's. Jim is a longtime desert rat who is a past Chair of the Sierra Club's Desert Subcommittee. In addition to being a recognized authority on the California desert, Jim is a rare combination of good writer and good organizer. Alas for the writing of this book, however, Jim is also an overcommitted Sierra Club volunteer. He just wasn't able to fit writing a book in between chairing the Angeles Chapter, chairing the Desert Subcommittee, and chairing the Southern California Regional Conservation Committee, among other things.

Realizing that it would be quite a while before he'd have the time to produce this much-needed guide to the California desert, several years ago Jim very generously suggested that the book might be an appropriate project for an underemployed writer and editor who was also a desert lover: myself. Together we generated the first outline for the book; then Jim wished me good luck and sped off in a cloud of Sierra Club memos to continue his commitment to overcommitment. And that's how it all got started.

Luckily, an editor and publisher for the project magically appeared almost overnight. Throughout the two and a half years *Adventuring in the California Desert* has been in preparation, Jim Cohee, senior editor at Sierra Club Books, has given me the kind of encouragement every writer longs for—never a discouraging word! If it weren't for Jim's foresight in recognizing that to know the California desert is to love it—and protect it—you wouldn't be holding the guide in your hand now.

Then there are the many knowledgeable contributors who did their best to provide me with up-to-date trip descriptions and accurate natural history information—and succeeded admirably. To these hardworking folks belongs the credit for most of the book's engrossing accounts of what to do, how to do it, where to do it, what it is, and what's important about it—in the California desert. I hope they understand how indispensable their assistance has been, because sincere gratitude (and their name in print below) is all I can offer in return for their labors.

Those who volunteered their professional expertise to help write and review the natural history chapters were: Oscar Clarke, retired botanist, University of California, Riverside ("Desert Plants"); Mark Dimmitt, Curator of Plants, Arizona-Sonora Desert Museum ("Desert Plants" and "What Is a Desert?"); and Karen Sausman, Executive Director, Living Desert Reserve ("Desert Wildlife"). Bob Sanders added some interesting bits about the fringe-toed lizard.

The desert rats whose painstaking descriptions of the California desert's wild places appear throughout the trip chapters are: Keith Axelson (Jawbone Canyon—Butterbredt Spring); Ron Jones (peak hikes, scrambles, climbs); Mary DeDecker (Eureka Sand Dunes); Joe Fontaine (Owlshead Mtns); Stan Haye (Inyo-Mono and Death Valley National Monument trips too numerous to mention); Bill Neill (Camp Cady); Barbara Patterson (Hidden Springs and Mecca Hills); and Dean Slaughter (Turtle Mtns, Old Woman Mtns, Chuckwalla Mtns, Palen-McCoy Valley, Panamint Mtns, Cima Dome, Granite Mtns, Kelso Dunes). My special thanks to Jim Cornett, Curator of Natural Science for the Palm Springs Desert Museum, who allowed me to use his descriptions of California desert native palm oases.

Much of the useful information in the "Desert Survival" and "Seeing the Desert by Foot and Car" chapters was contributed by Betty Tucker-Bryan, with a little help from Dean Slaughter, Lloyd Smith, and others. And, very importantly, the maps were painstakingly and professionally prepared by Pat Benn.

Fortunately for *Adventuring in the California Desert*, once the information had been written and edited into a semblance of order, Jim Dodson emerged from his cloud of commitments long enough to bring his expertise to bear on it. Because he managed to squeeze out the time to meticulously review and comment on the penultimate draft of the text, the manuscript's accuracy and consistency were vastly improved.

And, first and last, my greatest debt is to Lyle Gaston, past President of the Desert Protective Council, past Conservation Chair of the San Gorgonio Chapter of the Sierra Club, and past chair of the Sierra Club's Desert Subcommittee. Lyle allowed me to make use of his extensive collection of books, files, and hard-to-find reports concerning the California desert; he also acted as my personal desert tour guide and mentor during the years the book was in preparation, driving me several thousands of miles over roads describable and indescribable to many of his favorite desert haunts. In addition, he too reviewed the manuscript. My gratitude for his contribution goes far beyond that which these acknowledgments can begin to express.

Despite the best efforts of all concerned, there are bound to be errors here. Please let me know about them.

Introduction

The California desert — 25 million acres of open space — contains not only some of the West's most robustly magnificent wildlands, but also some of its most delicately beautiful ones. Here you can visit not just the kinds of places you expect to find in a desert (like 600-ft-high sand dunes and colorful badlands), but also a great many places you probably wouldn't expect to find in a desert (such as lovely waterfalls, spectacular granite peaks, extinct volcanoes, and mile upon mile of wildflower displays). In fact, this desert has little in common with most people's idea of "the desert as wasteland"; instead, it is one of the lushest, most scenic, and most diverse deserts in the world.

Of the California desert's 25 million acres, approximately 15 million acres are public lands. The largest holder of public lands in the desert is the federal Bureau of Land Management (BLM), which administers something approaching 12.1 million acres. In addition to BLM recreation lands, there are two national monuments in the California desert — Death Valley and Joshua Tree. Together, these monuments contain about 2.5 million acres. Also found in here are three state parks — Anza-Borrego Desert, Saddleback Butte, and Red Rock Canyon — several state recreation areas, and a number of regional county parks. These parks and recreation areas total nearly a million acres. The remainder of California desert lands are not public lands, but are held by the federal government — for example, as military reservations (3 million acres); by the state government, as school sections; and by various private individuals or business concerns for their own use.

Why This Book

Like other environments evolving on the fringes of biologic possibility, the California desert is fragile — every injury brings it just that much closer to destruction. And destruction of complex and valuable environments, like extinction, is pretty much of a "forever" proposition. If this is true, though, why this guidebook for the California desert?

Why not just leave well enough alone, rather than making it even easier for people to visit—and perhaps degrade—fragile and beautiful areas?

Of course it is true that any visitor is a potential degrader—but it is also true that it's possible to visit, enjoy, appreciate, have fun, photograph, explore, hike, tour, camp, stroll, picnic, plant watch and animal watch, and so on, *without* irreversibly injuring the desert. What we're talking about is *low-impact recreation*—recreation that uses the desert without consuming it. And so we come to the reason for putting together this guide to the California desert.

The primary purpose of *Adventuring in the California Desert* is to help people get acquainted with some of the unique, beautiful, and interesting features of this desert. In particular, to help them get to know and enjoy the desert responsibly—to take only pictures and leave only footprints (and to keep even those as inconspicuous as possible). People who become intimate with wildlands in this nondisruptive way come to respect and value what they have to offer—whether mountain or desert, sea or shore—and to protect such areas as best they can. It is in this spirit that this book is offered to you, its readers. (Keep in mind, though, that this guide is not intended to be a compendium of all existing California desert information. Instead, it is meant only to get you started exploring one of the West's most impressive landscapes.)

Who Goes to the Desert, and Why

The concept of *low-impact recreation* is an important one not only for the desert, but for all our other wildlands—because more and more people are visiting these lands each year. California desert visitation, for example, has increased 600% since 1958! Nowadays, over 8 million recreationists visit the California desert's national monuments, state parks and recreation areas, national wildlife refuges, regional and local parks, national natural landmarks, and BLM recreation lands each year—and their numbers are growing at an unprecedented rate. (There are no recent figures available on the numbers of visitors to the other several million acres of the desert; however, millions of people visit commercial resorts such as Palm Springs.)

This upward trend in desert recreation is, of course, not a surprising one. The automobile alone has made formerly remote desert lands accessible not only to millions of southern Californians, but to travelers from all over the United States and beyond. And, over the years, exploring the California desert by car has been made pretty easy—for it now has an amazing 15,000 mi or more of maintained roads and another 30,000 mi of unmaintained roads and ways. As a result, 95% of this vast and scenic desert is within 3 mi of a road! In addition, as population increases and the pollution and congestion of urban life continue to grow, more and more people will be seeking out opportunities for a variety of high-quality outdoor experiences free from urban pressures. And desert wildlands offer many such opportunities.

When Does a Use Become an Abuse?

Unfortunately for the desert, there are a fair number of seekers after *high-impact recreation* — which primarily consists of what is called off-road-vehicle (ORV) activity. ORVers get their desert enjoyment from driving dune buggies, all-terrain vehicles (ATVs), trail bikes, motorcycles, and four-wheel-drive vehicles (4WDs) across unroaded desert areas. This kind of high-impact recreation causes nonreversible degradation of fragile desert areas. Every injury of this sort to the desert's nearly untouched wildlands brings them just that much closer to destruction. Destruction, that is, in the sense of wildlands being lost to that kind of enjoyment that requires unspoiled land, solitude, beauty, and, more importantly, destruction in the sense of ruining, perhaps for all time, unique and important plant and animal habitats.

However, because the BLM allows ORV activity on most of their California desert lands (82%), thousands of acres are degraded by high-impact ORV recreation each year. And once an area is no longer beautiful, the ORVers usually move on to another area that still is. In this way, many of the California desert's loveliest lands are being ruined — virtually forever.

If such high-impact recreation were confined not only to suitable parts of California desert public lands, but to a percentage of those lands proportional to the percentage of desert recreationists interested in ORV activity (11%), this type of destruction could be minimized. But the BLM has a long record of favoring this small percentage of recreationists and of openly discouraging efforts to further the interests of the over 80% of low-impact recreationists, such as sightseers, campers, photographers, hikers, backpackers, educators, animal observers, rock-climbers, and picnickers. For example, during the 1970s the BLM classified 5.7 million acres of the 12.1 million acres of public lands they manage as meeting the criteria of the 1964 Wilderness Act. Yet, in their 1980 Desert Plan they recommended only about 2 million acres for wilderness — and this, despite the fact that a large majority of people, nationwide, supported the protection of California desert ecology, wildlife, scenery, and natural character.

High-impact recreation and the BLM's handling of it are, of course, not the California desert's only problem. There are many problems having to do with appropriate development of desert lands. How many utility corridors are necessary? How many microwave towers? How many toxic and radioactive waste dumps? How much grazing of domestic animals? How much mining? How much residential development?

How much energy production? Because the California desert is so vast, there actually is room for all these activities. But the desert is not limitless, and therefore great care must be taken in choosing where these activities can most appropriately take place and how much activity is really necessary. The BLM, though, often doesn't agree with this way of looking at possible desert developments. Most of the time it seems as if developers have only to ask and they receive—whatever they want in the way of desert to develop, regardless of whether the land to be developed is valuable wildland. That is, the BLM is still pursuing their long-established philosophy of developing and disposing of public lands for economic return. It is obviously going to be difficult to make this agency accept the responsibility of protecting public lands for future generations.

The California Desert Protection Act

The BLM's poor wildland protection record is a matter of public record. As a result, over the years, conservationists have become more and more concerned about the agency's repeated refusal to take seriously the responsibility given to them by congressional mandate to protect the wilderness-quality lands they manage in the California desert. Finally, in 1984, a number of conservation groups—including the Sierra Club, the Wilderness Society, the Desert Protective Council, and many others— banded together to work more effectively to protect the California desert's finest public lands. This alliance, the California Desert Protection League, worked closely with United States Senator Alan Cranston to produce the California Desert Protection Act, which was first introduced by Senator Cranston in February 1986. (It may, of course, take several years to get a bill such as this passed.)

The idea behind the bill is to identify the most appropriate kinds of protection for each part of the desert. For instance, several million acres of federal land are recognized as being suitable for wilderness, as national parks (Death Valley, Joshua Tree, Mojave), as state park expansion units, and as unique botanic and historic features. The aim of this carefully prepared, comprehensive bill (and its successors) is to secure lasting protection for California's unique and valuable desert lands— and to assure that their beauty and wildness are there for us to enjoy now and to pass on to succeeding generations. The California Desert Protection League hopes that when the occasion arises you will be among the supporters of this important bill! As with any piece of land protection legislation, this struggle is expected to last for years. (If you want to help now, contact the California Desert Protection League in care of the Angeles Chapter of the Sierra Club, 3550 W. 6th St., Los Angeles, CA 90020.

Using This Guide

For those of you who are new to the desert, it may come as something of an initial shock that although it is a definable area, the California desert is *nothing* like, say, a national park. For example, conveniences, amenities, facilities, trails, signs, and supermarkets do not lurk just around the corner from many of its most visitable places. Also, the California desert, at 25 million acres, is *much* bigger than any national park.

Because this desert is so large and undeveloped, visitors are pretty much on their own most of the time — which is one of the reasons why this book may be a helpful companion. After all, even when you're visiting a well-signed national park with almost all the conveniences of home close at hand, a guide of some sort makes sightseeing and exploring a whole lot easier and more rewarding. Actually, if this book is unique in any way, it's that it has tried to squeeze a whole California desert's worth of trips more or less conveniently into a single volume. (The trips are to places appropriate for low-impact recreation, naturally.) Hopefully, this grouping together will make getting acquainted with the surprising variety and singular beauty of this vast area just a little easier.

Up-Front Information

As you begin looking through this guide, you'll notice that Chapters 1 to 5 contain natural history information, Chapters 6 and 7 how-to information, and Chapters 8 to 16 the trip write-ups. If you take time to familiarize yourself with what's in these chapters — particularly Chapter 1 ("What Is a Desert?"), Chapter 4 ("Desert Plants"), Chapter 6 ("Desert Survival"), and Chapter 7 ("Seeing the Desert by Foot and Car") — *before* you start exploring the desert, you'll find the time will have been well spent.

Regions and Areas

Because the California desert is so large, for the purposes of this guide it has been divided into *nine* recognizable geographic regions, demarked primarily by freeways, paved roads, and dirt roads. The nine regions, from north to south, are: "Inyo-Mono Country," "West of Death Valley," "Death Valley and East," "The Western Mojave," "The Historic Eastern Mojave," "Around Joshua Tree," "The Southeastern Mojave," "Yuha Desert and Salton Sea," and the "The Colorado Desert."

There is a map showing the main roads and features mentioned in the trips given. Each region in turn is divided into several areas—three to six for each region, for a total of thirty-six in the whole desert. Each area then contains descriptions of several features or groups of features—the trips. This arrangement should make it easy for prospective visitors to readily find a trip or group of trips that suits their interests and available time. Trips, by the way, can be anything from an hour's stop at a desert museum to a weekend's (or a week's) car camp or backpack; there are trips to suit just about everyone's needs.

Many interesting and beautiful places have been left out of this guide—some to protect them from too many visitors, others because there simply wasn't room for them, and still others because they were overlooked. And, of course, there are those that could have been included, except for the fact that many of the most confirmed and expert desert rats were too busy going on trips to the desert to write up any trips for the guide! Perhaps it's just as well, though; those of you who eventually become desert rats will discover them for yourselves.

Different Kinds of Trips

There are three major kinds of trips in the guide: tours (including car camps); hikes (including walks, scrambles, climbs, and backpacks); and what you might call "destinations." Tours are taken in vehicles, may be one-way or loop trips, and include several points of interest; all can be done in a day or less, though this short time is not appropriate for many of the longer tours, which are better undertaken over a weekend (or longer). Walks, hikes, backpacks, scrambles, and climbs are, obviously, undertaken on foot; they can be one-way or loops; some may last an hour, others a morning or afternoon, a day, or a weekend (and longer). Trips to "destinations" usually involve visiting a single desert feature, including museums, perhaps while on your way to begin a tour or some other activity.

No matter what kind of trip you are taking, be sure to read *all* of the area introduction *and* the trip description; otherwise, you may miss important information you need to know *before* leaving, regarding roads, campgrounds, occasional permissions needed from landowners, etc.

Tours and Car Camps

In this guide, all tours are vehicle tours; total mileages range from about 5 mi to 150 mi, with the average being about 40–50 mi. If your time is limited, a tour can consist of merely enjoying the scenery from your vehicle. To get the most out of any tour, though, it's best to allow enough time for lots of stops to get out, stroll around, picnic, and really look at the desert close up. Most tours include suggestions for car camping along the way and are ideal for weekend (or longer) outings.

Hikes, Backpacks, Scrambles, and Climbs

Hikers will be interested to know that the majority of trails in the California desert are 4WD roads. These "roads" vary considerably in degree of use and state of decrepitude. Signed trails are usually only found in parks, national monuments, and officially designated recreation areas. This means that hikes are, of necessity, cross-country. However, cross-country doesn't necessarily mean difficult; you'll find that many of the trailless hikes described here are quite easy. Some of the not-so-easy hikes involve getting to the top of a peak; these trips are usually labeled "scramble" or "climb," rather than just plain "hike." The backpacks vary in degree of difficulty; some are easy, some strenuous.

There are two necessities for all hikes, scrambles, climbs, and backpacks: a compass and the knowledge of how to use it and United States Geological Survey topographic maps (USGS topos). See "Topographic Maps," below, for information on how and where to get these indispensable maps. For instructions on compass use, see the books under the "General" heading in "Recommended Reading".

To give some idea of their degree of difficulty, all hikes, backpacks, scrambles, and climbs are classified as follows in their one- or two-line opening summary headings. (There are several classifications of this sort in common use; the differences between them aren't important to hikers. Climbers know them, so they aren't detailed here.)

Class 1. Walking. Hiking on trail or easy cross-country. Likely to have steep portions. Any sturdy footgear is adequate.
Class 2. Scrambling. The terrain is rougher than for Class 1. Steps may be made between rocks. Hands are occasionally used for balance. Good hiking boots are advisable.
Class 3. Easy climbing. Handholds and footholds, usually large and easy to find, are used in the most difficult parts of the route. Climbing rope should be carried, as some hikers may wish to be belayed, usually across a short distance.
Class 4. More difficult climbing than for Class 3. Holds are smaller, and the exposure is greater. Belays are necessary. (No climbs of this class are included in this guide.)
Class 5. Like Class 4, but with smaller holds and more exposure. Climbing aids are used more often to give participants the same

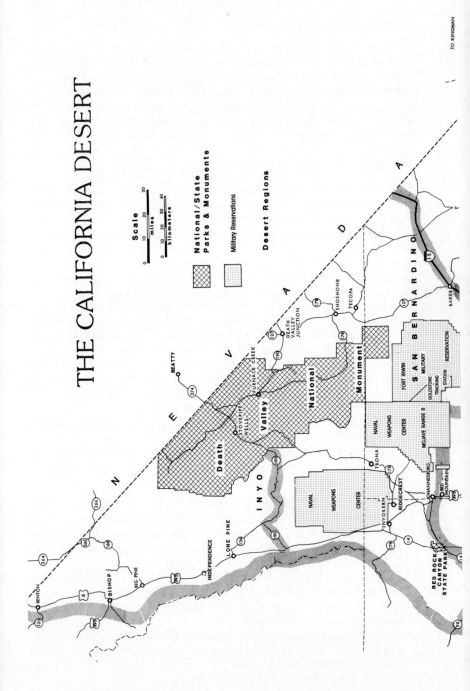

THE CALIFORNIA DESERT

Scale

miles

kilometers

National/State Parks & Monuments

Military Reservations

Desert Regions

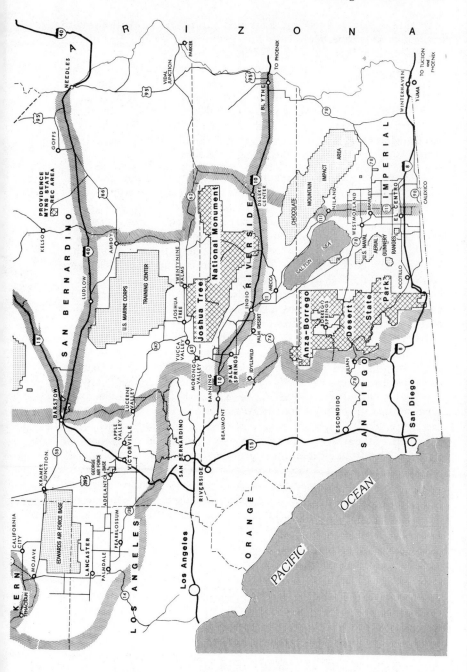

margin of safety. This class is divided into thirteen categories, with the highest number representing the greatest degree of difficulty. (No climbs of this class are included in this guide.)

Class 6. Artificial-aid climbing. Rock is so steep and smooth that stirrups (attached to other climbing equipment) are used to support the climber's weight. The one climb of this category in the book (Picacho Peak) has several short vertical rock faces that require proficient climbing rope management and special equipment. This climb is very much a fun climb for the adventuresome, but should not be attempted except with an experienced leader.

When reading the opening summaries of the hikes, scrambles, and climbs, notice the elevation given. This is the *highest* elevation reached in the description, *not* the elevation gain or loss. Where you begin a hike may depend on how far up a road your vehicle can get (or you choose to go) before you have to park. This means that elevation gains and losses for a single trip may vary from party to party—thus, they are not included. Check your topo for the elevation at which you are beginning a hike and compare with highest elevation figure to get an idea of elevation gains and losses. Also, there are no estimated times given for how long a hike may take. The reason for this is that individual paces vary too much for such an estimate to be useful. If you're a hiker, self-knowledge is the best source for this kind of estimate; if you're not, hikers' times may be considerably different than yours.

Hikers and peak climbers should keep in mind at all times that any traveling away from the roads can be dangerous (see Chapters 6 and 7—"Desert Survival" and "Seeing the Desert by Foot and Car"—for how-to and safety info). *Do not hike alone*; let someone know where you are going; always carry the necessary essentials, including the USGS topo map of the area; know how to use a compass; and remember that, unless otherwise indicated, hikes are *waterless*.

Quite a few trips to single features of the California desert are included in this guide. These can be anything from a stop at an extinct volcano just off the freeway to a tour of a museum or restored gold mine. These single-feature jaunts can often be fitted into your itinerary easily, as side trips on the way to somewhere else.

State and County Maps

Because California state maps show only major roads, you'll need county maps to help you get a good idea of what roads—paved and otherwise—actually exist in the desert. The best maps are published by the American Automobile Association (also known as Triple-A or AAA). Many of you (or members of your family) may already belong to this organization, which has chapters all over the United States. To find the chapter covering the California desert, look in the telephone book under "Automobile Club of Southern California." Maps are free to members.

If you do not have access to AAA maps, make sure the maps you use show such items as rest areas, campgrounds, elevations of towns and landmarks, and at least some topographic features. Also make sure you can read them without a magnifying glass most of the time! Incidentally, maps printed in this guide are not meant for navigation, but only to give you a general idea of how the California desert regions fit together and where the major features of the various areas are located.

Topographic Maps

For hikes, scrambles, peak climbs, and backpacks, you'll need the detailed topographic maps published by the United States Geological Survey (USGS topos). These useful maps also make exploring almost any area easier and more interesting. Topos come in two scales. The 7.5-minute maps cover an area of about 6.5 × 8.5 mi; the 15-minute ones cover an area of about 13 × 17 mi. (The "minute" referred to here is a measure of space, not time. The earth is viewed by mapmakers as a 360-degree sphere, with each degree covering about 70 mi of latitude or longitude at the equator. There are 60 minutes in each degree. Thus, the map dimensions.)

Topos for adjoining areas may vary in age by several decades, with some being as old as 1940 or so. As a result, the roads on them are often different from those on more recent maps. Fortunately for the users, topographic features—the ones you need for navigating your way cross-country—remain the same (barring catastrophe). Many sporting goods stores carry the USGS maps for their region. If they don't have what you need, an index and maps for areas west of the Mississippi can be ordered from the USGS Federal Center, Denver, CO 80225.

Directions

All directions given in this guide use "north," "south," "east," and "west" to describe which way to turn, rather than just "left" and "right," though these are occasionally included in tricky places. There are several good reasons for this. One is that the jumping-off points for many trips can be approached from several directions, and a lot of trips can be taken from one end or the other (or even from the middle). Under these circumstances, left and right become too confusing. What's right from one direction is left from another—and expressing something in between is very difficult. North, south, east, and west, however, remain the same no matter which way you are going to or coming from! You'll soon get the hang of thinking in these terms if you just pay attention to your maps and the landmarks around you. (Start by noting the little compass on every road and topo map. It tells you right away which direction is which.)

All the directions in the world won't do you any good, however, if you don't know how far it was from the last turn or how far it is supposed to be to the next one. Keep track of where you are when following trip directions, and get in the habit of checking your vehicle's odometer frequently. Most distances are given *between points* (landmarks, turnoffs, intersections, offramps, etc.) rather than being counted as miles from the jump-off point. When the latter mileage is used, it is noted in the text—so you shouldn't find this too confusing. Keep a pencil and notebook close by so that you can jot down important mileage readings as you go along.

Facilities and Camping

Despite the California desert's size, its 45,000 mi of roads ensure that even in its remotest corners the driving time to the nearest motels, restaurants, and supplies is usually no more than two hours; most of the time it's much less. Because facilities are not just around every corner, though, it is necessary to plan a little ahead when touring the desert. For example, if lunchtime arrives while you're comfortably ensconced at some scenic viewpoint, and you have a yen for a tuna sandwich and a long, cool drink, you'll have a much better chance of satisfying your yearning if you packed it all into your cooler before leaving home (or camp). And if nature calls when you're an hour from the nearest amenity, it helps to have the "eleventh essential" (and a trash bag) along. See Chapters 6 and 7 for detailed suggestions on what every desert traveler should have along—you'll be glad you did!

Camping in the California desert, you'll find, is one of life's most enjoyable experiences. If you prefer "developed" camping—that is, a campsite with table, barbecue or grill, water, and nearby restrooms—there are a number of such campgrounds scattered throughout the desert. A few of these campgrounds are less developed than others; at some, the only amenity is a portable toilet. Campgrounds that are developed in any way (even a pit toilet is sometimes viewed as a development) ordinarily charge a fee ranging from about $2 to $8 a day, with higher fees representing more amenities. An exception is national forest campgrounds, which are usually free. See "Public Campgrounds" in the Appendix.

For reasons of space, this guide describes only those developed campgrounds located on public land—no privately owned campgrounds are included. Look for a description of these public-land campgrounds in the Facilities section of the introduction to each of the thirty-eight desert areas. For descriptions of privately owned campgrounds, see the Rand McNally listing in "Recommended Reading". Privately owned campgrounds with full recreational vehicle hookups may cost as much as $15 per day.

Undeveloped or open-desert camping is allowed throughout the California desert on most Bureau of Land Management, national monument, national forest, and state park lands—even when developed camping is also available. (Regional county parks, however, prefer visitors to use their campgrounds.) If you have the right equipment and know that you are not on private land it's often possible to drive up some scenic dirt road, pull off at an attractive place, and set up camp. This is a privilege no longer offered to national park visitors. And it *is* a privilege—one that entails the responsibility of leaving the desert as you found it. This means using low-impact camping practices (see Chapter 7 for details). Please don't forget! The beauty and integrity of the California desert depend on your consideration.

And, whether you're camping in a campground or in the open desert, keep in mind that it's always BYOW—bring your own water (and wood). Even campgrounds with water sometimes run out; and, besides there is no such thing as having *too* much water when you are traveling in the desert.

Good Advice

On all trips, stop, get out of your vehicle and look, listen, walk—often. Don't just plunge on and on, trying to get somewhere. In the California desert, as in all the other wildlands of the world, it is the journey—the experiencing of a unique region—that matters, rather than your arrival at a specified point.

PART ONE

Getting to Know the Desert

1

What is a Desert?

The Physical Environment

What is a desert? The word can be variously defined, but all definitions focus on a single causal factor: water — or, rather, the lack of it. The simplest accurate definition of a desert is "a place where water is severely limiting to life most of the time." A more technical definition explains that "in a desert, the potential evapotranspiration (evaporation + water lost through plants) greatly exceeds precipitation." (Animals lose water, too, but they are an insignificant part of the total.) For example, Indio, California, averages about 3.2 in. of annual rainfall, while evaporation from the nearby Salton Sea averages about 12 ft per year. In other words, if it weren't for agricultural runoff from the Coachella and Imperial valleys, the Salton Sea would dry up in just two years!

The word *potential* is necessary in the latter definition because water can't evaporate if it isn't there — which is the situation in deserts most of the time. It's also easy to understand why the definition of deserts as "places receiving less than 10 in. average annual rainfall" doesn't work, either. For example, although the north coast of Alaska receives only 4 in. of precipitation per year, this area is not a desert — instead, it is perpetually waterlogged or icebound because of very low evapotranspiration.

Another major characteristic of desert climates is a large temperature range between day and night. Because water reflects infrared radiation (heat) and therefore retards heat loss into space, humid climates have small day-night temperature differences. A desert's low humidity and typical absence of clouds allow the sun to heat the ground all day long, but then up to 90% of this heat is lost to the night sky. Daily temperature fluctuations of 50° F are therefore common in deserts. A 70° F day can be followed by a 30° F night, a real hazard to unprepared travelers.

Desert rainfall is not only sparse but also highly irregular and undependable. The less the annual average, the greater the variation from year to year. Rarely does an average year occur. The climatic conditions that tend to prevent rain are fairly stable, and in most years rain-fall is less than the long-term annual average. When on occasion the system breaks down, storms roll in one after the other, resulting in a very wet year. Some of the more arid places in the California desert's Colorado region have gone two years without rain and have received two or three times the annual average in other years. A whole year's average of 3 or 4 in. may fall in a single storm!

Because most deserts receive insufficient rain to support substantial plant cover, desert vistas are dominated by geologic features. Most of the California desert is heavily studded with mountain ranges, which create a very rugged aspect. A large part of the California desert is also within the Basin and Range geologic province. In this province, except for some volcanic ranges, most of the mountains were formed not by uplift, but by subsidence of valleys due to stretching of the earth's crust. The land was stretched east–west, and the resulting basins and ranges trend north–south.

Desert soils are typically thin, alkaline, and contain very little organic matter. The lack of nitrogen (and, of course, water) is usually limiting to plant growth. The other minerals needed by plants are usually abundant, but the alkaline soil binds them so tightly that they may be nearly unavailable to plants, especially to nonnative (exotic) species.

The Living Environment

Most of the California desert has a low vegetation density, but an amazingly rich variety of both plant and animal species. There are 103 vascular plant families, and probably a thousand species. Despite its sparseness, the vegetation is quite diverse; some ten to fifteen major plant communities (associations of plants) have been described by different botanists. Several such communities will be described later in this chapter.

Animals are not classified into communities of their own and are rarely associated with specific plant communities. One reason is that they are more mobile and adaptable than plants, especially birds and mammals. Secondly, the important features of the habitat requirements of animals are usually (1) the soil and water conditions and (2) the height and density of vegetation, rather than particular plant species. The phainopepla's dependence on mistletoe is unusual; but even here it doesn't seem to matter to this glossy, black bird which mistletoe berries it feeds on. Thus, phainopeplas are common in two major plant communities that host abundant mistletoe: desert scrub and oak woodlands. More typical is the Scott's oriole, which breeds in dry woods—that is, open stands of small trees. It matters not to the oriole whether these trees are Joshua trees, scrub oaks, or pinyon pines. (Incidentally, communities containing both plants and animals are often called "biotic" communities.)

Change Through Time

Ecological succession is the orderly, progressive change in plant species composition that occurs on a site gradually, as when a lake evaporates, leaving a playa, or more quickly, as when a fire, flood, or landslide occurs. Eventually—in a few decades to perhaps a couple of centuries—a "climax community" develops that does not change until another disturbance occurs. Whether such classical succession occurs in deserts is a subject of much debate.

What is more important for desert recreationists to know, however, is that deserts recover from disturbance very slowly. An area in the California desert's Mojave region that was disturbed during construction of a gas line took thirty years to recover to approximately the original vegetation density; and when it did, the species composition was very different from that of the adjacent undisturbed desert. The estimated time for complete recovery is well over a century. A century or two is probably a reasonable estimate of recovery time for most of the California desert's habitats. The driest areas, though, probably require several centuries or even millennia to recover. Tank tracks made by General Patton's troops in the California desert's Colorado region during training missions in the 1940s still show clearly after more than forty years. A storm in 1976 did not appreciably erode the tread marks Patton's maneuvers left on stable desert pavement.

Vegetative responses to climatic changes over the geologic time scale may be as important as succession. The California desert expanded to its present extent only in the last few thousand years, which is just a moment ago in geologic time. At the close of the last Ice Age (about ten thousand years ago), the present Mojave region was occupied by a pinyon-juniper-oak woodland. The Colorado region in this cooler, wetter time was probably restricted to the extreme southeastern corner of the state. Presently existing desert biotic (plant-animal) communities have evolved over many millions of years; but the desert as a whole has expanded and contracted many times.

Life processes within desert communities may proceed very rapidly or extremely slowly, but nearly always irregularly—according to rainfall. The annuals making up the wildflower displays complete their life cycles in a few months, but only in years of ample rain. Some of the animals such as the smaller lizards and rodents are also essentially "annuals," living only a year or two. Barrel cacti and desert tortoises take five to twenty years to mature and may live for a century. The desert ironwood tree is long both in life and death. A large desert ironwood may be two hundred to three hundred years old, and when it dies its extremely hard wood takes a millennium to decay in the arid climate. And the nondescript-looking creosote bush reigns supreme in several categories—more about this amazing species later.

Desert plants grow and bloom only when there has been sufficient rain. Desert animals, whether they are herbivores (plant eaters) or carnivores (meat eaters), are dependent on plants; this means that both animals and plants are dependent on rain. Fringe-toed lizards eat insects near the ground—primarily those insects that feed on low-growing annual plants. In dry years when the annuals are not abundant, these lizards can find just enough to survive and don't waste time and energy reproducing. Quail eat a variety of plants and insects, but they need fresh, green vegetation in their diets to successfully reproduce. No rain, no green vegetation, no quail breeding. However, it may not be an all-or-nothing system. Many animals have more or fewer offspring, depending on the quality of their diet. In the desert, the quality of animals' diets depends directly on the rainfall. Little else matters in the desert.

California's Three Deserts

The California desert is actually made up of three different desert regions: the Great Basin Desert, the Mojave Desert, and the Colorado (Sonoran) Desert. The Mojave Desert region is unique to California, but both the Great Basin and Colorado (Sonoran) desert regions extend east and south outside of California.

The Great Basin Desert

The Great Basin Desert occupies almost all of Nevada, extends into parts of all the adjacent states, and has outposts in Colorado, Wyoming, New Mexico, and Washington. It barely enters California in the north end of the Owens Valley and the extreme northeast corner of the state.

The Great Basin Desert is the northernmost and highest in elevation of the North American deserts; most of it lies above 4000 ft. The winters are therefore extremely cold. This is the most important climatic factor distinguishing this desert from other deserts. Precipitation is distributed throughout the year, though in different parts of this very large area there are either winter or summer peaks. Because of the cold winters the growing season is limited to the summer months.

The combination of cold and dryness creates an environment that few plants can tolerate. A single life form dominates the whole area—the low shrub. There are almost no annuals (growing season too short), succulents (winters too cold), or trees (cold and dryness). The few species of shrubs are all densely branched, small leafed, and mostly deciduous.

Of these shrubs one species probably outnumbers all the others combined. This is the indicator plant of the Great Basin Desert: Great Basin sagebrush, also known as the big sagebrush (*Artemisia tridentata*). This shrub's characteristic silvery foliage tints the landscape, where it dominates and sometimes monopolizes huge areas of land. (When using Great Basin sagebrush as an indicator, look for these large stands. This widespread plant also occurs among junipers and pines some distance above and beyond the Great Basin Desert's boundaries.)

The Colorado (Sonoran) Desert

The portion of the Sonoran Desert that extends into California is known as the Colorado Desert. The Sonoran Desert, however, occupies a lot more than just southeastern California. It spreads from here to southern Arizona, over most of the Mexican state of Sonora, and most of the Baja California peninsula. Its characteristics are much different than those of the Great Basin Desert. For example, it is farther south in latitude and has much lower elevations, mostly below 2000 ft. Winters in the Sonoran Desert are mild and nearly frost free — which is tremendously important to the plants. Most of the rain falls in the summer months, except in the southeastern California section (the Colorado Desert), which gets most of its rain in winter.

The Sonoran is the most thoroughly studied of the North American deserts, particularly as to its climate and vegetation. Because of the mild winters, this desert has quite a variety of plants. It is the only desert with significant numbers of trees, especially species in the legume family. There are also many species of succulents, most of which are cacti. And, there are many annuals, shrubs, and herbaceous perennials. The indicator plants for the Sonoran Desert are of two types: legume trees (e.g., palo verde, desert ironwood, smoke tree, mesquite) and giant columnar cacti (e.g., saguaro, organ pipe, senita). The latter group is, however, all but absent from California because of insufficient summer rain.

Although the plants of the Great Basin Desert evolved from the northern, arctic flora, most of the Sonoran Desert's plants are derived from tropical relatives to the south. In fact, the southern end of the Sonoran Desert merges so gradually into tropical forest that it is difficult to draw a boundary line. (This boundary is traditionally thought of as being between Guaymas and Ciudad Obrégon, Sonora.) The Sonoran Desert is thus a tropical desert, and is quite literally a jungle that dried up.

The diversity of the Sonoran Desert has been organized by botanists into seven subdivisions based on vegetation and flora. The northwestern subdivision is the only one that extends into California. It is the largest subdivision and is also the lowest, hottest, and driest. This subdivision's official name is the Lower Colorado Valley; its California part is called simply the Colorado Desert. The official name comes from the fact that the desert surrounds the lower Colorado River valley, extending from Phoenix, Arizona, to Palm Springs, California, and from Needles, California, to one-third of the way down both coasts of Mexico's Gulf of California. The western boundary is sharply delineated by the Peninsular Ranges (for example, the Santa Rosa and San Jacinto mtns); to the north it merges confusingly with the Mojave Desert, very roughly along a sagging line between Indio and Needles. (The indicator plants of the two deserts grow together in this area.)

The Colorado Desert challenges Death Valley for the title of hottest and driest place in North America. El Centro averages less than 3 in. of rain per year; it appears to be even drier in adjacent Baja California, but there are no official weather stations there. Some places in the Colorado Desert have gone two years without rain! Summer temperatures often attain 120° F. Frost is rare, perhaps occurring only once every several years in most of this area.

Relative to the rest of the Sonoran Desert, the Colorado Desert is farther from the Gulf of Mexico—the moisture source for the typical summer rains. It is closer to the source of winter storms, which come from the Pacific Ocean. This explains why the Colorado Desert receives most of its rain in winter. Summer storms become sharply rarer as you go westward from the Colorado River, until they increase abruptly in the foothills of the Peninsular Ranges. In Tucson, Arizona, for example, half of the annual average of 11 in. falls in the summer months (June to September). Needles, California, receives almost one-third of its 5 in. in summer, and Indio gets only one-fifth of its 3 in. then.

The Colorado Desert's winters are so mild that most of the plants can respond to these winter rains. Ocotillo, for example, is always dormant from November to March in Tucson, but in the warmer Colorado Desert it will leaf out whenever it rains.

The Mojave Desert

In many ways the Mojave Desert is transitional between the Great Basin and Sonoran deserts, though it also has unique features. It is sandwiched between the other two, and its distinctive part is intermediate in elevation—between 2000 and 4000 ft. About one-half of it is below 2000 ft, and these parts are often difficult to distinguish from the Colorado Desert. The Mojave has the cold winters of the Great Basin Desert, though less extreme, and the hot summers of the Sonoran Desert.

The Mojave Desert is unique in being a winter rain desert, with most rain falling from November to March. This is especially true of the far western part; less than 1% of Lancaster's 5 in. and 8% of Victorville's 6 in. fall during summer. The eastern Mojave, however, gets one-quarter to one-third of its rain during the summer. Twentynine Palms, California, is almost Sonoran, in that nearly 40% of its 4.2 in. falls in summer.

Most of the Mojave Desert is in California. It also covers the southern tip of Nevada and extreme northwestern Arizona, and barely reaches the southwestern corner of Utah.

Although the Mojave's flora is largely borrowed from its two neighboring deserts, it also has many unique plants of its own. Plants in this area do have a problem with the cold winters and the rainfall pattern. Most plants are unable to grow in the winter when the largest amount of rain falls, and they also have to cope with a long, hot summer with little or no rain. As a result, many have adapted by producing a flush of growth in spring as the weather warms and before the soil moisture is depleted. Thus, the Mojave is justifiably famous for its spring wildflower displays.

The Mojave Desert has a greater diversity of plants than the colder Great Basin. Two kinds of plants dominate and show great variety: shrubs and annuals. Most of the annual species are shared with the Colorado Desert and make both deserts famous for spectacular wildflower displays. There are a few succulents and trees, although the primary indicator plant is a treelike member of the agave family — a yucca given the name Joshua tree. This giant yucca is almost synonymous with the Mojave. It occurs above 2000 ft throughout the area, and nowhere else!

THE LOWER MOJAVE DESERT. The large part of the Mojave that is below 2000 ft elevation is rather distinct from the higher Mojave Desert. Most of this area is in the northern Mojave, from about Baker north to the Death Valley region, where the land sinks below sea level. It is hotter and drier than the rest of the Mojave. Joshua trees and most other Mojave indicators are absent. The hotter, drier climate is more like that of the Colorado Desert, but it is either sufficiently isolated or there is enough frost for few Sonoran plants to have colonized it.

The Death Valley region is complex because of its numerous high mountains bordering deep, narrow valleys. The floor of Death Valley is very hot and arid; summer days frequently top 120° F, and the rainfall averages less than 2 in. But this changes dramatically as one ascends the mountains. From below sea level on the valley floor the bajadas rise to 2000 ft in a few lateral miles; these slopes receive much more rain and are clothed with fairly typical Mojave Desert vegetation. In a few more miles one has ascended to 5000 ft, where Great Basin Desert shrub endures snowy, bitter-cold winters, and only 25 horizontal mi from Badwater (in Death Valley) is conifer woodland at 11,000 ft. This rugged topography, combined with a similar diversity of rock and soil types, has produced a large number of endemic plants, some of which are found only on a single canyon or ridge!

Nondesert Islands

Within the California desert are several mountain ranges that are high enough to support nondesert biotic communities. These are true biologic islands because the desert around them is just as hostile to a forest plant or animal as is the water surrounding oceanic islands. The moderately moist conditions on the upper slopes of these ranges support communities that have been isolated at least since the last Ice Age. Since then, only the most mobile animals and plants (seeds) have been able to travel freely to and from them.

The highest desert ranges reach about 8000 ft and support pine and even white fir forests near their summits. Most of these ranges — the Providence, New York, Ivanpah, and Clark Mtns — are in the eastern Mojave Desert. Some in the Death Valley region are also forested, particularly the extensive Panamint Range, which reaches 11,000 ft. Several other desert ranges are high enough to support pinyon-juniper and/or chaparral communities.

The mountain islands have a significant effect on the desert biotic communities below, whether or not they have forested summits. They generate thunderstorms in the summer months when humid tropical air is forced up against them. These storms may then drift across the desert. Even if no rain reaches the desert floor, it flows down the desert washes — which carry the water many miles away from its source.

The California desert also has islands of wetlands. The Salton Sea is the largest, but there are several others — such as Carrizo Marsh (in Anza-Borrego Desert State Park), Afton Canyon (where the elusive Mojave River surfaces), Saratoga Springs (in Death Valley), the Amargosa River, San Sebastian Marsh, Darwin Falls, and a number of spring-fed native palm oases. The Colorado River probably qualifies, too.

These isolated biotic communities are important in many ways, not the least of which is that they add something to the desert's sum of biologic diversity. One of the ways such islands do this is by harboring plants and animals that are extinct elsewhere or are endemic to the particular location. Another way in which these rare wetlands add to the desert's diversity is by providing watering places for the many desert animals that are not able to exist solely on the moisture in their food or to manufacture it themselves. Without these few watering places, the desert's animal population would be much the poorer.

2

The Making of Deserts

Kinds of Deserts

Not everything that looks like a desert fits the natural historian's present definition of a desert. For help in deciding what is and is not a desert, scientists have developed guidelines. According to the present criteria, all barren lands are not desert, however desolate they might look. For example, some lands may have become barren because of overgrazing or other human mismanagement. Unfortunately, such mismanagement can provide the nexus for lands that not only look barren, but can actually by a self-expanding process become true deserts. This chain of events is a real danger in any dry parts of the world. The Dust Bowl phenomenon of the 1930s is an example.

According to natural historians, true deserts are defined most simply as tracts of land receiving less than 10 in. of precipitation each year. This cutoff point does not apply in all cases. For instance, a region getting 9 in. of rain, but having a temperate climate, might not be a desert at all. And a region receiving 13 in. of rain, but sustaining high temperatures, could very well be a true desert. Thus, say the scientists, lack of water (aridity) alone does not necessarily produce a desert. Variations in atmospheric pressure and sustained high temperatures are also determining conditions. And it just so happens that there are regions of the earth—30% of the continental surface, in fact—that, for a number of reasons, supply one or more of these conditions that encourage formation of true deserts.

SUBTROPICAL DESERTS. Careful study has shown that many desert areas lie within two superheated bands around the earth. These bands, one on each side of the equator, cannot escape the year-round, near-vertical rays of the sun because the inclination of the earth's axis of rotation (23.5 degrees) never changes. Thus, as the northern and southern summers exchange places each year, the areas between the southern Tropic of Capricorn and the northern Tropic of Cancer get very little respite from the blazing sun. These superheated bands on either side of the equator are referred to as the subtropics.

POLAR DESERTS. In contrast, the icy deserts of the North and South Pole regions never receive the sun's vertical rays, so they get very little respite from the chill of winter. These polar deserts are exceptions to the usual picture we have of deserts. The extremely cold (rather than hot) climate and the massive amount of water (trapped in ice and snow) that covers the areas would seem to disqualify the poles as desert lands. Not so; their actual dryness qualifies them for being at least desertlike. (Frozen water is about as available and friendly to life as hot sand!)

COASTAL DESERTS. With all that water right next to them, how can coastal regions be deserts? This seeming paradox is explained by the fact that huge currents of cold water from the polar seas are sometimes pushed to the ocean surface at the western edges of continental shelves, where the water is relatively shallow. When this happens, the winds blowing toward the coasts across the cold water masses are cooled quickly and lose their moisture before reaching the coast—which then becomes desert. The Baja California peninsula is an example of a coastal desert.

RELIEF DESERTS. Unlike other types of desert, relief deserts can form at any latitude where the topographic conditions favor them. The deserts of the western United States are, for the most part, young relief deserts— perhaps 1 to 5 million years old. As you can probably guess, these deserts result in great part from the West's numerous and dramatic mountain ranges. What happens is that the high ranges (such as the Sierra Nevada or the Rockies) intercept the rain before it can fall on the lands beyond them. As the rain clouds rise up and over the ranges, or up the slopes of high plateaus, they cool and drop their moisture on the nearest (usually the outermost) slopes—leaving the interiors nearly rainless.

The vast Great Basin Desert, which sprawls over several states east of California and the other two California desert regions, the Mojave and Colorado deserts, all fall into the relief desert category.

How Deserts Are Created

As you can tell from the above descriptions, deserts are pretty varied. Some, like the three parts of the California desert, are lush by desert standards. Others, like the Sahara, are nearly barren wastelands. One of the things that most deserts have in common, however, is that they are growing at more and more rapid rates. (One-third of the earth's surface is covered with desert or desertlike lands!) An interesting and important question has to do with why these deserts exist and why they are growing so quickly. Not surprisingly, climatologists, geologists, and ecologists all have come to some conclusions regarding why deserts form and grow. These ideas on the drama of desert formation fall into three groups: weather patterns and effects, changes in the earth's crust caused by internal pressures, and human mismanagement.

Weather Patterns and Desert Formation

The earth's climatic patterns are very complex, far more complex than can be dealt with here. The earth, on its constantly inclined axis of rotation, spins around the sun, creating temperature gradients from the equator to the poles. Atmospheric and oceanic currents are determined by this spinning. As a result, bands of high and low pressure circle the earth, helping give the regions below them their characteristic climates and providing the conditions that can result in the different kinds of desert.

The equatorial regions—for instance, the tropics—receive the near-vertical rays of the sun virtually all year. Yet these regions are not deserts. Very hot they are; deserts they are not. But why are the tropics not deserts? Well, they get lots of rain. And why is this? The answer is not simple. The general idea is that the very hot air masses there are continually on the rise, creating an area of low atmospheric pressure. As the hot air rises, it cools and releases its moisture—thus, the heavy rains in the tropics.

But that's only part of the story. After the hot air has risen and released its moisture, the now-dry air masses from the tropics fall to earth in the subtropics—thanks to the rotation of the earth and the powerful currents created by it. The subtropics, remember, are the two desert bands circling the globe on either side of the equator. This dry air warms as it falls, picks up the moisture it finds along the way (including what's on the ground), and creates dry, hot, high-pressure areas.

Between the subtropics and the Arctic and Antarctic regions lie more temperate regions. Not as hot as the tropics nor as cold as the poles, these are zones of low pressure. In these areas warm, moisture-laden air rises and cools, and rains fall. These lands have a wide range of summer and winter durations and temperatures, depending on their distance from the equator (and, thus, on the angle of the sun's rays in their region). Some of the richest agricultural lands in the world are found here.

In the Arctic and Antarctic regions, the cooled and somewhat dried air masses that have risen from the temperate regions fall to earth again. And when the cold air falls, it often gives up whatever moisture it has as snow, creating very cold, dry, high-pressure areas and icy deserts.

Heat, Cold, Wind, and Water

The desert landscapes we see and enjoy today have been produced not only by movements of the earth's crust and worldwide weather patterns, but by the long-term effects of local climatic conditions. Wind and water erosion, along with high and low temperatures, help produce many of the striking features we associate with deserts.

For example, the fine grains making up sand dunes were once massive, solid rock, perhaps part of a high mountain range. But when the violent thundershowers so characteristic of desert lands pound upon the rocks, leaching away minerals and weakening the rocks' structure, pieces break off and tumble away. With the aid of more water, and of the powerful winds that sweep across flat, mostly unvegetated areas, the pieces get smaller and smaller. Finally, sand begins to drift; eventually, drifts may turn into dunes. The California desert's Kelso Dunes, at 600 ft, are the tallest dunes in California.

Another striking desert feature is the bajadas. These huge, fan-shaped mounds are found skirting the edges of desert mountain ranges. These mounds—alluvial fans—are made up of gently sloping piles of debris washed out from the mountains behind. Fans melded together are called bajadas. Fans and bajadas are built up over the years from the bits and pieces of rock, gravel, sand, and soil washed pell-mell down off their parent mountains by brief, heavy desert cloudbursts. Near the top of the bajada are the largest boulders and pieces of rock; at the bottom, the smallest (the lighter the pieces, the farther they can travel down the hill).

Whatever water manages to reach the nearly flat desert floor rushes as best it can to the nearest, lowest point. The channels cut as the water flows across the desert are known as dry washes. These may be very shallow and only a few inches across, or they may be several dozen feet wide and several feet deep. The deepest ones are sometimes called arroyos. Waters rushing down these channels are known as flash floods; they are the reason that those nice, sandy desert washes are not good places to camp. (You may not be able to tell if thundershowers are occurring in nearby mountains. Because the water comes all at once, it doesn't have time to soak in—so great quantities are available to rush down the washes for some miles.)

If water from thundershowers collects at the bottom of a basin with no outlet, it can form a lake that usually lasts but a short time. When these lakes dry up, they often leave crusty salt deposits behind that make it impossible for most salt-tolerant plants to live there. Places where these transient lakes regularly form are often referred to as playas—which is Spanish for "beach." The large dry lake beds left over from wetter times in the California desert are also called playas. (Some of these are occasionally wet with an inch or two of water. Don't try to walk or drive across these deceptively firm playas—whether wet or dry—you may get irretrievably stuck!)

Temperature differences take their toll, too. Even the largest boulders can behave like ice cubes dropped into warm water—that is, heat can crack them into pieces. Even if they don't fall apart so drastically, high daytime temperatures and rapidly cooling nights can peel layers off even the toughest-looking of jagged mountain peaks. Some of the more granitic mountains have their layers peeled off and then wind-eroded in such a fashion that what remains is a graceful—but steeply piled—series of enormous rounded boulders. Granite Pass area of the California desert is such an area.

Another interesting desert phenomenon is desert pavement. This dark pavement of nicely fitted stones is formed when wind and water carry away the small particles of gravel, sand, and soil between successive layers of pebbles and rocks. As this happens, the relatively larger pieces settle together, forming the pavement. Desert varnish often gives the pavement a dark, shiny coat. This "varnish" is actually a thin coating of iron and manganese oxides formed on the stones as a result of weathering. You'll notice that only the top surfaces of the stones have this coating.

Fertile soil, often the end product of weathering in more temperate climates, is something the desert doesn't have in abundance. Lots of tiny particles are certainly present, but organic matter (dead plant and animal materials) is scarce bcause of the relatively small number of plants per unit area in deserts. This is true even in the California desert, which, compared to many other deserts of the world, is extremely lush.

In the subtropical deserts of the world, heat, cold, wind, water, and the near-vertical rays of the sun conspire to produce deserts that are truly barren. Here, the fringes of these beautiful but nearly lifeless deserts must be treated with great care. If the lands surrounding these deserts are mistreated, the deserts will continue to spread at a rapid rate, leaving famine, misery, and death in their wake. In the California desert there are forests, grasses, flowers, springs, rivers, and abundant wildlife. Yet even here—because there are also sand dunes, salt flats, lots of bare rock, high temperatures, much wind and water erosion, and almost no moisture—the organic matter that makes fertile soil possible is far from plentiful. The California desert's lushness is a very fragile lushness; it exists at the farthest reaches of adaptation, and must be enjoyed and appreciated with great care.

Floating Continents and Desert Formation

The forming of more relief deserts (and enlargement of present ones) is a trend in the earth's evolution as a planet. Interestingly, the earth's uppermost layers—the crust and, just below, the thicker mantle—are thin in comparison to the earth's total mass. The crust and the upper solid layers of the mantle are actually made up of a number of movable plates that geologists call "tectonic plates." These plates float about on the thick, molten magma of the mantle's inner layer. As a result of the plates' jostlings, the continental configuration we are familiar with today is but one in a continually changing series of arrangements.

Geologists think that the plates move because of convection currents resulting from temperature differences within the earth's molten interior. In places where the currents are rising, they push the plates apart; magma then oozes up into the enormous cracks, pushing them farther apart and forming new crust (as in the continental trenches). In other places, the currents push the plates together, lifting the crust higher, scrunching up folds, and producing mountains (as on the west coasts of North and South America). There are also places where the convection currents suck parts of the plates downward, thus balancing the places where the plates are pushed up. But all the ups, and downs, and slips of the plates are not random; they have distinct patterns—rather like a series of giant conveyor belts that recycle the same material over and over again. In a geologic sense, today's continent becomes tomorrow's molten magma, the next day's sea floor, and the following day's continent (again). And so the cycle continues.

In a somewhat more short-term geologic sense, the relatively light, floating continents are being folded accordionlike, at their edges, and thickened more and more. At the same time, the ocean basins have widened. With more and higher mountains forming at the edges of continents, less and less moisture from the oceans is able to reach the continental interiors. So, as the earth's evolution proceeds, this process produces an enlarging of the already existing relief deserts.

In the California desert, for example, there are many clues to the ebb and flow of desert lands both tens of millions and tens of thousands of years ago. When the continents were flatter, more rain was carried to the interior, and today's deserts were occasionally covered with glaciers or seas—and sometimes with lush forests and grasslands, which were dotted with freshwater lakes, crisscrossed by creeks and rivers, and teeming with large and small wildlife. And sometimes these lands were just plain deserts; they varied in size according to the climatic conditions. But the trend, overall, has been to increasing dryness for continental interiors, as mountain building continues and relief deserts enlarge.

Because of this pattern of geologic events, many geologists think there will be a time when desert once more covers all the earth's continents. If that happens, you can guess what the fate of our species will be. Unfortunately, it seems as if humans as a species are doing their best to aid and abet desert expansion. However much we love and appreciate the deserts we now have, it hardly seems in our own best interests to help them grow larger.

3

Reading the Rocks

As you cross the desert on foot or by vehicle, what earth shapes do you see around you? Mountains, of course, and plains. And, depending on where you are, perhaps sand dunes, cinder cones, valleys, dry lakes, washes, even a river. Put them together and you have a landscape characteristic of the desert region where you are. Take the landscape apart (figuratively) and what do you find? Landforms and the materials they are made of—rocks. These are the earth's history books, so to speak.

Rocks tell interesting tales, and you don't have to become a professional geologist to read them. All it takes is a willingness to look carefully around you and learn to fit the clues you find into logical (or maybe *geo-logical* is a better word) patterns.

Even seemingly featureless parts of the desert are filled with landscape features. Each of these landforms has a life history (as do the rocks they are made of). In some ways, landforms are elusive—in that they often blend into each other and overlap. At what point, for instance, does a mountain stop being a mountain and become a hill? A riverbed a creek bed? A trough a valley? A fault a crack? A sand dune a sand hill? An arroyo a wash? The idea here is not to worry about classifying landforms, but instead just to notice them, to try figuring out how and why they differ, and to begin discovering something about their life histories.

Knowing even a little about the materials that make up landforms (rocks, minerals), the structures that underlie them (bends, fractures), the forces that produce these structures (plate movements), and the processes responsible for their surface features (climatic, biologic) will add a new dimension to your appreciation of all desert landscapes.

Rocks Are the Root of All Landforms

Everything on nature's green (and brown) earth has to be made of something—and landforms are no exception. To state the obvious once more—they are made of rocks. And what are rocks made of? Again, the obvious—minerals. Here is where things can stop being obvious. As we all know, rocks and minerals come in a mind-boggling number of colors, sizes, shapes, origins, and chemical properties. Here, however, space and comprehension dictate that this vast realm of rocky possibility be reduced to a few simple (but useful) generalities and particularities.

To start out with, minerals are chemical compounds that are the earth's building blocks. What we think of as gems are certain kinds of somewhat scarce and beautiful minerals in a pure form. Salt is a mineral. So is a diamond. But only the latter is called a gem. Minerals are classified, quite complexly, according to certain physical qualities such as hardness, crystal form, color, specific gravity, and luster. (They are also classified according to chemical qualities.)

Rocks, though, are made up of two or more minerals and are classified according to their origins. Once you are able to tell rocks apart according to their origins, you are on your way to sorting out the geologic history of the landforms you see all around you in the California desert. Luckily, although there are hundreds of different kinds of rocks, there are only three recognized origin classifications—igneous, sedimentary, and metamorphic. Some folks like to add a fourth group: FRDK—"funny rock, don't know." (This category is quite useful.)

Igneous Rocks

Igneous rocks are minerals that have been melded together in liquid form as a result of heat. The earth's crust probably contains a higher proportion of igneous rocks than of any other kind. Active volcanoes can give you a glimpse of what liquid rock is like. Except when one is standing on the lip of a volcano, it's hard to believe that the seemingly solid earth is only a thin skin covering a great mass of very hot, thick magma. The magma is a mixture of liquid minerals, which when cooled forms igneous rocks (this liquid magma is called molten lava once it reaches the surface of the earth).

Igneous rocks can be either plutonic or volcanic. Plutonic igneous rocks are granular and contain easily seen crystals—an example is granite. Plutonic rocks are formed from magma under the earth's surface so they cool slowly, thus allowing large crystals to form. Volcanic igneous rocks form on the earth's surface from molten lava; they cool more quickly than plutonic rocks and are therefore more fine grained, even glassy. Examples are basalt and obsidian.

When a volcano erupts, gases are released from the molten lava. If there is little gas, the lava may ooze out slowly across nearby land. If there is quite a bit of gas, molten lava may be flung high into the air; when the lava pieces finally come down to earth, the fragments may be quite small. The smallest fragments are volcanic ash; later, the ash may become compressed into tuff, a volcanic rock. There are good examples of tuff at Red Rock Canyon, in the western Mojave. Slightly larger lava fragments are called cinders; some small volcanoes seem to have ejected nothing but cinders. There are many cinder cones in the California desert — for instance, Amboy Crater, in the eastern Mojave. (Such cones are sometimes mined for what landscapers call ornamental cinder rock.)

Molten lava that cools very quickly may become the dark, glassy rock known as obsidian. (Obsidian was much prized by the California Indians, who used it to make arrowheads and cutting tools.) Slower-cooling lava may become dark, fine-grained basalt. (If conditions are right, basalt sometimes forms impressively tall columns, like those found near Little Lake.) Other lava rocks are not uniform but may be made up of bits and pieces of quartz grains, dark glass, and ash, all cemented together into welded tuff.

Molten rock that has cooled before reaching the earth's surface can also be seen in some places. For instance, there are volcanic necks such as Mopah Peak. Batholiths are perhaps the most spectacular of the plutonic rock formations. These igneous rock masses are many miles deep and sometimes hundreds of miles long. The granitic, 400-mi-long Sierra Nevada is such a batholith. Erosion has almost completely exposed the formation in the southern Sierra; the northern Sierra is still capped in places with older rocks.

Sedimentary Rocks

Next to that of volcanic lavas, the origin of sedimentary rocks is probably the most obvious. The most common kinds of sedimentary rock are accumulations of pebbles, sand, and mud. These fragments have been eroded away from their original (or previous) location by wind and water, heat and cold, and then carried to some resting place where they gradually accumulate in layers. When you look at sediments, you'll notice that some have not yet been compacted enough to be called rocks. Also, there is a wide range of textures and hardnesses between loose sediments and sedimentary rocks. Once the sediments become hard enough to be chipped off in pieces, they are sedimentary rocks. These are usually classified as having been formed mechanically, chemically, or organically.

Sedimentary rocks such as sandstone and shale are made of bits of rock that have settled and accumulated until the pressure turns the layers into rock (mechanical formation). The fragments may come to rest in a valley, at the bottom of an ocean, or even on flat land. The wind may blow the bits there, or water may bring them. Other sedimentary rocks, such as some salt compounds and iron ores, are actually precipitated out of solution (chemical formation). Coal and some types of limestone can be produced when plant remains are subjected to pressure and chemical change (organic formation).

Most sedimentary rocks are soft (relative to igneous and metamorphic rocks) and show evidence of layering. Sedimentary rocks of all varieties contain much of the earth's fossil history. From these rocks we can learn about the plants, animals, and climates that existed millions of years ago. The many beautiful canyons in California's Colorado (Sonoran) Desert region are a good place to get acquainted with sediments, sedimentary rocks, and the fossils sometimes found in their colorful layers. Such layers are also found in the road cuts, arroyos, washes, and earthquake faults all over much of the rest of the California desert.

Metamorphic Rocks

As the name implies, metamorphic rocks are rocks whose original character has been changed—that is, metamorphosed in some way. The agents of geologic change are what you might expect—various combinations of heat, pressure, and chemicals dissolved in water. Veins of gemstones and precious minerals are sometimes laid down when molten rock comes in contact with hard, cool rock (contact metamorphosis). When great pressure is applied to sedimentary rocks such as soft limestones—as when rock layers fold—they can be changed to much harder marbles (dynamic metamorphosis). Petrified woods can be produced when water that carries minerals in solution "bumps out" some of the minerals in the wood and replaces them with others (replacement metamorphosis). Some wood is thus turned into beautiful forms of agate or opal.

Actually, any rock can become a metamorphic rock—if it finds its way below the surface of the earth far enough to be subjected to the heat, pressure, and chemical action that can recrystallize it without melting it (melted-down rocks become igneous rocks). What a rock is changed into depends on its original composition and texture, as well as on what happens to it. For example, shale (a soft, dull-appearing sedimentary rock made up of cemented silt or mud) can become the much harder metamorphic rock, slate, which is used for blackboards. In this metamorphosis, fossils have been destroyed, producing the small mica flakes that give mica a shiny appearance. If conditions are right, with temperature and pressure increasing, the metamorphosis of shale can continue from slate to schist to gneiss (pronounced "nice")—becoming ever coarser as it changes. The granitic-looking gneiss bears no resemblance to the original shale.

Metamorphic rocks are often found in and around the igneous rock masses called batholiths (see above). Contact metamorphosis takes place at interfaces between molten (igneous) rock and solid rock. In this kind of metamorphosis, chemical reactions between the molten and solid rock produce changes in composition. For example, ore veins (gold, silver, lead, etc.) are sometimes laid down at the interfaces between molten and solid rock. In another kind of contact metamorphosis, pressure and heat cause changes in large rock masses rather than just at interfaces. However, the new kinds of rock are formed from compounds already present in the old rock. So, although texture may change and different minerals may form, composition remains the same.

Rocks in General

All rocks, however ordinary looking, contain a goodly amount of information on the world's geologic history. Three things most rocks give clues to are their composition, the conditions that produced them, and what has happened to them since then. For example, careful examination of a rock may reveal if it has been weathered and fragmented, bent and broken, or squeezed and recrystallized.

As we find out what rocks are made of, how they are produced, and what can happen to them along the way, it becomes evident that rocks are far from eternal. In fact, rocks are being constantly recycled. The sedimentary rocks of today were the molten rock (magma), the metamorphic rocks, and the igneous rocks of tens or hundreds of millions of years ago. As these same sedimentary (or metamorphic or igneous) rocks of today continue their life cycles, they will sink beneath the earth's crust, be transformed, and rise again to the surface in who knows what rocky character tens or hundreds of millions of years from now. And so the stuff of which rocks are made will continue to shuttle back and forth between the earth's inner molten realm of magma and its cooler surface realm of landforms.

Rocks, then, are made of other rocks. Surprisingly, the number of compounds that go into rock making are few. In fact, it is the processes rock materials have been through, rather than their chemical composition, that give a rock the qualities we identify it by. For example, the minerals in some kinds of sandstone and granite are nearly identical, but the rocks certainly are not! Sandstone is a soft, often reddish, sedimentary rock that frequently contains fossils; granite is a hard, igneous, light-colored rock, with visible crystals. In other words, whatever kind of rock a particular specimen is at present—be it granite or sandstone, obsidian or limestone—has been determined by the most recent processes it has been through (recent in the geologic sense).

Landforms and the Earth's Restless Crust

The earth we stand on isn't as inert as it seems. Just a few miles below our feet it is virtually seething with activity—radioactivity, that is. And it's the heat energy released in the breakdown of radioactive compounds that, when transformed into mechanical energy, produces currents in the molten rock of the earth's interior. These currents in turn produce movements of the earth's crust, which result in the geologic structures underlying landforms all over the world.

Fractures, Joints, and Faults. The stresses and strains—the energy buildup—produced by movements of the earth's crust—are released when the crust fractures or bends. Some fractures stay put; these are simply called joints. Other fractures slip, with one or both sides moving in different

directions (right, left, up, down, horizontally). These moving fractures
are called faults.

As you probably already know, there are many famous faults in
southern California. Parts of the San Andreas, Sierra Nevada, Garlock,
Furnace Creek—Death Valley, San Jacinto, and several other major
faults are found in various California desert regions. You can get a pretty
good look at the traces of these faults on some of the trips in Chapters
8–16. In fact, each time you go through Cajon Pass, Tejon Pass, or San
Gorgonio Pass, you are traveling beside or crossing some part of California's largest and most well known fault—the 650-mi-long San Andreas
fault.

Southern California is also famous for its earthquakes—which result
from faults releasing stresses that have built up in the earth's crust. Fault
slippage doesn't just result in earthquakes, though. Once a fault has been
created, the earth's restless crust usually causes further heaving and
buckling. Horizontal sedimentary, metamorphic, and igneous rock beds
can become crazily tilted in all directions as large and small faults slip
up, down, right, left, and horizontally. Dramatic topographic features,
such as steep mountain scarps, are sometimes created by fault slippage—
for instance, the east side of the Sierra Nevada (Sierra Nevada fault),
the south side of the El Pasos (Garlock fault), and the south side of the
San Bernardinos (Banning fault). The San Andreas fault is even moving
Los Angeles and San Francisco closer together.

Bends, Folds, and Warps. Fractures, then, are referred to as joints (non-
moving) or faults (slipping). Bends, on the other hand, are folds or
warps. Upfolds are mountain and hill makers; downfolds are valley and
trough makers. Hills, ridges, and mountain ranges formed by upfolds
are somewhat easier to identify than the valleys resulting from downfolds. Such valleys are often so filled up with earth and rock washed
into them that they are unidentifiable. You can see smaller-scale foldings
in road cuts, badlands, and some canyons.

When examining rock folds, you'll notice they are mostly sedimentary
rock. Because of their relative softness and layered structure, sedimentary rock beds are more prone to folding than harder rock beds. Warping is the large-scale bending or tilting favored by huge, solid bodies
of metamorphic and igneous rocks (although they usually fracture when
stress is too great). Because of the large areas involved in warping, it's
difficult to see from ground level. Cima Dome, in the eastern Mojave,
is an example of warping you can actually see, from a distance.

An interesting fact about the California desert area is that, geologically
speaking, its often-dramatic topography is young. This striking scenery
is a direct result of various kinds of bending and fracturing.

In other parts of the continent, such upheavals took place long in
the geologic past; the topography of these areas today is mostly the
result of differences in weathering of hard and soft rock masses. Often,
these older landscapes are areas of low relief, with rolling hills, low-
lying, rounded mountain ranges, and broad, shallow valleys.

In southern California, however, you never know from one day to the next whether the earth beneath your feet is going to unexpectedly twitch! A fitting comment on this fact was once made by a well-known earthquake structural engineer, who said, "California, with all your faults, we love you still, only you don't stay still long enough."

Surface Sculpture

The desert landscapes we see today—indeed, all landscapes—are the results of several ongoing processes: movements of the earth's crust (which produce bends and fractures); climatic leveling processes (weathering and erosion); and biologic processes (in which living organisms change nonliving materials by making use of them). Bends and fractures in the earth's crust are responsible for such topographic features as mountains, domes, volcanoes, faults, troughs, valleys, and so on. Climatic leveling processes, however, are constantly at work on these ups and downs of landscapes, doing their best to reduce all relief to a uniform flatness by weathering rocks and eroding soil. Biologic processes both build up and break down landscape features. For example, some organisms layer their remains on sea or lake bottoms; others—lichens, for instance—nibble away at rocks, causing them to weaken and disintegrate.

Weathering. It seems, then, that a kind of contest is going on in all landscapes between the pushing-up forces and the breaking-down forces. Rocks and other solids (trees, bones, etc.) are broken down in several ways. Weathering is the chemical and physical interaction of solid substances with air (wind), water, heat, cold, and living organisms. This process ordinarily takes place slowly; and if conditions are right, weathering can turn even the hardest rock into a fine soil—eventually. A common kind of weathering involves water freezing and expanding in the cracks of rocks, thus weakening the rocks and making it easier for wind and water to erode and carry away rock pieces. And just as with everything else that has gone up, rock that breaks loose moves down. If it weren't for uplifting processes, all landscapes would finally become dull and featureless due to the effects of weathering.

Erosion. Whether by wind or water, erosion also carries any bits of solid material it can move—usually down. Wind erosion can create sand and sand dunes, as well as fantastically sculptured rock shapes. (Wind action is the only weathering process that does sometimes carry fine rock material uphill; for instance, it piles sand into dunes several hundreds of feet high.)

Wind is a rather constant desert feature, so it's not surprising that it plays a significant part in sculpturing the desert landscape. Water, though, is scarce in the desert—so it is surprising to learn that water erosion has a greater effect on the desert landscape than wind erosion. One of the reasons for water's greater effect is that, in desert areas, a year's allotment of rain often comes all at once in a monstrous thunderstorm. The many mountains, rocky bajadas, and barren badlands shed the vast sheets of water as fast as they fall, creating temporary but swiftly flowing rivers and creeks. These flash floods gouge out desert valleys, gorges, arroyos, gullies, washes, and canyons. They also pile huge quantities of rocky debris and mud into the impressive alluvial fans you often see at the mouths of desert mountain canyons.

Mass Earth Movements. After erosion and weathering have worked together long enough to result in large-scale disintegration of rock masses or to break down the soil structure in a wide area, gravity alone may cause huge quantities of debris to move downslope in what is referred to as mass movement. When this happens, the whole side of a valley or hill may actually flow downslope some distance. Such earth-flows may move very slowly, sort of creeping downward (mudflows); others may roar downhill (landslides). Such earth movements can change a landscape quite dramatically in a relatively short time.

Biologic Processes. Living organisms are responsible for more subtle contributions to the leveling and building up of the desert landscape. Instead of roaring down canyons or piling up sand dunes, various life forms quietly assimilate and break down rocks and minerals, making them more susceptible to weathering and erosion. Desert animals burrow under rocks. Plants sneakily slip their roots into minute cracks and pry away hunks of mountains. Microorganisms build up the landscape by helping create eerily beautiful tufa towers. And tiny water creatures leave behind layers of microscopic shells that are transformed into useful limestone, or scientifically valuable fossil beds.

Fossils — Rocks That Were Once Alive

Sedimentary rocks testify to the fact that in ancient times (600 to 200 million years ago) much of what is now the California desert was submerged in a sea. The sea came and went at least twice during this long time; later, over more millions of years, the land was pushed up and worn down, volcanoes started actively spewing out lava and ash, and yet more mountains were created by movements of the earth's crust. The volcanic activity continued until relatively recently; Amboy Crater, one of many similar craters in the desert, was still blowing out cinders about 10,000 years ago. In fact, today you can see evidence of volcanic activity in many parts of the California desert.

During the time of volcanic activity, the earth's restless crust was also thrusting up many of the desert mountain ranges we are familiar with today — the Transverse Ranges at the western edge of the Mojave Desert, the Peninsular Ranges at the western edge of the Colorado Desert, the Basin Ranges in the northernmost part of California's Great Basin Desert, and, last but far from least, the Sierra Nevada. This enormous mountain range, which effectively prevents Pacific Ocean moisture from reaching much of southeastern California, helped make the California desert regions the relief deserts they are today.

The many mountain ranges resulting from all this uplifting, along with the fact that the climate in those long-ago times was considerably more humid than now, produced a region dotted with lakes, flowing with streams and creeks coming from the mountains, and rich with plant and animal life. Some of this life can still be seen today as fossils.

Fossil Formation. As time went by, the climate continued to fluctuate between dry and wet cycles. During wet times the land was lush; during dry times it was much as it is today — desert. And all during this immensely long time — from the time of the great seas to the California desert of the present — countless creatures were living and dying. Some of these creatures, when conditions were right, had their shapes and even their minutest body structures permanently preserved. For fossils are formed when minerals dissolved in water replace the bodies of animals and plants trapped in layers of sediment. The mineral found in petrified wood, for instance, is often agate. Other minerals are known for their ability to replace even intracellular structures with great exactitude. Collophane, for instance, can perfectly copy ancient bone.

A Few Fossil Haunts. When ancient seas covered what are now the Marble Mtns in the eastern part of the Mojave Desert, primitive invertebrates such as trilobites, gastropods, and brachiopods were trapped in the sea floor sediments. These creatures are among the oldest (500 to 600 million years) fossils in the California desert. In some places they are easily seen, along with many fossils from later periods.

In Death Valley's Titus Canyon, paleontologists have located fossils of large mammals that date from about 40 million years ago. It's strange to think of primitive camels, rats, horses, and even a rhinolike animal as living in this now-desolate part of the desert. Look for these fossils in Death Valley's two museums.

The Calico Mtns area also is rich in fossil remnants dating back 15 to 20 million years. Some fossil animals found there include pronghorns, camels, three-toed horses, a small mastodon, dogs, cats, and insects. You can see samples of these fossils at the Calico Early Man Site. Much farther west, at Red Rock Canyon, similar fossils have been found — though these are somewhat more recent. The Red Rock Canyon State Park visitor center has some of these remains on display.

Old lake beds are often good hunting grounds for paleontologists, so it is not surprising that many fine examples of fossil animals only 10,000 years to 2 million years old are found in some of the many dry lake beds of the eastern Mojave Desert. These lake beds date from the times when glaciers were coming and going over much of the Northern Hemisphere, and the conditions were sometimes lush and wet. During this time animals were numerous; some of the dry lake finds include bears, wolves, turtles, tortoises, snails, flamingos, pelicans, ducks, and eagles. The San Bernardino County Museum, Riverside Museum, and the Los Angeles County Museum all have collections of these fossils.

Farther south, in the western part of California's Colorado Desert, a variety of fossils of similar age have been found. For example, in the Yuha area there are extensive oyster beds, indicating that the Gulf of California once extended much farther north; a good selection of marine invertebrates has been located near Split Mtn in Anza-Borrego Desert State Park; and in the Mecca Hills horses, camels, and other mammals have been found.

In addition, there are some California desert fossils that can no longer be seen as such. Most limestone and dolomite are composed of the limey shells and skeletons from ancient sea creatures, large and small. Limestone is soluble in water, so caves are sometimes formed in large deposits if conditions are right. Mitchell Caverns, in the Providence Mtns State Recreation Area, is such a cave system. Rangers give guided tours of the caverns nearly all year. If you spend much time in the desert, you'll probably notice that a number of the many large beds of both limestone and dolomite are being rather messily mined for cement.

These, of course, are only a few of the many places in the California desert where fossils can be found. See the "Recommended Reading" appendix for more information.

Getting Started on Rock and Mineral Hunting

People hunt rocks and minerals for a variety of reasons. Some are collectors (rockhounds) who enjoy observing, classifying, and arranging rock and mineral fragments as a hobby or avocation. Some not only collect but also polish and cut rocks and minerals into jewelry or decorative pieces (lapidarists, gemologists). Still others collect and observe rocks and minerals for scientific purposes (geologists). Then there are those who make a business of removing large quantities of rocks and minerals from the earth (miners).

Aside from the last category most rock hunters are motivated by a considerable amount of plain old curiosity. They want to know something about how the stuff of the earth was created, where it came from originally, how it got to where it is now, and what it is called and why. If you have a good bit of this kind of curiosity about rocks and minerals, the geologically active and varied California desert is a good place to exercise it. It's not necessary (or even desirable) to have the collecting inclination to be a rock and mineral hunter. Many very skilled hunters of this sort take only pictures (or notes and sketches) and leave only footprints — an excellent practice for the low-impact-minded!

Most people start their rock-hunting career by doing a little field guide and geology text reading as well as landscape looking. Unfortunately, there is not space here for a rock hunter's primer; as you may well imagine, that would be another whole book in itself.

As you travel about in the California desert, you can't help noticing a fair number of holes in the landscape. Most of these scars are the result of past or present mining activities. About 18 million acres of the California desert's 25 million acres are open to mining; the Bureau of Land Management (BLM) manages 64% of this land, and the rest is state or private land. Mining of gold, silver, lead, and borate began in the 1850s in several regions of the California desert. Since then, quite a number of other metallic and nonmetallic rocks and minerals have been exploited, including iron, limestone and gypsum, rare earths, talc, desert pavement, clay, sand and gravel, cinders, saline compounds, copper, and zinc.

Mines, however, need not scar the landscape indefinitely — if they are worked responsibly. The reasons for the many scars you see in the California desert are at least twofold: (1) nearly all this mining activity is surface mining, and (2) reclamation has been minimal. Unfortunately, it looks as if there are going to be more scars in the California desert's future, rather than less. This is true even though reclamation is now required by the Federal Surface Mining and Reclamation Act of 1977. But why? To illustrate this unlovely scenario, here are some figures from the BLM. The total acreage disturbance by mining between 1930 and 1980 was about 37,031 acres. The total acreage reclaimed during this period was between 9402 and 7161 acres — approximately 22% of the total disturbed lands. To say it another way — during these fifty years, on the average, there were about 740 acres per year disturbed and 165 acres per year reclaimed. Remember, during forty-seven years of this time there was no reclamation law.

Now, let's look at what's going to happen with the reclamation law. BLM's projection for mining and reclamation activities to take place between 1980 and 2000 goes like this: the total number of disturbed acres will be about 24,172; the total reclaimed acres will average approximately 3312, or 14% of the total disturbed. That is, during these twenty years, on the average, there will be about 1208 acres per year disturbed and 165 acres reclaimed. Remember, this is *with* the reclamation law; *without* the law, for some reason, the average was considerably higher: about 22% of disturbed lands per year were reclaimed!

It does seem more than a little strange that although the average acres per year disturbed by mining will be going from 740 to 1208 (an increase of 63%) between 1980 and 2000, the average acres per year to be reclaimed are projected to remain the same. It looks as if the reclamation law makes no difference whatever to the mining companies or to those from whom they lease land; repair and restoration of California desert lands mutilated by mining does not seem to interest them.

Reclamation does cost money—it can run from 0.5% to nearly 50% of the total cost of a mining project. Underground mines such as lead-zinc-silver mines are the least expensive to reclaim; limestone quarries and other open-pit mines are the most costly. Some of these costs can be reduced by use of more responsible mining practices. However, the expense of reclamation is one of the bills all mining companies (or individual miners) are morally obliged to pay (whether they do or not). In no way can the expense (or a strategic need for the ores) be construed as a legitimate excuse for scarring the land and then just walking away from it. If reclamation is unaffordable, then so is the whole mining operation. Scarring the land, like any other kind of pollution, should be remedied by those responsible for it.

Needless to say, the brief summary of a few interesting facts appropriate here does not do any kind of justice to the complexity of the task involved in reading the California desert landscape—and the rocks therein. Check the "Recommended Reading" appendix for books that will give you more detailed and concise information.

4

Desert Plants

Most of us are taught that deserts, whether in North America, Asia, or Africa, are nothing but vast, empty wastelands, devoid of all life except for a few poisonous animals and spiny plants. Looking out across expanses of windblown sand or over dry, rocky hillsides, it is indeed hard to understand how plants and animals survive the harsh environment.

But many do; a great many. So that, far from being an empty wasteland, the California desert is filled with life. In the desert lands of California there are over 2000 native plant species, including trees, shrubs, perennial herbs, annual wildflowers, and grasses. In addition, the California desert regions also have their share of introduced plants, such as filaree and tumbleweed (Russian thistle). To be successful desert residents, these many plants — both native and introduced — have had to adapt themselves to rather extreme environmental conditions; they have done this in a number of effective ways. (See Plant Lists in the appendix for the common and scientific names of plants mentioned in *Adventuring in the California Desert*.)

How Plants Have Adapted to the Desert

Chronic lack of water (drought) is the primary stress desert plants must cope with. Due to the desert's clear air and sky, plants also have to cope with intense solar radiation, frequent high daytime temperatures, and frequent rapid temperature drops at night — in addition to dryness. Most plant adaptations to drought fall into one of three categories: water storage, drought tolerance, and drought avoidance. Each of these strategies is quite different, and each has advantages and disadvantages.

Succulence — A Water Storage Method

Some plants take up large amounts of water whenever water is available (which is usually only for very short periods of time). They then store the water in leaf, stem, or root tissues for use during the longer dry periods. Such plants are called succulents. Most succulents in the California desert (and in the New World in general) are cacti; however, there are also succulents in five or more other California plant families. When they are fully hydrated after a rain, a typical cactus or agave can grow during several weeks of dry weather and survive for many months more. A large barrel cactus can survive at least a year without rain.

Several adaptations go hand in hand with succulence. Drenching rains are rather rare in the desert; light showers and brief downpours that wet only the upper few inches of soil are more common. The soil dries quickly following such minor wetting. Succulents are under selective pressure to absorb large amounts of water in a brief time, and nearly all species have evolved extensive shallow root systems. A 2-ft-tall cholla cactus may have roots radiating more than 30 ft, with none being over 4 in. deep. A quarter-in. of rain benefits such a plant, but not the deeper-rooted nonsucculents.

TYPES OF SUCCULENTS. There are three basic kinds of succulents. Cacti are stem succulents, and are leafless. (Prickly pear cactus pads are stems.) The elephant tree is also a stem succulent and has normal, nonsucculent leaves. The water storage tissue is what gives this tree's stems their strange, swollen appearance. In California, the elephant tree is found in the Anza-Borrego Desert, where a small finger of trees comes up from Mexico.

Agaves and dudleyas are leaf succulents. These plants are nearly stemless and have fibrous roots (young agaves have succulent roots, too).

Root succulents appear ordinary above ground. The coyote gourd, for example, has a typical gourd family vine — but this vine arises from a massive, turnip-shaped root. The vine sprouts in spring and can flower and fruit even if there is no summer rain.

CAM PHOTOSYNTHESIS. Perhaps the most remarkable desert plant adaptation is a special kind of photosynthesis called crassulation acid metabolism (CAM), which is used only by succulents. Most plants conduct gas exchange (intake of carbon dioxide and release of oxygen) in the daytime. During this process, water is lost through the plant's open pores (stomates) in a process called transpiration. CAM plants, however, open their stomates at night and accumulate and store carbon dioxide, which is then used for photosynthesis during the day. Because nights are cooler and more humid than days, much less water is lost through transpiration at night. Thus, a succulent's stored water lasts much longer than if the succulent had to transpire during the day like other plants. Almost all succulents have developed CAM.

Perhaps an even more important attribute of CAM plants is their ability to "idle." When nonsucculent desert plants experience water stress, they become dormant. It may take several weeks for some dormant plants to resume full growth when rain returns. When a CAM succulent becomes water stressed, it keeps its stomates sealed day and night so that the plant is nearly gas- and water-tight. But instead of going dormant, its metabolism merely slows to an "idling" level. The carbon dioxide released by normal respiratory activity is recycled into the photosynthetic pathway, and the oxygen released in photosynthesis is recyled into the respiratory pathway. In short, it becomes a closed system.

Much like an idling car engine, a CAM plant can resume full performance much faster than a dormant plant (which has a "cold engine"). Because only twelve to twenty-four hours are needed to resume full growth, the succulent can benefit from light rains that evaporate quickly.

Drought Tolerance

Succulents and nonsucculents have developed different methods for waiting out times of drought in the desert.

DORMANCY. To tolerate drought, most nonsucculent desert plants become dormant. In this condition they can withstand levels of dehydration that would kill most plants.

LEAF CHANGES. Some plants, like the creosote bush and brittlebush, respond to mild water stress by producing smaller and smaller leaves that are progressively hairier (brittlebush) or more resinous (creosote bush), responses that slow down water loss. Under extreme stress they drop all their leaves and may even shed branches, reclaiming their water content to sustain the all-important root system.

PERENNIAL GROWTH. Desert plants that do not die back to seed each year, but continue to put out new growth, are called perennials. These plants may have root systems that are shallow (though deeper than succulent roots), deep, or both. Because of their deeper roots and their long recovery time from dormancy, these shrubs require a more soaking rain to start their growth. There is a positive tradeoff, though—the deep roots can take up water long after the surface has dried out. Also, most desert shrubs can extract water from much drier soil than can succulents or other moisture-requiring plants.

Drought Avoidance

Drought avoidance is a strategy used by plants that die back to seed each year (annuals).

ANNUAL SEED PRODUCTION. Annuals are responsible for most desert wildflower displays and hold over as seeds during dry periods. (The dry periods can last from one to many years.) Seeds are extremely resistant to environmental extremes and germinate only in response to a precise combination of moisture and temperature, which ensures their survival even if no rain falls that year. This strategy is an excellent one for the desert, where rainfall is so undependable—and so critical to a plant's well-being.

CONTROLLED SEED GERMINATION. Because the Mojave and Colorado deserts both receive most of their rain in winter, most California desert annuals are adapted to that season. (The Great Basin Desert is too cold for winter growth and has few annuals.) The seeds usually germinate in response to fall rains, after the summer heat has broken but before winter cold begins. In the Mojave Desert, this season is approximately mid-September to mid-November. The seeds of many species have a chemical germination inhibitor that must be leached out; about an inch of rain is the minimum required to trigger mass germination. Other factors, some of which are poorly understood, also influence germination.

If these requirements are met and no further rain falls, the plants will be stunted; however, most will survive the winter and produce a few flowers and seeds the following spring. The more rain they receive, the larger and more flower-laden they will be in the spring.

In a land of little water, a juicy plant must protect itself from thirsty animals. Thus, most succulents — and many nonsucculents — are spiny, poisonous, or both. Some grow only on cliffs or other inaccessible places; a few have evolved camouflage, but none of these grows in the California desert.

Plant Distribution

In the arid Southwest the main determinants of plant distribution are temperature and precipitation, with soil type a distant third. Temperature in turn is determined by elevation and latitude. Precipitation is determined largely by elevation, distance from moisture sources (Pacific Ocean and Gulf of Mexico), and whether a site is on the windward or leeward side of a mountain. Other factors exert significant local influences: slope (south slopes are hotter and drier), soil texture (some soils hold water better than others), rock strata or earthquake faults (which may create springs), and so on.

Species of plants with similar ecologic requirements tend to occur together. These associations are called plant communities; the eight commonest ones in the California desert are described below.

Major Desert Plant Communities

SAGEBRUSH SCRUB. This community occupies most of the Great Basin Desert, where the namesake species occurs between 4000 and 9000 ft elevation and often in nearly pure stands over many square miles of valley floors and lower bajadas. In addition to Great Basin sagebrush (also called big sagebrush), a few other shrubs may be present: blackbrush, shadscale, Mormon tea, greasewood, and rabbitbrush. All these shrubs may occur in pure stands, where they are sometimes defined as separate plant communities. A few grasses are sometimes present, but almost no trees, succulents, or annuals.

Sagebrush scrub also occurs in patches outside the Great Basin Desert in cold, arid habitats, such as in parched valleys on the leeward sides of higher desert ranges and the Transverse and Peninsular ranges.

SHADSCALE SCRUB. This community occurs mostly in the extreme northern Mojave Desert, in heavy soils at elevations of 3000 to 6000 ft. It is similar in aspect to sagebrush scrub, but the variety of shrub species is greater. The dominant plant is usually shadscale; others include spiny hop-sage, winter fat, blackbrush, and more. Notice that shadscale is also an element of sagebrush scrub; it occurs in other communities, too.

Very few plants are entirely restricted to a single plant community. Nature is really a continuum; we need to keep this in mind as we attempt to comprehend nature by organizing plants into artificial systems.

JOSHUA TREE WOODLAND. Joshua tree woodland is the most easily recognized community in the Mojave Desert. It is found at elevations ranging from 2500 to 4500 ft, in better-drained soils than shadscale scrub. Beneath the overstory of Joshua trees are a variety of shrubs, including bladder sage, creosote bush, and buckwheat. Several species of succulents grow here: barrel cactus, chollas (especially buckhorn cholla and silver cholla), hedgehog cactus, and beavertail cactus. After wet winters there are also many annuals.

It is probably noncontroversial to claim Joshua tree woodland is the most picturesque plant community in the California desert. Certainly the Joshua tree is a candidate for the most striking plant in California, and a forest of them is a truly memorable sight.

CREOSOTE BUSH SCRUB. Creosote bush scrub is the most widespread desert plant community in North America. It occupies about half the Mojave and most of the Colorado Desert. Outside California, creosote bush occupies much of the rest of the Sonoran Desert as well as the Chihuahuan Desert and the Argentine Desert, where it originated.

The dominant plant in this community is (what else?) creosote bush; in the lowest, driest valleys (below 2000 ft) it forms pure stands or coexists with white bursage—often called burroweed—and/or brittlebush. On rocky bajadas and other less arid habitats more species enrich this community, such as ocotillo, barrel cactus (especially in the Colorado Desert), hedgehog cactus, teddy bear and buckhorn cholla, pincushion cactus, desert mallow, and numerous others. Because it is the driest desert community, it has the densest stands of annuals in wet years.

In California there is little difference between the creosote bush scrub of the Mojave and Colorado deserts; in fact, it is hard to draw a boundary between the two deserts in this community.

Creosote bush might be considered the most drought-tolerant perennial in North America, which explains its dominance in the driest valleys. This amazing species is also one of the earth's oldest living plants;

some creosote bushes near Phelan are thought to be over 10,000 years old. This means they could be nearly twice the age of the oldest known bristlecone pines!

DESERT DRY WASH WOODLAND. The plants making up the desert dry wash woodland form linear communities along major drainage courses. Dry wash woodland is essentially a Colorado Desert community; in the Mojave, washes have denser vegetation and different species than adjacent flats, but rarely enough trees to call the community a woodland. The dry wash woodland is the only California desert community — other than the Joshua tree woodland — having significant numbers of trees.

As is characteristic of the Sonoran Desert, the trees found in washes are mostly in the legume family: palo verde, desert ironwood, mesquite, and smoke tree. Desert catalpa (also called desert willow, though it is not a member of the willow family) is also common.

The trees and generally denser vegetation in the washes are a result of the greater water supply; washes collect runoff from adjacent areas. Even a tiny gully enhances the water supply for its plants; large washes drain hundreds of square miles. Contrary to common belief, most washes are not barren channels. Both small and large washes, particularly those on level terrain, have considerable vegetation cover. For example, quarter-mile-wide Milpitas Wash contains a near-forest of trees between its banks. Through these trees wind the wash's numerous braided channels, which sometimes surround islands of dense shrubs. These braided channels often support lush stands of annuals in years when there has not been enough rain to produce a show on the flats ouside the wash.

On the lower slopes of desert mountains and in valleys with deep, permeable soils, the wash trees can extend beyond the channels and form extensive woodlands. (This is the normal condition in the rest of the Sonoran Desert, which gets more rain.) One of the best such areas is in the valley between the Palen and McCoy Mtns, where a large desert ironwood forest exists. There is a less dense forest surrounding the Chuckwalla and Little Chuckwalla Mtns.

SUCCULENT SCRUB. The succulent scrub community occurs on many rocky hillsides in the Colorado Desert. Succulent scrub has most of the species found in creosote bush scrub, but differs in that dense stands of cacti and other succulents are the most noticeable plant groupings. It is the larger numbers of certain plants rather than the kinds of plants that make this community different from the creosote bush scrub.

The best examples of succulent scrub are found in the foothills of the Peninsular Range, such as along the grade west of Ocotillo on I-8. The diversity and density of cacti, agaves, and yuccas in this area are astounding. In the Sacramento Mtns west of Needles there is a 2-mi-square patch of teddy bear cholla that is almost too dense to walk through. There are also some excellent natural cactus gardens south of

I-10 between Desert Center and the Red Cloud exit. A slightly different version of succulent scrub is the dense stands of Spanish bayonet (also called Mojave yucca) in the Mojave Desert.

PINYON-JUNIPER WOODLAND. Technically, pinyon–juniper woodland is not a desert plant community, but there is so much of it in the desert mountains that it actually is an important part of the California desert. This community occurs in semiarid areas between 6000 and 8000 ft elevation. It is dominated by small trees, mostly single-leaf pinyon and one of two species of junipers. Scrub oaks are often present. There are also a variety of shrubs and perennial herbs, especially grasses.

RIPARIAN WOODLANDS AND MARSHES. These occur within any surrounding community, desert or not, along streams and other permanent or semipermanent water supplies. These watery places are rare in the desert and so are very special communities. Within the California desert, riparian woodland trees are mostly cottonwoods, willows, and mesquite. Sycamores and Arizona ash are sometimes present. Tamarisk is a frequent, and destructive, nonnative (introduced) invader. Dense thickets of shrubs and vines usually line the watercourses (with or without the above trees). Some examples are seepwillow, arrowweed, and grape.

The most extensive riparian woodlands are along the Colorado River and the Mojave River near Victorville, as well as in the canyons west of Death Valley. Smaller but still spectacular riparian areas are Coyote Creek in Anza-Borrego Desert State Park, Cottonwood Spring in Joshua Tree National Monument, Paiute Creek northwest of Needles, and the Amargosa River near Shoshone.

Palm oases are water-based biotic communities of the California desert's Colorado region. There are about one hundred in California, ranging from a lone tree to many hundreds in dense groves. The desert (California) fan palm is the only palm native to the southwestern United States; it is perhaps the western desert's biggest contribution to horticulture. This fan palm is one of the most popular landscape trees in the warmer parts of the world. There are far more planted in southern California alone than exist in the wild. The desert (California) fan palm occurs naturally only in California, except for two populations in Arizona and several in Mexico.

Wildflower Displays

A banner wildflower display requires that the rains begin early and continue at the rate of about an inch per month through March. Because the rainy season usually doesn't begin until November or December, and in most of the desert the average is only about 5 in., it's easy to see why good wildflower years are rare. Really good desertwide blooms occur about once in ten years, on the average—for example, 1964, 1973, and 1977 were particularly good years. In between there are usually some local areas that receive enough rain to put on a good show.

Although massive blooms are rare, annuals are largely a desert phenomenon. Annuals are not very good at competing with perennials;
they require open, sunny ground for growth. This means that most annuals occur in arid and semiarid habitats and reach their zenith in the
driest and warmest deserts. In the California desert as a whole, fewer
than half the plants are annual species; in its driest areas, though, nearly
90% of the plants are annuals.

California Desert Palm Oases

One of the California desert's most striking environments is the palm
oasis. Dominated by the often 50-ft-high desert (California) fan palm,
these plant communities are totally out of keeping with their arid surroundings. Through the blistering summer heat the desert fan palms
maintain their lush green crowns, in stark contrast to the leafless ocotillo,
brittlebush, and shriveled-up annuals of the surrounding desert.

The secret of the oasis is, of course, water; almost every palm grove
is situated around a permanent spring where fractures in the underlying
rock result in moisture rising to the surface. The abundant and permanent supply of water enables the palms to grow continuously throughout the year, regardless of annual fluctuations in precipitation. This is
not only crucial to the palms, and the mesquite and rushes that grow
beside them, but to the hooded orioles, bighorn sheep, and coyotes who
come to drink. Palm oases are usually a dependable source of water
and are therefore one of the best places to observe desert wildlife.

Prehistoric desert peoples were well aware of the permanent water
found at the oasis and were seasonal, if not permanent, residents near
most palm groves. The fruits of both the palms and mesquite were
nutritious and reliable foods. Palm fronds were used to make houses;
fibers from the leaves were used to make baskets. Potsherds, bedrock
mortars, and petroglyphs can still be seen today. These artifacts are
testimonials to the long association between prehistoric humans and
the palm oasis.

When visiting the palm oases, remember that these are important but
rare components of the desert ecosystem. Many animals in the vicinity
rely upon oasis water, but may be too frightened by your presence to
come in and drink. In most cases they have no other water source. After
visiting the heart of the oasis, move far enough from the water to allow
timid animals to drink. With respect to the palms, remember to make
no fires. The dry leaves that form the skirts of the trees are easily ig-
nited and the resultant fire destroys the virgin beauty of individual palms
forever. Finally, do not disturb artifacts; leave them for others to see.
If you find something unusual, photograph it and contact a museum.

(The above remarks on palm oases were contributed by James Cornett,
Curator of Natural Science, Palm Springs Desert Museum. Mr. Cornett
and the Desert Museum have kindly contributed all the trip information on palm oases appearing in *Adventuring in the California Desert.*)

Major Plant Groups

Popular field guides often use artificial categories to help their readers identify plants. Such guides may, for example, be broken up into sections by color or into groupings such as trees, shrubs, herbs, etc. Unfortunately, these artificial categories have little or nothing to do with the true relationships among plants. True relationships, unlike artificial categories, suggest evolutionary trends and can be discovered by comparing the various features of plants. Because true relationships make biological sense, the careful observer using this approach can more easily come to understand, retain, and use the knowledge acquired by studying plants than can users of artificial systems.

As you have doubtless already guessed, the point of this preliminary statement is to prepare you for the fact that this short guide to common desert plants uses the true-relationship approach. That is, closely related plants will be discussed in a cluster and in terms of their relations (as space permits). Keep in mind, though, that the evolutionary tree is three dimensional and doesn't actually fit comfortably into the two-dimensional (so to speak) organization of sequential book pages. In other words, there is no way to get around a two-dimensional, linear listing of plants. The best that can be done is to group the individual plants in the general order of their evolutionary appearance.

The names of the three major plant groups are descriptive of the way each produces its seeds. However, there is really no need to go into the details of seed production in the context of this short guide. For details, see the "Recommended Reading" appendix.

CONIFERS (GYMNOSPERMS). Conifers, also called gymnosperms ("naked seeds"), are the most primitive of the three plant groups. These cone bearers, such as the pinyon pine, are nonflowering plants.

MONOCOTS. Monocots are flowering plants with obvious parallel veins in their foliage. If you tear down a grass blade, for example, you can see the parallel veins quite clearly; you can also see them in segments of palm leaves. Flower parts in the monocots are usually in threes — often in two series of threes. In the desert lily, for example, the six petals are actually two series of three parts each. Monocot capsules, such as those of the yucca, burst into three distinct parts.

For the most part, monocot roots and stems quickly attain their largest diameter; for instance, a 3-ft-high desert (California) fan palm will probably have a trunk the same diameter as it would if it were 100 ft tall! The internal woody parts of monocots are bundles of fibers rather than the concentric rings of growth found in typical woods.

DICOTS. Dicots, like the monocots, are flowering plants. The leaves of dicots, however, are usually net-veined rather than parallel-veined. As the woody members of dicot plants enlarge, they keep adding cells to the periphery of trunks, twigs, and roots, thus producing what we think of as growth rings.

Dicot flowers are seldom produced in groups of three. The petals of dicots are sometimes separate, like those of the apricot mallow, and sometimes fused into tubes, like those of the ocotillo; they are generally in fours and fives.

There are a few logical groupings within the dicots. The structures of these groups suggest evolutionary trends. The most primitive flowers, for example, have petals free from each other, like the apricot mallow. The flowers found on the next step up the evolutionary scale have petals that have fused to form tubelike structures, like the ocotillo.

Incidentally, botanists believe that evolution of monocots and dicots has been nearly parallel.

Plant Descriptions

The descriptions and illustrations below primarily cover common desert plants having permanent and woody parts. Unfortunately, there isn't space to cover the many hundreds of lovely annuals that briefly carpet the desert with splashes of spring color in most years. See the "Recommended Reading" appendix for field guides containing descriptions of annual flowering plants.

Conifers (Gymnosperms)

Conifers (gymnosperms) are primitive, nonflowering, cone-bearing plants. Pines and their allies are perhaps the best-known gymnosperms throughout the world. Deserts, however, are considered marginal habitats for conifers in general.

PINE FAMILY (PINACEAE).
Pinyon Pine. Only one species of pine has become adapted to California desert conditions: *Pinus monophylla* (one-leaved pine), commonly known as pinyon pine. Unlike many pines whose winged seeds come whirling down in the wind, these pines have large, thin-shelled seeds that fall directly to the ground. They would soon become sterile in the hot desert sun if it were not for the animals such as jays and squirrels who gather and hide them. These "pine nuts" were also an important food for California Indians.

Juniper. A perhaps even better known conifer in the desert is the juniper. The California juniper, *Juniperus californica,* is probably the species most frequently encountered—especially at lower elevations. Its low, nearly horizontal branches are characteristic. Higher up is found a more erect form, the Utah juniper, *J. osteosperma.* The unnaturally heavy concentrations of junipers you see over much of the California desert's cattle range have been created by overgrazing.

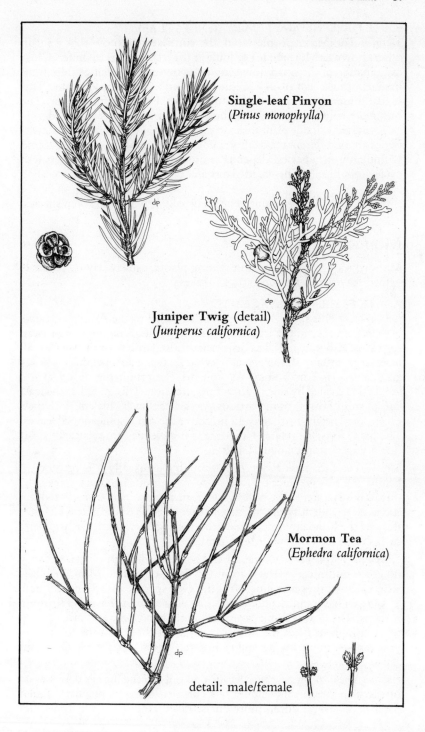

Single-leaf Pinyon
(*Pinus monophylla*)

Juniper Twig (detail)
(*Juniperus californica*)

Mormon Tea
(*Ephedra californica*)

detail: male/female

JOINT FIR (EPHEDRA) FAMILY (GNETACEAE).
Mormon Tea. Many people would be surprised to know that a shrub often known as Mormon tea or joint fir (*Ephedra* spp.) is a conifer. Close examination of the small flowering parts reveals this relationship. Joint firs (also called just plain ephedra) have male and female forms. This sexual dimorphism is very obvious when they are in full flower. The tiny male cones with their copious pollen are easily recognized.

When steeped, this plant makes a pleasant tea. People claim certain varieties are of different tea quality, but even greater differences are found within any one species, depending on vigor and stage in the growth cycle. Joint firs are long-lived plants and often form large clusters called clones.

In southern California this genus is usually broken into seven species.

Monocots

Monocots are single-seeded, flowering plants, usually having parallel-veined leaves and flower parts in threes.

AGAVE FAMILY (AGAVACEAE).
Joshua Tree. This spiny-leaved group, confined to the Americas, ranks high in frequency in the arid Southwest. Its Central and South American forms are also much used as ornamentals. Regardless of the species, all have large, usually showy, creamy white, six-petalled, pendulous flowers that are 1–2 in. across. As you drive through the desert, *Yucca brevifolia* is rivaled by few in attracting attention. This giant has the least conspicuous flowers of the various yuccas; its flower clusters, with their green-hued petals, rise barely 12 in. above the rigid, spine-tipped leaves. The name *brevifolia* refers to the fact that its leaves are relatively short (for a yucca) — only about 1 ft long.
Mojave Yucca (Spanish Bayonet). Although it is usually 6 ft or more in height, the Mojave yucca, *Y. schidigera,* never quite becomes a tree. The threadlike splinters that peel away from the margins of its 2-ft-long leaves clearly identify this species. In several areas of the Mojave Desert this and the Joshua tree are found growing together, particularly in parts of Joshua Tree National Monument.
Chaparral Yucca. These yuccas are not considered desert plants, but they do creep out into the desert from the San Bernardino Mtns and elsewhere, sometimes mingling with the two species already mentioned. *Y. whipplei* has long, slender leaves growing from its base and forming rosettes. The flower displays are strikingly handsome and often are up to 10 ft high. It takes the flower stalk about three months to mature; you can see the growing spikes in late winter — they look like giant asparagus stalks.
Banana Yucca. A blue-gray yucca found only in the higher desert areas in east San Bernardino County, *Y. baccata* forms somewhat circular patches of several dozen individuals, called clones, which sometimes

cover an area the size of a house. Its long leaves have splinters along their margins much like those of the Mojave yucca; the flower clusters usually don't rise above the leaves.

PALM FAMILY (ARECACEAE). The palm family is a tropical plant group of great economic importance. It is found in the equatorial zones throughout the world. Fiber and building materials (particularly thatch), along with several kinds of food and beverage, come from palms. The products we are most familiar with are probably coconuts and dates.

Palm seeds have a sweet coating surrounding a dense, round seed. Many animals are fond of this coating, so the seeds are well dispersed. Coyotes probably do the major part of the dispersing work, leaving seed-filled droppings throughout their large territories. Birds also help disperse the seeds, particularly those birds related to thrushes—bluebirds, mockingbirds, thrashers, and robins. Interestingly, birds regurgitate the naked seeds after digesting the sweet outer layer rather than passing them through their whole digestive tract as mammals do.

Desert (California) Fan Palm. Only one species of palm, *Washingtonia filifera,* is native to California. In its natural habitat it is confined to desert oases. (These are places that originate from fault zones where subterranean water is forced up to the surface.) So popular is this particular species that for every tree occurring naturally, there are at least one thousand trees planted in southern California.

Mexican Fan Palm. We often see this tall, slender palm (*W. robusta*) in roadside and highway plantings. It is closely related to the desert (California) fan palm, but is native to northern Baja California.

Dicots

Dicots are flowering plants having seeds that fall into two pieces, net-veined leaves, and flower parts usually in fours and fives.

OAK (BEECH) FAMILY (FAGACEAE).
Scrub (Turbinella) Oak. Oaks are not thought of as desert plants; however, there is a small, shrublike evergreen scrub oak—*Quercus turbinella*—that moves out into very dry areas. You usually find this scrub oak variety among the pinyons and junipers on the slopes of high desert mountains. Because oaks are highly variable, the exact taxonomic position of this species is disputed at present.

WILLOW AND COTTONWOOD FAMILY (SALICACEAE).
Slender Willow. Although willows are not desert plants, there is one species—*Salix exigua*—that can tolerate the harsh conditions of the desert and grow to a height of about 10 ft if it is next to permanent water. The slender willow's silhouette is not very willowlike, but the tree has the typical male and female catkins of the genus. The reddish roots you may see in the open water of a desert stream usually belong to the willow.

Fremont Cottonwood. The only other genus of this family found in the California desert is *Populus,* the cottonwood; specifically, *P. fremontii,*

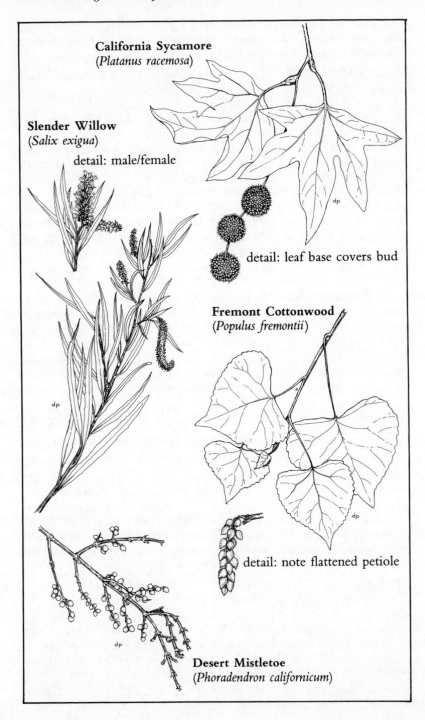

California Sycamore
(*Platanus racemosa*)

Slender Willow
(*Salix exigua*)

detail: male/female

detail: leaf base covers bud

Fremont Cottonwood
(*Populus fremontii*)

detail: note flattened petiole

Desert Mistletoe
(*Phoradendron californicum*)

the Fremont cottonwood, named in honor of Captain John C. Fremont. (In the mid-1800s Fremont made extensive collections of plants during his expeditions to what is now California.) This tree also needs to reach down into the water table, although it is somewhat less demanding of water than the willow.

This giant tree (it is often 70 or more ft high) produces male and female catkins similar to those of the willows, but much larger. This short-lived tree is the home of many birds and the feeding station for many insects. Its wood even supports many boring beetles. Obviously, the cottonwood is an important link in the complex ecological chain of California desert life. (The well-known quaking aspen, which is not found in the desert, is of the same genus as the cottonwood.)

SYCAMORE FAMILY (PLATANACEAE).
California Sycamore. The irregular trunk and peeling bark of this familiar and grand tree, *Aegeria mellinipennis,* are well known to most of us. (The eastern and oriental sycamores have straight trunks.) The California sycamore's shiny, whitish trunk and enlarged limbs have a darkened and rough surface when infested with the bark-boring larvae of a clear-winged moth, the western sycamore borer. Infestation by the larvae is confined to the bark on the lower portion of the tree's trunk.

When identifying this tree, examine a fallen leaf for a conical hole at its base. While the leaf is still on the tree, the bud of next year's leaf develops in this special structure. When the leaves fall in autumn, they leave behind the large dormant bud, which is easily seen. Look for the California sycamore in watercourses and other desert riparian areas.

MISTLETOE FAMILY (LORANTHACEAE). All mistletoes disperse their seeds similarly, in that they are usually eaten by birds. The seeds pass through the bird's digestive system without damage and are then deposited on twigs in the bird's droppings. Although several species of birds help disperse the seeds, the familiar phainopepla is the main broadcaster.

Desert Mistletoe. This mistletoe looks quite different from the kind used at Christmas. It is leafless, having densely grouped slender twigs fruiting with white berries that are pink on one side. The desert mistletoe, like other mistletoes, is a parasite; it must have a host plant to survive. This species—*Phoradendron californica*—preys almost entirely on the pea family, particularly the mesquite and screwbean. A mesquite shrub or tree full of mistletoe clumps is quite conspicuous. It seems amazing that the mesquite can survive such heavy infestation, but when you examine the victim (the host plant) closely you'll see that much of the mistletoe is dead. Mistletoe also attacks palo verde, catclaw, and desert ironwood trees.

Pine Mistletoe. This mistletoe—*Arceuthobium divaricatum*—is quite different from the variety described above. Rather than having viscous fruit like *P. californica,* it has inconspicuous, top-shaped fruit that disperses the seeds by explosively squirting them into the air. The twigs of the pine mistletoe are short, leafless, and often yellowish. This species is common in pine forests and is the only species of mistletoe that follows the pinyon out onto the desert.

SPINACH (GOOSEFOOT) FAMILY (CHENOPODIACEAE). The spinach (goosefoot) family is well represented in most deserts over the world. It is especially prominent in areas of high salinity. Some well-known members of this family are such crops as beets, sugar beets, chard, and spinach. Several other members are found in the California desert.

Saltbush. Various saltbushes belong to the genus *Atriplex;* a dozen or more species are found in the California desert. These hardy plants can grow in strongly alkaline, salty soil.

Desert Holly. The clean-looking, silvery, holly-shaped leaves make it easy to recognize this small, attractive bush. You can find desert holly (*A. hymenelytra*) in most parts of the California desert, though usually not in extensive stands like some other saltbushes.

Tumbleweed (Russian Thistle). This all too well known vagrant— *Salsola iberica*—calls attention to itself when it piles up against fences in the wake of autumn winds. (By the way, these pesky, prickly plants aren't thistles, but an aggressive weed that was accidentally let loose in the United States in the early 1800s.) Tumbleweeds are densest in disturbed soils; they cannot get a strong foothold in undisturbed natural areas because the native *Atriplex* and other similar plants dominate. Certain land management techniques that result in disrupting the fragile plant communities of the California desert regions have unnecessarily enlarged the tumbleweed's range.

Greasewood. Sarcobatus vermiculatus, commonly known as greasewood, is found mostly in the higher desert areas. In the Owens Valley, for example, it is very prominent and ranges east into Nevada, Utah, and elsewhere. When identifying the plant, look for its elongated, wormlike, male catkins (*vermiculatus* means "wormlike").

Spiny Hop-Sage. In the upper Mojave region of the California desert the spiny hop-sage— *Grayia spinosa*—is found throughout much of the desert scrub. This plant looks quite like an *Atriplex,* but differs slightly in the form of its fruit. In general, the genus *Atriplex* appears grayish, and *Grayia* is a more vivid green.

Winter Fat. Sprinkled through the same environment as *Grayia* and *Atriplex* is a beautiful little gray-white shrub called winter fat— *Euratia lanata.* This attractive plant is often more herbaceous than shrubby; the densely packed silvery heads of its seeds are eye-catching.

Iodine Bush. In the crusty lower deserts, with their crackly, salty surface soils, you can find vast thickets of waist-high, fragile dark shrubs called iodine bushes— *Suaeda fruticosa.* This plant is widely distributed throughout the California desert.

CACTUS FAMILY (CACTACEAE). Members of the cactus family are the most familiar succulents of the drier regions of the Americas; they are mostly confined to the Western Hemisphere. The various cacti readily hybridize, even among species that look remarkably dissimilar. Because hybridization has become an important subject in the western world, the number of described cactus forms is astronomical! Even in the natural world, where one to several species may intermingle their ranges, natural hybrid swarms contribute to the taxonomist's nightmare. Despite this confusion there are still many well-defined cactus species. Because there are many good cactus field guides with excellent illustrations available, only a few of the more prominent cacti of the California desert are described here.

Opuntia. The genus *Opuntia* stands apart from all other cacti in that these cacti have minute bundles of hairlike spines at the bases of their larger spines; these tiny spines are very irritating to the skin (hands off cacti!). The various *Opuntia* species usually reproduce from fallen sections, which are often carried far afield by animals unlucky enough to have come too close.

This genus falls into two natural groups: those cacti having flat stems and those having round stems. In the California desert, the best known of the flat group are the beavertail and prickly pear cacti; the most familiar of the round group is the cholla (*choy*-ya).

Beavertail Cactus. These flat-stemmed cacti are commonly represented in our deserts by one species, *O. basilaris*. This handsome, pink-flowered cactus differs from the other flat-stemmed cacti in that it has no large spines, but only very fine spines.

Silver Cholla and Deerhorn Cholla. These two cacti look much alike and often hybridize. The silver cholla (*O. achinocarpa*) tends to form a single trunk, while the deerhorn cholla (*O. acanthocarpa*) is more sprawly, often forming many branches near the ground. The latter also has less densely clustered spines.

Jumping (Bigelow's) Cholla. This species—*O. bigelovii*—is a single-stemmed cactus that branches only near the top. The very dark trunk makes it easy to tell the jumping cholla from its near relatives. This species rarely produces seeds, so it probably reproduces almost entirely from sections of branches that fall or are knocked off the parent plant. Jumping cholla also form dense colonies; there is an especially attractive colony in Joshua Tree National Monument's Cholla Cactus Garden (there are also many other cholla species in the garden).

Pencil (Darning Needle) Cholla. As you can tell from the common name, this cactus—unlike the other three chollas—has branchlets that are about the diameter of a pencil. The cactus has a profusion of these branchlets, a fact reflected in its scientific name—*O. ramosissima* (very much branched).

The above four round-stemmed *Opuntia* species have rather similar yellowish flowers that are open only in bright sunlight. An interesting feature of the chollas' bushy crown of blooms is that if you run your finger in around the pollen-bearing parts and then observe closely, within a few seconds they will all begin flexing inward.

MISCELLANEOUS CACTI. There are many other genera of cacti; none of them is individually as numerous or diverse as the above. Due to space limitations only two others will be mentioned here.

Barrel Cactus. This well-known cactus — *Ferocactus acanthodes* — has suffered such heavy losses from poaching that only a small fraction of its former population remains in its natural environment. However, now that there are more stringent protective laws, its numbers should begin to increase. It's easy to recognize this thick, squat, nonbranching cactus. Although it is usually not much more than 1 ft tall, older specimens may reach 4 ft or more. Its yellowish flowers form an attractive crown in the spring.

Mamillaria (Nipple) Cacti. There are several species of these very small cacti, which are less than fist size. They have tiny but beautiful flowers of various colors and little finger-shaped red fruit. Some have spines shaped like fishhooks.

BLAZING STAR FAMILY (LOASACEAE).
Sandpaper Plant. These small, woody-based, green-stemmed shrubs (*Petalonyx thurberi*) are covered with short, laid-back spines — even the leaves. The spines give the plant the texture of sandpaper; thus, its name. Found throughout the California desert, the sandpaper plant blooms profusely in summer. Its tiny cream-colored flowers are quite fragrant.

Blazing Star. Several species of *Mentzelia* are found in California's three desert regions. Most of the species are perennial and have conspicuously white stems with striking, bright yellow flowers. Leaves are sometimes hairy, but not stinging. The plants range from 3 in. to a yard in height and bloom from early to midsummer.

Sting Bush (Rock Nettle). This small, rounded shrub (*Eucnide urens*) has oval, gray-green, toothed leaves, well supplied with barbed, stinging hairs. It is found primarily in rocky places in and around Death Valley.

BOXWOOD FAMILY (BUXACEAE).
Jojoba (Goat Nut). No other native plant has attained as much commercial attention as the jojoba (ho-*ho*-ba). A very high quality oil-like wax can be pressed from the mature seeds, which are fingertip-sized, thin-shelled nuts. As a result, in recent years many thousands of acres in the Southwest have been planted with jojoba (*Simmondsia chinensis*); it remains to be seen whether the high profits hoped for will actually materialize.

This shoulder-high shrub has thick, oval leaves and is evergreen. The leaves are opposite each other and dull green; the plant appears quite opaque and dense. Because the jojoba is not a succulent plant it has a remarkable tolerance for dry conditions; it rejuvenates quickly after a soaking rain.

TORCHWOOD FAMILY (BURSERACEAE).
Elephant Tree. These trees are more common in Mexico, their natural home. In the California desert, they are found only in Anza-Borrego Desert State Park, east of San Diego. Visitors to this beautiful desert park soon find out that seeing the interesting elephant tree (*Bursera microphylla*) is a must. Once you see this unusual tree, you'll understand how it came by its common name!

The elephant tree is closely related to the pepper tree, which is so common all over southern California. Note that the elephant tree's leaves and pungent odor are very similar to the pepper tree's.

TAMARISK FAMILY (TAMARICACEAE). This family, although seen in many parts of the California desert, is an introduced one; it comes from the southern Mediterranean area. Only two species are commonly found here.

Salt Cedar. Throughout the Colorado River basin and many other watercourses are found vast thickets of salt cedar (*Tamarix ramosissima*). This small tree or shrub, usually about 9 ft high, displays tiny pale to deep pink flowers that are copious honey producers. The fine twigs bear pointed leaves that are minute and scalelike. At first glance, the tree looks somewhat like a cedar; hence, its common name, salt cedar.

Horticulturally and agriculturally, the salt cedar is considered a weed tree. Unfortunately, its seeds spread readily on the desert winds and put down roots whenever they land near a water source. Salt cedars grow rapidly and often choke out native vegetation, while at the same time they suck up what little natural water there may be in an area. Once they get started, salt cedars can ruin important and beautiful riparian areas in just a few years. To save some of these areas, eradication programs have been instituted in places such as Afton Canyon (Mojave Desert) and Eagle Borax (Death Valley).

Athel. The other member of this family found in the California desert is *Tamarix aphylla*. This species has lost its leaves totally, leaving no more than rings around the twigs—which give the twigs a jointed appearance. Flowers are whitish and inconspicuous, unlike those of the salt cedar.

Like some other salt-tolerant plants, the athel has what are called salt pumps. These are tiny glands in the foliage through which salt is excreted after it has been taken up in large quantities by the tree's roots. In time, the surface soil beneath these trees becomes very salty.

Unlike the salt cedar, this tamarisk does not spread on its own, but is found only where its canes (not its seeds) have been planted; the canes root easily. These trees are used extensively as windbreaks in windy desert areas.

OCOTILLO FAMILY (FOUQUIERIACEAE). Botanically, this group stands alone; all known relatives have long since died out.

Ocotillo. This 10-ft shrub with its bright red flowers does most of its branching from its base, which gives it a characteristic shape. The ocotillo we see in the California desert (*Fouquieria splendens*) has somewhat translucent, scaly bark and produces a fruit that at maturity opens into a three-valved capsule and releases its seeds. When the shrub is growing and elongating at each node, it has normal-looking leaves. These leaves are relatively short-lived; they fall as the soil dries out and water becomes unavailable. Suprisingly, though, the leaf stem and part of the midrib do not drop, but take on the appearance of a large, rigid, slightly curved spine.

When the ocotillo is not growing, soaking rains prompt the production of delicate, bright green leaves in just a few days, particularly in warm weather. These leaves fall from the plant when the earth again dries out. This cycle of leaf production and falling can be as short as a month. Unlike the primary leaves, all that is left after these secondary leaves fall is a minute scar.

This ocotillo is a Colorado Desert species that ranges into Baja California. There are several related species in Baja that, although somewhat different from the species found in the California desert, are readily recognizable as being of the ocotillo family.

CALTROP FAMILY (ZYGOPHYLLACEAE).
Creosote Bush. Everyone has heard of this plant (*Larrea tridentata*), but some are unaware that it has no connection with creosote, a wood preservative most of us are familiar with in connection with telephone poles and railroad ties. It's possible that the common name came about because people thought the plant's odor similar to that of the preservative.

Be that as it may, this good-sized (about 5 ft tall), rather open, light green shrub has the largest biomass of any plant in the Mojave Desert. A striking feature of this plant is the black bands at each node. The bands are a shellaclike secretion produced at least in part by a scale insect. Other interesting structures found on nearly every creosote bush are the round, rough, 1-in. galls that are produced by a gall-forming midge (an insect grouped with flies).

The creosote's distinctive, but pleasant, odor becomes quite noticeable just after a rain. Its five-petaled, half-inch yellow flowers have an interesting way of twisting their petals, giving them a sort of windmill effect. The flowers eventually give way to characteristic fuzzy little ball fruits that break apart at maturity into five wedge-shaped seeds.

Although you usually don't see the creosote bush in the Colorado Desert, it ranges widely—being very common in the Mojave Desert and swinging far south into Mexico and on into Chile.

PEA FAMILY (FABACEAE OR LEGUMINOSAE). The pea family is separated into three groups (tribes): Mimosoideae, senna (Caesalpinoideae), and pea (Faboidae). The chief feature separating these three forms is flower structure.
Mimosoideae Tribe. The flower structures of the three plants described just below are very similar in that all have showy, acacialike catkins; there are petals, but they are obscure.

Mesquite. For the most part, trees in the California desert are of the pea family. Of these several species, mesquite (*Prosopis glandulosa*) is one of the most prominent. The mature pods of the mesquite look like wax beans and were an important food of the California Indians. Overgrazing sometimes produces vast thickets of mesquite (in other areas, overgrazing can produce juniper thickets). However, these thickets are looked upon with favor by those country folks who find them a ready source of energy for cooking and heating.

Screwbean. This tree is *P. glandulosa*'s nearest relative; it is found in areas having a high water table, often growing along with the mesquite. You can tell the screwbean (*P. pubescens*) from its near relative by its shorter leaves, distinctive corkscrew pods, and more erect growth.

Catclaw (Wait-a-Minute Bush). The mesquite's next nearest relative is *Acacia gregii.* This considerably smaller tree (actually more like a bush) is well named: it has curved thorns that catch annoyingly on clothing and are difficult to extricate yourself from. This species is particularly late in producing its spring foliage and may be thought dead because other plants around it are in full bloom.

Senna (Caesalpinoideae) Tribe. The flowers of the two members of this tribe described below both have conspicuous yellow petals.

Palo Verde. Like the rest of the members of this tribe, the palo verde (*Cercidium floridum*) has flowers with conspicuous yellow petals; it is found throughout much of the lower desert. The name *palo verde* — which means "green twig" in Spanish — is apt, for the bark of this tree is an attractive and definite green, making it an easy plant to identify.

Cassia. This is a nearly leafless 2- to 3-ft shrub found in the Mojave Desert. During the spring flowering season, *Cassia armata* shows off vivid yellow flowers, which are very similar to the palo verde's blooms (and more easily examined).

Pea (Faboidae) Tribe. The members of this tribe have sweet pea–like flowers, which have a prominent upper petal, the "banner," and two lower petals fused at their lower margin to form a keel-like structure.

Desert Ironwood. This tree (*Olneya tesota*) has wood so dense it sinks in water. The flowers are a lovely, dusty violet and do not contrast sharply with the grayish leaves. Because flowers and leaves blend well, you usually don't notice a tree is in full bloom unless you are quite close.

Smoke Tree. The best known and largest of the several species of indigo bushes is *Parosela spinosa,* the smoke tree. This nearly leafless tree, with its gray twigs, from a distance indeed looks much like its trunk is surrounded by a smoky haze. Like the desert ironwood, the smoke tree has light blue flowers that contrast only slightly with its twigs and branches.

Indigo Bush. There are several smaller species of smoke tree–like plants that have small intensely blue-violet flowers. These indigo bushes (genus *Parosela*) have small, bright green leaves that contrast sharply with their deep-hued flowers. These are handsome and easily seen plants when in bloom.

Other Members of the Pea Tribe. Also in the pea tribe are countless herbaceous plants such as locoweed, lupine, lotus, etc., which make up a large part of the spring wildflower display.

MALLOW (HOLLYHOCK) FAMILY (MALVACEAE). The mallow family is a very useful one; most people are familiar with at least some of its members — cotton, hibiscus, and okra, for example.

Apricot (Desert) Mallow. The genus *Sphaeralcea* ("globe-shaped") is perhaps the most conspicuous of the mallow family. The desert mallow, one of *Sphaeralcea*'s members, is actually not just a single species, but a complex of several species in this genus. It's easy to recognize this 2-ft-tall, many-branched shrub that seems to like to show off along the disturbed roadsides during the spring and early summer. The mallow's brilliant apricot flowers are eye-catching even at highway speeds.

Rock Hibiscus. Oddly enough, there is a single species of hibiscus in the California desert. This small, inconspicuous shrub (*Hibiscus denudatus*) has yellow leaves and stems covered densely with branching hairs. Its flowers are whitish and about 1 in. across. You can find it in the Colorado Desert, particularly Palm Canyon in Anza-Borrego Desert State Park.

OLIVE FAMILY (OLEACEAE).
Leather-leaved (Arizona) Ash. Although the winged seeds of this tree (*Fraxinus velutina*) certainly do not remind you of an olive, the ash is actually a member of the olive family. The ash only grows in the moister parts of the California desert, usually in streams and canyons; it is found as far east as Utah.

NIGHTSHADE FAMILY (SOLANACEAE). The nightshade family includes such familiar plants as tomatoes, potatoes, peppers, eggplant, and tobacco. If you look closely at the seeds of the several boxthorns, you'll notice that they look like small tomato seeds.

Boxthorn (Thornbush). The boxthorns (genus *Lycium*) are a large group; over one hundred species are found throughout the world. There are about seven species of *Lycium* in the California desert. The most commonly encountered of these boxthorn species are the Anderson thornbush (*L. andersonii*) and the peach-thorn (*L. cooperii*). These thorny shrubs become bare and unattractive during times of summer drought and intense winter cold. In spring of reasonably moist years these waist-high shrubs can readily be identified. Anderson's thornbush is found in both the upper and lower deserts; its fruits are red, buckshot size, and as tasty as they look. The tubular flowers are usually lavender; those of the peach-thorn are white or creamy. The peach-thorn is found primarily in the Mojave Desert; its fruits are larger than the Anderson's, but remain greenish and inedible.

Tree Tobacco. This introduced plant, *Nicotiana glauca,* is established in many parts of the California desert and throughout the world. Its long, yellow, hummingbird-attracting flowers and sprays of drooping fruit make it easily identifiable. Unfortunately, the tree tobacco is a carrier of virus diseases that affect field crops; needless to say, farmers want to get rid of it! There are also two or three species of native wild tobacco. These have ill-smelling leaves and white tubular flowers that may open at sundown.

Western Jimson Weed (Datura). This sprawling, herbaceous native plant has giant, trumpet-shaped white to purplish flowers. You can often see *Datura meteloides* by the roadsides at lower elevations in the California desert; the reddish, prickly fruits are about 1½ in. in diameter. The Cahuilla Indians used this plant as a hallucinogen in some of their initiation rituals. *Note:* all parts of this plant are toxic.

MINT FAMILY (LAMIACEAE OR LABIATAE). Although we usually think of mint as growing in moist places, several members of this family are well adapted to desert conditions. When trying to determine if a plant is a member of this family, remember that all mints have single leaves situated opposite each other, and that most have square stems and are aromatic.

Desert Lavender. This grayish, 6- to 8-ft shrub (*Hyptis emoryi*) is the tallest of the desert mints. The plant is well named because it indeed smells like lavender, an Old World genus (*Lavendula*).

Clusters of the desert lavender's tiny, pale, blue-violet flowers open just before sunup and last but a day. When you look at these flowers closely, you will see that the upper lip stands erect and the lower lip remains folded over the pollen-bearing parts until triggered by a bee. The bee's touch flips the lower lip down, instantly exposing the pistil and four stamens and explosively dusting the under part of the bee with pollen. A nice trick! To actually see this interesting performance, though, you must get up ahead of the early bees; by midmorning nearly all the flowers have been triggered. This particular structure and behavior seem to be unique within the mint family.

Paper Bag Bush. The beautiful flowers of this 4-ft shrub have a white upper lip and a purple lower lip. *Salazaria mexicana*'s somewhat unusual common name, paper bag bush, is based on the plant's special seed-dispersing structure. The small leaves at the base of the plant's flowers enlarge many times during the seed-maturing process; they end up as distinctive round, papery bags. This globose structure breaks free and is rolled along by the winds, dispersing its four little free seeds (nutlets) along the way. At least a few of these little "bags" decorate the bush for a good part of the year, making this an easy plant to identify, despite the fact that it does not have the typical square stem and aromatic foliage that most of the mint family does.

Sage. These plants are of the genus *Salvia,* which is perhaps the biggest genus in the mint family. Every cook knows sage as a seasoning — though this is usually *Salvia officinalis,* an Old World native, rather than any of the many aromatic sages native to North America. Eight species of sage are found in the California desert. (See also *Artemisia*—sage-brush—below.)

Chia. This short, attractive annual (*Salvia columbariae*), with leaves springing from its base and tiered rosettes of tiny, blue-purple flowers, is perhaps the best known of the desert sages. This plant is remarkable for its nutritional value; chia seeds were a staple in the diet of several western Indian tribes. Chia is found up to 7000 ft from the coastal valleys to the higher, drier parts of the desert.

Purple Sage. The shrubby sages are also widespread. The most frequently seen desert species is *Salvia dorii,* sometimes called purple sage. After a rain, this shrub shows off its light blue flowers in tiers.

ACANTHUS FAMILY (ACANTHACEAE). The chiefly tropical acanthus family extends itself into southern California in only one form, the chuparosa. However, several species of the family are well known to the home gardener—for example, shrimp plant, jacobinia, and bear's breech. Some features of the acanthus family's flowers and fruits point to a true relationship with several near families, including the various familiar members of the catalpa family (desert catalpa, Cape honeysuckle, jacaranda, trumpet vine) and the figwort family (monkey flower, penstemon, and even the garden flower, snapdragon).

In general, this family's flowers have their petals fused into a tube. The blooms are produced horizontally, with each flower having an obvious top and bottom. The fruits mature into dry capsules that open by a central slit for seed release. Unlike many other families, the acanths have large seeds (usually four per fruit) rather than many small seeds.

Chuparosa. These 2- to 4-ft bushes (*Beloperone californica*) sometimes look like red mounds, with their profusion of tubular red flowers that catch the eye not only of people but of hummingbirds. The name *chuparosa* is appropriate for this plant, because chuparosa is one of the better-known names for the hummingbird itself (*chupa* means "to suck" in Spanish). In general, red flowers are bird attracters. Surprisingly, this flower is edible: it tastes like cucumber!

CATALPA FAMILY (BIGNONIACEAE).
Desert Catalpa (Desert Willow). This tree is the only member of the tropical catalpa family found in California. Botanists frown on the common name of desert willow because in no way is this plant a willow—it merely has narrow leaves and drooping branches that resemble a willow. Some other well-known members of this family are the various trumpet vines, the jacaranda, the catalpa, and the Cape honeysuckle.

The desert catalpa (*Chilopsis linearis*) grows best in arroyos, although single large specimens occur occasionally in very dry places. The tree's pale pink flowers structurally resemble those of the jacaranda so familiar to southern Californians.

Interestingly, the farther east toward Texas the tree grows, the more vivid and even dark pink its flowers become. The seeds of the desert catalpa are long (about 6 in.), slender, arched, and papery, with hairy margins. You can identify them easily, especially during the winter when the tree is leafless.

SUNFLOWER FAMILY (ASTERACEAE OR COMPOSITAE). Although the sunflower family got started on planet Earth in recent geologic times, few families of higher plants can rival the sunflowers in attractiveness and ubiquitousness. Members of this family are both common and diverse on all major continents. In good spring wildflower years no group lends more color to the scene than the countless annual members of this vast family. Yellow flowers certainly dominate, though creams and whites are not rare. Many forms darken into oranges and on into blues, lavenders, and purples, but true reds are absent.

Wonderful color displays seem to be the rule in this family, but there is an exception: the true ragweeds (*Ambrosiae*). This group has turned its back on beauty and shuns the successful insect-vectoring of pollen its colorful relatives indulge in. Instead, the ragweeds rely on the whimsical winds for dispersal of their copiously produced pollen. Fortunately, the western ragweed species do not seem to be nearly as allergy producing as the ragweed found in the "ragweed belt" stretching across most of the United States. In any case, human hay fever sufferers certainly wish the ragweeds had continued to rely on insects.

Ragweed Tribe. Our deserts commonly support two shrubby members of the ragweed tribe. During flowering time most ragweeds can be recognized by their differing male and female flowers. A dozen or more of male flowers form little pendulous, hemispherical heads that usually rise above the plant in spikelike series. The obscure female flowers are found singly or in small groups in the uppermost angles formed by the plant's leaf stems.

Burroweed. This low, rounded shrub (*Ambrosia dumosa*) covers vast areas of flat and rocky terrain in the Mojave Desert; in some areas it even vies with the creosote bush for dominance. As you might guess, it is a favorite forage plant of burros (and, unfortunately, sheep, too). It's not hard to pick out the usually whitish foliage of burroweed against the shiny green of creosote bushes (burroweed is only green for a short while in spring). This plant produces seeds with a covering of sharp prickles.

Cheese Bush. This somewhat straggly, 3-ft-high bush is found over much of the same range as burroweed, although it does get farther down in the lower desert. Locally, it tends to be densest in dry washes. Like burroweed, cheese bush (*Hymenoclea salsola*) has seeds covered with sharp prickles; on the cheese bush, though, the prickles are modified into wing forms.

Mayweed Tribe. The mayweed tribe can be thought of as the aromatic group of the sunflower family. Like chrysanthemums and chamomile, various members of this tribe's sagebrush-like genus (*Artemisia*) have

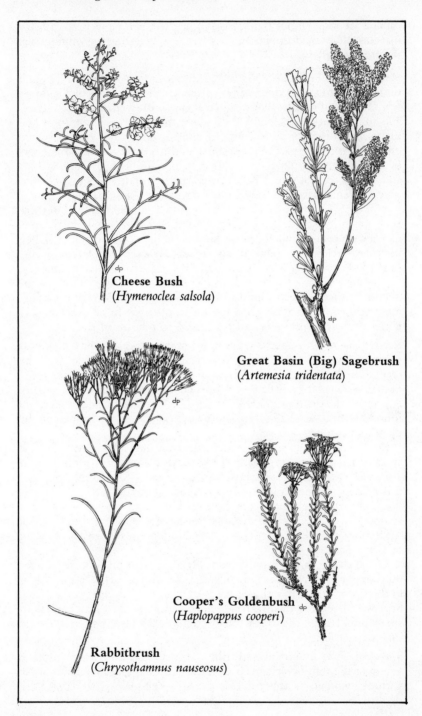

Cheese Bush
(*Hymenoclea salsola*)

Great Basin (Big) Sagebrush
(*Artemesia tridentata*)

Cooper's Goldenbush
(*Haplopappus cooperi*)

Rabbitbrush
(*Chrysothamnus nauseosus*)

strong and distinctly pungent odors when crushed. Note, however, that the word *sage*, used properly, alludes to the genus *Salvia*, a member of the mint family.

Great Basin (Big) Sagebrush. It is rumored that this species, *Artemisia tridentata*, is number one in biomass in the western United States. That is, if you marked off an area from Mexico to Canada and from the Great Basin to the Pacific, then weighed all plants found in that area, this 4- to 5-ft shrub would account for more of the total plant weight than any other! (This would probably still hold true if all the other species were weighed together rather than separately.) Great Basin sagebrush is so adaptable that it even reaches within a few miles of the coast in dry valleys and canyons.

As creosote bush and burroweed do in the southern desert, so does Great Basin sage in the northern deserts — that is, it often stretches as far as the eye can see in nearly pure stands. When you look closely at this bush's silvery leaves, you can see where it got its scientific name: the far end of each leaf is three-toothed — thus, *tridentata*. The leaf is very characteristic and makes the Great Basin sagebrush easy to identify. Don't look for many leaves in late summer, though; by this time they have usually all dropped, making the bush look rather straggly and unattractive.

This sage is another plant the Cahuilla Indians put to good use: they ground the seeds into a nutritious meal and made medicinal teas from the leaves.

Aster Tribe. In the California desert the aster tribe is primarily represented by two similar and hardly distinguishable genera: rabbitbrush (*Chrysothamnus*) and goldenbush (*Haplopappus*). With a few exceptions, most members of this large tribe flower in autumn.

Black-Banded Goldenbush. This 6-ft-tall, straggly, conspicuous shrub is a fall bloomer with yellow flowers. *Haplopappus paniculatus* is found in areas between the low and high desert.

Desert Rock Goldenbush. *H. cuneatus* is a small bush with roundish, bright green leaves and autumn-blooming yellow flowers. Look for it where the common name suggests.

Cooper Goldenbush. In spring, on the Mojave Desert, look for fields of bright yellow flowers made up of these small (1-ft) bushes (*H. cooperi*).

Linear-leaved Goldenbush. *H. linearis* is another spring-blooming member of the aster tribe. Look for a sturdy, roundish bush, 1 to 2 ft tall, with lots of showy yellow flower heads.

Mojave Rubberbrush. The herbage of these plants (*Chrysothamnus nauseosus mojavensis*) supposedly has a high rubber content — therefore, the common name. In autumn, look for a medium-sized, rounded shrub with light gray-green leaves and a profusion of attractive yellow blooms.

Brittlebush. *Encelia farinosa*, a low, hemispherically shaped bush, is widespread in the Mojave Desert. Look for this plant on rocky slopes; in spring, its large, bright yellow, daisylike flowers make a handsome show standing high above the bush's velvety, gray-green leaves.

Mule Fat. Baccharis glutinosa is a willowy bush with hairy, whitish heads found along watercourses.

Everlasting Tribe (Inuliae). Arrowweed. A slender plant with blue-violet flowers, *Pluchea sericea* forms dense thickets in the low, salty Colorado Desert. The tall, straight, 7-ft canes were used by California Indians to make arrow shafts. More recently, the canes have been used as supports for plastic sheeting to cover some of the Coachella Valley's winter vegetable crops.

5

Desert Wildlife

It is easy for those who are unfamiliar with the California desert to perhaps think of it as a kind of giant sandbox for motorcyclists or as a dangerous wasteland to be driven through as quickly as possible. In reality, however, the California desert is not an empty wasteland — instead, it is filled with life!

In the desert lands of California there are over fifty species of mammals, ranging in size from the quarter-ounce bat to the two-hundred-pound desert bighorn sheep. In addition, there are over two hundred species of resident and migrant birds, from the delicate hummingbird to the "tiger of the air," the great horned owl. The California desert regions also have their share of reptiles, from the 4-in. banded gecko to the 6-ft Western diamondback rattlesnake. Added to all these are desert fish such as the pupfish and, of course, thousands of invertebrate species — including creatures such as harvester ants and great hairy (nonpoisonous) scorpions.

Once you have some idea of how many animals (and plants) live and thrive in the California desert, it's easy to see that this desert is far from empty or uninteresting. Rather, it may at first seem that way because its biotic (plant and animal) communities and its climate are unfamiliar. But you'll find that, like many another first impression, the-desert-as-wasteland feeling wears off on closer acquaintance. To help improve that acquaintance, a little background information on a few of the California desert regions' more common inhabitants — those creatures you are most likely to see — is included here.

How Animals Have Adapted to the Desert

Life in the desert is filled with extremes of climate that native species have evolved to meet. On a summer day in the Mojave Desert, the ground surface temperature might soar to 160° F, yet that same area may be blanketed in snow in January! Some areas of the desert are buffeted by almost constant winds, which can dehydrate both animals and plants. The wind also may carry an abrasive load of blowing sand. Some areas, such as the center of a large dune system, seem incapable of supporting any but the smallest plants, which in turn provide very little food for the animals living there.

Perhaps the greatest challenge to desert species is finding and conserving enough moisture to survive. Life in the desert seems to alternate between long periods of extreme drought and violent moments of thunderstorms and flash floods. For an animal or plant to survive on the desert it must be able to adapt to extremes of temperature, desiccating winds, and long periods of drought.

Mammals

The wildlife of California's desert regions has adapted to meet harsh conditions by developing many unusual survival techniques. For example, one of the most fascinating of all desert animals, the kangaroo rat, never takes a drink of water. Instead, this animal lives on water garnered from the dry seeds he eats and the water manufactured within his body during the chemical process of turning food to energy. He is able to survive on this small amount of moisture because his body has evolved to conserve water in many different ways. For instance, the kangaroo rat does not waste water by eliminating great quantities of it in his feces and urine; instead, he concentrates both. Besides producing highly concentrated urine, he has a special chamber in his nasal passage that condenses moisture from the air he exhales and keeps the moisture in his body. Just as important as these physical adaptations is the fact that he is only active at night when it is cooler. During the heat of the day, this small creature is deep underground in a burrow where the temperature seldom rises over 80° F and where the air is more humid.

The two common species of ground squirrel found in the California desert, the antelope ground squirrel and the round-tailed ground squirrel, have evolved very different ways of surviving in the desert. The antelope ground squirrel (which looks like a desert chipmunk) is one of the few desert mammals that is active during the day. This squirrel has evolved to allow his internal body temperature to fluctuate radically. Rather than use precious moisture to cool his body while he is actively searching for seeds and plants to eat on a warm day, he simply allows his internal body temperature to rise up to 110° F. When he gets too warm, he simply retreats into the cooler environment of his burrow and remains there until his body heat is radiated into the cooler soil. Within a few minutes he will be out foraging again.

The round-tailed ground squirrel has quite a different approach to survival in the desert. He is only active in the spring and fall, when temperatures are more moderate and the greatest amount of food is available. During the winter he hibernates deep underground. In spring this squirrel surfaces to feast on flowers and seeds and to find a mate. During the heat of summer he goes into summer hibernation (estivation) and then appears again in the fall to take advantage of plant species that bloom after the summer rains.

Most small desert mammals are active only at night (that is, they are nocturnal). In this way they avoid the high temperatures and desiccating sun of day. Mammals too large to burrow into the ground spend the midday hours in the shade of plants or rock ledges.

Birds

Resident desert birds find much of the moisture they need in the seeds and insects they eat. However, because birds are more mobile than the other members of the animal kingdom, they usually travel at least daily to an open water source to drink. Also, a bird's natural internal body temperature is higher than that of most other animals, making birds somewhat preadapted to the desert's high temperatures.

Reptiles, Amphibians, and Fish

Reptiles—lizards, snakes, and tortoises—are unable to internally regulate their body temperature. Nonetheless, like all animal species, they have to maintain certain optimum body temperatures to function. Most lizards are active during the day, moving in and out of the sun to adjust their body temperature. Nocturnal species of lizards use heat radiating out of rocks warmed during the day by the sun. The majority of desert snakes are nocturnal and so avoid the lethal heat of midday.

During the winter most reptiles sensibly hibernate. The main reason for this behavior probably has to do with the fact that the cool days and cold nights of winter make snakes, tortoises, and the larger species of lizards sluggish, unsuccessful hunters. Why? Because they can't regulate their body temperatures, which become too low for efficient activity.

Although several common species of frogs and toads are found along the Colorado River, there are only two species of toads (and none of frogs) that are actually adapted to desert life and that can live away from the river. One of these is the tiny (3-in.) red-spotted toad, which can be found near permanent springs and seeps—usually in canyons. Fortunately for this small toad, as the wetter days of the past slowly disappeared, it developed a very useful water storage system. Now, when water is unavailable, the red-spotted toad can reabsorb its own urine. The other desert-adapted toad, Couch's spadefoot toad, evolved an equally clever, though quite different way of dealing with heat and lack of water. The spadefoot has a sort of extra "toe" on each of its hind feet; this protuberance makes it a very efficient digger and allows the toad to bury itself deep in the sand, where it is cooler and damper. The spadefoot is usually found only in the California desert's Colorado (Sonoran) region.

There are only a very few remnant fish populations in the California desert regions. The most famous of these populations, the pupfish, are found in and near Death Valley. These tiny fish, some only a little longer than a dime is wide, are thought to be leftovers from a Pleistocene river system. Surprisingly, they have adapted so well to desert life that they are able to live quite successfully in the waters of hot springs that are over 90° F!

Invertebrates

Of all the invertebrates found in the California desert regions, insects are the largest group. Because most insects look quite fragile, visitors are often surprised to find a great variety of these interesting creatures in almost every part of the desert. This is due to the fact that insects, like all other desert animals, have managed to develop some very ingenious adaptations that allow them to live successfully in the wide variety of desert biotic communities.

One of the ways some desert insects survive the seasonal heat and dryness when food and water are short is by retreating into a kind of suspended animation, or sleep, called estivation. Moths and butterflies seem particularly fond of escaping to this state, into which they may retire for months—or even years—until more beneficial conditions return. Other insects have evolved mechanisms allowing them to exist on dry food and without water for months at a time. Most of these creatures do not lose water from their body surfaces; in fact, they may even save water by excreting uric acid in a solid state rather than passing it as liquid. And when conditions are too harsh for some adult insects, they carry on with the business of life by leaving behind a considerable number of eggs. Many insect eggs, in the fashion of many plant seeds, are well adapted for surviving extremes of heat and cold, wind and water—while waiting for more favorable conditions in which to continue their life cycles.

One of the insects nearly every desert visitor comes across at one time or another is the Eleodes beetle, commonly known as tumblebug or circus bug (from its habit of standing on its head). These shiny, black, olive-shaped beetles seem to break almost all the rules of successful desert adaptation. They are black, which not only makes them easy to see just about anywhere but also means they absorb heat easily. If these beetles were nocturnal, this would make some sense—but they aren't; indeed, they are as active during the heat of the day as they are at night! They manage to not only survive, but flourish, by munching bits of organic matter that take up moisture when dew forms.

Ants are another highly successful form of desert insect life. The most numerous species are, not surprisingly, those that live on the desert's most reliable form of food: seeds. These ants extract the water they need from seeds and insects (some don't even mind preying on their fellows). Nests of the various kinds of harvester ants are easily found almost anywhere in the desert; just look for the circles of rejected seed hulls ringing the entrances to their tunnels.

There are also quite a few desert invertebrates that are not insects, and among these there are a fair number of interesting and successful spiders. Many spiders — for example, the harmless, if hairy, tarantula — deal with the heat by finding themselves a nice, cool tunnel into the cooler regions of the ground. During more temperate weather, it's fun to see how many different kinds of ingeniously constructed spider webs, pouches, and egg cases you can find in the vegetation.

One kind of invertebrate you probably wouldn't expect to find in the desert is a snail. Expectations notwithstanding, however, there are snails in the desert. These little vegetarians are left over from wetter times and now spend most of their lives resting under rocks, waiting for the rains. They manage to survive the heat and dryness by secreting a thick substance that becomes a tough membrane closing the opening into their shell. Look for them in the mornings and evenings during the wet season.

Animal Distribution

Within the 25 million acres of California desert lands each of the many plant and animal species attempts to live where conditions are most favorable to it. The rocky faces of the hillsides, the boulders and coarse soil of the alluvial plains, the gravel of the wash beds, and the fine, shifting sands of the dunes are all different habitats, each supporting special groups of plants and animals known as biotic communities.

But what determines the kinds of plants and animals living in these different habitats? Well, water — its availability and amount — is perhaps the primary determiner of plant and, thus, animal life. (No plants = no animals — that's the way the food chain works.) Soil composition is also very important; it controls where a desert plant may grow. In turn, soil texture determines how much moisture is available for vegetation and how long it will be available. Altitude and range of temperature are also elements determining who and what lives in each community.

The three California desert regions each have their own unique combination of determiners — amount of water, temperature range, altitude, topography, soil types, and so on. This means that each region also has its own unique set of environments, which in turn produce characteristic plant and animal communities.

THE COLORADO (SONORAN) DESERT. Going south from the Mojave Desert, elevations begin to drop, and the climate becomes even warmer and drier as you come into the low desert—the Colorado (Sonoran) Desert. In the Coachella Valley and the Imperial Valley (which borders on Mexico), rainfall is usually less than 5 in. a year and summer temperatures can routinely reach 115° F—and higher. Here, even in winter, it seldom freezes and even more rarely snows.

In the center of the Colorado Desert is a large, alkaline lake known as the Salton Sea, which—at 274 ft below sea level—is the second-lowest place in the United States. This lake was created in the early 1900s when the Colorado River flooded, followed irrigation channels into the Imperial Valley (rather than its normal route out to the Gulf of California), and partially filled an ancient lake bed. The reeds and marshes surrounding the Salton Sea provide yet another kind of habitat, one supporting an incredible variety of waterfowl that are either residents or migrate into the area along the Pacific Flyway. Here, in winter, you can see water birds such as the great blue heron, Canada goose, and green-winged teal.

THE MOJAVE DESERT. While most of the Mojave Desert lies at elevations between 2000 and 5000 ft, one section—known worldwide as Death Valley—contains the lowest point in the United States: 282 ft below sea level. On the floor of Death Valley and the surrounding hills are many species of plants and animals found only there. It is almost as if the Death Valley area is a land island. Interestingly enough, despite Death Valley's extremes of temperature and funereal name, several hundred species of animals are seen in and around it—including three hundred species of birds! Most of the Mojave gets only 1.5–5 in. of rain a year, which is not surprising considering that it lies in the rain shadow of several mountain ranges bounding it on the west and south.

The Mojave Desert's higher elevation and more northerly location—as compared with the Colorado Desert—also mean that you can expect snowfall several times in any winter and that summer temperatures rarely exceed 110° F. Although the Mojave is not as high as much of the Great Basin Desert region, the parts of it that are 3500–4000 ft and over are thought of as being high-desert country.

THE GREAT BASIN DESERT. The Great Basin Desert, the northernmost of the California desert regions, is just as different from the Mojave and the Colorado deserts as they are from each other. The Great Basin is the "cold desert" or the "high desert." Most of this region is above 4000 ft (some of its mountains are well over 10,000 ft), and its winters are long, cold, and snowy. Most of the Great Basin lies outside California; this small part of California is liberally sprinkled with alkaline lakes (mostly dry) and high mountain ranges (there are quite a few peaks over 10,000 ft in elevation). Despite its seemingly inhospitable environment, this scenic region is home to many well-adapted animals such as the sage grouse, whose spectacular courtship rites include a booming serenade!

Desert Habitats

WASHES. An example of a habitat is a wash—a watercourse that is usually dry. Many moisture-loving trees and shrubs thrive in wash beds because more water is received and retained there. Due to the extra moisture available, wash beds support a denser concentration of plants than any other desert habitat except an oasis. The large variety of plants in the wash provide food and shelter to a great number of animals—including many small rodents, reptiles, and birds. A quiet and patient observer will be able to see mice and ground squirrels foraging for seeds and fruits, and perhaps even gopher snakes, red racers, zebra-tailed lizards, or other reptilian predators hunting for small mammals. Somewhat easier to see are the yellow verdins, fast-moving hummingbirds, and other bird species that find food and nesting sites in the trees.

MOUNTAINSIDES. The high, rocky hillsides of desert mountains provide quite different living conditions than do the more well-watered gravels of the wash beds, with their dense plant communities. There are certain animal species that prefer living among the rocks on the hillsides—including the pack rat and the largest lizard in the California deserts, the chuckwalla. The chuckwalla uses crevices in rocks to escape extreme temperatures and predators. Slipping deep into the crevice, he then inflates his body until he is impossible to dislodge. Pack rats also use the rock crevices as bases for their fortresses of sticks and parts of cacti that form a protective mound for their nests.

ALLUVIAL PLAINS. Pack rats are also common on the alluvial plains (often called bajadas), where they build their nesting mounds out of cholla joints they pile up at the base of spiny ocotillos or other large shrubs or cacti. Alluvial plains are created by the action of water carrying debris out of the mouths of canyons. As water rushes down the canyon it picks up large boulders as well as smaller rocks and silt. Then, as the water empties out onto the plain, it slows and deposits its load of rocks, creating broad, sloping fans of rocks and boulders.

Many alluvial plains support dense stands of cacti, such as teddy bear cholla, as well as ocotillo and other shrubs. Collared lizards can be found basking on the boulders and hunting for small lizards and insects to eat. Well-vegetated alluvial plains can support a great variety of animals—including mice, rabbits, antelope ground squirrels, coyotes, gray foxes, cactus wrens, thrashers, and many reptiles.

CANYONS AND RIPARIAN AREAS. Large alluvial fans are formed at the mouths of all major canyons; however, once you move into the canyon itself, you are in quite a different habitat. The canyon floor may be scoured clean of almost all vegetation by frequent floodwaters or, if conditions are right, there may be dense thickets of mesquite, cottonwoods, willow, and even native desert (California) fan palms. The vegetation, the shade created by high canyon walls, and the movement of cooler air down from the higher reaches of the canyon make living conditions in the canyon less extreme than on the open plains and slopes. Many canyons have permanent sources of open water such as springs, intermittent streams, and natural rock basins that collect and hold flood- and rainwater. These permanent and intermittent water sources help create riparian areas — small, lush environments (sometimes called oases) in the midst of the desert.

Many species of animals make these canyons their home. Ring-tailed cats (which are related to raccoons, not cats) forage along the canyon walls for insects, small reptiles, and anything else they can overpower. Several species of bats roost in rock crevices, and bighorn sheep move in and out of the canyons to drink. If there are open pools or seeps on the canyon floor there are sure to be toads, tree frogs, and perhaps the rare desert slender salamander.

DUNES. The rolling dunes covering about 3% of California's desert lands provide a very different habitat from the relatively cool and moist canyons. Wind is responsible for the creation of sand dunes. Fast-moving winds pick up and carry fine grains of sand for long distances. As the wind strikes small hills or plants and begins to lose velocity, it drops its load of sand and a dune begins to form.

Surprisingly, the dry-looking dunes actually act like huge sponges. Under their windblown exterior they soak up and hold water. As a result, most dunes have grasses and other plants growing high up on their sides. At the base of dunes, in the sheet sand areas, mesquite and creosote collect little individual sand piles in their wind shadows. These minidunes are full of burrows of the animals that feed on the plants. Notice how much lusher plant life is in these sandy areas as compared to bare soil!

Despite the dunes' water-holding ability, life there is difficult. Animals and plants must be able to tolerate being dessicated by the winds as well as being abraded by the blowing sand. Only on the fringes of large dune systems can shrubs like creosote bush and burroweed survive. Yet there are several species of animals that prefer the dune habitat. Fringe-toed lizards and shovel-nosed snakes are well adapted to life in wind-blown sand. The shovel-nose, with its countersunk lower jaw and smooth scales, can move effortlessly through the sand searching for in-sects to eat. The long, traction-producing scales on the toes of the fringe-toe are just one of its many adaptations to life in the dunes. Sidewinders (rattlesnakes), pocket mice, kangaroo rats, and kit foxes are some of the other species inhabiting the dune environment.

Some Desert Animals You May See

You'll notice immediately that the selected list of birds found in Califor-nia's desert regions, though very brief, is considerably longer than the ones for reptiles, amphibians, fish, and invertebrates. The reason for this, as you may already have guessed, is that birds are more visible than most desert creatures. A great many species of invertebrates, for example, are not only tiny and well camouflaged, but spend most (if not all) of their lives underground, under rocks, under bark, under leaves, in flowers, and so on. All of which makes them not very easy to see, however interesting they may be. Despite the fact that, for the most part, the ubiquitous invertebrates—which include spiders, moths, butterflies, ants, bees, and many more very tiny creatures—must be sought out, they still seem to have many fans (including, perhaps, your own children).

Many of the mammals and reptiles are not only exceedingly shy, but are most active at night—which makes them not very seeable, despite their size (which is large compared to that of most invertebrates). The reptiles that are active both day and night are really the only desert creatures that approach the birds in visibility. This fact probably explains why lizard watching is nearly as popular a pastime as birdwatching in California's desert regions.

The lists of common amphibians and fish you may see in California desert areas are the shortest of all, because deserts provide few optimal habitats for these creatures. Those that do manage to live in the desert have adapted their life cycles to the lack of water in some very ingenious ways.

As there are many fine animal guides readily available, the various short lists are only included to jog your memory, spark your interest, and give you a small idea of the fine wildlife-watching possibilities in the California desert. See the "Recommended Reading" appendix for good field guides to help you identify the animals you actually do see in the desert. Be forewarned, though, that wildlife watching (and study) can be addicting. Once you've acquired the habit, you may find that trips to the library and bookstore begin to produce field guides in addition to the latest bestseller!

Mammals

Because our desert mammals are very shy—and primarily active at night—most of them are difficult to observe. An exception is the frisky antelope ground squirrel, the chipmunk of the desert. Although you can't get close to these speedy little creatures, you'll often see them whisking about their business of seed gathering just beyond camera range. If the weather isn't too hot, you may also catch a glimpse of some of the other numerous seed-eaters of the desert. Interestingly, about two-thirds of the California desert's mammalian species are mice and rats—rodents. These small, burrowing animals are for the most part seed-eaters, although some relish a nice juicy insect when they can get it. Because most of these dainty, large-eyed, nighttime seed-eaters aren't dependent on the usual sources of water for their moisture (some even manufacture their own water), they are among the most successfully adapted desert dwellers. Even if you never actually see most of them, it's easy to keep track of many of their nocturnal activities. Look for the footprints and lacily traced paths left behind from their many midnight passages in search of seeds.

As for the larger mammals, the coyote—though just as shy a night hunter as most of the rest of the desert mammals—is rather conspicuous because of its size. And this, of course, means you have a better chance of seeing one if it happens to be loping about in the daytime (which is not uncommon). And, if you're a hardy and observant hiker of certain of the California desert's mountain ranges, you may be so lucky as to see a desert bighorn sheep in the distance.

SOME MAMMALS OF CALIFORNIA'S DESERT REGIONS.
Antelope ground squirrel (*Ammospermophilus leucurus*)
Badger (*Taxidea taxus*)
Black-tailed jackrabbit (*Lepus californicus*)
Bobcat (*Lynx rufus*)
Coyote (*Canis latrans*)
Desert bighorn sheep (*Ovis cremnobates*)
Desert kangaroo rat (*Dipodomys deserti*)
Kit fox (*Vulpes macrotis*)
Mule deer (*Odocoileus hemionus eremicus*)
Ring-tailed cat (*Bassariscus astutus*)
Round-tailed ground squirrel (*Citellus tereticaudus*)
Western pipistrelle bat (*Pipistrellus hesperus*)
White-footed (deer) mouse (*Peromyscus* spp.)
Wood rat (*Neotoma lepida*)

Birds

The birds you see in the various desert regions change with the seasons. In spring many birds migrate north from the Southern Hemisphere, while in fall the reverse is true. So, at these times of the year, you can see many migrants, birds that do not live in the desert all year, but are just passing through. Some of these birds that come south in fall stay the winter (as do many people). This means that not all birds you see in the desert are necessarily resident desert birds—that is, birds that live there all year. In fact, some are passing through, some are seasonal residents, and some are even all-year residents. Your field guide will give you info on bird residential status.

A handy hint—with the exception of owls and a few other species, birds are most active in the daytime, with the prime times for bird viewing being early morning and late afternoon. A few of the birds you are most likely to see in the California desert are listed below; you are probably already familiar with at least some of them.

SOME BIRDS OF CALIFORNIA'S DESERT REGIONS
Black-chinned hummingbird (*Archilochus alexandri*)
Black-tailed gnatcatcher (*Polioptila melanura*)
Black-throated sparrow (*Amphispiza bilineata*)
Brown towhee (*Pipilo fuscus*)
Burrowing owl (*Athene cunicularia*)
Cactus wren (*Campylorhynchus brunneicapillus*)
Costa's hummingbird (*Calypte costae*)
Gambel's quail (*Callipepla gambelii*)
Golden eagle (*Aquila chrysaetos*)
Great horned owl (*Bubo virginianus*)
Ladder-backed woodpecker (*Picoides scalaris*)
Le Conte's thrasher (*Toxostoma lecontei*)
Loggerhead shrike (*Lanius ludovicianus*)
Mourning dove (*Zenaia macroura*)
Phainopepla (*Phainopepla nitens*)
Red-tailed hawk (*Buteo jamaicensis*)
Roadrunner (*Geococcyx californianus*)
Rock wren (*Salpinctes obsoletus*)
Sage grouse (*Centrocercus urophasianus*)
Sage sparrow (*Amphispiza belli*)
Scott's oriole (*Icterus parisorum*)
Scrub jay (*Aphelocoma coerulescens*)
Sparrow hawk (American kestrel) (*Falco sparverius*)
Turkey vulture (*Cathartes aura*)
Verdin (*Auriparus flaviceps*)
White-crowned sparrow (*Zonotrichia leucophrys*)

Reptiles, Amphibians, and Fish

Snakes and lizards—reptiles—are probably the most visible animals in the California desert (next to birds), partly because many of them are active both day and night. Lizards come in a bewildering variety of sizes, stripes, blotches, and colors; fortunately for the novice creature-identifier, though, their shapes are similar. Some lizards are seen pretty frequently, but are not always easy to identify—mainly because once they notice you they are off like a shot. If you're in the mood for lizard watching, moving slowly and quietly, then staying still for a while to observe will allow you to catch these desert animals in the act of being themselves.

There are many kinds of snakes in California's desert regions, but the ones desert visitors are likely to see are not as various or as numerous as lizards. Popular opinion to the contrary, it is always a real treat to get a glimpse of a snake—even if it is a rattler! (As long as you keep your distance, rattlers are nothing to worry about—and they are very handsome creatures.) Aside from the several species of rattlers found in the California desert, all other snakes found there are completely harmless if left alone—which, of course, they should be.

If you were to hold a desert reptile popularity contest, the winner would probably be the desert tortoise. These dignified, slow-moving creatures are found in several areas of California's desert regions. Unfortunately, careless drivers—both on- and off-road—have reduced desert tortoise populations considerably, as have those thoughtless folks who carry them home for pets. Although these large tortoises look indestructible, they are actually quite sensitive to human interference. Never attempt to tease or play with a tortoise; watch them quietly from a distance. If you disturb them, they may void the water they have stored against drought. Spring is the best time to observe tortoises; when the grasses and flowers are out, it's not unusual to find them munching contentedly away, their mouths and noses smeared stickily with bright yellow pollen. Tortoises are definitely one of the desert's most unforgettable sights.

There are several species of frogs and toads inhabiting the California desert, its mountain islands, and the date groves of the Coachella Valley. They are seldom seen, but their mating calls are often heard by people camping near water. Most of them are not really desert animals and are restricted to permanent or semipermanent water, including irrigated areas. There are only two genuine desert amphibians: the red-spotted toad and Couch's spadefoot toad.

Fish, of course, are the least numerous of all these groups, and are to be seen only in a very few California desert places. The few minnowlike species that have survived both the change of climate and destruction by humans now primarily live in very specialized habitats near Death Valley. Although this area is not exactly the place you'd expect to find fish, their presence there makes more sense when you consider that these desert fish are actually leftovers from cooler, wetter times of long ago. In those times—10,000 to 75,000 years ago—Death Valley was "Lake Manly," a body of water 600 ft deep and over 100 mi long that was the end of a chain of lakes fed by waters coming from as far away as the Owens Valley and the San Bernardino Mtns!

Below is a starter list covering some of the reptiles, amphibians, and fish you might be likely to see in the California desert—or that you might hope to see.

REPTILES
Lizards
Banded gecko (*Coleonyx variegatus*)
Chuckwalla (*Sauromalus obesus*)
Desert iguana (*Dipsosaurus dorsalis*)
Desert night lizard (*Xantusia vigilis*)
Fringe-toed lizard (*Uma* spp.)

Horned lizard (*Phrynosoma* spp.)
Side-blotched (brown-shouldered) lizard (*Uta stansburiana elegans*)
Whiptailed lizard (*Cnemidophorus tigris*)
Zebra-tailed lizard (*Callisaurus draconoides*)

Snakes
Desert rosy boa (*Lichanura trivirgata gracia*)
Gopher snake (*Pituophis catenifer deserticola*)
King snake (common) (*Lampropeltis getulus*)
Mojave rattlesnake (*Crotalus scutulatus*)
Sidewinder (horned rattler) (*Crotalus cerastes*)
Western (desert) diamondback (*Crotalus atrox*)
Speckled rattlesnake (*Crotalus mitchelli*)
Red diamond rattlesnake (*Crotalus ruber*)
Red racer ("coachwhip") (*Coluber flagellum*)
Western shovel-nosed snake (*Chionactis occipitalis*)
Striped racer (*Coluber taeniatus*)

Other Reptiles
Desert tortoise (*Gopherus agassizi*)

AMPHIBIANS AND FISH
Amphibians
Red-spotted toad (*Bufo punctatus*)
Spadefoot toad (Couch's) (*Scaphiopus couchii*)

Fish
Mojave chub (*Siphateles mohavensis*)
Pupfish (*Cyprinodon* spp.)

Invertebrates

The number of insects and other invertebrates in California's desert regions (as elsewhere) is very great. Unfortunately, most desert visitors tend to think only of the possibly dangerous species and do not pay any attention to the many other interesting and harmless "bugs." Of course, it is only sensible to be wary of a possibly dangerous creature such as the black widow spider, but it's not necessary to so generalize this wariness that you avoid all the other remarkable insects found in the desert—the other 99%. (True "bugs," by the way, are those creatures living on plant juices or the blood of animals.)

It's hard to know where to begin and end a brief list when the number of species is so great. To keep the list down to the handful there is space for, only a few of the more conspicuous invertebrates are mentioned.

INVERTEBRATES
Spiders and Their Relatives
Black widow (*Latrodectus mactans*)
Great hairy scorpion (*Hadrurus arizonensis*)
Labyrinth spider

Sun spider (*Erembates* spp.)
Tarantula (*Aphonopelma chalcodes*)
Wolf spider (*Lycosa* spp.)

Insects
Carpenter bee (*Xylocopa* spp.)
Desert termite (*Amitermes* spp.)
Harvester ant (*Messor* spp., *Pogonomyrmex* spp.)
Silver-spotted grasshopper (*Bootettix argentatus*)
Tarantula hawk (*Sphecius* spp.)
Tumblebug (circus bug, Eleodes beetle) (*Eleodes* spp.)
Velvet ant (*Dasymutilla* spp.)
Walking stick (*Timema* spp.)

6

Desert Survival

Emergencies can happen wherever you are—including the desert. In the city you usually have easy access to medical attention, vehicle repair facilities, food and water supplies, and so on. In the desert, this is often not the case. You may be many miles from nowhere when you run out of water, gas, food, or fan belts. This means that you should go to the desert prepared to meet possible crises as well as to enjoy yourself.

Planning Ahead

Any desert outing requires preplanning. It's just not smart to hop into the car with a candy bar and a soft drink and head for the wide open desert spaces. Even one-day trips to the desert should be undertaken with the help of a carefully thought out checklist. Grocery stores, gas stations, shade, and water are often in short supply among the oases, mountains, dunes, and bajadas. In other words, it can't be emphasized too often or too strongly that you are very much on your own in the desert. Keep this in mind whenever you're preparing for a desert trip.

The next chapter will give you some ideas on basic gear needed for car touring, day hiking, car camping, and backpacking. From these suggestions you can start your own checklists for the activities that interest you. Your lists will change with the season and your own interests and experience. Remember, the suggestions are not intended to be exhaustive, but only to cover most of the basics.

In the present chapter you'll find another list of basics, this one having to do with your vehicle. In addition, you'll find out a little about how to recognize, treat, and avoid a few of the more common hot-weather health hazards. Finally, there'll be some advice on plants and animals to watch out for in the desert.

This is a very important chapter. You could even say it concerns not just matters of comfort, but matters of life and death—specifically, your own! It is not intended to be a survival manual, a substitute for first aid training, or a course in auto mechanics, but only to offer some commonsense actions you can take to help prevent serious trouble from developing. This kind of preplanning will do much to ensure that your desert outing is both enjoyable and safe. See the "Recommended Reading" appendix for survival texts.

It goes without saying that everyone, not only desert travelers, should have some kind of first aid training. In addition, an American Red Cross first aid book, or at least a sheet of their emergency instructions, should be carried in every first aid kit (see Chapter 7 for first aid kit list).

Your Vehicle and the Desert

Preparing Your Vehicle

To be ready for the most common vehicle emergencies and breakdowns in the desert, check your vehicle over and make sure of the following before you leave.

1. Battery is strong, with terminals clean and cables tight; water is at appropriate level.
2. Cooling system works well; radiator has good hoses and is filled (coolant helps prevent overheating).
3. Fuel tank does not leak; tank is filled (try to keep it at least half full).
4. Transmission and crankcase are filled to proper levels.
5. There are no oil, gas, transmission, water, or air leaks.
6. Tires are in good condition and appropriately inflated (for whatever load you'll be carrying).
7. Vehicle has been recently lubricated.
8. Spare tire is in good condition and properly inflated.
9. Brake fluid reservoir is full (carry an extra can of brake fluid).

What to Take

To help you deal with the most common breakdowns in the desert, you might consider bringing along the items below. *Note:* all liquids should be in appropriate containers — never in glass! (Glass can break on rough roads.)

1. Sturdy, easy-to-use jack (and a 1-ft square piece of 1-in. plywood to put it on in soft sand or mud).
2. Extra fan belt and radiator hoses (even if there is a garage fairly nearby, they probably don't have the kind you need).
3. A set of jumper cables.
4. Several quarts of oil and opener.
5. Emergency flares.
6. Five gallons of water for the vehicle only.

7. Five extra gallons of gas.
8. A basic tool kit: pliers, large and small screwdrivers (Phillips head and regular), set of open-end wrenches, crescent wrench, wire cutters, small hatchet, tire iron, lug wrench, small hammer, bailing wire, electrical tape, duct tape, extra flashlight and batteries, siphon, cake of soap or cork (to plug pan punctures), air pressure gauge, funnel, vise-grip.
9. Spare set of keys.
10. Tire pump (heavy duty).
11. Fire extinguisher.
12. Spare fuses.
13. Gloves.
14. Radiator "stop leak."
15. Extra can of brake fluid.
16. Fix-a-flat air and sealant (good for thorn punctures).

But vehicle emergencies aren't limited to breakdowns; sometimes you get bogged down in sand, rocks, mud, or even snow. You'll probably find the following items helpful in getting you and your vehicle unbogged.

1. Tow chain or 50 ft of ¾-in. nylon rope.
2. Four 12-in. × 48-in. × ¾-in. pieces of plywood (for traction in getting out of sand, etc.) and/or four pieces of heavy old carpet (also 1 ft × 4 ft), chicken wire, or whatever; the plywood or carpet can be used as a floor in your vehicle's trunk or elsewhere.
3. Small shovel.

Desert Driving

For access to favorite desert haunts, desert buffs often rely on dirt roads left by mining and grazing operations. These roads usually haven't been maintained in years. Even experienced and well-prepared desert drivers occasionally grumble and sweat their way along these often-unpredictable roads, but on arrival at that secluded canyon are grateful for the solitude.

Proper preparation for desert driving begins with using a vehicle with better-than-average ground clearance, the widest tire option readily available, and premium-quality tires. For safe desert driving, your vehicle must be in good condition—as noted above. For desert breakdowns or emergencies, you may need any or all of the items mentioned above. To avoid damaging your vehicle or getting stuck in sand, soft dirt, mud, or on high-centered rocks or ruts far away from the main roads, you'll need to learn a few new driving techniques. Here are the most commonly used ones.

1. *Use Established Roads or Jeep Trails.* Going off-road damages the desert irreparably, as you can easily see when you examine the ugly ruts and erosion left by off-road-vehicle use. A single vehicle, driving once over

an area, can leave tracks that last for several decades or much longer, depending on the area! It is our responsibility to leave the desert as untouched as possible for those who come after us.

2. *Do Not Travel Alone.* Whenever you leave main roads, it's a good idea to travel in company with another vehicle, piloted by folks who have desert experience (if you do not). Next best is an experienced companion.

3. *Drive Slowly and Carefully on Rough Roads.* Aside from the maintained paved roads, you should count on averaging only about 30 mph while touring the desert. Keep this in mind when estimating how long it will take you to get from point A to point B. It's no fun to retrace your steps in unfamiliar territory after dark—or to set up camp then. It's a temptation to speed along at 40 mph on washboard roads (this makes them feel less bumpy than they do at 20 mph), but you sacrifice a lot of control for the comfort—you may find yourself flying off a curve quite unexpectedly, or hitting a washout that may put you completely out of control!

4. *Do Not Tailgate.* It's difficult to see road hazards when another vehicle is directly in front of you. Depending on your vehicle, you may need to take a run at some sand traps to get through, or you may need to detour around an obstacle (if you just do what the driver in front does, you may find yourself stuck or hung up).

5. *Check the Road Ahead for Common Hazards.* Never assume that because there is no sand trap under your wheels at the moment there is not going to be any. If the road looks questionable, get out and reconnoiter a bit. And while you're at it, have a look at the scenery—maybe even take a photo or look at a bird with your binoculars. But don't neglect to look for the hazards—for example, the following few:

Soft Road Shoulders. These can be a problem when you want to pull off or turn around. It takes less time in the long run if you back and fill a bit rather than taking a chance on getting stuck by swinging wide.

Sand. Sand probably accounts for more stuck vehicles than any other hazard. Shift into a lower gear before you enter a sandy wash; try to keep up your momentum as you go through, even if it means bouncing. Sometimes you can gain enough momentum to carry you across a small sandpit. Sometimes you can go around a short stretch of deep sand. Sometimes you have to change your plans.

The wider your tire, the better chance you have of getting through sand traps. Deflating your tires to as low as 12 to 18 pounds per square inch can also increase their surface area enough to get you out of or through soft spots. (You did bring the tire pump to reinflate them with, didn't you?)

If you do get stuck, do not gun the motor or spin your wheels. This will only dig you in deeper. Stop as soon as you lose traction. Putting your vehicle into reverse can sometimes get you out of a soft spot. Another technique that can sometimes extricate you is to alternately shift from low forward to reverse and back again, causing a rocking motion.

If none of these techniques works, and a little judicious shoveling and pushing doesn't work either, get out the jack. Jack up the drive wheels one by one (put jack on board), put boards or whatever under the wheels for traction, and either back out (if road looks just as bad ahead) or go forward, slowly – a little pushing won't hurt at this point, either. It helps to have companions! If this still doesn't work, unload the vehicle as much as possible, let some air out of the tires, and repeat.

When all else fails – or even before, if you're lucky – get someone to pull you out with tow rope or chain (properly attached to firm points on both vehicles). Don't let the rescuer get stuck, too!

Rocks and High Centers. When it looks like you may really get hung up, and you can't get around the obstacle, you'll probably have to spend some time building up or whittling down your chosen route of travel with rocks, earth, etc. If this isn't feasible, retrace your steps and change your route.

Steep and Side-slanting Roads. Know your own skills and your vehicle's capabilities. Don't take chances. Better to take your time or change your route than to slide or roll out of control to the bottom of a steep incline.

6. *Take Advantage of the Wind.* In warm weather, a tail wind can cause your vehicle to overheat if you're climbing a long or steep slope. If this happens, head the engine into the wind and keep the motor idling; this should help cool it down. If your vehicle is prone to vapor lock in warm weather, about the only thing you can do is wait for the engine to cool. A wet cloth wrapped around the fuel pump (with hood left up) can hasten the process.

How Your Vehicle Can Save Your Life

Even the most well prepared and experienced desert travelers can find themselves in serious trouble, so it's a good idea to think about how to handle such situations before they occur. If you follow the general suggestions in this chapter and in Chapter 7, you will be well prepared to meet most desert emergencies – including being really stranded.

If, then, for some unforeseen reason, your vehicle isn't going to move, period, what do you do? Most experienced desert people agree that what you shouldn't do is leave your vehicle. An exception, of course, is if you are just a short distance from certain help (say, 1–2 mi from a settlement or well-used road). Unless you are in a very out-of-the-way place, someone will probably come by long before you have exhausted your supplies of food and water.

Your vehicle itself is full of useful survival materials. For example, the average radiator holds six to twenty-one quarts of water. If there is no antifreeze or other additive in the radiator, that's enough water to last four people for four days. Hubcaps polished with sand can be used for signal mirrors. The honk of a horn carries as much as a mile. A quart of engine oil burned in a hubcap can make a smoke signal visible for miles. A sealed-beam headlight can be removed and used as a signal beam at night.

In short, don't panic. If your car breaks down in a remote area, stay with it. Use your imagination to make it a lifesaver. And even if you are in a truly far out area, those folks you left your itinerary with will soon have people looking for you—in the right places—if you don't return when you said you would. Far better to spend some time contemplating the desert from the safety of your vehicle than to risk heat exhaustion or being lost on foot.

Hot-Weather Hazards

No matter how hardy you are, no one is totally immune to heat exhaustion, heat stroke, sunburn, or dehydration. Fortunately, all it takes to avoid these miseries is common sense. If you are not used to exerting yourself in hot weather, you need to be extra careful at first. This means not doing too much, too soon. As with altitude, heat takes some getting used to. It's not always possible to spend several days becoming heat adapted—so if you aren't, don't try to keep up with those who are already adapted.

No matter how heat adapted you are, adequate water intake is a must. This could mean taking in a gallon or more of liquid each day if the weather is very hot or you are exerting yourself heavily. Even minimum activity in hot weather requires several quarts a day. Plain water is more thirst quenching than sweet drinks.

In addition, the salts you are sweating off need to be replaced—not just sodium (as in table salt), but equivalent quantities of potassium and magnesium. If you have chosen your foods carefully, salt replacement shouldn't be a problem. Some people, though, find buffered multi-mineral tablets very helpful (these should include approximately equal amounts of the minerals mentioned above and should be taken with a pint of water). Others feel that this supplementation is unnecessary. You might try both ways and see what works best for you.

Hiking in the hottest part of the day is not a good idea. This is a good time to relax in the shade and contemplate the view, drink water, chat with friends, or take a siesta. When you are in the sun, stay well covered with light-colored, lightweight cotton clothing, wear your wide-brimmed hat (plus sun lotion), and keep your water bottle close at hand. Keeping covered like this has been proven to slow down water loss caused by sweating and to help protect the body from heat gain by insulating it.

Following these suggestions will help keep your body's heat-regulating mechanism from overworking. This mechanism, though flexible, has rather narrow limits; it can stand only so much stress before it malfunctions. So, treat it with the respect it deserves and pay attention to its signals. Don't try to prove how much heat you can take—it isn't worth it. Anyone who's suffered from heat stroke, heat exhaustion, severe sunburn, or dehydration can tell you this.

HEAT EXHAUSTION. Heat exhaustion is the most common heat misery. However, if you pay attention to its warning signals, it need not be a dangerous one. Whenever your skin feels cool, clammy, and sweaty—and perhaps you are a bit nauseated or faint—*immediately stop exerting yourself*. Rest in the shade (lie down if possible), drink water, and do nothing until you feel better. Heat exhaustion is caused by the blood being directed away from the brain to the skin, accompanied by excessive sweating and loss of salts and water. After you've recovered, you can go on with what you were doing—if you take it a bit easier for a while.

HEAT STROKE. Heat stroke is a medical emergency; it can be fatal. Luckily, it is difficult to confuse heat stroke with heat exhaustion (which is much more common). A heat stroke victim will have hot, red, dry skin; he or she may be delirious or irrational. Early symptoms are dry mouth, headache, nausea, and dizziness. With heat stroke, the sweat glands shut down temporarily; when this happens, the body is no longer cooled by evaporation, and body temperature rises to dangerous heights. If it rises high enough (105° F or above), the brain's temperature-regulating mechanism may be permanently damaged.

When heat stroke is suspected, it is imperative to *lower body temperature*. Immerse the victim in water if possible; if this can't be done, put the person in the shade, cover with wet cloths (keep changing them), or massage arms and legs gently to increase blood flow and heat loss (keep head higher than body). *Do not give aspirin;* it interferes with the body's temperature control mechanisms.

A heat stroke sufferer should rest until feeling well again, then be accompanied home (taking the return trip in easy stages). The person should not try to complete the trip!

SUNBURN. As most of us know only too well, sunburn is caused by ultraviolet rays. When these rays are reflected from light-colored rocks and sand, their effect is greater than under ordinary conditions. You may have heard that a light overcast or even moderately cloudy skies do not necessarily protect you from these rays—and indeed this is correct! What will protect you are sunscreen lotion (see Chapter 7), wide-brimmed hat, and loose, light cotton clothing (long sleeves and trousers).

DEHYDRATION. The hotter it gets and the more you exert yourself, the greater the danger of depleting your body's water to a dangerous degree. Walking on the flat when the temperature is 100° F can cause you to lose a quart of water per hour. When resting in the shade, you'd lose only about a cup per hour (that's still six quarts a day). After losing only about 5% of your body's weight in water, you'll probably feel exhausted; at about 12% loss, body fluids become so thick that circulation is slowed and body temperature rises to a life-threatening level. You can guess the rest. Just mild dehydration can cause serious kidney problems and even permanent damage.

A warning that serious dehydration may be on the way is darkening urine. If you notice this, or if the call of nature is infrequent, increase your water intake immediately. During warm-weather hikes you may need a couple of quarts an hour to stay safely hydrated.

It makes good sense, then, to drink—even if you don't feel thirsty. The body's thirst-signaling mechanism lags behind the body's need for water; the amount it lags varies from person to person. You can't go wrong by taking a drink every half hour (at least eight ounces); more often is fine, too. After a few trips in warm weather you'll be able to gauge your needs fairly well. It's amazing how much more you enjoy yourself in the heat when you are well hydrated.

Plants and Animals to Watch Out For

The desert has the reputation of being full of dangerous and aggressive plants and animals that spend their lives lurking about, waiting to spring on the unwary traveler. It isn't so. The only time you will run into trouble is if you unnecessarily interfere with the natural course of desert plant and animal life. Learning who and what to watch out for and what to do in case of a painful encounter will do away with much of your uneasiness.

BLACK WIDOW SPIDERS. Black widows are fairly common, nonaggressive, and very poisonous spiders. The ½-in. female is easy to recognize—her abdomen is globular and shiny black, with a red hourglass shape underneath. The males are much smaller and quite nondescript looking. They are brown, have white lines on their sides, no hourglass, and are much less venomous. You'll probably see more black widows around your house and garage than you will in the California desert, but they are there.

To avoid the black widow, take considerable care when poking around shady, protected rock piles or old abandoned buildings. The spiders can be found even in wide open places—particularly during and shortly after a rain, when you may see them scuttling along near small animal burrows where they have taken up residence.

What to Do in Case of Black Widow Spider Bite. Though the fangs of this spider are sometimes too short to puncture human skin, don't count on it. Ounce for ounce the black widow's poison is much more potent than that of the rattlesnake. The effects of a black widow bite are immediate and always serious; they can be fatal, particularly to the very young or those in precarious health.

At first the bite is like a sharp pinprick, but within hours the pain can become severe. "Cut and suck" doesn't work for a spider bite. Your best bet is to first apply cold to the bite (and/or a constricting band, as for rattlesnake bite) to slow the spread of venom; then take the time between prick and pain to find medical help.

BURROS. Though not a native of the California desert, the now-wild (feral) burro has made itself at home in some of the desert's more mountainous areas. Standing about 4 ft at the shoulder, burros weigh from three hundred to five hundred pounds. They have excellent hearing, a good sense of smell, and fairly good eyesight. These qualities, combined with a strong territorial instinct and a willingness to fight for their territory, make the burro an animal to be reckoned with.

If while hiking you encounter a jack (male) burro snorting warnings, your best bet is to walk away slowly, making sure the burro realizes you are not threatening him. However cute they look, never allow a jack to get close enough to whirl and kick with those back feet! When given their rights, most burros are quite docile.

At night, take care not to bed down on top of a burro trail. Keep your food and all your gear together and be prepared to issue dire threats if one wanders into your camp. Yelling will usually discourage the camp moocher. Again, no matter how cute they are, never feed a burro — you will just create a demanding pest.

CACTI. Most cacti present little problem to the desert explorer. Some, though, have definitely earned their place in the ornery category. Chollas are beautiful cacti that often grow in thick stands. Some uncommon species are over 8 ft tall. The blooms produce only sterile seeds; propagation is by detached fleshy joints that seem to almost jump off the plant to root in the ground. (Thus the name *jumping cholla*.)

When you brush against one of these plants or detached joints, it will probably "jump" onto your clothes or shoes. To avoid having your fingers speared by the spines, do not use them to remove the stickery joints. Instead, use a comb, stick, or even a fork to flick the branch off. Then remove any remaining spines with tweezers or needle-nosed pliers.

Cacti in the prickly pear group (beavertail cacti) have large, pancake-like pads; often these pads grow close to the ground. More than one hiker has fallen into or over this cactus. Unfortunately, prickly pear cacti have many groups of tiny, stickery hairs. These hairlike stickers break off in your skin and are almost impossible to remove. They can cause considerable irritation until they finally wear away.

The only way to avoid painful encounters with cacti is to treat all of them with great respect!

CENTIPEDES. The centipede is a segmented, wormlike-looking creature with fifteen or more pairs of legs. These insect hunters are fast on their many feet. The species found in the California desert are yellowish to dark brown; they can be tiny or up to 6 in. long. The first pair of appendages behind the head are like claws and act as poison jaws. Centipedes can be found in rotting wood, around decaying buildings, and under rocks. As with black widows and scorpions, watch out when you are looking under things, and don't put your hands or nether regions anyplace unless you know it is unoccupied.

The centipede's bite is usually only painful, rather than being a medical emergency. Clean the wound thoroughly and use cold packs for the pain. Medical aid is occasionally required.

Millipedes are harmless centipede look-alikes with two pairs of legs on each round body joint. Centipedes have only one pair of legs on each joint; their bodies are flattish.

RATTLESNAKES. The deserts of the world have their fair share of poisonous snakes—enough to make most people wary. Also, most of us don't know the difference between a harmless snake and a poisonous one. So, rather than flaying the bushes with your hiking staff, trying to kill off every slithery thing that moves, you need to learn how to recognize the snakes you may come across in areas of the desert you visit.

In the California desert, the rattler is the only poisonous snake. The markings, colors, and temperaments of these rattlers vary, but all have diamond-shaped heads and rattles on the end of their tail. A good field guide will be of great help in sorting them out (see the "Recommended Reading" appendix). Not all rattlers buzz their rattles in warning, though; in some areas all the buzzers have been killed off, leaving only the silent rattlers.

During warm weather, snakes are more often seen in the cooler hours of early morning and around dusk. In cool weather, they are often out during the warmer daylight hours. Snakes are cold-blooded; that is, they do not have a temperature-regulating mechanism. Thus, they move between warm and cool areas to maintain a comfortable body temperature.

In general, rattlers move slowly (unlike some other snakes). When disturbed, they may buzz their rattles and coil to strike. They can only strike about half their body length and about a foot off the ground; they cannot jump.

To avoid being surprised by a rattler, take care to put your hands, feet, and posterior down only in places you can clearly see are unoccupied. When hiking, do not place your hands or feet on rock ledges you cannot see. Before jumping over or down from a rock, check the ground where you want to land. Keep an eye on shady areas under bushes as you walk along.

If, despite these precautions, someone is bitten by an unknown snake (most snakes are not rattlers), it will not be difficult to tell whether the snake was venomous. If it was a rattler, discoloration, swelling, and intense pain occur within ten minutes at the site of the bite. Treatment must start immediately.

What to Do in Case of Rattlesnake Bite. The bitten person should lie down at once, in the shade if possible, with the wound site lower than the heart. Next, a constricting band (not a tourniquet) should be placed between the bite and the heart and 2 to 4 in. away from the wound. This band is intended only to restrict the flow of lymph (and venom) near the skin, not to restrict blood flow. Check to make sure there is a pulse below the band. Keep moving the band to stay ahead of the swelling. Cold packs, if available, help greatly in slowing the spread of venom.

If you are near a vehicle, take the person to the nearest medical facility as soon as possible. If a vehicle is some distance away, send someone for medical help. In the meantime, keep the bitten person quiet, cool, and well-hydrated. Give water or dilute juice; *do not* give coffee, tea, alcohol, or painkillers.

If it will be more than a few hours before medical help can be reached, some of the venom can be removed using the "cut and suck" method — very carefully. To do this, sterilize the single-edged razor blade from a snakebite kit (use a match or disinfectant) and cut through the bite marks lengthwise relative to bones, arteries, and veins. Do not make cuts more than ¼ in. deep and ½ in. long. Make the cuts ooze freely (the fluid should be mostly lymph, not blood) by using the suction cup from the kit or your mouth (as long as you do not have any open lesions in it). If you use your mouth, spit after each suction. Loosen the band if suction does not draw out any fluid.

Antivenin is available and works well, but must be refrigerated to retain potency. Also, most antivenins are horse serums; some people are so violently allergic to these serums that they can go into shock and die within minutes. Because of this allergy problem (which can be tested for on the spot) — and because it has to be injected — antivenin should be administered only by trained people.

SCORPIONS. These nocturnal, eight-legged relatives of the spider range in size from 4 in. down to less than 2 in. In Arizona there are a couple of quite small species whose sting can be fatal, particularly to children or those in precarious health. The scorpions of the California desert usually have only mildly poisonous stings. Suprisingly, the largest scorpions are usually the least poisonous.

All scorpions sting with their tail, which they usually hold high and curved over their back. They are ordinarily not aggressive and only use their sting in a reflex action when they feel threatened. To avoid disturbing them, take care when turning over stones and logs, don't leave your clothes or supplies lying around on the ground, and shake out your boots and shoes before putting them on.

Scorpions are most active at night, when they foray out from their hiding places to hunt for food. Don't forget to use a strong flashlight when taking that last walk into the bushes before bedding down. Speaking of the latter, this is where a cot comes in handy if you like sleeping out under the stars. With a cot, you don't have to worry about unwelcome guests sharing your sleeping bag. Keep your campsite free of food crumbs; these attract the insects that are food for the scorpions.

If someone does get stung by a scorpion, cold packs help ease the pain and slow the spread of venom. This venom is neurotoxic and so may cause numbness and tingling in addition to pain, swelling, and heat.

SPANISH BAYONET. This spikey plant (also known as Mojave yucca) looks inoffensive until you get close to it. If you get too close, you'll get the "point" of this statement. The needle-sharp points on the tips of this yucca's leaves can do a considerable amount of painful damage to the unwary. This plant truly deserves its name!

TARANTULAS. These fat-bodied, furry spiders, with a leg span of up to 7 in., are easy to identify. Like the scorpions, they hunt at night and are rarely seen in the open during daylight. They favor homes under logs, rocks, and in unoccupied burrows of small animals. Like most other desert creatures, they are gentle and unaggressive; if goaded into defending themselves, their bite is somewhat painful, but not at all dangerous. Cleansing the wound with antiseptic is usually sufficient treatment.

Good Advice

Before Leaving Home, Tell Someone Where You Are Going. It's best to write down all the pertinent information as to your route, where you'll be camping, when you plan to return, and when to notify others that you have not returned on time (perhaps twenty-four hours after you are expected). Make a map if necessary. Then keep to your plan or notify your contact of any changes.

Take an Extra Two Days of Food and Water. Whenever you are planning a trip to a desert area that is off the beaten track, it's an excellent safety precaution to have along some emergency rations. People have been known to break an axle far, far, far from the nearest garage. A couple of days' rations will see you through until help happens by or a rescue party gets to you.

Be Observant When Traveling on Unfamiliar Roads. Check your topo or road map often. If the roads do not conform to the map or do not appear on them, carefully mark their actual place on the map. It sometimes helps to write down this information, too—including landmarks. After a while, desert roads can all begin to look the same.

Stay with Your Vehicle If It Breaks Down for Good. The exception to this rule is if you know that help is just a short distance away. Otherwise, you will be better off waiting (with your food and water) for help to appear. Even if no one comes by, you'll be rescued in good time if you took care to tell someone where to look before you left home.

7

Seeing the Desert by Foot and Car

Basic Gear for Desert Outings

What you need for the various kinds of desert outings (or, for that matter, outings in the mountains, seashore, or plains) falls pretty much into three categories—necessary, useful, and enjoyment-enhancing. The list of basics given here applies to any desert trip. This does not mean that you need to take all the items on every trip, but only that you may find most of them useful at some time. Water and the famous "ten essentials," however, should go along on all trips.

Necessary Items

TEN ESSENTIALS. Experienced outdoor people agree that there are certain items you should take along whenever you venture beyond the end of the road. (Actually, it seems a good idea to take them even on a car tour in the desert.) In an emergency these essentials could save your life. Of course, there are lots of other items each of us considers essential—for example, the most common "eleventh essential" is toilet paper! Here, however, are the standard ten:

To find your way	map of the area
	compass
	flashlight
For your protection	sunglasses
	extra food and water
	extra clothing
For emergencies	waterproofed matches
	candle or fuel tablets
	pocketknife
	first aid kit

1. *Map.* If you are going to be car touring only, you'll need a good California state map and appropriate county maps. (State maps show only the main roads.) The Automobile Club of Southern California (commonly known as AAA—Triple A) puts out good Imperial, Riverside, Kern, Los Angeles, and San Bernardino county maps. As yet, an Inyo County map is not available, but the AAA Death Valley map covers much of this county. If you are going to be day hiking or backpacking, you'll need United States Geological Survey (USGS) topographic maps for your specific area.

2. *Compass.* If you are never going to be off a main road, you will usually not need a compass. You should have one, though, as soon as you start doing even short day hikes, traveling desert back roads, or exploring roads that do not show on your maps. Compasses that are liquid damped and have a straight edge for map orientation seem most convenient for general use.

It's a good idea to attach your compass to a cord and wear it around your neck or attached to your belt. Even if you plan on staying within sight of your car you should get into the habit of carrying a compass. Always take a sighting from your camp or vehicle before leaving on a hike (see "Finding Your Car After Hiking," below, for details). The desert isn't as flat as it sometimes seems to be. Once you've gone over a couple of slight rises and around some rocks, things look pretty much the same. It is easy to become disoriented—an uncomfortable feeling, to say the least—and not all that difficult to get lost.

3. *Flashlight.* This is an emergency tool; maintain it with that in mind. Choose one with a switch that's not easy to turn on accidentally (for obvious reasons), or store it with batteries reversed. Carry extra batteries and bulb.

4. *Sunglasses.* These are a must. Sunglasses should block ultraviolet light and be polarized to cut glare. In addition to keeping the sun's rays from damaging your eyes, sunglasses protect your eyes from flying insects, dust, sand, and bush or tree backlash.

5. *Extra Food and Water.* Put extra food in a special container and keep it separate from your regular food supply. This emergency food should keep well and not take up much room; high-energy fruit bars and high-protein candy bars are suitable. Extra water means carrying about half again as much water as you think you'll need.

6. *Extra Clothing.* Something warm, something windproof, and something waterproof qualify. Many people find that a wool shirt, a nylon windbreaker, and an el cheapo rainjacket work fine.

Wool Shirt or Sweater. A medium-weight wool shirt or sweater, combined with a windbreaker, will probably keep most people warm enough on a cool evening or on a peak in spring or fall. In winter, you may need something a bit heavier.

Windbreaker. Wind is a fairly constant desert feature, so a windbreaker is always a good idea, even in hot weather. The nylon kind that has a hood and folds down into its own pocket makes a nice, compact package to slip into your day pack or backpack.

Rainjacket. Yes, it does rain in the desert, especially in winter. This rain is likely to be accompanied by that ever-present wind. A raincoat or rainjacket works better than a floppy poncho that bares your bottom half and catches on everything stickery.

7. *Waterproofed Matches.* Like extra food, these should also be carried away from your regular supplies. Waterproof your own with melted paraffin (or buy them that way), then put them in a waterproof container.

8. *Candle or Fuel Tablets.* These emergency wood-fire starters are not needed nearly as often in the desert as they are in the mountains or on the coast. However, as mentioned before, it does rain and get cold in the desert.

9. *Pocketknife.* Everyone needs to have this necessary, all-round tool. Even the fairly elaborate versions (Swiss Army knives) that provide can opener, scissors, corkscrew, tweezers, screwdriver, and awl are not all that expensive. Put the knife on a long nylon cord, then attach same to your belt or belt loop and put it in a convenient pocket. Pocketknives have a way of getting separated from their owners—with the knife winding up several miles away, up a looooong hill (at the lunch stop, perhaps).

10. *First Aid Kit.* When you need it—and even car tourers do—this is the most important essential. There are prepackaged kits of varying complexities and qualities on the market; check the contents carefully before purchasing. Most people eventually develop their own home-made kit—which needn't be extensive, but should cover personal needs adequately.

A useful all-purpose kit could consist of: large adhesive bandages; paper adhesive tape; several 2 × 3 Telfa sterile dressings; 2-in. roll of gauze; moleskin (blisters happen in the desert, too); elastic bandage; acetaminophen or aspirin; small scissors; tweezers (tapered to point); safety pins; needle threaded with heavy-duty nylon thread; antiseptic (Betadine or Zephirin type); insect repellent (50%–95% N,N,diethyl-meta-tolumide—DEET); snakebite kit (there is now some argument about the effectiveness of these—in any case, bring it only if you know how to use it); any personal medications; and an American Red Cross sheet of emergency instructions. Wrap tablets in plastic wrap; take small quantities of antiseptic, etc. Put everything into a small, waterproof container.

WATER. One gallon per person per day is a must. Never, never forget water when going on any desert trek! A one-quart water bottle is handy for carrying with you when you leave your vehicle.

FOOD. Keep it simple. In hot weather, avoid foods that may melt or spoil quickly. If preparing food outdoors is not one of your favorite activities, try bringing foods that require little or no preparation. Fresh foods, especially fruits and vegetables, are usually more appealing than canned or dried, though the latter do have their convenient place. The shorter the trip, the greater the proportion of fresh foods can be.

HAT. Take a hat that allows some air circulation between your sweaty skull and the hat top. The hat should have a brim wide enough to shade your face and neck (don't forget that the back of your neck needs protection, too). In warm weather, straw hats without sweatbands are the coolest and airiest. To keep your hat secured in the most capricious of winds, slip a sturdy leather or nylon thong or bootlace around the crown, push it through the brim, and fasten it under your chin. If you are addicted to the baseball cap, add some foreign-legion-style drapery to protect your neck.

LONG-SLEEVED SHIRT. This is another sun buffer. The shirt protects against too much sun or that breeze that's just a bit too cool. One hundred percent cotton is best in warm weather. One of the many advantages of cotton clothing is its ability to hold moisture for a while and thus act as an air conditioner (evaporative cooling type). If, and only if, you have plenty of water, pour some on your shirt; the cooling effect is immediate and wonderful.

WARM JACKET. It also gets cold in the desert, so for nights—except in summer in the low desert—you will need a warm jacket (or at least a heavy wool shirt) and possibly a wool hat and gloves. Remember that the desert is a land of contrast; the day and night temperature difference is often very great.

Useful Items

Walking Shoes or Hiking Boots. If you'll be doing most of your walking on trails or dirt roads, good tennis or running shoes will serve. (Sandals are not appropriate, even around camp—as people who have stubbed their toes on a cactus in the dark can attest.) Those who sometimes climb hills and wander off the beaten path may want to consider sturdy leather walking shoes or light hiking boots. The hardy peak-scrambler and heavy-duty cross-country hiker will need a medium- or heavy-weight pair of hiking boots.

Shoes and boots for desert walking and hiking should be sturdy and well ventilated. The combination of heat, sand, and perspiration can cause some pretty uncomfortable problems. For example, if your shoes have too-thin soles and the weather is hot, you'll probably find yourself with several painful blisters. For walking on sand or gravel, flat-soled boots or shoes work better than heavy mountaineering boots. For wading up canyons with streams, take along a pair of tennis shoes in addition to your regular shoes or boots. For peak scrambling and some other strenuous rock-related activities, lug-soled boots give good protection. Rock-climbers sometimes use specialized footgear designed just for climbing.

Before buying any hiking boots, do some research—ask friends about theirs, read magazine equipment reviews, and check out some of the sources in the "Recommended Reading" appendix. Boots are an important and often-expensive purchase.

Sunscreen. If you have sensitive or very fair skin, go for the high sun protection factor (SPF) rating; 15 provides the most protection. Remember, though, that some people's skin does not tolerate the higher-rated sunscreens; test your choice out before the outing. Also, many of the strong sunscreens can stain clothing; check the label. A rating of 6–10 is usually adequate for most people who are not terribly fair skinned. Don't forget sunscreen lip balm as well as lotion (same rating advice)—it's good for ears and nose as well as lips.

Enjoyment-enhancing Items

Binoculars. These are really a must if you are intent on seeing everything possible. No one wants to miss a closeup view of a rare bighorn sheep perched high on a craggy ridge. In fact, watching soaring hawks, fast-leaping jackrabbits, and feeding hummingbirds with the aid of magnification makes a desert trip all that more exciting and personal.

Camera. Photo equipment is indispensable for recording desert scenes in all their living detail. Be careful not to leave the camera in a hot car or in the sun; protect the lens from blowing sand and dirt.

Desert Information. If you are going to the desert for a specific purpose—such as hiking, petroglyph visiting, animal watching, or flower viewing—you'll probably enjoy your visit more if you bone up a bit beforehand. Your local library will have information on most desert subjects. After a couple of trips to the desert, you may want to buy a field guide or two. The Audubon, Golden, and Peterson field guide series are all excellent and well worth their price in the years of enjoyment they provide. These books cover identification of minerals, birds, mammals, reptiles, flowers, insects, animal tracks, trees, and several other subjects. See the "Recommended Reading" appendix.

Car Touring—It's for Everyone

There are two general types of car touring—organized group tours and informal self/family/friends tours. The first begins with a good leader. Tours can last an afternoon, a weekend, a week, a month, or even longer. A car tour lasting more than a day may involve car camping (or staying in motels); some tours include day hiking. Whether your trip is short or long, organized or informal, care in planning can make the difference between an enlightening and enjoyable trip and a less-than-satisfactory one.

Organized Group Tours

As a rule, group tours have a specific theme or objective. For example, the leader may key on gem or mineral collecting, fossil hunting, following an earthquake fault, birdwatching, or studying petroglyphs. Visiting ghost towns or gem and mineral areas is another activity many people enjoy. Or perhaps your group might want to learn the names of desert plants and find out why they grow where they do.

Whatever the reason for the trip, careful planning is needed to make it a success. Many groups have found that the best way to ensure careful and coordinated planning is to have one person do all the organizing — i.e., the administrative work. Another person may be responsible for scouting the trip — making sure of the route and determining whether the dirt roads and trails are passable. The scout will probably also lead the way on the roads and trails while the trip is in progress. Yet another may handle group food needs on either an individual or central-commissary basis.

For an overnight trip the group leader often must arrange ahead of time for a group campsite. In some areas you can just pull off the road (particularly if it is a dirt road) and camp. If you plan on making an open-desert camp, the group leader should check first to see if this is permitted in the area you will be visiting. The leader should also scout the camp area before the trip to make sure it will be suitable. See "Car Camping," below, for car camping information.

As part of the administrative work, the group leader should send each prospective participant an information sheet detailing the trip plans. Here are some important items that should be covered:

Directions to Meeting Place. The meeting place should be well defined, near a main route of travel, and in the general vicinity of the tour. Easy-to-find meeting places include grocery parking lots, park and drive lots, rest areas, and so on. If the meeting place is just off a roadway, make sure there is a turnoff area large enough to safely accommodate all the vehicles. Never drive onto the unspoiled desert; this destroys plants and the underground homes of small animals. Be specific about the location; generalizations such as "near the Kelso Dunes" will have people spread out all over the place searching for each other.

Time to Meet. Emphasize promptness; always leave within thirty minutes of the stated departure time. When choosing this time, make allowance for the people who have the farthest to come. People who have to drive three to four hours are not necessarily going to be enthusiastic about getting up at 3 A.M. to arrive by 6 or 7 A.M.

Time Tour Will End. People should be able to get home before they are overly tired. For example, if the tour is a weekend overnighter, have the activities over and done with by early afternoon on Sunday (assuming that no one has more than a four-hour drive home).

Equipment List. The amount and kind of gear you will need depends in large part on whether you are planning to be out for a day, for a weekend, or for a longer time. As mentioned above, equipment usually falls into three categories: necessary, helpful, and that which will make the tour more enjoyable. See "Getting Started," above, and "Day Hiking," "Car Camping," and "Backpacking," below, for equipment details.

Informal Touring

This second type of touring is just you, your family, or a few friends. Planning is done in much the same way as for organized group touring, except you are more on your own. If you go by yourself, for example, and your car breaks down, there is no one right there to ask for a ride. (Make sure your car is in good running order! See "Your Vehicle and the Desert" in Chapter 6 for details.)

Day Hiking

One of the best ways to experience the desert close up is to explore it on foot. It is only by wandering unencumbered by your vehicle that you will feel free to stop and watch the tiny Lucy's warbler feeding on the underside of an acacia leaf or get down on your hands and knees to look eye-to-eye at a desert tortoise. When you are on foot there is time to read the story of a coyote who chased his prey across a rain-soaked playa—the tracks now captured in the curling, dried clay—or to admire the tenacity of a weather-beaten shrub.

As a stroller, walker, hiker, or peak climber, you can enjoy the vast, seemingly endless desert expanses. There is plenty of room to roam over pebble-strewn flats and into brushy basins. There are sinuous sand dunes, barren salt flats, and alkali-encrusted playas to wander in. The ambitious will find plenty of peaks to scramble up. A walk across black volcanic rocks will remind you of ancient earthly rumblings and eruptions, just as seeing petroglyphs will make you think of the people who created them long ago.

In the higher desert there are tall, aromatic sage, junipers covered with knobbly blue berries, and pinyon pines drooping with cones. It is here that you often flush quail as you walk along. You may see mule deer on the flat-topped mountains. If you are very lucky, you may spot powerful bighorn sheep on the steep, rocky sides of the higher mountains.

To enjoy sights such as this (as well as sounds and smells), some people take off on a day hike with nothing more than a canteen of water and a banana. But there are a few items that can make things so much more comfortable, safe, and enjoyable it seems only reasonable to take them.

Equipment

For day hiking, you might want to add the following to whatever items you feel you need from the basics list in "Getting Started," above.

Small Day Pack. This catch-all is great for carrying a quart or two of water, windbreaker, pocketknife, sunscreen lotion, a bit of toilet tissue, your lunch, a few adhesive bandages, a pair of tweezers (cacti are sometimes rather aggressive), and some of the rest of the items on this short list.

Bandanna. This versatile piece of cloth deserves a lot of praise—it can be used to keep the wind out of your ears, the dust out of your nose, or your hair out of your eyes. You can use it for a tablecloth, washcloth, napkin, towel, bandage, or sling. It can even be used as originally intended—to blow your nose on.

Baggie or Small Paper Bag. This can serve as a trash container for those after-lunch leavings. Never toss orange or other citrus peels out into the desert for the animals. The peels turn into dried, gnarly looking things; animals ignore them, and they may not biodegrade for decades. Haul them out, along with any other trash or garbage you create (used toilet paper, feminine hygiene items, etc.) or find along your way.

Clothing. Desert hikers are an individualistic bunch. It follows that their ideas of what to wear vary. As a rule, beginning desert wanderers wear shorts, T-shirts, tennies, and a hat. As their time in the desert accumulates over the years, the outfit changes. The shorts yield to long, comfortable pants. The T-shirt is layered over by a long-sleeved cotton shirt, and feet find comfort in high socks (sometimes wool ones) and protection in hiking boots. The hat takes on a character of its own; dented, mashed, lop-eared, and loved. The result equals an outfit that is comfy and protective.

Small Ripstop Nylon Tarp. You might want to at least try this. It can be used as a sunshade when you want to spend some time in one place—such as when having lunch. A hiking staff can aid in holding the tarp.

Hiking Staff. Once you use a staff, it will probably become a permanent part of your equipment. Bamboo is lightweight, unbelievably strong, and will last for years. Hairline cracks will eventually appear; when the cracks get too treacherous looking, simply wind some sturdy tape around them. Occasionally you may find a stick that will make a decent hiking staff. It should be sturdy, so it won't bend or break under your weight. It should also be fairly long, within 6 in. or so of your height so it can serve as a third leg and aid you in going over rocky areas or down steep grades. If you enjoy early morning and early evening walks in warm weather, a staff is good for poking under rocks and into bushes for snakes (they are usually active during these times).

The equipment list is necessarily brief, for reasons of space. For detailed information and advice on selecting and using gear, see the "Recommended Reading" appendix.

How Not to Get Lost When Hiking

If you are planning on doing any amount of hiking away from your vehicle in unfamiliar desert territory, study guidebooks and USGS topo maps before the trip. Get a good idea of what your route will be, from beginning to end. Practice the basics of compass use near home until you have mastered them. (See the "Recommended Reading" appendix for books on compass use.)

In warm weather, walking and hiking are most enjoyable in the cool of early morning or late afternoon. In cool weather, any time of the day is fine. Exploring should be done at a pace that the whole party can maintain and enjoy. Unless you have a sufficient number of experienced leaders, it's best if the group remains together. Visibility is poor when you are walking in flat, brushy, or rocky territory; there are few topographic features such as creeks to use as landmarks or leads. Under such conditions, it's not difficult for an inexperienced person to get disoriented or even lost. To minimize your chance of getting lost, take a moment every now and then to consult your map, check the landmarks, and assure yourself that you know where you are and what is coming next on your route.

Distances can be very deceptive in the desert, particularly when it's warm. What looks near may be quite distant — for instance, an interesting rock formation that looks to be strolling distance away ("I won't bother taking a canteen because I'll only be gone a few minutes") can be many miles away instead. Also, that lake or pond "just ahead" may really be the light refraction called a mirage. Never wander away from camp without a plan — not to mention a canteen, map, etc.

It's easy to get lost on foot in widespread sand dunes where there are few landmarks to note. Sometimes you can follow your footprints back to camp; however, if a wind comes up and covers your footprints or it gets dark and you have no flashlight, you could be in trouble. Here's another occasion when a compass is handy.

Twisting canyons with many side canyons can also be a potential problem if you're not paying attention while exploring. When walking up canyons, note which turns you make (write them down!) — especially if the ground is so hard you don't leave prints. Continually check on your general direction from camp.

When visiting ghost towns or mining areas, beware of abandoned structures, tunnels, and mine shafts — they can be deathtraps. Many are well disguised by rocks, plants, or old lumber. If you're not careful, a building could collapse on you, or you could fall through a floor or down a deep shaft. Even if you're with a group, this could mean serious injury or death.

Despite what maps may indicate, desert trails (and 4WD roads) often become obliterated or barely recognizable without notice — either owing to the actions of nature or of inconsiderate vehicle drivers. Roads and trails also have a tendency to divide, and divide again—without this fact showing on maps. If no one in your group knows the trail well, take care to write down your route (and sketch landmarks) as you go along. Alternatively, choose a well-known trail.

And, of course, do not go out on foot all alone in remote areas. If you were to have a bad fall in a rocky area, for example, it might be several fatal days or weeks before you could be located.

These suggestions may seem at first to paint the desert as a dangerous place. But when you consider them, you'll see that they are only common sense—not some set of difficult, technical, and arbitrary rules. In fact, such commonsense precautions apply to almost any outdoor activity area, not just to the desert.

Finding Your Car After Hiking

Ordinarily you won't get lost while driving, as you can usually retrace your tracks. Note landmarks such as tall rocks, twisted trees, bushes in bloom, etc., as you are driving along in unfamiliar country.

Locating your car after hiking in desert valleys requires more skill. A common mistake is walking past a bend in the road or past the end of the road where your car is parked. Even when you do locate the road again, you are still faced with the problem of which way to walk to find your car. Problems of this sort can be solved with the aid of a single compass bearing. Here's how you do it.

When leaving your car, take a compass bearing on a nearby hill, preferably one located sharply to the left or right of the road. Sketch the landmark's profile on a piece of paper (the back of your topo map is a handy place). Recheck the profile as you move away. You may be startled by the change in aspect. Also note the general direction of your movement away from your car. Sketching is a useful technique, even without a compass.

Upon returning to the road, the compass bearing will tell you whether to walk left or right. If the road is not readily found (because it made a bend or ended), a single compass bearing will tell you whether to look to your left or right to find the road. If these instructions don't make sense to you, check the "Recommended Reading" appendix for books containing instructions on using map and compass.

Car Camping—With the Comforts of Home

If you are a desert novice (and all of us are, at one time), one of the best ways to improve your acquaintance with the desert is by weekend car camping. Those who are used to car camping in primitive settings can probably start right out by exploring some of the better dirt roads and plunging right into open-desert camping. Those who have not car camped before might start by trying one of the campgrounds with facilities, listed in Chapters 8–16.

Open-desert camping means just that—the campsite you select will have only the open desert around it. No facilities, no supplies, no water, no shelter—except what you bring with you! But although facilities will be lacking, the desert will not. Even if it seems like you are spending most of your time figuring out how to camp at first, it will be time well spent. And you'll be surprised at how much enjoyment you can get out of learning about desert animals, plants, and scenery within just a few hundred yards of your campsite.

Equipment

In addition to the basics listed in "Getting Started," above, you'll need a few extra necessary items for car camping. After going out a few times, you'll be able to customize these basic lists to suit your own needs.

Sleeping Quarters. If you have a camper of some sort, your sleeping arrangements are well in hand. A camper certainly isn't necessary, though; many car campers use tents or other shelters. And quite a few people like to sleep out under the stars.

For sleeping out you need a *ground cloth* or *tarp*, a *small air mattress* or *closed-cell foam pad*, and a *sleeping bag*. Some folk like to use folding cots (don't forget to put a foam pad on the cot for insulation). However, the clear, cold nights of winter can seemingly suck every bit of heat from your sleeping bag, so it should be a fairly warm one at this time of year. In warm weather, even a lightweight bag can be more than warm enough. If you've never owned a sleeping bag before, talk to friends about what they like and don't like about theirs. Then do a little shopping around before purchasing one.

Actually, because it's often windy, winter desert camping is usually more comfortable with a *tent* of some sort. Tents come in all shapes and sizes; even a small one will do (unless you have a large family). Before buying a tent, talk to several tent owners and (again) shop around before purchasing one.

Kitchen. You'll need a *cook stove* of some kind (either the single-burner type used for backpacking or the two-burner Coleman type. Both these kinds of stoves have models that use different kinds of fuels—usually white gas, kerosene, propane, or butane. If you don't own a stove, try out a few before buying one. Friends are usually quite willing to lend a stove. Sterno is not very satisfactory, though it's better than nothing in an emergency. Cooking over an open fire is neither easy nor safe for most people.

If you find yourself going desert camping regularly, it saves time to have a *camp box* in which you always keep a set of kitchen essentials. Your camp box might consist of second-hand knives, forks, spoons, large saucepan, small saucepan, small frying pan, plates, cups (thermal cups are good for keeping things either hot or cold), can opener, small cutting board, hot pad, small dish towel, biodegradable dish soap, napkins, spices, and a few emergency canned and dried foods like fruit, cocoa, juice, tuna, stew, crackers, milk, and granola. Also, make sure that food transport containers are insect- and camp-robber-proof if you plan to leave them unattended or sitting around on the ground in camp.

Another useful box (especially for car camping) is an *icebox*. Like tents, iceboxes come in all sizes and shapes. The very inexpensive styrofoam ones with no plastic covering usually leak after a few uses. The small, expensive, bright-colored ones are fine for one-day outings. If you plan on weekend or longer outings, the larger Coleman-type icebox that holds a ten- or twenty-pound block of ice is better. An icebox expands your fresh-food options considerably.

Food. Keep it simple. Avoid greasy foods and those that create thirst. Foods with a high protein or sugar content (including alcohol) require a lot of water for digestion, as do fats and oils.

Breakfast can be cereal (cold or hot instant), hot drink, fruit (canned or fresh), and milk. If you are feeling ambitious, bacon and eggs or pancakes are not much trouble.

For lunch, a sandwich (or something like crackers and cheese or sardines), fruit, cookies, and a cool or warm drink are enough for most people.

If you plan to car camp overnight, prepare something for your evening meal before leaving home; keep it in an icebox (if necessary) until you're ready to eat. Or concoct something from canned foods; use your imagination. (One-dish meals are very popular with camp cooks!) In winter, a hot evening meal is welcome; in warm weather, you may want to dispense with cooking.

Wood for Campfire. If you're planning a campfire, bring your own wood. Desert growth, dead or alive, should never be used. Plants not only offer protective homes for small insects and animals but will eventually decay and nourish the soil.

Be sure to check with the Bureau of Land Management (BLM) or the Forest Service in advance to find out if you need a campfire permit or if there might be danger because of high fire hazard. During dry periods the fire hazard can be extreme. Building any kind of fire during periods of high fire hazard is not only dangerous but dumb.

Don't make a circle of rocks for your campfire. They serve no real purpose, and the soot-blackened rocks create a longtime eyesore. Instead, either use an area that has already been used or one that is clear of plant debris for several feet all around.

Before bedding down for the night, saturate the fire pit with water and cover it with soil or sand. Unless you do this the night winds could scatter the hot coals and start a fire where one isn't wanted.

Personal Kit. This might contain whatever it takes to make you feel human. For example, soap, small cotton towel, toothbrush and toothpaste, shaving gear, dental floss, hand lotion, comb, etc. If you are the type who gets eaten alive by every insect that moves, take a repellent that contains 50%–95% N,N,diethyl-meta-tolumide (DEET).

Clothing. General clothing needs for the desert are listed above. For overnighting, you might want to add a watch cap and warm jacket for cool evenings — it's amazing how cold it can get when the sun goes down in winter, early spring, and late fall. (Did you know that your head loses more heat than any other part of your body?) Sometimes a pair of mittens or gloves is welcome.

Miscellaneous. A couple of very handy items for car camping are folding chairs (for lounging around by the campfire or in the shade) and a small folding table (for meals and general clutter-holding).

Finding, Making, and Breaking Camp

When selecting a car camping spot, make sure it isn't on private property or in a wilderness area (no cars are permitted in the latter). There are many small campgrounds, primitive and otherwise, scattered throughout the desert. (See Chapters 8–16 for descriptions and directions.) There are also a multitude of places you can simply pull off into and camp. Many times you can drive up an old dirt road to a nice bare sandy or gravelly site where you can camp without destroying fragile desert vegetation.

In any case, make your camp away from piles of rocks and plant debris, abandoned buildings, etc.; these areas are favored by rattlers, black widow spiders, and scorpions. Don't camp directly under large Joshua trees, desert ironwoods, or smoke trees if it's windy or stormy. The heavy limbs could break off and fall on you.

When selecting a campsite and setting it up, and when breaking camp, remember to use techniques having the lowest possible impact on the land. Although regulations vary from place to place, low-impact camping techniques are always in order. (See "Backpacking" and "Good Advice," below, for more tips on low-impact practices.)

Try to find your campsite at least two hours before dark. This allows time to set up camp, cook, and wash the dishes in a leisurely fashion while it's still light.

If you camp where no one else has camped before, make every effort to leave the site as you found it. If you camp in an already-used area, try to leave it in better shape than you found it. If there are no trash cans (or if they are full), take all your trash and garbage with you.

Backpacking

Knowledgeable backpackers have given themselves the gift of freedom. They have extended their homes to include some wild areas and are as familiar with the native inhabitants as they are with their city neighbors. To experienced backpackers, the outdoors is a safe, familiar, and fascinating place. Backpackers can wander from season to season and place to place, sampling from each and enjoying each for its unique characteristics.

Water — How Much Is Enough? Being prepared for all the desert has to offer takes competent planning. First and foremost you must consider your water supply. If the weather is temperate and you will not be scrambling every peak in sight, you will be able to comfortably carry all the water you will need for a weekend overnight hike. A gallon per person will be enough — if used only for drinking and food preparation. (Point of interest: a gallon of water weighs eight pounds.) If you plan a strenuous weekend or if the weather is quite warm, you'll need a gallon per person per day.

Learn to drink a cup of water every half hour. Dehydration can creep up on you before you become thirsty, so don't wait until you feel thirsty before taking a drink. Dehydration is dangerous. (See "Hot-Weather Hazards" in Chapter 6 for details.)

Caches. For a trek longer than a couple of days you will probably have to cache your water, unless you plan on not taking any food, clothing, tent, or sleeping bag. If you are going to be close to a supply point during your trek, another possibility is hiking out to fetch more water.

Caching water takes considerable preplanning. Check your hike route on a USGS topographic map; mark where you expect to be on your second night out. Plan on having hiked about 15–25 mi at this point. Always underestimate how far you will go. To cache your water, drive as near as possible to where you expect to be on alternate nights and hike in with it.

While caching the water you might want to also leave replacements for any supplies you may have used up, such as stove fuel, toilet tissue, matches, batteries, or food. The water should be in tightly sealed, heavy plastic bottles. Bleach bottles are excellent for this purpose. Don't rely on flimsy milk containers. Any food or equipment should go into rodent-proof containers.

A cache is best made above ground; put it out of sight among large rocks or pile rocks over it. Take a photo of the site, showing the surrounding area as it will look when you approach. Mark the site on your topo and take a compass reading to at least two significant topographic features. (See the "Recommended Reading" appendix for books containing instructions on map and compass use.) Mark all the information on the photo backs and number them in order of usage.

Once the cache has been used, return the rocks to a natural pattern. Tie your empty bottles to your pack and carry them out.

Equipment

Make a list of what you will need for your backpack. Your gear should suit the occasion. In addition to appropriate basic gear items listed in

"Getting Started," above, you may need some or all of the following:

Backpack. If all your hikes will be single-nighters, an inexpensive backpack may suffice. For an extended trip, you will want one that is well made. Do some reading and talk to other backpack owners before purchasing one. Like hiking boots, this is an important and sometimes expensive purchase.

A Wilderness Home. This includes a *nonbulky sleeping bag* (lightweight or warm, depending on the season), *small closed-cell foam mattress, ground cloth*, and *tent* or *tarp shelter*. Talk to tent owners and then shop around. Get the lightest-weight tent you can find. Make sure it will be stable in the wind, has a waterproof "bathtub" floor, and is easy to erect on rock or sand.

Kitchen. Unless you plan on subsisting on fruits and nuts, you will need stove and fuel, cookpot with lid, "Sierra" cup, spoon, jackknife, water bottle, and matches. The pot lid can serve as your plate.

For cleaning up, take half a scouring pad (those without soap are easier to deal with), a small towel, and biodegradable soap. The soap can be used to clean the dishes and your hands. Some people even manage very well without soap (for the dishes). Remember that washing dishes uses precious water, so be frugal.

Food. Keep it simple. Some people get so involved with food that they spend half their trip cooking and cleaning up the mess. Others get very simple, and take only dried fruits, seeds, and nuts. They seem to graze their way down the trail. The proverbial happy medium suits most backpackers.

Try taking foods that are easy to prepare and will fit into one pot. Meat is almost impossible to take along (fresh meat weighs too much and freeze-dried meats are both expensive and not very tasty). Quick-cooking grains, noodles, dried vegetable flakes, instant soups, pasta and packaged sauces, raisins and other fruits, nuts, granola, dry milk, etc., are all inexpensive and available at most grocery stores. These items will keep your food bill lower (and may taste better) than if you purchase freeze-dried foods. If the weather is cool, fresh fruits and vegetables will keep well enough on a short trip.

Clothing. Once more, the layer method is best. Take just enough clothing to keep yourself comfortable. Windbreaker, sun hat, watch cap, warm jacket, T-shirt, long pants and long-sleeved shirt, hiking boots, and rain gear (if necessary) will cover all the elemental variables.

Personal Kit. As with car camping, this consists of whatever it takes to make you feel human. It could include toothbrush (skip the toothpaste), floss (without the container), small piece of soap (in baggie), old cotton diaper (lightweight and dries fast), small quantity of hand lotion in tiny plastic bottle, comb, nail clippers, and toilet paper.

The equipment list is necessarily brief, for reasons of space. For detailed information and advice on outfitting, see the "Recommended Reading" appendix.

Finding, Making, and Breaking Camp

As was mentioned under "Car Camping," above, one of the most important parts of low-impact travel in the outdoors has to do with the appropriate choice, setting up, managing, and cleaning up of campsites. Anything said in that section applies when you are backpacking, as well as when you are car camping.

When you're backpacking in the desert, particularly in wilderness areas, you may often have to select a pristine area, rather than an already-used one, for your campsite. Your responsibility is great when you choose an untouched site; you will need to make every possible effort to leave the land just as untouched as you found it (not always an easy task).

When choosing an untouched site, find a place where foot traffic does the least damage to vegetation. Desert vegetation may not look fragile, but it is. Sand, gravel, and rock make the best campsites for backpackers concerned about using low-impact techniques. It's OK to move a few small rocks and sticks for your tent or bed site, but do not rearrange the natural landscape. Tie your tent or tarp lines to rocks, if possible; do not dig holes or trenches; do not build fireplaces with rocks.

In the desert, an acceptable campsite will be at least three city blocks from any water source. This is a particularly important precaution in the desert, because the few watering spots are vital to the area wildlife. You can seriously disrupt the lives of many animals by casually camping too near their water.

When choosing a campsite, also keep in mind that cool air flows downward at night. A camping area on a hill or even a small rise will be several degrees warmer than a lower one. In warm weather you may prefer a lower camp, in cool weather a higher one. Take care not to camp in any wash, canyon, or arroyo that shows signs of flash flooding (steeply cut banks, mounds of debris left by high water, etc.). Even if the weather is good where you are camping, a thunderstorm in nearby mountains could result in unexpected and potentially dangerous flooding in the mountains' drainage area.

Good Advice

Wind. Wind is the one thing you can usually count on in the desert. Usually it is welcome, but there are times when it definitely is not. Sunglasses, a windbreaker, bandanna, and hat can make a windy day an enjoyable one, rather than a miserable one. Also, if you have a choice, it's best to start a hike by going into the wind—your return trip will be much easier with a tail wind.

Compass. Due to the fact that many desert areas lack trails, most of your hiking will have to be done point-to-point cross-country. It is therefore imperative that you know how to use USGS topographic maps and a compass. Practice many times until you are positive you know how to get from A to B — *before* you hike alone or with inexperienced companions. See the "Recommended Reading" appendix for information on compass use.

Road Information. If the road you want to travel is indicated on the map by a faint or dotted line, it's always best to inquire locally about its condition before turning off the paved or well-maintained road. In the desert, a storm or high wind can change road conditions overnight.

Low-Impact Reminders

Keep Your Group Small. Impact on the desert is more manageable if people travel in groups of no more than eight to ten and camp away from other groups.

Avoid Making Trails. When hiking cross-country, spread out, rather than walking single file; this spreads your impact over a larger area.

Be Unobtrusive. Be as invisible and inaudible as possible. Leave pets and radios at home.

Do Not Smoke. Smoking in the clean air of the desert, as with everywhere else, is unnecessary and unhealthful; it can also cause fires.

Camp on Bare Ground. Whether camping on an untouched site or a well-used one, make use of ground that is already bare; do not increase the bare area. Move only small rocks.

Use a Stove. Leave desert plant materials where you find them; do not try to cook over an open fire. If you want to have a campfire, bring your own wood and observe the precautions noted under "Car Camping," above.

Pack It Out. Always carry out all of your garbage and trash.

Do Not Camp Near Water Sources. Desert waterholes are few and far between; your presence near them keeps desert creatures away. Most animals will not remain in areas where they have to compete with people for water.

Dispose of Human Wastes Properly. Pack out all toilet paper, tissues, and feminine hygiene items. (Carry a plastic baggie for this purpose.) To dispose of solid waste, use a trowel to dig a small hole no more than 4 in. deep (decomposition of organic matter takes place in the top few inches of soil); replace soil, covering wastes carefully and leaving as few telltale signs of human use as possible.

Respect Life. The desert may look like it can't be damaged (what can you do to sand and rocks?), but this is definitely not true; instead, desert ecosystems are fragile and easily disrupted. Brush, rocks, and cacti are the homes of many desert creatures. When vegetation is damaged, its already-slow growth is slowed even more. Carelessly trampling ground, digging fire pits, and moving rocks can lead the way for wind and water erosion to turn an area into a truly barren wasteland, devoid of plants and animals. So, take care not to damage desert plants; respect the homes of the animals. Remember that *you* are the visitor.

Use the Desert Without Consuming It. The desert will repay you with beauty, knowledge, and adventure.

PART TWO

Adventuring in the California Desert

CHAPTER TWO

Adventuring in the
California Desert

8

Inyo-Mono Country

Saline Valley

ABOUT THE AREA. The Saline Valley, along with the Eureka Valley, is one of the most remote and spectacular places in the California desert. Together these valleys add up to an expanse of more than 500,000 acres of roadless area. Indeed, many feel that both valleys are of national park caliber.

An Offering of Solitude. The Saline Valley offers the visitor a tangible sense of isolation—a sense that is becoming increasingly rare, even in the California desert. The valley's topography is responsible for much of its faraway feeling. Around it the Inyo Mtns rise 11,000 ft to the west, the Saline and Last Chance ranges reach 6000 ft to the east, and there are high passes at the north and south ends of the valley. In addition, rough roads make the trip into the valley a long one, regardless of where you start.

What to Do and See. However long the approach, though, it's worth it, for there is much to do and see in the valley—historic sites to be visited, wildlife to be watched, hills and canyons to be explored, peaks to be hiked (see Saline Peak and Manly Peak hikes, below), and views to be admired and photographed. A good way to take in most of it is to make a loop trip through the valley from the last gas at Big Pine to the next gas at Lone Pine, a distance of 132 mi (see Saline Valley loop trip, below). About half of this 132 mi is on good gravel roads (albeit a bit washboardy in places). The loop includes such places as Marble Canyon, Lower Warm Spring and Palm Spring, the Salt Tram, and Beveridge and Hunter canyons.

Ups and Downs (Otherwise Known as Topography). Elevations in the valley range from 7200 ft at North Pass (the head of Whippoorwill Canyon) to 6000 feet at South Pass (the head of Grapevine Canyon). The floor of the valley is around 1100 ft. Roads can become impassable at any time, at any season of the year, due to dust storms, snow, or flash floods. North Pass is usually closed by snow in winter; it is not plowed (check local sources for current conditions). South Pass at the top of Grapevine Canyon is usually open all winter but is subject to flash floods and deep snow. An example of the unexpected was when this pass was closed by snow for three days over Thanksgiving 1981, making all travel to or from the valley impossible even by 4WD vehicle. Be careful to check the weather forecast before traveling in this area.

The Hot and Cold of It. Because winter temperatures can get down to 20° F or below, with light snow on the floor of the valley, and summer temperatures of over 120° F are not uncommon, the best times to visit the valley are spring and fall. If you like cool weather, winter is also a good time to make a trip here.

FACILITIES. If you are coming from the south, the last gas and supplies are at Olancha on US 395 or at Trona on CA 178. If you are coming from the north, last gas and supplies are at Big Pine. There are *no* services in the valley. Big Pine and Trona have motels and restaurants; there is also a restaurant and small market at Olancha.

Camping. There are no official established campgrounds in Saline Valley, although there are unofficial, user-maintained campgrounds at Lower Warm Spring and Palm Spring, off the Saline Valley Rd (see Saline Valley Loop Trip for directions). All other camping is open desert.

The nearest developed campgrounds are in Death Valley National Monument (DVNM). Emigrant Campground is just off CA 190 7.5 mi inside the west boundary of the monument. Wildrose Campground is just off the Trona-Wildrose Rd 4 mi inside the east boundary of the monument. For information on other DVNM campgrounds, see the DVNM "Facilities" section.

Saline Peak Hike
Class 1/elev. 7063 ft/USGS topo *Dry Mtn*/9 mi RT/cross-country

TO GET THERE. Take US 395 to Olancha, then CA 190 east about 30.6 mi to the posted Saline Valley turnoff east of CA 190 (between Owens Lake and Panamint Springs). Drive north on this road (BLM 1385)—which is paved for a short distance and then graded—for about 4 mi to a Y, where you should bear left. Ten miles farther on, take the west fork leading down Grapevine Canyon into the Saline Valley (don't go east to Hunter Mtn). Go past the old salt works to North Warm Spring Rd, about 48 mi from CA 190. Turn east at Painted Rock and go 7 mi on the good dirt road past Lower Warm Spring to Palm Spring. High-clearance and 4WD vehicles can continue about 11 mi up the very rough road (BLM 1864) to near the 3300-ft elevation. (This road may need "gardening.")

ABOUT THE HIKE. If you look around after having arrived at the road's end (3300 ft), you may find some obsidian, sometimes called Apache tears. This mineral was much sought after by the native Americans in the Southwest; they used it to make tools, weapons, and ornaments.

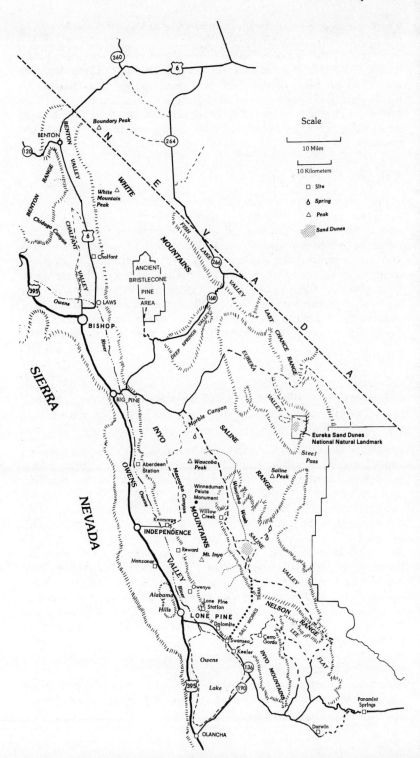

Scale

10 Miles

10 Kilometers

□ Site
◊ Spring
△ Peak
▒ Sand Dunes

Eureka Sand Dunes
National Natural Landmark

There is also an absolutely spectacular view of Dry Mtn to the east (it can be climbed from this point).

To reach 7063-ft Saline Peak, hike up the obvious east ridge shown on the *Dry Mtn* topo; continue on to the high point. This summit is the top of the Saline Range. The view from the top is awesome and totally unspoiled by the sight of any human activities. The Sierra Nevada can be seen to the west over a low spot on the crest of the Inyo Range. Remember, this is a desert peak; there is no shade or water along the route.

Saline Valley Loop Trip

TO GET THERE. To start this loop from the north, take US 395 to Big Pine, then take CA 168 east. To start the trip from the south, follow the directions for the Saline Peak hike. (If you choose the southern approach, you'll have to reverse the order of the various north-to-south points of interest described below.) If you make the trip from south to north, be advised that the Whippoorwill Canyon grades are steep. Once you leave CA 168 or 190, roads are generally dirt or gravel; most are graded. Some are not. Vehicles with good clearance are recommended, as the conditions vary from good to fair on the valley's main roads. Check road conditions locally before setting out on any trip into this area. If you plan to do any exploring off the main roads, a 4WD vehicle is definitely in order.

GETTING YOUR BEARINGS. There is no good county map for this area; instead, bring along the AAA "Eastern Sierra" and "Death Valley" maps. For the Hunter Canyon hike (a side trip), you'll need the USGS topo *Hunter Mtn*.

ABOUT THE LOOP. This loop totals about 132 mi, not counting side trips. The dead of winter is not the best time to make this trip because snow may close the passes into the valley. If you don't like hot weather, the dead of summer is also not a good time (Saline Valley can be very hot in summer). This leaves about eight months of the year to explore in.

To start the loop, go east on CA 168 from US 395, and turn south on the Eureka Valley Rd 2.3 mi later. This road will take you up to the top of the Inyo Range (7500 ft) in 16 mi. At this point, turn south on an unsigned (usually) gravel road. (The Eureka Valley Rd continues east through the valley and on over the Last Chance Range to Death Valley National Monument.) The gravel road will take you through several long flats and then (at about 24 mi from US 395) will drop down into Marble Canyon. The cabins and this section of the canyon are private property.

■ *Marble Canyon (Side Trip).*
This canyon contains placer gold claims. The placer mining shafts go down about 60 ft and then drift up and down the canyon more or less

horizontally, following an ancestral stream (now buried by alluvium) and its placer gold deposits. The area was most active in the 1920s and during the Depression.

The dirt track that continues west down the canyon ends at a private mining claim in a short distance. A road that goes south up a side canyon off this track can be followed on foot or by 4WD out onto Jackass Flat, where it divides into several branches, all dead ends. This is a pleasant, easy hike of about 1.75 mi from the lower end of the canyon. Park off the road in the flat dirt area where the track begins.

LOOP CONTINUES. Continuing on the main road past Marble Canyon, you'll climb out of a branch canyon, you'll cross Whippoorwill Flat and then a long, pinyon-covered slope at the head of Whippoorwill Canyon. The area to the north and west is the Pinyon Pine Study Area of the U.S. Forest Service; pinyons are protected in this area. The pinyon slope and the top mile of the steep canyon on the other side are impassable in winter (and sometimes late into spring) owing to snow; the road, however, is sometimes plowed. From the top (6000 ft), at about 29 mi from where you started (at the US 395/CA 168 junction), the road drops steeply into Saline Valley through a narrow, steep canyon and, later, goes along alluvial fans above Waucoba Wash, which is to the east. The original road was located in the wash.

At 32 mi you'll pass the spur road to Waucoba Spring, and at 44 mi you'll come to the bottom of Saline Valley (2300 ft) at Willow Creek Camp (a private mining claim). Help for true emergencies is available here, but casual visits are definitely discouraged.

Continue on by taking the curve to the east and go past Bad Water Spring, visible to the west, to Painted Rock (1400 ft), at 50 mi.

■ *Lower Warm Spring and Palm Spring (Side Trip)*.
To get to the springs, follow the dirt track from Painted Rock east and south around the sand dunes (the east side of the dunes is a good place for camping). At 4 mi turn east (left) to the springs, which are another 3 mi farther on. The other branch of this road (to the west) goes to the artesian well and back to the county road. The well road is very rough and dusty; during the rainy season it is sometimes wet where it crosses the edge of the usually dry lake.

These springs are popular primitive camping areas that are maintained by users. Over the years, regular visitors have diverted the water from the springs to several large concrete-lined tubs, creating hot pools that are somewhat spalike. (By common consent of the users the hot pools are clothing optional.) Users have also constructed primitive sanitary facilities and a shower area.

These campgrounds are often very crowded; needless to say, the surrounding area has been heavily impacted. Although this is not an official BLM campground, a BLM campground host usually lives at Lower Warm Spring; the host maintains and operates a sheriff's radio.

LOOP CONTINUES. Continuing on from Painted Rock, the first road to the east (at 50.7 mi) leads to the north side of McElvoy Canyon; the next road (at 51 mi) leads to the canyon's south side.

- *McElvoy Canyon Hike (Side Trip).*

Either the north or south road can be used as access for a hike up the canyon. The north road dead-ends at a cabin (if you get that far); the south road goes up the mountain to a mine. Stop before the switchbacks (if you get that far). In any case, drop down into or walk up into the canyon to the west and just keep going. Not too far up is a beautiful mossy waterfall — a very refreshing shower on warm days. The canyon can be hiked farther, until a waterfall is reached that can't be gotten up without climbing equipment.

LOOP CONTINUES. The sand dunes you see to the east at this point are closed to vehicles, but short roads lead to their edge, where camping is possible. Beware of soft sand on these roads. Follow the main county road as it loops to the west; the road closer to the dunes may have a bad soft spot.

At about 55 mi, at a place where the road curves east from its south course, you'll come abreast of Beveridge Canyon, to the west.

- *Beveridge Canyon Scramble (Side Trip).*

This is definitely a hike for those who like scrambling over steep rock. For those who don't, there is a nice waterfall not too far into the narrow canyon where you can halt if you wish.

To reach the canyon mouth, look for the creek outflow above the road. As you follow the outflow to the canyon entrance you'll come to some buildings. The entrance is almost hidden in a dark, rocky cliff. Here you'll find a faint trail on the north side of the creek. Not too far along this trail is the waterfall and pool.

From here on it is possible to go another couple of miles up this narrow cleft in the Inyos, but be prepared for some steep clambering around and over waterfalls (it's a good idea to take along a climbing rope on this one). Although there is an impassable waterfall about 2 mi up-canyon, hardy and experienced hikers can probably make their way out onto the flanks of the Inyos by going up the talus slope below the second waterfall. The nonhikeable waterfall is the fourth one; for this one you need climbing equipment.

Despite its difficulties, this hike is both interesting and beautiful. The canyon's rock walls are impressive and colorful; and riparian plant and animal communities are always worth attending to — even if your boots are wet and squishy (which they probably will be).

LOOP CONTINUES. The area with the large tamarisk tree (athel) in the mesquite at about 55 mi is private property (no camping). The road junction at about 56 mi is the Artesian Well Rd, which goes to the east.

The next road junction, at 57 mi, is with the Hunter Canyon Rd, which leads to a private mining claim to the north.

■ *Hunter Canyon Hike (Side Trip).*
Hunter Canyon also has water. If you'd like to hike directly up into the impressive face of the Inyos, just park opposite Hunter Canyon on the main road, as indicated on the topo map, and walk cross-country to its mouth. Here you'll find a private mining claim, complete with leftover buildings and the inevitable junk. Please respect the privacy of any occupants.

As you walk up the canyon by the small creek, you'll come to some modest falls surrounded with welcome greenery. If you manage to get around the trickiest of these falls by carefully edging along some ledges and assisting yourself over a drop by hanging onto a small metal ring, the going will get easier. You'll have to push your way through some places that are quite lush with thickets of willows and grasses, but in other places the walking will be quite easy.

At about 3 mi from the canyon mouth, at a fork in the canyon, you'll be able to catch a view of the Inyo Range. If you decide to go farther toward the Inyos (about 5000 ft up and 4–5 mi ahead), note that the main canyon follows the south fork.

LOOP CONTINUES. The next junction is with the Saline Marsh Rd, at 57.4 mi. The road is under the gateway in the fence to the east. At about 58.4 mi you'll come upon the towers and ponds of the Salt Tram.

■ *Salt Tram (Side Trip).*
The tram was built in 1913 to transport salt up Daisy Canyon (to the southwest of the road) and over the Inyo Range to Swansea, near Owens Lake. The salt, harvested from ponds visible east of the road, is nearly pure, so pure that it was sold without further refining.

The tram was never a success, probably due to a slight engineering error. The salt was to be harvested, shipped over the top, and dried at Tramway, near Swansea. Unfortunately, the tram was designed to transport dry salt. The extra weight of the wet salt reduced the tram's capacity to the point at which operation proved impractical.

It is also reported that miners rode the buckets over the mountain. It must have been quite an experience, swinging hundreds of feet over the steep, deep canyons!

LOOP CONTINUES. Beyond the tram is a long stretch of washboard across the flats of the valley, then the gradual ascent into Grapevine Canyon. As you ascend the fan, you may see a road to the east—this is the Lippencott Lead Mine Rd; it should not be attempted beyond where it goes over the first ridge, as it then becomes very steep, narrow, and rough.

Grapevine Canyon becomes narrower and more angled as it approaches the top, where it crosses Hunter Mtn Rd at 82 mi.

- *Hunter Mountain Road (Side Trip).*
This road curves east around pinyon-covered Hunter Mtn, gradually deteriorating and dropping down to some abandoned cabins at Gold Belt Spring in Death Valley National Monument (DVNM) (10.7 mi). From here the road runs north to Teakettle Junction (another 15.2 mi); 17.5 mi farther north it eventually changes to pavement at Ubehebe Crater in DVNM. Just before the road enters DVNM, you can turn north (left) on a mining road that follows a ridge for 3–4 mi to a spectacular view of Hidden Valley and the Racetrack. Hunter Mtn, by the way, is a good place to avoid during deer season.

LOOP CONTINUES. Elevation here at the top of Grapevine Canyon is 6000 ft. Bear south and continue on the main road. Now you will skirt the north end of Panamint Valley and, at a pulloff, have a spectacular view south into Panamint Valley. In the valley, CA 190 can be seen running east and west, with the Panamint Valley/Trona-Wildrose Rd running south. The Panamints are to the east; the tallest mountain visible is Telescope Peak (11,049 ft). On the west side of the valley is the Argus Range.

LOOP ENDS. After winding around through the hills and crossing Lee Flat (stay left), you'll reach an oiled road—the first pavement for 73 mi! Go south on this road (north goes to Cerro Gordo Rd junction and the Bonham Talc Mines) to CA 190 at 98 mi. There are no gas or supplies at Darwin or Keeler, so continue to Olancha or Lone Pine, both at about 132 mi from the beginning of the loop mileage.

Owens Lake–Panamint Dunes

ABOUT THE AREA. Owens Lake (actually now a dry lake salt flat) is the southern Owens Valley's most prominent feature (if you exclude the mountain ranges). Like the Salton Sea, Death Valley, Panamint Valley, and the Searles Basin, in ancient times it was a large, deep lake. In fact, at the north end of the present lake bed you can still see the ancient Lake Owens shorelines, which are as much as 200 ft higher than the shorelines of the early 1900s, when the Los Angeles Aqueduct was built.

Living off the Lake. In times somewhat less ancient than those of the surprisingly high shorelines, Owens Lake was very important to native Americans. These people, the Paiutes, lived in the area for thousands of years before explorers and settlers arrived. They depended on Owens Lake for some of their most important food supplies. One food item — the pupae of a tiny salt marsh fly—may not sound too appealing to modern folks, but it was a very nutritious staple.

As the climate continued to become more arid and the Owens Lake level slowly fell, the Paiutes made use of another lake product—salt.

As the water receded, the accumulated salts of many thousands of years eventually crystallized out. These salt layers are an incredible 9 ft deep. That's a lot of salt! The crystals, formed into balls of an easily carryable size, were a trade item much coveted by the peoples on the Sierra's west side (where salt was scarce).

Discovery of the Valley. At the time the Owens Valley was first "discovered" by Joseph Walker (of Walker Pass fame) and his fellow beaver hunters in 1834, the lake was still something over 30 ft deep. Although the Walker group found no beaver, they did find a route from the Great Salt Lake to the Humboldt country of western California. This route later became an important part of the California Trail.

Mining the Mountains. Gold and silver seekers began to spill into the valley in the 1860s. The famous Cerro Gordo ("fat hill") silver mines, high in the Inyos above the lake, were touted as "rivaling the Comstock." It took a lot of ingenuity, hard work, and hardship to carry on the various mining activities around Owens Lake over the years. If you make a loop around the lake, stopping at the different sites where these activities took place, you perhaps can begin to capture at least a little of the feeling of what life was like in those days.

Cerro Gordo was far from being the only successful mining operation in this mineral-rich area. Darwin, another well-known mining enclave, is located south of CA 190 between Owens Lake and Death Valley. Rich lead–silver deposits were found here in 1875, and the Modoc Mine continued to operate intermittently until a few years ago. One of the roads to the mine goes up Darwin Canyon, passing by a side canyon containing a desert country rarity — a year-round stream that makes its way through the canyon over several lovely waterfalls (see Index).

As you approach the Darwin Canyon Rd from the west on CA 190, you'll pass by the site of one of the old stage stations used by the freight companies serving the mines (this station is the site of the Pioneer Grave). You'll also pass the Saline Valley turnoff (to the north), and soon you'll come to one of the best places to take photographs of the north end of Panamint Valley and its dunes: the Padre Crowley Viewpoint.

From Lake to Salt Flat via the Aqueduct. By the early 1900s, the Owens Valley was well settled. Mines boomed here and there, and agriculture was off to a prosperous start. Then came the Los Angeles Aqueduct. Before 1913, when the aqueduct began carrying Owens Valley water to Los Angeles, Owens Lake covered about 100 square mi and was 30 ft deep. Now, water rarely reaches the "lake"; when the wind blows, the visitor gets a faceful of alkali dust rather than a view of deep blue waters ruffled with whitecaps. For a view of the waters of Owens Lake nowadays, one must visit the swimming pools of Los Angeles. Fortunately, the wind blows only occasionally — and the rest of the time there is much to do and see in the lower Owens Valley.

Outing Possibilities Galore. As you will see, even this small area of Inyo-

Mono country offers a wide variety of outing possibilities—from the Pleasant Mtn peak walk to a leisurely loop by car around Owens Lake (see below). There are also ghost towns to be visited, old mining equipment to be examined, dunes to be explored, spectacular views to be enjoyed and photographed, and solitude to be savored—to name but a few of the pleasures in store for the visitor.

FACILITIES. Gas, a restaurant, and some groceries at Olancha; motels, restaurants, gas, and all supplies at Lone Pine. No store or gas in Darwin; no supplies or gas between Owens Lake and Stovepipe Wells in Death Valley National Monument (DVNM).

Camping. See the Lone Pine–Independence–Big Pine–Bishop "Facilities" section for info on developed campgrounds near Lone Pine. Also see the Death Valley National Monument "Facilities" section for info on Emigrant campground (west side of DVNM).

Open-forest camping (i.e., undeveloped—no water or other facilities) is available both north and south of Olancha off several dirt and paved roads that lead west off US 395 into Inyo National Forest north and south of Olancha. For example, if you take Sage Flat Rd (about 3.6 mi south of Olancha) west toward the Sierra for 5 mi or so, you'll find several good camping areas just off the road (which is paved, though a bit bumpy, to this point). Take care to avoid private property.

Owens Lake Loop

TO GET THERE. Take US 395 to CA 190 at Olancha or to CA 136 just to the north of the Interagency Visitor Center on the south edge of Lone Pine.

GETTING YOUR BEARINGS. There is no good county map for this area. Instead, you'll need the AAA "Death Valley" map.

ABOUT THE LOOP. This trip can be made almost any time of year. The valley can be quite cool in winter (plan your trip for midday) and quite hot in summer (plan your trip for early morning or late afternoon). In any case, don't attempt it when there is a strong wind. The great clouds of sand and alkali dust that blow up in a good wind from the salt-flat-that-used-to-be-a-lake are not friendly to your lungs, eyes, nose, or the paint on your car.

From Lone Pine, this loop will take you to the Interagency Visitor Center and then into the past, via the Owens River (a dry bed in this location); the terminus of the Saline Valley salt tram; the site of Swansea (of smelter fame); the remains of the Carson & Colorado Railroad (which got to Keeler, but not to the Colorado River); the Old West town of Keeler (not quite a ghost town, yet); the Olancha Sand Dunes (scenic); the site of Cartago (where steamers docked); the Cottonwood Landing charcoal kilns (which served the mine smelters); and back to Lone Pine.

The total mileage for the loop is about 53 mi (not counting any side roads you decide to explore). The main roads are all paved, but most of the side roads are not (their usual condition is noted in each description).

To start the loop, park at the Interagency Visitor Center, located at the junction of US 395 and CA 136. The center is open seven days a week, during business hours. Here you can get a good introduction to Inyo-Mono country by taking a few minutes to look over the interpretive displays of local plants, animals, and geology. The friendly people who staff the center are always willing to answer your questions, so don't be afraid to ask. There is also a good selection of field guides and local history books. Detailed maps of the region are for sale at nominal prices. Don't forget to identify 14,495 ft Mt Whitney while you're taking a break here—it's just across the road (and up). It's not every day you get to see the highest peak in the continental United States!

Owens River Bed and a Short History of the Los Angeles Aqueduct. About 2 mi east of the visitor center on CA 136, the road crosses the now always-dry Owens River bed. Pull off the road here to contemplate the scene and bring yourself up to date on why the once briskly flowing river is no more.

From the 1870s to 1913, when the Los Angeles Aqueduct was completed, the valley—with its abundant water supply from the east side of the Sierra and good land—was a rich farming area. Farms and ranches yielded alfalfa, apples, corn, wheat, grapes, butter, and many other products.

As the big mining ventures waned in the early 1880s and the money they brought to the valley dwindled away, times were a bit hard for a while. But by 1883 the railroad had come to the valley, sizable irrigation projects were in place, and the now-healthy farm economy promised a prosperous future for the 4500 settlers.

Their future only lasted a few decades, though. The beginning of the end of Owens Valley agriculture came in 1904, when William Mulholland, the Los Angeles water superintendent, visited the valley with an eye to the possibilities of tapping into its abundant water supply to help his city grow. (Mulholland was tipped off to the Owens River's possibilities by a Federal Bureau of Reclamation employee who later defected and became a leading official of the aqueduct project.)

Soon, options on key lands were secretly bought up by Los Angeles officials posing as ranchers and cattle buyers (1905–1906); then plans for the aqueduct were drawn up; and in 1907 many millions of dollars were voted by the citizens of Los Angeles for the aqueduct's construction.

Valley farmers and ranchers were not consulted during the initial planning stages. They first found out about the plans when the *Los Angeles Times* printed the story in July of 1906. This announcement began a twenty-five-year battle with the city of Los Angeles and its Department of Water and Power (LADWP).

Some valley residents sold out willingly; others were tricked into selling their lands. Promises by Los Angeles to allow the valley sufficient water for its residents' own agricultural uses were not honored. Valley residents did not initially object to some of their water going to Los Angeles faucets; what they did grudge was the amount of water Los Angeles wanted for its irrigation projects—projects that were to go forward at the expense of Owens Valley crops!

With Los Angeles's continued refusal to grant them any reasonable water rights, many valley citizens took up a new hobby—sabotaging the aqueduct. Despite dynamitings and other retaliatory acts, the 233-mi aqueduct was finally completed in November 1913, amidst sighs of relief from the drought-belabored Los Angeles agriculturists and howls of outrage from the citizens of Owens Valley (what there was left of them).

Not satisfied with draining most of the valley, Los Angeles then commenced to buy up lands along the river's tributaries, all the while refusing to consider paying the valley farmers and ranchers damage claims (for loss of livelihood). Eventually, the city even bought up most of the lands surrounding the towns, along with as much of the valley's town lands as it could lay its hands on.

The broken promises of the city of Los Angeles have continued down through the years; today little has changed. It doesn't take an expert to see the dead and dying trees, empty river and stream beds, blowing alkali dust—the creeping desertification of the once-lush valley. And yet the draining continues; trees die, crops wither, and lakes empty so that swimming pools may fill.

Believe it or not, though, this water-draining drama actually has had at least one good side to it. That is, because so much of the land—watershed and river—is owned by Los Angeles, it behooves it to keep the water flowing. Thus, the Owens Valley, though it is being drained of much of its water, has remained relatively undeveloped and relatively unpopulated. As a result, the valley is a place many love to visit for its own sake, as well as for its being a portal to some of the finest (even if heavily used) backcountry in the West.

Despite the dry riverbed here at the north end of Owens Lake, you can still enjoy the few pieces of the Owens River and some of its tributaries that are still flowing relatively briskly, beautifully, and fishily farther north in the valley.

Swansea. Traveling east on CA 136 from US 395, you soon (3.3 mi) come to the Dolomite Loop Rd going off to the northeast. This road meets up with CA 136 again in another 3.3 mi. Follow the Loop Rd for about 2.9 mi to the turnoff to Dolomite and continue another 0.5 mi along CA 136 (7.5 mi from US 395) to the site of Swansea, just north of the road. About all that can be seen here is a piece of a stone foundation near the historic marker. This was the site of one of the three Cerro Gordo silver-lead smelters—the only one not controlled by the Cerro Gordo owners. It was built by the Owens Lake Silver-Lead Company in 1869 and did well for several years, even carrying bullion across the lake in a steamer, the *Bessie Brady* (named after the little daughter of one of the company's owners).

Unfortunately, the Cerro Gordo owners did not approve of the smelter's success and tried to drive it out of business. It seems that the "barons on the hill" were very possessive about the toll road they controlled. This road, the Yellow Grade, had been built jointly by many of the miners in the region, but once it was finished the barons took it over and charged an arm and a leg for its use.

The smelter company also owned one of the three principal mines and did so well that it could afford to begin buying up some mines in the Cerro Gordo area. However, the barons retaliated by trying to keep the Silver-Lead Company from using the toll road. First, they raised the toll to an unreasonable amount; then they made the road nearly impassable.

The company responded by initiating a lawsuit—and so ensued a long, expensive legal battle over the toll road. The Silver-Lead Company quite rightfully had public opinion on its side; it won the case. But the victory came too late—just a few months later the smelter was buried by a massive landslide, in 1874, and its owners hadn't the money to rebuild. Such were the misfortunes of Swansea.

Keeler, the Carson and Colorado Railroad, and the Cerro Gordo Road. Continuing southeast along CA 136 for another 4.1 mi (11.6 mi from US 395) brings you to the old, but not deserted, town of Keeler. Believe it or not, this was a bustling metropolis for several decades. When the Cerro Gordo mines—high in the Inyos above the town—were going strong during the 1860s and 1870s, it was an active milling and supplies center. Business was expected to pick up even more in the 1880s, when it seemed that the area might contain more rich silver mines.

On the strength of these hopes, the narrow-gauge Carson & Colorado Railroad was built from near Carson City, Nevada, over Montgomery Pass, and down the east side of the Owens Valley (where the mines were) to Keeler (then called Hawley). The C & C arrived in Keeler in 1883; its builders planned on eventually extending it to Mojave and on to the Colorado River.

However, the silver strikes never materialized. So the C & C and Keeler fell on hard times, despite the fact that the railroad's early years were profitable—it hauled everything from apples to corn, gold to granite, lead to salt, sheep to soda (borax), and talc to zinc. Indeed, the times were so hard that the C & C was sold to Southern Pacific in 1905—just in time for it to become a moneymaker again with the discovery of large silver and gold deposits in Tonopah and Goldfield, Nevada.

Before financial difficulties set in, the train was interestingly described as "a passenger train, freight train, and a milk train run each way, every day, but in order to economize, one engine is made to pull all three. . . . The tourist who travels in the cars of the C & C RR is not unlikely to wonder which is the more interesting, the road or the desert region." According to old accounts of travel on the line, it had a very utilitarian kind of schedule. The engineer was prone to stop so the crew could take a swim, or to pick up any prospective passengers strolling the tracks, or just to chat with friends and acquaintances.

After the C & C's acquisition by Southern Pacific, the old narrow-gauge tracks began to be replaced with standard gauge (to make the Tonopah connection), and SP connected the Owens Valley with Mojave by 1908 (the better to build the aqueduct). At about this time, an unforgettable nickname was coined for the popular narrow-gauge steam engines—a name that pointed up the line's narrow-gaugeness. Today, even those who never saw the old engines in operation can remember this name: the Slim Princess.

After Tonopah went bust, the aqueduct was built, highways improved, trucking became more economical than shipping by rail, and the railroad went into a long decline. Between 1930 and 1961 the old C & C narrow gauge was nibbled away little by little, its branch lines torn up one by one and its passenger service dropped. The last 70-mi segment between Keeler and Laws limped along financially by carrying loads of nonmetallic minerals and sheep. In 1957 the Keeler station was closed (but it's still there—have a look).

Finally, in 1960, the last engines were parceled out to museums and civic organizations, and the last tracks were torn up. By 1961, all that was left of this pioneer railroad were the original stations at Laws, Lone Pine Station, and Keeler, and the long roadbed you can now easily see on the east side of the valley. A rather spectacular segment of switchbacks and a tunnel can be seen in the Montgomery Pass area. You can also see the Slim Princess and other early railroad memorabilia at the city park in Independence and at the Railroad Museum in Laws (see below).

Keeler is also the jumping-off place for another interesting area: Cerro Gordo (see below). Without the Cerro Gordo mines, there very likely would have been no Keeler.

After leaving Keeler, it is 4.9 mi to the CA 136–CA 190 junction. Take CA 190 to the right around the south side of the lake (instead of to Death Valley). In 9.9 mi you'll come to a spur road leading north to the lakeshore, 26.4 mi from where you started at US 395. As you continue west from this point on CA 190 toward Olancha and the junction with US 395 (4.7 mi away), you'll see the Olancha Sand Dunes just south of the road.

Olancha Sand Dunes. The dune area is a good picnic and walking-around place when the wind isn't blowing. In spring the sand-loving wildflowers make a nice display among the hummocks.

Cartago Landing. Just about 3 mi north of the CA 190–US 395 junction at Olancha (where you turned right again), and on the east side of US 395 (35.1 mi from the loop's beginning), is the town of Cartago (originally called Dante's Landing). In the area's mining heyday, this was the landing where thousands of silver ingots were unloaded from the steamers bringing them from Swansea and reloaded onto mule-pulled wagons for shipment to Los Angeles. As many as eighty wagons sometimes left Cartago for Los Angeles each day! When the wagons returned from Los Angeles, they were loaded with supplies and machinery that were to be off-loaded and steamed across the lake to keep the mines and miners going. Cartago was, to say the least, a busy place.

Driving north on US 395 from Cartago, you'll come to the signed spur road for the charcoal kilns in another 6.1 mi (41.2 mi from your starting point). The sign, like all historical landmark signs, is small, with brown lettering on a tan background. Look carefully for it on the east side of the highway.

■ *Cottonwood Charcoal Kilns (Side Trip).*
Depending on the condition of the spur (usually a good gravel road), either drive east on it to the kilns or walk in to them from the highway. It's only a short distance — about 1 mi.

Still standing here at Cottonwood Landing are the remains of two beehive-shaped charcoal kilns used to fire cordwood to make charcoal bricks for the silver-mine smelters. The wood was logged off the mountains up Cottonwood Canyon, which goes northeast up the face of the Sierra just across US 395; you can see it easily from here. The logs were brought down the mountainside by way of a flume — a V-shaped wooden trough into which some of the waters of Cottonwood Creek were diverted.

After being fired to charcoal, the bricks were ferried across the lake and used by the smelter at Swansea or hauled by mule up to the Cerro Gordo smelter via the infamous Yellow Grade. The charcoal even went as far as Darwin (see above), for kiln operators had already burned all available nearby pinyon trees — as had the Cerro Gordo managers. Most of those trees have never grown back, which is why Buena Vista Peak (now called Cerro Gordo Peak) looks so barren. If you look northeast across the now-dry lake to the peak, you can see this for yourself.

LOOP ENDS. Continue north on US 395 to the junction with CA 136 south of Lone Pine (about 12 mi from the kiln spur). You might want to stop at the visitor center again and take another good look at (and some photos of) 14,495-ft Mt Whitney. This is a sight few ever tire of. There are not many places where you can see a group of peaks over 15 mi long, with a half-dozen of them being over 14,000 ft. The center of Lone Pine is 1.5 mi farther, making a grand total of approximately 53 mi for the loop.

Cerro Gordo Ghost Town and Mines Tour

TO GET THERE. *Route 1:* take US 395 to CA 190 at Olancha, then go northeast 14.6 mi on CA 190 to its junction with CA 136; turn left and take CA 136 northwest 4.9 mi to Cerro Gordo Rd.

Route 2: take US 395 to CA 136 just to the north of the Interagency Visitor Center on the south edge of Lone Pine; follow CA 136 southeast for 12.6 mi to Keeler and the Cerro Gordo Rd junction.

Route 3: from the Trona area, take the Trona-Wildrose Rd 30.6 mi north to the Panamint Valley Rd; take this road north 14.4 mi to CA 190; go west on CA 190 32.7 mi to the junction with CA 136; take CA 136 straight ahead northwest 4.9 mi to Keeler and the Cerro Gordo Rd junction.

From the junction with CA 136, go northeast on Cerro Gordo Rd for about 7.5 mi to the townsite. The road is an Inyo County–maintained gravel road; it is usually in fair condition and negotiable by the average vehicle with decent clearance. It is a good idea to check the road's condition locally before making this trip (ask at the visitor center or sporting goods stores), as the road is subject to washouts. Also, snow may make the last mile or two impassable in winter. The grades are steep, which means that if you have an automatic transmission you need to be quite careful when coming down.

There are some areas flat enough for dry camping along the road up to the town.

Note: The Cerro Gordo area is private property — check with the caretaker before walking around.

ABOUT CERRO GORDO. "Fat Hill" (the English translation of the Spanish *cerro gordo;* the hill — 9184-ft Buena Vista Peak, now called Cerro Gordo Peak — was "fat" in silver) is a ghost town delight. Calico Ghost Town may be fun, but Cerro Gordo is all original and real. A trip here will take most of a day, for there is much to be seen on the steep (and slow) road on the way up, a lot to be seen at the site, and many new views to be appreciated on your careful way down again.

Discovery Brings the Barons. Silver deposits were first discovered here at about the 8500-ft level on the west slope of Buena Vista Peak by one Pablo Flores in 1865. When word of the rich ores leaked out, Mortimer Belshaw of San Francisco and Victor Beaudry were among the men attracted to the new mining camp. Eventually, the two men bought up the claims that became the principal mines. (Theirs were not the only mines on the hill; at one time there were nearly a thousand claims on the books.)

These mining "barons" of Cerro Gordo controlled not only the major mines, but also the smelters (except for the one at Swansea — see Owens Lake loop trip, above, for that saga), the toll road (the infamously steep Yellow Grade, which much later became the county road you came up on), the water supply, and a large freighting company. Some folks said that one of the reasons they did so well with the mines was that their business practices were notoriously unfair. For example, although other miners had participated in building the toll road, they were charged for the use of it just the same as those who had not. And the tolls were excruciatingly high!

Steamboat Days. Although the town of Cerro Gordo was in full swing by 1871, processing lead and zinc as well as silver and having a population of nearly 2000 (most of whom lived in tents), the mines still had serious transportation problems. Ingots were being produced in such large numbers that the freighting company could not ship them out to Los Angeles by fourteen-mule teams fast enough to keep up with the output. In 1872 the steamer *Bessie Brady* was put into operation. *Bessie* was a considerable 85 ft long and 16 ft wide and was able to ferry the bullion from the east shore of Owens Lake to the west shore, thus saving four or five days of hauling around the lake's north end.

Before *Bessie* started her runs it took at least three grueling weeks to get the heavily loaded ore wagons from the mines to Los Angeles; the bullion ferry shortened the haul considerably. Of course, the wagons were equally heavily laden on the return trip—with machinery for the mines, fodder for the pack animals, and food and supplies for the mining town residents. As you might guess, Los Angeles owes much of its early growth to the infusions of silver from the Cerro Gordo mines.

Houses Built of Silver. However, this great improvement in transportation led to other problems. By January 1873, there were 18,000 silver bars piled up at Cartago and Swansea awaiting shipment to Los Angeles. These bars averaged a hefty eighty-seven pounds apiece and were valued at $335 each. There were so many of them that the workers used them to build huts, which they roofed with canvas, for protection from the cold winter winds. By May of that year 30,000 bars had collected. Something had to be done.

That something was finally accomplished late in 1873, when Beaudry, Belshaw, and a new partner, Nadeau, formed the large-scale Cerro Gordo Freighting Company. By buying up the small freight companies (and the *Bessie Brady*) and arranging for stations only a day's haul apart all the way to Los Angeles, they got the ingots moving at the rate of 700 tons per month. But the problem parade just kept marching on.

Moving Trees and Water. Next to be solved were the problems of where to find more charcoal to feed the ravening smelters and more water to cool the smelters' jackets and the throats of the townsfolk. Answer: form more companies. By 1876 the Inyo Lumber & Coal Company was sending enough lumber to keep the smelters going, using a flume from Cottonwood Creek to the kilns at Cottonwood Landing, on the lake's west side, north of Cartago. Colonel Sherman Stevens, the company's owner, even built another steamer, the *Mollie Stevens*, named after his daughter, to carry the lumber or charcoal across Owens Lake. Meanwhile, in 1874, the Cerro Gordo Water & Mining Company began pumping 90,000 gallons per day of water through 10 mi of pipe up to 1800 ft from the east side of the Inyos. (This was quite a change from the meager 1300 gallons per day the town had been existing on until then.)

Just Rewards. It was in this year, 1874, that Cerro Gordo reached its peak, producing 5300 tons of bullion worth $2 million. From here on, though, little seemed to go right for the Cerro Gordo barons. For just as they had brought their operations to the point where things were running rather smoothly and profitably at a high level (by dint of combination of much conniving, cleverness, hard work, and meanness), the ore gods deserted them. The lawsuits they instigated to subdue their rivals dragged expensively on and on. Production fell off. Veins of silver began to dwindle. The Darwin and Coso mines began to pick up. Bodie began to boom. Miners moved on to these more silvery fields. By 1879 Cerro Gordo's silver days were over, and the barons drifted into well-deserved obscurity (not soon enough to suit most folks, though).

Number One Again — in Zinc. There were still a few boomlets to come for Cerro Gordo. In 1879 zinc was discovered there. Soon the town of Keeler was laid out, the *Mollie Stevens* was put back in action again, and zinc production began. Now it was this rather unromantic mineral that brought in the dollars — not nearly as many as in Cerro Gordo's silvery heyday — but still enough to keep the mines going until 1883. Between 1883 and 1906, despite the coming of the Slim Princess (the narrow-gauge railroad) to Keeler, there ensued a long period of financial nothingness. But the mines were to be revived yet once again — to become the primary source of high-grade zinc in the United States!

From 1906 to 1936, in fits and starts, with the help of an aerial tramway (now gone), Cerro Gordo gave up its zinc, quite a bit more silver-lead from mine tailings (left over from the early days, when the recovery rate was only 90%), and even some limestone. The total value of all its ores over the years has been estimated at $15 million in preinflationary values. (In 1902, silver was at a low of $.53/oz, vs. $6/oz today. However, a good day's wages were $4 and a good dinner only $.50.) Some think no other group of mines in California has matched Cerro Gordo's output of zinc, silver, and lead. After this period "Fat Hill" again gradually became dormant and so far has not revived.

What to See in Cerro Gordo Today. As you come into Cerro Gordo today, the first building on the right is the elegant two-story American House, built in 1871. It has two dormitories and two private rooms upstairs, and a dining room, kitchen, and private dining room downstairs. In addition, there are a lobby, an office, and another private room. The ice plant west of the hotel was added in 1916, when the power line from Owens Valley reached town. At this time the electric tram was also built. The tram was an impressive 29,560 ft long and had a capacity of sixteen tons per hour. In the 1940s the tram was sold to a company in Nevada. After dismantling it and carting it away, its new owners didn't use it — instead, they let it rust to pieces at its new location.

Other 1916 vintage buildings (which can be identified by their corrugated iron exteriors) include the bunkhouse, which is across the road to the north, and the commissary, up the hill to the east. The store, the two-story house (built by Beaudry), and the other dilapidated frame buildings date mostly from 1871. The remains of Victor Beaudry's smelter may also be seen north of the American House, across the road. Up the hill to the east, the Union Mine dumps are prominent; above them are the Union shaft and buildings, which include the change room, machine shops, and smelter. All these, along with the equipment, date from either 1871 or 1916.

As you leave Cerro Gordo to return to the valley, drive slowly and carefully. The road is treacherously steep and often rough. In the old days, freight wagons sometimes had their wheels chained so they couldn't turn, in order to slow their descent. It is said that some teamsters quit right after their first trip down. After your first trip down you'll know exactly how they felt!

Pleasant Mountain Hike

Class 1/elev. 9690 ft/USGS topo, *New York Butte*/7 mi RT/part trail, part cross-country

TO GET THERE. Follow the directions for the Cerro Gordo trip, above.

ABOUT THE HIKE. This peak is located about 3 mi north of the Cerro Gordo Mine, once the richest silver mine in California. The mine area is on private property, and permission to visit must be asked of the caretaker. However, the old buildings can be viewed from the hiking route.

To get to the jumping-off point, go as far north up the steep, graded road to the Cerro Gordo townsite as possible (hopefully, 7.5 mi). This should bring you to about 8100 ft. Now you can hike northwest along the lower dirt road leading from the townsite. After about 1.25 mi you'll be on a faint trail that follows a nearly level course for another 1.25 mi. To reach the 9560-ft peak, traverse up the steep, slatey slopes.

Views from the top are outstanding. You can look out over Owens Lake southwest, the Saline Valley northeast, and the abandoned salt tram leading from Saline Valley to the shores of Owens Lake. (For more info on the tram, see the Owens Lake loop trip, above.)

Owens Lake to Panamint Dunes Tour

TO GET THERE. To begin the tour from the CA 190–CA 136 junction, just east of Owens Lake, take CA 136 southeast from US 395 for 17.5 mi (the CA 135–US 395 junction is 1.5 mi south of Lone Pine), or take CA 190 northeast from US 395 (at Olancha) for 14.5 mi.

GETTING YOUR BEARINGS. There is no good county map for this area. Instead, bring along the AAA "Death Valley" map.

ABOUT THE TOUR. This is a good fall or spring outing, although it can also be pleasant enough in summer if done in the early morning or late in the day. Winter is fine, too, if you choose your weather forecast carefully and tour during the middle of the day.

From the junction, on CA 190 going east, the tour will take you first to Pioneer Grave Historical Site, then to Father Crowley viewpoint, by Panamint Springs, and finally to the lovely Panamint Dunes. There are open-desert camping areas near the dunes.

One-way mileage for the tour (beginning at the CA 136–CA 190 junction) is about 41 mi, not counting any side roads you decide to explore. The main road is a good paved road, but the road to the Panamint Dunes is dirt for 6 mi, to where it curves east to the Big Four Mine. This road varies from good to execrable — depending on the time of year, the number of people who have traveled it, and the number and severity of washouts.

Pioneer Grave. The first stop on CA 190, 6 mi east of the junction with CA 136, is at Pioneer Grave. This site (on the northeast side of the road) is that of a stage station active in the mid- to late 1800s. The graves are those of two small children who died in a diptheria epidemic in 1876. However, it wasn't until the 1940s that a private citizen marked the graves. The cross was put up later by two highway workers, and Cal Trans workers still maintain the site. Pause for a minute to think about the McKellup family, who came to this spot over a hundred years ago and kept the stage station. At that time, theirs was the only house within a day's ride in any direction!

Father Crowley Point Monument. As you continue east on CA 190, you will reach this spectacular viewpoint in about another 15 mi (21 mi from the junction where you began the tour). From here, as you look northeast across the Panamint Valley, you get perhaps the best view of the rugged Panamint Range that is to be found anywhere in the region. Get out your map and see if you can identify the peaks. The tallest, often snow-covered, is 11,049-ft Telescope Peak, in DVNM. Look down into the valley for a bird's-eye view of the Panamint Dunes. If you see a haze of sand around the dunes, perhaps you'd better plan your visit to them for another, less windy time. If the sand seems to be behaving itself, continue on down the road and become better acquainted with the dunes at a closer range.

Before you do that, though, be sure to read the monument's short description detailing Father Crowley's importance to the Owens Valley area.

Panamint Springs. About 8.2 mi farther east on CA 190, you'll come to Panamint Springs Resort. This is a privately owned restaurant, motel, and traveler's rest area — and when open, it is a pleasant place to stop (don't count on it being open, though).

Panamint Dunes. Another 5.3 mi east brings you to the Panamint Dunes Rd (on the north side of CA 190). The road is on the left within the first ¼ mi after you leave the lake bed. Actually the road should be called the Big Four Mine Rd, because it was put in some years ago to give access to that mine. If the road is in pretty good shape, follow it toward the dunes until it turns to the right and goes up a steep, rocky slope to dead-end at the mine. Do not drive to the mine; park at the junction and walk the rest of the way to the dunes, following an old jeep track (if you can find one). The road (such as it is) from CA 190 to the junction skirts the edge of a now-dry lake bed (closed to vehicles). You'll pass a onetime island (now known as Lake Hill)—it will be to the west of you, about 3 mi from the paved road. You should be able to get within 4 mi or so of the dunes, which are about 8–9 mi from the paved road. The walk will be worth it!

The compact, star-shaped Panamint Dunes are counted among the most beautiful dunes in the California desert. Some of them loom a magnificent 250 ft high. If you are in decent shape, don't resist the urge to climb to the top of the nearest dune. From there (if the light is right) you'll be able to get some unforgettable photos of the dunes, the valley, the surrounding mountains, your antlike companions below, and—if you're lucky—clouds.

Dunes, though they may look lifeless to the casual observer, actually support a varied and unusual community of plants and animals. Here in the Panamint Dunes, for example, are not only such common species as the kangaroo rat and tumblebug (Eleodes beetle), but also the much less common Mojave fringe-toed lizard and kit fox. These dunes also have their share of truly rare creatures (for their own protection, all such creatures shall be nameless here and elsewhere in *Adventuring in the California Desert*).

As you clamber about on the dunes, take note of how the wind has patterned the sand, of the tiny tracks dune-dwellers have left as they went about their daytime and nighttime business (these tracks have some dramatic tales to tell the careful observer), and, in spring, of the delicate beauty of the dune flowers. Also notice that dune grasses grow almost to the top of the dunes' north side. You may even find evidence (mostly flakes) of prehistoric people around the dunes. When water, vegetation, and desert animals were more plentiful in the region, this was a well-used area.

Lone Pine–Independence–
Big Pine–Bishop

ABOUT THE AREA. This is the Owens Valley! Here at the valley's south end, the imposing Inyo Mtns are to the east, the Coso Range is to the south, and the glorious Sierra is to the west (how could you miss it!). Although the Owens Valley is sometimes called the Land of Little Rain, it still gets more moisture than most of the California desert—even though far less than the Sierra's west side. This means that, in general, the country hereabout is quite lush by desert standards.

As you drive up into the valley from the south, what you see—besides very imposing mountains to the left and right of you—are carefully cultivated fields of alfalfa (beginning with Rose Valley, north of Little

Lake). There are also islands of fertile riverbottom grasslands (from Olancha to Bishop). These alfalfa fields and grasslands are interspersed at nearly every turn with crisp, vigorous, gray-green sagebrush communities. The landscape is one of the most varied and beautiful in the West.

Ups and Downs (Otherwise Known as Topography and Geology). As you go farther north in the valley, the Inyos will blend into the White Mtns at Westgard Pass—while the 400-mi-long Sierra continues on northward long after you have left the Owens Valley and Owens River behind. The Owens River flows the length of the valley, from its headwaters north of the valley (over Sherwin Summit, near Crestview) to Los Angeles. Of course, the Owens is often diverted from its natural bed at Tinemaha Dam into the aqueduct that carries its water to Los Angeles. In recent times, before the aqueduct, the river flowed as far as Owens Lake; in earlier, wetter times the Owens went as far as Indian Wells Valley (the China Lake area), the Searles Lake basin, and Panamint Valley.

As you look from the Sierra crest in the west to the Inyos in the east, it's not difficult to understand that, geologically, the Owens Valley is a long, narrow block of the earth's crust that has slipped downward due to faulting at the bases of the surrounding mountain ranges. (Geologists refer to this kind of valley as a *graben*.) Owens Lake is the lowest point in this block, and thus is a natural collecting place for most of the streams flowing into the valley. Before 1913, when the aqueduct began carrying Owens Valley water to Los Angeles, the lake covered about 100 sq mi and was up to 30 ft deep. Now, water rarely reaches the lake; it is a salt flat.

The mountain ranges just 20 mi apart on either side of the Owens Valley each have their own distinctive characteristics. The Sierra has a crisp, gray, pinnacled look about it; the Inyo-White Mtns have rounded contours and earthier tones. Both ranges sport many peaks of 13,000 to 14,000 ft. The high point of the Sierra, Mt Whitney, rises 14,496 ft above Lone Pine (it's the highest peak in the continental United States). The Inyo-White Mtns' high point is 14,426-ft White Mtn, which lies north of Bishop and just above the Ancient Bristlecone Pine Forest Natural Area. The rocks in both ranges are moderately old—150 to 500 million years.

When Was the Owens Valley Not a Valley? Tens of thousands of years ago most of what we now call Owens Valley was actually Lake Owens. From approximately 100,000 years ago to 10,000 years ago, this ancient Lake Owens was one in a chain of several huge pluvial lakes in east California (Panamint Valley and Death Valley were each under water, too).

During this period, the region east of the Sierra was cooler and got a lot more rain and snow than it does today. The freezing temperatures of the last Ice Age then transformed much of this moisture to glaciers. When these great ice streams slowly melted, the water flowed down into the Owens Valley and helped create 200-ft-deep Lake Owens. When the waters in Lake Owens became high enough, they flowed south over Fossil Falls (see Index) into Indian Wells Valley—that is, into Lake China and Lake Searles. These last two lakes sometimes flowed together to make a body of water nearly 400 mi in area—hard to imagine nowadays!

Even harder to imagine is that when Lake Searles reached a depth of 640 ft, it flowed east and north around the south end of the Slate Range and into 60-mi-long Lake Panamint. But that is not the end of this amazing series of events. When Lake Panamint reached a depth of 1000 ft it, too, overflowed (through what is now called Wingate Pass) into another basin—Death Valley. The 100-mi-long body of water created there was 600-ft-deep Lake Manly.

As the Ice Age tapered off, and the climate became warmer and drier, these lakes dried up. However, we can still see the telltale signs of their ancient presences in Death Valley, Panamint Valley, Indian Wells Valley, Searles Valley, and Owens Valley. For example, at the northern end of today's Owens Lake you can still see the ancient Lake Owens shorelines. These sandy and pebbly beaches are as much as 200 ft higher than the more recent, preaqueduct shorelines.

The Valley's Original Inhabitants. Native Americans had been living in the Owens Valley area for some thousands of years before explorers "discovered" the valley and emigrants came to settle there. As mentioned above, the valley's climate had once been much wetter and cooler than that of today. In those times, fish, shellfish, game, and vegetable foods were abundant. Trees dotted the grasslands, streams and rivers flowed freely, and lakes were deep and fresh. The valley must have been an ideal place to live for the tribes who wandered into it in ancient times—and stayed.

Not much is known about the area's first inhabitants; they left little behind to tell their story. Estimates of when they came to the area vary. Some experts feel they could have come there as long ago as 40,000 years; others feel that 10,000 to 13,000 years ago is a better estimate. In any case, these ancient peoples apparently led a simple life and left behind only some primitive pebble tools and hearths. Most experts agree, though, that those tribes who lived in the area by around 10,000 years ago were producing an impressive array of "points." These sharp-edged arrowheads and knives were used in hunting large and small animals, as well as in preparing vegetable foods. In those times, near the end of the last ice age, large mammals like the mastodon and bison still roamed the grasslands. Food was easily come by.

As the climate became drier, much of the grassland disappeared—along with the large lakes and a lot of the fish and large game. Native Americans began to depend more on vegetable foods such as pinyon nuts; on small game such as lizards, rabbits, and birds; and even on the larvae of the hosts of little flies that flourished on the shores of the now-alkaline lakes.

Unlike the tribes in Arizona and New Mexico, the Paiutes (for so they called themselves) used little pottery; instead, they developed basketmaking to a fine art. Excellent examples of their baskets can be seen in the Eastern California Museum at Independence (see below). Like some other California tribes, the Paiutes also left behind interesting (if untranslatable) designs on rocks, called petroglyphs. These designs were pecked and scraped on rock surfaces in quite a few locations in the Owens Valley (see the Chalfant Valley petroglyph loop trip, below). Their meaning is obscure, but some feel the designs were associated with rituals designed to ensure successful hunting.

Such was the life of the valley's original inhabitants until the explorers, prospectors, and settlers came to the valley. An account of what happened then would take far more space than can be afforded here. Suffice it to say that the Paiutes were just as cruelly and insensitively treated as had been the other native American tribes all across the United States. For them, the "discovery" of the valley was a tragedy that resulted in total disruption of their way of life—though it need not have been so.

Beaver Hunters Discover the Valley. The Owens Valley was first "discovered" by Joseph Walker (of Walker Pass fame) and his fellow beaver hunters in 1834. Although the Walker group found no beaver, they did find a route from the Great Salt Lake to the Humboldt country of western California. This route later became an important emigrant trail—the California Trail. From this time on, settlers and prospectors began to make their way into the valley. Native Americans were displaced (and worse), lands were homesteaded, claims staked, wagon trails cleared, fields plowed, and crops planted; towns sprang up—development had come to the valley.

Farmers' Paradise. In desert regions, water is the key to everything—the indispensable element for survival. With abundant runoff from the Sierra's east side and good land, the Owens Valley residents seemed to have an assured future in farming and ranching.

By 1910, there were 4500 settlers in the valley. The McNally and Bishop Creek ditches (irrigation canals), the Big Pine Canal, the Owens River Canal, and others had already been built to irrigate hundreds of thousands of acres of valley land. Farms and ranches produced alfalfa, grapes, apples, corn, wheat, butter, and potatoes. The latter even won prizes at the California State Fair. A healthy farm economy was in place.

What happened next in the farmers' paradise is an all-too-familiar story to many small farmers and ranchers all over the West. First, so the story goes, employees of the U.S. Bureau of Reclamation who were planning an irrigation project for the valley were suborned by city of Los Angeles officials. The city officials also secretly bought land (ostensibly for reclamation), bribed a few Owens Valley officials, and managed to push through their Owens Valley–Los Angeles aqueduct project.

As the aqueduct siphoned off the Owens River waters, the Owens Valley was turned into a desert. The residents—business people, farmers, ranchers—were ruined; many were forced off the land their grandparents had settled. The city of Los Angeles justified this use (and ruination) of the valley as being "the greatest good for the greatest number." (They were right about the "greatest number.") This destruction of Owens Valley agriculture was well described by one of its farmers, Will Parcher, in this way:

Dry ditches
In a bleaching land.
A broken pane,
A swinging door,
And out upon
A withered field
Where blue blossoms
Once nodded in the sun,
A rusted plow,
Deep furrowed
In the crusted sand.

Visible proofs that the valley was once very different than it is today are everywhere. Two of the more visible casualties of the Los Angeles Department of Water and Power's ruinous water policies are Mono Lake and Owens Lake. Although Mono Lake is now included in the Mono Basin National Forest Scenic Area, and as such receives some small degree of protection, Owens Lake is gone; a salt flat has taken its place. There are many who feel this is not a fair exchange.

The Valley of 1000 Visits. As you can tell, the valley's terrain is not the only thing that is varied! The history of the area is western history in a nutshell (a pinyon nutshell, that is). If you want to visit ghost towns, rough it in the wilderness, revel in solitude, have all the comforts of home, expand your natural history knowledge, climb (or walk up) peaks, take prize-winning photos, or just plain enjoy some of the most spectacular scenery in the West, the place to come is the Owens Valley. Even 1000 visits will not begin to exhaust the area's possibilities for the highest quality of low-impact recreation.

About the only industry in the valley nowadays is what is popularly called the tourist trade. There are very few "dirty" industries in the valley, though there are some undesirable ones—ones that either destroy nonrenewable resources or make no attempt to renew the renewable ones they destroy in the service of economic gain. There are small towns, where life still moves at a human pace (if you don't count those tourists who are in a hurry). There is clean air to breathe (98% of the time), there are wide open spaces to look across, and, above all, there are the mountains. Need I say more?

FACILITIES. Motels, restaurants, gas, and all supplies are located at Lone Pine, Independence, Big Pine, and Bishop. Olancha also has gas, limited supplies, and a restaurant.

Camping Near Lone Pine. To get to Tuttle Creek, a Bureau of Land Management (BLM) campground, go about 3.5 mi west on Whitney Portal Rd off US 395 out of Lone Pine; then 1.5 mi south on Tuttle Creek Rd. A national forest campground, Lone Pine, is located 7 mi west of the town of Lone Pine off US 395 on Whitney Portal Rd. There are also two Inyo County campgrounds in the Lone Pine area — Portagee Joe (turn west off US 395 on Whitney Portal Rd and go 0.5 mi to Tuttle Creek Rd; turn south and go 0.2 mi to the camp) and Diaz Lake (on US 395 2 mi south of Lone Pine).

All these campgrounds have tables, water (stream water must be boiled or purified), and toilets (of various kinds); some have grills or fire rings. Swimming is allowed at Diaz Lake. Altitudes range from around 3800 ft (Diaz, Portagee Joe) to 6000 ft (Lone Pine, Tuttle).

Also see the Owens Lake–Panamint Dunes "Facilities" section for info on camping near Owens Lake, Darwin, and Olancha.

Camping Near Independence. To get to Independence Creek, an Inyo County campground, turn west off US 395 on Onion Valley Rd (in Independence). Go about 1 mi, then look for the campground on the north (right) side of the road. There are three Inyo National Forest campgrounds near Independence. Lower and Upper Gray's Meadow (6000 and 5800 ft) are 5.0 and 5.5 mi west on Onion Valley Rd off US 395 in Independence. To reach Oak Creek, go 1.5 mi north on US 395 from Independence, then turn west on Mt Whitney Fish Hatchery Rd and go 4 mi to the campground (5200 ft).

Again, all these campgrounds have tables, water (stream water must be boiled or purified), and toilets (of various kinds); some have grills or fire rings.

Camping Near Big Pine. There are four Inyo County campgrounds near Big Pine. Taboose Creek is 14.5 mi north of Independence and 2.5 mi west on Taboose Creek Rd (3900 ft). To reach Tinemaha campground, turn west on Fish Springs Rd 7 mi south of Big Pine (19.5 mi north of Independence). Then go 0.5 mi south to Tinemaha Rd and turn west; follow the road 2 mi to the campground (4400 ft). Baker Creek campground is located 0.5 mi north of Big Pine and 1 mi west on Poplar St (4100 ft). Big Pine Triangle campground (4000 ft) is 1 mi north of Big Pine, right on US 395 — at the turnoff to the Ancient Bristlecone Pine area (CA 168, Westgard Pass Rd). This camp has piped water. Goodale Creek, a BLM campground, is 14.5 mi north of Independence on US 395 and about 2 mi west on Goodale Creek Rd.

All these campgrounds have tables, water (stream water must be boiled or purified), and toilets (of various kinds); some have grills or fire rings.

Camping Near Bishop. There are two Inyo County campgrounds near Bishop. Pleasant Valley is 7 mi northwest of Bishop on US 395 and 1 mi east on Pleasant Valley Rd (4200 ft). To get to the Millpond Recreation Area, go 6.5 mi northwest of town on US 395, turn south on Ed Powers Rd and go 0.2 mi, then go west on Sawmill Rd for 0.8 mi to the park (4100 ft). Both these campgrounds have piped well water, toilets, tables, and grills. Swimming is allowed at Millpond. Horton Creek, a BLM campground, is located 8.5 mi northwest of Bishop on US 395 and 3 mi west on Round Valley Rd. This campground has tables and toilets; stream water must be boiled or purified.

There are several national forest campgrounds near Bishop, at somewhat higher elevations. For information on these campgrounds, check at the Forest Service office in Bishop or the Interagency Center in Lone Pine.

Lone Pine to Independence: A Scenic and Historic Tour

TO GET THERE. You can, of course, follow this route in either direction—north to south, or south to north. To get to a starting point, take US 395 to either Lone Pine or Independence.

Total mileage for the tour is about 32 mi, not counting any side roads you decide to explore.

GETTING YOUR BEARINGS. Bring along the AAA "Eastern Sierra" map. There is no good county map for this area.

ABOUT THE TOUR. This route, which is mostly on the west side of US 395, will take you from Lone Pine to Independence via the 1872 earthquake scarp, through the Alabama Hills (on Movie Rd) and by the site of Manzanar (the World War II internment camp for American Japanese).

1872 Earthquake Scarp. There are several places to view this scarp. Some are along US 395 north of Lone Pine, but this particular location is not only more spectacular, but more convenient if you are on your way to the Alabama Hills. To find this part of the scarp, go 1.8 mi north on US 395 from the junction with CA 136 (at the Interagency Visitor Center) to Whitney Portal Rd. Turn left and travel west on Whitney Portal Rd for about 0.5 mi. After crossing the aqueduct, go north (right) on a dirt road. After about 0.3 mi you will come to a light gray ridge of boulders around 20 ft high. If you climb to the top of the ridge, you will see that the scarp has cut into the alluvial fan that spreads out west from the east side of the Alabama Hills.

The 1872 earthquake was at least of a magnitude equal to that of the earthquake that destroyed much of San Francisco in 1906 (8.25 on the Richter scale). It was only because the valley was sparsely populated that so few people were killed. Indeed, the twenty-nine people killed were a goodly percentage of Lone Pine's total population. At the time of the earthquake, most of the buildings in the community were built of adobe (dried mud) bricks, put together with more mud as mortar. The buildings, unfortunately, were far from earthquake proof; most of the deaths occurred when the buildings were shaken apart and crumbled on top of their terrified occupants in the middle of the night. The frame buildings in Independence held up much better; there were no deaths there.

According to geologists, the main fault-line movement of the 1872 earthquake took place along the Alabama Hills fault, not in the fault that runs along the main eastern Sierra front. The Alabama Hills fault existed long before this earthquake, but in 1872 many fault scarps were created—including the one described here. These fault scarps can be seen here and there all the way to Big Pine. Faults, as you know, are cracks in the earth's crust, evidence that the crust sometimes cannot withstand the great pressures that build up beneath it. When the pressures become too great to be contained, the blocks of rock and earth release the pressures by moving horizontally or vertically (becoming a scarp). Sometimes long and/or wide cracks appear that extend the fault line. At other times the two sides of the fault slide past each other in opposite directions, causing stream beds, glacial moraines, and even fence lines to zig-zag when they used to be straight. The 1872 quake caused land on the Alabama Hills fault to drop 4 to 21 ft!

A very visible local example of the 1872 earthquake's work is Diaz Lake, which you probably noticed on the west side of US 395 as you came into Lone Pine from the south. This lake, known geologically as a sag pond, is cupped by two fault scarps formed in 1872; the area between the scarps sank, allowing formation of the lake. One side of the fault scarp is easily seen along the west side of the lake's north end, where it forms a bank about 15 ft high.

Alabama Hills. To find the hills, retrace your path from the 1872 earthquake fault back to Whitney Portal Rd and go west on it toward the Sierra for about 2.0 mi to Movie Flat Rd; turn north (right) here. At this point you may see a sign indicating that this is the Alabama Hills Scenic Route. The road is a good, graded gravel road, usually negotiable by any passenger car in decent condition. Stay on the main road at all times; some of the side roads can be rough and confusing.

About 1.5 mi along Movie Flat Rd, continue around the curve to the northeast (right) at a junction and cross the big gulley; at another junction 3.7 mi farther on, continue around the curve to the right (northeast). Travel another 0.4 mi and then turn north (left) at the T intersection. Nine-tenths of a mile on, go north (straight ahead) at the junction of Hogback Rd and Moffat Ranch Rd; go down beside Hogback Creek to Old Highway 395 in 0.7 mi (there is a swimming hole on the right as you cross the creek). At the old highway, go south on pavement across the cattle guard and aqueduct for 0.2 mi, then turn east to US 395, 0.1 mi away (there are undeveloped camp spots on Old 395 by the creek).

At present, the Alabama Hills are managed by the BLM; they cover about 30,000 acres. Despite a long-standing local folk tale (started by a traveling medicine man as an advertising stunt), the hills are not "the oldest in the world." Instead, they are just as old as the Sierra—about

200 million years. Interestingly enough, though, the Inyo Mtns (just across the Owens Valley to the east) are 500 million years old. In the White Mtns, a bit farther north, some rocks are nearly a billion years old. In addition, Death Valley (not satisfied with merely containing the lowest point in the United States) encompasses some rocks as much as 1.8 billion years old. Now, that's old!

The reason the hills don't look like they are part of the Sierra mountain block is that several million years ago they slipped away, en masse, from the main block. However, they didn't slip as far as did what is now the lowest part of the Owens Valley; they are about midway between the eastern foot of the Sierra and the valley's lowest point. Boulders, rocks, gravel, sand, and soil washed down from the Sierra have filled in the spaces between the hills and the Sierra and have covered and built up the floor of the Owens Valley. The true floor of the valley lies 9000 ft below today's floor—6000 ft below sea level. In other words, the Alabama Hills are just the "tip of the iceberg." In this case, the tip is the top of a bedrock scarp nearly 10,000 ft high! Pretty astounding, but true, figures, particularly when you take a moment to contemplate the Sierra rising another 10,000 ft above the Alabama Hills—it gives you an appreciation for the forces of nature.

The hills were named after—of all things—a Confederate cruiser: the *Alabama.* This came about during the Civil War when some Confederate sympathizers found placer gold in the area. Over the years the whole range of hills took on the name. In retaliation, the mines west of Independence were named Kearsarge, after the Union ironclad that sank the *Alabama.*

Although the hills are the same age and of much the same rock materials as the Sierra, they look quite different. While the Sierra crest is crisp, gray, and pointed (for the most part), the Alabama Hills are much weathered, rounded, and colorful in the good old southwestern tradition of rich browns and russets. The reddish colors come from metavolcanic rocks containing iron that has oxidized to rust.

If, as you travel along, you notice that the scenery looks familiar, this is probably because you've seen it before—in the movies and on television. When the stage was held up and the Three Musketeers, Cisco Kid, or the Lone Ranger headed the bad guys off at the pass, very often this is where it happened. Many westerns and commercials, including John Wayne's last one for Great Western Savings, were shot here. The hills have been a popular filming place for several decades; hence, the road's name—Movie Flat.

You'll also notice that there are plenty of places to picnic, take photos, and explore as you go along this scenic road. The rock formations and scenery—including views of Mt Whitney—are unexcelled, and kids love to climb in the rocks and explore the caves. There are even some side roads where you can get far enough away from other sightseers to make camping out pleasant.

Manzanar. To reach the present-day entrance to the site of Manzanar,

go north 4.4 mi on US 395 from where you just came in (at the end—
or beginning, if you are doing it from north to south—of the Alabama
Hills Scenic Route). The entrance is on the west side of the highway,
just past the Manzanar-Reward Rd, which goes east.

Around the turn of the century the settlement of Manzanar was a
prosperous farming community; its apple and pear orchards even required a large packing shed. The settlement got its name from the
Spanish word for apple. Manzanar was abandoned when the city of
Los Angeles first bought up the land and then put in the aqueduct, which
drained off most of the water that had made the valley ideal farmland.

During World War II the Manzanar area was put to use once more,
but this time in what is now a highly controversial way. The United
States government designated it as an internment/detention camp
(known, at the time, as a "relocation center") for over 10,000 American
citizens—who happened to be of Japanese origin. About all that remains
of Manzanar today are a pair of ornamental stone gateposts, a large
garage (formerly the camp auditorium), and a monument in its cemetery.
The garage, gateposts, and gatehouse can be seen near the highway (on
the west side) about 3.6 mi north of the Moffett Ranch (the northernmost Alabama Hills turnoff). To see the monument, go west at the
present-day entrance for 1.1 mi, then south for about 0.4 mi.

The dirt entrance road now leading into the site breaks up into several
more roads; some of these lead to the Inyo National Forest (about 6
mi), and one goes south toward the Alabama Hills. If you decide to
explore any of these, make sure your vehicle has good clearance, as the
road conditions vary and there are some very soft, sandy spots.

From the Manzanar entrance it is only 5.3 mi north to Independence.

Mount Inyo Hike

Class 2/elev. 11,107 ft/USGS topo *New York Butte*/10 mi RT/trail, cross-
country

TO GET THERE. In Lone Pine, 0.7 mi north of Whitney Portal Rd, turn
east off US 395 on Lone Pine Rd (paved); the road will be signed "Lone
Pine Station." After about 3 mi, the road will turn north and parallel
an abandoned railroad embankment. The road continues paved for about
3.2 mi and then becomes graveled. About 5 mi from where the road
turned north, go east on a steep, fairly good dirt road toward the Silver
Spur Mines. Go as far as is practical for your vehicle, which should
be at least 1.5 mi. This will bring you to the 4400-ft level. The road
continues on from this point.

ABOUT THE HIKE. Mt Inyo is the high point of the Inyo Range; its
peak affords grand views of the Sierra Nevada and Owens Valley to
the west and the Saline Valley to the east. The peak got its name as
a result of a climb made by members of the Sierra Club's Desert Peaks
Section in 1956. The Section successfully proposed the name, "Mount
Inyo," to the U.S. Board of Geographical Names.

This peak is usually climbed as a backpack with an overnight stop at Bedsprings Camp, located just below the Inyo–Keynot peaks saddle at about 9500 ft. There is wood, but no water at this camp area. Both Inyo and Keynot peaks can be climbed in a very long day hike.

To get to the peak, follow the use trail up the canyon. (This trail is mostly on the south side of the canyon.) When you get to the saddle, hike north along the ridge to the Mt Inyo summit.

Mt Inyo is also climbed from Saline Valley via the ridge between Beveridge Canyon and Keynot Canyon; the ridge leads up to the Keynot Mine and Keynot Peak. It has also been climbed from Saline Valley via the ridge north of McElvoy Canyon.

Eastern California Museum, Independence

TO GET THERE. Take US 395 to the center of Independence. Just across from the County Courthouse (two blocks south of Dehy Park and its very visible Locomotive No. 18), go west on Center St for two blocks to Grant St. The museum and Little Pine Village will be right in front of you. There is plenty of parking. For info on hours, call 619-878-2010.

GETTING YOUR BEARINGS. The AAA "Eastern Sierra" map is helpful.

ABOUT THE MUSEUM. This is but one of several fascinating museums found in the California desert area. Founded in 1928, the Eastern California Museum has several exceptional collections and interpretive displays of native American and pioneer artifacts, photographs, documents, scientific data, natural history, and railroad and mining memorabilia. One of the most interesting collections is of Paiute-Shoshone baskets, beadwork, featherwork, and arrowheads. The natural history exhibits contain Inyo fossils, rocks and minerals, birds' nests and eggs, and pressed plants and flowers.

Just behind the museum is Little Pine Village, a historic building preserve made up of several original structures moved here from around Independence. Also included is a Paiute-Shoshone grass shelter. Some of the buildings have been reconditioned to serve as general store, millinery shop, livery stable, beauty and barber shop, and blacksmith shop. These buildings are furnished with hundreds of historical objects appropriate to the buildings' function. The blacksmith shop is even operational! This Old West village is called Little Pine because that was one of Independence's earliest names.

To the south of the main museum building you'll notice a large collection of historic farm and ranch equipment. Take some time to pick up the self-guided tour instructions and wander about among the old harvesters, planters, plows, wagons, buggies, and threshing machines. It helps give you an appreciation for what life must have been like in the West in the early days.

The museum also cares for several historic sites in Independence. You can visit the Commander's House (ca. 1872), the Edwards House (the oldest house in the Owens Valley, ca. 1865), and the No. 18 Locomotive (narrow gauge). Please check with the museum for the hours when the buildings are open.

While you're visiting there, don't forget to look carefully through the book and gift section. Here, you'll find friendly volunteers to answer your questions and a good selection of paperback and hardcover books on local and California history, as well as native American craft items, stationery, and music box records.

There's so much to see in this museum that you need to allow yourself most of a morning or afternoon to browse through it.

Independence to Big Pine Tour
via the Inyo Crest ("The Hard Way")

TO GET THERE. In Independence, 0.4 mi south of Onion Valley Rd, go east on Mazourka Canyon Rd off US 395.

GETTING YOUR BEARINGS. In addition to the AAA "Eastern Sierra" map, you'll need the USGS topos *Independence* and *Waucoba Mtn*.

ABOUT THE "HARD WAY" TOUR. First, don't let the name put you off. This top-of-the-Inyos trip is well worth the nonfreeway driving required. Second, only attempt the complete trip with a 4WD vehicle having good clearance (passenger cars with decent clearance can easily go as far as the communications site viewpoint at about 20.5 mi). And third, traverse this route from south to north, starting at Independence. (If you do it the other way around you'll probably not find the steep grades and poor traction to your liking.) Also, the trip is best done in two days—one day does not allow enough time for maximum enjoyment. Plan on a dry camp, as there is no water along the route. Warm clothes are a must, even in summer, as the best campsites are at 8800 ft. Also, don't forget to check locally on road conditions before starting out.

The tour will take you across the Owens River, by the sites of Bend City and Kearsarge, to the foot of the Inyos, up into the Inyos via Mazourka Canyon, past many old mining claims, through Badger Flat, out to Mazourka Peak viewpoint, out to an Inyo summit viewpoint, to Papoose Flat, past some good campsites, through Squaw Flat and Marble Canyon (optional), out to the Eureka Valley Rd, and back to Independence. The total mileage is about 50 mi (excluding forays off the main road to the viewpoints, side trips, any dead ends you find, or extra exploring you do).

On the Way to Mazourka Canyon. To start the tour, go east on Mazourka Canyon Rd (located at the Shell station, just south of town). At 0.7 mi you'll cross an old canal, evidence of the agricultural activity in the Owens Valley before the city of Los Angeles diverted most of the area's water. At 1.5 mi, notice the dead vegetation south of the road; this, too, is a result of the water diversion. Just south of the road at 1.9 mi is an artesian well—an excellent supply of water when it is flowing. You'll cross the 1872 earthquake fault at about 3.2 mi and the Owens River at 3.7 mi. From here, if you look east and slightly north, you can get a good view of Winnedumah, a natural, 80-ft finger of granite pointing skyward almost on the crest of the Inyos, at 8369 ft.

Winnedumah is sometimes called Paiute Monument. According to one version of a native American legend told of Winnedumah, the Waucobas of the Sierra and the Paiutes of the Inyos were once warring when a Waucoba brave saw two Paiute brothers coming down from the Inyos. The Waucoba shot an arrow across the valley (15 mi!) and hit one of the brothers, whose body turned to stone. The Waucoba then commanded the other brother, "Stay where you are!" (*"Winnedumah!"*)— and the Paiute was immediately transformed into a shaft of granite. Since then, the Owens Valley Paiutes have looked upon the rock as a symbol of faithfulness.

At 4.3 mi, you'll pass the site of Bend City—near the transmission tower—and at 4.4 mi the paved road ends. Here, just after crossing the abandoned railroad embankment, is the site of Kearsarge, one of the stations on the old narrow-gauge Carson & Colorado Railroad, which ran from Keeler on Owens Lake to near Carson City, Nevada. At this point, a dirt road goes north; 3 mi up this road is the site of San Carlos, one of the earliest towns in the Owens Valley.

After passing the turnoff to San Carlos and continuing east (the paved road ends here and a dirt road continues on), you'll cross the road north to the Snow Caps Mine at 5.7 mi. At 7.1 the road east to the Whiteside Mine and west to the Copper Queen Mine will appear. The Whiteside tunnel, on the south side of the road, near the mouth of Mazourka Canyon, is so large and safe that it once was approved as an emergency shelter—though it never succeeded as a mine. Many of the tunnels and shafts in the canyon are dangerously unmarked and open; be very careful when exploring any diggings!

At 8.3 mi you'll cross the road east to the Black Eagle and Betty Jumbo mines; the road you are on will be changing its course from east to northeast during these last couple of miles. Mazourka Canyon is unusual in that it runs primarily north and south, paralleling the Inyo crest, whereas most of the other Inyo canyons run east and west. According to the geologists, the canyon runs north and south because a layer of metamorphic rocks (now the middle of the canyon) that was between two layers of granite (now the sides of the canyon) was more susceptible to erosion than the granite and so was worn away more quickly when the range was uplifted.

Mazourka Canyon. As you approach the mouth of Mazourka Canyon from near the sites of Bend City and Kearsarge, you can see that the metamorphic rocks are colorful shades of russet, tan, brown, and dark gray. When you are in the canyon, you'll also be able to tell that parts of the Inyo Range were formed at the bottom of an ancient sea. The layers of sediments have since been squeezed and changed (metamorphosized), rumpled, cracked, folded, and otherwise rearranged—even upended—by nature into what you now see.

The Inyo National Forest boundary is at 8.9 mi from US 395. (The name *Inyo,* by the way, is said to mean "dwelling place of a great spirit," according to the native Americans of the Owens Valley.) You'll come across some primitive mining claims at 9.3 and 11.6 mi, and at 12.4 mi you'll encounter the Santa Rita Flat Rd leading to the northwest (good gravel; about 3 mi to its end—it loops back on itself). From Santa Rita Flat there is an excellent view northeast across Badger Flat to the Inyo crest, as well as west to the Sierra. You'll notice on the topo map that the stretch you travel after you pass the Santa Rita Flat Rd is called Al Rose Canyon. (By the way, no one seems to know who Al was, but this place-name probably dates from the 1860s.)

All the mines mentioned above also date back to the 1860s, and a few are still being worked today. The claims in Mazourka Canyon, Santa Rita Flat, and Pop's Gulch to the north are all gold placer mines. They were worked by dry washing or by hauling the gravel to a water supply for washing. Pop's Gulch was especially active during the Great Depression years when the jobless could wash enough gold out of the gravel for beans and bacon.

Badger Flat and Mazourka Peak Viewpoint. At about 16.7 mi you'll see the first of the pinyon pines; at 16.8 mi the better road is to the west, up the side of Al Rose Canyon, rather than in the canyon bottom. At 18 mi you'll come up onto Badger Flat. Here, at 18.5 mi, is a junction. Follow the main gravel road north (ahead) a short distance, where it then curves west and south, climbing 9441-ft Mazourka Peak (which is unnamed on the topo and called Barber Peak on the AAA map; locals call it Mazourka). The end of the road, at the communications site, is 2.7 mi from the junction.

This is an outstanding place to look over the Owens Valley and the Sierra crest. From here you can even see the shapes of the canyons. The steep-sided, V-shaped canyons were cut by briskly flowing water; the round-bottomed valleys and basins were gouged out by glaciers. The viewpoint is also used for world-class hang-gliding competitions each summer. Take your time here; the views are worth it!

An Inyo Range Summit. After you return to the road junction, the dirt road leads east to the Blue Bell Mine (at 18.9 mi). From the junction on, a 4WD vehicle with good clearance is necessary; the road is rough, rocky, and narrow, with steep grades and a bad side hill, but is safe in a good vehicle, properly driven. At 19.0 mi a dirt road leads south, eventually rejoining the Badger Flat Road; do not take this road, but continue straight ahead, keeping to the right at 19.5 mi.

At 20.8 mi, a steep drop off the ridge leads down into a small valley to the north and a T intersection at 21.1 mi. This valley and the one to the west are reminiscent of the "parks" at the top of the Panamints.

From the T the road leads 2.5 mi east (right) to the summit of the Inyos (10,292 ft), where there is a spectacular view east down Waucoba Canyon, across Waucoba Wash, to the Saline Range. Side Hill Spring, aptly named, is 1100 ft below the crest. The jeep track continues north along the crest to just below Waucoba Peak (11,123 ft).

■ *Waucoba Peak Hike and Bristlecone Walk (Side Trips).*
Follow the jeep track north along the crest until you can scramble up Waucoba Peak. This is an easy hike of about 6 mi, round-trip.

The jeep track also runs south a short distance and dead-ends in a bristlecone pine area. To protect the bristlecones, please do not drive down this road (walking is fine).

Although gathering firewood (wood that is both dead and down) is legal in this area, any cutting of live trees should be reported to a Forest Service office (Lone Pine or Bishop). In fact, because a nearby area has been proposed for wilderness, it is advised that all resource damage be reported to the Inyo National Forest office in Bishop (behind the Sizzler).

TOUR CONTINUES. After returning to the T intersection in the valley, continue straight ahead to the northwest over a low saddle, through the next valley, and to a good campsite at 23.1 mi. There are several other campsites scattered over the next 0.75 mi. This is a good stopping place when you are doing the trip in two days. Beyond the dry campsites the road drops steeply into Papoose Flat, with its picturesque rock formations.

On to Eureka Valley Road. At 24.5 mi, there is a dim dirt track to the east, and at 24.6 mi you will come to a junction with a well-used dirt road to the east (right). The best and shortest road is straight ahead to the north. This road climbs a low divide and continues down a set of switchbacks on out to the Eureka Valley Rd at 35 mi. Big Pine is another 14 mi to the west.

Tinemaha Wildlife Viewpoint

TO GET THERE. The viewpoint is located a short way northeast off US 395, about 7 mi south of its intersection with CA 168 in Big Pine. The turnoff is not well signed (a sign appears some distance before the turnoff, but there is no sign at the turnoff itself), so watch carefully for the road going east off US 395. Once you get on the road (good dirt), directions to the viewpoint are easily seen. About 0.2 mi from the highway, you'll turn north and go 0.9 mi around and up a small hill to the high point. There are no facilities except some garbage cans.

GETTING YOUR BEARINGS. The AAA "Eastern Sierra" map is helpful.

ABOUT THE VIEWPOINT. There is an excellent view north up the Owens Valley from this little point. It's a good place to compare the mountain ranges to the west and east, and to see their relation to the valley itself. Unfortunately, some of the interpretive signs have been removed by vandals for their private collections.

If you visit the viewpoint in the early morning or late afternoon, you may see some tule elk feeding near the Owens River in the lush valley below you. Once, before California was settled by emigrants from the eastern United States, large herds of tule elk roamed the state's Central Valley and coast ranges. By the late 1800s, though, the elk had been pushed out of much of their natural habitat and hunted nearly to extinction.

In the early 1930s, about fifty tule elk were brought to the Owens Valley from California's Central Valley. The elk prospered and are now the largest free-roaming herd in California. The California Fish and Game Commission feels it necessary, however, not to allow more than four hundred elk in the valley. One of their means of keeping the herds "under control" — "controlled hunting" — is controversial. However, elk are also taken to new areas.

Rutting season is in the fall, and if you are fortunate you may see males locking their impressive antlers in competition for the cows. As with some other members of the deer family, tule elk males collect harems of cows during the breeding season. Males shed their antlers late each winter; calves (one or two) are born in the spring.

There are two other places in southern California where tule elk are being protected after reintroduction and can be seen: Tule Elk Reserve State Park (near Tupman, west of Bakersfield) and San Luis–Merced National Wildlife Refuge (west of Merced).

Chalfant Valley Petrogylph Loop

TO GET THERE. Take US 6 north out of Bishop from its junction with US 395 at the north end of town. After 1.4 mi you'll have to decide whether you are going to make the loop clockwise or counterclockwise from this point (the intersection of US 6 with Five Bridges Rd). Here, the trip will be described in the clockwise direction — which means you'll need to go north (left) on Five Bridges Rd.

The north leg of the loop will be on good dirt roads and the south leg on US 6 (paved). Total mileage for the loop is about 40 mi from this point.

GETTING YOUR BEARINGS. You'll need the AAA "Eastern Sierra" map. The topographically minded will probably want the USGS's *Bishop* topo.

ABOUT THE LOOP. The petroglyphs in this loop are the largest group in this part of the state. These rock markings were done some hundreds of years ago by ancestors of the native Americans (Paiutes) who still live in Owens Valley. Some of the designs were lightly scraped into the rock, while others were pecked or deeply gouged out. (If they had been painted they would be called pictographs.) Most of the rock draw-

Chidago Canyon petroglyphs, north of Bishop, near Chalfant Valley.
Photo by Stan Haye.

ings are found near where water used to be—at springs, streams, or lakes—for these places were where people gathered. There is seldom any water near the petroglyphs now.

Some of the petroglyphs you will see are what appear to be abstract designs (spirals, mazes, undulating lines), but some are clear images of deer, bighorn sheep, snakes, insects, and human and animal footprints.

Although even prehistorians are not certain, it may be that some of these designs had religious significance, while others may have been meant to serve as signs telling people where to find water or trails. Some may represent important events. Almost all of the petroglyph sites are on early native American hunting trails, so some prehistorians feel that many of the drawings could be meant to magically bring good hunting. (And, like today, some are probably grafitti.)

Fish Slough. Follow Five Bridges Rd north for about 1.7 mi and west for about 0.7 mi. Here the paved road ends, just about as you cross the Owens River. At this point you will see three dirt roads — one going west, one northwest, and one north. Take the last (the rightmost): Fish Slough Rd. After about 6.8 mi, turn west on a short dirt road to the petroglyph area. There may or may not be a BLM sign — depending on whether you got here before the most recent group of vandals.

As you wander around the rocky area, you will easily be able to find several large flat-topped rocks with good-sized, uniformly shaped, shallow holes in them where early people ground nuts and seeds. There may still be a few obsidian chips on the ground, left over from making tools and arrowheads. Some years ago pottery shards, shells, and circles of stones marking shelter outlines could also be seen. If you do find any artifacts, please leave them at the site. The more that is carried away, the less there is for the next person to see.

Of course, you will also see some petroglyphs, though they are not as numerous or complex here as they are at some of the other sites.

Chidago Canyon. About 4.0 mi farther north on Fish Slough Rd, turn east on another short spur road to the next group of petroglyphs. These are located on the faces of a great pile of boulders and rocks. One of the rocks is so crowded with the rock drawings that it is called Newspaper Rock.

Although some of the drawings have been stolen or otherwise defaced, and other visitors have tried their hands at creating petroglyphs, this is still a fascinating site to visit. It will take you some time to look carefully through the large number and variety of designs and figures. If the light is right it is possible to get some good photographs (photographing is permitted at all these sites). For the best photos, use a polarizer; if you don't have one, be careful of reflections on the desert-varnished rocks the petroglyphs are worked on.

Panorama View. This area is about another 2.9 mi on from the Chidago site. As the name implies, there is a good view from here. You are on the eastern edge of a volcanic tableland. As with so many other places, the signs have long been removed for souvenirs. The view, however, is still there!

Red Canyon. To reach this site, travel another 2.7 mi north on Fish Slough Rd from the viewpoint to a turnoff going northwest. Walk along the ridge on the south side of this road — there are many petroglyphs scattered along it. Plan to spend some time in this area, as there is much to be seen.

Chalfant. From the Red Canyon site the road bends sharply southeast, arriving back at US 6 in 3.6 mi; go south (right) here. In about another 2.2 mi, take a dirt road going generally southwest for approximately 0.9 mi to the Chalfant site. Here there are some circle designs 5 ft in diameter; these are very unusual, as petroglyph designs go. To find the circles, hike north by the canyon wall. Other petroglyphs are located within a quarter-mile radius of the parking area.

Returning to the Start of the Loop. Continue south on US 6 for about 13 mi. This will bring you to Silver Canyon Rd, the turnoff to the Laws Historical Site and Railroad Museum. Here US 6 bends sharply west and brings you back to Five Bridges Rd in another 2.4 mi. The junction of US 6 and US 395 on Bishop's northern edge is just 1.4 mi farther south.

Laws Pioneer Exhibits and Railroad Museum

TO GET THERE. From Bishop, take US 6 3.8 mi north and east from its intersection with US 395 to Silver Canyon Rd. Go east on Silver Canyon for about 0.5 mi to the museum (south side of road).

GETTING YOUR BEARINGS. The AAA "Eastern Sierra" map covers this area well.

ABOUT THE MUSEUM. Laws is situated at the foot of the spectacular White Mtns and looks out over the upper Owens Valley to the equally imposing Sierra crest. On the 11 acres of museum grounds are not only the restored Laws Railroad Depot, but several buildings from the old pioneer community of Laws. You can visit an old-time doctor's office, a country store, the railroad agent's house, a library and arts building, an old Wells Fargo building, a blacksmith shop, and the former Laws Post Office. All these buildings have been restored and refurbished with antique local furnishings. In addition, there are exhibits of native American artifacts, rocks and minerals, old bottle collections, antique bells from Bishop schools (you can ring them), farm wagons and machinery, and mining machinery. And don't forget the gift shop—it has a good selection of books on local history, a supply of engineer's caps and handmade sunbonnets, and a selection of railroad memorabilia.

The Laws Railroad Depot sits in the middle of the museum grounds and contains all kinds of railroad and pioneer relics. There you can also see a display of western tack, a working model-train (with sound effects), and exhibits of branding irons and barbed wire. Beyond the depot you can climb aboard the Slim Princess, one of the narrow-gauge locomotives that ran the rails from Keeler (on Owens Lake) to near Carson City, Nevada. Here you'll also find one of the famous Death Valley Railroad cars, a boxcar village, and an old railroad water tower, turntable, and pump house.

The town of Laws was incorporated in 1880; the first train came to Laws from Nevada in early 1883, and the narrow-gauge Carson & Colorado was completed to Keeler in mid-1883. Between that time and 1960, when the last train arrived at Laws, the Slim Princess was the eastern Sierra's link with the outside world. In 1912 the Southern Pacific Railroad took over the Carson & Colorado Railroad, and the Laws-Keeler branch of the Southern Pacific became the last operating narrow-gauge public carrier west of the Rockies. Because of its railroad connections, the town was an important commercial and cultural center for the farmers, ranchers, and miners of the eastern Sierra. Via the railroad, they shipped ore products and the food and livestock grown in the valley to population centers outside their area. Over the years, Laws played an important and constructive part in the history of the eastern Sierra.

The restoration and preservation of this historic site is being accomplished by the devoted members of the Bishop Museum and Historical Society. These people have selflessly donated not only their valuable time but their money to uphold their society's aim, which is "to discover, procure, and preserve whatever may relate to the natural, civic, literary, and ecclesiastical history of our area." Be sure you take time to visit this museum's excellent exhibits, both outdoor and indoor—they help make the Old West come alive!

By the way, the museum is open seven days a week, from 10:00 A.M. to 4:00 P.M.

White Mountains–
Last Chance Mountains

ABOUT THE AREA. The White Mtns–Last Chance Range area well represents California's Great Basin country. The Great Basin—which lies between the Sierra Nevada and the Wasatch Mtns (near Salt Lake City)—is so called because this region does not drain to any sea; that is, it is a basin. In fact, the Great Basin region is itself a subprovince of the Basin and Range province, which covers much of the western United States.

Basin and Range. This larger province is made up of long, narrow, mostly north-south-oriented mountain ranges separated by equally narrow valleys or by wider basins. From good viewpoints you can get some idea of the overall structure of the Great Basin—as you look out over the serried ranks of alternating mountains and valleys, as far as you can see.

California's share of the Great Basin is a rather triangular part, stretching from the White Mtns in the north (the triangle's apex) to the Silurian Hills (near Baker) in the south; and from the Sierra Nevada in the west to the Grapevine and Funeral Mtns (on the Nevada border) in the east. That is, it basically covers southern Mono County and all of Inyo County.

How to Tell the Great Basin from the Rest of the World. It's not necessary to travel widely in the Great Basin to get its flavor. A trip or two in this area will acquaint you fairly well with the basin's main distinguishing features. One of the features of most of the basin ranges is that they rise steeply from their valleys, giving the region a very high relief.

A good example of this reach-for-the-sky tendency in Great Basin country is found in the northern part of the Owens Valley. Here, the western foot of the Whites is around 4500 ft—and the Whites rise nearly 10,000 ft above the valley! (White Mtn has an elevation of 14,246 ft.) By contrast, the mere mile-high escarpment of the Last Chance Range, as it rises up over the Eureka Valley, seems hardly worth mentioning. As you will see when you visit it, even this small part of the Great Basin is definitely a haven for immensities—in the geological sense. (This high relief means, of course, that you can stay warm in winter by camping in the valleys and cool in summer by camping high in the mountains—like the native inhabitants once did.)

Fans. The valleys and basins themselves are ordinarily filled with the rocks, earth, and sand (alluvium) that wash down from the steep mountains surrounding them. When you travel to Eureka Valley (and other valleys in the region) you will see excellent examples of how the alluvium gracefully fans out into the valley's dry lake flats (playas) from steep, cleftlike canyons in the nearby Last Chance Mtns. Although these fans appear to have a very gentle grade, you (and your vehicle) will notice as you walk or drive up them that they are considerably steeper than they look.

Although rainfall is scant, a few inches may fall on a small area in a few hours. Such downpours can result in floods that move tremendous amounts of earth and rock. Many western towns have been wiped out by such floods. In 1985, for example, the Cerro Gordo Rd and the town of Keeler (on Owens Lake) were badly damaged by a flash flood. Thus, travel and camping in narrow canyons and wash bottoms should be undertaken only when the region's weather is clear and dry.

Sometimes so much sand collects in basins of this region that over the years, dunes are formed by the frequent strong winds—as in Eureka Valley, where the sand mountains are so unique that they have been named a national natural landmark.

Mines. The White Mtns–Last Chance Range area is no exception when it comes to having been heavily prospected for minerals. As with most of the mountain ranges in this part of the Great Basin, though, no huge mining operations have taken root. However, although this is not a boom area, a number of minerals have been profitably mined from time to time over the years. In the Last Chance Range you'll come across a large sulfur mine (closed since the 1940s). You'll also see small prospects, in various stages of past and present development, scattered through both ranges.

What to Do at the Top of the Triangle. Despite their remoteness from large population centers and their rugged, somewhat forbidding looks, both the White Mtns and the Last Chance Range have much to offer the low-impact recreationist. Whether you are interested in touring this scenic and unusual area on four wheels or on two feet, you'll not be disappointed.

Here you can easily visit one of the largest enclaves of the earth's oldest life forms — the bristlecone pines, located at 10,000 to 11,000 ft in the White Mtns. A trip to some of the West's highest sand dunes, through some of the Great Basin's most varied country, is also a possibility. And if it's peak walking you want, there's lots to choose from: White Mtn, Montgomery Peak, Boundary Peak, Mt Dubois, and Last Chance Mtn — to name only the hikes described here.

FACILITIES. There are motels, restaurants, gas, and supplies at Big Pine and Bishop. Gas and supplies at Benton. Gas, food, motel, and Nevada entertainment at Montgomery Pass. Gas and a restaurant at Scotty's Castle (east of Ubehebe Crater, near the northern border of DVNM).

Camping. For camping near Big Pine and Bishop, see the Lone Pine–Independence–Big Pine–Bishop "Facilities" section. Grandview, an Inyo National Forest campground, is located on the road to the Ancient Bristlecone Pine Forest. To get there, take CA 168 east off US 395 from Big Pine; a sign directing you north to the bristlecones is 13 mi ahead. After turning north, go about 5.4 mi to the campground — which has tables and toilets, but no water (be sure to bring your own). Off-road camping is not allowed in the Ancient Bristlecone Pine Forest; you must use the campground.

All other camping is open desert (or open forest, as the case may be). Some good undeveloped camp areas are described in the various trip write-ups. When planning a camping trip in this area, keep in mind its remoteness. There is often no water or shade for many miles, and in spring or fall the high elevations can be quite cold and windy — with some passes even closed by snow. Come prepared for all eventualities, because in this country help can sometimes be a long time coming.

Ancient Bristlecone Pine Forest

TO GET THERE. In Big Pine turn east on CA 168 (Westgard Pass Rd) from US 395. At 2.3 mi the Eureka Valley Rd goes southeast; keep to the northeast at this junction. The paved road to the bristlecones goes north off CA 168 13 mi out of Big Pine.

The distance from Big Pine to the end of the road (the Patriarch Grove, at 11,000 ft) is about 35 mi. Any vehicle in decent condition should be able to make this drive, although some may cough and choke a bit because of lack of oxygen. If you are hauling a trailer or are driving a large RV, it's not a good idea to go farther than Schulman Grove

(10,000 ft). Big rigs just do not do well at high altitudes! Keep in mind, too, that there are no services between Big Pine and the end of the road.

GETTING YOUR BEARINGS. A California map will show the main roads in this area; hikers, though, will probably want to consult the following USGS topos: *White Mtn, Mt Barcroft,* and *Blanco Mtn.* The AAA "Eastern Sierra" map is helpful when you want to identify Sierra peaks from the viewpoints in the White Mtns.

ABOUT THE BRISTLECONE FOREST. The bristlecone pines are thought to be the world's oldest living trees; some of them are more than 4000 years of age! You can see bristlecones in other parts of the Great Basin, even as far east as Utah, but those here in the White Mtns are the largest and oldest groves of trees. To protect these unique living things, the 28,000-acre Ancient Bristlecone Pine Forest was set aside in 1958.

Due to the rigors of their environment, the bristlecones are rather unusual looking trees. They are not tall—most are under 25 ft—nor are they lushly green. Instead, over the centuries, they have become beautifully gnarled and polished, often having graceful serpentine shapes—which make them ideal photographic subjects. It is almost impossible not to take a good photo of a bristlecone, as they are quite striking from any angle. Often, only a small strip of rich, russet bark and a few needle- and cone-tipped branches reveal that a bristlecone pine is indeed alive, well, and reproducing itself.

As you might guess from looking at and handling its mature cones, the bristlecone got its name because of the short, sharp, curved, and fragile spikes on those cones. The young cones are a striking deep purple in color; you can't really mistake them for either young limber pine or pinyon pine cones (these are the other two pines found in the area). The mature bristlecone cones are a bristly 3 in. long, chocolate in color, but with a purple tinge. The limber's cones have scales that lie down fairly smoothly and are about 5 in. long. And the ubiquitous pinyon's cones are untidily open and a mere 2 in. long (all measurements approximate).

Because most of each bristlecone is barkless and polished, some have called the trees living driftwood. This is actually quite an appropriate nickname, as both bristlecones and driftwood get their unique appearance from having been thoroughly worked over by wind, water, sand, heat, and cold. Unlike the mature trees, young bristlecones are straight and wandlike, as are most other pines. It is because they grow so slowly—less than an inch in diameter each century—that the elements have a chance to mold and shape them into such interestingly beautiful forms. Even a tiny tree may be several hundred years old—and there are many tiny trees, testimony to the bristlecone's hardiness and fertility.

It's hard to believe that any tree could thrive under the harsh conditions of the high White Mtn slopes: poor soil, meager rainfall (usually less than 10 in./year), and long, cold winters. Yet the bristlecones do. They are apparently well adapted to the weather conditions and to the alkaline limestone soil from which it is so difficult to draw nourishment. In fact, the bristlecones are so well adapted that they seemingly refuse to grow in richer soil and more congenial climate. However, some scientists think they probably could grow under better conditions—if they could survive the competition from other more vigorous trees and shrubs. Be that as it may, bristlecones seem to thrive in their rarified environment.

The best time to visit the forest is in the summer. The road to Schulman Grove (the lower one, at 10,000 ft) is usually open from late June until sometime in October. To visit at other times, you need skis. Summer in the high reaches of the White Mtns is as good as spring in other places; even in August and September you'll find many wildflowers blooming. Look especially for the several colorful kinds and sizes of paintbrush and for the profusion of tiny, soft-colored belly flowers (so named because you have to get down on your belly to properly appreciate them).

The bristlecone forest is a truly remarkable place. The vast open spaces of these upper slopes and high plateaus of the White Mtns give you the feeling that you are indeed on top of the world. There aren't many places so easily accessible that can give you this feeling. No words can really describe what you'll find there—you'll just have to go and experience it for yourself.

From Cedar Flat to Grandview Campground. As you drive up this road (which starts out at about 7200 ft), you'll shortly come to the Cedar Flat entrance station. Here, you can pick up a map and information on the bristlecone forest. Next, at 3.5 mi from CA 168, you'll come to the Pinyon Picnic Area at 8000 ft (no camping).

At 5.4 mi from CA 168, you'll come to the Grandview Campground (about 8200 ft), on the west side of the road. Even if you don't plan to camp here, take some time to drive west to the end of the campground road and then follow a short trail (0.25 mi) to a viewpoint near a large pile of boulders. (The trail may or may not be marked.) This is one of many good places to watch the sunset or sunrise, as you can see both the Inyos and the Sierra crest from it.

As you continue north up the main road, you'll cross into the forest in about another 3.4 mi (8.8 mi from CA 168). This is the beginning of the area designated as the Ancient Bristlecone Pine Forest. No camping is allowed inside this area, and this includes trailers and RVs. There are several roads that lead off the main road and outside the bristlecone area to where you can camp in Inyo National Forest. (There are, however, no other developed campgrounds besides Grandview—which, by the way, has no water. All other camping is open forest.) To find the roads leading outside the bristlecone area, consult an Inyo National Forest Visitor Map—obtainable at any of the Owens Valley Forest Service offices and at the Schulman Grove visitor center.

Sierra View. A couple of miles beyond Grandview Campground, on the west side of the road, is one of the all-time best viewpoints in the eastern Sierra — aptly named Sierra View. Here, at 9000 ft, in addition to the incredible views, there are a small parking lot and restrooms. The interpretive displays will help you identify what you are seeing. Suffice it to say here that to the west you can see from Tioga Pass to Mt Whitney, and that to the southeast you can see as far as Death Valley! This, too, is an excellent place to watch the sunset (or the sunrise). Early morning and late afternoon (sun time) are the best times for photography.

Schulman Grove. At about 10 mi from CA 168 you'll come to Schulman Grove (10,000 ft), named in honor of Dr. Edmund Schulman, who first determined how ancient the bristlecones are. There are a picnic area and restrooms here at the grove, as well as a small visitor center. The ranger-naturalists staffing the center give several short, interesting programs each day during the summer. Inside the center you'll find several small displays of local flora and fauna, a selection of guide and field books, and maps of the area. An Inyo Forest Visitor Map is a handy thing to have if you are planning to explore a bit. Ask for one at the center; there is a nominal charge. Outside the center is an interpretive display explaining how the bristlecones are dated.

You should allow enough time to walk at least one of the two trails in the Schulman Grove (sometimes known as the Methuselah Grove). The Discovery Trail is a short, self-guided, loop trail that nevertheless will give you fine views. Somewhere along this trail is Pine Alpha, which, at 4300 years of age, was the first bristlecone over 4000 years old that Dr. Schulman identified. To protect it from vandals, the tree is no longer marked.

The Methuselah Trail is an easy 4.5-mi loop hike through some of the thickest parts of the grove, down into and back out of a canyon (on a gentle grade), up onto a ridge where you can see the Inyo and Last Chance ranges, and then back to the visitor center. There are even benches along the way at various viewpoints.

This longer trail is not one to plan on doing quickly. Not only is there a lot to see, but most people who come up to 10,000 ft without taking a couple of days to acclimate find the altitude slows them down somewhat (even those in good shape). Unless you are used to the altitude, don't try to go too fast — or you may find yourself with a headache and nausea. Just take it easy, see what there is to see, and you'll enjoy yourself mightily. (For maximum enjoyment, allot a half day for this hike.)

Patriarch Grove. About 13 mi beyond Schulman Grove is the Patriarch Grove, at 11,000 ft. From Schulman to Patriarch, the road is a good gravel road. Beware, though, if you travel it early or late in the season; several portions are steep enough to be extremely difficult when muddy, icy, or snowy.

When you arrive at the parking area you'll find an interpretive exhibit and two self-guiding nature trails, both quite short — and both well worth doing. The Vista Trail leads to a ridge overlooking the meadows of Cottonwood Basin. From here you can also see the timberline, which on this side of the Owens Valley is generally above 12,000 ft. On the west side of the valley, timberline is about 1000 ft lower. The Patriarch Trail once led to the largest bristlecone in the preserve, the Patriarch. This tree is 36.7 ft in circumference and is still but a baby of about 1500 years old. Unfortunately, visitors persisted in vandalizing the tree, so to protect it the trail was changed and the Patriarch is no longer identified as such.

The Patriarch Grove is, if possible, even more photogenic than Schulman Grove. Mid- to late afternoon (sun time) is the best time for capturing the bristlecones and their incredible backdrop of bright blue sky, huge white clouds, and high mountain peaks. Don't forget to try some close-ups to record the graceful lines and interesting textures of the bristlecones' bare trunks and limbs.

Beyond the Bristlecones. The gravel road continues another 4.6 mi beyond the Patriarch Grove to a locked gate below the University of California laboratories on Mt Barcroft (12,470 ft) and White Mtn (14,246 ft). The hardy may want to start from here and try the 15-mi hike (round-trip) to the summit of White Mtn (see below).

White Mtn is the third highest peak in California. (Mt Whitney, at 14,496 ft, is the highest; Mt Williamson, at 14,375 ft, is the second highest.) The area between the locked gate and White Mtn is the White Mountain Scientific Area. No camping is allowed within this area, which is devoted primarily to research on effects of high altitude on humans.

White Mountain Hike
Class 1/elev. 14,246 ft/USGS topos *White Mtn Peak, Mt Barcroft*/15 mi RT/dirt road, trail

TO GET THERE. See directions for Ancient Bristlecone Pine Forest tour and the last section, "Beyond the Bristlecones." It is about 27 mi from CA 168 to the locked gate where this hike begins. The road is paved to the Patriarch Grove (about 14 mi from CA 168) and gravel from there on (about 4.6 mi to locked gate). In early summer and late fall the gravel road may be in poor condition due to snow or rain. Check with local sources before driving it. Last services are in Big Pine.

ABOUT THE HIKE. White Mtn is the highest desert peak in California. From it you can enjoy wonderful views of Mono Lake, northern Owens Valley, and the Sierra.

To reach the peak, begin walking at the locked gate (signed "White Mountain Scientific Area") and follow the road 2 mi to the area of the University of California's Barcroft Laboratory. The folks here usually have time to answer visitors' questions, so don't hesitate to stop and chat for a few minutes. Most of the lab's research is on the effects of high altitude on humans. By the way, the elevation even at the lab is about 12,470 ft; so, as you might guess, this hike can be chilly and windy even in high summer—be sure to bring along appropriate gear.

As you continue along the rough road to White Mtn peak, about 5.5 mi on, you'll notice that you are definitely above the tree line and are traversing a high plateau having little vegetation. The relative barrenness, wide open spaces, and clean, sharp air all combine to give most hikers a real top-of-the-world feeling that is well worth the effort to experience.

Eventually, when the peak is towering above you, you'll begin a series of switchbacks up the final slopes. At the peak the views are outstanding (you did bring your camera, didn't you?). Your maps will help you identify what you are seeing. There is also a small stone summit hut, which can be welcome shelter on a cold and windy day.

If you and your companions are experienced hikers and still have lots of energy left, you might want to explore a bit farther on along this spectacular range. Take care to keep an eye on the weather, though; this is no place to be caught in an electrical storm. Also, leave plenty of time to get back to the gate before dark.

Mount Patterson Hike
Class 1/elev. 11,673 ft/USGS topo *Fales Hot Spring*/8–12 mi RT/cross-country

TO GET THERE. *Approach 1:* from Bridgeport, drive 12.4 mi northeast on CA 182 to the Nevada state line, then 6.3 mi north on NV 338 (to Sweetwater Ranch), then another 3.4 mi to Sweetwater Summit. Turn west here on a dirt road that angles at about 150 degrees and drive about 5.3 mi to some cabins—or as far as practicable (you'll be crossing back into California). At this point, you'll be at about 8200 ft.

Approach 2: a popular alternate route is from Swauger Canyon. To reach the canyon, drive about 10 mi north of Bridgeport on US 395 to a road leading north and signed "Swauger Canyon." Follow this as far as practical—at least to about 8400 ft.

ABOUT THE HIKE. Mt Patterson is considered by some to be the northernmost high peak in the California desert; it is located east of the Sierra in Toiyabe National Forest. The summit looks out over the Sierra south of Lake Tahoe and western Nevada; the views are breathtaking.

For approach 1, hike up Sweetwater Canyon and gain the ridge to the south leading directly west to the summit. The final 2000 ft are on a colorful, nearly alpinelike ridge; only near the summit are there traces of recent mining exploration. The hike is cross-country, 8 mi round-trip.

For approach 2, hike up Swauger Canyon, swing to the east, gain the plateau, and then go north to the summit. The hike is cross-country, 11–12 mi round-trip. Wheeler Peak, only 9 ft lower than Patterson, stands nearby to the east.

Montgomery Peak, Boundary Peak, and Mount Dubois Hikes

Class 2/elev. 13,442; 13,140; 13,559 ft/USGS topo *Benton*/10–13 mi RT/ cross-country

TO GET THERE. From Big Pine, take CA 168 northeast from US 395 for 37 mi to the junction with CA 266 (near Oasis Ranch). Go north on CA 266 for about 27 mi to the Trail Canyon Rd (CA 266 will become NV 264 when you cross into Nevada); turn west here. Follow the main dirt road, keeping right at a fork about 7.2 mi from NV 264. Stay in the canyon bottom, and after about 13 mi of careful driving you will reach the end of the road in a sometimes-wet meadow by a stream. Park here (about 8700 ft).

ABOUT THE HIKES. These peaks can be done as a group or separately. It all depends on how much time and energy you have to spare.

Montgomery Peak (Approach 1) and Boundary Peak (Approaches 1 and 2). To begin, hike west on the trail about 3 mi to the "springs" in Trail Canyon (shown on the topo at 9600 ft); the springs have water only in wet years. Some hikers prefer to backpack to here and set up camp before going farther.

Ordinarily, hikers will climb Boundary Peak before climbing Montgomery Peak. Boundary Peak is the highest point in Nevada (13,140 ft) and lies just east of Montgomery Peak—which is in California. The route to Boundary can be via the Trail Canyon saddle and then south to the summit.

An alternative route to Boundary is to climb the easy slopes on the northeast side of the ridge (5 mi one way, from where your vehicles are parked). Montgomery Peak (302 ft higher than Boundary) can then be reached by traveling along the connecting ridge southwest of Boundary. Stay on the use trail on the west side for a Class 2 route to the saddle, then continue on nearer the ridge line (13 mi, round-trip, from where your vehicles are parked).

Montgomery Peak (Approach 2). Montgomery can also be climbed more directly from Middle Creek, the next major drainage south of Trail Canyon (this route bypasses Boundary Peak). The turn west from NV 264 is the same as for Trail Canyon, but to get to the next drainage you'll need to take the left fork to Middle Creek at 7.2 mi (there is a sign). From the fork, drive about 11.5 mi from NV 264 to about 8200 ft.

Hike up the canyon toward the area of the springs shown on the topo at 7900 ft. The springs are near the center fork of Middle Creek (a year-round stream). Continue up the easy Class 2 slopes southeast of Montgomery to the summit (10 mi, round-trip).

Mount Dubois. Another Class 2 climb that can be made from the Middle Creek roadhead is to Mt Dubois (13,559 ft). For this climb, hike to the Jumpoff shown on the topo, then turn south and walk to the peak on an almost level plateau.

Montgomery Peak (Approach 3). Yet another way to climb Montgomery Peak is to start from the site of Montgomery City near Benton and go up via the west ridge.

Last Chance Mountain Hike
Class 1/elev. 8456 ft/USGS topo *Magruder Mtn*/7 mi RT/cross-country

TO GET THERE. In Big Pine, turn east off US 395 onto CA 168. After 2.3 mi go south and then east on Eureka Valley Rd for about 49.5 mi to a primitive dirt road leading north to Last Chance Spring. The turn-off is at the very north end of Death Valley, at the bottom of the grade from the Last Chance Range. It is signed "Crankshaft Junction" and features one or more (you guessed it) crankshafts. Drive as far as possible on this road (about 2 mi). Eureka Valley Rd is paved for about two-thirds of the way and graveled the rest of the way.

Alternatively, this road to Last Chance Spring can also be reached from the north end of Death Valley, 2 mi east of the turnoff for Ubehebe Crater. This is the south end of BLM road 1856, Eureka Valley Rd; from this point it is about 21.2 mi north to the Last Chance Spring Rd.

ABOUT THE HIKE. The drive to the jump-off point for this peak is worth paying close attention to because you'll be going through the Eureka Valley. As you go through the valley, look for its remarkably beautiful and massive sand dunes to the south. At 43 mi also note the old sulfur mining camp of Crater, on the south side of the road.

To get to the peak, hike to the spring by going about 1.5 mi up the canyon leading west. This will take you past some small mines. Then, gain the ridge to the north and hike west to the peak.

Eureka Sand Dunes
National Natural Landmark Tour

TO GET THERE. From Big Pine, go east off US 395 on CA 168, the Westgard Pass Rd, for 2.3 mi. Take the south fork, Eureka Valley Rd (signed "Death Valley" and shown on the topo as Waucoba Rd), and follow this paved road as it winds up the canyon for about 16 mi. Pass the unsigned Waucoba/Saline Rd turnoff to the south and continue straight ahead on what is called Loretto Rd on the topo, but is either unsigned or signed as "Eureka Valley Rd." The road descends into Little Cowhorn Valley and skirts Joshua Flats before turning south to descend even farther before climbing over Lime Hill 24.1 mi from where you took the Death Valley fork. From this summit the road descends Loretto Wash to Eureka Valley. The pavement ends here and the remainder of the route is over graded gravel roads, crossing Eureka Valley almost to the Last Chance Mtns. About 12.3 mi from Lime Hill (38.8 mi from US 395), the South Eureka Valley Rd comes in; take this road south. (The present route of the South Eureka Valley Rd does not follow the old route shown on the topo.) It is approximately 10 mi from this point to the Eureka Dunes. (See below for points of interest along this route.)

Mileage from Big Pine to the dunes is approximately 49 mi. There are *no* services between Big Pine and the dunes. In summer the temperatures can reach 120° F, so beware of traveling then.

Although some surfaces may be a bit washboardy, vehicles with decent clearance should have no trouble with this route. Sometimes, however, storms can cause washouts—so check locally regarding this possibility before setting out. Most of the ungraded side roads require a 4WD vehicle.

Return Options. Route 1. Return the way you came. Mileage back to Big Pine is 49 mi; no services.

Route 2. Return to Eureka Valley Rd, go east and ascend Hanging Rock Canyon in the Last Chance Mtns. This is a scenic route up a colorful desert canyon on a paved road. At the top, where the pavement ends, is the crater, an open-pit sulfur mine. The mine closed some years ago when the dry sulfur dust exploded and burned the mill. You'll be able to smell the sulfurous odor near the mine. From this point a graded dirt road winds down the canyon until it comes out at the north end of the Death Valley drainage. From there it trends south for miles, entering DVNM and continuing about 7 mi more until it meets the road to Ubehebe Crater. Services are at Scotty's Castle, about 8 mi east of where you come into the paved road.

Route 3. Return to Eureka Valley Rd, go west, and travel 0.7 mi to the North Eureka Valley Rd. Turn north and follow this road to the dramatic Cucomunga Narrows. This is a scenic area of colorful outcrops and badland erosion of ancient granite. Then follow the main traveled road northwest into Fish Lake Valley. On the far west side of the valley you will come to CA 168, a paved road. Turn west on CA 168, go over Gilbert Pass (6373 ft), through Deep Springs Valley, over Westgard Pass (7313 ft), and back to your starting point in Big Pine at US 395. Mileage back to Big Pine is about 70 mi; no services.

GETTING YOUR BEARINGS. Maps covering the rather large area of this trip are: (1) AAA's "California" (doesn't show the 10-mi road to the dunes), "Death Valley," and "Eastern Sierra"; (2) USGS topos—*Big Pine, Waucoba Mtn, Waucoba Spring, Soldier Pass,* and *Last Chance Range.* (The Eureka Dunes are on the latter.)

ABOUT THE DUNES. The Eureka Sand Dunes (2880 ft) are located in remote, virtually waterless Eureka Valley, which is situated between Owens Valley and Death Valley. Although not directly accessible from DVNM, the dunes are only 6 mi west by air from the northwest corner of the monument. They are managed by BLM as an Area of Critical Environmental Concern (ACEC). They were designated a national natural landmark in 1983.

Points of Interest on the Way to the Dunes. On your trip from Big Pine to the dunes, there is much to be seen. Some of the main points of interest are listed here:

Miles from US 395	Point of Interest
1.6	Owens River—fishing and swimming.
2.0	Greasewood scrub—a valuable plant community because these plants tolerate heavy soil, some alkali, temperature extremes, and other unfavorable conditions that most plants would not tolerate; dependent on groundwater.
4.5	Layers of ancient lakebed deposits—on north side of road.
10.6	Devil's Gate—a narrow slot through folded metamorphic rock formations.
15.0	Open summit with mountain sagebrush scrub—a splendid view of the Sierra Nevada; about 7200 ft elevation.
15.7	Road to Saline Valley—turns off to the south; this is the north route into the valley.
16.4	Pinyon-juniper woodland—good picnic area in the lower portion where roads turn off.
17.5	Little Cowhorn Valley—a small flat, much of it covered by winter fat, a low whitish shrub.
20.3	Joshua Flats, a Joshua tree woodland—old man cactus and good flower displays in late spring of good years.
26.7	Lime Hill—pale gray or buff to white dolomite (limestone) cliffs; specialized plant species occur here; about 5700 ft elevation.
27.0	Loretto Wash—outstanding flower displays in good years; chuckwallas may be seen surveying their territories from boulders in the granite area north of the road; traces of the rock walls of the Loretto mining camp may be seen along the south side of the road.
30.0	Eureka Valley—the pale form of the Eureka Dunes may be seen in the distant southeast; most of the route through Eureka Valley is in the creosote bush scrub plant community.
38.8	Turnoff to the Eureka Dunes—the alluvial fan above this junction is a good cactus garden.
48.5	The Eureka Valley Dunes!—the dunes are situated on the bed of a Pleistocene lake. The shoreline is well

defined northeast of the dunes. The playa northwest
of the dunes is sometimes filled with water, reflect-
ing Inyo Mtns peaks. The Saline Range forms the
south wall of Eureka Valley, and the Last Chance
Mtns are the spectacularly banded wall on the east.
The Inyo Range encloses the remainder of the valley.
Early May is the best time to visit the dunes to see
flowers. The sand mountain in the foreground is
triangular in shape, covering approximately 4 sq mi.
Beyond it a series of transverse dunes, about a third
as high, cover about 5 sq mi. A sand sheet surrounds
the dunes on all sides except on the playa. The whole
is an island of sand; a unique ecological unit.

When to Visit the Dunes. Fall, winter, and spring all have their charms
for the desert lover. Summer, in general, is just too hot for real enjoyment. Spring has flowers (and sometimes rain, which can mean road
washouts). Fall has warm days and cool, but not cold, nights (also a
few flowers — and little rain). Winter can get pretty cold at night (but
this is the clearest, driest time of the year in the desert — excellent for
photography). In short, almost any time other than the hottest part of
the summer is a good time to visit the desert — and the Eureka Dunes.

If you do decide to make the trip when the weather is still a bit on
the warm side, don't forget your hat (broad brimmed) and canteen (take
it on even a short stroll). In winter, don't forget your long underwear —
just because this is the desert doesn't mean that the nights can't get down
to freezing! At any time of the year, don't forget your binoculars,
camera, day pack, and a $10 \times$ hand lens (to look at the insects and flowers
with, of course).

The Sand Mountain. The Eureka Dunes are noted for their massive
sand mountain nearly 700 ft high, at their north end, and the unusually
rich flora of the dune system. The sand mountain, located just west of
a prominent mountain wall (the Last Chance Mtns), catches more
moisture than most dune systems. There is no runoff, so any rain or
snow falling on the dunes gradually percolates downward. Thus, even
in dry years, some moisture is reaching the dune plants. The storage
capacity of this great ridge of sand is unique.

Very Special Plants. Over fifty species of plants occur in these dunes,
including three endemics that are limited to southern Eureka Valley.
These are the Eureka dunegrass, the Eureka evening primrose (look for
large, white showy flowers), and the Eureka milk-vetch. Endemic
beetles are also present, in addition to an unusually rich fauna.

Exploring the Dunes. These dunes rank high in aesthetic appeal. The
pale sand forms against the richly banded Last Chance Mtns make a
scene of dramatic contrasts. The rhythmic patterns of the dunes are
enhanced by shadows in the late afternoon and morning hours. It is
a photographer's paradise.

A favorite morning pastime is to study the tracery of activity on the sand—a graphic record of dune life during the night. If you look closely you will see the footprints of tiny mammals and reptiles, the undulating trail of snakes, the abstract patterns made by large insects, and the traces of other human visitors.

Few can resist climbing the dunes, although not all make it to the top. A barefoot, toes-in-the-sand experience tunes one in on this dune world. Children can safely enjoy sand play at any level. Those who climb to the higher crests may hear the dunes "sing." Only a few dunes can boast this feature. Cascading sand creates a vibrating sound comparable to a bass viol!

Those who enjoy challenging hikes may want to climb canyons slashed in the Last Chance Mtn wall. The way may be blocked by dry falls or cliffs, however, so caution is advised. There are no trails other than animal routes.

Camping Near the Dunes. On the final approach to the dunes, an ungraded road goes east to the barren clay surfaces on the north side (near the interpretive signs), which are commonly used as campsites. You can safely drive straight ahead to the northwest corner of the dunes, but beyond that point there is danger of getting stuck in the sand.

There are no developed campsites at the dunes, and thus no water, no firewood, and no restrooms. Group campers should go prepared to furnish a toilet.

9

West of Death Valley

Red Rock Canyon–Randsburg

ABOUT THE AREA. Here, in the space of about 60 mi, you can go from one of the California desert's best birding and wildlife areas, Butterbredt Canyon; to one of its most unique scenic features, Red Rock Canyon; and to one of its most outstanding historic features, Rand Mining District. And to get between the last two, you travel along yet another important feature, this time a geologic one—the Garlock fault. That's quite a few features for one small area!

The El Paso Mountains Are the Garlock's Fault. The El Pasos are the southwesternmost of California's Great Basin Ranges. Their elevation ranges from about 2000 ft at their southern foot to the 5244-ft summit of Black Mtn (an extinct volcano) to the north and to the 4578-ft El Paso Peaks to the east; the mountains cover about 50 sq mi.

Geologically, the height of the El Pasos is the result of great vertical and horizontal displacements of earth and rock: a continual faulting and folding of the earth's crust. In this the range is like most of the other striking topographic features in the West. More specifically, the El Pasos are a block pushed up by the actions of the Garlock fault. This fault forms the southern geologic boundary of California's Great Basin (and the northern geologic boundary of the Mojave Desert).

The Garlock fault is a huge one, stretching from Tejon Pass near Lebec to the southern end of Death Valley. It cuts off the Basin Ranges from the Mojave Desert with imposing, several-thousand-foot-high vertical displacements of ancient rocks and sediments. The horizontal displacements are even more imposing—stretching to as much as 30 to 40 mi. Unfortunately, you usually can't see the horizontal displacements from the ground as easily as you can the vertical displacements unless you know just what to look for (which most of us don't).

As you drive along the Red Rock–Randsburg Rd and the Garlock Rd between CA 14 and US 395, you are following the fault trace and two of its products: the El Paso Mtn range and the Fremont Valley. This valley (actually a closed basin) was probably formed as the mountains were pushed up and the basin floor sank. (About 8.5 mi south of China Lake Blvd on US 395 or 5.5 mi north of Johannesburg you can clearly see the 50-ft fault scarp where it intersects US 395.)

Mining Was a Mixed Bag. Early miners and prospectors had a hard time of it in the Butterbredt Canyon, Red Rock Canyon, and El Paso Mtns region. A few good strikes were made in the late 1800s, but lack of water in the El Pasos and the playing out of the ore in the canyons discouraged larger, more permanent mining operations such as flourished in the Rand Mining District for many decades.

The Rand District got its start in 1895, when gold—and a lot of it—was found on the site of what was later aptly called the Yellow Aster

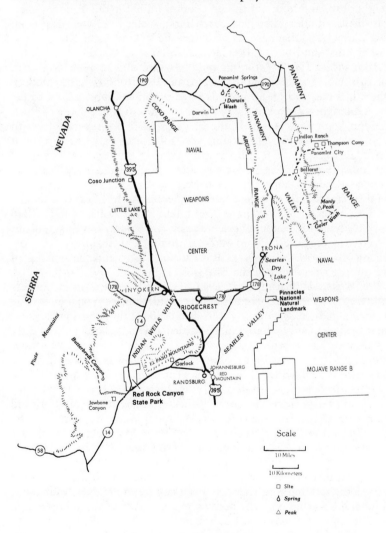

Mine. Later, silver and tungsten were also profitably mined nearby at Red Mtn and Atolia. Johannesburg was the area's supply town, first as a major freight service stop and later on as a railroad stop. Nowadays, Randsburg is one of those rare places: a living ghost town.

When you visit Randsburg, you'll still be able to see some of the original buildings and mining remnants. There is also an excellent Old West museum, administered by Kern County. The townspeople are friendly folk and will supply you with antique stores to browse in, a restaurant, and even a place to try an old-fashioned phosphate.

The town of Garlock, which initially did so well as a water supplier, freight stop, and home of the first stamp mills for the Yellow Aster, was displaced after just a few years. First, water lines were laid from Iron Canyon to Johannesburg, and then the Yellow Aster built its own stamp mills—and poor little Garlock couldn't compete.

A Rockhound Haven. Although mining wasn't able to get a long-term and profitable foothold in the El Pasos and Red Rock Canyon, modern mineral, fossil, and photo hounds have certainly found plenty to interest them there. Most of the El Pasos are open to collecting; Red Rock Canyon State Park is not. In the El Pasos there are several places to look for petrified wood (though you sometimes have to dig for it nowadays), jasper-agate, bits of gold-bearing ore, and various good mineral specimens. (See Strong's excellent book, listed in the "Recommended Reading" appendix, for details.)

Fossil fans find these areas interesting because some of the oldest non-marine fossils in the West have been found in the El Pasos and in Red Rock Canyon (for example, ancient camels and horses, as well as remains of very tiny creatures). Photo buffs can do pretty well amongst the colorful badlands of the canyon's Ricardo formation and the remains of old mining operations in the El Pasos.

Red, White, and Brown Lake-Bottom Cliffs—In Red Rock Canyon. Lookers and photographers alike are bound to consider this canyon a must. The accordion-pleated, grotesquely crenellated cliffs of the Ricardo formation are indeed eminently photographic, particularly in the long light of early morning or late afternoon. However, if cameras bore you, join those who prefer wandering and looking. There is no way to see all of this miniature Grand Canyon in just one visit (even if you wander all the time), so don't wear yourself out trying. Instead, take time to try your hand and eye at identifying some of the desert and mountain flora and fauna that live in this scenic transition zone. Plan on coming again.

A Place to Meet Desert Creatures Face-to-Face. Bird people will not want to miss the Butterbredt Canyon tour. In this area, with its year-round water supply, at least two hundred species of birds are seen each year! Many other desert creatures also live there, including large mammals such as the rare bighorn sheep, bobcat, coyote, mule deer, and an occasional mountain lion. Whether you prefer to ride or walk, you're sure to see many desert creatures in action.

Decisions, Decisions. Choosing where to go first—when several points of interest are presenting themselves—can sometimes be a problem. Because this area is an easily accessible one, though, and has a centrally located campground (for those who aren't ready for open-desert camping just yet), it shouldn't be too difficult to get started exploring. If you really can't decide, start at the top of the list and go from there.

FACILITIES. Motels, restaurants, gas, and supplies at Mojave, California City, Ridgecrest, and Inyokern; gas and minimal supplies at Johannesburg and, farther south (off CA 14), at Jawbone Canyon Store; cafe at Randsburg.

Camping. There is a developed campground at Red Rock Canyon State Park (see directions below). Tables and pit toilets are available; no water. Also see Indian Wells Valley–Little Lake "Facilities" section, below.

All other camping is open desert, where permitted—for example, most parts of Butterbredt Canyon and the El Pasos (Bureau of Land Management lands).

Red Rock Canyon (State Park)

TO GET THERE. Drive north on CA 14 from Mojave about 25 mi. Turn northwest (left) in the heart of the canyon, at the sign to the campground, onto a good paved road—Abbott Dr—into the park; follow this road for about 0.75 mi to the ranger station/visitor center and campground turnoff. If you plan on exploring any of the back roads (dirt), check with the rangers at Ricardo Ranger Station about whether your vehicle is suitable.

GETTING YOUR BEARINGS. Deciphering landmarks will be easier with the USGS topo *Saltdale*. For a good general map of the area, try the AAA "Kern County" map.

ABOUT THE CANYON. The first thing people notice about Red Rock Canyon is the rock formations. As you approach the canyon from the south, the colorfully layered cliffs can be seen for several miles. As you go through these badlands, look for a dark layer among the pinks, whites, reds, rusts, and browns. This is one of the lava flows left over from more volcanic times.

If you enter the canyon from the south, you'll pass through a narrow, steep-walled gorge. The walls of this gorge are made up of old, hard, crystalline rock, in contrast to the younger, softer materials of the richly colored, accordion-pleated cliffs farther on. Soon you'll emerge from the gorge, leaving the old rock behind, and come into a wide bowl edged both east and west by sharply dissected, spectacular palisades. Notice the pink volcanic materials in the center of the bowl and the dark lava capping the cliffs on the west side of the road.

To better explore the canyon's features, stop at the visitor center and pick up some maps of the park's roads (mostly dirt) and information on how best to get to the two preserve areas (Hagen and Red Cliffs) and other interesting formations. Access to cliffs and preserves is by foot only. The 4000-acre park stretches for some distance on either side of CA 14 and has several sets of dirt roads, so you really do need more information on how best to see the area than there is room for here.

It's not just spectacular rock formations that make Red Rock Canyon interesting, though. There's also the fact that it lies in a biologic transition zone between the Mojave Desert (south) and the Sierra Nevada (west) — and in a geologic transition zone between the Mojave Desert and the Great Basin (north). This means that you can have a very interesting time of it just trying out your natural history skills by identifying which flora and fauna represent which province. Then there is the area's geologic and paleontologic history, in which a deep, ancient lake, 7000 ft of sediments, active volcanoes, and saber-toothed cats figure. But let's not forget the Old People who lived here perhaps 20,000 years ago, and the gold miners of the 1800s.

The time span involved does make it hard to comprehend how much can happen in a single area like this. But let's give it a try by looking over a few of the area's geological, prehistorical, and historical bits and pieces. There's so much to see at the canyon that even a little background will do wonders for your appreciation faculties.

From Sediments to Palisades — The Ricardo Formation. Ten million years ago the crenellated cliffs of the Ricardo formation you admire today were forming at the bottom of a landlocked lake. When you look at the cliffs you can see that the various layers are mostly sand, silt, clay, and gravel, mixed with various kinds of volcanic leftovers. What you see here is only a small part of the Ricardo formation; its total depth is nearly 7000 ft! The many-colored lower layers of the formation visitors see today have a high volcanic content. Also, some of the ridges are topped with a dark, lava-flow layer.

Actually, two different lava flows are identifiable in the canyon. These lava layers are much harder than the sediment layers, which is why they often cap the palisades. Without these caps, there would be no striking palisades; the mostly soft sedimentary layers would wear down more evenly. It is this combination of soft (Ricardo formation) and hard (volcanic) layers that make the striking ins and outs, ups and downs, of the Red Rock badlands possible. However, not all volcanic material is hard and dark. For example, in the middle of the bowl (or amphitheater) mentioned above, there is a thick, relatively soft bed of what was once hot volcanic ash. This tuff is a lovely pink; you can't miss it.

From Saber-toothed Cats to Coyotes. In among the layers of the Ricardo formation are fossil reminders of a time several million years ago when Red Rock Canyon was on the shoreline of a freshwater lake, surrounded by fertile grasslands and open forests. In those times, the rainfall was probably about 15 in. a year — three times what it is now. Munching on the grasses (and, of course, on each other) were such creatures as mastodons, rhinos, saber-toothed tigers, tiny horses, and wolves.

This interesting menage browsed on the rich grasses and hunted among trees such as locust, oak, cedar, acacia, palm, and even fig. Some of these animals considerately left behind their bones and teeth for us to marvel at. One can't credit the trees with such foresight, but nevertheless they, too, left behind some of their substance—in the form of petrified wood.

Then there are the more modern wildlife inhabitants of the area. Here, as in many other places in the California desert, you may see creatures such as ring-tailed cats and kangaroo rats, desert iguanas and leopard lizards, burrowing owls and hermit thrushes, and, of course, our old friends the fuzzy, cuddly tarantulas.

From Old People to Moviemakers. As far as the prehistorians can tell, people first lived in the Red Rock Canyon area about 20,000 years ago. A few petroglyphs in the El Pasos and a village or religious site on Black Mtn are about all these ancient canyon dwellers left behind. Who, if anyone, lived in the area between the time of these Old People—as they are called—and the Mojaves is not definitely known.

The Mojaves, however, lived in the area for several hundred years before Europeans "discovered" the western United States. As did many of their relatives throughout the Great Basin and other parts of the southwestern deserts, these native Americans traveled seasonally from place to place in search of food. In the Red Rock Canyon area they left behind rock mortars that were used for grinding seeds and other plant parts, along with other implements also used in day-to-day activities.

In historic times Red Rock Canyon experienced its share of the mining mania that gripped the West from the mid-1800s on. Most of this activity did not begin until gold was found in a big way at what came to be called, first, Rand Camp and then Randsburg. Of course, minor gold finds in the El Pasos also helped encourage prospectors to explore the Red Rock area.

When gold fever was raging in the area, a Mr. Hagen took the enterprising step of buying up much of the land in and around the canyon. He even named the little community that grew up around the mining operations after his son, Richard. Now, you can find the park headquarters on the site of Ricardo and the Hagen name on one of the park's major preserves.

In the human sense, Red Rock had an even more important function than the grubstaking of a few miners. Its dry wash and springs made it an ideal stopping place for the stages and freight wagons shuttling back and forth from Los Angeles and Bakersfield to the Owens Valley, the Panamints, Randsburg, and other towns and mining operations. Here, people could get out of the summer sun and winter winds, fix their wagons, feed and water their stock (and themselves). As a way-station, it was a busy place for many years.

The railroad, however, put an end to the canyon's days as a bustling way-station. But it wasn't long after this happened that Red Rock was "discovered" again—this time by moviemakers. If you have a feeling of déjà vu when you first visit the canyon, it's probably well founded.

Remember all those Saturday afternoon westerns you used to happily munch your way through when you were a kid? Well, not a few of those exciting scenes were filmed at Red Rock Canyon!

Still Famous After All Those Years . . . Nowadays the canyon is famous in another way—as a unique and spectacular desert park and preserve. It is unique not just because of its geology or beauty, but because—as mentioned before—it is a geologic transition area between the Mojave Desert and the Great Basin provinces and also a biologic transition area between the Mojave Desert and the montane Sierra Nevada region. This means that the plant and animal communities you see here can be a mixture of those usually found in the respective provinces and life zones (see Chapters 4 and 5 for details).

By the way, the canyon hasn't always been a state park. It was made a state recreation area in 1969; it only became a state park in 1980 after a long fight by local conservationists. Much of the area still shows scars of the off-road-vehicle use that used to occur here.

What to Do in the Canyon. First, visit it any time but high summer. Like many parts of the high desert (over 4000 ft), the canyon is often unpleasantly hot in summer. Plan to spend a couple of days—the campground makes car camping easy. Don't forget binoculars and camera. (The best times to get photos of the rock formations are early morning and late afternoon, when shadows define the shapes and colors are at their most intense.) Visit the small but well-planned interpretive center. Finger the rock display there, look through the flower photos, and ask the park rangers for the plant and animal lists compiled especially for the canyon (the birds are especially numerous and interesting). Also ask the rangers how to best explore the preserves and get to the must-sees—and then go out and explore them!

You say all this should take you about a week, at least, and you have only two days—well, do the best you can.

Butterbredt Canyon Tour

TO GET THERE. Take CA 14 north from Mojave for 20 mi; turn west on Jawbone Canyon Rd (paved) and go 6.3 mi, then bear north on a dirt road and travel approximately 6 mi farther. This will take you up and out of Hoffman Canyon. The turnoff to Butterbredt Canyon is heralded by a battered white range sign describing private boundary regulations. Twenty yards farther, on the right side of the entrance road, is a more recent wood sign designating Butterbredt Spring as a wildlife sanctuary. The spring is down this road another 0.9 mi. The Butterbredt Canyon Rd continues northwest from the spring entrance.

GETTING YOUR BEARINGS. The following maps will help you get the most out of this tour: AAA "Kern County"; USGS topos *Cross Mtn, Onyx, Emerald Mtn, Breckenridge,* and *Isabella.*

ABOUT THE CANYON. Butterbredt Canyon was named after Frederick Butterbredt, a native of Germany who settled here in the 1860s. He married a native American woman and produced a large family. When the U.S. Geological Survey mapped the Mojave quadrangle in 1912–13, the surveyors misspelled the name, setting it down as Butterbread (this error has been corrected on recent maps).

The Jawbone-Butterbredt area consists of approximately 153,000 acres of BLM-administered public land and about 58,000 acres of private land. Butterbredt Spring and Wildlife Sanctuary is supported by the National Audubon Society and the Onyx Ranch. The land on which the spring is located is privately owned, and vehicle travel and hunting are restricted.

An End to Misuse by Motorcyclists? In 1976 an agreement was reached between BLM and private landowners in which off-highway vehicles could continue to use the public acreage in designated areas and ranchers could use other areas for grazing. The area was also declared an Area of Critical Environmental Concern (ACEC) by the BLM.

I hope Butterbredt Canyon's misuse by motorcyclists and others will eventually cease now that all motor travel is restricted to the existing main road. No motorcycle trails crossing the canyon have been designated. Only the existing Butterbredt Canyon Rd and the rough Gold Peak Rd in the northwest of the canyon are designated roads.

There are no facilities of any kind in the Jawbone-Butterbredt area — it is considered primitive. Although the land is a checkerboard of public and private ownership, some open-desert camping is permitted under BLM regulations. If you camp in the area, please remember that the desert here will not support wood gathering of any kind.

Butterbredt Canyon is enjoyed by many people. A log book atop Butterbredt Peak (elevation 6000 ft) lists great numbers of hikers with enough stamina to have been rewarded with the seemingly endless view from the highest rocky point. Wildflower fanciers find an abundance of colors and species each spring. And those whose preoccupation is birds just can't find enough time during spring and fall migratory periods to spend searching for the unusual in the cottonwoods and willows lining Butterbredt Spring. Such popularity is not surprising, as there aren't all that many riparian areas in the California desert, and few that are as easily accessible — and as varied — as this one.

A Haven for Birds and Bird Lovers — The Canyon as Flyway. The area is made up of many complex habitats — ranging from riparian (willow and cottonwood trees, tules, rabbitbrush, and other typical shrubs), to thick, impressive stands of Joshua tree, to mixed juniper and pinyon pine forests at the higher elevations. Thus, the canyon contains valuable protective cover and critical nesting habitat for many species.

In fact, the most important aspect of this canyon is probably its use as a natural flyway for migratory birds erupting north in spring up Butterbredt Canyon and on to the Sierra. Careful counts have shown that the canyon supports over 230 species of migratory and resident birds, not to mention a variety of other wildlife!

What to Do in the Canyon. For birders, there are perhaps too many choices! If you aren't in the mood for hiking, spend some time in the Audubon Wildlife Sanctuary at Butterbredt Spring. It's not a large area, but lots of birds like it. From here you can also walk down the canyon, where during migration times you may spot Scott's oriole, or get an unexpected glimpse of a chukar or mountain quail. Be sure to study the seeps for migrant warblers and vireos. The gray vireo is found here in spring.

Other birds to look for near the spring or in the canyon are ladder-backed and Nuttall's woodpeckers, cactus wren, Le Conte's thrasher, and Brewer's, black-chinned, and black-throated sparrows. Also be on the lookout for long-eared, great horned, and barn owls roosting in the trees growing in the wash.

A leisurely drive through Butterbredt Canyon (see directions below) will reward you with excellent high-desert scenery and add to your bird list. The canyon opens into a broad, bowl-like valley filled with Joshua trees. Here the Scott's oriole nests in profusion — also the blue-gray gnatcatcher. The golden eagle is seen regularly, as are cactus wren and Le Conte's thrasher.

If you take the side trip to Kelso Creek while driving through the canyon, take some time to walk along the rich creek bottom and some of the canyons to the west of it (directions below). This is a good place to see all kinds of wildlife.

For those in the mood for hiking, rather than walking, sitting, driving, or strolling, there are several choices. As mentioned above, Butterbredt Peak (6000 ft) is a popular destination. There is also a log book on Kelso Peak (5090 ft). Check your topo maps for best routes. Part of the Pacific Crest Trail crosses the northeast part of Butterbredt Canyon; you can easily get on it from Kelso Creek (see general directions below).

TO BEGIN THE TOUR. Go northwest from the spring on the poorly maintained Butterbredt Canyon Rd, which follows the base of the canyon and winds to the summit pass (5220 ft) in 5.6 mi. Beyond, the canyon drops to the paved Kelso Valley Rd in 3.0 mi. This last stretch has some interesting narrow spots at the lower end that sometimes require careful rock-crawling. This road can be navigated by most passenger cars. It should be considered rough, but passable with caution.

- *Kelso Creek (and Peak) (Side Trip).*
Turn right on Kelso Valley Rd for a side trip to nearby Kelso Creek. Follow the paved road 3.8 mi to an area surrounded by massive cottonwoods and willows on the creek's east side. Turn left through the opening in the old fence and proceed for 150 yds to the bank above the creek. This should place you near a historic willow tree growing where the road becomes level.

Walk along the rich creek bottom for 0.5 mi north and 0.25 mi south. Look for warblers, vireos, flycatchers, and woodpeckers. A yellow-billed cuckoo and an American redstart were seen here in September of 1975. The evening grosbeak is a regular fall visitor. If time allows, walk up some of the canyons that flow to the west, keeping an eye out for black-chinned sparrows and pinyon jays.

If you feel like taking a hike to see the view from on high, Kelso Peak (5090 ft) is just to the west. Consult your topos for the best route. There is a log book to sign at the summit.

TOUR CONTINUES. *Exit Option 1:* Kelso Valley Rd continues north, reaching Weldon on CA 178 in 6.2 mi. To end the tour at this point, continue on to Weldon and then go east and back to CA 14 in about 30 mi. This route will take you down over Walker Pass (5250 ft). This pass played an interesting part in early California history. If you like adventure tales, you might want to hunt up the story of Captain Joseph R. Walker, for whom the pass is named. A good place to start is with Farquhar's *History of the Sierra Nevada* (see the "Recommended Reading" appendix).

On to Unnamed Summit. If you decide not to exit, retrace your route from Kelso Creek 3.8 mi back past the Butterbredt Canyon Rd exit, take the southwest fork, and proceed to the high point in 1.2 mi. The pavement ends here, but the road is well graded beyond. An 18-mi segment of the Pacific Crest Trail crosses Kelso Creek Rd at this summit and passes northeast across part of Butterbredt Canyon.

At the summit (4850 ft) you see Kelso Creek stretching before you. The Paiute Mtns are to the east and a part of the southern Sierra Nevada to the west. The northern Tehachapi Mtns are to the south. Joshua trees are thick in this valley; Brewer's sparrow is known to nest here. Close to the base of the Paiutes, you can expect to see montane species such as the white-headed woodpecker, Williamson's sapsucker, and Clark's nutcracker.

A Bird Stop. As you continue down into Kelso Valley, note the cattle chute at 3.9 mi and, just beyond, a house among some willows and cottonwoods. A little farther on (0.2 mi) there are three ponds on the right, about 100 yds below the road. Stop and walk to the fence to search for shorebirds, ducks, geese, and many passerines. You never know what you might see! (It's a good idea to announce your birding intentions to the people at the ranch house.)

Exit Option 2: On down the road another 1.3 mi you will meet up with the Jawbone Canyon Rd again. If you go east you will get back to CA 14 in 19 mi, again passing the Butterbredt Canyon turnoff en route (6.9 mi from CA 14).

■ *Paiute Peak via Jawbone Canyon (Side Trip).*
If you want to continue exploring, go west on Jawbone Canyon Rd and follow it through the fields, watching for horned larks, mountain

plovers, northern harriers, and longspurs (in winter). A rare snow bunting was found in these fields in December 1978. (The road beyond this point is not maintained during the winter.)

About 7 mi up this road, you'll find yourself climbing up the east side of the Paiute Mtns and entering a portion of Sequoia National Forest. The highest point in this part of the forest is Paiute Peak (8432 ft)—which you'll come to about 19 mi from where you turned on to Jawbone Canyon Rd. You can actually drive nearly to the top of this peak; the last few hundred yards require a 4WD vehicle or willing feet.

To return to your starting point near exit option 2, just retrace your steps.

Rand Mining District and Randsburg Desert Museum

TO GET THERE. To get to Randsburg: (1) take US 395 to Johannesburg and follow the signs 1 mi southwest to the town, or (2) take CA 14 north from Mojave 20.3 mi to the Red Rock–Randsburg Rd and go east 21 mi to the town.

GETTING YOUR BEARINGS. Bring along a good Kern or San Bernardino County map.

ABOUT THE MINING DISTRICT. It was 1895 when gold was discovered at the base of what was later called Rand Mtn, and the boom towns of Randsburg and Johannesburg began to blossom around the Yellow Aster Mine. During World War I, in 1914, rich tungsten ore was found nearby, and Atolia became a part of the district's second boom. In 1919 horn silver began to be mined on Red Mtn, just a couple of miles southeast of "Joburg," and yet another mining community was added to the area.

The district was named after the famous and rich Witwatersrand mining area of South Africa, and for a time it certainly did live up to its name. For example, the Yellow Aster Mine is said to have turned more than a cool $25 million during its forty-seven years of operation. Also, this mine's very successful presence helped encourage the development of more than a hundred other mines, many of them at least modestly profitable for some years.

The Rand area continued to ride the boom-and-bust cycle between World War I and the 1950s, and as prices of gold, tungsten, and silver rose and fell, so did production of these ores. All in all, between 1895 and 1924 the total money brought in for all metals is estimated to have been over $35 million; the eventual total production may be over $50 million! Perhaps not in the Comstock Lode class, but quite a tidy little sum for such a small area.

As with most mining districts, these monetary ups and downs have been the story of Rand's life. Unlike some other areas, though, the district has never gone completely bust. Today, there are still several mines operating in the area—though none of them produce enough ore to make the district boom as it did at the turn of the century. It's hard to believe that at that time more than fourteen thousand people lived in and around Randsburg. Many of the people who live in the district now, though, prefer it as it is—a quiet, out-of-the-way, friendly, Old West–New West community.

The Blooming of the Yellow Aster. Surprisingly, Randsburg was never one of those wide-open, lawless mining towns. Instead, it was a company town—even during its glory-hole days. The Yellow Aster Mine was not only rich in ore, but had owners who weren't just out for the fast buck. Because the proper running of the mine required a large and complex operation, they took the wise course of treating their workers well and of maintaining good relations with the towns that supported the mine. They even "invited" lawbreakers to leave the area.

One of the events that helped keep the towns from going the way of Bodie was the advent of the railroad. A spur line was built from Kramer (27 mi south of the town of Red Mountain) to Johannesburg so that heavy machinery for the Yellow Aster could be brought from Los Angeles. (Kramer was—and is—on the Santa Fe's main line.) As a result, Randsburg—with its giant stamp mills—was transformed into a large (fourteen thousand people), busy mining town. Johannesburg, just a mile away, became the mining area's transportation center. The railroad supplied whatever the communities needed for both day-to-day living and mining. And in those days there were other mining communities besides Randsburg that needed supplies—primarily those in the Argus, Slate, and Panamint ranges to the northeast, such as Trona, Ballarat, and Skidoo.

What to Do in Randsburg. There aren't very many authentic gold-mining communities in the California desert that haven't become ghost towns, but Randsburg is one of them. Here you find both old and new—and here most of the new is in keeping with the old. At the moment (1986) there are no gas stations, motels, or hotels open in the town. There are, however, many other places to visit. For the shopper there are several antique and gift shops; for the hungry, a restaurant and a general store; for the travelers behind on their postcards, a post office; and for the history buff, an excellent small museum. All these are on the main street, Butte Ave.

Even without its Randsburg Desert Museum (a branch of Bakersfield's Kern County Museum), this historic and picturesque town is well worth a visit—but with the museum, it is a must for anyone interested in Old West and mining memorabilia. The building itself may look small and unimposing, but it is crammed with remnants of the old days. Outside the museum is perhaps its most impressive exhibit: a collection of mining machinery from the district's earliest days. After examining these massive pieces of equipment, some put together with wood and leather, you begin to really appreciate the kind of hard work involved in living in and mining the Old West! (The museum is open from 10:00 A.M.

to 5:00 P.M. on weekends and long weekend holidays—except for Thanksgiving, Christmas, and New Year's Day.)

Although most of the original buildings have been destroyed by fire, some of them still stand between Rinaldi's Market, the museum, and the White House. There are enough false-front buildings, weathered cabins, mines, tailing piles, and mine waste dumps to give you a fair idea (if you use a little imagination) of what it might have been like here a score of decades ago.

So, next time you're traveling from here to there (or vice versa) near Randsburg/Johannesburg/Red Mountain, take the time to go just a little out of your way and into the Old West for a while. Swing over to Randsburg, stomp on the museum's stamp mill, have a phosphate at the general store or a meal at the restaurant, sort through some antiques, look for color in some mine tailings, and speculate on what it must have been like to live here in the glory-hole days.

Indian Wells Valley–Little Lake

ABOUT THE AREA. Contrary to the opinion of some blasé travelers, the Indian Wells Valley and Little Lake area are not just blanks on the map, to be driven through as quickly as possible on one's way to somewhere else (e.g., Mammoth or Death Valley). Far from being a blank, this corner of the California desert has its own personality—the result of a particular combination of biologic, geologic, and human history.

Biologically, this part of the western Mojave Desert is wedged between the sagebrush communities of the Great Basin Desert on the north and the creosote bush communities of the Colorado (Sonoran) Desert to the south. So, as you might guess, there is something of an unusual mixture of animal and plant associations here.

Geologically speaking, the valley lies just north of the Garlock fault, which marks the boundary between the mostly flat western Mojave Desert province and the rugged, many-mountained Basin and Range subprovince. This circumstance is partly responsible for the fact that the area is geologically older, has been more volcanically active, and was once more well watered and lush than the desert lands to the immediate south. Which means that the lay and layers of the area's land are also distinctive—if you take the time to examine them.

Regarding the valley's human history, you might say it's similar to that found in most areas of the Far West. That is, there is enough of the good, the bad, and the ugly to fill at least a dozen epic novels— none of which we have space to write here. What we do have space for, though, is a once over lightly; which, hopefully, will be enough to send you off to do more investigating on your own.

A Valley at the Bottom of a Sea. It's hard to imagine, but this region was once under a lot of water. That was about 500 million years ago. Geologists know this from examining and dating rocks from this period, which lasted at least 200 million years. For the most part, the deposits of that time were limestone and shale — some of which contain marine fossils paleontologists are still studying.

Then, 200–300 million years ago, land appeared above this sea, along with a considerable number of volcanoes. Volcanic activity pushed up great masses of molten rock through the ocean sediments, changing (metamorphosizing) the sediments in the process. Limestones were re-crystallized into white marble, and the muted colors of the shales were transformed into minerals in shades of white, rust, and green.

Where the Ores Came From. It was during the period when these molten rocks were cooling that tungsten and gold, as well as other minable minerals such as silver, lead, and zinc were deposited in the area that later became Indian Wells Valley. At the same time, huge masses of granite were formed from the cooling of still more vast quantities of magma. This is the granite that forms so many of the mountains surrounding the valley — and the 400-mi-long Sierra Nevada.

Faulting = Mountains and Valleys. The area started to take on a more valleylike shape about 11 million years ago, when faulting began to lift mountains up from the rolling plain and the plain began to subside. (During this period, the Red Rock Canyon area, to the south, was at the bottom of a large lake. The sediments laid down then later became what we know as the Ricardo formation.)

Not until 1 to 2 million years ago, though, did faulting lift the Sierra Nevada and surrounding mountains to anything like the elevation we see today. And while faulting was defining the perimeter of Indian Wells Valley, water was washing more and more rocks, earth, and sand down into its bowl. Obviously, all this didn't take place overnight, but over hundreds of thousands of years. During this time, many kinds of animals — including mastodons, saber-toothed cats, and giant ground sloths — roamed the fertile, well-watered valley. These creatures eventually left their bones behind to be covered with yet more mud and gravel, thus enriching our fossil record.

Underwater Again. From about 100,000 to 10,000 years ago, during the wind-down of glacial times and when the yearly rainfall was considerably more than it is now, a great chain of interconnected lakes formed between the eastern Sierra and Death Valley. When Lake Owens overflowed, the water went on to Lake China in the Indian Wells Valley; from there, as each lake overflowed in turn, the water flowed into Lake Searles, then into Lake Panamint, and finally into Lake Manly, in Death Valley.

These large lakes slowly became dry lakes (alkali flats) as the climate changed from cool and moist to warm and dry. (An exception is Owens Lake, which was hurried to its end by the Los Angeles Department of Water and Power in the early 1900s.) A number of nonmetallic minerals are mined from these old lake beds—potash, boron, and lithium salts, as well as common salt (Searles Lake), borax (Death Valley), talc (Panamints), and so on.

Geologic processes are, of course, still going on in Indian Wells Valley—they don't belong only to ancient times. Earth and gravel are moving down from the mountains into the valley (bedrock is several thousand feet down from the present valley floor); fractures in the earth's surface, called faults, continue to slip and slide up and down and back and forth, pushing up mountains, pushing down valley floors, changing watercourses, and causing earthquakes; water and mud still bubble at hot springs, live steam and heated gasses are still venting in geothermal areas, and new volcanoes may even be forming!

Arrowheads of Obsidian. Some prehistorians feel that people first came to the Indian Wells Valley region as much as 40,000 years ago, but the first substantial evidence suggests that people were certainly living in the valley about 4000 years ago. These Pinto people led a simple life, living in small, circular huts and foraging for their food. During those times the valley was still quite lush and had year-round streams, lakes, grasses, and trees. Small game, fish, and plant foods were plentiful. These people made and used a variety of tools—obsidian arrow and spear points, manos and metates, and rock scrapers, knives, and hammers. They were fortunate in having a good supply of obsidian (a black, shiny, glasslike volcanic mineral) close by, at Coso Hot Springs. (This interesting area is, alas, off limits to the visitor, because it is part of the China Lake Naval Weapons Center reservation.)

About 1000 years ago, as the Pinto people faded away (why, it is not known), the Basketmaker people came into the area. Later still came native Americans of Shoshonean origin, and it was these people who were in the valley when it was "discovered" by Joseph Walker in 1834. The many petroglyphs in Big and Little Petroglyph canyons—the largest collection in the eastern Sierra area—are probably of Shoshonean origin. These stylized drawings, pecked into the rock with rock tools, are thought to be connected with hunting rituals. If petroglyphs interest you, a trip to these canyons is a must.

Pickaxes and Stagecoaches. Joseph Walker, a well-known and intrepid explorer, came upon Indian Wells Valley after successfully locating the relatively low pass (later named after him) from the western to the eastern Sierra. (All the other passes known at the time were much higher and more difficult to cross.) Between 1834 and 1849 only a few parties came through the valley—on their way to the west side of the Sierra via Walker Pass. In the 1850s prospectors began to explore the area in search of gold and silver. It wasn't until the early 1860s, though, that gold and silver mining got a good hold in the Coso and Slate ranges and mining towns began to spring up.

Quite a few people started coming through the valley in the 1870s, when Owens Valley mining really got going, and farmers and ranchers began to settle permanently in the Owens. By the early 1870s, thanks to all the mining operations, the freighting business was going strong. Scores of fourteen-mule, three-wagon teams plodded up and down the valley as fast as they could (usually about 2 mi per hour!)—and there were several busy stops in Indian Wells Valley. A passenger stage also went through the valley three times a week—on its way from Los Angeles to the Owens Valley. Indian Wells Valley was on the map.

As for mining in this valley, after the big Coso strikes played out in the early 1870s, small-scale mining operations came and went until most of the Coso Range and the northern half of Indian Wells Valley was taken over wholesale by the military in 1945. A lot of people—native Americans, local residents, prospectors, visitors—were not at all happy about this land withdrawal. The Coso area, in particular, was important to many. To native Americans the hot springs had been a sacred place for centuries; the springs were also popular soaking places for health seekers and the hot-tub crowd of those days. And many of the prospectors and miners who had claims in the Coso Range felt that their chances for a good strike had been unreasonably snatched away. One does wonder whether such enormous land withdrawals are really necessary. All of which brings us to . . .

Where Not to Go. Unfortunately, many of the best places to view some of the old lava flows, cinder cones, and other scenic areas are within the boundaries of the nearby Naval Weapons Center (NWC). (Some old maps designate this area as NOTS—no pun intended; the translation of this acronym is Naval Ordnance Test Site.) This huge area is off limits to all but authorized personnel, so mind the signs when exploring the back roads east of US 395.

NWC and the other military installations have arrogated to themselves a goodly hunk of the California desert. There are some limited exceptions to the off-limits rule, one of which is the prearranged, escorted group tours (two or more people) to Big and Little Petroglyph canyons allowed on China Lake NWC. Another exception is the group tours of the facilities at the Goldstone Tracking Station.

Not all of the Little Lake area, however, is part of the NWC; there are places where you can easily see extensive lava flows and several cinder cones, in addition to a deep and beautiful gorge cut into a lava flow by the glacial Owens River.

Let's face it—people don't come to Indian Wells Valley (1) for highrise hotels and interminable limo rides, (2) for the ninth wave and bumper-to-bumper traffic, (3) for star-studded nightclub acts and crowded sidewalks, or (4) for the opera and long waits in line. What they come for is (1) highrise mountains and drives with a view, (2) the first peak (or the hundredth) and uncrowded trails, (3) quiet campsites and a view of the stars, and (4) the songs of the birds (no waiting required). And in addition (no admission), visitors can also take in as many of those ever-popular standby acts on human, natural, and geologic history as they have time and inclination for. And all of this within about a 40-mi radius. Yes, it's true, all right—Indian Wells Valley (like the rest of the California desert) is definitely a place to be gotten to, not a place to be gotten through!

FACILITIES. Cafe in Randsburg; supplies (minimal) and gas in Johannesburg; restaurants, motels, supplies, and gas in Ridgecrest and Inyokern; gas and restaurant at Little Lake.

Campgrounds. At the far south end of Indian Wells Valley, there is a campground at Red Rock Canyon State Park (see the Red Rock Canyon–Randsburg "Facilities" section). At the south end of the Sierra there is a BLM campground, Chimney Peak, 15 mi west of US 395 on Nine-Mile Canyon Rd (this road is 10 mi north of the CA 14–US 395 junction). About half the distance is paved and the rest is good graded dirt; look for the BLM sign directing you south at about mile 10, near the fire station. Elevation at the campground is about 6000 ft. There are tables and pit toilets, but no piped water (stream water must be boiled or purified); the many pinyons make this a nice, woodsy place.

All other camping is open desert/forest, where permitted—as in the West Side Canyons trip, below.

West Side Canyons

TO GET THERE. The series of canyons described from south to north below are on the west side of CA 14 or US 395 north of Walker Pass. The first canyon is Indian Wells Canyon on CA 14, 2.3 mi north of the junction of CA 178 and CA 14. Next is Short Canyon, 1.4 mi farther north, off US 395 (0.4 mi north of the junction of CA 14 with US 395). Grapevine Canyon is 1.1 mi north of Short Canyon, and Sand Canyon is another 3.4 mi north from Short Canyon. Nine-Mile Canyon is 4.6 mi north of Sand Canyon.

With one exception, all canyons briefly described below have dirt roads leading into them. (The exception is Nine-Mile Canyon, which is paved for about 7 mi.) These roads vary considerably as to condition. Some are suitable for the average vehicle all the way; others require a 4WD vehicle. Because—as with so many desert roads—the road conditions change with each heavy storm, it is not possible to give accurate info about their condition here. Check with the BLM office in Ridgecrest or the Red Rock Canyon State Park rangers for current info. Whenever you have any doubts about whether your vehicle can make it on these roads, do your exploring on foot (you see more that way, anyway).

GETTING YOUR BEARINGS. You'll find the following maps useful when exploring these canyons: USGS topos *Inyokern* and *Little Lake*; AAA "Kern County" and "Death Valley" maps.

ABOUT THE CANYONS. Each of these canyons has a number of spots suitable for picnics and walks to enjoy the desert scenery. In spring, whole mountainsides are sometimes covered with brilliantly colored wildflowers. Summer is usually too warm to make visiting the canyons a pleasure. Again, an exception is Nine-Mile Canyon Rd, which is partly paved and climbs up to a cool and piney 6000 ft; it's a good place to get out of the valley's summer heat. Some of the other canyons also reach up to cooler elevations, but either their roads don't go high enough to get above the heat or they cannot be followed that far. Aside from Nine-Mile Canyon, Indian Wells Canyon is the next most likely candidate for getting you out of the heat. Starting elevations at the highway are appoximately 3000 ft.

Indian Wells Canyon. About 0.3 mi south of the turnoff to this canyon, there may be a historic marker on the west side of the road. This marker commemorates the old Indian Wells watering place, without which many a thirsty emigrant would never have reached their destination. The road west up the canyon leads toward Owens Peak, which, at 8475 ft, is the highest peak in the immediate area. The road forks in several places; keep to the most well traveled. When you stop to explore, pull your vehicle off the road (make sure there is room for another vehicle to pass your parked car).

Short Canyon. The road to this canyon goes west just south of Brady's Cafe; about 1.3 mi up the road you'll come to a fork. The left fork terminates at a trail. If you follow the trail over the hill, you'll come to a stream. In spring there is a 20-ft waterfall upstream; to reach it, just clamber up a short distance beside the stream. There may even be some watercress along the edge. There will be large beds of wildflowers to admire if it's a good year; but even in bad years you'll find enough to make the excursion worth your while.

If you go right back at the fork in the road, the track will take you farther up the mountain and end in a place where you can park. Here you'll find a trail that goes up a rise and then follows the stream bed.

Grapevine Canyon. The road up this canyon will take you toward some evergreens on the mountains ahead. When the road becomes impassable, walk toward the foot of the mountains along the canyon floor.

Sand Canyon. Part of this road follows a stream where you can find nice picnicking places. As usual, there are plenty of places to explore.

Nine-Mile Canyon. If you are traveling the Indian Wells Valley in hot weather, this is a fine place to get up out of the heat for a while. The road is paved for about 7 mi and then becomes a graded dirt road. At about 9 mi (at 6000 ft) you'll cross the eastern Sierra crest and reach a junction; a fire station and heliport are nearby. The dirt road south from this junction leads to several BLM campgrounds (see "Facilities" section, above). You can follow this road on up into the southern Sierra to Kennedy Meadows and points beyond—but that's another book.

Even if you don't need to get out of the heat, this is a drive you should take. As you go higher and higher you can watch the desert shrubs and grasses give way to mountain plants and evergreens, primarily the useful and beautiful pinyon pine. Looking closely at the changing plant communities while moving up through the different life zones sharpens one's awareness of the uniqueness and complexity of both desert and mountain environments.

Big and Little Petroglyph Canyon Tour

TO GET THERE. Visits to these petroglyph canyons inside the China Lake Naval Weapons Center (NWC) are possible only on weekends or holidays. They usually begin at the main gate of the NWC or at the Maturango Museum, near the NWC (see below). The easiest way to visit the canyons is to go on a fall or spring tour escorted by knowledge-able Maturango Museum volunteers. For info on the tours, call the museum at 619-375-6900.

You or your group may be allowed to visit the petroglyphs on your own (without the museum people, but still with an NWC escort); how-ever, arrangements must be made ahead of time with the NWC's Secur-ity Department community liaison assistant. To make these arrangements, call 619-939-3481 some weeks before the weekend you want to visit the petroglyphs. The lead time to get on a tour can be very long because the demand is high.

The trip to Little Petroglyph Canyon can be made in any vehicle in good condition with fairly high clearance. To visit Big Petroglyph Can-yon, however, a 4WD vehicle is necessary. One of the advantages of the museum tours is that you can carpool in 4WD vehicles if you don't have one.

To reach the NWC's main gate, either take China Lake Blvd northeast off US 395 for 5 mi and continue to follow it for 3 mi after it bends to the north, or take CA 178 (Inyokern Blvd) east from CA 14 for 14.3 mi.

GETTING YOUR BEARINGS. USGS topos *Coso Peak* and *Mountain Springs Canyon;* AAA "Kern County" map.

ABOUT THE TOUR. This is a 90-mi round-trip, about half of which will be on rough dirt roads; there are a few steep grades. As with all desert travel, make sure you and your car are properly prepared for the kind of emergencies that can arise any time you travel to remote areas.

The canyons are at about a 5000-ft elevation, so even if it is warm at Ridgecrest's 2200 ft, it may be cooler up there. Keep this in mind when planning what to take along. Speaking of which, don't forget your binoculars and camera. Your escort will tell if there are any areas it is verboten to photograph.

Most groups have a guide who points out interesting features of the petroglyphs, so we won't take the space to describe any here. Of course it wouldn't hurt to do a little reading on this variety of rock art before you take the tour. The Maturango Museum has several interesting books and brochures on these petroglyphs in particular; you might want to visit the museum before you take the petroglyph tour. Your public library will have a number of informative general works.

All visits to the petroglyphs, whether group or individual, are escorted. There are picnic tables and pit toilets at the petroglyph area; please be careful to carry out all your trash.

11,000 Petroglyphs! Scattered throughout the California desert there are thousands of petroglyph sites, some having only a few of the designs scratched or pecked on rock and other sites having a great profusion. These two canyons on the NWC, Renegade and Petroglyph (now commonly called Big and Little Petroglyph canyons), contain what is perhaps the greatest concentration of this prehistoric art in the whole desert.

But why here? There are perhaps a number of reasons. For one, these canyons have miles of large, more or less flat, basaltic rocks—the kind that take well to scratching and pecking. Long before these designs were created, from several hundred to several thousand years ago, these dark basaltic rocks had accumulated a coating of oxidized minerals called desert varnish. This dark, shiny varnish coating, which you can see in many places in the California desert, was the canvas on which the primitive artists pecked their designs. As they scratched away the varnish, the somewhat lighter color of the rock came out in dramatic relief. And although more layers of desert varnish have been laid down over the drawings, the designs still show up clearly.

What Are These Rock Drawings About? We'll never know the answer to this question for sure, of course, because the artists are not around to explain them to us—but prehistorians have made some educated guesses about their purposes. For instance, they are inclined to think that because so many of the drawings are of game animals and human hunters with their weapons, they had magical and/or ritual significance for hunting. Perhaps they were meant to bring success to the hunters. There are many representations of bighorn sheep, which were probably much-sought-after and hard-to-kill game. Deer and antelope were more plentiful and easier to kill, which may account for there being fewer rock drawings of them.

Some of the other petroglyphs seem to be designs rather than representations of people, utensils, animals, or plants; they don't resemble anything we are familiar with. And although these, too, may be of magical or ritual significance, it may also be that not all of the drawings were meant in this way. Some of them may have been clan symbols; others may have been created to please the artist; some of them may even be humorous; some may be doodles; and some may be maps or records of trading activities. There are all sorts of possibilities: it's unlikely that we'll ever know which of our guesses hit the mark.

Tour Mileages. Whether you go on a group tour or not, your escort will know the way to the canyons. However, it sometimes makes a drive more interesting if you know something about your route and what to expect along the way. Here is a brief description of the route to the Big and Little Petroglyph canyons.

Mile	Location and Directions
0	At NWC main gate, go east on Halsey Ave to first stop sign; turn north (left) on Lauritsen Rd and go four blocks to guard station (the weekend entry point). Continue to four-way stop and go east (right) on Knox Rd. After another 0.1 mi, take the north (right) fork at a Y intersection and travel past the China Lake Golf Course and B Mtn. At a Y marked "Dangerous," go north (left) and continue on left until you come to some railroad tracks.
5.9	At the railroad tracks, bear northeast (right) on G-2, Tower Rd.
17.6	Pass Wilson Canyon Rd. Look to your left along here and notice the huge volcanic caldera between you and the Coso area to the west.
23.0	At the locked gate, where the road becomes a dirt track, go east (right) on Mountain Springs Canyon Rd.
24.3	At another junction, go right into the mouth of Mountain Springs Canyon. (This route was once followed by a mining road leading to Darwin.) When you get to a locked gate, your escort will have a key.
28.0	Come to a road leading to ruins of Mammoth Mine. At one time, this gold mine was the largest in the valley. You might want to take a little time to explore the area.
30.8	Turn left (north) on Coles Flat Rd. As you drive along here, you will go through a fairly thick Joshua tree forest.
33.0	This area used to be a prospector's camp, but is now a picnic area.
38.1	At Divide junction, go left.
42.9	Stay right on the main road.
44.5	Arrive at parking lot and picnic area in Little Petroglyph Canyon.

Maturango Museum

TO GET THERE. The museum is in the city of Ridgecrest at the intersection of Las Flores Ave and China Lake Blvd, about 1 mi south of the Naval Weapons Research Center at China Lake. To reach the museum, take China Lake Blvd northeast off US 395 for 5 mi and continue to follow it for 3 mi after it bends north.

GETTING YOUR BEARINGS. Bring along a good Kern or San Bernardino County map.

ABOUT THE MUSEUM. The museum, a nonprofit organization, was founded in 1961 by a group of people determined to help preserve the valuable prehistoric, historic, and natural heritage of the Indian Wells Valley. A large part of the museum's function is education. The organization tries to, as they put it, "promote the increased diffusion of knowledge about, and appreciation for, the cultural and natural history of the upper Mojave Desert."

The museum volunteers and staff plan and offer a variety of educational events, including public tours, lectures, field trips, school programs, and exhibits. There is also a gallery for changing displays. A small bookstore is maintained at the museum, where visitors can find a number of excellent publications on local history and prehistory (some of them published by the museum itself).

When you visit the museum, you will find exhibits telling the story of the upper Mojave Desert. Here, you can learn about the ancient animals who once roamed the lush lakefronts of the area, about rich gold and silver strikes, and even about the space shuttle. The museum's collections include fossilized bones of extinct animals such as the mammoth; petroglyphs, arrowpoints, and many other native American artifacts; gemstones collected locally; desert shrubs, trees, and wildflowers; not to mention scorpions, tarantulas, and other denizens of the upper Mojave. And don't forget to check out the 4100-year-old section of bristlecone pine.

If you are on your way to or from the petroglyph canyons (see above), don't forget to stop and take in the museum. In fact, any time is a good time to visit the museum—whether you are exploring the Indian Wells Valley, driving near Ridgecrest on your way to somewhere else, or just need a rest stop.

For information on the museum's current hours and days, please call 619-375-6900 or write to P.O. Box 1776, Ridgecrest, CA 93555.

Fossil Falls

HOW TO GET THERE. About 20 mi north of the junction of CA 14 with US 395 (approximately 3 mi north of Little Lake) go east off US 395 on Cinder Cone Rd (signed). (You can't miss the cinder cone, locally called Red Hill.) Continue east for around 0.5 mi, then turn south (right) on a dirt pole line road and go another 0.3 mi to a road heading east (left). Take this road to the parking area, about 0.5 mi on. There should be BLM signs at each of these turns that indicate the route (vandals sometimes remove these signs, so you can't count on them). The roads are good dirt, unless they have been recently flooded.

Look around the parking area for some splotches of yellow or orange paint at the trailhead; follow the splotches and the trail to the falls, about

0.25 mi away. There are two sets of falls—the second set is a couple of hundred yards south of the first one; just walk along the edge of the gorge until you get to them. *Note:* if you have young children with you, keep them under very close supervision. You will be walking on the top of a high, steep, treacherous-to-the-unwary cliff!

GETTING YOUR BEARINGS. Peak and valley watchers will need the USGS topo *Little Lake* and the AAA "Death Valley" map.

ABOUT THE FALLS. Let's begin not with the falls, but with the approach to them from Little Lake. It isn't every day you get to cross a large volcanic field!

What to See Between Little Lake and Fossil Falls. Going north on US 395, about 17 mi from its junction with CA 14, you'll come up a rise to the Little Lake Hotel (plus restaurant and gas station). As you approach the rise, notice the cliffs of black lava to the east. Soon you'll go through a narrow gap in the volcanic field and come first to the hotel (on the west side) and then to a little lake. There is quite a bit to see in the next few miles, so you might want to get into the slow lane.

Little Lake. This lake in the old Owens River bed was created by damming natural springs; it is usually crowded with migrating waterfowl in spring and fall. Here, among the many hundreds of birds, you may see several kinds of ducks and geese, along with some pelicans. This lake and the springs that feed it have been a regular stopping place for people traveling up and down the Owens Valley for many thousands of years.

On the east side of the highway, near the north end of the lake, you may see a fence and a sign with blue lettering proclaiming "Great Basin Foundation." The foundation is affiliated with the Los Angeles Museum of Natural History and helps finance wildlife research projects in the Little Lake area as well as other important desert studies. The lake is off limits to all but authorized visitors.

As you pass the lake, Red Hill comes into view straight ahead, about 3 mi farther on. This hill—actually a small, extinct volcano topped by a pile of volcanic cinders—is being slowly eaten away by mining operations that sell the cinders and pumice for use in building blocks, concrete, landscaping, running tracks, and roadbuilding (note the red patches in the highway). Cinder cones like this are built up when small pieces of porous lava are exploded out of a volcano.

Postpiles. While you are continuing north to the Cinder Cone Rd turn-off, look across the valley to the east toward the Coso Mtns to see more cinder cones and low cliffs of now-hard, dark-colored lava flows. Some of these lava cliffs are made up of columns of basalt; these jointed structures formed as the huge lava flows cooled. Devil's Postpile National Monument, near Mammoth Lakes northwest of Bishop, is a much larger example of this phenomenon.

If you look northeast (right) about 1.5 mi north of the hotel you may see part of the Owens River gorge through the lava field—the same gorge you'll be seeing at Fossil Falls. At this point you can also see more examples of the basalt columns directly east. There are also some good columns just south of the hotel turnoff on the west side of the road.

Flowers. In spring, this area north of Little Lake is often a sea of wild-flowers. There are a number of places to pull off and look more closely at the flowers, to photograph them, or to identify them.

Red Hill. At about 3 mi north of Little Lake you come to the Cinder Cone Rd turnoff, with Red Hill and its mining operations on its north side. Follow the directions given above in "How to Get There," and soon you'll be on the (sort of) trail to the falls.

The Falls Trail. As you walk along, look out for your toes—lava is very knobbly and can trip you up neatly. This knobbliness is due to many, many little holes left over from the gas bubbles that were in the molten lava. Once you get to the falls themselves, feel how very smooth the lava flow is where the silty, fast-flowing water sanded and sculptured its surface. The large, rounded holes in the lava were caused by small whirlpools in the rushing river and later were made larger by having rocks tumble around in their hollows.

How the Falls Happened. The very presence of these rather impressively high falls immediately tells us two things about the history of this area: that great quantities of lava once flowed here and that a good-sized river later cut its way through the hardened flows. But when did this take place? Well, according to geologists, volcanoes were still active here, pouring their lava into the Owens River channel, as recently as 20,000 years ago. And, at about the same time, the Owens River waters (which cut the enormous channel and the falls you see at your feet) were rushing headlong from Lake Owens through this outlet and down to Lake China in Indian Wells Valley and beyond.

This older version of the Owens River continued its brisk flow for thousands of years, cutting the gorge and cascading down the falls, until the climate began to become drier. By about 5000 to 6000 years ago, the Owens no longer flowed, and the large lakes that had formed during the wetter climatic cycle had dried up. Around 4000 years ago, the climate had moderated a bit and become pretty much as we know it today. But the falls stayed dry, the lakes did not return, and though the Owens River was once more flowing, it flowed only as far south as Owens Lake (and that far only until the Los Angeles Department of Water and Power diverted it from the lake to Los Angeles in the early 1900s).

Life Around the Falls—From Mammoth, to Pinto, to Paiute. While the volcanoes, the falls, the river, and the lakes were coming and going, other things were also happening. Two to three million years ago—before the period of volcanic activity that produced the lava flows the falls are carved through—large, now-extinct creatures roamed the grasslands around the lakes and rivers: short-jawed mammoths, camels, hyena-like dogs, saber-toothed cats, even horses. Some of these animals survived the Ice Ages into more recent times, to about 10,000 to 20,000 years ago. (In this part of the world, the Ice Ages lasted from about 1 million years ago to about 20,000 years ago.)

Some prehistorians believe it was between 10,000 and 20,000 years ago that the first humans probably came to the Fossil Falls–Little Lake area. Human tools of this approximate age have been found in seeming association with mammoth bones along ancient river and lake shores in the Little Lake region. By about 6000 years ago, the weather had become even drier than it is now. As the water disappeared from the lower areas, taking with it the rich grasslands, the animals either died off or wandered to greener pastures. The changing climate probably also resulted in the earliest people moving camp to the mountain uplands, or perhaps farther north, where water, plant foods, and game animals were more abundant.

It is not known whether the Pinto people who lived in the area around 4000–5000 years ago were descended from those earlier inhabitants. These later people, however, developed a way of life that enabled them to make good use of the available food sources in this now drier, but still quite hospitable, land. They were nomadic and traveled from place to place with the seasons — gathering a wide variety of plant foods such as chia seeds and pinyon nuts, catching fish, shooting waterfowl, trapping small game, and collecting and drying insect larvae. They built circular huts, thatched with grasses and brush; fashioned some clay utensils; and made many kinds of obsidian tools unique to their culture (obsidian is a dark, glasslike, volcanic rock). They also pecked and scratched some of the rock art — the petroglyphs — that can be seen in several places around the Little Lake region.

During the Pinto people's occupation of the lands around Little Lake, the Owens River was still flowing down to Indian Wells Valley. And although some of the earlier large lakes to the south and east had been transformed into playas — dry lakes that sometimes partly refilled — there was still plenty of water flowing down off the Sierra and enough lakes to attract waterfowl.

Somewhat later, the Pinto people either became or were supplanted by a Shoshonean people, the Paiutes. The Paiutes had their own distinctive methods of tool- and utensil-making — for example, they made beautiful and intricate baskets. However, they continued living off the land in much the way the Pinto people had until explorers and, later, emigrants came to the Owens Valley.

Artifacts — Part of Everyone's Cultural Heritage. While you are exploring the falls area, you may come upon some rock rings, remainders of the circular huts the Paiute built. Also, there are still some obsidian chips to be found along the edges of the Owens River gorge near the falls. If you find oblong basins on the tops of good-sized rocks or rock slabs, there's a good chance that these were worn there in the process of grinding up wild seeds and nuts by hand with a rounded chunk of stone. The shallow, oblong hole in the rock is usually called a metate, and the hand-held stone a mano. Remember, though, these artifacts belong to everyone, and are to be left where they are so that others can enjoy seeing them and prehistorians can study them. Collecting is prohibited. The Eastern Sierra Museum, in Independence, has an excellent collection of native American artifacts and pioneer objects.

The Falls Today. Nowadays, the Fossil Falls area is visited primarily by tourists, who come to see the evidence of the earth's past so well displayed here. In addition to seeing the massive, once-molten lava flow and the remarkable effects of water's cutting force over the centuries, you may also get a chance to watch rock-climbers practicing their skills on the gorge's sheer walls.

Panamint and Searles Valleys

ABOUT THE AREA. From about 100,000 years ago to 10,000 years ago, these two valleys were lakes: Lake Panamint and Lake Searles. During those far-away times, glaciers were forming and melting and the climate was cooler and wetter. Between runoff from the Sierra Nevada, runoff from the several Basin Ranges surrounding these two valleys, and overflow from Lake Owens, water sometimes accumulated to a depth of over 600 ft in Lake Searles and nearly 1000 ft in 60-mile-long Lake Panamint! And the water didn't stop there, but continued on to fill Lake Manly. We know Lake Manly today by another name—Death Valley. This last lake in the chain—through which water flowed from Lake Owens to Lake China to Lake Searles to Lake Panamint to Lake Manly—was sometimes 600 ft deep.

As the climate fluctuated—changing for the drier and warmer and back to the wetter and cooler, through cycle after cycle—these lakes became more and more saturated with salts. Lake Searles in particular became a cauldron of chemicals and elements that would later prove to be valuable in the modern world.

Thar's Salts in Them Thar Lakebeds! Searles Valley's principal claims to fame are its almost improbably large saline deposits and its tufa towers, the Pinnacles. The vast salt beds were left behind by that series of lakes that came and went over tens of thousands of years. In the 1870s, when gold and silver were being discovered in nearby Panamint Valley, mineral salts were first being mined from Searles Lake. Today, Kerr-McGee Chemical Corporation (whose plants can be seen near the town of Trona) is still profitably extracting minerals such as borax, potash, soda ash, lithium, bromine, and just plain salt from the now-dry lake.

The Pinnacles. The tufa towers at the south end of Searles Lake are thought to be the best examples of their kind in the United States; they have been declared a national natural landmark. These pinnacles are composed primarily of calcium carbonate; they formed in the lake 10,000 to 25,000 years ago. A visit to this weirdly beautiful Cathedral City (so called by early people in the area because of the towers' spirelike appearance) is not to be missed (see below).

Panning a Mint of Gold and Silver. Enclosed by the Panamint Mtns on the east and the Slate Range on the west, central Panamint Valley has not been a candidate for wilderness status, though the parts north of CA 190 and south of Ballarat Rd have been. The reason for this is that human impact is evident over much of the area. Over 100 years ago, silver and gold were discovered here in large quantities, and mining for these and other minerals continues in much of the valley today.

However, for those who enjoy exploring historic remains such as ghost towns and old mines, who are in search of spectacular desert scenery, and who (perhaps) have a 4WD vehicle, Panamint Valley is one of the finest areas of the California desert to visit. There are no hordes of aimless off-road drivers in the valley (the topography pro-hibits this)—in fact, there aren't too many people, period. However, this wasn't always true.

The Panamint area probably had its largest number of citizens in the mid-1870s, when Panamint City, Ballarat, and Lookout were all sup-plying their respective nearby mines, processing ore, and trying to ship their gold and silver bullion out to the big cities without having it stolen. Around this time, Panamint City alone had a population of about 5000, with nearly 700 men working in the Panamint Mining District, and a reputation for violence and lawlessness that nearly rivaled Bodie's! (Regarding Bodie's reputation, it has been reported on good evidence that one prospective resident of that city, when informed by her parents that they were to move there, exclaimed: "Goodbye, God—I'm goin' to Bodie!" Some witnesses to this incident, however, disagreed about how the phrases had been rendered, swearing that what the youngster had really said was: "Good, by God—I'm goin' to Bodie!")

The Panamint City boom, though quite a profitable one, didn't last long. By the late 1870s, the town was nearly empty. Other Panamint strikes came and went up through the 1890s; after that time, most miners who had come to "pan-a-mint of gold" had gone on to richer panning places, and once-busy Ballarat and Lookout became all but deserted by the early 1900s. For the past few decades, what with faster means of transport to supply centers outside the area and the less profitable nature of the mines now operating, no more Panamint Cities, Lookouts, or Ballarats have sprung up.

The Miserable Panamints? Just twenty-five years before the first big strike and the great influx of people, the only people who had visited the area (other than native Americans) had been a few unfortunate pioneers who got lost in Death Valley, came west over the Panamints, and eventually barely made their way alive to the Owens Valley. The second party in the area may have been a USGS survey party in 1850 or so. They supposedly camped near Ballarat while reconnoitering part of the Panamints. Reportedly, neither of these groups had much use

Upper Pleasant Canyon at the southwest end of the Panamint Range.
Photo by Stan Haye.

for the Panamint Mtns or valley. They apparently thought the area a
pretty wretched place—almost waterless, too hot (or too cold), dusty,
barren, windy, and nearly lifeless. But you can hardly blame them; after
all, they weren't prospectors on to a "big one" or visitors looking for
a nice, quiet, umpopulated, spectacular place to recreate in.

What to Do in the Valleys. In Searles Valley, don't forget to see the
tufa towers at the Pinnacles, just south of Trona. In Trona, stop by the
town recreation hall and see if there are any rockhounding activities
scheduled; take a guided tour of the chemical plant (make arrangements
in advance); drive around town and look for some of the old buildings;
stop at the Valley Wells State Historical Monument (just north of the
Trona Airport) and learn a little more about the history of the area.

If you're in the mood for some desert mountain scenery and not in
the mood for crowds, the accessible remoteness of the Panamints may
be just what you are looking for. There you can spend your time exploring riparian areas, watching the animals, hiking the canyons, touring the back roads, climbing the dunes, or just smelling the Panamint
daisy.

Oh, and by the way, don't do any of these things in the middle of
the summer if you can help it. (Unless you're one of the lucky ones
who are perfectly comfortable in roaringly hot weather!)

FACILITIES. Motels, restaurants, supplies, and gas at Trona; supplies
and gas at Stovepipe Wells in Death Valley National Monument (DVNM).

Camping. The nearest developed campgrounds are in DVNM (see "Facilities" section for DVNM in Chapter 10). All other camping is open desert. Most lands in this area are managed by BLM; camping is allowed. Do not camp on private land without permission. There is limited camping (undeveloped) at the Darwin Falls Trailhead (see below).

Darwin Falls Hike

Class 1/elev. 3100 ft/USGS topo *Darwin*/14 mi RT/cross-country, use trails, dirt road

TO GET THERE. *Lower Darwin Falls Approach.* Get on CA 190 either by going east from US 395 at Olancha or by going west from the Panamint Valley Rd (to get to this road, take the Trona-Wildrose Rd north out of Trona for about 30.6 mi to a Y; take the west arm and go 14.4 mi to CA 190). The Darwin Canyon Rd turns south from CA 190 about 44 mi east of Olancha or 3.2 mi west of the Panamint Valley Rd junction where CA 190 starts to climb steeply out of the canyon. After turning south to stay in the canyon on the Darwin Canyon Rd (good dirt), go about 2.5 mi to a more primitive dirt road that turns southwest again, where the main road starts to climb steeply. Turn right onto this road for about 0.5 mi to a dead end at a rock barricade. Just to the left of the barricade there is an open spot used for parking and open-desert camping (no facilities). Be sure to check road conditions locally before driving Darwin Wash.

Upper Darwin Falls Approach. Follow the directions above to where the more primitive road goes southwest. Instead of taking it, stay on the better road going south; it will climb steeply to the heights on the southeast of the main drainage. In about 4 mi the road makes a sharp hairpin turn first one way and then another to keep in the main wash. Despite its unmaintained appearance, the route is normally passable for passenger cars with decent clearance. Another 1.5 mi more brings you to the upper entrance to Darwin Canyon (look for sign) and to the willows, old cabins, and spring-fed pool of China Gardens.

ABOUT THE FALLS. Hidden in the rugged, seemingly barren mountains on the east side of Panamint Valley is a truly special place—the canyon oasis at Darwin Falls. The same ancient bedrock that creates the spectacular scenery found here also forces a permanent stream of life-giving water to the surface, creating a sparkling stream and refreshing waterfalls amid cottonwoods and willows. This is a true desert oasis.

You can hike into the canyon from either the lower or the upper end. For the intrepid (those with rock-climbing skills and a climbing rope) it is possible to hike on through the canyon, for the distance is not too great. The steep rock faces surrounding the waterfalls tell you immediately that going all the way through the canyon is not in the cards for the average hiker.

From either direction, start by signing in at the Bureau of Land Management (BLM) visitor book (there will be no ranger, just a trail book). This is both for your own safety and so the BLM can keep count of how many are enjoying the area. On your way out, add any comments you think might help the BLM do a better job of providing management.

From the lower end, you will park at a row of big boulders that the BLM has placed across the canyon to discourage off-road vehicles from going farther. After walking about 0.25 mi you will round a bend and hear the first roar of water. The canyon narrows sharply here, willows begin to grow thick about you, and soon you encounter the first sheer drop, where a steady stream falls more than 15 ft to a sandy pool. This is a nice place to picnic; at midday you can also get some good photos here (it's too dim the rest of the time). Even the average hiker can scramble up some of the ledges surrounding the falls to get a better view. Just use your judgment and don't go up what you can't get safely down!

From the less-visited upper end you first encounter a brimming pool of water and some old mining buildings (private) at China Gardens. Going past the pool and buildings, while staying to your right, you quickly come to another barricade, this one made of pipe. Again, a quarter mile of walking around a couple of sweeping horseshoe bends will bring you to the first thickets of willows. The trail stays to the right as you go down-canyon, and finally gives you a spectacular view down into the heart of the gorge. A little boulder-hopping and stream-jumping puts you in the middle of that scene, with water-polished stone and beds of watercress at your feet and sheer volcanic walls surrounding you on all sides. At this point, you can get some attractive photos of small scenes — rocks, shadows, water, and greenery — if you don't mind crouching on some of the ledges above them.

Unless you and your companions have a climbing rope and know how to use it, clambering down to the falls at the lower end of the canyon is not advised. Instead, explore the upper end and then retrace your steps to the end of road.

East Panamint Valley Tour

HOW TO GET THERE. Take CA 190 east from US 395 in Owens Valley (or west out of Death Valley) to Panamint Valley Rd; go south on this road for 14.4 mi to the Trona-Wildrose Rd (paved). Or, you can go north from Trona on the Trona-Wildrose Rd 30.6 mi to this intersection.

Most of this tour can be handled in a vehicle with good clearance. For extra exploring up some of the old canyon roads a 4WD vehicle is necessary.

GETTING YOUR BEARINGS. In order to get a good idea of what you're looking at in this area, you'll need the USGS topos *Telescope Peak, Manly Peak,* and *Emigrant Canyon*; also the AAA "Death Valley" map.

ABOUT THE TOUR. In some ways, all of the west-facing Panamint canyons are similar. Most have water — sometimes only a few springs, sometimes a mile or two of running water and extensive riparian vegetation. Most have seen mining activity and have rough, steep, rocky dirt roads leading up to them. Exceptions to this rule among the major canyons are Middle Park Canyon (which has no road) and Wildrose Canyon (which usually has a paved road). Vegetation in the canyons is also similar, varying from sage and mesquite at the lower elevations to pinyon and juniper at the higher elevations.

The condition of the various canyon roads on this tour can change without notice. The canyons are all steep, and even moderate flooding can wipe out several miles of good road in minutes. It's a good idea to check with local sources if you are planning on serious exploring.

Wildrose Canyon. To drive this canyon, turn northeast on the Trona-Wildrose Rd. In about 4.8 mi you will enter DVNM, and 4 mi farther on up a narrow canyon you will come to Wildrose Campground and Mahogany Flat Rd. This road takes off east (right) and goes to several campgrounds (see "Facilities" section for DVNM in Chapter 10). From here, Wildrose Rd winds through the scenic canyon, crosses Nemo Canyon and El Nemo Crest (5547 ft), goes over Emigrant Pass (5318 ft), and down into Emigrant Canyon. As the road winds through Emigrant Canyon, several side roads (gravel or dirt) lead off east to points of scenic and historic interest. After about 30 mi, the road ends at CA 190 and the Emigrant Ranger Station and Campground.

The Wildrose Canyon Rd, along with several other Panamint Canyon roads, was washed out in the winter floods of 1984–85. It will be repaired by the time you read this.

Although this canyon is actually in DVNM, it is a typical Panamint canyon. And like the canyons farther south, Wildrose is very scenic. Because the road through the canyon is usually a paved road, it is a good choice for visitors who are either on their way to DVNM or who don't have the equipment or inclination to make the rougher trips in the Panamints. Be sure to travel this route slowly and stop often to look at your surroundings, walk around, and explore.

Jail Canyon and Indian Ranch. Go south on the Trona-Wildrose Rd from our starting point at the South Panamint Valley Rd for about 1 mi to Indian Ranch Rd (graded dirt); turn left here and follow the road east 4.2 mi to Jail Canyon. There is a road up this canyon to the Corona Mine, which is a private mining claim. This is a good canyon to pass by, though, for it is relatively uninspiring, as Panamint canyons go. If it's a weekend and you're out of cold drinks, continue east (passing the turn where Indian Ranch Rd goes south to Ballarat) to Indian Ranch, about a mile beyond the Jail Canyon turnoff. Here, at Indian Ranch, you can sometimes buy cold drinks; however, there are no overnight trailer spaces, camping, or gas.

Surprise Canyon. Follow Indian Ranch Rd as it turns south about 4.7 mi from the Trona-Wildrose Rd. The road up Surprise Canyon takes off northeast in about 5.4 mi. The road is roughly graded (maintained by Inyo County) for about 3 mi to Chris Wicht Camp.

The road used to be a lot better, but the "hundred-year flood" of late 1984 pretty well wiped out all of it. Eyewitnesses say the recent flood made the ground literally shake 100 yds from its edge at Chris Wicht Camp and that the noise of the water made ordinary conversation impossible. (Glad I wasn't there!) The historic records indicate that this flood was probably bigger than the one a hundred years ago that wiped out much of Panamint City. By the time you read this, the county may have repaired the road—but, then again, it may not have. Road repair is expensive, especially in remote, steep canyons. If the local folks say it's still impassable, believe them—and get out your hiking boots.

Anyway, if you make it to Chris Wicht Camp—actually a private mining claim, with a stone mill on the north side—look for the road that used to cross the creek and go up a rough, rocky, wet narrows (similar to those in Pleasant and Happy canyons). Beyond this pitch, as you go up toward Panamint City, the road was just plain rough, rocky, and steep—fit mostly for high-clearance vehicles. Now it could still be just plain gone (don't forget those boots if you want to be sure to get to Panamint City).

Springs on the canyon walls help maintain the year-round creeks in Surprise Canyon. This also makes it a good place to see birds and other wildlife and to browse among the many kinds of trees, shrubs, and flowers found here. Some lucky people have even seen bighorn sheep up the canyon's steep side walls.

■ *Panamint City and Thompson Camp (Side Trip).*
About 6 mi from Chris Wicht Camp and 9.5 mi from where you turned up into Surprise Canyon, you come out of the narrows into a small, attractive basin surrounded by pinyon-covered hills. Ahead is Panamint City's tall, brick chimney. This 65-ft chimney, built in 1872, is all that remains of a huge ore smelter. The elevation at Panamint City is about 6300 ft. This is a pretty good climb from the valley, which has an elevation of about 1000 ft!

Panamint City's claim to fame, silver, was first discovered in 1873 by outlaws who were using the canyon as a hideout. The ledges of silver ore there were reported to be "wide enough to drive a wagon through." Their outlaw status presented problems for the discoverers, who did eventually manage to sell their claims to Nevada senators John P. Jones and William Stewart through an intermediary. These government officials were newly rich from the Comstock Lode, and hoping to become even richer.

In keeping, so to speak, with its discoverers and its isolation, Panamint City had a brief, violent life. It developed into a stereotypical western mining boomtown, where arguments were stilled with a gun and Boot Hill in Sourdough Canyon never lacked for occupants. By 1875 the town had a population of 1500 and over two hundred stone houses on its Main Street. This street was a mile long—there being no room in the narrow canyon for side streets—and was 1000 ft higher at one end than the other.

Outlaws were waiting eagerly for the ingots to start being shipped out, but the town was so rough that Wells Fargo refused to service it. Senator Stewart, however, found a solution: he shipped the silver out in wagons, unguarded—but in 750-pound balls, which were impossible to carry off on horseback!

In 1876 two flash floods wiped out much of the town, killing almost 200 people; by 1877 the boom was over. Supposedly, more than $2.5 million in ore (silver and copper) had been produced in the boomtown's brief heyday. Rich ore was still to be had then, and still is now, but the metallurgic processes necessary to recover silver at a profit are so complex as to make the recovery economically unfeasible. Senators Jones and Stewart spent $2 million trying—and perhaps broke even.

Since 1877 there have been small-scale attempts to work the mines. An attempt in 1982 resulted in the extensive bulldozing of the old townsite and construction of a new mill. However, this effort had no more success than those which went before.

The Panamint City townsite is privately owned, and there are many patented claims in the vicinity. Please check with the caretaker before sightseeing.

On the far (east) side of Panamint City, in about another mile, the road ends at Thompson Camp (about 7000 ft). The most notable thing that ever happened to Thompson Camp was Shotgun Mary. In the 1950s, Mary would greet unwanted visitors (everybody) with a shotgun blast close enough to discourage further investigation! In recent years, though, the camp has been abandoned.

TOUR CONTINUES. The ruins of a stage station are visible from about 0.3 mi south of where you turn off to Surprise Canyon. A sandy track leads off to the west (right) of the road for several hundred yards to the rock walls of one room, about 3 ft high. This station probably dates from the Panamint City boom, which in turn predates Ballarat.

Happy Canyon. As you continue south on the Ballarat Rd from the Surprise Canyon junction, in about 0.8 mi you'll come to a 4WD dirt road leading up the canyon. This canyon is similar to Pleasant Canyon in that it has a rough, steep, wet narrows area. The lower part of the road, which goes through a narrow inner canyon with a mesquite-covered bottom, is reminiscent of some Anza-Borrego canyons. Mining activity is not nearly as extensive here as it is in most of the other canyons; and, scenically, Happy Canyon is one of the loveliest of the Panamint canyons.

Ballarat. About 1.1 mi south of Happy Canyon on the Indian Ranch Rd is the site of Ballarat. This mining town, vintage 1897, is located just west of the intersection of Ballarat Rd (which leads back to the pavement at Trona-Wildrose Rd) and Indian Ranch Rd. The town was named after the Australian Ballarat gold district and was primarily a supply center for the many mines in the area at that time. Excruciatingly hot in summer and bone-chillingly cold in winter, the site had little to offer but a location convenient for working the mines or supplying them.

Ballarat prospered until about 1905, when mining began to wind down. When Ballarat was on the upswing, it had three general stores, more than three times that number of saloons (of course), a school, a boarding house, a Wells Fargo office, a stage station, a jail, and even a two-story hotel—but no church. At one time it was even southern Inyo County's government seat. Its fortunes, though, were tied to the mines—and when the mines went under, so did little Ballarat. By 1917 its post office had to close its doors.

The ghost town of Ballarat became a state historical site in 1949, but for two and a half decades after that little was done to preserve the site. Weather, vandals, and collectors have pretty well stripped the old town. Despite the fact that much is gone, there are still picturesque ruins—a few buildings, some partial walls and foundations, and the cemetery (west of town).

Ballarat is privately owned, so please ask permission at the "store" (no gas or supplies) before camping or sightseeing around town. Also, if you are planning to travel up any of the canyons, the caretaker will usually have good information on road conditions and other people in the area; in addition, the caretaker will keep track of you. This last may seem unnecessary, but some areas in the Panamints are so rough, isolated, and dry that anything—a slight misjudgment in driving, mechanical problems, illness—could result in your being stranded for days or weeks if no one knows where you are. Always check back when you return, so that search parties don't go out looking for you.

Post Office Spring. At Ballarat junction, Indian Ranch Rd ends and South Panamint Rd begins. One-half mile south of Ballarat is Post Office Spring. This spring got its name because the outlaws who frequently hid out in the Panamint canyons during the late 1800s used to meet and leave messages here. Their "message tree" was situated so that they could approach from the elevated bench to the east and be sure there was no ambush waiting for them.

Gold Bug Mine. About 1.3 mi south from Ballarat is the Gold Bug Mine Rd. This road is private and not open to the public. In the old days, supplies and materials—including a disassembled Model A auto— were brought up to these mines on the south rim of Pleasant Canyon by cable tramways, which still exist. From the Gold Bug Mine, Clair Camp (in Pleasant Canyon) is clearly visible at about the same elevation (4500 ft). This road was built all the way up to the old mines in the 1950s; it is very steep and narrow in places. The mines are presently active, and the road is used by large ore trucks.

Lower South Park Canyon. You'll find the road leading east into lower South Park Canyon about 2.5 mi south of the Gold Bug Mine Rd. If you are driving a 4WD vehicle, this canyon is passable up as far as the Suitcase Mine (about 4 mi). The upper part of the canyon is accessible from the upper part of Pleasant Canyon. The road once went all the way through the canyon, but was deliberately closed to help prevent vandalism. (There are ruins of several mines and mills in the canyon.) Because there was a road from the canyon's top (6400 ft) to its bottom (1050 ft), the fact that part of it is closed shouldn't stop intrepid hikers from exploring in either direction.

Arrastre. About 2.6 mi south of the road into lower South Park Canyon, look for a doughnut-shaped ring of rocks east of the road. These are the remains of an arrastre, a simple, if primitive, contraption (imported from the Mexican mines) for grinding ore. It worked by means of a beam (now missing) that extended from a center pivot out over the edge of a trough. Rocks were fastened to the part of the beam over the trough, and mules, oxen, or even men, dragged the beam around the trough, pulverizing ore placed in the trough. Stamp mills, jaw crushers, and rod or ball mills — all of which can be seen in the Panamint area — are the somewhat more modern equivalents of the arrastre.

Redlands Canyon and Manly Falls. Beyond the arrastre about 1.2 mi south is the entrance to Redlands Canyon. Manly Falls, about 1.5 mi east up the canyon, is now a highly developed mining area. The road into Redlands Canyon above the falls reportedly does not go very far; it is not open to the public.

Goler Wash and Beyond. Seven miles south of Redlands Canyon is Goler Wash, where a good dirt road goes east into the Panamints to the Keystone Mine and on into DVNM. This private claim is also known as the Lotus Mine; it is presently being worked. When the mine is not being worked, the road deteriorates to 4WD only. After the Keystone, the road becomes 4WD anyway, and passes Sourdough Spring (the Keystone's water source), a road junction leading south (right) to an unnamed canyon (where there is good camping), and another road junction south (right) to the Myers and Barker ranches (private property). It finally goes on over Mengel Pass (4200 ft) and into Striped Butte Valley (in DVNM).

Inside DVNM the road gradually improves, although it stays rough and rocky (it was widened to permit removal of burros by truck). Eventually the road joins with the Warm Springs Talc Rd and finally with the Death Valley West Side Rd. This is the only road across the Panamints south of Townes Pass that is open to the public; it's a very interesting 4WD route!

TOUR ENDS. A few miles south of Goler Wash, Wingate Rd enters the Naval Weapons Center reservation, which is off limits to the general public. This means you need to return to the Trona-Wildrose Rd by retracing your route to Ballarat and then going west on Ballarat Rd for about 3.6 mi. From here you can go northeast into Death Valley National Monument or northwest to CA 190 and then west to Owens Valley. Or, you can go south to CA 178, Trona, and US 395.

West Panamint Valley Tour

TO GET THERE. From US 395, 0.9 mi north of Red Mountain, take CA 178 north about 35 mi to Trona, then continue on the Trona-Wildrose Rd (paved) for about 14 mi to Slate Range Pass (signed). Alternatively, take CA 190 (east from US 395 in Owens Valley or west out of Death Valley) to Panamint Valley Rd; go south on this road for 14.4 mi to the Trona-Wildrose Rd (paved). Continue south on this latter road for about 17 mi to Slate Range Pass.

Most of this tour can be handled in a vehicle with good clearance. For exploring up some of the old canyon roads, though, a 4WD vehicle is necessary.

GETTING YOUR BEARINGS. Unfortunately, there is no good Inyo County map; the AAA "Death Valley" map covers this area.

ABOUT THE TOUR. This short tour of about 30 mi, including the side trip, will take you from Slate Range Pass to the Shotgun Rd and an onyx mine (with gift shop), then by Lookout Mtn and one of the Hearst family's mines, and finally to a point where you can easily pick up CA 190 (and other trips). From the south, the Trona-Wildrose Rd enters the Panamint Valley over Slate Range Pass, about 14 mi north of Trona.

Nadeau's "Shotgun" Road. On both sides of Slate Range Pass, rockwork of the original Nadeau Trail can be seen. At the top of the pass, you can see a dirt road going straight north up the west side of the valley. This is a good place to stop and stretch your legs. While you're doing this, look for some rock terraces on the north side of the pass. These were constructed by Chinese laborers when the road was first built. The builder was Remi Nadeau — a successful teamster who plied the Owens, Indian, Searles, and Panamint valleys — and who believed that the shortest distance between two points was a straight line. Thus, he had this "shotgun" road constructed in the late 1870s to service the Modoc and Minietta mines. The road was one of the first in the desert to be surveyed. (In this case, Slate Range Pass and the Modoc mines were the two points.)

■ *Nadeau Road (Side Trip).*

Near the bottom of the pass, in the Panamint Valley, about 16 mi from Trona, the Whittaker Iron Mine is to the north, marked by rusty red outcroppings of iron ore. Farther down the pass, at a junction about 17.4 mi from Trona, take the Nadeau Rd (not the original) north (left fork). This road eventually leads to the Kerr-McGee Limestone Mine at the end of the road, 11 mi on. The limestone is trucked to Westend, south of Trona, where it is used in processing the brine from Searles Lake. About 3 mi north on the Nadeau Rd, the Shepherd Canyon Rd (dirt) goes west. A drive of about 3 mi up Shepherd Canyon on a dirt road will bring you to the Onyx Mine, where you can buy gift items made of — onyx.

Various of the canyons in this part of the Slate Range have roads into them, but most lead to privately owned mining claims; some claims have cabins and are occupied.

TOUR CONTINUES. After you return to the junction and continue north on the Trona-Wildrose Rd, the Ballarat turnoff to the east comes up in about 4 mi. There is a radar station at this junction that is tied into similar sites in the Searles Lake Valley and Owens Valley; the central computer is at Edwards Air Force Base. These stations are used to keep track of small aircraft that may wander into the areas used by fast, low-flying military jets on training missions.

The Modoc Mine and the Beginning of the Hearst Dynasty. On the Trona-Wildrose Rd, about 13.3 mi north from the Nadeau Rd junction, turn northwest (left) onto the Panamint Valley Rd at the T. In another 6.7 mi, the Minnietta Mine Rd turns west (left) to the Minnietta and Modoc mines and the site of Lookout. This town near the top of Lookout Mtn is privately owned, and the Modoc Mine is in the process of being reopened. Visitors are not encouraged—which is too bad, for there is an excellent view of the Panamint Valley from the mountain.

Silver was discovered in this area in 1875, and for the next few years Lookout was a fair-sized town. To provide the charcoal needed for the mines' reduction furnaces, ten charcoal kilns were built in Wildrose Canyon. The Modoc Mine—owned by George Hearst, father of William Randolph Hearst—produced about $2 million worth of ore, getting the Hearst fortunes off to a good start.

What to Do Next. From this point it is only 7 mi north to CA 190, where you can go west to the Owens Valley, east to DVNM, or north to the Panamint Dunes. Alternatively, you could go south to the Panamint Valley east-side canyons and on to Pinnacles National Natural Landmark.

Trona, Searles Dry Lake, and Pinnacles National Natural Landmark

TO GET THERE. To get to the Pinnacles, take CA 178 north from US 395 (near Red Mtn) for about 29.3 mi; you will descend a winding canyon and approach the floor of Searles Valley. As the terrain opens up, you will find a dirt road intersection on the right. Turn southeast here and go 0.5 mi to a fork. Continue south via the right fork, cross some railroad tracks, and continue for about 5 mi to the tufa pinnacles. There are several roads coming and going in the tufa area; if you're lucky, there'll be someone ahead of you who knows the best way to get to the pinnacles. If not, you'll just have to keep trying until you find the best road. The best road sometimes changes according to the weather, so these directions can't be more explicit. It's not advisable, however, to visit the pinnacles if the roads are wet. You could get yourself into a nasty mudhole.

To get to Trona, just continue north from the Pinnacles turnoff for another 7 mi.

GETTING YOUR BEARINGS. The AAA "Death Valley" map is useful in this area. (No good county map exists.) Topo watchers will want the USGS's *Searles Lake*.

ABOUT SEARLES LAKE. When approaching Trona from either the north or south, you can easily see all that remains of Searles Lake—a vast, dry- and wet-patched salt flat. Yet, this alkali basin was once a huge, 640-ft-deep lake. At the end of the last Ice Age, Lake Searles was part of a chain of lakes that began with Lake Owens. When this highest lake overflowed, the water rushed through the Owens River gorge, over Fossil Falls, and down into Indian Wells Valley, 1500 ft below, filling Lake China and Lake Searles. When these basins overflowed, the water flowed on to Lake Panamint and Lake Manly (in Death Valley). However, during much of this time, Lake Searles was the end of the chain. (To distinguish the prehistoric lakes from the modern lakes, geologists and natural historians generally refer to the older lakes as Lake _____ and the lakes we know today as _____ Lake.)

In those days, tens of thousands of years ago, the climate was cooler and wetter, the lakes were set in fertile grasslands, trees dotted the plains and mountains, and many animals roamed the area. But the climate changed for the drier and warmer, the trees and grasslands disappeared, the animals moved on or adapted, and the lakes slowly evaporated. Because Lake Searles had been the end of the chain for long periods of time, it became the final resting place for many valuable minerals—in layers up to 70 ft thick! Many of these minerals are so pure they need almost no processing.

The Most Outstanding Tufa Towers in the United States. Mono Lake, north of Bishop, isn't the only place you can see a weirdly beautiful tufa landscape—in fact, the Pinnacles National Natural Landmark, about 13 mi south of Trona, is recognized as being the best example of these oddly imposing spires and towers in the United States. Some mineralogists think that the calcium carbonate that makes up these tufa towers was laid down by blue-green algae of prehistoric times, living in freshwater hot springs in and around Lake Searles. The algae combined the calcium from the springs and the carbonates from the lake, forming the calcium carbonate deposits that make up the tufa towers. The towers have central channels through which the water bubbled up. Some of these pinnacles are as much as 140 ft high.

Cathedral City (as the old-timers called the Pinnacles) is yet another place in the California desert that has been discovered by the movie industry. If you are a science-fiction film fan, some of the scenery may look quite familiar to you.

Mining the Lake's Salts. Until the 1870s the area that is today known as Trona was just another dry lake to be crossed as quickly as possible. Then, in 1873, John and Dennis Searles built a small borax plant, laid claim to a square mile of the lake surface, and began producing borax. Their first year's production was reputed to have been 1 million pounds! Needless to say, the borax was shipped out by twenty-mule teams. The Searles' plant was sold to Pacific Coast Borax Company in 1895, but ceased operating the very next year. No one managed to make a success of mining the lake until 1916, when another company, using a new process, began producing potash. In 1926 the American Potash Chemical Company bought the plant and operated it until 1967, when yet another company (Kerr-McGee Chemical Corporation) purchased it.

Trona — A Fittingly Salty Name. What is now the town of Trona was first referred to as "somewhere near thirty-five buildings forming in itself a small town in the heart of the desert." So commented Dennis Searles, in writing of a summer vacation at Searles Lake in about 1890. The next period of development started in 1914, when Trona acquired a railroad. Many of the buildings constructed during that time — some of which are still in use — had wide porches and asbestos shingle exteriors for coolness (evaporative coolers did not arrive until 1937). Because the town was company owned, troublemakers were not tolerated — company policy was to remove whoever was causing problems. After World War II, the company gradually sold its houses to employees; now, although the town is not company owned, it remains company dominated.

Trona was always a civilized place, even in the old days. It had an ice plant, a social hall where movies were shown, a doctor, churches, and several stores. Today it even has a recreation complex at Valley Wells, which includes one of the largest saltwater pools in the United States. Because water is ever a precious commodity in the desert, the pool does double duty as swimming pool and reservoir.

Trona, by the way, is the name of the predominant mineral found in Searles Lake (a double salt — sodium carbonate/sodim bicarbonate). The trona minerals are used in such products as glass, cleaners, baking powder, bleaches, soaps, and fire extinguishers.

Advice from an Old-Timer. According to Dr. O. N. Cole in his book *Trona,* "You've been in Trona too long when . . . you think the West-end Plant is beginning to smell like lilacs . . . [and] you start thinking of Trona as the garden spot of the universe."

10

Death Valley and East

Calico

ABOUT THE AREA. The Calico Mtns area is tucked into the southwest corner of the "Death Valley and East" region, just east of Barstow, north of I-15, and south of the Fort Irwin military reservation. The location makes access easy for most desert travelers. Also, because the Calico area's points of interest are so close together, it's both a good destination for a day or two and a convenient place for a morning or afternoon visit on your way to or from somewhere else.

The Calico Early Man Site offers guided tours several times a day—or you can take a self-guided tour. Here's a chance to get a closeup look at a real dig and to see firsthand the tools early people in the California desert used to make their way. There are sights and entertainment for all ages at the Calico Ghost Town Regional Park—a bit of the Old West come to life again! And the Mule Canyon scenic drive, with plenty of places to see the unadorned desert and get away from it all, nicely rounds out anyone's visit to the area.

FACILITIES. Motels, restaurants, gas, and supplies are available in Barstow. In addition to the possibilities mentioned below, see the "Facilities" sections for the surrounding areas.

Camping. There is a large, well-appointed campground at Calico Ghost Town Regional Park; for details, see trip of that name below. There are opportunities for open-desert camping in Mule Canyon.

Calico Early Man Archaeological Site

TO GET THERE. Take I-15 14.6 mi east from its intersection with I-40 in Barstow to the Minneola exit (gas and minimart). Go north on a good dirt road at the exit and follow the signs 2.5 mi to the site.

GETTING YOUR BEARINGS. Bring along a good San Bernardino County map.

ABOUT THE SITE. Almost everyone is curious about how prehistoric people made and used tools. Perhaps that's why the Calico Early Man Site is so popular. Here you can see some of the nearly twelve thousand tools that have been excavated since 1958. The tools found here — for example, scrapers, choppers, hand axes, perforators, and stone saws — have been dated to 200,000 years old, plus or minus 20,000 years, by means of the uranium-thorium technique.

The First People in North America? It is this dating of the tools at about 200,000 years that makes Calico such a unique archaeological area. Until the uncovering of this site, archaeologists did not think humans had been in this part of the Northern Hemisphere that long ago. Many, in fact, believed that early Indian peoples were the first humans in the area — and that they came only about 10,000 to 20,000 years ago. Archaeologists who have compared the tools found here at Calico with those found in China, Korea, and Siberia think that these much earlier humans were not Indians, however, but probably an earlier species — perhaps late *Homo erectus* or early *Homo sapiens neandertalensis.*

The Calico region where these early people lived was much lusher than it is today. In those ancient times the shores of a large Pleistocene lake — Lake Manix — were very near. Animal and plant foods were abundant. Many waterfowl and other birds flew, strutted, swam, and sang in and around the lake. Horses, camel-like creatures, short-faced bears, sloths, mammoths, and even saber-toothed cats roamed among the tall grasses and live oaks, junipers, and pines. The climate was temperate. Many minerals were easily available for toolmaking — jasper, chalcedony, chert, petrified palm wood. So, it's not surprising that people chose to settle here.

Dr. Leakey Comes to Calico. The findings at the Calico site were so interesting that in May of 1963 Dr. Louis Leakey came to look them over. He was so impressed that he managed to get funding from the National Geographic Society to begin extensive excavations. From 1964 until his death in 1972, Dr. Leakey was project director for the Calico Early Man Archaeological Site.

Today's visitor center and museum was yesterday's Camp Leakey — and day-before-yesterday's miner's shack. It was there that Dr. Leakey baked his bread (as he did everywhere he went) and where a great deal of archaeological work was done. Be sure to make time to examine the displays at the center and to check out the free desert information brochures available there.

Tours — Guided/Self-Guided. Calico Early Man Site is open Wednesday through Sunday from 8:00 A.M. to 4:30 P.M. Guided tours of the dig are offered by the Friends of Calico on the hour, beginning at 8:30 A.M. and ending at 3:30 P.M. (no tour at lunchtime — 12:30 P.M.). The site is closed on Mondays and Tuesdays, as well as on January 1, July 4, Thanksgiving, and December 25. (This schedule is subject to change over time, of course.)

You can also give yourself a tour. Just pick up the self-guided trail

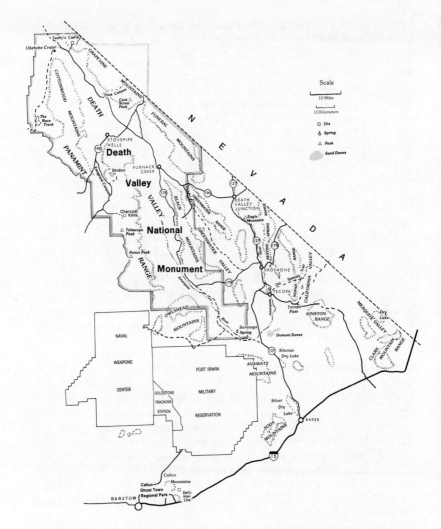

Scale

10 Miles

10 Kilometers

□ Site
◊ Spring
△ Peak
░ Sand Dunes

information at the visitor center and set off on the labeled walkways through the site. Don't forget to bring along your San Bernardino County map; it will help you identify the topographic features of the area that are pointed out in the self-guided trail information sheet.

Calico Ghost Town Regional Park

TO GET THERE. Take I-15 east from its intersection with I-40 in Barstow for 7.6 mi to the Ghost Town Rd/Solar Information Center exit. Follow the signs north for 3 mi to the park. (If you miss this exit, there is another—Calico Ghost Town Regional Park—about 2.8 mi farther east.)

GETTING YOUR BEARINGS. Bring along a good San Bernardino County map. For exploring, try the USGS topo *Daggett.*

ABOUT THE GHOST TOWN. Around 1881, prospectors in the Calico Mtns struck it rich. Practically overnight, Calico grew into a prosperous — and wild — mining town with a population of several thousand. Supposedly there were more than twenty saloons in Calico, as well as a good-sized Chinatown. (Surprisingly, there were also a dancing school, literary society, and temperance league.) But when the ever-fickle price of silver took a precipitous drop in 1886, so did the town's prosperity — although not before over $86 million in silver, gold, and other minerals had been taken out of the multicolored "calico" hills.

When the money ran out, many of Calico's silver miners moved on to richer mining areas. Others gave up mining and went to work for the railroad companies, whose lines were catching up on the desert mining boom and had converged on Waterman Junction (now Barstow). Soon the railroads changed sleepy little Waterman Junction into a bustling commercial town.

All was not lost just yet, though — in 1889 "Borax" Smith extended his lucrative borax operations from Death Valley to the Calico Hills to take advantage of the rich deposits there. As it turned out, Smith's Pacific Coast Borax company — and its unglamorous mineral — earned almost as much money for Calico as the silver had! Alas, the big profits in borax, like those in silver, didn't last forever. By the turn of the century the dismantling of the all-important narrow-gauge railroad from Daggett to Calico indicated that Calico's boom days were over. The boom-and-bust cycle had busted again. By 1935, the once-bustling streets were deserted — Calico had become a true desert ghost town.

However, in 1960 Walter Knott, of Knott's Berry Farm fame, had the idea that there could very well be tourist gold in them thar Calico hills. In pursuit of that gold, he began restoring Calico to its original Old West self. Perhaps Calico didn't prove to be quite profitable enough for Mr. Knott, or perhaps he was very public-spirited — in any case, he deeded the land to San Bernardino County in 1966, and the town became the popular regional park it is today.

Nowadays, during Calico's fourth boom, visitors can experience a little of what it must have been like in the old days. You can walk through the general store, see the schoolhouse, look over the pottery works, take a ride on the Calico-Odessa Railroad, wander through headstones of the town's picturesque cemetery, and explore the Maggie Mine, one of the West's most well known silver mines. And if you happen to be visiting Calico during one of their famous celebrations in March, May, October, or November, you may get to see dancing girls, shootouts, old-time vaudeville, gold-panning exhibitions, melodramas, country western music shows, and other frontier entertainments. Check with the park for dates. (Park hours are from 9:00 A.M. to 5:00 P.M.)

Base Camping at Calico. This ghost town has a few amenities that the old prospectors would have welcomed. For instance, a large, comfortable campground in a secluded, tree-lined canyon just below the town. Here you'll find water, tables, fireplaces, toilets, and shade—everything you need for a pleasant stay. This is an excellent location from which to foray out into the surrounding desert for anything from leisurely sightseeing to ambitious exploring.

Baker–Death Valley Junction

ABOUT THE AREA. California's Hwy 127, between Baker and Death Valley Junction, goes through some of the West's most starkly beautiful desert country. In the seemingly waterless lands off this highway you see many things you might expect to see—for example, the ancient shorelines, dry lakes, and playas that are evidence of cooler, wetter times long past. However, quite surprisingly, you can also see a small lake, lushly fringed with green and teeming with wildlife—and a river, with waterfalls, which flows year round, waiting for you to hike it, upstream or down.

In addition, there are peaks to climb, canyons to explore, "white gold" to investigate, mining camps to visit, Ice Age fish to find, minerals to hunt, and lots of unforgettable scenery to photograph. And all this on good roads (though not all are paved). Here, as in most parts of the California desert, the visitor's greatest problem is deciding what to do first!

FACILITIES. Motels, restaurants, gas, and supplies in Baker, Tecopa, and Shoshone—Death Valley Junction has a rather special hotel.

Camping. A couple of miles north of Tecopa you'll find Tecopa Hot Springs County Park (Inyo). It has spaces for tents and RVs, but no power hookups. For details, see the Tecopa–Valley Wells tour, below. For other developed campgrounds, see the Death Valley National Monument "Facilities" section. There are many opportunities for open-desert camping off the highway on any of the trips in this area; take care not to camp on private property, though.

Baker–Shoshone Tour

TO GET THERE. From the intersection of I-15 and I-40 in Barstow, take I-15 east 62.5 mi to CA 127 at Baker.

GETTING YOUR BEARINGS. You'll need a good San Bernardino County map along this route. If you plan on any exploring off the main highway, the following USGS topos may be helpful: *Baker, Silurian Hills, Avawatz Pass, Tecopa,* and *Shoshone.*

ABOUT THE TOUR. As you travel the 58 mi north on CA 127 from
Baker to Shoshone, for the first 30 mi or so—until you reach the
Amargosa River—you'll be following the approximate route the Mojave River took in prehistoric times. From at least 100,000 to 10,000
years ago, the Mojave flowed north from its headwaters in the San Bernardino Mtns, angled east below today's Barstow, and ran to the south
of what is now I-15 to empty into Soda Lake. But in those ancient times,
at a point just a little west of Baker, it then turned and went north to
eventually empty into the Amargosa River—which in turn emptied into
the southern end of Death Valley.

A Little Desert Time Travel. If you have already visited Afton Canyon,
(see Index), you may remember seeing the wave-cut beach ridges of
prehistoric Lake Manix just west of the canyon. This immense lake
covered 200 to 300 sq mi and was about 200 ft deep. The Mojave River
filled and emptied Lake Manix several times during a period of
fluctuating rainfall lasting from approximately 75,000 to 10,000 years
ago.

When the climate was particularly wet and the lake level was high,
the water cut a channel at the lake's east end (now called Afton Canyon). This channel allowed the river to flow east and fill what are now
Soda Dry Lake and Silver Dry Lake (just west of Baker) on its way
to the Amargosa River. In those times, Silver Lake probably also included Silurian Dry Lake (now 10 mi north of Silver Dry Lake). That
is, what we now see as a chain of dry lakes—Soda, Silver, and Silurian—
were all included in a single body of water: ancient Lake Mojave. This
huge lake drained an area of over 3500 sq mi.

At first it may be difficult to imagine the Death Valley area as a lush
region of lakes, streams, abundant wildlife (even flamingos!), grasslands,
forests, and (of course) people. After you've visited some of the desert's
riparian areas, seen several ancient shorelines, have perhaps found some
freshwater fossils, you'll begin to get a sense of how it once was—and,
who knows, may even be again. In any event, learning to pick out even
a few evidences of the past is bound to enrich your perception of the
California desert's present.

As you drive north out of Baker to start the tour, the mountains on
the skyline to the northwest are the Avawatz Range. In about 3.5 mi
you'll notice that Silver Dry Lake is just to the west, a short distance
from the highway.

Silver Lake—Past/Present. As you travel along, look carefully at the
hills on Silver Dry Lake's west shore for a waterline indicating what
was once the edge of ancient Lake Mojave. (To get a good view, stop
and pull off before you reach the power lines, about 6 mi out of Baker.
Binoculars work better when your vehicle isn't moving!) Many artifacts
have been found indicating that prehistoric Indians lived on the
lakeshores over a long period of time, beginning more than 10,000 years
ago.

About 6 mi north of Baker a powerline road goes west from the highway across the tip of Silver Dry Lake; at this point you can see the ancient shoreline quite well near the bottom of the hills on the west side of the lake. Stop here and look back the way you came to get a good idea of how this remnant of ancient Lake Mojave fits into the landscape.

At this intersection you may still be able to see a foundation or two left from what was once the railroad town of Silver Lake. The Tonopah & Tidewater Railroad, which operated from 1905 to 1940, did not chug along between the towns it was named for, but did manage to ply the rails between Ludlow and Beatty (Nevada). The town of Silver Lake was a supply center for nearby miners; its depot had a telegraph, and there was even a post office in town. In its heyday, one of the companies in town sold over $150,000 in goods per year. The little community hung on until about 1933, when it admitted defeat and had its post office moved to Baker. Besides Silver Lake, quite a few other towns sprang up along the T & T's route—most of them hoping to get in on the borax boom of the early 1900s. All the other nearby railroad townsites— Riggs, Renoville, Valjean, and Sperry—have no ruins left for their ghosts to haunt.

In another mile, watch just off the west side of the road for a long hump—actually an old beach ridge—which once had a pond on its north side. When you reach the second powerline road about 0.25 mi beyond this shoreline, see if you can identify an even older, higher beach ridge under the power lines.

On to a Mojave River Gorge. As you continue north, keep an eye out to the northwest for the Avawatz Mtns again. Looking west across an unnamed dry lake about 5 mi from the first powerline road (or about 11 mi from Baker) you should be able to clearly see the enormous alluvial fans that spread east from the base of these mountains. Thus— with the help of wind, water, cold, heat, and gravity—do mountaintops find their ways to valley bottoms. How many sets of fan surfaces can you pick out?

On the east side of CA 127, as you continue north, look for the Silurian Hills just a few miles off and the impressive Kingston Range on the horizon. If the weather is good, you may be able to see Nevada's snow-capped Charleston Peak (11,918 ft) about 60 mi away on the far horizon, at the north end of the Kingstons.

The playa to the east of the highway about 17 mi from Baker (11 mi from the first powerline road) is Silurian Dry Lake. You can now see the Dumont Dunes, an ORV area, about a dozen miles to the north. After traveling about 5 mi farther, start looking for a narrow opening in a ridge lying a couple of miles east of the highway. Here, as in Afton Canyon, the Mojave River waters cut their way out of an ancient lake— in this case, ancient Lake Mojave (at Afton it was ancient Lake Manix). Once the gap was made, the Mojave flowed on to empty into the Amargosa River, which in turn emptied into ancient Lake Manly in Death Valley.

To see this gap at close range, turn east on a dirt road about 24.5

mi from Baker (before passing a good-sized knob just to the west of CA 127) and go 0.3 mi. It took a lot of water to cut this gorge through the granite. The area certainly wasn't a desert then!

Death Valley from the South. The dirt road west that you come to about 30 mi north of Baker leads to the southernmost entrance to Death Valley National Monument (DVNM); the Harry Wade Exit Route State Historical Monument should be clearly visible at the turnoff, if someone hasn't carried it away. It's about 26.5 mi north to CA 178 in DVNM. This road also leads to Saratoga Spring and the Owlshead Mtns; for trip details see Saratoga Spring–Owlshead Mtns tour, below.

Crossing the River of Bitter Waters. A couple of miles on from the DVNM turnoff, CA 127 crosses the Amargosa River (look for a sign). In years when there is a high spring or winter runoff, the river sometimes has a considerable flow—enough to wash out the highway for days at a time. (The Amargosa's headwaters are in the Spring Mtns in Nevada, about 90 mi north.)

About 4 mi from the DVNM turnoff (31.5 mi from Baker), you'll come to the Dumont Dunes turnoff. Before the advent of ORVs, the dunes were a beautiful and interesting place to visit. Unfortunately, the high-impact, mechanized recreation permitted in the dunes by the Bureau of Land Management has changed their character considerably—and not for the better.

Over Ibex Pass to the Tecopa Lake Badlands. At Baker the elevation was 923 ft, and by the time you arrive at the Harry Wade turnoff to DVNM it has dropped to around 500 ft; now the highway begins to climb fairly quickly along the east edge of the Ibex Mtns toward Ibex Pass (2090 ft). The pass is about 12 mi north of the DVNM turnoff (or about 39 mi from Baker) and straddles the San Bernardino/Inyo county line; once over the pass, you're in Inyo County.

A mile or so down the north side of the pass, begin to look at the valley floor ahead for the eroded badlands that were once soft sediments at the bottom of ancient Lake Tecopa. When you check your maps, it's not difficult to see that this long-ago lake was fed by the Amargosa River's flow from high mountains to the east, in Nevada. Here, just as in many other parts of the California desert, a soft, easily eroded ancient lake floor has been transformed over thousands of years into a dramatically dissected badlands area.

The two high, layered mountain ranges looming over the Tecopa Lake basin are made up of even more ancient sediments—ranging from 300 to 600 million years old. Even more amazing than their age is the over 2-mi depth of the sediments composing each of the ranges. The Paleozoic inland seas in which those layers built up were far larger than the much later lakes such as the Mojave and the Tecopa—and far longer lived. Try finding the names and orientations of these striped ranges on your maps.

As you come down the north side of the pass toward the badlands, about 2.5 mi from the top you can see the broad Greenwater Valley ahead. At this point the valley is bordered on the east by the Dublin Hills (more stripes from the Paleozoic) and on the west by the Ibex Hills.

By the time the pass is 4.5 mi back, you'll find yourself in the eroded badlands of the Tecopa Lake bed. Notice the festoons of dark gravel that were deposited on top of the light-colored sediments before they began eroding. Can you find some cliffs that remind you of a miniature Afton Canyon?

The Old Spanish Trail, about 5.7 mi north of Ibex Pass (about 45 mi from Baker), is the first turnoff to the little town of Tecopa—which is approximately 4 mi east. Gas, supplies, food, motels, campgrounds, and hot springs are available in and around Tecopa (see the Tecopa–Valley Wells tour, below).

A Bit About the Desert's White Gold—Borax. About 2 mi on north from the first Tecopa turnoff, look for some badly eroded adobe ruins on both sides of the highway. These are all that are left of the Amargosa borax operation of the 1880s. The elevation here at Amargosa (about 1500 ft) is considerably higher than in Death Valley (below sea level), which means it doesn't get quite as hot here as in Death Valley. So, in the old days, when the summer temperatures at Death Valley's borax works got so high that the borax crystals couldn't crystallize out of solution, mule teams brought the "ore" to Amargosa to be processed.

The story of "white gold" in the California desert is a long and interesting one. A fair number of fortunes have been made from this noncharismatic mineral. See Death Valley National Monument, below, for details of how it was discovered, what it's used for (besides Boraxo), how it is mined, where it came from, what it's worth, etc.

On to Shoshone and Tour's End. The second Tecopa turnoff is about 3 mi north of the first one. If you want to go to Tecopa, but missed the first turnoff, go southeast here—it's only a little over 2 mi to Tecopa. As you continue north on CA 127, you'll come to Shoshone in a little less than 7 mi from this second turnoff. Gas, supplies, food, and accommodations are available here, too.

Like so many of the little towns in this part of the California desert, Shoshone got its start courtesy of borax—as a Tonopah & Tidewater Railroad stop. Unlike most of the other small mining-oriented communities, though, little Shoshone has managed to corner enough of the tourist trade to keep it from becoming a ghost town. (Nearby Tecopa and Death Valley Junction also share this distinction.) From Shoshone it's only 58 mi to Furnace Creek's visitor center and museum, in the heart of Death Valley.

Saratoga Spring–Owlshead Mountains Tour

TO GET THERE. Take the Baker turnoff from I-15 and go north 29.7 mi to a dirt road on the west side of the highway, signed "Saratoga Spring." (Also look for the Harry Wade Exit Route historical monument at this turnoff.)

GETTING YOUR BEARINGS. You'll need a good San Bernardino County map for the general area. For more detail, bring along the USGS topos *Leach Lake, Quail Mtns, Wingate Wash,* and *Confidence Hills.*

ABOUT THE TOUR. The Owlshead Mtns area is a large rectangle of land (approximately 12 × 19 mi) lying between Death Valley National Monument (DVNM) on the north and east, the Fort Irwin military reservation on the south, and the navy's Mojave Range B on the west. A maintained road crosses the south one-third of the area from east to west, starting west of Saratoga Spring in DVNM and ending at a telephone company microwave relay station near the west edge of the area. There is a rough mining road running north from Owl Hole Springs for about 5 mi. (Check your maps for the lay of the land.) The rest of the area is roadless; motor vehicles are prohibited.

What's in a Name? The Owlsheads got their name because when seen from a high altitude the terrain roughly resembles an owl's head. The two playas, Lost Lake and Owl Lake, are the owl's eyes. The surrounding mountains form the rest of the head. A relatively flat-topped ridge between the "eyes" is the "beak." The two playas are scenic focal points and are surrounded by jagged peaks and ridges that are mostly of volcanic origin. The overall impression for most visitors is one of flat playas surrounded by dark, rugged peaks and ridges standing out against a clear, powder blue sky.

Local Inhabitants. There are no perennial surface streams in the area, but an occasional spring is a pleasant place to stop along the road or destination for a day hike. Water promotes the growth of interesting plant communities and attracts many kinds of birds, particularly during the spring and fall migration seasons. The three most common plants in the area are creosote bush, black brush, and saltbush. In spring, if the winter rains have fallen at the right time and in the right quantities, there can be dazzling wildflower displays.

The Owlsheads offer a variety of habitats for desert wildlife. If you're lucky, you may see the shy desert bighorn or the unselfconscious desert tortoise — both of which are on California's protected species list. Feral burros also visit the area — but if efforts to remove these destructive munchers and tramplers in DVNM and nearby military reservations are successful, the Owlsheads may escape the devastating impacts burros have inflicted in those areas.

An Owlshead Wilderness? The Bureau of Land Management (BLM) once inventoried the Owlshead Mtns for possible wilderness designation and determined that the entire area — except for a corridor for the road and the area around the Black Magic Mine — qualifies for wilderness classification, according to the 1964 Wilderness Act. The BLM is required to maintain all areas it identifies as potential wilderness in roadless condition so that wilderness qualities aren't diminished. Presently, although there has been some off-road trespassing by ORVs, the Owlsheads are relatively pristine and unscarred. The area has few minerals of commercial value — which means that little mining has taken place.

Vital Statistics. There are no developed facilities in the area. Cars must be parked along the road. Be sure to fill up with gas at Baker or Shoshone (on CA 127). Round-trip mileage is about 100 mi, including Saratoga Spring and the mine area. The roads are good dirt; ordinary, well-maintained cars having good tires should have no trouble unless there have been recent storms.

There are no trails in the area; all hiking is cross-country. Day hikes are, of course, the best way to visit areas away from the road. Hiking is generally easy. Experienced hikers who want to get a bit further afield may want to try overnight backpacks — but remember, all water must be carried!

Saratoga Spring, actually a large pond, just inside DVNM's south boundary, is the best place to start your visit to the Owlsheads. The easiest approach to the springs is from the south via CA 127, rather than from the north, through Death Valley National Monument (the DVNM road is often impassable because of deep, soft sand where it crosses the Amargosa River). The dirt road that turns off CA 127 to the spring (and to DVNM) is well marked; it will also be on your San Bernardino County map. When you get to the road, turn northwest on it and go about 5.9 mi to a fork. Go north (right) at the fork and travel 2.6 mi to another fork. At this point, bear west (left) and go about 1.3 mi to the spring's parking area.

Saratoga Spring — A Desert Oasis. The lush vegetation and wide variety of wildlife here are in stark contrast to the surrounding grand but nearly waterless desert lands. The spring is a day use area only — overnight camping is not permitted. There are plenty of open-desert camping spots along the road a few miles away from the spring.

It's hard to believe that just a few years ago this lovely riparian environment was totally choked with the invasive exotic, tamarisk. It took several years of hard work by the National Park Service and volunteers to remove the tamarisk and restore the spring to its rightful riparian beauty and function.

This is pleasant place to have a snack, get out your binoculars, and wander around a bit. If you enjoy taking color photos, there are some good opportunities here. The color contrasts are quite remarkable. Take care, though not to walk into the green, marshy area or on the mounds around the pond — this is a very fragile environment, with many wildlife species depending on it. There are even fish in the pond! These are the well-known pupfish, two other species of which are found in the Amargosa River and DVNM's Salt Creek.

After your break, return to the road to Death Valley and follow it northwest 5.8 mi to a fork. Take the arm of the fork leading southwest (left); the north arm (which often requires 4WD) goes up to CA 178, which continues north through DVNM.

Checking Out the Rocks at Black Magic and Owl Hole Springs. In about 10 mi, at Owl Hole Springs, there will be another fork. To explore the Black Magic Mine area, go north (right) at this fork and keep west (left) at the next fork (1 mi on). About 3.1 mi from this last fork you'll come to the mine. The road is rough and steep in spots, but can be negotiated with care in an ordinary vehicle. From the mine area you can get a good view of Owl Lake. Rock fanciers may want to examine the mine dumps for iron-containing minerals.

Another place to look for interesting rocks is just above Owl Hole Springs. To try this site, retrace your route to the intersection at the spring and look around a bit. Some minerals you may find at this site and the next include sagenite, agate, geodes, manganese, quartz, opal, and chalcedony. You'll need to know something about minerals and will have to search diligently to turn up any prizes.

To find the next mineral-rich site, take the south fork at the Owl Hole Springs junction and go about 5–6 mi to a ravine on the left side of the maintained road as it drops into the Owl Lake watershed. Look for the ravine at the point where you leave the exposed bedrock of the mountains and begin to enter the alluvial fan at the base of the mountains. (By the way, if you happen to be in the Owlsheads in cold, windy weather, the ravine is a sheltered camping spot.)

A Word of Warning. There is a bombing range at Leach Lake in Fort Irwin military reservation just 3–4 mi south of Owl Hole Springs. At this point, the road passes through the military reservation for a short distance. During the week you may actually see aircraft using the target range on the dry lake bed. Some of the ordnance is scattered across the terrain in the Owlshead Mtns, mostly south of the road. Although the ordnance consists mostly of empty shell casings, there are some duds and other items that could explode. The best rule is not to touch any piece of metal you find lying around. It's particularly important to make sure children understand this; children too young to understand should be supervised at all times.

Hiking in the Owlsheads. There are many day hiking—and overnight backpacking—opportunities in this area. You might enjoy hiking across relatively flat terrain to one of the playas or trying something more strenuous, like scrambling up one of the numerous peaks for a view. If solitude is what you want, it can almost be guaranteed if you are willing to walk away from the road. There are no trails, so all hikes— except those on 4WD or abandoned roads—are cross-country. This means you need to be an experienced hiker: one who can use a compass, plot a route using a USGS topo, and deal with possible desert hazards.

An example of a day hike you might want to try is the following to Quail Springs.

Quail Springs
Class 1/elev. 4100 ft/ USGS topo *Quail Mtn*/6–8 mi RT/cross-country

ABOUT THE HIKE. From the Owl Hole Springs junction (see above), take the south fork of the road and go 13–14 mi. Park by the side of the road (elevation approximately 2900 ft) and hike across the alluvial fan. Use the topo to plot your cross-country route—there is no trail. Round-trip time for this hike is about 5–6 hours. From the springs you have an impressive view to the north, with both Telescope Peak and Badwater (in DVNM) in sight.

On to the End of the Road and the Tour. At the Owl Hole Springs junction, take the west fork and go about 20 mi to road's end at a microwave station. Although the road is maintained for access to the station, the area is subject to sudden flash flooding that can make roads impassable. The road is usually repaired as soon as possible, but be prepared to find it closed if there have been recent desert storms.

The end of the road—at about 3300 ft—is a good viewpoint. However, there's an even better one from a nearby unnamed peak to the northeast (elevation 4666). If you're feeling energetic and have the time, it takes only an hour or two to hike up to the peak and back. From the top you can see 11,049-ft Telescope Peak to the north, the south end of DVNM, and—at your feet—Lost Lake (dry, of course).

When you've come to the end of your time in the Owlsheads, return to CA 127 by retracing your route; a loop trip isn't possible.

Eagle Mountain Hike
Class 3/elev. 3806 ft/USGS topo *Eagle Mtn*/4 mi RT/cross-country

TO GET THERE. From I-15 at Baker, take CA 127 north approximately 78 mi; from Death Valley Junction, take CA 127 south about 8 mi. At this point, CA 127 crosses the Tonopah & Tidewater Railway right-of-way (long since abandoned). Turn north here and go 0.25–0.5 mi on a dirt road paralleling the right-of-way.

ABOUT THE HIKE. Eagle Mtn is not hard to recognize from here; at this point it is a solitary sentinel alongside the Amargosa Rvier. To reach the mountain, park off the road (this is also a good place to camp) and hike east across the Amargosa River bed toward a prominent white boulder at its base. If you are making this trip during the wetter winter months, it may be necessary to wade; the river is usually underground during the drier months. Occasionally the river is very high and dangerous. Do not attempt to cross on foot at such times.

Once at the base, climb up the steep but solid limestone slopes. Somewhat more than halfway up, cross south at the head of a large wash overlooked by a cliff. Here, rock "ducks" will mark the way south across a couple of washes. Enter the second wash and follow it up to the summit area.

A bit of tricky route-finding is necessary to reach the summit, which is a rocky area. To get to the top, some hikers may want the comfort of a rope. The views of the Greenwater, Resting Springs, and Nopah ranges from the summit are dramatic (check your maps and figure out which is which).

Shoshone-Tecopa and East

ABOUT THE AREA. Most of the triangle lying between CA 127 and the Nevada border is true basin-range country, with rows of steep, rocky mountainfronts rising from the edges of broad, low valleys. Through this difficult territory emigrant wagon trains once rolled on trails we can still clearly see today. The people who came through this part of the California desert in the 1800s were mostly on their way to somewhere else—to the goldfields of the western Sierra, to the temperate farming lands in the central valleys, and to the growing cities of commerce on the coast. Miners were about the only folks who settled in this rough country—and there aren't many of them left now.

But for the travelers who want to get away from the teeming cities and suburbs, such emptiness is good news! For this area is one of the best places in the California desert to get away from just about everything—except clean air, fine vistas, interesting plants and animals, nearly unlimited places to camp, and solitude (which is pretty scarce nowadays).

FACILITIES. Gas and supplies can be found at both Shoshone and Tecopa.

Camping. A couple of miles north of Tecopa is Tecopa Hot Springs, an Inyo County park. This is a developed campground, complete with tent spaces and RV electric hookups (but no sewer connections). Tenters will find tables, grills, restrooms, and showers. All may enjoy the hot springs for free in separate men's and women's bathhouses. All other camping in the area is open desert—and there's plenty of it! See area trips for suggested camp spots.

Motels and Restaurants. There are motels, cabins, and small restaurants in both Tecopa and Shoshone.

Tecopa-Valley Wells Tour

TO GET THERE. From I-15 at Baker, take CA 127 north 50 mi to the first Tecopa turnoff at the Old Spanish Trail. Go east here for 3.9 mi to Tecopa.

GETTING YOUR BEARINGS. This area is in Inyo County, but because there is no good Inyo map, you'll need the AAA "San Bernardino County" map (which covers this part of Inyo, too). To help you understand the topography around the southern end of the California Valley, you might want the USGS topo *Tecopa.*

ABOUT THE TOUR. This scenic tour will take you east on the Old Spanish Trail, south through California Valley to the Tecopa Pass area, then east around the north side of the Kingston Range, and, finally, south to Valley Wells, at I-15, on the edge of the East Mojave National Scenic Area. For the most part, the roads are oiled; however, even the few miles of dirt and gravel roads are suitable for ordinary vehicles. Total mileage for the tour is about 80 mi.

A Look at Tecopa. In 1907, Tonopah & Tidewater Railroad officials named this little desert town after a Paiute Indian chief, Tecopet, who had saved the Pahrump Valley settlers from being killed by Indians in the 1870s. (Tecopet means "wildcat.") Although the T & T line was dismantled long ago, and borax no longer rides the rails through Tecopa, the town still lives pleasantly on.

One of Tecopa's attractions is Tecopa Hot Springs County Park, located on a paved side road to CA 127 just 2 mi north of town. The hot mineral springs at the park have been popular since prehistoric times, and boast a fairly large number of regular users. If you'd like to indulge, the price is right—that is, it's free! There are men's and women's bathhouses and a private pool for the handicapped. (Park rules require that no bathing suits be worn in the baths.) All are open seven days a week. In addition, the park has a large campground with electric hookups for RVs (modest fee required), air-conditioned community center (open 9 A.M. to 9 P.M.), restrooms, and showers. For more information, call 619-852-4264 or write to P.O. Box 158, Tecopa, CA 92389.

Another reason Tecopa hasn't become a ghost town is that there are many good rockhounding places nearby. For info, inquire around Tecopa and/or consult your rockhounding guides.

Exploring the Old Spanish Trail. In Tecopa, by the Miners' Diner, go east on the Old Spanish Trail Highway. After about 1.5 mi, you'll pass Furnace Creek Rd (which goes south—and which you will join later) and begin a slow, scenic climb to Emigrant Pass (elevation 2624 ft), 9 mi away.

This road, as its name implies, more or less follows the old trail's route. About 3 mi from where you first get on Old Spanish Trail Highway, look to the north for the trees and buildings of Resting Spring. No, despite its name, Resting Spring is not yet a real estate subdivision—though it is private property. Actually, it is an aptly named oasis once used by weary travelers on the Old Spanish Trail and the Salt Lake Rd. At the pass, on the crest of the Nopahs, a gravel road turns north a short distance to an overlook. Here, if the weather cooperates (which it usually does), you'll be able to look east to Nevada's snow-capped Charleston Peak (elevation 11,918 ft), about 35 mi away. To the west is the Amargosa River valley; the mountains rimming Death Valley are on the western horizon. This is a good place to get out your maps and brush up on your map-reading skills. How many ranges can you identify?

From the viewpoint, the jeep trail you can see heading north along the ridgetop is actually a trace of the historic Salt Lake Rd, which stretched all the way from San Bernardino to what is now Salt Lake City, Utah. Other traces of this trail can be seen down the canyon to the west and dropping off the ridge to the east.

Further north, where the ridge ends against a hill, a white monument—inscribed "Old Spanish Trail, 1829–1850"—marks where this trail crossed the ridge. The Spanish Trail was but a single track that made its long and difficult way from Los Angeles to Santa Fe, New Mexico. This trail, unlike some others, was primarily a commercial trade route where horses and mules, rather than wagons, were used.

These trails, unused for over a hundred years, are excellent examples of how long human scarring of the desert can endure. In a hundred years, nature has been unable to wipe away any significant portion of these rather primitive traces. Just imagine how long it may take nature to efface the large-scale mechanized damage being done to many parts of our fragile and beautiful desert.

California Valley Camping. As you come down from the summit viewpoint and continue east, look for a good dirt road going south — signed "Mesquite Valley Road" — in about 2.5 mi (about 13 mi from Tecopa). This road will take you south through spacious California Valley to the Furnace Creek Rd (which you passed on your way out of Tecopa to the Old Spanish Trail Highway).

If you're thinking of doing some open-desert camping, there are several nice camp spots along the Mesquite Valley Rd. At about 2.5–3.0 mi from the turn onto Mesquite Valley Rd, keep your eye out for a side road leading west to some low hills. There is a nice campsite at the edge of the hills. Another good campsite is at Davis Well, about 3.4 mi from Old Spanish Trail Highway. To find this one, look to the east of the main road for a short side road leading to a clump of trees.

Looking east to Nopah Range from Davis Well in the California Valley. *Photo by Stan Haye.*

As you continue south through California Valley, after about 6.7 mi you'll see a dirt road—South Mesquite Valley Rd—come in from the east. There may also be some campsites up this good road. The places just mentioned are not the only possible camping spots, of course. There are many side roads to explore. Just take care to examine the roads before driving down them; some may not be good enough for your vehicle. It's no fun to have to back for a mile or so if you come to a big hole or sand pit and there's no place to turn around!

Along here, at the interface of two natural provinces, take time to see if you can find some Great Basin and Mojave Desert plants. It's easy to find creosote, mesquite, and desert holly, but what else can you pick out?

On to a Nameless Summit. It's 8 mi from Old Spanish Trail through California Valley to the intersection of Smith Talc Rd (which goes east) and Furnace Creek Rd (which goes west). These latter two roads are basically the same road, but with different names. Furnace Creek Rd goes to Tecopa, and Smith Talc goes southeast along the north side of the Kingston Range, crossing an unnamed summit of about 5100 ft. At this intersection, go east (left) on Smith Talc Rd. The road will climb gently, reaching about 3000 ft in another 4 mi (at this point, look for some nice barrel cacti to the west of the road and some yuccas to the east). The Kingston Range is just ahead, on the south side of the road; over the next 15 mi or so, the road curves around the range's north side before finally heading south toward Cima Dome.

About 5 mi from Mesquite Valley Rd, the paved road will become a good dirt road. After you get to the dirt road and have gone another 1.5 mi, look for a talc mine and its dumps north of the road. In spring also look for wildflower displays. The north side of the Kingstons is well known for its nolinas, which look like very large yuccas. In late spring, look for the nolinas' impressive white pillars of blossoms. You are now at approximately 4000 ft. Just a short distance past this mine, some humorist of dubious artistic taste has created a "whale rock" on the south side of the road. The mine headquarters are a couple of miles beyond the dumps (8.5 mi from Mesquite Valley Rd).

In another 1.5 mi or so, you'll cross a 5100-ft summit where the pavement resumes. Look for a side road leading north to a knob with a small communications tower on top. This is a good place to pull off, walk around a bit, "admire" the ugly gravel pit operation below, and get out your maps. What *are* all those bumps out there on the horizon—not to mention those right in front of you?

Along Excelsior Mine Road to Tour's End. On the main road again, coming down off the summit and continuing east (the road is again paved), you'll pass a cattle-ranching outfit—a water tank, corral, small ranch house, and (not surprisingly) cattle. Cattle are allowed to graze all along here. They bring in pieces of cholla, which take root and grow into thick stands in areas where the fragile desert forage has been overgrazed. Lower down, watch for the many fine nolinas and yuccas.

About 2.7 mi from the summit, look for evidence of more talc mining on the slopes ahead. Clark Mtn (7929 ft) is ahead on the northeast horizon when you have come about 5.5 mi from the summit; Mesquite Valley is to the north. Look ahead and west of Clark Mtn for Cima Dome and its little Teutonia Peak after having come some 11.5 mi from the summit. Cinder Cones National Natural Landmark is on the far horizon and to the west of the dome, the Shadow Mtns are west of the road, and the Mesquite Mtns are to the east. For a good photo of Clark Mtn with a clean foreground, try stopping about 14.5 mi from the summit.

Notice how the vegetation keeps changing as you get lower and lower. At about what elevation do the Joshua trees appear again? By the time you reach the site of Valley Wells and I-15 (and this tour's end), about 30 mi from the summit, the elevation will be 3707 ft. Here, on the south side of I-15, Excelsior Mine Rd becomes Cima Rd, which leads into the East Mojave Scenic Area.

Pahrump Peak Hike
Class 2/elev. 5704 ft/USGS topo *Stewart Valley*/9 mi RT/cross-country

TO GET THERE. From I-15 at Baker, take CA 127 about 56 mi north to its junction with CA 178; then, go only about 5.5 mi northeast on CA 178 into Chicago Valley—to the vicinity of the 2337-ft benchmark shown on the topo. Park off the highway on the shoulder of a dirt road going east at this point.

ABOUT THE HIKE. The view from the summit of Pahrump Peak, located in the Nopah Range east of the town of Shoshone, is perhaps the grandest of any peak in this part of the desert. Winter and spring vistas are considered the most spectacular. At these times, the snow-capped White Mtns (to the north), 11,049-ft Telescope Peak (to the west), and Nevada's 11,918-ft Charleston Peak (to the east) all stand out against a clear sky.

To start the hike, walk east off CA 178 into the canyon on the dirt road near the 2337-ft benchmark noted above. Seen from here, the summit is the southernmost of the two high points on the ridge. (Before this area was recommended as wilderness, people drove up this road about 2 mi—heavy rains have now cut the road at the first large wash.)

As you follow the road into the canyon, be sure to make a sharp left turn at about 3800 ft. Continue on to the small fork at about 4200 ft and hike up the right-hand canyon trending east and then north. This canyon ends on the ridge leading southeast from the summit at a point a few hundred feet below the top.

Follow the ridge up, staying generally on the north side. The route leading to the summit is marked with occasional rock ducks. There are several possible choices near the top; careful route-finding is necessary. It's a good idea to carry a short rope.

Death Valley National Monument

ABOUT THE AREA. Death Valley is one of the best places in the world to get a good look at the earth's naked crust. All around you in the valley are immense landforms, colorful landscapes, and puzzling phenomena—all fairly begging you to unravel their histories. From whence come the valley's lovely 14-sq-mi dune system, crusty 200-sq-mi salt flats, snow-capped 11,000-ft mountains, wavecut shorelines, volcanic craters, many-hued hills and canyons, racing rocks, finely crafted arrowheads, fault scarps, Ice Age fish, huge fans of rocky debris? These are questions worth asking, for the explanations will enable you to see Death Valley for what it really is: not a static, barren wasteland where rattlers leap snarling from under every fiery rock, but an ever-evolving landscape, a constantly changing display of our planet's life history.

The visitor center at Furnace Creek can provide you with what you need to begin understanding what you see in Death Valley. On your first visit, though, don't spend too much of your time trying to sort things out. But do spend a lot of time really looking at the valley's outstanding features—and not just from the window of a speeding car. Whenever you can, examine what interests you by pulling off, stopping, then walking, standing, or sitting. Sort of soak up the local color (of which there is an unlimited supply). On future visits you'll find it easier to absorb the how-it-got-this-way and where-it's-going information and apply it to what you're seeing. (By that time you'll have looked over the various bits of information you are bound to collect on your first trip.)

As you use this section to tour Death Valley, keep particularly in mind that the information here is but a small start on what there is to do, see, and know about the valley. See the "Recommended Reading" appendix and your friendly Death Valley visitor center ranger for the rest.

FACILITIES. There are motels, restaurants, supplies (including propane, white gas, charcoal, firewood, and ice), and gas at Furnace Creek and Stovepipe Wells (restaurant at Stovepipe Wells closes in summer); gas at Scotty's Castle. Nearest diesel fuel is at Beatty, Lone Pine, Olancha, and Las Vegas. The post office in Stovepipe Wells operates from October 1 through May 15; the post office at Furnace Creek is open all year.

Camping. There are nine campgounds in Death Valley. Those at Furnace Creek (Furnace Creek, Texas Spring, Sunset) and Stovepipe Wells (Stovepipe Wells) are quite large and have water, flush toilets, and fireplaces. Furnace Creek and Texas Spring also have tables. Texas Spring, Sunset, and Stovepipe Wells have RV sanitary stations. Furnace Creek is open all year; the other three are open November through April.

The smaller campgrounds are Mesquite Spring (near Scotty's Castle), Emigrant (near Emigrant Ranger Station); Wildrose, Thorndike, and Mahogany (all three in Wildrose Canyon); all of these campgrounds have tables. Emigrant, Mesquite Spring, and Wildrose campgrounds also have water and fireplaces. Emigrant and Mesquite Spring have flush toilets; the rest have pit toilets. There is an RV sanitary station at Mesquite Spring. Mesquite Spring and Wildrose are open all year; the other three are open October through April. The road to Wildrose (4200 ft), Thorndike (7500 ft), and Mahogany (8000 ft) is not suitable for trailers, campers, or motor homes. (Mahogany Campground, at 8000 ft, can be quite cold in early spring and late fall.)

Note: (1) Fires are permitted only in the fireplaces provided in designated campgrounds. All wood collecting is prohibited. (2) The best time to visit Death Valley is between October and May. The most crowded times to visit are on three-day winter weekends, the second week in November (Forty-niners celebration), Thanksgiving weekend, Christmas–New Year's week, and Easter week. (The summer months are the least crowded, but for good reason! This is a good time to visit the high country in the Panamints and the Cottonwood Mtns.)

The gas station, store, restaurant, and some motel units (all air-conditioned) stay open all year at Furnace Creek Ranch. Stovepipe Wells also operates in the summer, though with reduced hours. The gas station and store stay open, and a few motel rooms are usually available.

Emigrant Canyon Tour

TO GET THERE. There are several ways to approach this tour.

Access 1: From Trona, take CA 178 (the Trona-Wildrose Rd) north about 39.5 mi to Mahogany Flat Rd and the Wildrose Ranger Station and Campground. The Wildrose Rd is partly gravel, but quite passable unless there has been recent flooding.

Access 2: If you have already been touring inside DVNM, you can do the tour in reverse by taking CA 190 west to Emigrant Ranger Station, at the intersection with CA 178/Wildrose Rd (this road will take you through south Emigrant Canyon).

Access 3: If you have been touring the Owens Valley area, take CA 136 southeast 17.5 mi from US 395 to CA 190 and the latter 32.7 mi east to Panamint Valley Rd. Go south 14.4 mi on Panamint Valley Rd to CA 178, then northeast 8.8 mi to Mahogany Flat Rd and the Wildrose Ranger Station.

GETTING YOUR BEARINGS. Unfortunately, there is no decent Inyo County map, but for DVNM and vicinity, there is a good AAA map. The USGS topos *Emigrant Canyon* and *Telescope Peak* are handy for those who plan on doing some hiking or visiting some of the points of interest around Emigrant Canyon.

ABOUT THE TOUR. From the Wildrose Ranger Station and Campground, the steep Mahogany Flat Rd takes you up Wildrose Canyon, past the charcoal kilns (see below for a hike to Wildrose Peak from here), and up to Thorndike and Mahogany Flat campgrounds (see below for a hike to Telescope Peak from the latter). After returning to Wildrose Rd, you'll continue north, cross the Emigrant Pass and then have the chance to visit the site of Harrisburg (once a mining town), to make a trip up to a high, spectacular viewing area (Aguereberry Point), and to indulge in a final "detour" to Skidoo ghost town — all this before you reach Emigrant Junction, 21 mi away!

The total mileage for this tour will depend on how many of the local attractions you decide to see. The round-trip to the end of Mahogany Flat Rd is about 15.5 mi; to Aguereberry Point, 14.5 mi; to Skidoo ghost town, 14 mi. If you visit them all, the total distance will be about 65 mi. Wildrose Rd (CA 178) is paved; the side roads are dirt and are usually safe for ordinary cars. When there have been severe winter storms, the dirt roads can be rough. Check with a park ranger if you have any questions about the roads.

Wildrose Springs — A Welcome Stop. As with nearly all the longtime spring areas in the California desert, the true natives, the Indians, were the first to find and make use of the springs later named Wildrose. Archaeologists believe early peoples may have lived in the Death Valley region as long ago as the late Pleistocene, when the region was considerably more well watered than it is now. It is, however, quite certain that groups of Indians occupied the area from time to time — with their numbers depending on climatic conditions — beginning about 10,000 years ago and continuing right up to the time when non-Indians arrived in the region and began to appropriate the Indians' ancestral lands. After miners moved in, it was the usual story — a conflict of interests between the newcomers and the old inhabitants. Needless to say, the old inhabitants got the short end of the stick.

From the 1870s to the 1930s, on and off, the Wildrose Springs area saw a fair amount of activity, mainly as a stage station. It was a long, hot, treacherous 25 mi or so across the Panamint Valley from the Water Canyon stop at the foot of the Argus Range up to Wildrose Springs. It's not hard to imagine that the teamsters freighting supplies to the mines up Emigrant Canyon in wagons hauled by up to ten pairs of mules were only too happy to stop at the Wildrose oasis. Not only did the springs have plenty of water, but the 3600-ft elevation made camping considerably cooler than in the low-elevation Panamint Valley at 1200 ft.

A Look at a Charcoal Factory. The distance to the end of the Mahogany Flat Rd up Wildrose Canyon is a little under 8 mi; the elevation gain is around 4000 ft, so your vehicle should be in good condition for the climb.

To see the "charcoal factory," drive about 7 mi east up the canyon (on a paved road that becomes good dirt) and watch for a rather amazing sight. On the north side of the road are ten stone structures that look very much like huge beehives. These are the charcoal kilns that kept the Modoc Mine silver smelters across the Panamint Valley, up on treeless Lookout Mtn, in business. These imposing kilns are about

30 ft across and 30 ft high. The kilns burned wood in the absence of air, to produce charcoal. Like many other projects requiring hard physical labor — e.g., railroads — the kilns were built by Chinese laborers; Indians cut the pinyon pines used to make the charcoal; mule teams freighted the charcoal across the valley. Senator George Hearst was one of the principal mine owners; the Hearst family fortune really started here.

Mahogany Flat — The Top of the Road. As you continue up the canyon from the kilns, you'll pass Thorndike Campground and then come to Mahogany Flat Campground. The road ends just a short distance beyond the latter, at about 8 mi from Wildrose Rd. (For campground info, see "About the Monument," above.) The elevation here is about 8130 ft; this is as high as you can get in an ordinary car in DVNM.

A look around, here at the end of the road, will tell you why this was a favorite pinyon-nut-gathering spot for the Indians. Nowadays this upper part of the canyon attracts quite a few campers and hikers who find the summer-hot valleys below not to their liking. (Between November and March, though, several feet of snow often cover the area up here.) Besides trees and a haven from summer heat, you can also find the trailhead for Telescope Peak (see the Telescope Peak hike, below). If you like hiking, be sure to plan on a trip to Telescope; the panoramic views have to be seen to be believed.

Emigrant Pass — A Forty-niners' Escape Route? To continue on up Emigrant Canyon, retrace your route back to Wildrose Rd and turn north. Don't hurry along the canyon here; take time to enjoy the scenery. After about 7 mi you'll cross Nemo Crest (5547 ft) and, a little farther on, Emigrant Pass (5318 ft). This is the famous pass that some of the Forty-niners may have used to make their way out of the vast, salty sink they found when taking a shortcut to the California goldfields.

Actually, only one Forty-niner died in what we now call Death Valley. Most of the emigrants survived because they were making their way through the valley in winter — had it been summer, it's doubtful that many would have made it. But how did these folks happen to find themselves in the alkali wilderness of the valley? As you'll see, it may have been because many of them were so eager to reach the goldfields of central California that any shortcut, even through an unknown area, seemed like a good idea.

The remarkable journey of the Forty-niners began in September of 1849 at Salt Lake City. Here, a group of over a hundred wagons started out on the Old Spanish Trail for California. Not far out of Salt Lake, a passing pack train leader told the group of an Indian route — one that would supposedly cut 500 mi off their trip. After this news, it wasn't long before the would-be gold miners started feeling that things just weren't moving fast enough to suit them. Quite a few of the party began thinking seriously about trying this shortcut that went more directly west, rather than taking them south all the way to San Bernardino first, as the Old Spanish Trail did.

As it turned out, for a while only a handful of wagons continued to California via the originally planned route; a hundred wagons set off on the shortcut. (A fair number of these emigrants decided the rough new route wasn't for them and soon rejoined the little party making its more conventional way down the Old Spanish Trail.) Several separate parties made up the few dozen wagons still taking the shortcut. One of these was a group of bachelors calling themselves the Jayhawkers. The other groups were a mix of old and young, families and single people, friends and strangers.

On Christmas Day, 1849, after considerable hardship crossing Nevada's steep border ranges and near-barren desert, this brave, and foolish, motley group came upon what we now call Death Valley: entering through Furnace Creek Wash, they found themselves in an inhospitable salty sink that was once a deep freshwater lake (prehistoric Lake Manly). Once the shortcutters arrived in the desolate wasteland of this unknown valley, they couldn't agree on what route to take. (One thing they did all agree on was that they wanted to get out of the area as soon as possible.) So, once again, the party decided to split and go their own ways.

The Jayhawkers went north up the valley, camped in the vicinity of what is now Jayhawker Spring, slaughtered their oxen and burned their wagons to smoke the meat, then hiked out via Emigrant Canyon (or Towne Pass, depending on which historian you consult).

The second group of Forty-niners, the Bennett-Arcane party, decided to head toward the valley's southern end. They got as far as Tule Spring, at the foot of the Panamints (so some historians say, though there is some disagreement about this), before they realized they couldn't make it out without more supplies. Fortunately, two of the single men (John Rogers and William Manly) volunteered to go for help. Unfortunately, help was a lot farther off than they thought. Instead of being just over the Panamints, relief was 250 mi away — at Tejon, only 30 mi from Los Angeles. But they made it, and in just a few weeks (26 days, to be exact) they were back to lead the rest of their party through the rocky canyons, over the mountains, and out of the place where they had suffered so many hardships. It was at the crest of the Panamints that one of them, looking back at the scene below, gave the area its name by spontaneously saying, "Goodbye, Death Valley."

Aquereberry Point — Pete's Favorite View. But we are far from ready to say goodbye to Death Valley. So, when you're ready to move on, start looking for the sign showing the way to Aguereberry Point about 9.2 mi from the Mahogany Flat Rd; turn west here on a dirt road. The viewpoint is a little over 7 mi ahead.

Pete Aguereberry was a Basque sheepherder turned prospector. An acquaintance of his was a semilegendary character known (for good reason) as Shorty Harris. Five-foot-tall Shorty had a talent for being in the right place at the right time, and supposedly found and lost more good prospects in his lifetime than most confirmed prospectors ever dream of (for example, he discovered Rhyolite). One of his finds was made in the summer of 1906 (or 1905, depending on your source). At that time, according to Pete, he and Shorty were on their way to the lively annual Fourth of July celebration in Ballarat, when they camped one night on the flat that's on the south side of the road you're on, about 1.5 mi up.

Prospectors will be prospectors, so the next morning Pete and Shorty had a look around. What they found made them immediately stake out their claims. When the other gold seekers in the area found out about this new prospect (which was almost immediately — Shorty couldn't bear to keep his finds to himself), a tent town sprang up almost overnight. Its name: Harrisburg. The little community had a short life; a few weeks later, a better ore vein was found over the hill to the north. And as Skidoo's star rose, Harrisburg's fell. Shorty could see that his find was going nowhere fast and sold out his interest in the mine; eventually, Pete did the same.

But after the buyers had abandoned the mine, Pete came back. He worked the mine — with modest success — all by himself, for many years. Pete was a real desert lover, and one of the things he loved most was the view of Death Valley from the top of the Panamints a few miles east of his mine. He even scratched out a road up to it — thus, the viewpoint's name.

On a clear day, Aguereberry Point is a wonderful place from which to take panoramic photos of Death Valley, especially in the afternoon. It's also an ideal place to get out your maps and try to figure out which mountain ranges and landmarks you are seeing. The elevation at the viewpoint is a little over 6400 ft; the floor of the valley is about 6600 unobstructed feet lower. No wonder the view is so good!

Twenty-three Skidoo to You, Too! If you're game for one more dirt road excursion after returning to Wildrose Rd, continue north for another 2.3 mi to the Skidoo Rd. Turn east here and wind up Tucki Mtn for 7 mi (from about 4900 ft to 5700 ft) to what's left of one of the California desert's more successful mining towns. Gold was discovered here only a few days or weeks after Pete and Shorty made their modest find at Harrisburg in 1905 (or was it 1906?). Anyway, as a result, most miners and prospectors lost interest in Harrisburg and moved north to try their hand at Skidoo's richer lode.

The original discoverers of Skidoo's golden possibilities quickly sold out to Bob Montgomery, who evidently had the wherewithal to make the area pay. The new owner began by having 23 mi of 6-in. water pipe laid from Birch Spring up on Telescope down to the mines; he continued by having a fifteen-stamp mill built to process the ore. These were no small tasks — the pipe and the stamp mill parts were cast iron! The water wasn't just for drinking, though; to be successful, large gold mining operations need lots of water. You can still see the pipeline trace; hardy hikers have even followed it all the way to Birch Spring.

Skidoo was what you might call a company town, in that it was owned and controlled by one person. The community had a population of about seven hundred — a number that included a great many families. It also had a respectable number of general stores, a telephone and telegraph office, school, and (of course) several bars. One story of how the town got its name was that someone connected the 23-mi length of the town's pipeline with a popular, slangy, off-putting saying of the time—"twenty-three skidoo for you!"—and christened the little settlement Skidoo.

Despite its rather lively name, Skidoo, like most company towns, was not a particularly lively place—no shades of Bodie here. But the town did make money—over $3 million, net, came out of the ground around Skidoo. This fact alone also makes Skidoo unusual; most Death Valley mining operations were dismal failures at profitmaking. And the mining operation at Skidoo kept bringing home the bullion until about 1917, when the veins seemed to be played out. During hard times in the 1930s a few folks tried their luck at reworking some of the mines; some were still there as late as the 1950s. Since then, the relic robbers and arsonists have pretty well reduced Skidoo to a few foundations, a mostly burned mill, a barren cemetery, and shards of broken glass. Despite this vandalism, the town is still worth a visit. It takes only a little imagination to envision something of what kind of life miners and their families had here early in the century.

Last Stop—Emigrant Ranger Station. Once you get back to Wildrose Rd, it's only 9.5 mi on north up Emigrant Canyon to the ranger station and CA 190. From here you can set off on any one of a number of DVNM or Owens Valley tours. There is usually a friendly ranger on duty here to answer questions and dispense brochures. If you'd like to know what weather is coming up, check the weather report on the bulletin board. Emigrant Campground is just across the highway.

Telescope Peak Hike and Backpack

Class 1/elev. 11,049 ft/USGS topo *Telescope Peak*/14 mi RT/signed trail

TO GET THERE. Follow the directions for the Emigrant Canyon tour, above, to Wildrose Canyon. Drive to the end of the road at Mahogany Flat, a little less than 8 mi. The road is paved for about half the distance; the rest is dirt, but OK for ordinary cars (usually). The last few miles are pretty steep; your transmission and cooling system should be in good condition.

ABOUT THE HIKE. The Panamint Range and its highest peak, Telescope, are as much a source of Death Valley's unique character as is the Devil's Cornfield on the valley floor. This mountain is the highest point in DVNM; it rises more than 11,000 ft above the Death Valley floor (to the west) and almost 10,000 ft above the Panamint Valley floor (to the east). The well-maintained trail from the Mahogany Flat roadhead to the summit offers one of the finest hiking experiences of a lifetime. Both Badwater, the lowest point in the United States, and Mt Whitney, the highest point in the lower forty-eight states, are visible along the trail. The best times to make this hike are May-July and September-October. (The peak is often snow capped until Memorial Day.) Ordinarily, wildflower displays are at their finest during late June and in July. As with desert hikes in general, there is no water on the trail; be sure to carry plenty.

Due to its 3000-ft elevation gain, the 14-mi round-trip climb all the way to Telescope Peak can be tiring for some folks. For those who have the time, the hike to the peak makes a good overnight backpack. You can shorten the hike by just going as far as the Panamint crest—a 3.5-mi, 2000-ft ascent. At this point (and at the peak), get out your maps and try identifying the landmark peaks and ranges of this basin-and-range country.

At both the crest and the peak, the colorful language of a John Muir is needed to describe the view to the east. In its awesome desolation, reaching to the horizon, Death Valley conjures up images from William Lewis Manly's account, *Death Valley in '49*. Manly, as you may remember from the Emigrant Valley tour, was one of the two men who hiked out of Death Valley and returned with supplies to bring out their stranded party—the first group of settlers to go through the valley. (See the "Recommended Reading" appendix for details on Manly's book.)

If you have been wise enough to choose a cool, breezy day in late spring or early fall, you will also be rewarded with views to the west—Mt Whitney and the Sierra Nevada, with a hint of Saline Valley to the north. And no matter which way you look, you'll probably agree with the reason the first person who reached the peak (in 1860) supposedly gave when he named it: "You can see so far it's just like looking through a telescope!"

An Alternate Route for the Hardy. The peak is also occasionally climbed by a hearty (or masochistic?) few from Shorty's Well (−252 ft) via Hanupah Canyon. This route is a twelve-plus-hour test of strength!

Wildrose Peak Hike
Class 1/elev. 9064 ft/USGS topo *Emigrant Canyon*/8 mi RT/trail

TO GET THERE. Follow the directions for the Emigrant Canyon tour, above, to Mahogany Flat Rd at the mouth of Wildrose Canyon, and then on up the canyon to the charcoal kilns.

ABOUT THE HIKE. If your time is limited, but you'd still like to hike a trail famous for its views, try this jaunt to Wildrose Peak. You'll find the trail at the west end of the charcoal kilns. On the way to the summit, look for excellent panoramas of both Panamint Valley (to the west) and Death Valley (to the east). Also notice the differences between plant and animal life at lower and higher elevations. For example, what are the most common trees near the trailhead? Near the summit?

Stovepipe Wells, Scotty's Castle, and Ubehebe Crater Tour

TO GET THERE. From Towne Pass, on CA 190, continue about 17 mi east to Stovepipe Wells Village. From Furnace Creek Inn, follow CA 190 north and west for about 26 mi to Stovepipe Wells Village.

GETTING YOUR BEARINGS. You'll need a good Death Valley and vicinity map. Walkers may want the USGS topos *Stovepipe Wells* and *Ubehebe Crater*.

ABOUT THE TOUR. From Burned Wagons Point, east of Stovepipe Wells Village, the tour will take you to the famously photogenic Death Valley sand dunes and the arrowmaker's delight, the Devil's Cornfield, before turning north and continuing to Death Valley Ranch (now known as Scotty's Castle) and vast Ubehebe Crater. Total mileage is about 45 mi.

The Forty-Niners Stopped Here. Take time to find Burned Wagons Point, just east of Stovepipe Wells Village. Here, you'll find an interesting historic marker describing how one party of Forty-niners got together enough supplies to enable them to leave Death Valley. For the story of the Forty-niners (the first parties of emigrants to successfully cross Death Valley on their way west), see the Emigrant Canyon tour, above.

At Stovepipe Wells Village there is a motel, dining room, swimming pool, grocery store, and gas station. Just across the highway to the north of the village is the campground, complete with fireplaces, tables, water, restrooms, RV disposal station, lots of sand, and no trees. (Restaurant is not open in summer.)

The original well for which the village was named is actually some miles northeast and can be reached by means of the same road that takes you to the sand dunes.

Photographers and Sand Fans Stop Here! As you go east from Stovepipe Wells on CA 198, the sand dunes will be to the north of the road. To get a good look at the dunes, look for a well-maintained gravel road going north about 6 mi east of the village. A little way before you reach the gravel road, look to the south of the highway. What you see (amongst other things) are not bundles of cornstalks, but clumps of arrowweed growing high on pedestals carved out by wind and water erosion. The plant got its name from the fact that Indians found the straight stalks ideal for arrow shafts. (To bypass the dunes and head directly for Scotty's Castle, continue east past the gravel road 1.2 mi to CA 190; turn north here — it's about 33 mi to the junction with Ubehebe Crater Rd. At this point, just follow the signs northeast on CA 190 to Scotty's Castle.)

When you reach the gravel road, turn north and continue slowly along the edge of the dunes until you find a good stopping place. There are tables and portable toilets where the road turns east. The best times for taking photos are in the early morning or late afternoon. As all sand dune photographers know, the biggest problem with sand dunes — including this striking 14-sq-mi sweep — is the surfeit of subjects they offer. Just about the time you think you've finally captured that nearby and far-off curve, shadow, and ripple, you notice the beautifully intricate tracks a shiny black olive with legs is making right in front of your toes, and you're off again.

You may well wonder — if you run out of film and find yourself with time on your hands — where all this sand came from. A quick, though limited, explanation goes something like this: By the time the Death Valley region became arid, much bedrock granite was exposed. Over long periods of time, the strong prevailing winds from the south and west picked up the hard quartz bits left from the weathering away of the softer granite parts and moved them north and east, around the flanks of Tucki Mtn — which you can see south of CA 190 (check your map). Here, the winds were (and are) bounced back and forth by the surrounding mountains until their energy was pretty much spent. The tiny bits of quartz went no further, but piled up and up into the dunes we see now. Today the winds are still building and shifting the dunes — and will continue to do so for some time, say the geologists.

When you eventually manage to tear yourself away from the dunes, continue north on the dirt road (the road is about 3.5 mi long and connects CA 190 with the Death Valley North Highway — the road to Scotty's Castle). Keep your eye out to the west for signs of the original Stovepipe Well. The piece of stovepipe once used to mark the well for thirsty travelers in the late 1800s is, of course, long gone.

Once you're back on North Death Valley Highway, it's another 30.5 mi north to the highway's junction with the road to Ubehebe Crater. To get to Scotty's Castle, turn east at the junction and go about 3 mi up Grapevine Canyon.

Death Valley Scotty and His Castle. The why of this famous mansion in the desert is tidily put by Ruth Kirk, who says in her guide to Death Valley: "Two men thought Death Valley a fine place for a Moorish mansion with eighteen fireplaces and a 185-ft swimming pool; one of them had enough money to build it." The man with the money was Albert Johnson, an insurance executive from Chicago. It seems that in the mid-1920s Johnson's doctor advised him to move to a warm, dry climate for his health. While casting about for a likely place in the California desert, Johnson met Walter Scott, a former Buffalo Bill's Wild West Show trick rider, sometime prospector, and enthusiastic promoter of his own best interests.

Unlikely as it may seem, the two men became fast friends and together conceived the idea for the Death Valley Ranch, which came to be called Scotty's Castle. The builders started on the $2 million Moorish mansion in about 1925; construction stopped about 1931, when the Depression unfavorably affected Johnson's finances. The pool, formal gardens, and landscaping remain unfinished. From 1931 until he passed over to the great desert in the sky, "Death Valley Scotty" earned his keep in the best way he knew how—by his wits. He was, by all accounts, perhaps the most accomplished tall-tale teller and self-promoter Death Valley has ever known. The tales, the friendship, and the desert air must have agreed with Johnson, for he lived until 1948—his seventy-fifth year. The desert didn't do too bad by Scotty either; he was eighty-one when he died in 1954.

When you tour the "castle," it'll become evident that the $2 million didn't all go into construction. There are costly and beautiful antiques and reproductions throughout the mansion, along with artfully wrought ironwork, massive beamed ceilings, a huge pipe organ, an indoor waterfall and fish pool, collections of paintings and ceramics, and much more. In such a place, with such company, and at 3000 ft, Death Valley summers were probably quite tolerable.

Besides tours, the castle offers gift shops, water, snack bar, picnic area, shady parking lot, and gas station. South and west of the castle about 5.5 mi is Mesquite Spring Campground, which has water, fireplaces, tables, restrooms, and a dump station.

From Scotty's Castle it's only 8 mi to Ubehebe Crater. To get there, return to the junction 3 mi west the way you came, then follow the signs northwest 5 mi to the crater parking lot.

More Desert Volcanoes. Geologists can't seem to agree on Ubehebe Crater's age. Some say only a few hundred years, some a thousand, and still others vote for 10,000 years or more. All agree, however, that the group of small craters on its south side, including Little Hebe, are very young—perhaps only three hundred years old. Geologists also agree that all these craters, including Ubehebe, were formed by volcanic explosions, rather than meteorites or lava extrusions. The force of the explosion creating Ubehebe must have been tremendous, for it is shaped like a huge upside-down cone rather than a right-side-up one like many other volcanoes are.

Ubehebe's vital statistics are about as follows: width at top, 0.5 mi; width at bottom, 450 ft; depth, 800 ft. The crater walls were cut so cleanly by the force of the explosion that 800 ft of many-colored layers can be clearly seen. Can you tell anything about what the Death Valley area was like in times past from examining some of the layers? To get a closer look at the layers, try the trail to the bottom of the crater. Another trail leads along the rim to Little Hebe.

Ubehebe is a rather unforgettable name, but its Indian meaning is another thing people can't seem to agree about. Some say it stands for "basket in the rock." The following account (again from Ruth Kirk), however, indicates this may not be correct. According to Kirk, the Indians said the crater used to be a basket, so they somewhat humorously called it after an Indian woman living nearby. (She must have been a famous carrier!) Their name for the crater, "Duh-vee'tah Wah'sah," meant "Duhveetah's carrying basket." Ubehebe, then, is a somewhat altered version of the name Duhveetah.

What Next? From tour's end here at Ubehebe you can easily go south again to see more of Death Valley, or you can foray north into Inyo-Mono country.

Porter Peak Hike and Backpack
Class 1/elev. 9101 ft/USGS topo *Telescope Peak*/7–16 mi RT/trail, cross-country

TO GET THERE. *Access 1:* In Death Valley National Monument, take the Furnace Creek Rd south about 4.3 mi from Furnace Creek to its junction with Badwater Rd. Go south on Badwater Rd 6.1 mi to its junction with the West Side Rd (good dirt). Take the West Side Rd southwest about 21 mi to another dirt road leading into Johnson Canyon; go west on this road. Drive up the canyon about 11 mi, to a point near a fork at 3500 ft. This latter road can sometimes be impassable; be sure to check with a ranger before attempting it.

Access 2: See the East Panamint Valley tour in Chapter 9 for directions to Ballarat. From Ballarat, take the rough road (usually 4WD only) about 6 mi up Pleasant Canyon toward the Cooper Mine. How far you go will depend on your vehicle.

ABOUT THE HIKE. Porter Peak is a seldom-climbed summit overlooking the ghost town of Ballarat in the Panamint Valley to the east and southern Death Valley to the west.

The Easiest Approach (Access 1): As you travel south on West Side Rd, look for the Bennett's Well marker. Some historians think this is where the Bennett Forty-niner party waited for William Manly and John Rogers to bring the supplies they needed to make the journey out of Death Valley. (See the Emigrant Canyon tour, above, for details of the Forty-niners—the first emigrants to cross Death Valley.)

The hike to Porter Peak is a fairly long one; most people prefer to make it an overnight backpack. That way, you don't have to hurry but can enjoy the scenery, take photos, botanize, or whatever. To begin the hike (after driving up the road into Johnson Canyon to the fork at about 3500 ft), take the north fork. The trail will take you past a spring and some ruins at about 3800 ft and on to Hungry Bill's Ranch, a pleasant place to camp.

Truck Farming in the Old West. At Hungry Bill's you can still see massive stone walls and terraces, along with some hardy apple, walnut, and fig trees. These are the remains of what was once a flourishing fruit, nut, and vegetable farm. But why here? Well, according to the records, the farm was the bright idea of several people who wanted to take advantage of the fact that in the mid-1870s it was a loooong way from the mining camps of the western Panamints to any kind of fresh food. You can hardly blame folks for not wanting to pay $1.20 for a head of cabbage coming all the way from the Los Angeles area. (And $1.20 was a lot of money in those days!) The Hungry Bill farmers thought they could do better than that—and they did. (Hungry Bill, by the way, wasn't one of the farmers, but a Shoshone Indian whose family had spent their summers in the canyon for many generations. He was luckier than most native Americans, in that he managed to get official homestead papers on some of the canyon land after the farmers left.)

Porter Peak and Beyond. If you weren't already on your way to Porter Peak, you could follow the old fresh-vegetable route by continuing up Johnson Canyon to Panamint Pass (sometimes called Sentinel Gap because of its proximity to Sentinel Peak) and then down to the old mining town of Panamint City, about 10 mi away. Or, instead of going down to Panamint City, you could descend east from the pass on a good trail back to Hungry Bill's and the roadhead.

Backpackers staying at Hungry Bill's can day hike southwest up the old mining trail shown on the topo map (it's obscure in places) and up the easy slopes to the peak. Ambitious hikers wanting to see more of the crest can hike north from Porter Peak 6 mi to Sentinel Peak (9636 ft), down to Panamint Pass, and then back to Hungry Bill's on the trail described just above. For an even longer hike, continue north on the crest from Panamint Pass to Telescope Peak (Class 2 route) and down to Mahogany Flat in Wildrose Canyon. (For this you need to set up a car shuttle.)

Another Route to Porter Peak (Access 2): The rough, 4WD road east up Pleasant Canyon takes you past a lot of old mining equipment, several ore trams, Clair Camp, the Radcliffe and World Beater mines, and on toward the Cooper Mine. (If you stop to examine some of this equipment, you'll be forcibly reminded that mining was not, and is not, easy work.) From the Stone Corral at 5881 ft, about 6 mi from Ballarat and about a mile below the Cooper Mine (see your topo), the peak is a 7-mi round-trip. To reach the summit, hike up the trail to the saddle (8240 ft) just east of the peak and then along the west ridge to the peak itself.

Corkscrew Peak Scramble

Class 2/elev. 5804 ft/USGS topos *Grapevine Peak, Bullfrog, Chloride Cliff*/8 mi RT/cross-country

TO GET THERE. In Death Valley National Monument, travel 7 mi northeast of Stovepipe Wells Village on CA 190 or 19 mi north of Furnace Creek Inn on CA 190, then take North Highway north for 0.6 mi. At this point, turn northeast on Mud Canyon–Daylight Pass Rd and continue for 8.5 mi to a sign on the north side of the road pointing out Corkscrew Peak; park here. (If Mud Canyon–Daylight Pass Rd sign has arrows but no name, the arrows point to Beatty, Nevada.)

ABOUT THE SCRAMBLE. Corkscrew is a popular, showy, little peak whose spiral lives up to its name when viewed from the south. To reach the peak, hike northwest past Hole-in-the-Rock Spring, toward the saddle west of the peak, and on up the broad ledges east to the summit. Views from the top include Titanothere Canyon and Thimble Peak to the north.

An interesting descent can be made via the eastern ridge to the narrow, north-south-bearing canyon about 1 mi away. Enter this canyon at about 4400 ft and hike down to your vehicle. This peak is an easy day's climb.

Mosaic Canyon Hike

Class 1/elev. 2000 ft/USGS topo *Stovepipe Wells*/3 mi RT/use trail

TO GET THERE. Follow the directions to Stovepipe Wells Village above. Take the good dirt road going south past the west side of the village; in about 2.4 mi you'll come to the mouth of the canyon. Park here.

ABOUT THE HIKE. Mosaic Canyon is an hourglass (or wineglass) canyon. That is, its head is wide, but it funnels down to a deep, narrow gorge. During storms, huge amounts of water are collected on the broad slopes at the canyon's head and roar down through the deep gorge. The tremendous force of the water carries huge boulders, as well as rocks, pebbles, and sand, down to the canyon's narrow mouth. Here, the water is forced to spew out its load of debris into a fan. As you have probably noticed, Death Valley — and much of the mountainous California desert — has many such canyons and alluvial fans. You drive across one as you approach the mouth of Mosaic Canyon.

As for the hike itself, the first 0.5 mi takes you through the canyon's mouth — a very narrow stretch, worn smooth by water rushing through it. Then, over the next mile or so, the canyon floor widens. As you amble up the canyon, look closely at the rock layers. What kind of a story do they tell? The sedimentary layers in which rock fragments are embedded in a sandy matrix are called breccia. In Mosaic Canyon, these layers are particularly colorful and attractive — thus, the canyon's name. There is white marble in the canyon, too. See if you can find some.

Eventually, the wash narrows again and the going gets quite steep. After a total of about 1.5 mi, some hikers will feel the going is getting too steep for comfort. Hardy, experienced hikers may want to continue farther toward the canyon's head, about 5 mi on (at approximately 4000 ft).

Sand Dune Junction–Dante's View Tour

TO GET THERE. Sand Dune Junction is in the approximate middle of Death Valley National Monument, where CA 190, North Death Valley Highway, and Daylight Pass Rd come together (almost). More specifically, it is 7.3 mi east of Stovepipe Wells Village, 36 mi south of Scotty's Castle, and 19 mi north of Furnace Creek Inn.

GETTING YOUR BEARINGS. The AAA DVNM map is a must. In addition, exploring types might find the USGS topos *Stovepipe Wells, Furnace Creek,* and *Funeral Peak* handy.

ABOUT THE TOUR. The first stop south of the junction will be at Salt Creek's Fish of the Desert exhibit and nature trail. Next, at the Harmony Borax Works, you'll explore the life and times of that useful mineral, borax. Then comes the visitor center, where you can find out just about anything you want to know about DVNM; and still more about borax, complete with machinery, at the Borax Museum; and Zabriskie Point's superb badlands views; and, finally, from high up on Dante's View, a spectacular panorama of the mountains rimming DVNM on the west. Total distance is approximately 43 mi.

Ice Age Fish. About 4.5 mi south of Sand Dune Junction, go west 1.1 mi on a signed, well-maintained dirt road to a parking area near Salt Creek. Believe it or not, this creek flows all year. Even more incredible is the fact that there are fish in it! But these aren't your average, everyday fish—these tiny pupfish (only 1 in. long, give or take a few millimeters) are some of nature's leftovers from the last Ice Age. During that time, ancestors of today's pupfish made freshwater Lake Manly their home. You can also see pupfish at the Saratoga Spring pond, in the Amargosa River, and at Devil's Hole in Ash Meadows, a part of DVNM in Nevada. Although the average visitor probably can't tell the difference, each location harbors a different species of pupfish.

In the cooler, wetter Ice Age times, Lake Manly filled Death Valley to a depth of 600 ft or more. As climatic cycles slowly moved toward the warmer, drier part of the weather spectrum, Lake Manly's level fell and rose several times—and eventually disappeared. While the lake's level was slowly falling, some of its inhabitants were adapting to the water's increasing salinity. The pupfish adapted well and still manage to survive in a few warm, salty places—despite the actions of people who feel that any species but their own is quite dispensable.

Take time to browse through the exhibit and to walk the 0.25-mi self-guiding boardwalk trail along the stream (don't forget to pick up an information booklet). The purpose of this handy walkway is to protect the fragile riparian environment, rather than for the convenience of visitors. Notice that even here, in a salt basin, several species of plants seem to be doing quite well.

A Short History of Borax. To begin your education on the subject of that uncharismatic but interesting mineral borax, continue south on CA 190 for about 10.4 mi from the Salt Creek/Fish of the Desert turnoff. At this point, take the paved and signed Harmony Borax Works Rd west a short distance to the adobe ruins.

In the California desert, more money has been made from that unglamorous mineral borax than from that glamorous and glittering mineral gold. You can't wear a nugget of borax on your keychain or pan it out of a cool, scenic, mountain stream, but if you're in the right place at the right time you sure as Borax Smith can make money on it! And that's just what enterprising folks have been doing since the days of the Babylonians, several thousand years past.

Borax began making its way west via that famous globe-trotter and adventurer, Marco Polo. Yes, indeed, one of the many riches the famous explorer brought home with him from the wilds of Mongolia was none other than the mineral we most commonly think of as being useful in removing "ring around the collar." In Marco Polo's part of the world, these precious little white crystals were much coveted not by the local launderers, but by goldsmiths and ceramic glaziers. Without borax to use as a flux, the goldsmiths could not, for example, create the many-jeweled crowns so essential to the well-dressed ruler in those days. Nor could the fine-porcelain makers produce their world-renowned wares without borax to use in the delicate glazes.

Cottonballs — The White Gold of the Desert. Out here in the Old West, though, Death Valley's first borate entrepreneur, Aaron Winters, quite likely had no knowledge of such delicacies. Winters started the Death Valley area run on borax in 1880 by staking an extensive claim in the area that later became the Harmony Borax Works. (He had heard that the United States' growing glass industry needed borax, so he rightly deduced that there was likely to be a tidy profit in the crystals.) After a short time, however, an even more enterprising Mr. Coleman came along and offered Winters $20,000 for the claim. Winters apparently had found life as a borax miner not to his liking, because he snapped up the offer and was off like a shot to buy a ranch at Pahrump.

It was Coleman who, with the help of abundant water from the springs up Furnace Creek Wash and cheap Chinese labor, actually developed the Harmony Borax Works. At first, the mineral didn't even have to be mined; the white clumps of crystals — called cottonballs — were right on the surface and could be shoveled up by Coleman's Chinese laborers and hauled to the works. Here the cottonballs (a mixture of sodium and calcium borates) were dumped into tanks filled with a mixture of water and sodium carbonate and boiled. When this mixture was cooled, calcium carbonate settled to the bottom of the tank and the sodium borate (borax) was left in the liquid to crystallize out on iron rods. One of the problems with this process was that when summer temperatures in Death Valley were high, the borax would not crystallize out. When this happened, Coleman had the cottonballs hauled over to the Amargosa Borax Works to the east. The elevation at Amargosa is about 3000 ft, so temperatures didn't get as high there — and the borax could be crystallized.

Coleman did his best to make a profitable operation out of Harmony Borax Works, but by 1888 his financial difficulties were so severe that he had to give up the business to F. M. "Borax" Smith. Smith became what you might call a borax tycoon. He managed to buy up several going operations — the Harmony, the Lila C. (near Death Valley), the Borate (at Calico), and others — and to found the Pacific Coast Borax Company. As borax from the California desert became a readily available commodity, foreign competition began to slack off. Why buy from overseas when the domestic product was just as good? And so, although

California gold mines were still glittering, borax became a fairly important economic asset for California.

The Harmony operation was but one of several borax ventures in the Death Valley area that continued to be successful over the next five decades—until 1928, when massive deposits were found east of the town of Mojave, in an area now called Boron. Most of the borates used in the Western Hemisphere today come from the Boron area. Despite the rise of Borax Smith and, later, the success of the Boron works, William Coleman's name has not been forgotten: ever hear of colemanite (a crystalline form of calcium borate)?

Twenty-Mule-Team Days. Whatever borax lacked in luster for the general public of the late 1800s was more than made up for by the popularity of the twenty-mule teams that at first hauled the profitable white stuff across the California desert to the nearest railhead at Mojave. And Mojave wasn't just around the corner, but two weeks or more away over 180 mi of rough and almost waterless country. At Harmony you see one of the famous wagons, and at the Borax Museum there are some fine photos of the teams with their enormous wagons. The wagons had wood-and-iron wheels 5–7 ft in diameter; an empty wagon weighed almost four tons, and a full one weighed nearly sixteen tons. Each overworked team pulled two wagons and a water tank for a grand total of over thirty-six tons—almost a ton and a half per animal!

It wasn't until 1899 that any of the poor mules got some relief. That was when the Daggett & Borate Railroad was constructed from near Barstow to Mojave. The Death Valley area mules couldn't retire until the Tonopah & Tidewater Railroad arrived, which didn't happen until about 1907, when it reached Zabriskie. Although this railroad never quite lived up to its name, by 1908 it had managed to get all the way from Ludlow (a stop on the coast-to-coast Atlantic & Pacific line, now the Santa Fe Railroad) to the vicinity of Beatty, Nevada (with Tonopah still some distance to the north). There was even a spur line over to the Lila C. (borax) Mine and on to New Ryan in Furnace Creek Wash. Needless to say, this line made life easier and more profitable for all the various mining operations in the region—gold, copper, silver, and borax.

Life After Borax. To continue your survey of the life and times of borax, travel south toward Furnace Creek Ranch another 2 mi to the Borax Museum. The mining machinery and paraphernalia here will give you some idea of the back-breaking labor that was involved in early borax mining (admission is free).

Not all borax operations in the Death Valley area were successful, though. For example, the Eagle Borax Works—which had good deposits and lots of water, but a bad manager—failed miserably. Although there's not much to be seen of the old works, this site is worth a visit, should you be passing by. Eagle Borax is located on the east side of West Side Rd, 2 mi south of Hanupah Canyon Rd.

The springs here, used long ago by the borax operation, eventually became choked with the invasive exotic tamarisk. These trees use so much water that they actually lower the water table in areas they take over. As a result, native plants in the area die off and wild animals are forced to find other water sources—if they can. However, this sad story has a happy ending, thanks to the National Park Service, the Sierra Club's Desert Committee, and the Desert Protective Council. Volunteers from the two conservation groups, along with others, worked along with the National Park Service for several years in the early 1980s to rid the springs of tamarisk. Now, when you visit the old Eagle Borax area, you find lovely ponds fringed with green reeds and cattails—and lots of wildlife, including waterfowl. The Saratoga Spring area, at the southern end of DVNM, is another tamarisk-removal success story (see the Saratoga Spring–Owlshead Mountains tour, above).

Meanwhile, Back at the Visitor Center. Now that you've learned as much as (or more than) you ever wanted to know about borax, it's time to back up just a little—to the monument's fine visitor center. You probably noticed the sign on CA 190 a few hundred yards north of the Borax Museum. Here you can fill your water bottles, pick up a number of free informational brochures about DVNM, watch one of the hourly slide shows, examine the natural history displays, buy or just browse through many interesting books, picnic, and ask the rangers any questions you may have about the monument. If you're looking for a campsite, you'll have to make a choice—because there are three nearby: Furnace Creek, Sunset, and Texas Spring. Furnace Creek is in the mesquite next to the visitor center. Sunset is for RVs, and is located on the flats across CA 190. Texas Spring is up a small canyon a short distance farther south.

On to Zabriskie. It's only about 4 mi or so south to one of DVNM's most scenic spots—Zabriskie Point. Be sure to take the east fork (CA 190) at the junction by Furnace Creek Inn; the west fork, Badwater Rd, is covered in the next tour.

If your camera isn't loaded when you get to this viewpoint, it soon will be—particularly if you visit Zabriskie in the early morning or late afternoon. Although the point is a mere 710 ft high, it overlooks a striking badlands panorama of sharp-featured, mustard-colored mud hills that are lakebottom sediments laid down 2 to 12 million years ago. Notice the mud flows spreading out from between these easily eroded hills. Once these flows covered Badwater Rd to such a depth that it was easier to build a new road on top of them than to try clearing the road! Also look for remnants of lava flows.

If you feel like taking a short hike, try the trail leading from Zabriskie Point past the small peak of Manly Beacon and down to the road in Golden Canyon, which comes out on Badwater Rd. Distance from the point to Badwater Rd is about 2.5 mi.

Where the Borax Museum Came From. When you're ready to make your way south to Dante's View, about 20 mi on, consider taking a little side trip off CA 190 to the west to see 20 Mule Team Canyon. Look for the turnoff approximately 1.2 mi south of Zabriskie Point. The one-way road into the canyon loops back to CA 190 after 2.7 mi.

Despite its name, some say that twenty-mule teams never hauled borax through this canyon, though the white gold was mined here. The canyon, however, was home to quite a few miners over the years. In fact, the miners' boarding house—once located midway through the canyon—was the first frame building in Death Valley. Today, you can still visit this historic building—it was moved to Furnace Creek and is now the Borax Museum.

The best time to drive through the colorful mud hills of this canyon is late afternoon. Looking west, notice the contrasts between the dark-layered Black Mtns and the canyon's white-, yellow-, brown-, and orange-hued clay hills. Before being faulted, uplifted, and covered with lava, these many-layered mountains were flat lake beds, similar to the ones you can see on the floor of Death Valley.

Once you're back on CA 190, it's only 4.5 mi to the junction where you'll take the west fork (paved) leading to Dante's View, a little over 13 mi on. Look for evidence of old mining activities along the way in the Funeral Mtns (to the east) and the Black Mtns (to the west).

A View Fit for a Poet. Like most viewpoints, the best time to visit this one is in early morning or late afternoon—when the light is low, bringing out the area's remarkable colors, and shadows define the layers of hills, flats, and mountains stretching to the skyline. From mile-high Dante's View you can see the true vastness of the alluvial fans flowing out from canyon mouths and of the sparkling, barren salt flats. But even Death Valley has oases. Try getting out your maps and looking for Bennett's Well, Eagle Borax Works, Furnace Creek Ranch, and others. To the west, as you look over the ranks of sharply dissected canyons and the flat valley floor, are the massive Panamint Mtns, topped by snow-capped, 11,045-ft Telescope Peak. Beyond the Panamints, on the horizon, is the Sierra Nevada—the "snowy range."

At Dante's View you have the unique opportunity of seeing the highest and lowest points in the "lower forty-eight" at the same time. To get to this overlook, take the short footpath to the right—the Whitney View Trail. The path will take you to a point where you can see Badwater, the lowest point, more than a mile below you, at 280 ft below sea level, and Mt Whitney, on the western horizon, the highest peak, at 14,495 ft.

Don't hurry away from Dante's View. Take some time to wander around, to enjoy the wide open spaces, the colors, the patterns, the clear air, the mountains' silent presence.

Manly Peak Hike

Class 1/elev. 7196 ft/USGS topo *Manly Peak*/5 mi RT/cross-country

TO GET THERE. Take CA 190 into Death Valley National Monument from the west side or CA 178 or 190 from the east side. Once in

DVNM, go east on the Warm Spring Canyon Rd. This road turns off the Death Valley West Side Rd about 5 mi north of the Ashford Mill ruins (the ruins are located in the south end of DVNM, about 11.5 mi west of the east boundary). About 14 mi from the turnoff, at a Y, bear left up the wash on the minor road, which will take you past an area of talc mining and on into Butte Valley. Park near the stone cabin at Anvil Spring (about 24 mi from the Ashford Mill site and 7 mi from Warm Spring Canyon Rd). 4WD vehicles are recommended for the road into Butte Valley.

ABOUT THE HIKE. In Butte Valley you will easily be able to see the imposing eminence of 4773-ft Striped Butte (an easy scramble). Recently the National Park Service has been successfully conducting a burro capture program in Butte Valley.

Manly Peak is the first named peak in the Panamint Range south of Porter Peak. As with all the peaks in this varied range — each of which is unlike any of the others — Manly has its own unusual scenery and features.

To reach Manly's 7196-ft summit, hike up either the east or the northeast ridge (consult your topo).

Salsberry Pass–Furnace Creek Tour

TO GET THERE. From I-15 at Baker, take CA 127 north for about 60 mi to CA 178 (a couple of miles north of Shoshone). Next, go west on CA 178 for about 11 mi, to Salsberry Pass (3315 ft).

GETTING YOUR BEARINGS. You'll need the AAA Death Valley and vicinity map. For hiking and exploring, try these USGS topos (south to north): *Avawatz Pass, Confidence Hills, Funeral Peak, Bennet's Well,* and *Furnace Creek.*

ABOUT THE TOUR. After going over the low Salsberry and Jubilee passes, CA 178 (Jubilee Pass Rd) curves north and becomes Badwater Rd just before it passes the Ashford Mill ruins. On its way north, the road skirts the fault scarp that is the western edge of the Black Mtns, traverses a number of alluvial fans, and eventually passes Mormon Point and Badwater. The latter, at about 280 ft below sea level, is the lowest point in the United States. North of Badwater, the highway passes a spur leading to a natural rock bridge and one leading to the Devil's Golf Course and the Salt Pools. There is also a very colorful loop trip on a paved road off CA 178 called Artists' Drive. Finally, a little way before you reach the junction with Furnace Creek Rd, you'll come to a spur leading into Golden Canyon, where there is a trail heading up to Zabriskie Point. This is probably one of the most scenic drives you'll ever take! Total mileage is a little less than 65 mi.

Two Low Passes. As you climb out of the broad Greenwater Valley up to Salsberry Pass (3315 ft), watch the south side of the road for dark, crinkly lava flows and light areas of compacted volcanic ash called tuff. About a mile west of the pass, notice that the road is crossing an alluvial fan. Where is the fan coming from?

The highway crosses the DVNM boundary about 4.5 mi from Salsberry Pass; at about 7 mi from the pass, notice a high, red cliff close by the south side of the road. After you come around the cliff, look ahead for Jubilee Mtn, a good-sized, darkish, rather pointed peak. At this point, you can look down Rhodes Wash and see the floor of Death Valley, with the rounded Confidence Hills just beyond to the west.

A little over 8 mi from Salsberry Pass, you'll top Jubilee Pass (1320 ft). The mountain just north of the pass is Desert Hound Peak. The rock the peak is made of is from the earth's Precambrian era—it is 600–3600 million years old. This ancient rock making up the peak is at one end of the core of a massive, uplifted, rock fold (an anticline) that stretches all the way to Mormon Point, over 20 mi north. At Mormon Point, as you will see, the anticline plunges below the surface of the valley. Also to the north is a fine view of Epaulet Peak.

About 1.4 mi west of the pass, keep an eye out on the south side of the road for a ridge made up of many angled red sandstone layers, along with some dark volcanic layers. Also look for some smooth-appearing pink and white layers of tuff 0.25 mi or so farther south, away from the highway. These layers are all more than 2 million years old (which is young, geologically speaking).

The Sad Tale of Ashford Mill. A little less than 5 mi west of Jubilee Pass, the road turns north and you can now see the steep, faulted front of the Black Mtns on the east side of the road, stretching north toward Furnace Creek. In another 2 mi, look for the concrete remains of an old mill on the west side of the road. The mill was built during World War I, when Death Valley mining enjoyed a brief comeback.

It all started with the three brothers Ashford, who staked a large gold claim up nearby Scotty's Canyon, in the Black Mtns. Seemingly, the Ashfords must not have had much faith in their claim, because they soon sold it for $60,000. The new owner then turned around a couple of times and sold it again—this time for a whopping $105,000, which was a lot of money in those days. It was this last set of owners who hopefully built the large mill. Unfortunately, the success they hoped for never materialized.

Some Death Valley Shorelines. A couple of miles west of Ashford Mill is a black, basaltic hill (elevation 648 ft) called Shoreline Butte. For a mile or two north from the mill, in the early morning or late afternoon—when the low-angled light brings out contours invisible at midday—you can easily see several different wave-cut horizontal lines on the butte's northeast side. These ancient shorelines are left from a cooler, wetter time 10,000 to 75,000 years ago when Lake Manly filled Death Valley. This Pleistocene lake was about 600 ft deep and over 100 mi long; from the west it was fed by meltwaters from the Sierra Nevada (which came through Wingate Pass), and from the south by the combined Amargosa and Mojave rivers. (Check your maps for the locations of these old water entrances.) You will see other Lake Manly shorelines north of Badwater at Manly Terrace.

On the Way to Mormon Point—Scarps and Layers. Mormon Point is 11 mi north of the Ashford Mill site on Badwater Rd (CA 178). About 2 mi north of the mill, the Death Valley West Side Rd (dirt) comes in from the west. Southwest from this junction you can see Wingate Pass on the horizon. West of the junction, on the Death Valley floor, look for a small cinder cone—you'll see it again a few miles up the road, from a different angle.

As you continue north on Badwater Rd (the east arm of the junction), after about 3 mi look west again for the cinder cone. Now you can see it has been cut by fault movement. The steep face of the Black Mtns to the east is also the result of fault movement. Look for more evidence of fault scarps and scarplets in the mountains and alluvial fans as you travel north.

Other features to look for as you travel north are the differences between the fans on the east side of the valley and those on the west side. You can see right away that the fans on the west side are much larger and more gently sloping than those on the east side. This is partly because the Panamint Range in the west is not only higher and more massive than the Black Mtns, but also traps more water from Pacific weather systems. In addition, however, the western fans are larger because the huge block of the earth's crust supporting the Panamint Range and the Death Valley floor is tilted downward to the east. This tilt forces the valley's west side fans to extend themselves by flowing eastward. The east side fans, because of the steep fault scarp at their canyons' outfall areas and the flow of valley debris from the west onto the foot of the Black Mtns, are cone-shaped rather than fan-shaped. These east side canyons, with their wide headwater areas, stemlike gorges, and flat bases are sometimes referred to as goblet, hourglass, or wineglass canyons.

It's not hard to figure out that the floor of Death Valley you see today is but icing on a geologic cake. That is, the fans, the salt flats, the mud hills, and so on, are sitting on many more layers of alluvium washed down from the surrounding mountains. These layers add up to 3000 ft or so. Below these relatively recent layers are many more layers of very ancient lakebed sediments and of volcanic debris as much as 70 million years old. These layers may be as much as 6000 ft in depth. And as long as gravity continues to operate, and some vast cataclysm does not intervene, the floor of Death Valley will continue to accumulate layers.

When you stop to think about it, it's not hard to believe that in a cooler, wetter time the hot, salty, arid Death Valley of today was filled with fresh water. Because, after all, water does run downhill and Death Valley is—and has been for many, many millennia—the lowest point in a vast, mountainous area. Even today, despite its rather stark appearance, the valley harbors more creeks and springs per square mile than most of the desert around it.

Mormon Point to Badwater—Turtlebacks and More Shorelines. Take time to stop near the Mormon Point sign; here is where the "nose" of the huge mass of Precambrian rock that stretches from Jubilee Pass to here plunges into the valley floor. If you look north along the face of the Black Mtns at this point, you can see where younger, more colorful, sedimentary and volcanic rocks begin. Layers like these, from the earth's Tertiary period (2–70 million years old), once covered the ancient, now-exposed core—the turtleback. When the Precambrian rock underlying the newer layers was uplifted into the kind of gigantic fold geologists call an anticline, the overlying softer layers became very vulnerable to erosion. Wind and water—with the help of heat and cold—wore these young layers away, exposing the ancient core we see today.

As you curve around Mormon Point and continue north toward Badwater, start looking for the Copper Canyon turtleback; you should be able to see this grayish Precambrian rock core (600–3600 million years old) ahead after about 1.5 mi. (Can you find its nose?) The road will begin curving out and around the sizable alluvial fan issuing from the mouth of Copper Canyon about 5 mi north of Mormon Point. As you drive across the fan—or, better yet, stop for a closeup look—notice that some of the first small, cone-shaped piles of debris are coated with desert varnish. The older the varnish is, the darker it is. (This coating is composed of iron and manganese that has been oxidized by weathering.)

Here, above the varnished cones, is another good place to see if you can find more Lake Manly shorelines. If you also look back from here at the north side of Mormon Point, you should see more shorelines cut into the somewhat eroded Pleistocene fanglomerates—hardened alluvial fans—at the foot of the point. (The fans formed during the Pleistocene are as much as 2 million years old and had had time to consolidate somewhat by the time the waves of Lake Manly started cutting shorelines.)

Between Copper Canyon and Badwater, you'll travel over and around several more fans at the base of the Black Mtns. The large fans, as you might guess, probably drain large areas. The good-sized rocks making up some steep fans indicate that the bedrock of the canyons above is probably pretty hard; canyons having gently sloping fans of finer materials are likely to be bedded with softer stuff.

About 10 mi from Mormon Point, you'll be able to see that the valley's salt flats are beginning to ease over toward the foot of the Black Mtns. By the time you're 15 mi from the point, the salt flats are right up against the mountains' base. Because the valley floor tilts east, as mentioned earlier, the salt flats have been sort of slopped up against the edge of the mountains.

Badwater—The Lowest and the Hottest. If you pull off at Badwater (about 18 mi from Mormon Point) for a look north at the glistening salt flats, you may wonder where all the salts have come from. Where else but from the lakes that have come and gone in Death Valley for millions of years. Lake Manly, the valley's last large lake, left behind its share of the many layers of minerals as its waters rose and fell for 65,000 years. By about 10,000 years ago, the increasingly arid climate had transformed the once 100-mi-long, 600-ft-deep lake into 200 sq mi of salt flats.

Here at Badwater, a short walk west out into the flat will bring you to places where the sometimes-muddy, sometimes-dry ground is broken up into rather large polygons. A close look at these platelike structures reveals that their edges are covered with salt crystals. In fact, it is the crystallization of these salts that creates the plates. Rocks, too, are flaked and cracked by growing salt crystals.

From out on the flats you should be able to pick out more old Lake Manly shorelines on the mountainfront. You'll also be able to see the turtleback that rises high above Badwater, just a little to the north. The fault running along the front of the Black Mtns has caused the turtleback to slip down and away from the main mountain mass, along with the rest of the ever-subsiding valley. (Badwater, at 280 ft below sea level, is the lowest point in the United States.) Both the Badwater and Copper Canyon turtlebacks are made of rock from the Precambrian era (600–3600 million years ago); this means they are some of the oldest rocks in the world.

Although the scene before you looks all but lifeless, a surprising variety of living things have successfully adapted themselves to the demanding conditions here. For instance, Badwater Pool and the area around it harbor not only algae, but several species of invertebrates, including a water snail able to thrive in a saturated salt solution! Around the salty pool live several plant species—desert holly, salt grass, pickleweed, iodine bush, spurge, and others. Can you tell which is which? By the way, the water in the pool comes from the surrounding mountains. Rain and meltwater trickle down the cliffs and into the valley's underground water system, then seep into the pool.

Supposedly, Badwater was inadvertently given its name when a surveyor whose mule refused to drink here wrote "bad water" on the edge of the map he was working on. The water isn't poisonous, though, it's more like a concentrated solution of Epsom salts—and has the same predictable results. No wonder the mule refused to drink!

Today's travelers, however, are more likely to be searching for a "good shot" rather than a drink when they visit Badwater Pool. Photography buffs will find that midmorning is the best time for catching snow-capped Telescope Peak reflected in the pool. Remember, too, that summer is definitely not the time to visit Badwater—the summer temperatures here are the highest in the world. (Highs average 116° F in July.)

Natural Bridge—A Monument to Erosion. A short drive of about 3.5 mi north will bring you to the turnoff for Natural Bridge. Go east at the sign for a couple of miles to the end of the steep dirt road. To find the bridge, walk a few hundred yards up the canyon and around the turn.

This 50-ft-high arch is composed of Tertiary sediments (2–70 million years old). It was carved out by water rushing over the lip of the dry falls you can find behind the bridge and pounding against whatever was in its way. The softer and less consolidated formations were washed away, leaving the bridge. The water-cut ledges on the canyon walls show the wash floor's earlier levels. To effectively show the scale of Natural Bridge, be sure to have someone standing under the formation when you photograph it. If you walk farther up the canyon, you'll find it peters out in some badland terrain. As you leave the canyon, look south for a good view of the Badwater turtleback.

Salt, Salt, and More Salt — The Devil's Golf Course. Just a little over 2 mi north of the Natural Bridge turnoff, you'll come to the Devil's Golf Course turnoff. Go west at this point for about 1.3 mi on a dirt road to a parking area. Here, where the valley's salt pan is particularly deep (over 1000 ft thick), you can easily see that its very rough surface consists of spikey formations of salt crystals. Wind, rain, erosion, and continual dissolving and recrystallizing of the salts in the old lake bed have produced this forbidding landscape.

The crystals forming 95% of the salt pan's top layer are nearly pure sodium chloride — the same kind you use at home. Sodium chloride is more soluble than the other salts in the pan and so is drawn up to the surface by capillary action whenever enough water is present. The sodium carbonates at the edge of the pan are the least soluble of the pan's salts and were the first to be redeposited as the valley's last small, shallow lake evaporated a couple of thousand years ago. (You know these carbonates as baking soda.) Between these two layers is a salt of intermediate solubility — magnesium sulfate, as in Epsom salts.

If you feel like checking out the salt towers and pinnacles at closer range, your rambles may take you by a salt pool. The crystal formations in these pools can be quite fascinating. Also, some say you can actually hear the hard, mineral-caked crust crack and the salt towers softly clink as they expand or contract when the temperature changes.

Artists' Drive — A Desert Rainbow. About 2.5 mi north of Devil's Golf Course, take the paved road east (signed). This one-way, 9-mi loop takes you through a rainbow-hued badland made up of mud hills eroded from lakebed sediments and layers of colorful volcanic debris. In the background is an immense cliff — actually a fault scarp. As the road climbs up the fan, across narrow washes, and above the valley, be sure to look southward for an excellent wide-angle view of the salt flats.

About midway in the loop is Artists' Palette, where everyone without a camera wishes they had one! The colors of the piled-up hills here are outstanding and range from softly tinted pastels to deeply hued and brilliant primaries. The great variety is partly a result of oxidation — for example, the blacks are probably manganese oxides, the greens are chlorides, and the russets, oranges, yellows, and reds are all different shades of iron oxides. To catch both the contrasts and the colors at their best, late afternoon is the time for photography here.

Golden Canyon—Three Short Trails to Choose From. After exiting Artists' Drive, you'll come around some dark basaltic hills at the foot of the Black Mtns. There are some wave-cut lake shorelines on these hills, but unless the light is just right they aren't easy to see from so close up. The flat-topped point you come around at the northern end of these hills is Manly Terrace. Archaeologists think this point may have been one of the first places in Death Valley used by Indians. As you round the point, look ahead on the east side of the road for an unusual basalt formation called Mushroom Rock. This rock is another good example of the erosional power of wind, water, heat, and cold.

North of the Artists' Drive exit about 2.8 mi is the Golden Canyon turnoff. Go east on this dirt road for 1.5 mi to its end. From here it's a half hour's walk to Cathedral Wall, a natural amphitheater, or to the foot of a small peak called Manly Beacon. If you're heading for the beacon, look for the self-guided geology tour markers along the way. More ambitious walkers may want to continue past the peak to Zabriskie Point, about 2.5 mi from the roadhead (see above). This is a relatively flat walk.

If you come to Golden Canyon looking for the expensive yellow mineral, you'll be disappointed. However, if you're looking for a pleasant and scenic place to spend the late afternoon, this will suit you nicely. And when the sun drops low in the sky, you'll find out why this steep, narrow canyon is called golden. As with Artists' Palette, the wide range of colors—from soft buff to vivid orange—in the clay hills comes from iron oxides. When you leave the canyon, explore the area around its mouth to see if you can find the red clay deposits Indians used in compounding face paint.

On to Furnace Creek and Tour's End. From the Golden Canyon turnoff, it's only a little over 2 mi to Furnace Creek Inn and the junction with Badwater Rd. Even if you never stay at Furnace Creek Inn, don't forget that you can tour the gardens and grounds for free.

11

The Western Mojave

Tehachapi Mountains–Antelope Valley

ABOUT THE AREA. The broad Antelope Valley—which forms most of the western part of the Mojave Desert—lies south of Kern County's Tehachapi Mtns and northwest of Los Angeles County's San Gabriel Mtns. (The Tehachapi mountainfront indicates where the western end of the Garlock fault lies; the Coast Range fronts are, of course, on the infamous San Andreas fault.) Here you'll find (among many other attractions) flaming poppy fields, large, slow-moving desert tortoises, gold mines, historic railroad towns, and graphic evidences of what earthquake faults have accomplished over millions of years of geologic time. And just over the Tehachapis, above the western edge of the Mojave, you'll find a refreshing mountain retreat.

Where Have All the Antelope Gone? Before the railroad was pushed through this western Mojave valley, many thousands of pronghorn antelope roamed the area. According to anecdotal evidence, at that time even the most persevering antelope-counters used to give up after they had counted seven thousand or so in a day! But the antelope and the railroad didn't mix. After the rails were laid through the area in 1876, the antelope refused to cross them as they migrated to their traditional grazing grounds—so hundreds starved to death. (In other parts of the California desert, the bighorn sheep refuse to cross paved roads.) A severe winter in the 1880s finished off thousands more of the antelope. In the early 1900s, ranching, farming, and fencing eliminated the last hardy few. Now, all that's left of the antelope is the valley's name. (Within the last few years, however, some antelope have been brought from the Rocky Mtns area and released on the Tejon Ranch in the Tehachapi Mtns.)

Tortoise Watchers, Take Note! There are probably few better places to meet the object of your interest than the Desert Tortoise Natural Area just north of California City. The interpretive center supplies information on these increasingly rare creatures, and the trails take you deep into tortoise land. This is a good place to start honing your wildlife photography skills—the tortoises are very cooperative.

FACILITIES. Gas, supplies, restaurants, and motels can be found in Palmdale, Lancaster, California City, Mojave, and Tehachapi.

Camping. There are several developed Angeles National Forest campgrounds near Littlerock Reservoir, a short distance out of Littlerock. To find Lakeside, Juniper Grove, Rocky Point, and Joshua Tree campgrounds, take Eighty-second St south of Littlerock for about 0.5 mi to Fort Tejon Rd; go southwest on this road for 1.4 mi to Littlerock Cutoff Rd. Follow the cutoff 3.5 mi west to the road leading south into the campgrounds. These campgrounds have tables, fireplaces, water, and chemical toilets. Swimming and fishing are allowed in the reservoir, and there are hiking trails nearby. Outside Tehachapi is Kern County's Tehachapi Mountain Park. The sites there have tables, fireplaces, toilets, and water. The park also has hiking trails and a public corral. Saddleback Butte State Park has campsites with tables, fireplaces, and chemical toilets. Water is trucked in. For directions, see the trips below.

Open-desert camping is allowed on Bureau of Land Management (BLM) lands in the Antelope Valley. Because there is so much land under private ownership in the valley, it's a good idea to check with the BLM's Ridgecrest Resource Area Office at 619-446-4526 for information on the best places to try.

Mojave-Tehachapi Tour

TO GET THERE. From the intersection of CA 138 with CA 14 in Palmdale, take CA 14 north about 20 mi to Rosamond Blvd. Go west on Rosamond Blvd for 3.1 mi to the Mojave-Tropico Rd; turn north here and go about 1 mi to the Tropico Gold Mine.

GETTING YOUR BEARINGS. You'll need a good Kern County map.

ABOUT THE TOUR. This short, easy tour of the Mojave Desert's westernmost reaches will take you from a gold mine at Rosamond (just a few miles south of Mojave), through the historic town of Mojave, over Tehachapi Pass (where the Mojave Desert officially ends) to the little community of Tehachapi, and up into the foothills of the Tehachapi Mtns. Total mileage is about 43 mi.

Relive the Gold Rush in Rosamond. Before you look over the Tropico Mine, consider for a moment how gold mining got started here. Unlike Mojave, Sand Creek (today's Rosamond) initially depended on farming and ranching for its livelihood rather than on the business brought by the railroads. In the 1870s, however, a Mr. Crandall began mining clay from what is now Tropico Hill and shipping it to Los Angeles to a Mr. Hamilton's pottery and tile company. By the 1890s a depression had hit the country, and Hamilton's pottery business in Los Angeles

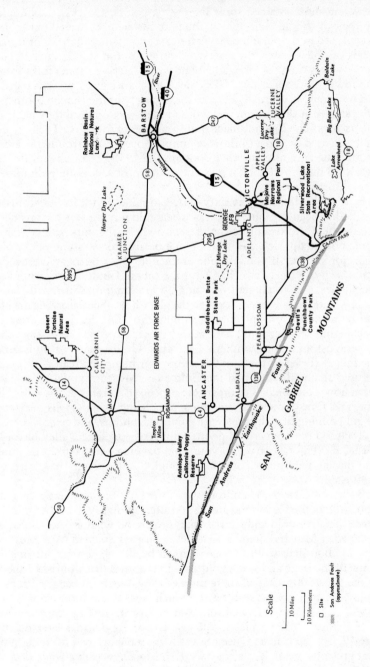

was pretty slow. At about this time Hamilton discovered that the clay he was using contained some interesting colors. Quickly, he bought up the clay-riddled hill, which, much to his delight, turned out (quite literally) to be a gold mine. Several years and many hundreds of thousands of dollars later, the now-well-off Hamilton sold his mine. The new owners then sold it again about a year later—to some folks from the town of Tropico near Glendale. Thus, the mine's present name.

The Tropico eventually became the property of the Burton brothers, who started at the bottom and worked their way up until they became the owners. The Burtons made quite a success of the mine. Their stamp mill was used by most of the small mining operations around the area. In the long run, after another boom in the 1930s, the mine produced nearly $8 million in gold; it was one of the most successful gold mines in California history.

Here at the Tropico, the sixty-year-old mine—with its 900-ft main shaft—has been kept just as it was when gold mining was big business around here. According to the present owners, the mine still contains some potentially rich ore veins. You'll be able to see some of the old veins for yourself if you take one of the hour-long tours given several times each day (there is a charge for the tours). Guides explain mining techniques, and you'll get to see mining tools and machinery in place, as they were actually used—even in the glory hole. (Special arrangements can be made for group tours. Call 805-256-2644 for information.)

The gold recovery mill here at the Tropico was for some time the largest custom mill in southern California. Unfortunately for visitors, the mill is closed to tours now because it is being renovated so it can be used again. However, at the Gold Mine Museum you'll be able to learn how gold and silver ores were processed to remove the valuable minerals. One of the museum's most interesting exhibits tells the story of gold mining in California with paintings, photos, and relics. There's also a good newspaper and photo exhibit of Antelope Valley history. You can even practice up on your gold panning—in a tank! The mine and museum are open Thursday through Sunday from 10:00 A.M. to 4:30 P.M.

Back in the 1890s, Hamilton wasn't the only one to make a success of mining in the Rosamond area. Soon after his discovery, other miners made lucrative gold and silver strikes nearby on what are now known as Soledad Mtn and Standard Hill. As you pass Soledad Mtn, west of CA 14 about halfway to Mojave, you'll be able to see the remains of some of the large and small gold and silver mines that flourished there in the late 1800s. One of these mines—the Golden Queen (still active today)—can easily be seen on the north side of the mountain. In its heyday, this mine was sold to a South African mining company for $3.5 million. A few miles to the east and a few decades later (in the late 1930s), the Cactus Queen Silver Mine gave up over $6 million of that precious metal. The sleepy western Mojave wasn't always sleepy!

On the Way to Mojave. Tropico Hill is on the southwestern edge of the Rosamond Hills. When you return to CA 14 and start north toward Mojave, about 13 mi away, notice that the hills ahead are many colored. You may be even more familiar with the volcanic bits and pieces making up these hills than you think: the rocks are quarried for ornamental and roofing purposes.

The formation making up the Rosamond Hills stretches east to Boron, where it yields up what is probably the world's richest deposit of borates. (After 1925, when production began, most of the other borax mining operations in the United States had a hard time making ends meet. One of the reasons for this is that about 70% of the borates mined at Boron are pure sodium borate—and so need little processing.)

About 6 mi north of Rosamond Blvd, Soledad Mtn (4183 ft) will be to the immediate west of CA 14. The materials making up this mountain were forced into the older surrounding granite many millions of years ago. When the newer (very hot) materials met the old, various minerals were formed—among them, silver and gold, which explains why the mountain was home to a number of successful silver and gold mining operations. It's estimated that as much as $25 million of ore was mined here.

Mojave—Child of the Railroad. Unlike some other small western towns, modern Mojave hasn't retained much of its historic flavor. But the desert still surrounds it, and with the help of a little imagination and a few facts, you should be able to get a whiff of the old times. For example, consider the fact that in 1876, when the San Joaquin Valley's Central Pacific Railroad (now Southern Pacific) finally managed to get through the Tehachapi Mtns and down to the Antelope Valley (on its way to Los Angeles), all the immediate area could boast was an old stage station called Cactus Castle. It wasn't long, though, before the townsite of Mojave was laid out a couple of miles northeast of the "castle" and soon grew into quite a respectable-sized community—thanks to the railroad.

Southern Pacific, however, was still looking for new railroad worlds to conquer. So, beginning in 1882, SP started pushing its rails from Mojave toward the Colorado River (it reached Barstow—then called Waterman Junction—the same year, and the Colorado River the next year). Before the railroad reached the mining operations farther east, though, these operations were obliged to haul their wares to the nearest railroad—at Mojave. From 1884 to 1889, twenty-mule teams were hauling their immense loads of borax the grueling 165 mi from Death Valley's Harmony Borax Works to Mojave. (The wagons, by the way, were built in Mojave.) Freight wagons also brought the "white gold" to Mojave from the Searles Lake and other borax mining areas. After 1889, the railroad—not the mule teams—brought the borax to Mojave. As the years rolled by, more and more railroad business went through Mojave on its way to Los Angeles, making the little town a pretty busy place. Nowadays, though, the railroad business isn't as good as it used to be—and Mojave is, well, sleepy (except for the huge, expensive, diesel-belching trucks that now carry goods the railroads used to haul more cheaply).

Through the Tehachapis to a Mountain Park. To get from Mojave to the town of Tehachapi via the back way, rather than by the more prosaic freeway, take Oak Creek Rd west from the center of Mojave for 10.5 mi to its intersection with Tehachapi–Willow Springs Rd. At about this point, the Oak Creek Rd takes you over the original Tehachapi Pass.

The names of passes, like the names of towns and roads, are of course mutable. In this case, once the railroad made it through the Tehachapis and down to the desert in 1876, the powers that be must have thought it more politic to "move" the pass over to what was obviously going to be the more well traveled road. So today the official summit (4065 ft) is on CA 58 just as you come into the outskirts of Tehachapi. A look at your map to get the lay of the land will tell you that the Tehachapi Mtns hold a rather privileged position, in that they not only mark the southern end of the San Joaquin Valley, but form a link between the two ranges defining that vast valley: the Sierra Nevada and the Coast Range.

To continue, follow Tehachapi–Willow Springs Rd 5.4 mi northwest to Highline Rd. Go west on Highline (left) 5.3 mi to Water Canyon Rd; turn south and go about 3 mi to Tehachapi Mountain Park (Kern County). Altitudes in this 490-acre park range from 4000 to 7000 ft, making it a fine place to go in summer when you want to get away from the heat of the low desert. The park has over five dozen individual campsites, a large group camping area, lots of excellent mountain spring water, and—for the horsily inclined—a public corral. There are hiking trails in and near the park. In winter, snow play (sledding, etc.) is popular; there is no downhill skiing.

About Tehachapi. The first people to settle in this area, as in most of the California desert, were native Americans. The Kawaiisu were an offshoot from the Chemehuevi (southern Paiute) people. By the 1850s, settlers began drifting into the area, attracted by possibilities for cattle raising, farming, and lumbering. Aside from the rich limestone deposits (which could be turned into that useful and lucrative product you know as cement), there wasn't much to attract miners in the Tehachapi area.

During the first settlement years, several tiny communities sprang up—Williamsburg, Tehichipa, and Greenwich. It wasn't until the Southern Pacific Railroad came through in 1876, however, that a townsite—Summit Station—was laid out. This name was as changeable as most other western town names, and eventually was transmuted into Tehachapi (certainly a memorable name). The coming of the railroad made larger-scale livestock raising and agriculture possible. Today Tehachapi is a small, pleasant town that has fulfilled some of the agricultural hopes the earliest settlers had for it.

By the way, if you have a little time to spare while you're touring in and around Tehachapi, stop in at the Tehachapi Heritage League Museum.

Desert Tortoise Natural Area

TO GET THERE. From Mojave, in southeast Kern County, take CA 14 northeast 3.9 mi to California City Blvd. Go east on the boulevard about 9 mi, through California City, to 20 Mule Team Parkway. Take the parkway northeast (left) for about 1 mi to Randsburg-Mojave Rd, which bears a bit farther north. The interpretive center for the natural area is approximately 3 mi up the road.

GETTING YOUR BEARINGS. You'll need a good Kern County map.

ABOUT THE NATURAL AREA. The Desert Tortoise Natural Area was established in 1974 by the Desert Tortoise Preserve Committee, Inc., in conjunction with BLM. The BLM now manages the area with the assistance of unpaid volunteers from the committee. The purpose of the preserve is to protect the unique tortoise habitat and keep it in its natural state by freeing it from conflict with other land uses.

The committee is a self-perpetuating, incorporated group of people from various organizations (schools, conservation groups, government agencies, turtle and tortoise groups, garden clubs) who are working together to protect the dense and valuable tortoise populations near California City. These volunteers have raised thousands of dollars to help the government buy private lands for the preserve. Committee volunteers also give guided tours for interested groups of children and adults from schools and organizations.

The area has been closed to vehicle use since November 1975, and grazing on public lands within the area is not permitted. The wire fence (30 mi of it) was installed in 1978 to help enforce these proscriptions.

However, the boundaries of this natural area contain only a small percentage of the desert tortoises near California City. And these, in turn, are only a small percentage of the total California population. These creatures are found in a number of other areas in the California desert — areas that are, unfortunately, not protected from careless humans by appropriate land management actions. In fact, most desert tortoise populations and their inhabitants seem to be ignored in land management plans. So, the tortoises are not doing as well as they should be — their numbers are decreasing. Let's work for more preserves, wilderness areas, and parks to ensure that this trend is not allowed to continue. Each tortoise killed or not allowed to reproduce and live in peace diminishes the biological diversity on which all creatures (including ourselves) depend for their well-being.

Meet Gopherus agassizi! Did you know that the desert tortoise is the California state reptile? Well, despite this claim to fame, *Gopherus* is a shy, retiring creature who leads a very quiet life (if possible). The best time of the year for observing desert tortoises is probably in the spring, March to June. During this time they are at their most active — munching succulent spring flowers and grasses, mating, and laying eggs. In the heat of the summer they usually spend their time sensibly in individual,

Desert tortoise in the Desert Tortoise Natural Area, north of California City. *Photo by Lyle Gaston.*

shallow burrows, protected from the heat of the sun (to which they are quite sensitive). These burrows are often found under perennial shrubs or bushes, where the roots help stabilize the soil and the foliage provides cooling shade. As you might guess, tortoise burrows are half-moon shaped to accommodate the high, rounded hump of their shell.

The Tortoises of Winter. The burrows in which tortoises hibernate during the cold winter months are larger, deeper, and more elaborate than their summer ones. To construct their winter burrows, tortoises dig into the ground at an angle, using their forefeet to make a tunnel 5 to 7 ft long. From this point they excavate branching tunnels, which sometimes are as long as 20 ft or more in the colder parts of the tortoise range. These burrows are often used regularly for many years by up to a dozen tortoises at a time, unlike the summer burrows—which are usually used by individuals. The energy and water the tortoise stores during the months of plentiful plant food sustain it during its winter hibernation.

What Habitat Is Good Habitat? Because tortoises cannot survive without the shelter and protection of their burrows or without a good supply of suitable plant foods in the spring, not all areas of the desert are suitable tortoise habitat. Some areas are too soft and sandy to safely support the burrows; other places have soil that is too hard or rocky for digging; and still other areas do not have enough of the right kind of plant cover. This means that it is important to protect not just this bit of desert tortoise habitat, but as many other areas of good habitat as possible. (Speaking of the desert tortoise's range, it covers a surprisingly large geographic area. The tortoise is found not only in a number of places in California, but in small regions of Utah, Nevada, Arizona, and northwest Mexico.)

Silver-Dollar Tortoises. Like others in the genus, the female desert tortoise lays eggs—and leaves her eventual offspring to fend for themselves—in late spring to early summer. When the three to five young hatch sometime in September, they are very tiny; so tiny that two months after hatching they are still no larger than a silver dollar! If these small, soft-shelled creatures manage to survive the many predators who consider them a tasty mouthful, their shell may eventually measure up to about 13 in. when they are full grown at fourteen to twenty years of age.

Tortoises at Work and Play. Somewhat like people, tortoises prefer to spend much of their time sunbathing, sleeping, eating, and (at the right time of the year) making more tortoises. They must also, of course, make a living—that is, provide themselves with food and shelter. They manage the former in the course of slowly but purposefully searching for food as they travel over the few acres they have selected as their individual range. The latter they take care of by methodically digging new and better protective burrows or refurbishing their old ones.

Unlike most other desert wildlife—which usually, if you can find them, will not stay still long enough for you to take their likeness—*Gopherus* is an ideal photographic subject. If you keep your distance, and move slowly, you should have no trouble in getting some excellent photos of this impressive reptile. You may even be so lucky as to snap a close-up of one with its brilliantly yellow-irised eyes wide open.

What to Do at the Desert Tortoise Natural Area. Walk (there are several trails). Look (carefully). Bring plenty of water (there isn't any at the preserve). Don't forget your camera and binoculars (all the better to see the inhabitants with). Wear a hat with a brim (even when the weather is cool). Breathe deeply (of clean desert air). Do not touch the tortoises (or disturb them in any way). Relax (it's good for you). Walk. Look.

Antelope Valley California Poppy Reserve

TO GET THERE. In Lancaster, take West Ave I west from CA 14 about 10 mi to Lancaster Rd; follow this road about 3.8 mi to the reserve.

GETTING YOUR BEARINGS. A good Los Angeles and vicinity or Los Angeles County map will be helpful. Hikers may want the USGS topo *Lancaster West*.

ABOUT THE RESERVE. The best time to view the flowers the area is famous for is during the March–May period. During that time, the unusual, energy-efficient visitor center is open every day. [The reserve is open year round, but the visitor center (staffed by volunteers) is only open during the peak flower time.]

It was not an easy job to make the reserve a reality. Although as early as 1970 the California Department of Parks and Recreation recognized the need to set aside a part of the best poppy-bearing land in southern California, funds for the land's purchase were not available at that time. But thanks to the California State Parks Foundation (a private organization) and the many concerned citizens who volunteered their time, enough money was raised to qualify for matching grants from state and federal sources. Once the land was acquired, the 1630-acre reserve became a reality in 1976. After a lot more hard work, the visitor center was opened in 1982.

When you visit the reserve, take time to admire the many ingenious, energy-saving features of this award-winning visitor center. Notice, for example, that three sides of it are buried in a hill and that several design features help keep the interior warm in winter and cool in summer. You might even find a feature you could retrofit on your own house! Also, don't forget to view the excellent slide show, which covers a year in the life of the reserve.

If you have the good fortune to be at the reserve in spring, when the flowers are in bloom, see if you can tell the tidy tips from the coreopsis, the gold fields from the cream cups, the lupine from the brodiaea, the locoweed from the dandelion, and so on. And keep an eye out for desert tortoises — one of the desert's great thrills is a look at a tortoise blissfully munching a mouthful of succulent spring wildflowers.

There are four short loop trails (1.2 to 1.7 mi) in the reserve, some of which lead to fine viewpoints near the Antelope Buttes. Elevations range from about 2700 ft to about 2900 ft. There is also a picnic area. If you want to find out whether the reserve visitor center will be open when you plan to visit (or would like to have a brochure and map even if it's not), call the California Department of Parks and Recreation at 805-942-0662.

Devil's Punchbowl Regional Park

TO GET THERE. From CA 138 on the east edge of Pearblossom, take Los Angeles County Rd N6 (Longview Rd) south about 7.5 mi to the entrance of Devil's Punchbowl Natural Area Park. Watch the highway signs carefully, because this route jogs left on Tumbleweed Rd, then right on Devil's Punchbowl Rd; it is also confusing in its intersections with Fort Tejon Rd.

GETTING YOUR BEARINGS. Take along a good Los Angeles County map. Hikers may want to have the USGS topos *Juniper Hills* and *Valyermo*.

ABOUT THE PUNCHBOWL. Like so much of the California desert, the Devil's Punchbowl area was once at the bottom of an ocean (perhaps about 60 million years ago) and later at the bottom of a lake. The enormous, tilted slabs of sandstone you see here are layers of sediments that accumulated in those bodies of water over many millions of years. In fact, the sediments were once almost 2 mi deep! These sediments have since been squeezed, dried, faulted, and pushed up as the earth's crust has adjusted itself to the vast movements beneath its mantle.

The bowl-shaped depression of the area, with its sharply angled sandstone slabs, is a result of continual activity of the two faults it lies between: the infamous San Andreas fault (north side) and the San Jacinto fault (south side). A good way to get a feel for the bowl's topography is to hike down into it on the 1-mi loop trail that begins at the rim next to the nature center.

This interesting geologic formation has been protected with park status since 1963 and is a very popular day-use area. Because the park rises to 4500 ft, summer temperatures are usually quite pleasant; hikers should take note, however, that winter can bring subfreezing temperatures. One of the park's notable features is the network of well-planned hiking trails criss-crossing its 1310 acres; there are even several self-guided nature trails. When you're walking the trails, keep an eye out for the plant and animal life characteristic of different elevations. On some trails you can watch pine forest plant and animal communities change to desert scrub communities — or vice-versa.

For Bird Fanciers — A Side Trip to Hamilton Preserve. Just a short distance outside Devil's Punchbowl is Hamilton Preserve, 40 acres of pinyon-juniper woodland set aside as a wildlife sanctuary since 1964. Here, along a seasonal creek and a dammed-up pond, is a fine riparian area where many bird (and other) species can be observed. For an attractive fact sheet on the preserve — including directions on how to find it — call or write the Nature Conservancy at its southern California office, 849 S. Broadway, Suite 660, Los Angeles, CA 90014, 818-962-9111.

Saddleback Butte State Park

TO GET THERE. From CA 14 in Lancaster, take Ave J (County Rd N5) east about 19 mi to the park's main entrance. The park can also be reached from US 395 by going west from Adelanto on Crippen or El Mirage Rd for about the same distance. Check your San Bernardino County map for directions (there are several right-angle turns).

GETTING YOUR BEARINGS. A good San Bernardino County map will be useful. Hikers might like to take along the USGS topo *Alpine Butte*.

ABOUT THE PARK. Spring is the best time to visit this high-desert park. Beginning in February and continuing through May, you can usually see fine displays of native wildflowers in many places throughout the Antelope Valley, but it's not everywhere that you can camp comfortably as close to them as you can at Saddleback Butte State Park.

The butte for which the park is named rises about 1000 ft above the valley. There is a 2.5-mi trail leading to its 3651-ft summit. From the top of the butte you'll have good views of the Antelope Valley all around; the Angeles National Forest's impressive San Gabriel Mtns are to the south. (The butte is actually the top of a granite mountain—as are the other buttes in the area.)

Thanks to the hard work of many concerned citizens and the state park service, the area was declared a park in 1960—to protect nearly 3000 acres of typical high-desert plant and animal life. Here you'll find stands of Joshua trees, as well as many species of reptiles, mammals, insects, and birds. The area was first named Joshua Tree State Park, but that was changed because of confusion with the national monument. Don't forget to look for some of the smaller creatures, such as horned larks and alligator lizards, as well as for the more easily seen residents like desert tortoises and golden eagles.

The campground has several dozen sites with tables and stoves. Unlike many desert sites, water is available here—there are usually two tanks in the campground. Near the park headquarters there is also a picnic area (tables, stoves, toilets) with a good view of the butte.

Just Next Door—A Museum at Paiute Butte. When you visit the park, don't forget to stop in at the newly renovated Antelope Valley Indian Museum. To get to the museum, take 170th St 3 mi south from the park to Ave M. Go west here for about 1 mi to the museum sign. Unfortunately, the museum is only open to the public without appointment during the second weekend of each month (except July–September, when it's closed). At other times of the month, you can often arrange for a tour by calling ahead to the State Department of Parks at 805-942-0662.

How the museum came to be is a long, interesting story—which you can hear when you visit it. Suffice it to say here that its various southwestern collections are certainly worth seeing.

And Around the Corner—A Wildlife Sanctuary. An interesting way to extend your high-desert knowledge is to visit some of the many wildlife (and wildflower) sanctuaries near the park. The Alpine Butte Wildlife Sanctuary is just a few miles farther south than the Indian Museum. To find it, go south on 170th St from the park for 5 mi, to Ave O; go west here for about 3.5 mi. At about this point a dirt road goes south along the east side of the sanctuary. Drive down the road and park well off it. From here you can walk into the sanctuary. A church on the south side of the sanctuary marks the boundary in that direction.

There are no trails in the sanctuary, but the country is open and easy to find your way around in. A patient observer can find much evidence here of how desert creatures lead their lives. For example, look carefully at the rock outcroppings for the telltale signs of favorite perching spots. Under the perching spots you often come across remains of the local residents' previous meals. The best time to visit is in spring or on early summer mornings and evenings. Camping is not allowed.

For a fact sheet on the various sanctuaries in the area, call the Los Angeles County Department of Parks and Recreation at 805-259-7721.

Cajon Pass–Victorville

ABOUT THE AREA. To the uninitiated, the part of the Mojave Desert stretching north from the San Gabriel and San Bernardino Mtns may look relatively uninteresting at first glance. However, closer acquaintance reveals a number of rather unique features in the area. For example, here are found the headwaters of the Mojave River, one of the three largest rivers in the California desert; the Mojave flows north out of the San Bernardino Mtns and out into the desert for almost 150 mi—mostly underground. If it weren't for this river, which supplies water for the folks who live in this part of Mojave Desert, there wouldn't be nearly as many thriving little communities between Cajon Pass and Barstow.

Then there is the infamous San Andreas fault, which is responsible for there being a Cajon Pass and two mountain ranges—the San Bernardinos and the San Gabriels—instead of one range, with no pass through it. For the adventurous, and their audience, there are places for sand sailing and soaring. And of course there are a number of lovely drives from the mountains to the desert and vice-versa. So, as you'll be able to see, there is more to experience in this area than is evident at first glance—and it's all easily accessible.

The Hot and Cold of It. Like most of the other lower parts of the California desert, though, it's best to visit here in spring or fall. Summer can be quite sizzling. And except for the over-5000-ft parts of the mountain drives, winter can also be a good time to tour this part of the Mojave.

FACILITIES. Supplies, gas, restaurants, and motels are available in Hesperia, Victorville, Apple Valley, Adelanto, and, to a more limited extent, Lucerne Valley.

Camping. Almost all the camping in the area is developed camping. On the south side of Cajon Pass, there is Glen Helen Regional Park (San Bernardino County), which is reached by taking the Devore–Glen Helen exit off I-15 or I-215 about 13.5 mi north of either the I-10/I-15 or I-10/I-215 interchange. This 500-acre park has campsites that each have a barbecue, table, and trash can; some sites have shade ramadas. There are also restrooms, showers, a dump station, and trails for hikers and horseback riders.

To find the Applewhite Campground (San Bernardino National Forest), check your San Bernardino County map for an exit about 1.7 mi north of the Devore–Glen Helen exit from I-15. The map will show you how to reach the campground, which is about 9 mi away (though not that far as the crow flies).

Silverwood Lake State Recreation Area is located about 11.5 mi east of I-15 on CA 138 (go east on CA 138 at Cajon Junction, about 8 mi north of the Devore–Glen Helen exit on I-15). Campsites here have barbecues, restrooms, and showers. Hikers and bicyclists will find 12 mi of paved hiking; the park also offers opportunities for boating, swimming, picnicking, and fishing.

To get to Mojave River Forks Family Recreation Park (San Bernardino County), follow the directions to Silverwood Lake SRA, but go east on CA 173 at its intersection with CA 138 about 8.5 mi from Cajon Junction. The park is about 6.5 mi northeast of this turn. Hesperia Lakes Park (city of Hesperia) is another 4.5 mi north of Mojave River Forks Park.

Just outside Victorville is Mojave Narrows Regional Park (San Bernardino County). To reach this park, take the Bear Valley Cutoff exit east from I-15 for about 4 mi; then follow the signs north for about 2.8 mi to the park. In addition to campsites with tables, barbecues, and nearby restrooms, the park offers horse rentals, hiking and equestrian trails, picnicking, and boating.

If you are interested in open-desert camping in this part of the Mojave Desert, check with the BLM Way Station at 831 Barstow Rd in Barstow for approved areas (619-256-3591). Even here, most of the open desert you see is privately owned.

Cajon Pass–Baldwin Lake Tour

TO GET THERE. Go north about 13 mi on I-15 from its intersection with I-10 just south of San Bernardino; this will bring you to the tour's starting point at the Devore–Glen Helen Regional Park exit. Do not exit, but note your odometer reading.

GETTING YOUR BEARINGS. Bring along a good San Bernardino County map. Those interested in the San Andreas fault may want the USGS topo *Cajon*.

ABOUT THE TOUR. After crossing the San Andreas fault and historic Cajon Pass, the tour will traverse several western Mojave Desert valleys. First, it will lead north along the eastern edge of Victor Valley, then east across Apple Valley and Lucerne Valley. Next, from the small town of Lucerne Valley, you'll switchback up out of the desert on Cushenbury Grade, and finally find yourself at scenic Baldwin Lake, in the cool forests of the San Bernardino Mtns. Total mileage is about 65 mi.

A Short History of Cajon Pass. As you ascend to Cajon Summit and the western Mojave Desert on today's broad, smooth freeway, it's easy to forget the struggles of those early travelers who made their way across this division between the San Gabriel Mtns and the San Bernardino Mtns. For one thing, these early travelers confronted not a nicely graded path, but a steeply walled box canyon (*cajon* is the Spanish word for "box"). The "box" faced south, so those coming from the Mojave Desert found themselves looking down a precipice; those coming the other way had to contend with a towering cliff.

Native Americans, of course, were the first to traverse this area; one of their well-used prehistoric trade trails from the Colorado River made its way to the Mojave River sink (about 150 mi to the northeast of the pass area), followed the Mojave to its headwaters in the San Bernardino Mtns (8 mi east of the junction of I-15 and CA 138), went over the San Bernardino crest at a point between Devil and Cable canyons, and then continued on southwest via Cucamonga and San Gabriel to the Pacific Ocean. The crossing didn't seem to give the Indians too much trouble, though. Even after the San Bernardino and San Gabriel valleys were settled (first by the Spanish from the south and later by emigrants from the eastern United States), the Chemehuevis managed to regularly make off to the Mojave Desert with a considerable number of the settlers' cattle and horses!

Before settlers from the east arrived, however, the Indians had escorted that famous padre-explorer, Garces, across the San Bernardinos in 1776 and later did the same for the intrepid Jedediah Smith in 1827. It's been said that Smith's extensive explorations did for California what those of Lewis and Clark did for the Pacific Northwest. (The trip that opened the San Bernardino and San Gabriel valleys to settlers was but a small part of his accomplishments.) Only four years after Smith's trip, the Spanish Trail—which was to serve Santa Fe–to–Los Angeles trade caravans for over two decades—began pushing its wagon road over the San Bernardinos from the mouth of Cajon Canyon. Initially, those traveling the route had to take their wagons to pieces at one particularly steep point, lower them down a steep defile, and then reassemble them after the going got easier. Not quite the experience of today's traveler!

Once the Spanish Trail (also called the Santa Fe Trail) was in operation, other routes were opened up across the San Bernardinos at various points within not too many miles of today's route. Soon the rich valleys were well settled. By 1885 the pass even had a railroad: the Santa Fe made it through after a route was found that required making only a large cut and not a tunnel. And so it went, right up to today's high-speed freeway—which enables travelers to get over the once-treacherous route to the Mojave Desert in a matter of minutes. If you're not in a hurry, though, take the route at a leisurely pace and try to get a feel for what it must have been like in the early days.

Cajon Pass and Its Geologic Claims to Fame. The pass area is often used by geologists to demonstrate the action of faults—those cracks made in the earth's crust as it adjusts itself to the tremendous forces at work underneath the relatively thin "skin" we are familiar with. The pass, which is the major break dividing what we call the San Bernardino Mtns (to the east) and the San Gabriel Mtns (to the west), was produced by the action of one of the world's most active faults: the San Andreas. To understand how this has happened, it helps to know how faults behave.

According to geologists, faults fall into three main categories—lateral (right or left), up-down, or horizontal (thrusting). The San Andreas, which stretches 650 mi from the Mexican border to Cape Mendocino (north of San Francisco), is a right-lateral fault. This means that if you were to stand on one side or the other of the fault as it moved, the opposite side would appear to move to your right. Some geologists think that the total displacement the San Andreas has caused amounts to hundreds of miles — with the average over the last hundred years being about 2 in. per year. An interesting, if not too useful, fact is that this means San Francisco (on the fault's east side) and Los Angeles (on its west side) are getting closer and closer together. The San Gorgonio and Tejon passes are also products of San Andreas fault action.

What to Look for on the Way Up to the Desert. As you approached the Devore–Glen Helen turnoff you may have noticed that for several miles the freeway was already climbing slowly. This is because I-15's route up to the pass begins by ascending the Cajon Creek's large alluvial fan. At this point, you can see other, smaller, fans at the base of the San Bernardino Mtns to the northeast of the freeway. Because the San Andreas fault runs along this base, some of the fans show fault scarps. Cajon Creek also parallels the freeway here, but on the southwest side. Yet another creek — Lytle Creek — parallels Cajon Creek to its southwest and marks the trace of another very active right-lateral fault, the San Jacinto.

About 3.5 mi on from the Devore–Glen Helen exit, the freeway comes out into what is called the Cajon amphitheater. Here, just as you come into the amphitheater, you cross the San Andreas fault. To get a good view of the fault trace, look northwest here up a long, straight canyon — Lone Pine Canyon. The San Andreas runs up this gap. A mile or so into the amphitheater you can see the railroad lines cutting across Cajon Creek; on the hillsides almost straight ahead are large, pink sandstone deposits (the Cajon formation). These sediments were laid down about 15 million years ago at the bottom of a large inland sea. Similar beds are found at Devil's Punchbowl (see above), 23 mi northwest of the amphitheater. Geologists believe the beds have been separated by the San Andreas fault's movement over the past 15 million years.

How the Cajon amphitheater itself came to be is rather interesting. It seems that the rocks on the San Andreas fault's northeast side are quite soft and easily eroded, while the rocks on its southwest side are hard. Cajon Creek flowed down out of the San Gabriels northwest of what is now the amphitheater, eventually wore its way through the hard rock on the fault's southwest side, and then began easily scooping out the softer rock formations on the fault's northeast side, forming the amphitheater. The point where Cajon Creek entered the amphitheater area is about 8 mi from the Devore–Glen Helen exit, where CA 138 crosses I-15. Here, CA 138 goes northwest up Cajon Canyon.

As you climb out of the amphitheater to Cajon Summit (4260 ft), the highway angles across some of the eaten-away rock formations. The top layers of these bluffs are actually made up of gravel from the alluvial fans that once stretched all the way back to the San Bernardino and San Gabriel Mountains. Once over the summit, the freeway route begins to gently descend into the western Mojave Desert across what is left of the alluvial fans.

On to Victorville. While traveling the 22.3 mi from the summit to the CA 18 turnoff at Victorville, Victor Valley is to the west. Along here, you'll see some typical western Mojave Desert scenery. Nowadays, however, the scenery includes not only wide vistas, Joshua trees, animals, and (in spring) flowers, but considerable evidence that people like living in this area. Today, Victorville is not the supply town for prospectors and miners it once was, nor even the busy rail town it became in the mid–1880s, but a fully modern agricultural and industrial city of medium size — and one of the fastest-growing communities in the state. (Victorville's name honors a Mr. Jacob Victor, who brought the Santa Fe's route over Cajon Pass to link San Bernardino and Barstow, thus putting them on the second transcontinental railroad route in the United States.)

As you approach Victorville, look for white areas in the surrounding hills. Some of these are mining operations that quarry limestone and marble for Victorville's cement plants. The clouds of dust and smoke on the city's skyline are mostly from these plants. In Victorville, take the CA 18 turnoff to the east. As you follow CA 18 east, the Mojave River channel is just to the north of the road and very shortly, in about a mile, the road crosses it at the Apple Valley Bridge.

The Mojave River has its headwaters in the San Bernardino Mtns to the south and flows underground for most of its length — except for a few places where rock formations force it to the surface. Here in Victorville, for a couple of miles on either side of I-15, bedrock forces the underground river to the surface. On both the east and west sides of the freeway the river had to cut through granite ridges that were in its way as it flowed north. These are the upper narrows and the lower narrows of the Mojave River. One of the places you can actually see the river at your leisure is at the upper narrows (on the east side of the freeway), near Mojave Narrows Regional Park (see "Facilities," above). At the lower narrows on the west side of the freeway, the Spanish Trail crosses the river (this trail was also known as the Mojave Trail and the Santa Fe Trail).

From Apple Valley to Lucerne Valley. About 8 mi east of I-15 on CA 18 lies a town that's already led two lives: Apple Valley. Although the area had been ranched for some time, the community didn't earn its name until the late 1800s. At that time, a local resident convinced her neighbors that the valley would be a good place to grow apples. And she was right! By the turn of the century, the orchards were flourishing — and apple products from Apple Valley were selling well. Alas for the apples, though; first, World War I took away most of the orchard tenders, and later disease, frost, hail, and heat finished off the famous trees. Today's town was laid out after World War II by developers who saw the area—with its abundant Mojave River water just under the surface—as ripe for a good resort-type venture.

As you continue east from Apple Valley, look for the craggy Granite Mtns on the north side of the road. Some 20 mi from I-15, CA 18 intersects Bear Valley Cutoff Rd at Deadman's Point. The point, a picturesque jumble of granite, is on the south side of the road just beyond the cutoff. If the rocks look familiar, it may be because you've seen them as the good guys were heading the bad guys off at the pass. (This was once a popular place—not being too far from Hollywood—for shooting western movies.)

Six miles east of Deadman's Point, look for Rabbit Dry Lake on the north side of the highway (actually, the highway goes across the south end of the lake itself). If you're in luck there may be some sand sailers whipping across it, colorful sails bellied in the wind. At the east of Rabbit Dry Lake is a small agricultural town that had its beginnings around the turn of the century: Lucerne Valley. The fields of alfalfa along here are hard to miss. In Lucerne Valley, CA 247 splits off to go north to Barstow and east to Yucca Valley and Twentynine Palms, while CA 18 bears southeast and begins its climb up into the San Bernardino Mtns to Baldwin Lake, a little over 14 mi away.

Up Cushenbury Grade to Baldwin Lake—One of the Desert's Finest Views. It'll come as no surprise that this road was initially chopped out in the 1880s to allow hauling of cement and other items necessary for building the dam at Big Bear Lake. Needless to say, the original road was nothing if not steep and rough. The upper—and steepest—part was called the snubbing-post grade because wagons sometimes had to be lowered down by snubbing them to trees with ropes! In winter, the grade was the only access to the Big Bear Lake area and so was also called the sunshine route. It wasn't until the mid-1930s that the road was finally paved.

Today the road is a good one, fit for any car with a radiator that works. As you switchback up the grade, take time to pull off at a turnout or two to admire the view to the north and to notice the different species of plants characteristic of the changing elevations. As you approach Baldwin Lake (6720 ft), keep a sharp eye out for the Pacific Crest Trail marker and parking area a mile or so east of the lake. Pull off here and walk north on the trail to view the Mojave Desert basin. If the weather cooperates, you'll be able to see nearly 100 mi northwest to the southern Sierra Nevada and east to several mountain ranges in Nevada. Get out your maps and see how many Mojave Desert features you can identify.

For information on recreational opportunities in the San Bernardino National Forest (which you entered about halfway up the grade), follow CA 38 from its intersection with CA 18 at Baldwin Lake along the north shores of Baldwin Lake and Big Bear Lake for about 8 mi to the

Fawnskin Ranger Station. The station is approximately 3 mi east of Fawnskin, so if you get to the town before finding the station, just retrace your steps back to the station.

Mojave River Tour

TO GET THERE. Take I-15 to its intersection with CA 138, just south of Cajon Pass. Go east on CA 138.

GETTING YOUR BEARINGS. Bring along a good San Bernardino County map.

ABOUT THE TOUR. From the CA 138 offramp, this route will pass through Summit Valley, along the north side of Silverwood State Recreation Area, bear north down the Mojave River drainage, and then follow the Mojave's channel through Hesperia, Victorville, and Oro Grande to the outskirts of Barstow. Because it gets pretty hot in this part of the Mojave Desert in summer, plan on taking this tour during some other season. Spring and fall are the best times. Total distance is about 70 mi.

The Mojave—An Underground Desert River. To reach an area near the Mojave River's headwaters, take CA 138 east from I-15 at Cajon Junction. A couple of miles east from the turnoff, look north for the summit over which the rail lines pass. Coming down off the summit, the road passes through the ranching country of Summit Valley (3800 ft) for the next 8.5 mi or so. The valley and the San Bernardino National Forest land, which lies just a short distance north of it, are all part of the headwaters area of the Mojave River's west fork. The relatively low elevation of this north-facing mountain area keeps its rainfall low, so that chaparral covers most of the open area and trees are primarily found in stream courses. From the top of the cliffs on the valley's northern side, alluvial fans stretch down into the Mojave Desert. In the past, a stream flowed across an unstable slope resulting from an east-west fault line in the mountainside and cut Summit Valley into the fans.

About 8.5 mi from I-15, CA 138 goes south around the west side of Silverwood State Recreation Area (see "Facilities," above) and then on up into the mountains. At this point, continue east on CA 173. Soon, you'll be passing the 249-ft Cedar Springs Dam on the north side of Silverwood Lake; this dam blocks the west fork of the Mojave River. About 2.5 mi beyond the CA 138/CA 173 intersection, CA 173 turns north near the channel of the Mojave River's west fork; in spring, despite the dam, there will probably be some water on the surface here. Notice that the abundance of water draining down this slope produces quite a concentration of trees and bushes. How many can you identify? (Look for manzanita, juniper, oak. Also notice how the vegetation changes as you come down into the desert proper.)

A little less than 15 mi from I-15, the road (CA 173) comes to an area called the Forks where you should turn north. Here, the west fork of the Mojave River meets with Deep Creek, which comes from the east. Together, the two form the Mojave River, which flows out—and under—the desert. Here also is the Mojave River Forks Recreation Park (San Bernardino County). The park has campsites with tables and barbecues (including equestrian sites), RV sites, restrooms and showers, a store, and hiking trails nearby. A short distance beyond the Forks, the road goes over a rise where you can get a good view of the upper part of the Mojave River valley. Notice the huge fans—cut by water into cliffs, particularly to the west—stretching north out of the San Bernardino Mtns 25 mi or so into the desert. See how far you can trace the Mojave's floodplain as it winds its way toward Barstow.

It's not hard to understand why the inland mountain ranges of southern California have less rainfall than those ranges nearer the coast—and that the rainfall gets less and less the farther into the desert the mountains are. Surprisingly, though, creeks, rivers, and year-round water sources are pretty scarce even in southern California ranges having a pretty good rainfall. Keeping this in mind when you look out over the Mojave Desert from the northern side of the San Bernardino Mtns, it's a bit hard to believe that the Mojave, a pretty good-sized river, actually flows from them and out over the desert to the north and east for almost 150 mi!

From the Forks to Oro Grande. As you continue north, CA 173 (Arrowhead Lake Rd) generally follows the Mojave's main channels (though they are sometimes a little distance from the highway). After about 4.3 mi you'll pass Hesperia Lakes Park, a Hesperia city park where there are campsites, restrooms, etc. About 5.8 mi on from this park, go west for approximately 0.4 mi on Main St, then north on Peach Ave for 4 mi to Bear Valley Cutoff. Go east here and in about 0.7 mi you'll find yourself crossing the Mojave River again. (What does it look like here?) After crossing the bridge, continue about 4 mi to Navajo Rd, then north 2 mi to CA 18 in Apple Valley, where the route goes west once more. On CA 18 another 7 mi will take you over a ridge, into Victorville, and then across the river at the upper narrows before you go under the freeway on National Trails Highway. If you have time, stop off the road and find a place to look at the narrows.

At this point, be careful you don't get on the freeway (I-15), but instead go under it, by following D St/National Trails Highway and the Oro Grande signs as the road bends northwest and follows the railroad tracks. A couple of miles west of the freeway, you'll cross the river again, at the lower narrows—and now it will be on the west side of the road all the way to Barstow. Pull off the road and have another look at the river. Is there surface water?

In your passage through Victorville, it's hard not to see the smoke from the cement plants that dot the city's periphery. Most of the cone-shaped hills nearby are of limestone (calcium carbonate), which is used in cement—which makes limestone quarrying and processing a big business in the area. The large limestone deposits indicate that in very ancient times this whole region was once under a sea. (Limestone is made up of what were once shells and coral.)

From "Big Gold" to Tour's End. It was here at the lower narrows that wagons, horses, and footsore travelers on the Spanish Trail (Santa Fe Trail) crossed the Mojave River. In the mid-1800s there was even a store there. Settlers began to drift in, and when the railroad came through in the 1880s, a small community of a few stores and saloons quickly developed. As the community grew, it moved across the river to the present site of Victorville.

Before the railroad came through, though, another small community had already developed a few miles to the northwest of what was to become Victorville. This was Oro Grande—"Big Gold"—the town that got its start as a result of a sizable strike made in 1868. The proprietor of the original claim got together the Oro Grande Mining & Milling Co., and then a ten-stamp mill was constructed by some other enterprising folks. A few years later, silver was also discovered in the area— and then marble and limestone. It was in one of the silver mines that the first rich limestone deposit was found. Today, limestone—like that other unglamorous but profitable mineral borax—is still going strong, while gold and silver are pretty much history.

Beyond Oro Grande, National Trails Highway follows the Mojave River in a sweeping circle to the north. Notice how the river has eaten away the fan materials on its west bank and has created gently sloping open areas to the east. About 18.5 mi up the road from Oro Grande, take Hinkley Rd north to where it crosses the river. What do you see here that indicates there is water not too far below the surface? Spend a few minutes examining the river bed, looking at plants, and trying to imagine the pleasant riparian area this must have been when the river flowed above ground all year.

For a view of the country to the north and west, continue on up the road to the top of the rise ahead. Here, look north toward the mountains to see part of the route the twenty-mule teams traversed on their way from Death Valley to the railroad terminus at the town of Mojave. Get out your maps and see how many of the nearby—and far-off—landscape features you can identify.

From here you can easily return to the National Trails Highway; Barstow is only about 7 mi to the northeast.

El Mirage Dry Lake

TO GET THERE. From I-15 just south of Victorville, take CA 18 east about 13.4 mi to Sheep Creek Rd; go north here for 5 mi to El Mirage Rd. Take El Mirage 1.5 mi west to a dirt road leading north 1.3 mi to the soaring center. You can also follow the signs from Adelanto on US 395.

GETTING YOUR BEARINGS. Take along a good San Bernardino County map.

ABOUT THE DRY LAKE. El Mirage Dry Lake is one of the most popular soaring centers in the southwest. On a good day you'll be able to see dozens of gliders catching the drafts. The lake is also a sand-sailing center. A jaunt over here to watch the acrobatics on land and in air is always a treat.

Rainbow Basin

ABOUT THE AREA. The part of the Mojave Desert where you find colorful Rainbow Basin is tucked in south of the off-bounds Naval Weapons Center's Range B and north of CA 58 just to the west of Barstow. One of the first things you notice about the general area when you look it over on a San Bernardino County map is that it contains several lakes—dry lakes, that is. During the Pleistocene epoch (2 million–11,000 years ago), Lake Harper, Lake Cuddeback, and Lakes Superior, along with the streams feeding them, helped make today's desert a lush, tree-studded grassland, teeming with wildlife. Even longer ago, during the Miocene epoch, a much larger lake covered the area. At that time, 12 to 16 million years ago, the creatures living on the lakeshores were rather exotic—three-toed horses, small camels, rhinos, mastodons, dog-bears, and incredible insects.

Luckily for us, a great many specimens of these wonderful creatures were preserved in the lake sediments. And you can see these very sediments, and the fossils they contain, when you visit scenic Bryce Canyon–like Rainbow Basin. If you take the time and trouble to examine the colorful layers making up the canyon walls, you may well be rewarded by a fossiliferous glimpse into the distant past. (Please leave all fossils in place for others to see.)

Visitors can get another glimpse into the past by visiting Inscription Canyon, where there are a number of fine petroglyphs. These are not nearly as ancient as the fossils of Rainbow Basin, but attract us for different reasons. The petroglyphs can help you see a little into the minds of the prehistoric peoples who successfully made the California desert their home for many thousands of years before Europeans arrived in North America.

A trip to Rainbow Basin can occupy a weekend (preferably) or an afternoon (if your time is limited). However, it's better to allow a full day for a trip to Inscription Canyon, as a little route-finding is sometimes involved, as well as a few more miles.

FACILITIES. Gas, supplies, motels, and restaurants are available in Barstow.

Camping. Owl Canyon Campground (BLM) is located in Rainbow Basin (see following trip for directions and details of amenities). Also check the "Facilities" sections for the Calico and Barstow–Baker South areas.

Rainbow Basin
National Natural Landmark

TO GET THERE. Locate CA 58 in Barstow on your San Bernardino County map. From CA 58, take Fort Irwin Rd north 5.5 mi to Fossil Bed Rd; go northwest (left) on Fossil Bed Rd a little less than 3 mi to Rainbow Basin National Natural Landmark.

GETTING YOUR BEARINGS. You'll need a good San Bernardino County map. Hikers and those interested in how the canyons lie may want to have the USGS topo *Opal Mountain.*

ABOUT THE BASIN. Here at Rainbow Basin, many fossils of ancient animals are exposed in the colorful sedimentary layers making up the canyon walls. Some of the remains discovered here include mastodons, large and small camel-like creatures, rhinos, and dog-bears. The insect fossils are some of the best-preserved in the world. (Please leave all fossils in place for others to see.)

In addition, the folded and faulted canyon walls are considered excellent examples of how the earth's crust behaves under stress. It is these very qualities that resulted in this site being declared a national natural landmark in 1972. Among other attributes, such landmark areas are chosen because they best illustrate particularly important geologic and ecologic characteristics of the United States. Other national natural landmarks in the California desert are the Cinder Cones in the eastern Mojave Desert and the Pinnacles, near Trona. Rainbow Basin is also a BLM-designated area of critical environmental concern (ACEC).

When to Visit, Where Not to Stay. Because this area is at about 3000 ft, it is not quite as hot in summer as lower parts of the desert (though still pretty warm). If you do visit in summer, take care not to camp in washes; summer thundershowers sometimes cause dangerous flash floods.

Owl Canyon Campground, just off the scenic drive, a little north of Fossil Bed Rd, has sites with tables, shade ramadas, fire rings, grills, chemical toilets, and water. There is also a primitive campground for use when the main campground is full. As in all parts of the California desert, there is no wood available for fires; bring your own.

BLM permits off-road vehicles in some parts of the natural area, which means your stay may sometimes not be as quiet and peaceful as you would wish. However, despite this drawback, colorful Rainbow Basin is well worth visiting.

Seeing Rainbow Basin. There are no signed trails in the natural area, but there are many interesting washes to explore. One of the most popular is Owl Canyon Wash, which starts near Owl Canyon Campground. As you walk up this wash, watch for the changing geologic formations that represent millions of years in the area's evolution. (Do not attempt to scale the mud cliffs; you will probably find your footholds crumbling beneath you.) There is also a 3-mi, one-way, scenic drive through some of the most spectacular and colorful badland areas of the basin. The drive begins on Fossil Bed Rd (look for the signs).

Inscription Canyon 4WD Loop

TO GET THERE. Follow the directions for Rainbow Basin National Natural Landmark above, but continue northwest past the turn into the basin proper for about 12.5 mi on the graded dirt road. At this point, go north on Black Canyon Rd (dirt, with some deep sandy spots) for about 11.8 mi to the BLM's Inscription Canyon petroglyph site (signed). See details of route below before starting.

GETTING YOUR BEARINGS. Bring along a good San Bernardino County map. In addition, the terrain will make more sense if you have the USGS topos *Fremont Peak* and *Opal Mtn.*

ABOUT THE LOOP. This loop will take you west from the intersection of CA 58 and Fort Irwin Rd, past Rainbow Basin National Natural Landmark, north up Black Canyon to BLM's Inscription Canyon petroglyph site, then east across Superior Valley, and, finally, south on Copper City Rd back to your starting point. Total mileage for the loop is about 65 mi.

Note: The several deep, sandy places on the Black Canyon Rd mean you may need to have a 4WD vehicle in your group, just in case someone gets stuck. High clearance is also nice, but you can get along without it if you're careful.

Getting the Best of Black Canyon. The directions given above sound simple, but following them can be something of an adventure. The reason for this is that there are many side roads coming into the main Black Canyon road, and much of the time it's difficult to tell which road is main and which is side. But don't let these possible complications scare you off. The drive up Black Canyon is beautiful as well as interesting, with many places along it being well worth stopping to explore. In spring there are wildflowers, and at most times of the year you'll see quite a few bird species — including chukar and various birds of prey.

If you note your odometer reading at the turnoff into Rainbow Basin National Natural Landmark proper, the following route details may be of some help. About 0.75 mi west past the turnoff, bear right at a Y; at 7.1 mi past the turnoff, pass the road on the right to Opal Mtn/

Pumice Quarry; at 10.1 mi, continue west past a road coming in from the south; at 12.5 mi, go north on Black Canyon Rd.

Note odometer reading again at Black Canyon turnoff. At about 2.4 mi up Black Canyon, watch for a stretch of deep sand and bear right at a fork. Bear right again about 0.2 mi on. Look for a marker on the south side of the wash about 3 mi from the Black Canyon turnoff (note the modern graffiti). At about 6.6 mi from the turnoff, bear right at a fork; 1.3 mi beyond the fork, pass the entrance to a loop road (camp spots on loop, which is about 1 mi long). Bear right again at 8.7 mi from the Black Canyon turnoff. Don't despair—just a bit more than 3 mi farther (about 12 mi from the turnoff) and you've reached Inscription Canyon (signed). Congratulations!

Looking at Rock Art. Four different kinds of native American rock art are found in the California desert: petroglyphs, pictographs, intaglios (also known as geoglyphs or rock alignments), and ground paintings. Petroglyphs, such as you see here in Inscription Canyon, are the most numerous. These designs were pecked and scratched into the rock many years ago by people who followed the seasons across different parts of the California desert, hunting and gathering their food along the way.

Some of the designs are realistic; the ones of people and animals are the most easily identified. Other designs are abstract; at present, no one is able to reliably interpret such art. Of course, it's possible to identify, in a general way, what some figures—such as bighorn sheep—represent, but what they mean is something that can't be determined. About the only information on meaning scholars today have is from accounts of native Americans in historic times. Various of these people have said that petroglyphs often give information on such practical matters as distance to the next water hole and location of food and campsites. In addition, some are said to illustrate legends or catastrophic happenings, while others represent magic symbols intended to help the group be successful in hunting. Look closely at the art in Inscription Canyon. Can you get any idea of what some of the various designs represent?

Rock art experts are not certain how old many of the petroglyphs are, but some in the Colorado Desert (the southeastern part of the California desert) have been reliably dated by the carbon-14 method as being over 9000 years old. Another dating method being developed involves analysis of the desert varnish, a thin, dark layer of carbonates, sulfates, and oxides that forms over time on the surface of rocks in arid environments, perhaps with the help of microorganisms.

Fortunately, even without the help of such sophisticated analyses, there are a number of petroglyph locations where the untrained observer can tell that some petroglyphs are older or younger than others—for example, at the Coso petroglyph site. At such locations some of the designs may be very light and new looking, while others are covered with such a dark layer of desert varnish that they are almost invisible except when observed with the help of a Polaroid lens or Polaroid sunglasses.

(Be sure to use a polarizing lens when photographing petroglyphs.)

Across Superior Valley and on to Loop's End. To finish the loop and return to Fort Irwin Rd (and thence to Barstow), continue east past Inscription Canyon and across Superior Valley on a good dirt road for about 9.7 mi to Copper City Rd (you can visit the sand sailers at Superior Dry Lake by turning north here and traveling about 1.6 mi). To reach Barstow, go south on Copper City Rd for about 16.5 mi to Fort Irwin Rd, then continue south for another 6.2 mi to CA 58 in Barstow.

12

The Historic Eastern Mojave

ABOUT THE AREA. The history of the eastern Mojave Desert is not easily divided up into the histories of its parts. The "parts" themselves — the five areas: Barstow–Baker South, Kelso, Providence Mtns, New York Mtns–Lanfair Valley, and Cima Dome–Clark Mtn—have been more or less arbitrarily decided on for the traveler's convenience. Most people have limited time when visiting the desert—particularly those parts of it that are not near a large urban area. Each of the designated areas, then, has been delimited to be about as large as can comfortably be looked over in two to four days. And the term *looked over* is actually what is meant. No part of the California desert can actually be thoroughly explored in that amount of time. It takes many visits to even a single area to get to know it well!

Because the histories of the eastern Mojave areas are actually much of a piece, that's the way they will be treated here—as one big area: the historic eastern Mojave.

Everybody's Piece of Pie—And Park? A quick glance at the base map for the eastern Mojave shows that the region looks a lot like a piece of pie. Its outside rim is the California-Nevada border, with the southeast corner being formed by the Colorado River. The south side is I-40, the north side is I-15, and the apex of the pie is Barstow. Most of this vast piece (about 1.4 million acres of public lands) is presently being managed by the Bureau of Land Management (BLM) as the East Mojave National Scenic Area. The title is impressive, but unfortunately it has conferred little actual protection on the eastern Mojave's outstanding scenic, historic, and prehistoric values. Many people hope that passage of the California Desert Protection Act sometime in the next few years will protect the region's unique qualities permanently—as Mojave National Park.

From Coast to Colorado—A Popular Pathway. For thousands of years before explorers from other parts of the world first stumbled across the California desert, Indians were beating tradeways from the California coast to the Colorado River — via the Mojave Desert. Perhaps their most popular path went from the coastal Indian villages right through the middle of the eastern Mojave, following the Mojave River and linking various springs and Mojave Indian villages — from Camp Cady to Afton Canyon, Marl Spring, Camp Rock Spring, Fort Paiute, and finally to the Colorado River.

By the late 1700s the Indians had guided explorers and Spanish missionaries across the Mojave via this trail. And by the mid-1800s the U.S. Army had made the trail into a wagon road, now variously called Old Government Rd and Mojave Rd. Stagecoaches, wagon trains, the army, prospectors and pioneers, and mail wagons went back and forth on the road from near Los Angeles to Prescott, Arizona — making it one of the most well used and famous roads in California.

Then, in the 1880s, the railroads made their California desert debut. Eventually, the wagon routes began to follow the rail routes, as did the automobile routes that sprang up in the 1900s. You can still visit picturesque Kelso Station, a crew change and rest point for the main railroad station for the Union Pacific and the Mojave area from about 1920 on. It wasn't until 1985 that the station was closed. It may eventually become an interpretive center for Mojave National Park.

As a result of railroad development, the Mojave Rd fell into disuse; today, its interest is primarily historic. Thanks to a group of people called Friends of the Mojave Road, however, this important historic trail is certainly not being forgotten. Those of you who are interested in California desert history — and particularly in the history of the Mojave region — may want to contact the Friends: P.O. Box 307, Norco, CA 91760. This group leads many interesting outings in the eastern Mojave. Their founder, Dennis Casebier, has written several books on the Mojave.

Making a Living in the Mojave. There aren't too many ways to support yourself on desert lands. Over the years from the 1860s through 1919 (particularly from 1900 to 1919), a number of mining entrepreneurs in the eastern Mojave managed to make a modest go of digging out silver, lead, copper, zinc, and even a little gold. Most of the now-deserted little townsites you pass in the Mojave sprang up during this period — Hart, Rock Spring, Barnwell, Vanderbilt, Providence. One of the biggest mines of the 1880s was the Bonanza King (Providence was its town), which is said to have produced over $60 million in silver.

Of course, some folks worked for the railroads that served the mines. Construction sites and tiny railroad towns grew up at various sidings and crossroads — Ivanpah, Cima, Kelso, Goffs, Fenner, Essex, Lanfair. And still others tried their hands — mostly unsuccessfully — at ranching and farming. A few wet years beginning in about 1912 encouraged homesteading in the Lanfair Valley area. Water is always an unpredictable quantity in the desert, though, and in just a few years it was too dry to farm successfully. Ranchers had somewhat better luck. Several

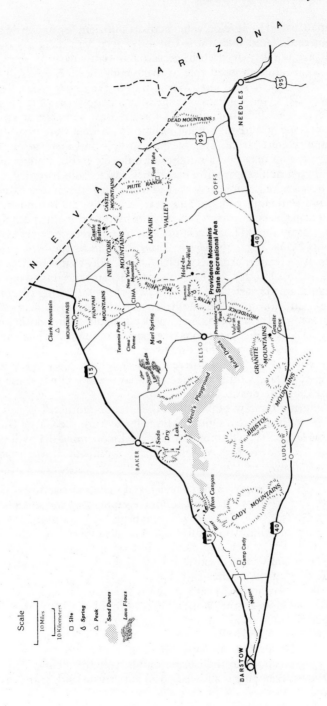

Scale

10 Miles

10 Kilometers

□ Site
◊ Spring
△ Peak
▨ Sand Dunes
▨ Lava Flows

of them managed to develop water sources sufficient for variously sized herds of cattle. And since cattle can move to where the grass is, and the Mojave is relatively rich in grasslands—particularly in the Cima Dome area—graziers were able to make ends meet. A few still do.

Big Guns Come to the Desert. War games in the desert? Alas, yes. In the early 1940s General Patton ranged over a good part of the eastern Mojave, training his troops for the North African campaigns. Then in 1964 over one hundred thousand military personnel were involved in Operation Desert Strike. This means that here and there throughout the Mojave you may find a number of unlovely military souvenirs—snarls of communication wire, blank shell cases, radio batteries, tank-chipped rocks, indiscriminately slashed roads, and piles of miscellaneous rusty, unidentifiable garbage and gear carelessly left behind during military maneuvers. Fortunately, very little live ordnance has been found recently; if you should find any suspicious objects, report them to BLM.

What to Do and See in the Mojave Today. Nowadays the Mojave's big business is recreation. And it's not hard to see why that is so. The Mojave has colorful buttes and canyons, spectacular sand dunes and cool mountains, a wide variety of lovely flowers and interesting plants (including cacti), forests of unique desert trees, many lush, year-round riparian areas and spring-fed oases, moderate temperatures during most of the year (and higher elevations to escape to in summer), historic and prehistoric sites almost without number, and abundant wildlife. In the Mojave you can camp in a different and delightful place every night for a year and take a different hike each day—and still not come near to exhausting the possibilities.

In exploring the few points of interest suggested here—places like the Mojave River, Kelso Dunes, Mitchell Caverns, the Castle Buttes, and Cima Dome—you'll come across several score more that will repay a return visit. The historic eastern Mojave is difficult, if not impossible, to exhaust.

FACILITIES. Gas, supplies, restaurants, and motels at Barstow, Baker, Amboy, and Needles. Gas and minimal supplies at Mountain Pass, Ludlow, Goffs, Essex, Cima Rd offramp from I-15, and at the I-40/US 95 intersection. Minimal supplies at Cima; no supplies at Kelso. Rest areas with toilets, water, and picnic tables off I-15 just west of Afton Canyon exit and Cima Rd exit; off I-40, about 30 mi east of Barstow and just west of the Fenner exit.

Camping. There are BLM campgrounds at Afton Canyon, Mid-Hills (5600 ft), and Hole-in-the-Wall (4200 ft). Providence Mtns State Recreation Area (4300 ft) also has a small campground. The BLM campgrounds have chemical toilets, tables, and fireplaces; Mid-Hills and Afton have water. The Providence Mtns SRA has chemical toilets and limited water. For directions to the campgrounds, see trips below.

Open-desert camping is allowed on all but private lands in the eastern Mojave.

Barstow-Baker South

Barstow Way Station

TO GET THERE. In Barstow, take the Central Barstow exit off I-15. Go one block north to 831 Barstow Rd (east side of road).

GETTING YOUR BEARINGS. Bring along a good San Bernardino County map.

ABOUT THE WAY STATION. The Barstow area is known as the Gateway to the Mojave. To get the most out of your visit to this vast and scenic region located between I-15, I-40, and the Colorado River, take time to stop at this well-appointed information station run by the Bureau of Land Management (BLM).

Here you'll find friendly folks ready to answer questions on camping, hiking, weather, and roads. You can also pick up a variety of maps and brochures on the Mojave, as well as on other parts of the California desert. And don't forget to look over the interesting desert displays. From these you can learn about prehistoric Indian rock art, desert geology, how not to get in trouble in the desert, edible plants, wildlife, and — of course — cacti.

The way station is open Monday through Friday from 8:00 A.M. to 5:00 P.M. When funds permit, it is also open on the weekends — but don't count on it. Parking is free. If you have a large group, contact the station for information on group tours and talks.

Camp Cady and the Mojave River

TO GET THERE. From the I-40/I-15 divergence in Barstow, go east 20 mi on I-15 to the Harvard Rd exit; go south here for 2.7 mi to Mojave Trail. Take this improved dirt road east along the south edge of the Mojave River floodplain for 2.1 mi to the Camp Cady entrance (signed). Turn north here and go about 0.5 mi to a parking area along a fence between a long, unpainted barn with a sheet metal roof and a yellow house.

GETTING YOUR BEARINGS. A good San Bernardino County map will be helpful. Those interested in the Mojave River should bring along the USGS topo *Newberry*.

Note: You need an appointment to visit Camp Cady. If you don't have one, the entrance gate will be locked! To make an appointment, call the Camp Cady Reserve office at 619-257-0900. If that number is inactive, contact the California Department of Fish and Game's regional headquarters in Long Beach to get the new number.

ABOUT CAMP CADY. Here at Camp Cady is one of the finest riparian woodlands of cottonwood, desert willow, and mesquite still remaining in the deserts of the Southwest. Here also, the nonnative tamarisk (salt cedar) is unfortunately beginning to spread and push out plants native to the region. This woodland is on a part of the Mojave River floodplain where bedrock close beneath the river alluvium forces groundwater to the surface. Upstream and downstream from Camp Cady the river channel is usually dry and does not support cottonwood and willow trees.

Camp Cady got its name during the 1860s, when it was an encampment site on the Mojave Rd. An army fort was built here in 1860 to protect wagon trains from Indian attack; the fort was occupied sporadically until 1871. In 1913 the military reservation land was subdivided and auctioned off. The Camp Cady area was then used for hunting and grazing. A 3.5-mi-long tract of river bottom land was purchased for habitat preservation by the California Department of Fish and Game in 1979.

Walking the Floodplain. It's not every day you get to visit a floodplain (unless your home is built on one!). At Camp Cady, an easy, 1-mi walk on sandy dirt roads will enable you to see a number of the interesting and beautiful features around this part of the Mojave River's path. To get started from the parking area, go north on a levee crossing the main river channel. The channel is about 300 ft wide at this point, and carpeted with grasses and cattails. Beyond the levee is a dense stand of young willow and cottonwood trees, also about 300 ft wide. The grove is cut by several narrow flood channels. The remainder of the floodplain — about 1000 ft across — is an open woodland of screwbean mesquite and large, dispersed cottonwoods and desert willows.

While you're walking, keep an eye out for some of the many bird species found hereabouts. Some of the larger birds you might see include the barn owl, great blue heron, and turkey vulture. Migrating ducks and geese also visit during the winter months when surface water is abundant.

At the end of the road, by the north edge of the floodplain, turn east (right) and go 900 ft to a road intersection near an abandoned truck and some buildings. Now turn left for a short excursion through a typical desert creosote forest to the top of the bluff. Up on top, there's a panoramic view of the Cady Mtns to the east, the Newberry Mtns to the south, and the vast swath of riparian woodland in the foreground.

Return to the road intersection and continue south along an old fence across the mesquite woodland to a T junction. Go east (left) here for 600 ft, passing several abandoned buildings; then turn south (right) after passing a tall, broken cottonwood stump. Now, as you cross a second levee, you'll pass some mud flats and shallow ponds surrounded by cattails. When you reach the south bank, turn west toward the old barn and return to the parking area.

Camping at Camp Cady. You can arrange for your group to camp here by contacting the reserve office at the number mentioned above. The camping site is west of the parking area. An old bunkhouse with a kitchen, flush toilet, and shower is available for campers who have reserved ahead of time.

Afton Canyon

TO GET THERE. From the intersection of I-15 and I-40 in Barstow, take I-15 east for about 33 mi to the Afton turnoff. Follow a good dirt road southwest for about 3 mi to the Afton Campground and the Mojave River.

GETTING YOUR BEARINGS. Take along a good San Bernardino County map; for exploring the Afton Canyon area, the USGS topo *Cave Mountain* is a help.

ABOUT THE CANYON. Afton Canyon is one of the few places in the California desert where there is year-round flowing water. The Mojave River has its headwaters in the San Bernardino Mtns near Lake Arrowhead and flows east to the Mojave River Sink, or Mojave River Wash, which stretches east from Afton Canyon toward Soda Dry Lake and Baker. In some places—such as the Mojave Narrows, Camp Cady, and Afton Canyon—the river is forced to the surface. In areas like these you'll find trees, grasses, abundant wildlife, and people.

Afton Canyon along the Mojave River bed in the eastern Mojave. *Photo by Lyle Gaston.*

As you drive into the canyon from the interstate, look southwest of the highway. This basin is part of what's left of now-extinct Lake Manix, a 200-sq-mi freshwater lake that dried up 15,000–18,000 years ago. If you look carefully, you can still see some of the lake's old shorelines.

This immense lake was fed by the Mojave River during the Pleistocene epoch. At that time, as it does now, the Mojave River brought water all the way from the San Bernardino Mtns to the Lake Manix area — about 140 mi. But in those more well watered times, the river flowed above ground, rather than mostly underground as it does now. Finally, the lake's rising waters cut a channel at its east end, and the Mojave River continued flowing east to Soda Dry Lake, and then north to Silver Dry Lake and Silurian Dry Lake, eventually emptying into the Amargosa River, just east of the southern tip of Death Valley National Monument. (Check your San Bernardino County map to get a better idea of the river's route.) This gorge cut by the Mojave River in ancient times is today's colorful, steep-walled Afton Canyon (also sometimes called Cave Canyon).

Afton Canyon is sort of a miniature Grand Canyon of the Mojave. Over many thousands of years the Mojave River has been carving this canyon, so that now its walls tower several hundred spectacular feet above the visitor. Because the canyon is a pleasant spot, it is also a popular one. Unfortunately, many of its visitors are interested in ORV play — which means that quiet is not one of the amenities the area usually offers. Despite the noisy machines (and the night trains), though, Afton is still worth a visit.

Find a place to park, get out your topo map, and wander up some of the twisty, colorful side canyons. Walk on through the canyon for a mile or two and see if you can find the cave of Cave Mtn fame. (The cave and river were a popular camping and watering place for Indians traveling the Mojave Trail from the coast of California to the Colorado River in prehistoric times and for settlers traveling the Mojave Rd — which was basically the same route — in the mid- to late 1800s.)

If you're lucky in your choice of weekends and aren't ready to try open-desert camping just yet, Afton is also a good place to camp. There are ramadas (shading the picnic tables), chemical toilets, drinking water (usually), and fireplaces. (The unlucky hit the campground when it's full of ORVers!)

Kelso

Kelso Dunes

TO GET THERE. At Baker, about 60 mi northeast of Barstow on I-15, take Kelbaker Rd (just stay on the pavement) south for about 34.5 mi to the town of Kelso. Continue through Kelso on Kelbaker Rd for another 7.2 mi to a signed dirt road (just before a big natural gas compressor station) leading west (right) to the main part of the dunes. Follow this dirt road for about 3 mi to a parking area. The closest approach is to park at the far end of the dirt landing strip in the road. (To get some good photos of the dunes from higher up, turn east instead of west off Kelbaker Rd and drive up the powerline road toward the Providence Mtns.)

GETTING YOUR BEARINGS. A good San Bernardino County map is helpful in this area.

ABOUT THE DUNES. The Kelso Dunes are not as extensive as some other dune systems in the United States, but at 500–600 ft are the second highest (after the Eureka Dunes) in the California desert. The sand forming these gleaming white dunes is blown across the windswept plain of the Devil's Playground from the Afton Canyon area, 35 mi to the west. Winds from the north, south, and east balance these strong westerly winds here in this part of the Mojave, causing the sands to accumulate in a dune formation second only to the Great Sand Dunes National Monument in Colorado. (The best view of the dunes as a whole is from Kelbaker Rd, about 3 mi north of Kelso.)

Because the winds shift in a circular fashion here (which is why the dunes are where they are), you'll notice that the tips of the tall grasses have often swept a full 360-degree circle on the sand. Hikers often vie with each other to see who can find the biggest circle. Be sure to bring plenty of film to the dunes!

The Living Dunes. If you think of dunes as nothing but piles of sand, you'll be in for a surprise when you start exploring the Kelso Dunes on foot. In spring, look for the delicate and showy yellow and white to blush desert primroses (they close at dusk), brilliant pink sand verbena, and bright yellow desert sunflowers in the lower reaches of the dunes. Look also for the "birdcage" remains of last year's primroses, a gracefully curved set of dried stems around what was once a central flower spike. These and many other sun-loving annual plants set seed when climatic conditions are right. The wind then gathers and carries the seed for miles (and for years). Some seed falls to earth and germinates; some is used as food by the many creatures who make the dunes their home.

If you're lucky, you may see some sidewinder tracks. The sidewinder is a rattler that leaves behind a unique track of parallel S's as it loops gracefully sideways. And where there are snakes, there are rodents and other small mammals. The lower dunes support a fairly luxuriant growth of grasses that help provide food — and water — for rodents, beetles, and crickets, among others. As these small creatures pursue the dramas of their everyday lives, they leave behind many fascinating track records. In the heat of the day, these tracks are about all you'll see, for most desert reptiles and mammals (for example, the fringe-toed lizard and the kangaroo rat) hide in burrows or holes to avoid high ground temperatures. At night they foray out, looking for food—insects, seeds, etc.

It is interesting that the several species of rats and mice living in the dunes each eats a different size or kind of seed, so there is little competition for food. Also, the larger animals that live in and around the dunes—such as kit foxes, skunks, coyotes, snakes, and owls—all for the most part hunt a certain size and type of smaller animal. So the plant and animal communities of the dunes are nicely balanced—as long as humans do not interfere.

It takes only a single dune buggy or all-terrain vehicle (ATV) to irreversibly damage the delicate balance between dune plant and wildlife communities. Our California desert dune communities are too precious and unique to be used up by high-impact recreation activities. (Fortunately, the BLM has now closed these dunes to motorized vehicle use.)

A Climb to the Top. Climbing to the top of the highest dune is not as difficult as you might think at first glance. It takes most people no longer than about an hour and a half, round-trip (longer for photography, lunch munching, etc.). Hike toward the low saddle located to the right of the high point, then walk along the crest to the high point. If you try to take the shortest route by attacking the crest frontally, you'll find yourself going two steps forward and three back—it's very tiring!

For efficient sand-walking, try to walk flat-footed on the crust without breaking through (don't dig in your heels or toes). Thin people with large feet may now gloat over their well-muscled friends!

When you're up on top of a dune, shove some sand down the lee side and listen for the low rumble, suggestive of a distant airplane. The vibration extends deep into the dunes. This sound has led these dunes to be called "singing" dunes.

Don't let your breakfast, dinner, or camping chores interfere with dawn or sunset dune photography. Break out of your routine: humankind does not live by bread alone!

Granite Mountains Hike
Class 1–2/elev. 6786 ft/USGS topo *Flynn*/6 mi RT/old 4WD road, cross-country

TO GET THERE. Take I-40 east from its intersection with I-15 in Barstow to Ludlow (about 52 mi); continue another 28 mi east on I-40 to Kelbaker exit—go north here. In about 3.5 mi, if you look west (left), you'll see the Granite Cove Area. This area used to be quite popular with rock climbers before it became part of the Granite Mountains Natural Reserve, which is owned by the University of California and is used for research purposes.

About 6 mi from where you left the freeway, the road will become good, graded dirt (for several miles). The reason for this is that the desert bighorn sheep frequent the area and need to cross the road to get to water. They will not cross a hard-surfaced road—thus, the dirt.

About 8 mi from I-40, just over Granite Pass, look for a microwave station on the road's east side. Go past the station about 1.8 mi, and then go left on a dirt road. (Ordinary cars with good clearance are usually OK on this road.) A number of road options soon present themselves, but following along the foothills will eventually lead you into Cottonwood Wash, a major interior valley and cattle grazing site.

The hike is in that part of the Granite Mtns. Nat. Res. managed by BLM and the Univ. of Calif. Hiking is allowed; camping is not. Please obey signs indicating closed areas.

ABOUT THE HIKE. There are numerous "Granite Mtns" in southern California; this one offers a very easy climb of the northernmost peak via an old mine road. The peak will give you an inspiring, panoramic view of the Kelso Dunes and Devil's Playground.

Finding the Trail. At the upper end of Cottonwood Wash, about 3–4 mi from Kelbaker Rd, park and look for an old mine road (not shown on the topo). Follow this fair to poor trail up the slope to the right. In about 3 mi (2000 ft gain), including an easy rock scramble over the last 0.25 mi, you'll come to the peak. This is the highest point in the northern section of the Granites. Look around for the Sierra Club Desert Peaks sign-in sheet inside the stone cairn. To return to your car, just retrace your route.

Note: The BLM leaseholder in Cottonwood Wash would like you to believe that you are on private property; he justifiably resents the use of his water tanks for target practice. At all times avoid the appearance of souvenir hunting and vandalism. If you should encounter the leaseholder, keep your temper and courteously explain your reason for being in the area.

Providence Mountains

Providence Mountains State Recreation Area and Mitchell Caverns Natural Preserve

TO GET THERE. Take I-40 east from its intersection with I-15 in Barstow for about 80 mi to the Essex Rd turnoff. Go northwest on Essex Rd for 16 mi to the state recreation area (SRA). At 10 mi there is a complex intersection, with Black Canyon to the north and the poleline road to Foshay Pass to the west. Just continue straight ahead and slightly to the left.

GETTING YOUR BEARINGS. A good San Bernardino County map is a must. Those who plan on doing some hiking will probably want to have the USGS topos *Flynn* and *Colton Well*.

ABOUT THE RECREATION AREA. The views from the visitor center at 4300 ft are really exceptional. From this eastern slope of the Providence Mtns you can see several 7000-ft peaks, as well as dunes, buttes, mesas, rocky crags, and wide-open bajadas and desert valleys. Although the SRA — at not quite 6000 acres — is a rather small place by desert standards (the California desert, remember, is about 25 million acres), it packs a lot of interesting sights into its limited area.

For example, very few visitors leave without touring El Pakiva and Tecopa caves, some large limestone caverns filled with complex and beautiful rock formations. Needless to say, in summer the 65° F caverns are a popular attraction! (In summer guided tours are given only on weekends and holidays; during the rest of the year, daily.) In addition, near the visitor center there are an excellent self-guiding nature trail; a nice hike up into the Providence Mtns via Crystal Spring Canyon; a snack bar and gift shop; a viewpoint and parking lot; a small (six spaces), primitive campground; and restrooms.

The caves were first "toured" by a least one ground sloth — a Pleistocene animal that roamed the area some 15,000 years ago. The sloth's remains were found in the cave. Later, Indians used the caves for several hundred years. Archaeologists have discovered a number of Chemehuevi food caches, fire pits, and tools in the caves.

It was not until the early 1930s that Jack Mitchell, a sometime silver prospector from the Los Angeles area, had the idea that the caves might have tourist potential. With tourists in mind, he built a road to the caves and put up several stone buildings to use for accommodations. (The headquarters building is one of his original ones.) Mitchell and his wife stayed open for business — offering food, lodging, and guided tours of the caves — until 1954. The area became an SRA in 1959.

The geologic story of how the caves were formed is an interesting one. Don't forget to pick up the SRA brochure explaining the process.

Providence Peak Hike
Class 2 or 3/elev. 7171 ft/USGS topo *Flynn*/5–6 mi RT/cross-country

TO GET THERE. Take I-40 about 101 mi east from its intersection with I-15 in Barstow or about 44 mi west of Needles to Essex Rd. Go north on Essex Rd 9.7 mi.

Approach 1: Continue straight ahead at the paved intersection of Essex Rd with Black Canyon Rd (which leads to Hole-in-the-Wall Campground). Continue about 6 mi to the end of the road at the Providence Mountains State Recreation Area Campground. Near the campground is Mitchell Caverns, an interesting limestone cave; rangers give guided tours to the caves every day (see trip above).

Approach 2: If you're opting for the longer route to Providence Peak, stay on Essex Rd for another 0.8 mi after reaching the Black Canyon Rd intersection. At this point, take the north (right) fork (signed "Blair Brothers Ranch — 6 mi") for 5 mi to an old Department of the Interior sign reading "Bonanza King Mine." Bear left here and go about 1.3

mi to another fork. Again take the left road (the right goes to Bonanza King Well) and continue for about 0.5 rough mile to the Bonanza King Mine (an interesting place to explore in its own right).

ABOUT THE HIKE. The Providence Range is a mass of limestone rock — solid and sure to climb on, but sharp and abrasive to soles of boots, clothing, and skin. For this reason (and also because there are many fine specimens of cacti flourishing on the mountain), stout clothes and boots are recommended for this climb.

There are several obvious routes on ridges leading northwest from the campground area to the summit of Providence Peak. Washes should generally be avoided, as they usually contain a lot of loose rock and may have dry waterfalls that may be difficult or impossible to climb — up or down. Choose a ridge and give it a try.

A Longer Route. Experienced route-finders might like to try a longer variation on this hike, starting at the old Bonanza King Mine. From here, follow a faint mining trail and ascend the canyon to the northwest. Then climb to the ridge and make the Class 3 traverse south to Mitchell Peak (7048 ft) and over to Providence Peak.

Hole-in-the-Wall

TO GET THERE. *Access 1:* Take I-15 northeast from its intersection with I-40 in Barstow to the Cima Rd turnoff, about 89 mi. Go south on Cima Rd to Cima, about 17 mi, then make a right at Valley Wells and continue south 4.4 mi on the Kelso-Cima Rd to the Cedar Canyon Rd (signed for Hole-in-the-Wall and Mid-Hills). Pull off here for a few moments and look west from the white signpost at the Mojave Rd (also known as the Old Government Rd). In the mid- to late 1800s, part of this famous wagon route went from Fort Paiute (about 20 mi southeast) to Marl Springs (about 10 mi west). Check your map for the Marl Mtns, which can be seen to the southwest. Now, go east on Cedar Canyon 6 mi to Black Canyon Rd (also signed). Go south on Black Canyon Rd about 8.3 mi to Hole-in-the-Wall Campground, Fire Station, and Information Center. Once you get on Cedar Canyon Rd, all the roads are good, graded dirt and gravel suitable for all vehicles.

Access 2: Follow the directions for the Providence Mtns State Recreation Area trip (see above), but at the intersection of Essex Rd and Black Canyon Rd (9.7 mi north of I-40), take Black Canyon Rd north 8.5 mi to Hole-in-the-Wall.

GETTING YOUR BEARINGS. Take along a good San Bernardino County map; hikers will probably also want the USGS topo *Mid-Hills.*

ABOUT THE AREA. Many parts of the California desert were once volcanically active. You will probably have already noticed the many cinder cones and volcanic plugs scattered throughout those parts of the Mojave you have already visited. For example, about 20 mi northwest of here lies the 25,600-acre Cinder Cones National Natural Landmark — a group of thirty-two cinder cones. The colorful rock towers and caves around Hole-in-the-Wall are also of volcanic origin. A look through the binoculars at some of the nearby mountains will reveal several different volcanic layers and basaltic caps, in addition to layers of sediments left from an ancient lake that once covered the area. (Check your topo map for Wild Horse Mesa, Table Mtn, the Colton Hills, and the Woods Mtns.)

For an interesting hike to Bonshee Canyon, first find the fenced view area in the campground's upper loop. From here you can climb a twisted and spectacular canyon with the help of iron rings set in the rocks. After a few hundred yards, the volcanic rock formations open into an enclosed canyon (a box canyon). From here you should have an excellent view of Wild Horse Mesa.

The country around Hole-in-the-Wall is ideal for photography, bird and animal watching (look especially for large birds of prey, such as golden eagles), plant study, hiking, and just plain relaxing. Elevation is about 4200 ft, so in warm weather it's a bit cooler here than in the desert lowlands. The campground has chemical toilets and water (usually); it can accommodate groups nicely. Kids will enjoy exploring the rock formations.

Mid-Hills

TO GET THERE. *Access 1:* Follow directions for the trip to Hole-in-the-Wall (see above), but when you turn south on Black Canyon Rd, go only 2.8 mi to Wild Horse Canyon Rd and then turn west at the sign. The entrance to Mid-Hills is 2 mi ahead.

Access 2: Follow directions for Hole-in-the-Wall trip, but turn northwest on Wildhorse Canyon Rd just south of Hole-in-the-Wall. Follow Wildhorse Canyon for about 9.7 mi to the Mid-Hills entrance.

GETTING YOUR BEARINGS. Same maps as for the Hole-in-the-Wall trip (see above).

ABOUT THE AREA. This is one of the best places in the California desert to camp in the summer. At 5600 ft, you're above the heat that can make desert lowlands an oven in summer. And there are trees! Lots of pinyons and junipers—and shade. This is a very pleasant campground, with tables, chemical toilets, fireplaces, and water. Some of the campsites have fine views north to the Cima Dome area. Be sure to bring your own charcoal; woodcutting is absolutely forbidden.

Why "Mid-Hills"? Well, perhaps because this area lies midway between the Providence and the New York mountains, which march right up the center of the East Mojave Scenic Area. Despite the fact that the area has had little use historically, it's easy to get to. Because it's had little use, it is a nearly unspoiled wilderness—an ideal spot for hiking, wildlife watching, photography, camping, and enjoying the solitude it's becoming increasingly hard to find, even in the desert.

A short hike (0.5 mi) to the west from the campground will bring you to some spectacular granite spires and a breathtaking view out across Kelso Valley to Cima Dome and the Marl and Kelso mountains.

New York Mountains– Lanfair Valley

Castle Buttes Tour

TO GET THERE. Take I-15 east from its intersection with I-40 in Barstow for 102.5 mi to the Nipton Rd exit; go east 3.5 mi to the Ivanpah Rd. Now, take the Ivanpah Rd south for about 16.8 mi to Hart Mine Rd and the Barnwell site, where you will turn east. The paved road ends and becomes good graded dirt and gravel about 4.8 mi before the Hart Mine Rd comes in. If you plan on taking the back way to the Buttes (see below), it's a good idea to have a 4WD vehicle – or at least one with good clearance.

GETTING YOUR BEARINGS. Bring along a good San Bernardino County map. If you plan on doing any exploring or hiking, the USGS topo *Crescent Peak* will be a help. (The Castle Buttes are called Castle Peaks on the topo.)

ABOUT THE BUTTES. If you really want to get away from it all, Castle Buttes country is about as far away and as unpopulated a place as you'll find in the California desert. These spectacular red volcanic buttes are located just west of the Nevada border and about 15 mi southeast (as the proverbial crow flies) of the Nipton Rd exit off I-15. This location makes them the Far East of the Mojave.

As you begin searching southwest from the Nipton exit on a map, you'll find the Castle Buttes embedded in the southwest-northeast trending New York Mtns. Both the New Yorks and the Buttes have been designated wilderness study areas by the BLM. The pinyon-juniper, white fir, and oak woodlands in the New York Mtns make up some of the most important wildlife habitat in the Mojave Desert.

In the Castle Buttes area you may see some of the animals that already have or may soon attain the dubious distinction of the threatened, sensitive, or endangered species lists. These creatures include the desert tortoise, bighorn sheep, Swainson's hawk, gray vireo, rock squirrel, golden eagle, Panamint kangaroo rat, prairie falcon, Panamint chipmunk, and mule deer.

The area also contains a great many prehistoric sites – a village, rock art, rock shelters, and trails. In addition, there are historic remains of mining camps, railroads, and towns. The New York Mtns figure largely in the origin tales of the Mojave Indians; some parts of these mountains are still used as traditional hunting areas by the Mojave and Chemehuevi.

The hiking is good throughout this area. Like many other parts of the California desert, there are no marked trails, but plenty of 4WD roads and opportunities for cross-country walking.

If you enjoy taking photos, the Castle Buttes are ideal subjects because they stand somewhat separate from the body of the New Yorks and so rise steeply and starkly against the horizon from almost any angle or compass point. Because this area is on the far edge of the Mojave, it is a good choice for a leisurely and varied three- or four-day trip. Binoculars and field books are a must for this area, which is rich in wildlife, interesting plants, and geologic formations.

On the Road to Castle Buttes — The Front Way. At the intersection of the Ivanpah-Lanfair Rd and the Hart Mine Rd, look for several houses and a white signpost. Go east on Hart Mine Rd. The 4808-ft Castle Buttes can be seen to the north. After about 5 mi you'll pass a road going south to the site of Hart (4 mi away). There are several windmills along the road here. In another mile there will be a crossroad. The road north leads to the Castle Buttes area and ends in 6.6 mi. If your time is limited, this is the more direct route to the Buttes. (The road south also goes to Hart.)

On the Road to Castle Buttes — The Back Way. From the crossroads mentioned just above (where the "front way" road takes off to the Buttes), continue straight along the railroad road (Hart Mine Rd). As you look east along here, note a large clay mine on the horizon; the white next to it on the southeast is a talc mine.

If you look behind you about 8 mi from where you turned onto the Hart Mine Rd from the Ivanpah Rd (about 1.5 mi on from where you saw the clay mine), there is a good view of Table Mtn to the southwest and the high part of the New Yorks to the northeast. All along this road, be alert for birds. There are many shrikes, horned larks, flycatchers, Gambel's quail, red-tailed hawks, and California thrashers here.

About 10 mi from the beginning of the Hart Mine Rd, go north on the railroad road. Parts of this road are narrow and raised; the tracks are gone, though you pass in washes several sets of old pilings that are left over from bridges. In another 0.3 mi, go west up a short, steep rise on a road leading off the railroad road, then northeast at a fork leading to Coats Spring.

As you go along the road to Coats Spring after the last fork, you'll pass crossroad in about 0.6 mi. To the east this road leads to Searchlight, to the west back to the railroad road. Continue toward Coats Spring. In another 0.5 mi you'll pass a road going east to the site of Juan; continue northwest just above the windmill at Stagecoach Spring. Look west for a view of the Castle Buttes close up. This is a good photo point.

About 1 mi beyond the good photo point, the road goes through a gate; be sure to close it after going through. At the fork just beyond the gate, continue northwest past a road going west (it goes to Indian Spring). Right here is an excellent view east to many ranks of mountain ranges in Arizona and west to the spectacular red volcanic Castle Buttes and New York Mtns.

A tenth of a mile farther, just above the windmill at Malpais Spring, the road becomes rutted and descends steeply. Turn northeast at the fork, onto the road going to Talc Spring. After another 1.6 mi, go northwest at a corral to continue on the road to Talc Spring.

Continue about 1.2 mi to a place where a wide (40-ft) wash crosses the road; go west up the wash toward the Castle Buttes. There are trees and good camping spots along this wash, some of them sheltered (depending on which way the wind is blowing). The wash becomes impassable in about 2 mi (depending on your vehicle). Elevation here is about 4600 ft; you are about 16 mi from where you first turned on to the Hart Mine Rd.

From here you can hike cross-country toward the buttes, or just wander around admiring the Mojave yuccas, junipers, Joshua trees, chollas, beavertails, barrel cacti, desert willows, paper flowers, ruby-crowned sparrows, white-crowned sparrows, ladder-backed woodpeckers, etc. You may even stumble into a badger hole!

To return to the Ivanpah Rd, just retrace your route.

New York Mountain Scramble

Class 2–3/elev. 7532 ft/USGS topos *Ivanpah, Mid-Hills*/3–5 mi RT/cross-country

TO GET THERE. Take I-15 102.5 mi east from its intersection with I-40 in Barstow; get off on CA 164 (Nipton Rd) and go 3.5 mi east to Ivanpah Rd.

Access 1: Take Ivanpah Rd 24.2 mi south, by the site of Barnwell, to New York Mtn Rd. (Ivanpah Rd will turn to good dirt/gravel after about 12 mi.) Turn west (right) on New York Mtn Rd and proceed for about 5.5 mi to Caruthers Canyon Rd (unsigned); go north into the canyon as far as is practical—at least 1.5 mi.

Access 2: Take Ivanpah Rd 17.9 mi south (1.2 mi beyond the Barnwell site), then go west into Live Oak Canyon. Drive past Lecyr Well and into the canyon as far as your vehicle will allow.

ABOUT THE SCRAMBLE. On the drive into Caruthers Canyon you'll notice many good campsites under the trees. If it's a nice weekend, you'll notice that this is a popular family camping area. (See Caruthers Canyon trip, below, for details.)

Route 1: From where you parked, hike up the dirt track to the Giant Ledge Mine (copper). Follow a gully west from the mine, past the south side of the prominent east pinnacle. Ascend to the summit ridge just south of the top. When you gain the ridge, turn west and then north to follow a scrambling route diagonally up across the west face. The final 30 ft is Class 3.

Route 2: To climb the peak from the east, follow access 2 directions. Climb the steep east slopes of New York Mtn, circling north around to the west side and joining the summit route as described in Route 1. This second route is only about 3 mi round-trip.

Caruthers Canyon

TO GET THERE. Follow the directions for the Castle Buttes trip to the intersection of Lanfair Rd and Hart Mine Rd. Continue south on Lanfair Rd 7.9 mi to New York Mtn Rd; turn west on New York Mtn Rd. After 5 mi, go north on Caruthers Canyon Rd.

GETTING YOUR BEARINGS. If you're planning on doing some hiking, take along the USGS topos *Mid-Hills* and *Ivanpah* in addition to a good San Bernardino County map.

ABOUT THE CANYON. As you drive into the canyon, you'll notice several roads leading off to good campsites, many of them sheltered by trees. The main road continues on through the canyon, eventually becoming impassable before it reaches a mine at its end.

An interesting fact about Caruthers Canyon is that the vegetation here is a relict stand of coastal chaparral from the old, wetter days of the Mojave. This now out-of-place vegetation has survived in the sheltered microclimate of the canyon much as the white fir forest on Clark Mtn has. This unique biotic community needs your help to remain intact for all to continue enjoying. Please drive only on the main roads, do not cut or collect wood for campfires, and always take all garbage and trash with you when you leave.

If you come to Caruthers Canyon when the weather's nice, you'll find it is a popular family camping place. The camping here is undeveloped — there are no restrooms, tables, or other amenities. The campsites, however, are spacious and well appointed by nature. A look around will reveal live oaks, jojoba, manzanita, hedgehog cactus, Joshua trees, old man cactus, beavertail cactus, and many other trees and plants at home both in the desert and mountains. The elevation is about 5500 ft in the canyon.

The canyon is a fine base from which to explore a good bit of the Mojave Desert. For the hardy, there's the New York Mtn Scramble (see above), which can be started right from Caruthers Canyon. If you're not up to anything quite so strenuous, there are plenty of 4WD roads and use trails to walk about on. And it's only a half hour to an hour's beautiful drive to such places as Kelso Dunes, Fort Paiute, Hole-in-the-Wall, the Lanfair Valley, Cima Dome and the Cinder Cones, and even Providence Mtns State Recreation Area and Mitchell Caverns.

If it's rest and relaxation you're after, though, there's absolutely no reason to stir from the canyon. Nowhere is it written that you have to drive or hike anywhere at all. It's perfectly legal to just lie about and enjoy the scenery, fresh air, and birdsong.

Fort Paiute Hike

Class 1/elev. 3400 ft/USGS topos *Lanfair Valley, Homer Mtn*/4.5 mi RT/cross-country, use trails

TO GET THERE. *Access 1 (from the north):* Follow the directions for the Castle Buttes trip, above, then continue south for 13 mi on Lanfair Rd from its intersection with Hart Mine Rd to where it crosses Cedar Canyon Rd. Go east here for 3.4 mi to a fork; keep southeast (right) and continue for 4.2 mi to a crossroad. Continue straight on (southeast) for about another 2.4 mi (if you cross a low pass and start to descend, you have gone too far). At this point, just before you come to a fence, turn north. In about 0.1 mi your road crosses the Old Mojave Rd; in another 0.2 mi, you'll pass a corral on the west; 0.4 mi more will bring you to the vicinity of the trailhead at the edge of the gorge. Park in this area and look for the trail.

Access 2 (from the south): Follow the directions for the Providence Mtns State Recreation Area trip, above, but do not get off at the Essex Rd exit. Instead, continue east on I-40 for another 7.4 mi to the Fenner-Goffs exit. Go 9.8 mi northeast to Goffs; in Goffs (small store and gas station), take Lanfair Rd north about 15.2 mi to where it intersects Cedar Canyon Rd. Go east here, following the directions for access 1.

ABOUT THE HIKE. Paiute Creek has been one of the Mojave's most important watering spots since prehistoric times. Like Camp Cady and Afton Canyon, Paiute Creek was on the Mojave (Indian) Trail. As mentioned above, this trade trail stretched from the coast of California to the Colorado River and even on into Arizona.

All around the creek area evidences of Indian occupation can be found. Some of the most obvious remains are petroglyphs; there are several easily found examples of petroglyphs near the Fort Paiute end of Paiute Creek. Archaeologists have also found huts, sleeping circles, food caches, tools, and other artifacts. The Indians may have used the area for thousands of years before explorers and, later, settlers entered the area. Thus, like other permanent riparian areas in the California desert, Paiute Creek is a museum in the wild of Indian art and life.

When non-Indians began traveling the Mojave Trail and then started settling down in country the Indians looked upon as theirs, there was usually trouble. Unfortunately, it can't be said that the intruders were very understanding of the Indians' point of view. In places where the Indians wouldn't just quietly allow their lands to be taken from them, it was deemed necessary to put up army outposts to protect travelers and their wagons on what became the Mojave Road.

Paiute Creek, with its 150,000-gallon-a-day flow, was an important link in the chain of watering places along this major wagonway. So, in 1867, when the Indians in the Paiute Creek region became a little too "troublesome," a small outpost at Paiute Creek was put up by the Army Corps of Engineers to house a few soldiers who acted as escorts for travelers. There is some difference of opinion about how long the out-post was manned—some say six months, others say two to three years. The rock walls at the east end of Paiute Creek are the remains of the outpost—now called, somewhat grandiosely, Fort Paiute. Notice that the rock is volcanic, and that mud mortar was used.

Although Indian "troubles" were infrequent, the army had a hard time persuading soldiers to serve out their terms of duty at Fort Paiute. It seems that the lure of gold and silver in nearby mining communities, along with the isolation and monotony of life at the fort, led to a high desertion rate.

Later, in the 1880s, when the railroads came to the Mojave and the major transdesert wagon roads moved to follow them, the Mojave Rd and its watering places fell into disuse. The Mojave Indians, however, lost no time moving back into the area—and who can blame them?— they didn't want to leave in the first place. Nowadays, the BLM manages Fort Paiute and the Paiute Creek area. Both are valued for their historic and prehistoric remains. In fact, the outpost is now on the National Registry of Historic Places.

When viewing the area's historic and prehistoric remains, please take care not to disturb them. Leave them as you find them for others to study and enjoy.

On the Trail to Fort Paiute. From the trailhead in Lanfair Valley on the lip of Paiute Gorge, follow an old pack trail as it winds down about 500 ft into the gorge. In the gorge, bear right into a dry wash (there should be a cairn here). Follow the main wash through the gorge for about 1.75 mi to Paiute Spring. The scenery is really lovely along the way, no matter what time of year it is. (It can be very hot in summer, though.) In spring there are usually some nice wildflower displays in the sandy wash.

You'll recognize Paiute Spring easily; the wash becomes choked with trees and bushes, and the creek bed is full of water. It's not always easy to make your way along here. A little perseverance will bring you out on the other side of the spring, about 0.75 mi from Fort Paiute. Con-tinue to follow the creek for another 0.25 mi, as the canyon walls lower and you enter a steep-sided valley.

At this point, if you spend a little time looking up the side canyons on the south side of the creek a couple of hundred feet west of where the "trail" crosses over to the north side of the creek, you should be able to discover the one where the Mojave Rd comes down from Paiute Hill to the creek. (The road then follows the "trail" on to Fort Paiute.) You may be able to recognize the side canyon by some stretches of red rock in it. When you start walking up the canyon, look for the old wagon ruts. There are also some petroglyphs on either side of the road. It's not hard to imagine the difficulties of driving a wagon over this road, even under the best of weather conditions!

After exercising your imagination on the Mojave Rd wagon ruts, follow the "trail" across to the north side of Paiute Creek and make your way on to the Fort Paiute ruins. Keep to the left at most of the forks. If you get off course, just backtrack and take the other arm of the fork. As you near Fort Paiute, keep an eye out for petroglyphs. There are several fine ones along the way.

To return to Lanfair Valley, just retrace your route. For a slightly more strenuous return with some fine views, go back to the side canyon with the Mojave Rd and follow it up over the ridgeline. From there you will be able to see your vehicle, and it's an easy cross-country walk back to your starting point.

Cima Dome–Clark Mountain

Cima Dome Hike

Class 1/elev. 5700 ft/USGS topo *Mescal Range*/RT mi varies according to your inclination/use trails, 4WD roads, cross-country

TO GET THERE. Take I-15 northeast from its intersection with I-40 in Barstow for about 89 mi to the Cima Rd exit at Valley Wells. Get off here and travel southeast 6.8 mi on Cima Rd, then turn on the dirt road leading due south to the Valley View Ranch in 3.2 mi. As you near the ranch, take the road southwest toward Deer Springs. (This is a confusing place with several roads. The road you want is a turn to the left as you enter the developed ranch area; this road goes uphill by a windmill. If you find yourself at the main ranch house, you've gone past the road.) Park at the cattle fence 2–3 mi from the ranch. (The fence represents a grazing lease on public lands.)

ABOUT THE DOME. Cima Dome, though very close to the cinder cones described below, is not of volcanic origin. Instead, this huge (10 mi in diameter), gently sloping, nearly symmetrical dome was once a large mass of molten rock. As this rock cooled it became quartz monzonite, a rock similar to granite. Unlike masses of granite, which erode into craggy, steep-faced peaks and eventually crumble into huge piles of boulders, quartz monzonite erodes smoothly when conditions are right. So, over the years, the mass that became Cima Dome was eroded away into a large, low, convex mass. (Cima, by the way, is Spanish for "summit.") Most of the original rock (bedrock) is under the erosional debris, but there are still a few outcroppings here and there. Teutonia Peak, at 5755 ft, is the largest of these (see below).

Besides having an unusual geologic history, Cima Dome has another claim to fame. It hosts one of the world's finest and most extensive Joshua tree forests. The Joshua trees on the dome (*Yucca brevifolia Jaegeriana*) are a slightly different species than the ones in Joshua Tree National Monument. To the casual observer, the differences lie in *Jaegeriana*'s larger size and great number of bi-symmetric branches. (The Mormons named these primitive trees Joshua trees because they reminded them of the biblical Joshua, with his arms raised in supplication to heaven.)

A Nearby Attraction. If you look south as you are driving northeast along I-15 from Baker to the Cima turnoff, you can't miss either the Mojave Cinder Cones National Natural Landmark or Cima Dome. There are thirty-two colorful, rounded cinder cones in the 25,600-acre national landmark. It's sometimes hard to believe, today, that this region — and many other parts — of the California desert was once so volcanically active as to produce such an impressive cluster of cones.

The cones closest to I-15 (near Halloran Summit) are the most ancient — about 10 million years old. The crisper-looking cones to the south near the Old Dad Mtns (check your map) are considerably younger — only about 1000 years old. Geologists think there is a possibility these young cones could become active again.

The lava and other volcanic debris found in the Cinder Cones National Natural Landmark area are primarily made up of a type of basalt — a dark rock made up of magnesium, calcium, and iron. Unfortunately, this rock is much in demand for decorative and roadbuilding purposes. The Bureau of Land Management, which manages the landmark, is allowing these cinder cones to be mined — for profit, of course. Those who would like to have our national landmarks preserved rather than carried off are not happy with this kind of management.

These cinder cones are only one example of past volcanic activity in the California desert. As you travel anywhere in the desert, keep an eye out for the many cones (and their mines), lava flows, volcanic plugs, and layers of volcanic ash interspersed among the sedimentary and rocky layers of canyons and mountainsides. You'll soon get the idea that the California desert is no stranger to geologic change.

On the Trails of Cima Dome. From where you parked, the dome is your oyster, so to speak. You can hike on the unsigned dirt roads, follow cattle trails, walk cross-country, or whatever. As you look up Cima Dome, the small, bare peak to the east is Teutonia Peak. Perhaps its quartz was a little harder than that of the rest of the original mountain, so it survived as a small crag. There are several other smaller crags scattered about the dome. There are good campsites near some of these.

Spring (late April to early June) is a particularly pleasant time to visit Cima Dome; the wildflower displays are often superb. Even in summer the elevation (over 5000 ft) makes the area quite a bit cooler than the surrounding lowlands. The dome is an ideal location for short, overnight backpacks. Because of the gentle slope and visible landmarks, the dome is a good place for beginners to try out their backpacking and compass skills before venturing into more rugged territory. Of course, you sometimes have to share your wide open spaces with some cattle — but they are, for the most part, quiet and considerate companions.

If you are out exploring the east Mojave in warm weather, Cima Dome is a good place for car camping. Although there are fences, the land is still public land; just be sure to close all gates when you are exploring the roads for a good place to camp—and there are many of them. Even though the freeway is only a few miles away, up on Cima Dome you can spend the night in relative solitude, watch the Milky Way pursue its lazy way across the sky, and rise at dawn to photograph the chollas or the upraised arms of the Joshua trees as they catch the rising sun.

Clark Mountain Tour

TO GET THERE. Take I-15 northeast from its intersection with I-40 in Barstow about 107.5 mi to the Cal-Neva–Yatec Well exit (there are a gas station and restaurant here). The roads will be good graded dirt and gravel for most of the tour; the last leg will be paved.

GETTING YOUR BEARINGS. You'll need a good San Bernardino County map; hikers and explorers will want the USGS topo *Clark Mtn.*

ABOUT THE TOUR. Clark Mtn (elev. 7929 ft) is the highest peak in the Mojave Desert. Because it is somewhat isolated from the Clark Mtn Range just to the north of it, Clark is easy to see for some miles around in any direction. As you explore it, you will easily see why the mountain is well known for its plant and animal life. One of the unusual features of the mountain, and one that makes it a kind of island in time, is the small white fir forest near the peak.

Like many another fine mountain in the California desert, Clark has been the object of many miners' affections. In the late 1800s, several silver mines were quite successful on Clark. One, on the east side of the mountain, brought in over $4 million between 1872 and 1885. Between about 1900 and the present, various mining ventures—mostly for copper and turquoise—have come and gone. As you will see, even now, in the late 1980s, the Las Vegas Metals Company is busy uglifying beautiful Clark Mtn in hopes of striking it rich. The Bureau of Land Management, the land manager for the Clark Mtn area, seems to feel that mining is the best of all possible uses for this lovely region. Not everyone agrees—though the miners doubtless do.

On the Powerline Road in Search of Clark Mountain. When you come off I-15 at the Cal-Neva–Yatec Well exit, cross over to the west side of the freeway (on the east side you can see Ivanpah Dry Lake). Next, turn northeast on a good gravel road that parallels the freeway and go about 5.1 mi; bear north for another 0.9 mi, then west (left) on what is obviously a powerline road. (Alternatively, you can get off at the next exit, Stateline, and catch the powerline road there.) In about 14.5 mi this road will take you up to Keany Pass, at 4906 ft. From here there is a good view west over several broad valleys and rugged mountain ranges. Now is the time to get out your map and try to figure out just what you are seeing out there. Clark Mtn, of course, is looming quite close to the south—you can't miss it. (If you're hungry, this is a good lunch stop—even if the only shade is a power tower, the view is great.)

As you continue west, make another stop in about 1.7 mi at the point where the Mesquite Pass Rd comes in from the north. Here, if the weather cooperates, you can look northeast all the way to 11,919-ft Charleston Peak, about 60 mi away, in Nevada. The Mesquite Pass Rd, not surprisingly, leads to Mesquite Dry Lake (about 8.5 mi away). This dry lake is closed to ORVs, which means that its sand dunes are a pleasant place to visit. The road to the lake varies from good to poor. It's a good idea to check locally before attempting it in anything but a 4WD vehicle.

Winding Among the Mines. Continue past the Mesquite Pass Rd for about 0.6 mi to a road going south toward Clark Mtn and signed for the Taylor and Green mines. Take this road, which winds upward among pinyons, junipers, Joshua trees, beavertail and barrel cacti, and—check your plant guide. In about 3.4 mi you'll come to a fork signed "Juniper Claims, 1 mi"; bear left here (notice the leftover mine ruins). After 1.5 mi you'll approach the Las Vegas Metals operation and the Green's Well cattle ranch area. In another 0.6 mi you'll come to the top of Coliseum Gorge, where there is an excellent view to the south of Clark Mtn (now quite close above you) and of Coliseum Gorge falling away steeply to the east. In the future, the views may be considerably less appealing—if the proposed Coliseum Mine project actually gets started. It's quite possible that this operation, which will strip-mine a rhyolite plug nearby to the north, will virtually bury this whole valley in tailings.

To the Top of the Gorge. The road you are on continues down the gorge and back to the gravel road paralleling I-15—sometimes. Unless you are an experienced 4WD operator, don't try it! And even if you are going to try it, be sure to check with the locals before doing so. The nonadventurous (or perhaps the sensible) will want to stop here for the view, but then return the way they came.

As you look around, notice the several dirt roads leading up the mountain. These are good for hiking; just be sure to respect gates and No Trespassing signs. One of the roads used to go around the east side of the mountain and down the south side, coming out at what is now the Mountain Pass exit onto I-15 (check your topo). Strong, experienced hikers might want to arrange a car shuttle and try to hike this road around to the other side of Clark and down to the Mountain Pass area.

What's Rare About Mountain Pass? The Mountain Pass area at the southern foot of Clark Mtn is renowned for its production of rare earths—a group of elements classed together because of their chemical similarities. Contrary to what their collective name suggests, rare earths are not all that rare; in fact, they make up over 15% of all known elements. A number of the rare-earth elements are used in the manufacture of high-tech products such as catalysts, sparking alloys, color TV tubes, etc. The Molybdenum Corporation of America (also known as Molycorp) handles the Mountain Pass rare-earth mines.

Camping Out or Winding It Up. Meanwhile, those who are still sitting back at the top of Coliseum Gorge might want to continue their tour around Clark Mtn. This can easily be done by returning to the powerline road and continuing west for 5.5 mi to the (paved) Kingston Mine Rd. If you are planning on some open-desert camping, go north on this road for about 3.3 mi to a good dirt road signed "Kingston Rd," which bears northeast. Take this road and go about 6.3 mi to a road leading west. There are some nice campsites 0.25 to 0.75 mi up this road.

To return to I-15, turn south on Kingston Mine Rd (instead of north to the campsites); in about 8.2 mi you'll be at the Cima Rd interchange. As you drive toward the freeway, don't forget to admire the view of Cima Dome straight ahead.

13

Around Joshua Tree

Joshua Tree National Monument

ABOUT THE MONUMENT. In 1936, Joshua Tree National Monument (JTNM) was created to protect a large, nearly untouched tract of land located between the California desert's Mojave and Colorado regions—a unique transitional area where the characteristics of both types of deserts mingle. For example, on the monument's west side, you see a great many Joshua trees—those unforgettable hallmarks of the high (Mojave) desert. In addition, the monument harbors several of the California desert's loveliest palm oases—each of which can be visited. All in all, JTNM includes about 850 sq mi of spectacular California desert landscape that many feel should have the added protection and recognition of national park status (467,000 acres—730 sq mi—of the monument have already been designated as wilderness by Congress).

Settlers Old and New. Looking at today's ruggedly spectacular desert scenery in the monument, with its jumbles of warm granite and forests of primitive-looking Joshua trees, it's hard to believe that a wide river once flowed through what is now arid Pinto Basin. In those times, many thousands of years ago, the basin was green and verdant; trees and grasses grew thick and lush, horses and camel-like creatures roamed the meadows. Later, the area's first human settlers wandered into the basin—and stayed. As the climate grew warmer and drier, the river flowed no more, and eventually early peoples clustered around what are now the monument's oases—particularly the Oasis of Mara (where the Twentynine Palms visitor center is located).

In the late 1860s the Colorado River Chemehuevis were forced out of their ancestral lands on the river by the Mojaves. A number of those who escaped followed the trade trails to the Twentynine Palms region and settled among the already-resident Serranos. The Serrano and the Chemehuevi cultures were similar, so the two groups peacefully mingled, each culture adopting some of the ways of the other. The river dwellers, for instance, were farmers who knew how to use irrigation;

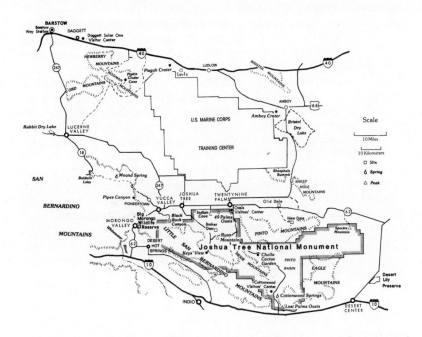

they taught the Serranos how to go about setting up gardens near the oasis. The two cultures blended so successfully that by 1900 they were considered one: Chemehuevi.

When the first nonnative miners and homesteaders came to what is now the monument area during the 1870s, the Indians were still at the oasis, leading the same hunting, gathering, and—more recently—farming life they had lived for the past several hundred (perhaps even several thousand) years. A small gold strike was made near the oasis in 1873, causing a flurry of activity that soon petered out along with the ore vein. Then, in the early 1880s, more substantial gold strikes were made just a few miles away, in what became the Dale District. Now, a flood of miners and ranchers streamed into the Dale and Twentynine Palms areas. Houses were built, cattle grazed, mine shafts dug, stage stations opened—and the Chemehuevis, of course, were displaced. By 1913—as in so many other parts of the California desert—both the Indians and the pronghorn antelope were gone from the area.

TO GET THERE. I-10 goes by the south boundary and CA 62 takes you the few miles from I-10 to the north boundary. If you're coming from I-40, you pick up the National Trails Highway or Kelbaker Rd, come south to Amboy Rd, and soon find yourself right at the main entrance. Actually, JTNM has several entrances, not just the one. The west entrance road (Park Blvd) takes off, fittingly, from the little town of Joshua Tree on CA 62. The main entrance road, the one that takes you to the primary visitor center (Oasis), takes off from the quite sizable town of Twentynine Palms, also on CA 62. And the southern entrance road (Cottonwood Spring) takes off from I-10 a little over 20 mi east of the town of Indio. Each time you visit JTNM, try a different entrance—they all have their scenic charms. The entrance roads for two of the campgrounds—Black Rock Canyon and Indian Cove—end at the camp areas and do not connect with the rest of the monument.

What to Do First. Jog to the top of the nearest peak? Tour the viewpoints? Stake out a camp spot? Picnic? Relax in the shade of a granite boulder while sipping something cool? Wander up a wash with binoculars and field guide? Watch the rock-climbers? Suggestion: head for the nearest visitor center. There are three: Oasis (the main one, at the Twentynine Palms entrance), Cottonwood (at the south entrance), and Black Rock Canyon (at the campground southeast of Yucca Valley; check your county map—as noted for the trips—for directions). After taking time to peruse the brochures, books, and maps at one of the centers, you'll have a much better idea of where you want to start. (Maybe it'll be at your ice chest!) Remember that the few trips suggested here are only a sampling of many possibilities.

FACILITIES. Gas, supplies, motels, and restaurants are plentiful near the northern end of JTNM. Try Twentynine Palms, Joshua Tree, and Yucca Valley—and points between. At the monument's south end, the nearest amenities—and plenty of them—are at Indio, about 22 mi west of the Cottonwood Spring Rd exit (where you get off I-10 to approach the south entrance).

Camping. There are nine *developed* campgrounds in JTNM: Black Rock Canyon, Hidden Valley, Indian Cove (some group sites), Ryan, Sheep Pass (group), Jumbo Rocks, Belle, White Tank, and Cottonwood. All the campgrounds are not always open; some of the satellite areas are used only when demand is high (for example, Belle and White Tank are overflow areas for Jumbo Rocks). The main visitor center will be able to give you current campground information; you can even call them before you leave home. In any case, several campgrounds are open year round.

Many of the campgrounds have sites among large, attractive rock formations. All campgrounds have tables, fireplaces, and toilets, but *no water* (except for Cottonwood) or firewood. Please bring your own! Check your county map or the JTNM map you picked up at the visitor center for directions to the campgrounds. (Two of them—Black Rock Canyon and Indian Cove—can be reached only from CA 62, not from inside the the monument, unless you have a 4WD vehicle.)

Oasis Visitor Center

TO GET THERE. The most common route to the Oasis visitor center in Joshua Tree National Monument (JTNM) is via I-10 to its intersection with CA 62 (about 47 mi east of San Bernardino and Riverside). When you reach CA 62, go north and east for about 43 mi to the JTNM turnoff (signed) in the town of Twentynine Palms. Follow the signs a short distance to the visitor center.

GETTING YOUR BEARINGS. You may need both the San Bernardino and Riverside County maps.

ABOUT THE VISITOR CENTER. Before beginning to explore JTNM (or any other park or monument, for that matter), make it a point to stop at the visitor center. Here, you'll find an excellent selection of free and low-cost fact sheets, brochures, books, posters, and maps to help

Joshua tree in snow. *Photo by Lyle Gaston.*

you better understand and enjoy what you'll be seeing in the monument. There are also several interesting exhibits, a slide show, and some friendly folks who'll do their best to answer any questions you may have about the area.

The visitor center is located alongside one of JTNM's four palm oases—the Oasis of Mara (also known as Twentynine Palm Oasis). For many hundred years before the arrival of settlers in the area, native Americans lived here at the Oasis of Mara—the "place of little springs and much grass." In those days, before the area was heavily settled, the water table was higher and area was lusher. The native residents had a good life; in season, they gathered foods, hunted animals, and provided themselves with clothing and shelter from materials nearby. They also made trips to other areas to gather foods and materials not found near their oasis.

When gold was discovered in the Dale area just to the east in the 1880s, though, it wasn't long before the lands around Twentynine Palms Oasis were settled. Soon, cattle grazed on the abundant grass, stage stations and ranches sprang up, and the native Americans were driven from their longtime home. The new residents, however, didn't understand the connection between the Indians' periodic burning of the oasis and the "much grass." And when the oasis was no longer regularly burned over, the shrubby plants you see here today took over. The burning had kept the shrubs under control and produced conditions ideal for the growth of grass and the edible plants having deep, starchy roots. (The Indians probably didn't understand the exact connection either; they burned the oasis to remove dead palm fronds, where evil spirits were thought to lurk.)

Today the oasis, with its many shrubs, provides a fine home for birds, small mammals, and other wildlife. Don't forget to take a few minutes to wander around the nature trail near the visitor center area and make their acquaintance.

Cottonwood Spring Visitor Center

TO GET THERE. This southern entrance to Joshua Tree National Monument (JTNM) can be reached by taking I-10 about 60 mi west of Blythe or 22 mi east of Indio. At this point, take the Cottonwood Spring Rd exit (also signed for JTNM) north about 7 mi to the visitor center and campground.

GETTING YOUR BEARINGS. Bring a good Riverside County map.

ABOUT THE VISITOR CENTER. Here at Cottonwood Spring Oasis you'll find a small visitor center with displays, informational brochures, and a ranger on duty to answer your questions. There are also a picnic area and well-appointed campground, with water, tables, and fireplaces. Across the road is a short, self-guided nature trail that will help acquaint you with the plants in the area.

This oasis, like the other three oases in JTNM, owes its existence to faults in the earth's crust. The very active San Andreas fault runs near JTNM's southwestern boundary, making the whole area somewhat unstable and creating numbers of smaller faults. These faults sometimes reach down into reservoirs of underground water and allow the water to come to the earth's surface—thus, the oases. Unlike the other oases in JTNM, Cottonwood Spring is primarily manmade. In prehistoric times, there were no palms or cottonwoods, just the flowing springs. The vegetation around the spring today makes the area a good place to observe wildlife of all kinds, but particularly birds.

Fortynine Palms Oasis Hike
Class 1/elev. 2800 ft/USGS topo *Twentynine Palms*/3 mi RT/trail

TO GET THERE. From the Twentynine Palms visitor center (see above) near the north entrance of Joshua Tree National Monument (JTNM), go north 1 mi to CA 63, then west 5 mi to Canyon Rd. Follow this road about 1.8 mi to a parking area. Look for the trailhead sign.

ABOUT THE HIKE. This oasis, like most others, is a good place to observe desert wildlife—from a discreet distance. Remember, the oasis is their home; you are only a visitor. The trail is classed as moderately strenuous by the JTNM folks; the elevation gain is about 400 ft. For details on the trail's conditions, etc., check with the visitor center.

Cholla Cactus Garden Nature Trail

TO GET THERE. From the Twentynine Palms visitor center (see above), go south 9 mi to a fork; at this point, bear east and travel about another 9 mi to the Cactus Garden sign. The garden is on the south side of the road.

GETTING YOUR BEARINGS. Bring along a good Riverside County map.

ABOUT THE NATURE TRAIL. Be sure to pick up the Cholla Cactus Garden brochure at the visitor center. This guide will help you become acquainted with the interestingly desert-adapted plants and animals you'll find along the self-guiding nature trail. On the trail you'll find out why chollas "jump," what makes a cactus a cactus, and which plants and animals can successfully live with desert extremes of heat and cold—and how.

Queen Valley–Little San Bernardino Mountains Geology Tour

TO GET THERE. From Twentynine Palms visitor center (see above), go south 9 mi to a fork in the road; turn southwest (right) here and continue for a little under 5 mi to Geology Tour Rd (signed). This car tour is a loop; the roads are good dirt. To begin the tour, go south.

GETTING YOUR BEARINGS. Bring along a good Riverside County map. The USGS topo *Lost Horse Mtn* will be a help in seeing how the ups and downs of Joshua Tree National Monument (JTNM) fit together.

ABOUT THE TOUR. First, you'll need to pick up the Geology Tour brochure at the Twentynine Palms visitor center. This folder takes you through the tour step by step, explaining the desert landscape as it is now and as it was in the distant past—and giving you some idea of how now relates to then. You can learn how valleys are formed, where alluvial fans come from, what kinds of rock you're seeing, how precious metals are deposited, why dry lakes are dry, and many other interesting details of JTNM's geologic evolution. What you find out on this tour will help you understand the geologic processes shaping the rest of the California desert. Total mileage is about 18 mi.

Ryan Mountain Hike
Class 1/elev. 5461 ft/USGS topo *Lost Horse Mtn*/3 mi RT/trail

TO GET THERE. To reach the trailhead from CA 62, you may enter Joshua Tree National Monument either from the western entrance on Park Blvd in Joshua Tree (6 mi east of the intersection of CA 62 and CA 247) or from the main entrance on Utah Trail (or Adobe Rd) in Twentynine Palms.

Access 1 (from Joshua Tree): Follow Park Blvd southeast for about 15 mi to a fork; go east here for about 2.8 mi to the turnoff for Sheep Pass Group Campground (signed). Follow the signs 0.5 mi to the campground and trailhead.

Access 2 (from Twentynine Palms): Follow Utah Trail past the Twentynine Palms visitor center (taking time to stop for info, of course) for about 9 mi to a fork in the road; go west here for about 8 mi to the turnoff for Sheep Pass Group Campground. Follow the signs 0.5 mi to the campground and trailhead.

ABOUT THE HIKE. From the top of Ryan Mtn there are fine views of Lost Horse, Pleasant, Hidden, and Queen valleys—so don't forget your camera and binoculars! The elevation gain is about 800 ft. For details of trail conditions, check with a ranger.

Lost Horse Mine Hike
Class 1/elev. 5100 ft/USGS topo *Lost Horse Mtn*/3 mi RT/trail

TO GET THERE. See above for directions to Ryan Mtn hike.

Access 1 (from the west entrance at Joshua Tree): Continue south 2.5 mi past fork going east. At this point, go southeast on a graded dirt road for 1 mi to the trailhead.

Access 2 (from the main entrance at Twentynine Palms): Continue west past the Sheep Pass Group Campground turnoff for about 2.8 mi to a fork, signed "Keys' View"; go south here for 2.5 mi, then southeast on a graded dirt road for 1 mi to the trailhead.

ABOUT THE HIKE. This is a good hike for those interested in the area's gold mining history. At the mine you can see a stamp mill, various building foundations, and the treeless slopes left behind by the mine operators. (The hills were once covered with junipers, Joshua trees, and pinyon pines. But the boilers for the steam engines driving the stamp mill required a lot of fuel.) The Lost Horse was a pretty good claim; it's said that it made $3000 a day during the years 1893–1895, and a total of about $350,000 between 1896 and the turn of the century. In those days, that was a lot of money! Unfortunately for the miners, the rich vein eventually hit a fault, and although the search went far and wide, no one could pick it up again.

The elevation gain for this hike is only about 450 ft, making it a relatively easy one for most people. For details of trail conditions, check with a ranger.

Keys' View

TO GET THERE. To find Keys' View via the shortest route, come into Joshua Tree National Monument (JTNM) via the west entrance in the town of Joshua Tree. Here, turn south off CA 62 onto Park Blvd and travel about 21 mi to the viewpoint.

GETTING YOUR BEARINGS. You'll find a good Riverside County map useful.

ABOUT THE VIEWPOINT. This high point (5185 ft) is thought to offer the best views in the monument. On a good day you can even see to the Salton Sea, nearly 40 mi away. At the viewpoint, consult your maps and try to identify the mountains, valleys, and other landmarks laid out before you. From here you can get some fine photos that well represent the California desert's superb landscapes.

Like a number of other sites in the desert, this one was named for a longtime early resident of the area. Some miles to the north of the viewpoint are the Desert Queen Mine and the Desert Queen Ranch, which were owned and managed by Bill Keys and his family from the early 1900s to the time of Bill's death in 1969 at the age of eighty-nine. Bill, like many another gold miner, was something of a character. Unlike many other "characters," however, he was also a hard worker. Over the years he and his wife not only successfully raised a family of five in the far-away outback of what is now JTNM, but managed to make a success of mining, too. But Bill, like all of us, had his weaknesses — and one of them seems likely to have been an over-quick trigger finger.

It seems that Keys and a neighbor—one Mr. Bagley—disagreed violently one day about a right-of-way. And Mr. Bagley was the permanent loser. For this unneighborly action, good old Bill went to the penitentiary for five years. But he returned to his ranch and mine as energetic as ever and continued with his beloved improvement projects for another twenty years (history is silent as to whether he repented of his rash action).

If you'd like to visit the "scene of the crime," the Desert Queen Mine, and the Keys ranch, check with the rangers for directions. The mine is a moderate hike of about 6 mi round-trip, but the "scene" is just a short walk from the road.

Whitewater River– Yucca Valley

ABOUT THE AREA. Like Joshua Tree National Monument (JTNM), much of the country in this area is in transition between California desert's higher Mojave region to the north and the lower Colorado (Sonoran) region to the south. Partly because it is higher, the Mojave Desert gets more rain, is somewhat cooler, and has denser and more varied plant life than the Colorado Desert; Joshua tree forests are a prominent feature. The lower, warmer, and more arid Colorado Desert has a sparser plant cover, with much more creosote, and many spectacular vistas featuring colorful, dramatically eroded canyons, cliffs, and mesas. This dramatic landscape is the result of sudden summer storms, which cause this type of erosion.

In addition to the Mojave-Colorado transition, this area between JTNM and the San Bernardino Mtns features a desert-mountain transition and a true desert riparian community—all of which makes observing the plant and animal life in this part of the California desert not only interesting, but particularly challenging. So, whether you are meandering up the Whitewater River Valley into the San Bernardino Mtns, wandering down Big Morongo Creek, switchbacking up Burns Canyon to Baldwin Lake, or driving from I-10 to Yucca Valley, take time to notice the many changes in the terrain and the plant-animal communities as you move from one type of landscape to another.

FACILITIES. Gas, supplies, restaurants, and motels are available in Morongo Valley and Yucca Valley. (And also, of course, in Banning and Twentynine Palms.)

Camping. See the JTNM "Facilities" section for developed campgrounds in JTNM. Open-desert camping is allowed on Bureau of Land Management (BLM) lands in this area. Call the BLM's Barstow Way Station (619-256-3591) for info on the best places to try.

Whitewater Canyon–
Pacific Crest Trail Hike

Class 2/elev. 2100–3100 ft/USGS topos *Whitewater, Palm Springs*/1–10 mi RT/
cross-country, trail

TO GET THERE. The Whitewater Canyon Rd exit off I-10 is about 40
mi east of San Bernardino. Go north here on the canyon road for a little
over 4 mi to a parking area just before the road crosses the river.

ABOUT THE HIKE. The Whitewater River Valley contains part of the
Pacific Crest Trail (PCT), which stretches from the Mexican border
to the Canadian border. South of the valley the PCT crosses the San
Jacinto Mtns; north of the valley it crosses the San Bernardino Mtns.
The Whitewater portion of the PCT is still under construction, as you
will notice while walking up the valley. (Look for the trail on the east
slope of the valley.) Just a few miles north of here, the PCT climbs out
of the Whitewater drainage and continues on up Mission Creek into
the San Bernardino National Forest. Once in the national forest, hikers
are on one of the completed portions of the trail. It won't be long before
the Whitewater–Mission Creek part of the trail is also completed; right
now (mid-1987), Sierra Club volunteers are working with the Bureau
of Land Management to finish the last few miles. In the meantime, PCT
hikers are having to exercise a few of their route-finding skills in using
the temporary route to get out of the river valley, over to the Mission
Creek drainage, and then up to the completed part of the trail in the
national forest. There are some signs, though.

How far you want to hike up the river valley is, of course, up to
you. If you stay in the valley, the hiking is almost level, rising only
about 400 ft in 4 mi—though you do have to clamber over quite a few
rocks in some places. Some distance from the starting point, you'll come
to a road on the west side of the valley; you can walk this "trail" for
a considerable distance up the valley. If you're an experienced hiker and
would like to try following the PCT out of the valley and up into the
Mission Creek drainage, be prepared for an elevation gain of another
1000 ft—which will get you over the saddle to the north of Red Dome,
across the west fork of Mission Creek, and up to the north fork of same.
Let your map, your feet, and your skills be your guide if you attempt
this.

Here, in the Whitewater River Valley, you are on the western edge
of the California desert and nearly at the interface of the Mojave and
the Colorado portions of the California desert, in addition to being close
to a desert-mountain transition. As you walk up the valley, see if you
can find plants characteristic of both desert regions. If you climb out
of the valley to higher elevations, look for plants commonly found in
our southern California mountains. When do they start to appear? Also
notice how the river has carved out the valley and how the valley

changes as you travel from the river's outfall toward its headwaters. As you return to your starting point, take a slightly different route than you did going up; it's pretty difficult to get lost in a river valley.

Big Morongo Wildlife Reserve

TO GET THERE. From the intersection of I-10 and CA 62, 15.5 mi east of Banning, go north on CA 62 for about 9.5 mi to a sign for Covington Park. Turn east at the sign and go a short distance to the road leading north into the reserve parking area.

GETTING YOUR BEARINGS. Bring along a good Riverside County map. Hikers may want the USGS topo *Morongo Valley*.

ABOUT THE RESERVE. The part of Big Morongo Canyon that is included in this 3900-acre reserve contains several springs and one of the few year-round creeks in the California desert. The creek's headwaters are in the mountains northwest of Morongo Valley, but it is primarily here, where the water is forced up by nonporous rock layers, that it comes to the surface. On either side of the reserve, the water flows underground through layers of sand (much like the Mojave River does, farther north). This relative abundance of water has produced a lush riparian area of great beauty, where many desert animals thrive. Bighorn sheep, for example, sometimes come down into the canyon to drink. The reserve is particularly popular with birdwatchers, because a number of unusual — even rare — bird species (for example, the vermilion flycatcher) stop here to rest during the fall and spring migrations.

Any area in the California desert having a year-round water supply usually has a long human history, and Big Morongo is no exception. For thousands of years before the settlers of historic times arrived, the hunting and gathering peoples who lived in the California desert used the canyon as a stopping place in their seasonal journeys. However, when settlers came to this part of the desert in the mid-1800s, the native Americans were forced off the land and into reservations. From then until 1968, the canyon became the property of homesteaders and ranchers.

The present management history of the canyon began in 1968, when 80 acres of this valuable desert riparian area were sold (and partly given) to the Nature Conservancy. Shortly thereafter, San Bernardino County acquired another 160 acres of land, and the Big Morongo Wildlife Reserve became a reality. Finally, in 1982, the Bureau of Land Management designated another 3600 acres of land around the reserve as an area of critical environmental concern. All of which means that the reserve we all enjoy so much today, like so many other protected special areas, didn't just happen all by itself. Instead, it is the result of years of hard work, planning, and working together by many people.

The reserve has several trails, a natural history display at the main trailhead, and even a resident Nature Conservancy caretaker. If you enjoy walking, there's a very pleasant 6-mi hike down Morongo Canyon to the vicinity of Mission Lakes Country Club. It's easy to arrange a car shuttle back to the reserve from there; all you have to do is leave a car there on your way to the reserve so you can drive back afterward (park on Indian Ave where it crosses the Colorado River aqueduct a couple of miles north of the country club entrance). If you're really energetic, you can hike there and back, of course.

Check the natural history display for trail information, recent wildlife sightings, and suggestions for where to see what. Early morning and late afternoon are the best times for birding, but you can usually sight some interesting creatures even at midday. Take your time here — there is much to see. Also, Covington Park is right next door, so to speak, and is a fine place for picnicking. There are restrooms and water near the reserve parking area. Camping is not allowed.

Yucca Valley–Baldwin Lake 4WD Tour

TO GET THERE. Take CA 62 north and east from its intersection with I-10 east of Banning for 20 mi to the town of Yucca Valley. Turn north here on the old Pioneer Pass Rd (also signed for Pioneertown).

GETTING YOUR BEARINGS. Bring along a good San Bernardino County map. Explorers may want the USGS topos *Morongo Valley, Old Woman Springs,* and *Lucerne Valley.*

ABOUT THE TOUR. This drive will take you from the high-desert country of the Mojave near Yucca Valley (about 2500 ft); up several scenic rocky canyons; past a number of interesting side roads leading to old mining operations, springs, and an observatory; onto what was once the Rose Mine Rd in the foothills of the San Bernardino Mtns; and finally to cool, pine-fringed Baldwin Lake (6725 ft). Total distance is about 25 mi.

Pioneertown Daze? About 3.8 mi up the paved road leading out of Yucca Valley is what looks like a ghost town — but isn't. No pioneers ever lived here, in what some failed entrepreneur hoped would become a filming site for westerns! Pioneertown was constructed in about 1947, when western moviemaking was at its height. A fire in the 1960s destroyed part of the "town," but there are still a number of "old" buildings standing — a saloon, restaurant, store, etc. — that visitors can stop to explore. Today, the area around Pioneertown has been built up into a tiny, but thriving, community of about 550 people — and not a ghost among them.

Burns Canyon–4WD Country. About 3 mi northwest of Pioneertown, the paved road turns west at almost a ninety-degree angle — and then turns to dirt. Depending on how the weather has been during the past winter or two, this road can be either pretty good or pretty bad. The going doesn't get really steep for about another 6 mi, though, so now is the time to enjoy the scenery. When you check your San Bernardino County map, you'll see that there is a side road leading north to the Farrington Observatory at about 6 mi from where the road became dirt; just a little beyond that road is another leading to Mound Spring. If you're in the mood to explore, try these. (Mound Spring has some huge Joshua trees.)

Now comes the steep, winding part of the road—with a mountain on one side and deep Rattlesnake Canyon on the other. After about 4 mi of twists and turns, you'll top a rise and be able to see the remains of various old mining operations. The largest of these was the Rose Mine; look for the piles of ore debris on the north side of the road (which is sometimes still called the Rose Mine Rd).

On to Baldwin Lake or Pines to Palms Highway and Tour's End. From the Rose Mine area to CA 18 at Baldwin Lake is a little over 8 scenic mi. There are several side roads along the way you might want to explore. One of them, which goes off southwest just beyond the mine, leads across an attractive meadow area called Broom Flat to CA 38, the Pines to Palms Highway, in a bit more than 5 mi. The elevation is about 8000 ft when you reach the highway just north of Onyx Peak.

If you stay on the Rose Mine Rd, take the south fork of the road as you near CA 18; near where this fork comes into the highway, the Pacific Crest Trail crosses CA 18 (look for the trail post). Take time to pull into the parking area and walk north on the trail to Mojave View. From here, on a good day, you can see all the way to both the southern Sierra and to the mountains in Nevada. (And don't forget your camera!)

Lucerne Valley–Ludlow

ABOUT THE AREA. This part of the Mojave Desert, tucked in between CA 247 to the south, I-40 to the north, and the off-limits Twentynine Palms Marine Corps Training Center to the east, is crisscrossed with 4WD roads. There is nary a paved road to be seen for many miles north of the little town of Lucerne Valley. Unfortunately for those folks who go to the desert to enjoy the peace and quiet, however, there is a very large open area (Johnson Valley) for ORVs that stretches south from the Rodman Mtns almost down to CA 247 and leans right up against the marine corps base. Despite this seemingly great drawback, though, there are still some nearly unfrequented places to be explored here.

You can get some idea of what's out there if you try the 4WD tour to the Rodman Mtns petroglyphs described below. For ideas on how to explore, say, the Newberry Mtns, check with the Bureau of Land Management (BLM) Barstow Way Station (831 Barstow Rd, 619-256-3591). In addition to the outback roads, there are places just off the freeway that are well worth a visit—or a scramble. For example, there's the unique Solar One visitor center, where you can see the clean-energy world of tomorrow come to life. And a stop at Pisgah Crater, a recently active volcano, is a fine leg-stretcher. Once you've sampled these, however, the real dilemma presents itself—i.e., which area do you visit next? Will it be Amboy–Desert Center, Barstow–Baker South, Calico, Rainbow Basin, Joshua Tree National Monument, or . . . ?

FACILITIES. Gas, supplies, restaurants, and motels are available in Lucerne Valley to a limited extent and plentiful in Barstow.

Camping. For information on the nearest developed campgrounds, see the "Facilities" sections for the following areas: Death Valley and East, the Western Mojave, and the Historic Eastern Mojave.

Except on private property, open-desert camping is allowed throughout the area, much of which is managed by the BLM.

Rodman Mountains 4WD Tour

TO GET THERE. Take CA 18 or CA 247 to Lucerne Valley, a town about 22 mi east of Victorville and 33 mi south of Barstow. Approximately 5 mi east of the intersection of CA 18 and CA 247 in Lucerne Valley, the latter highway crosses Camp Rock Rd; go north here.

GETTING YOUR BEARINGS. Bring along a good San Bernardino County map. The USGS topos *Ord Mtns* and *Rodman Mtns* will also be helpful in figuring out the lay of the land as you go along.

ABOUT THE TOUR. Don't be too surprised if you make a couple of unexpected side trips while on this tour—there are a lot of dirt roads out where you're going. If all goes well, the tour will take you northeast out Camp Rock Rd to a viewpoint near Pipkin Cinder Cone, down to a petroglyph area at the edge of the Rodman Mtns, then through ruggedly beautiful Box Canyon, and finally up to I-40 at the Fort Cady exit. The roads are generally good dirt and passable by ordinary vehicles, but because there are a few places that can be pretty rough if winter storms have been unusually heavy, the tour is recommended only for 4WD vehicles. There are plenty of opportunities for open-desert camping along the way. Total distance is about 42 mi.

On the Way to Pipkin Cinder Cone. About 4 mi north on Camp Rock Rd, you'll come to a Y with Harrod Rd; go northeast here. After another 9.8 mi, Camp Rock crosses a powerline road; 4.3 mi beyond the powerline road, at a crossroads, go east (right). (Follow the "Cinder Pit" sign; Camp Rock Rd goes left to Daggett here.) Keep to the main road, bearing north toward the Cinder Pit at another sign about 2.2 mi from the last one. After another 3.5 mi, pull off at a viewpoint.

From here, at about 5000 ft, you can see north not only to Pipkin Cinder Cone and the extensive mining operation going on there, but also to some extensive lava flows on the slopes of the Rodman Mtns. Pipkin Cinder Cone, along with Amboy and Pisgah craters, is what's left of a volcano that last erupted quite recently, geologically speaking— perhaps only 3000–4000 years ago. After you've visited Pisgah and another cone or two, you'll see that cinder cone mining is very popular in the California desert; almost every one is being eaten away by a company eager to sell the volcanic fragments for decorative or construction purposes. What do you think about this practice? Is it necessary? Unnecessary? Does it improve the desert or degrade it? You be the judge.

The Rodman Petroglyphs. To reach the petroglyphs, continue on from the viewpoint, bearing east away from the cinder cone at a Y in about 1 mi. After another mile, you'll pass a road going north that may have a "Wilderness Study Area" sign (if vandals haven't removed it). Just beyond this road, bear southeast (right) at a Y. In another 0.5 mi, pass a road coming in from the north (left) and start down into a wash (if you look left along here, you may see a small petroglyph on the rocks close by). In another 0.25 mi, bear left at a crossroad (there's a fence to the left) and come upon a sandy dip. Check out the dip before venturing across; if you aren't sure you can make it, just park and walk from here—the petroglyphs are only 0.25 mi away.

The Bureau of Land Management has fenced the main petroglyph displays to discourage vandalism. Walk to the right up the dry creek to see others. For more information on petroglyphs, see the Index.

Through Box Canyon to Tour's End. Return to the crossroad on the other side of the sandy dip and bear southeast—not on the road going sharp right, but on the one going right at about a forty-five degree angle. (Notice that chollas, yuccas, barrel cacti, and creosote bushes are mingled here.) After about 2.8 mi, the road will T into a powerline road; go northeast (left) on the powerline road (it's sandy here, but passable). Look for Box Canyon Rd in another 0.8 mi; go north on it (it, too, is somewhat sandy at this point). After about 4 mi the canyon walls begin to close in; look for smoke trees, pigmy cedars, and—in spring—many different kinds of wildflowers.

About 6 mi from where you turned onto Box Canyon Rd, you'll come out of the canyon and have a good view of the mountains ahead (and the freeway below). Pull off and check your maps—what are you seeing? At 9 mi from the beginning of Box Canyon Rd, go west at a T for 0.25 mi, then north at another T for 2 mi, then west again for 3.1 mi to Fort Cady Rd. Go north on Fort Cady for 1.9 mi to I-40. Whew!

Solar One Visitor Center

TO GET THERE. From the intersection of I-15 and I-40 in Barstow, take I-40 east about 7 mi to the Daggett exit. Get on the frontage road on the north side of I-40 and continue east about 2.5 mi to Solar One visitor center (follow the signs), which is a bit east of the plant.

GETTING YOUR BEARINGS. A good San Bernardino County map is helpful.

ABOUT THE VISITOR CENTER. Although Solar One isn't a scenic wonder of the California desert, it's a good illustration of one way the desert will probably be used in the future. Solar One is a 10-megawatt solar thermal pilot plant operated by the U.S. Department of Energy, Southern California Edison, Los Angeles Department of Water and Power, and the California Energy Commission. Here, you can learn something about the different methods that may one day be used on a large scale to transform the sun's energy into the energy we use every day. At the visitor center there are several interesting exhibits and talking displays, as well as movies, free brochures, and models of solar energy projects. And, of course, there is the chance to see the nation's first experimental solar "power tower"! Restrooms and picnic facilities are available.

Pisgah Crater

TO GET THERE. Go 34.5 mi east on I-40 from its intersection with I-15 in Barstow. Take the Hector/Pisgah exit to the frontage road on the south side of I-40. Drive east on the frontage road for about 4 mi to Pisgah Rd (dirt), then turn south and go as far as you can toward the crater. If the crater is being mined, there will be a locked gate somewhere along the road. You can pull off and park near it.

GETTING YOUR BEARINGS. You'll need a good San Bernardino County map.

ABOUT THE CRATER. This part of the California desert—and Pisgah Crater—has been volcanically active within the last few thousand years. Which means that this 250-ft volcano and the lava flows surrounding it are just youngsters, geologically speaking. Pisgah, along with the nearby Amboy and Pipkin craters, is a cinder cone. Small, steep-sided cones like these are created by what are called central eruptions—as opposed to fissure eruptions. In central eruptions, as you might guess, lava, gas, ash, and cinders are pushed up through holes in the earth's crust that are pipelike, rather than through cracks, as are the fissure eruptions common to volcanoes in Hawaii.

Like many other volcanic cones in the Mojave, Pisgah has been extensively mined for its cinders, which are used for decorative purposes and for road building and other types of construction projects. (The cinders that make up the cone are small pieces of very porous volcanic rock.) As mentioned above, there may be a locked gate on the road up to the crater. However, you can park off the road near the gate and then walk out over the lava flows and even up to the rim of the crater if you wish. Notice the extensive flows stretching south from the crater for several miles. From the rim you can see Lavic Dry Lake, a low spot just beyond the south end of the lava flow. If you feel like exploring the lava fields, don't go very far south, as the boundary of the Twentynine Palms Marine Corps Training Center is only about a mile away from the crater. Also take care to stay as far away as possible from all mining activities.

Amboy–Desert Center

ABOUT THE AREA. When you travel from Amboy to Desert Center, you go from the Mojave region of the California desert to the Colorado region. Along the way you can visit another young volcano, Amboy Crater, and the extensive lava fields surrounding it. Going south from Amboy, on your way to a scenic hike up Sheephole Mtn, you'll cross Bristol Dry Lake and the extensive chloride works, where once stood a large freshwater lake surrounded by verdant grasslands. Even if you decide not to saunter up the mountain, you'll surely take a break at Sheephole Summit (2368 ft), where the view north to some of the Mojave's striking mountain ranges can't be passed up. South of Sheephole Summit, the Pinto Mtns and Joshua Tree National Monument (JTNM) come into view. However, mining buffs won't want to just view this part of the area—instead, they'll doubtless plunge right into a tour that will take them in search of Old Dale, New Dale, and other long-deserted mining points beyond, right down into JTNM's Pinto Basin, site of yet another ancient lake. The truly hardy, though, may not be in the mood for touring, but will head for a scramble up an eerily named peak on the east side of JTNM—Spectre Mtn.

And, of course, as in most parts of the California desert, there'll be plenty of places to explore other than those suggested here. What about those sand dunes over there? The flower-filled wash across the road? That little volcanic plug just over the hill? But no matter what parts of this area you choose to become better acquainted with, in spring don't fail to either begin or wind up your visit with a stop at the Lily Preserve, just north of Desert Center.

FACILITIES. Gas, supplies, restaurants, and motels are available in Twentynine Palms. Amboy has gas, a post office, a motel, and Roy's Cafe, a breath out of the 1950s and "Route 66." Desert Center has gas, limited supplies, and a cafe.

Camping. For developed campgrounds, see the JTNM "Facilities" section. Open-desert camping is allowed on Bureau of Land Management lands throughout this area.

Amboy Crater

TO GET THERE. Go east on I-40 from Barstow for 52 mi to the Ludlow exit. Get on the National Trails Highway (old Hwy 66) and travel southeast about 28 mi to this highway's intersection with Amboy Rd.

Take Amboy Rd south and begin looking for a dirt road leading west toward the crater, which is only a little over 2 mi away. Park here. To approach the crater from the north, pull off on a spur located next to the first bridge west of Amboy Rd on National Trails Hwy. Park here and walk south to the crater.

GETTING YOUR BEARINGS. You'll need a good San Bernardino County map.

ABOUT THE CRATER. Amboy Crater, like Pisgah Crater, is a young volcano that was created by what are called central eruptions, as opposed to fissure eruptions. The crater and its vicinity are a BLM wilderness study area; so although there is a road of sorts to the crater, vehicles are not allowed. The roads to the cinder cone cross an extensive lava field, but still make good footpaths. No matter which way you approach the crater, you may get sidetracked onto a road or two that doesn't lead up close to it, but just keep trying—you can't really get lost, as the highway and the crater are in view all the time. Once you get near the crater, look for the trail that leads up to the rim. It's a short hike up to the top (the crater's rim is only about 250 ft higher than its base), where you can look down into the volcano's maw and also get a good view of the surrounding countryside. It's not often one gets to do this. Don't forget to take your map (for identifying mountain ranges), binoculars, and camera with you on this short walk. If you're in a hiking mood, though, take care not to stray too far west—the off-limits Twentynine Palms Marine Corps Training Center boundary is only about 1.5 mi west of Amboy Crater.

Sheephole Mountain Hike
Class 2/elev. 4613 ft/USGS topo *Dale Lake*/6 mi RT/cross-country

TO GET THERE. In Twentynine Palms, take Amboy Rd east, then north, about 23 mi to Sheephole Summit. You can't miss the summit— there is a microwave relay station there, and a large pull-out with adequate parking.

ABOUT THE HIKE. The Sheephole Mtns are located between the towns of Twentynine Palms and Amboy, just north of the east end of Joshua Tree National Monument. The range is sparsely vegetated, but its washes support a nice show of wildflowers after a season of good rainfall. Many small desert mountain ranges can be seen from the summit of Sheephole Mtn; the sharp spires of the Coxcombs to the southeast are especially interesting. To the north you can see Bristol Dry Lake. Those ponds of intensely blue water are used by the National Chloride Flaking Company as part of their processing operations.

Will the Real Summit Please Stand Up! Hike southeast from the microwave station, following an old mining road into a canyon about 0.25 mi away. Swing into the canyon and follow it past the meager remains of activity from the old Sheephole Mine. Climb up the mostly sandy wash for about 1.5 mi to the first prominent canyon to the northeast. Turn into this canyon and proceed up it, staying to the east side until you reach the ridgeline at about 3700 ft. Climb east about 300 yds across the head of another canyon to the main ridgeline at about 4000 ft. Ignore the peak with the fine rock cairn some distance away to the northwest. Instead, continue east along the ridge to the true summit, bypassing a false summit guarding Sheephole Mtn.

Dale Mining District 4WD Tour

TO GET THERE. From the center of Twentynine Palms, at the intersection of Utah Trail and CA 62, take CA 62 east about 14 mi to Gold Crown Rd. Turn south here.

GETTING YOUR BEARINGS. Bring along a good Riverside County map. Explorers may want the USGS topos *Valley Mtn, Dale Lake,* and *Pinto Basin.*

ABOUT THE TOUR. This trip up Gold Crown Rd (dirt) passes near the sites of several deserted mining communities—Old Dale, Dale number two, and New Dale (Dale number three)—and then into Joshua Tree National Monument (JTNM). Here, at a good viewpoint, the road becomes Old Dale Rd (still dirt) and continues south into Pinto Basin, where it connects with the Pinto Basin Rd about 7 mi north of Cottonwood visitor center and campground (which, in turn, is only about 6 mi north of I-10). Total distance from CA 62 to Pinto Basin Rd is about 25 mi.

If you like looking around old mining operations, you'll find plenty to entertain you on this tour—but do not attempt it in anything but a 4WD vehicle! As you wind your way through the Dale District, you'll come across many side roads—some of which are passable and some of which are not, even for 4WDs with high clearance. When in doubt, walk. And when you're walking, keep a sharp eye out for old, uncovered mine shafts. If you do find any shafts, stay clear of them; your first fall could be your last. Unfortunately, treasure hunters have carried off just about everything that is portable from the various now-silent sites, but there are still some heavy items left for mining buffs to examine.

The Dale District. Mining in what is now the JTNM area began in the 1870s, near Twentynine Palms. About the time these operations hit a slump in the early 1880s, placer gold was discovered east of them—near what became the town of Virginia Dale (later, Old Dale), which quickly acquired a population of one thousand! The center of the old townsite is approximately on the spot where CA 62 and Gold Crown Rd intersect. A little later, in 1885, after Dale number one's mining business had slowed down, Dale number two grew up around a mine also called Virginia Dale, about 4 mi or so south of the original town. The mine area is just a short walk from Gold Crown Rd.

A couple of miles farther south on Gold Crown Rd from the road to Dale number two is another track leading to what was once the Supply Mine. The strike made here in the early 1900s was so good that the folks from the lagging Dale number two area decided to move the town to a location more convenient to the new mine. And so Dale number three — New Dale — sprang up about a mile south of the mine. Check your topo to locate its site and road. According to local historians, this mine kept producing until about 1917, bringing in a total of about $1 million in gold. (If you're interested in learning more about the area's mining history, the visitor centers in JTNM have several booklets and brochures on the subject — including descriptions of how the ores were extracted.)

On to Pinto Basin and Tour's End. As Gold Crown Rd continues on south past the New Dale turnoff, there will be a number of other tracks leading off in various directions to yet other mine sites. After about 8.5 mi, the road passes through a low point in the Pinto Mtns and approaches the JTNM boundary. Just about at the boundary, there's a wonderful view south over Pinto Basin. Take time to pull off here and check your maps; see if you can identify the features spread out before you. Pinto Basin, like many such low points in the California desert, once contained a lake and was fringed with verdant grasslands. As little as 10,000 years ago, large mammals grazed here and early people lived by the lake's edge. Later, the lake cut its way out of the basin, leaving a river to flow through it. As the climate became increasingly arid, the river disappeared. Today, water is found only at a few oases in JTNM — all of which are open to visitors.

The drive from the viewpoint down Old Dale Rd to the paved Pinto Basin Rd in JTNM is not long or difficult. About 3 mi south of the boundary you'll cross Pinto Wash in the vicinity of several old wells. This is a good place to make another stop — this time for a walk up a desert wash. What plant species do you see here? Birds? Take time to enjoy the solitude of this little-visited area of the monument. From the wash area it is about 10 mi to the paved road.

Spectre Mountain Scramble
Class 2–3/elev. 4400 ft/USGS topo *Cadiz Valley*/6 mi RT/cross-country

TO GET THERE. *Access 1 (Northern):* From Twentynine Palms, take CA 62 east about 40 mi to a dirt road about 0.2 mi west of county highway marker SB 73. This is also about 10 mi west of the intersection of CA 177 and CA 62. (This access point gets you higher up and closer to the peak than Access 2.) Go south on this road for about 3.5 mi to a concrete slab and faint signs of old mining activity. Park here.

Access 2 (Eastern): From Twentynine Palms, go east on CA 62 to a dirt road 7 mi west of CA 62's intersection with CA 177. Drive south on this road, turning southwest at about 1.9 mi or where the road becomes too sandy to drive.

ABOUT THE SCRAMBLE. On your topo, Spectre Mtn is that unnamed high point in the Coxcomb Mtns. It lies just inside Riverside County and just inside the northeast corner of Joshua Tree National Monument, 0.5 mi southwest of benchmark Agua (4416 ft).

Spectre from the North. From the parking area by the concrete slab, walk up the large wash to the east. Cross the saddle ahead and descend the other side for about 300 ft, to the point where a canyon comes down from the southwest. Ascend this canyon, pass through two small bowls, and enter the third. Spectre Peak is in view nearby, south and slightly to the east. Climb the easy rocks to the summit.

Spectre from the East. Walk up the canyon before you. There are some low third-class rocks in this canyon before it ends at an intersection with a larger, shallow canyon. Turn northwest here and go about 0.75 mi to a large gulch (sometimes ducked) that enters from the west. Proceed up this wash for 0.5 mi past the south side of benchmark Agua, and you'll enter the third and final bowl mentioned in the northern route. Ascend the summit as described for that route.

Desert Lily Preserve

TO GET THERE. From the intersection of I-10 and CA 177 at Desert Center (23 mi east of the Cottonwood Spring Rd exit to Joshua Tree National Monument), go north about 8.5 mi. The signed and fenced area of the Desert Lily Preserve is on the east side of the road. There are plenty of wide pull-offs nearby. Look for the entrance near the highway. (There are no roads into the preserve; only foot traffic is allowed.)

GETTING YOUR BEARINGS. You'll need a good Riverside County map.

ABOUT THE PRESERVE. In general, the best time to visit the Desert Lily Preserve is February-April. It's hard to predict when the finest displays will be, as this depends on the previous months' weather patterns. Some years, when conditions haven't been to the plant's liking, there are very few blooms—in other years, the dunes and sandy areas of the California desert's southern region may be thickly dotted with the lily. When the lilies are blooming, you'll notice that the whole area surrounding the preserve has just about as many flowers per square meter as does the preserve.

These plants, with their large, white blossoms, erect stalks, and ruffly, straplike leaves, are easy to identify. The stalk sometimes reaches a height of over 3 ft, and the striking flowers have a lovely fragrance. Like many members of the lily family, the bulbs of the desert lily—which are usually found 1–2 ft below the surface of the sand—have a garlic/onion flavor and are edible. (Do not, however, sample them!)

14

The Southeastern Mojave

Palen Mountains–Colorado River

ABOUT THE AREA. Here in the southeasternmost corner of the California desert's Mojave region there is a lot of wide-open, nearly unused space that stretches from the Palen Mtns to the Colorado River. (Needless to say, this southerly part of the California desert is best visited in spring, fall, or winter. Summers are usually pretty scorching!) The mountain ranges in this area are bronzed and rugged, with broad plains sweeping between them. The Rice Valley sand dunes bound the area's northeast side, and the Palen Dunes the southwest side. But despite all the granite and sand, this is where you can find what is perhaps the largest and most luxuriant desert ironwood forest in the world.

The place to look for this unusual forest is the valley between the Palen and the McCoy mountains, which is filled with a network of intricately dissected washes—and groves of desert ironwoods, along with mesquite, palo verde, and smoke trees. All these trees are members of the bean (legume) family and favor sandy washes with good drainage from nearby mountains, warm winters, and lots of sun—which is why they are found in such great abundance here, in this protected valley on the edge of the California desert's Colorado region.

The desert ironwood was a particularly useful sort of tree in prehistoric times. For example, its hard and heavy core—from whence comes its name—was used by the native peoples of the area for tools and weapons (its seeds were a staple food item, too). Today, the wood is so much prized by woodworkers that ironwood poaching in the Bureau of Land Management's (BLM) wilderness study areas is a serious problem. Surprisingly, this gnarly, rough-barked tree bursts into clouds of lovely purple and white blooms in late spring and early summer.

Another of the more unusual attractions in this part of the Mojave—some giant Indian ground figures—can be found along the Colorado

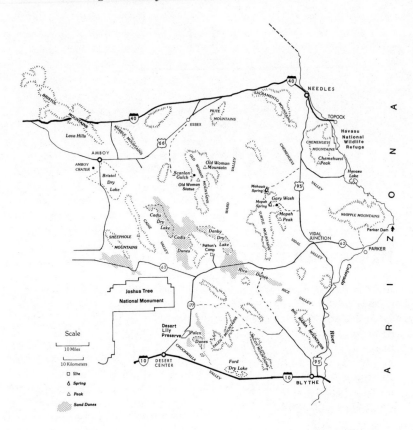

River, north of Blythe. These enormous patterns were "carved" in the desert floor by moving the surface layer of rocks and gravel to expose the lighter, sandy layer beneath. One of the figures is over 160 ft tall! There are several other examples of this kind of rock art up along the Colorado between Ripley and Fort Mojave.

To really get a good feel for the contrasts in this far corner of the Mojave, you might try a loop tour that begins and ends in Blythe, taking you up the Colorado River and down through the Rice Valley. On this route, you'll go by the ground figures and the roadhead to the Palen-McCoy Valley. (Of course, the loop can be done in reverse order, too.) The loop is not described below; you can easily do it with the aid of a Riverside County map.

FACILITIES. Gas, supplies, restaurants, and motels are available in Blythe; there are gas and water at Vidal Junction.

Camping. There are two developed Riverside County parks in the Blythe area. For info on McIntyre Park, see the Blythe-Winterhaven

"Facilities" section in Chapter 16. To find Mayflower Park, go north on US 95 from I-10 at Blythe about 3 mi; at this point, go east on Sixth Ave, then north on Colorado River Rd. Campsites are under large trees on the river; restrooms and water are in the camp area.

Open-desert camping is allowed on BLM lands throughout this area. The Palen-McCoy Valley has many excellent sites.

Palen-McCoy Valley

TO GET THERE. From I-10 in Blythe, take the Lovekin Blvd exit north; go about 6 mi to Midland Rd and continue northwest for 13 mi (about 24 mi from I-10) to the Inca turnoff.

Note: The roads in the valley vary greatly in quality from year to year; for real exploring, you need a 4WD vehicle—although sometimes you can drive an ordinary vehicle to all the points mentioned below. However, even when the roads in the valley are bad, the road to the edge of the valley is usually good to a point about 7.5 mi west of Inca—and from there the valley is easily accessible on foot.

GETTING YOUR BEARINGS. Bring along a good Riverside County map. If you plan on exploring some of the dirt roads in the valley, the USGS topos *Midland, McCoy Spring,* and *Palen Mtns* are useful. (This valley between the Palen and McCoy mountains is not named on any map, but both mountain ranges are.)

ABOUT THE VALLEY. This valley, located between the Palen and McCoy mountains, carries a closely grouped, braided array of washes heavily forested with desert ironwood and palo verde trees. BLM studies done between 1976 and 1980 identified this area as an outstanding example of desert ironwood forest worthy of preservation as wilderness. This lovely forested part of the California desert provides exceptional habitat for desert wildlife, including rabbits, mice, kangaroo rats, coyotes, kit foxes, and many birds. For an area accessible by ordinary vehicles, it offers a great many more opportunities than most for nature study, easy hiking and backpacking, and car camping away from ORVs. Because the entry road is well traveled and the washes are easy walking, in this area you have an excellent opportunity to take the advice of the late Edmund Jaeger, dean of California desert naturalists, to "enter into a profitable intimacy with nature. Go alone on your walks if you can, but if you must take a companion, choose one who will appreciate with you the desert's great silence."

From Midland Road to the Valley. The good dirt road to Inca from Midland Rd is marked by a large white rock; go west here. After about 1.4 mi, at Inca, the road crosses the Atchison, Topeka, & Santa Fe Railroad tracks and, as Arlington Mine Rd, is paved for the next 5 mi or so. Look for desert pavement on either side of the road along here. (The Inca operation, by the way, bulldozes desert pavement to sell for decorative purposes.)

At about 5 mi from the railroad crossing, the Superior Gypsum Rd will come in from the north. Notice the long scrapes, like fingers, on the slopes of the Little Maria Mtns to the north where desert rock has been harvested. From this point on, you'll see roads going off up washes from time to time; most of the washes offer a number of good camp spots.

Into the Ironwood Forest. Beyond the mine road about 3 mi, bear northwest at a Y; just south from here is the old Arlington Mine. In about another 1.1 mi the road enters the ironwood forest; there's a track into a particularly nice wash for camping about 0.2 mi ahead of this point (go north into it for a short distance). Another 0.2 mi west past the wash road is another Y; the arm going west will take you across the forested valley to the foothills of the Palen Mtns. The south arm will take you along the western edge of the McCoy Mtns for a couple of miles.

If you're feeling energetic, take the south arm and pick a spot along it to climb on foot up to a ridge in the McCoys. From there you can get good photos of the valley's intricate structure of washes and the vastness of its ironwood forest. Palen Mtn, across the valley to the west, is thought by many a desert buff to be the most colorful peak in the California desert.

The Far Side. The drive west across the valley to the foot of the Palen Mtns (using the other arm of the Y) may take you a while because there is so much to see. Don't rush across; take your time; stop and explore some washes. What plants other than desert ironwood and palo verde can you identify? (In spring the ironwoods are a mass of purple blossoms — which the green-barked palo verde tries to outdo by flaunting its own clusters of butter yellow blooms.) Look overhead for raptors (hawks and other birds of prey). Keep an eye out for lizards and small birds.

About 2.4 mi from the Y, there'll be a road coming in from the southwest. See what's up it or continue on toward the Palens, where the road goes up, up, up to an old copper mine. Don't try driving up the road to the mine! Stop and park where there's a good place to turn around, then explore on foot. This is a good place to take photos of the surrounding mountains.

There are, of course, many other possibilities for exploring the valley. Check your topos and county map for ideas. For example, you could take the road leading to Palen Pass, stop at the foot, and climb up to a ridge on the western side of the valley, as you did on the east. Then there are the endlessly interesting washes — each one is different (don't forget your binoculars and field guides). Or how about a weekend car camp, on which you do nothing in particular but enjoy the solitude and catch up on your cloud watching? And so on. As you can tell, this valley is one of the many places in the California desert you'll want to come to again and again.

Giant Indian Ground Figures (Intaglios)

TO GET THERE. From Blythe, take CA 95 north for about 15.5 mi to a well-signed road leading about 0.5 mi west to the figures.

GETTING YOUR BEARINGS. Bring along a good Riverside County map.

ABOUT THE INTAGLIOS. Four kinds of rock art are found in the California desert: petroglyphs, pictographs, intaglios (also called geoglyphs or rock alignments), and ground paintings. The prehistoric rock figures here, on some Colorado River terraces near Blythe, were made by pushing the dark, top layer of rocks and gravel away, leaving the lighter layers of sand underneath clearly visible. The shape of the figures isn't easily seen from ground level, but some careful walking around will enable you to recognize what appear to be a human figure, a spiral design, and a four-legged animal. The largest figure, the anthropomorphic one, is over 160 ft long! It is from the air, of course, that the figures are seen to their best advantage. (Imagine how the Indians who built these viewed them.)

Aside from several sites located throughout southern California, there are only a few places in the world where large ground figures similar to these are found. Archaeologists are not sure whether such figures were intended as art objects or if they served ritualistic purposes. These, near Blythe, are only one of several sets found along the Colorado River (on both the California and Arizona sides) between Ripley and Fort Mojave. For more information on intaglios, check with the Bureau of Land Management office in Needles at 641 Front St, Suite B, CA 92363 (619-326-3896), and see the "Recommended Reading" appendix.

Needles–Colorado River South

ABOUT THE AREA. The Colorado River dominates this far eastern area of the California desert's Mojave region. Whether you're standing on a summit in the Chemehuevi or the Whipple mountains or exploring Havasu National Wildlife Refuge, one of the first things you are likely to see is the river.

If you decide to hike to the summit of Chemehuevi Mtn, you'll find that the peak has plenty of company. No less than seventeen other peaks make up the geologic menu of the Chemehuevis. The Whipples, to the south, contain some of the California desert's most memorable landscapes. Here you'll find dramatic spires and pinnacles, washes leading up canyons of red-striped rock, and rugged, russet mountains framed against a bright blue sky. Also, as in the surrounding areas, there are plant species characteristic of both the Colorado and the Mojave desert regions. And if you've always thought that saguaros didn't grow in California, think again—as you examine the mountains' eastern slopes. If you don't bring a camera to the Whipples, you'll wish you had!

If peak scrambles and hikes up colorful canyons aren't on your pre-ferred itinerary, there's still plenty to do—like exploring 44,746-acre Havasu National Wildlife Refuge. Topock Marsh, at the refuge's north end, is a haven for the magnificent Canada goose and many other kinds of waterfowl in winter and, for other species, an important stop along the Pacific Flyway's spring and fall migration routes. If you're not much of a walker, there are a number of places in the marsh area where you can observe birds without going too far from your vehicle. Walkers will find to their liking the several roads into the marsh where vehicle traffic is prohibited.

The Bill Williams River Delta section is at the refuge's south end. This area shelters the largest variety of wildlife and plant life in the refuge. You can drive a good gravel road almost the length of this sec-tion, stopping to explore on foot many of the interesting delta byways.

If water sports are something you enjoy, there'll be plenty to tempt you along the Colorado—canoeing, boating, swimming, etc. Inciden-tally, Topock Gorge, the middle section of the refuge, can only be visited by water. There isn't room to give any information on water-oriented activities here, but you'll be able to get it just about anywhere in the river's vicinity. See Havasu National Wildlife Refuge, below, for infor-mation on how to contact the refuge manager.

FACILITIES. Gas, supplies, restaurants, and motels are available in Needles and in Parker, just across the river from Earp. Gas and limited supplies can be found in Topock, Havasu Lake, and Earp.

Camping. For developed camping, try Moabi Regional Park (San Bernardino County). To find the campground, follow I-40 south from Needles; just before the freeway crosses the river, take the Park Moabi exit and follow the signs north to the park. The campground has hot showers, supplies, and even a laundry. To get to Havasu Landing Resort (Riverside County), go south on US 95 for about 20 mi from I-40 to Havasu Lake Rd. Take this road southeast for about 16 mi to the town of Havasu Lake. The resort is east of the road, near the river. Amenities include hot showers, groceries, restaurant, and gas. No camping is allowed in the refuge except at the concessions (private) in the Topock Marsh area and on the Arizona shoreline south of the entrance to Topock Gorge.

Open-desert camping is allowed on the Bureau of Land Management (BLM) lands west of the Colorado River. For suggestions, check with the BLM's Needles office at 641 Front St, Suite B, CA 92363, or call them at 619-326-3896.

Whipple Mountain Hike

Class 1/elev. 4131 ft/USGS topos *Whipple Mtn SW, Parker NW, Parker*/9 mi RT/cross-country

TO GET THERE. From Vidal Junction on US 95, take CA 62 east toward Earp, on the Colorado River. About 2.2 mi west of Earp and

Whipple Wash in the center of the Whipple Mountains, west of Parker Dam on the Colorado River. *Photo by Lyle Gaston.*

1.6 mi east of the road leading south to the town of Big River, go northwest on a graded dirt road for 1.5 mi, to an intersection. Continue straight on for 2.7 mi to the Colorado River Aqueduct; about 1 mi after crossing the aqueduct, the road leads into a moderately sandy wash. Proceed up the wash no farther than 2 mi before parking (beyond this point, wilderness values should be preserved).

ABOUT THE HIKE. To find the route, cross the low ridge to the west (on which the mine sits) and drop down into the wash beyond. Follow the wash about 2 mi to a fork in the canyon; take the left fork and climb a steep slope into the wash above. (If you stay in this wash when you come down from the peak, you'll come upon a very high, dry waterfall below. Backtrack to your point of descent into the wash and continue down to the right of the waterfall.) On the ascent, continue up the wash to an obvious saddle and around to the west toward the summit.

Whipple Mtn can also be climbed from Chambers Well to the southwest and from Whipple Well to the northwest.

Chemehuevi Peak Scramble
Class 2/elev. 3697 ft/USGS topo *Chemehuevi Peak*/5.5 mi RT/cross-country

TO GET THERE. Take US 95 south from Needles for about 23 mi or north from Vidal Junction for about 27 mi to a dirt powerline road leading southeast. The Havasu Lake Rd leading east to Havasu Lake lies just south of this road. Drive about 4 mi southeast on the powerline road and park.

ABOUT THE SCRAMBLE. The Chemehuevi Mtns lie south of Needles and overlook Lake Havasu, the Topock Gorge, and the Chemehuevi Valley. It is a rather barren limestone range calling for stout boots and clothing. As you hike toward the summit, there are distant vistas of the Whipples, the Mopah Range, the Turtles, and the Stepladders.

To reach the peak, hike northeast from the road across small washes and enter the big wash coming from the saddle northwest of Cheme-huevi Peak. Follow this wash all the way to the saddle, then turn right up some easy Class 2 rocks to the summit.

Havasu National Wildlife Refuge

TO GET THERE. *Topock Marsh Access:* Take I-40 east to Needles, then follow it south and east across the river to the Topock offramp. Exit here and drive north on the Oatman-Topock Rd (US 95).

Bill Williams River Delta Access: Take CA 62 east to Earp, then continue northeast along the river on the California side for 15.3 mi to Parker Dam. Cross the Colorado here and go 1.5 mi to AZ 95; go northeast on this highway 2.1 mi to Planet Ranch Rd (gravel). Turn southeast here.

GETTING YOUR BEARINGS. You'll need a good San Bernardino County map. The AAA Colorado River map is also helpful.

ABOUT THE REFUGE. When Parker Dam was completed in 1938, the Colorado River inundated thousands of acres of wildlife habitat, much of it used by waterfowl migrating on the Pacific Flyway. Floodplains were transformed into bottomlands, leaving birds, mammals, and other wildlife to find new homes as best they could. In 1941 the refuge was established to offset these habitat losses. Today, its total acreage, including the recently acquired Needles Peaks on the Arizona side of the Colorado, is 44,746 acres. Most of the refuge is on the Arizona side of the Colorado River—but that needn't deter California desert explorers. There's not a whole lot of difference between the desert scenes on either side of the river.

The refuge stretches from Topock Marsh east of the river at Needles, through Topock Gorge to Lake Havasu (which is not part of the refuge), then extends east into the Bill Williams River Delta from near Parker Dam. From north to south, the marsh is about 12 mi long, the gorge about 16 mi, and the Bill Williams River section is approximately 11 mi. The area contains over 300 mi of river shoreline.

Although the primary recreational activities along the Colorado River are, as you might expect, water oriented, there are a number of places where car touring, walking or hiking, and wildlife watching are popular.

Naturally, if you also enjoy boating, canoeing, swimming, and fishing, there will be just that much more to attract you to this area. And if all this recreational furor strikes you as being not quite what you might expect in a wildlife refuge, you have plenty of company. However, the refuge rules and regulations allow it all (along with some hunting, to boot) — and perhaps if they hadn't been written that way, there would be no refuge at all, just untrammeled recreation and waterfowl hunting.

For birdwatching, hiking, and car touring, the best times to visit the refuge are in winter or spring. Water recreation is most popular in warm weather. For information on all kinds of recreation in the refuge, contact the refuge manager, Havasu National Wildlife Refuge, P.O. Box A, 1406 Bailey Ave, Needles, CA 92363, or call 619-326-3853. There are several free brochures (with maps) and wildlife checklists available.

Exploring Topock Marsh. A couple of miles or so north up the Oatman-Topock Rd (see above for directions), follow the signs west to Catfish Paradise. Here you'll find picnic facilities and a small concession where you can get information on the refuge. Back at the road, continue north about 2.5 mi to a Y; follow the signs saying "Five-Mile Landing" (you'll now be on the Bullhead-Topock Rd — still US 95). The turnoff to this concession is about 2 mi or so ahead. Continue north from the Five-Mile turnoff for another 4 mi, then follow the signs to the parking areas for Pintail Slough, a popular winter and spring birding area. There are several tracks here to wander around on while wildlife watching.

Back on US 95, continue west for about 4 mi to the turnoff north to Bullhead City; go south here for a mile or so; after passing Plantation Dr, the road will turn to gravel and follow the east side of the Colorado River. Watch for the signs to the Topock Farm Observation Tower after about 3.5 mi or so. Turn east here to visit Topock Farm Goose Management Area.

Here, as in the Salton Sea Wildlife Refuge, succulent greenery is cultivated for the express use of these magnificent birds — in this case, most of the greenery is Bermuda grass. Each year over two thousand Canada and snow geese feed and rest here. The Canada even overwinter. You can see them at the farm from September through March. It's easy to tell Canada geese from other geese — they have a black neck and head, with a white cheek patch extending under the chin. Hearing the unique and stirring call of these "honkers" is an unforgettable experience. Several other less common species of geese are also seen here each year.

From the Topock Farm, the road continues south and dead-ends after about 6.5 mi. There are several roads leading off from it along the way; these tracks are closed to vehicle traffic, but you may explore them on foot. When you come to the end of the road, you'll be almost across from your starting point — but you can't get there from here! Retrace your route to the start or exit at Needles.

Exploring Bill Williams River Delta. Parker Dam, which you just crossed, was completed in 1938; without it there would, of course, be no Lake Havasu — and no 241-mi Colorado River Aqueduct bringing water to the swimming pools of Los Angeles at the rate of about 1.1 million acre-ft per year.

The Planet Ranch Rd into the delta follows the south side of the river in the refuge for about 7 mi, before bearing south away from it. Stop here and there as you go along to see if you can pick out the different kinds of habitats in this area. What plant species do you see? Animals? The best way to see this area is on foot, so don't forget your walking shoes, binoculars, and field guides.

Cadiz Valley–Old Woman Mountains

ABOUT THE AREA. The broad Cadiz Valley, with its attractive buff-colored dunes stretching alongside what was once a large freshwater lake, lies only a few miles southwest of the ruggedly scenic Old Woman Mtns. Both can be reached via roads leading off either the National Trails Highway (old Highway 66) in the north (from Essex or Cadiz) or CA 62 to the south (from near Granite Pass or Iron Mtn).

This part of the California desert's Mojave region, like Joshua Tree National Monument to the southwest, shows some signs of merging with the lower, hotter Colorado region found farther south. Throughout this area you'll find plants characteristic of both the Mojave and Colorado desert regions. One of the reasons for this phenomenon is that the broad, low, north-south valleys like the Cadiz Valley have over the millennia served as pathways for plant "migration." Plants have gone both ways—south from the more northern reaches of the Mojave and north from the Colorado region. And so it is that here in this area the respective groups characteristic of each region are mingled. In fact, many botanists think that perhaps only about 25% of all plants in the Mojave region are endemic—that is, are found only in the Mojave. This transitional character makes the area a particularly interesting one to explore. (Check Chapter 4 for the different kinds of plants you might expect to find here.)

The Cadiz Dunes and Old Woman Mtns have a lot to offer visitors bent on hiking and car camping. There are quite a few old mining roads into canyons on both the east and west sides of the Old Womans. And although there are no trails as such, the old roads serve very well—when you can't safely drive any farther, you just make camp and start exploring on foot. Once you get up above the valley, you'll find no dearth of inspiring vistas. As for the dunes—again, no trails, but who needs them? And who can resist climbing to the top of the nearest one?

If you are a wildflower fancier, you'll be happy to hear that much of this area is noted for its fine spring displays. At the dunes you can see acres of verbena and primroses, along with many other equally lovely flowers. In the rock-walled canyons of the Old Womans you'll find cactus gardens brilliant with striking hot pink, yellow, and red blooms — as well as more delicately beautiful shows in the washes.

History buffs may find something to interest them in this area, as well — in the ruins of what is commonly called Patton's Camp, just north of Granite Pass. A stroll around this now-protected area will give the sensitive observer some idea of what it must have been like for the thousands of young World War II recruits who spent several scorching months here before going off to North Africa — perhaps never to return.

This area, then, offers a little something for almost everyone who likes to see things close up: flowers; gracefully contoured dunes, enticingly soft underfoot, and low enough to be climbed with relative ease; narrow, winding, colorful canyons, with side canyons just asking to be explored; and, for the hardy, view-topped peaks to climb. What more could you ask?

FACILITIES. Gas and limited supplies in Essex. Gas, motel, and cafe at Amboy. Nearest motels and restaurants in Twentynine Palms and Needles.

Camping. For developed campgrounds, see the "Facilities" sections for Joshua Tree National Monument and the Historic Eastern Mojave. Open-desert camping is allowed throughout this area and is what most visitors opt for.

Cadiz Dunes

TO GET THERE. Take I-40 east 80 mi from its intersection with I-15 in Barstow to the Kelbaker Rd exit. Or take I-40 west from Needles 66 mi to the same exit. Go south on Kelbaker Rd 11 mi to National Trails Highway; turn east on National Trails and go 5 mi to Cadiz Rd.

A somewhat more scenic way to approach Cadiz Rd is to get on National Trails Highway going south 29 mi west of Needles at Mountain Springs Summit or 52 mi east out of Barstow at Ludlow. These routes get away from the freeway, so you can better see the desert.

However you get to Cadiz Rd, turn southeast on it. After about 3.3 mi, Cadiz Rd will jog east for 0.8 mi, then cross the Atchison, Topeka, & Santa Fe Railroad tracks and go south again (the southern tracks T with the east-west tracks right near here — see your San Bernardino County map). At about this point, the pavement ends and a graded dirt road begins; the railroad tracks are now on the west side of the road. In about 2 mi or so, a poleline road crosses the road and you'll have to jog west across the railroad tracks to keep on it (the tracks will now be on the east side of the road). About 6.5 mi farther down the road, look for a dirt road going southwest toward the dunes.

Although the roads (both north and south) leading into the dunes' east side are usually passable by ordinary vehicles, a 4WD with high clearance is required to drive the connecting north-south road running close to and paralleling the dunes (not on county or topo maps). However, this shouldn't keep you from visiting the dunes; exploring on foot is more satisfying, anyway.

To reach the dunes from Cadiz Rd, drive southwest on the dirt road about 2.5 mi. At this point there is an informal camping area (no facilities). Unfortunately, although these dunes are closed to ORVs, ORV enthusiasts sometimes camp here in groups, so you may have to hike away from them for a bit to enjoy the dunes. If you have a 4WD with high clearance, you can drive south about 6 mi on the dirt track paralleling the dunes to a road that leads east back to Cadiz Rd. The southern end of the dunes is less visited, so it's usually quite nice down there.

Initially, you can also approach the south end of the dunes by continuing southeast on Cadiz Rd past the first road to the dunes for another 5.5 mi or so to another dirt road and going toward the dunes from there. It's about 5 mi from Cadiz Rd to the dunes. This is the road the dirt track described above connects with.

GETTING YOUR BEARINGS. You'll need a good San Bernardino County map. The USGS topo *Cadiz Lake* is also good to have along, although it doesn't show the more recent roads carved out by recreationists.

ABOUT THE DUNES. Sand dunes are a very rare and unusual type of habitat where there is an amazing abundance of life. Although on the surface dunes may sometimes look waterless and nearly lifeless, this impression is usually false. Actually, only the top layer of sand is dry; not too far beneath the surface the sand is moist with water it draws up by capillary action from below the dune. Desert animals do not live in the top layer of sand, but frequent it in search of food when the ground temperature is not too high for comfort. The layer of sand under the dry dune surface is only a little damp, but this dampness cools the sand enough to allow many species of desert animals to live quite successfully. (Ground temperatures of over 100° F can kill desert reptiles in seconds.) The rare fringe-toed lizard, for example, "swims" through this damp layer in search of its food—crickets and other insects—which it detects by pressure sensing. Beneath this merely damp layer there is another, wetter layer, where microorganisms live. And, at the "bottom" of dunes is often a rather waterlogged layer of sand and water.

Besides the animals living "in" the dunes, there are many desert creatures that make their homes in, under, and around the shelter of plants at the dune edges. These sandy open spaces around dunes, where water is often not too far below the surface, make good habitat for sun-loving annual plants. In spring, the displays of sand verbena, desert lily, and other showy flowers are well worth making a special trip to see. Sprinkled among the annuals are the perennial shrubs, such as creosote and burroweed. The seeds from these wildflowers and shrubs, and from other plants in surrounding areas, are a necessary part of the dune communities' cycle of life. Daily, the winds forming and reforming the dunes carry the seeds (and sand) to the dune crests, where they are dropped to the surface in the weaker eddies of the wind's lee.

These seeds are the province of the dunes' seedeaters — pocket rats and mice, and kangaroo rats and mice. Most dunes have several species of each. One of the remarkable facts about how these tiny creatures lead their lives is that they do not drink water! Evolution has supplied them with the means to break down the carbohydrates locked in seeds and reassemble them as water — metabolic water. Yet another amazing fact about these small seed-gatherers is that each species is a different size and each subsists on different kinds and sizes of seeds, so there is no competition as such. Every species has its own pretty-much-uncontested niche.

A similar pattern obtains among the larger animals that prey upon the mice and rats. Each stalks the prey that suits its own size, so that the kit foxes, skunks, snakes, owls, and even the coyotes are not really competing for the food they hunt at the dunes' edge. Almost all this important activity takes place at night, when the sand surface is cooler, so if you want to see something more than tracks you'll have to lurk quietly in the dunes after dark with an infrared light. When reading tracks in the early morning light, though, you can give free rein to your imagination — this can be a lot of fun!

The unique sand dune communities are highly and completely adapted to their difficult environment — and this means that the slightest disturbance can cause great, perhaps irreparable, damage. When you visit the dunes, keep this in mind. *In particular, do not drive off the roads.* When sand dunes are compacted by wheels, vegetation and some animals are killed directly; and indirectly, the plant-animal food chain is altered, perhaps forever. Some effects on plant-animal life cycles are: compaction causes sand to hold more heat, so sand and air temperatures become too high for seeds of spring flowers to germinate; animal burrows are destroyed; moisture content in sand is reduced because of density increase; and plant-animal communities are disrupted, if not completely destroyed. Enjoy the dunes carefully!

Patton's Camp

TO GET THERE. Take CA 62 east for 52 mi from Twentynine Palms to its intersection with CA 177; stay on CA 62. About 1.1 mi east of the intersection, near Granite Pass (1550 ft) look for a gravel poleline road on the north side of the road. Turn northeast here and go about 2.5 mi to a sign and fence marking the camp area. Continue east 0.3 mi along the road indicated by the sign to a turnstile in the fenced area (there are others farther along).

GETTING YOUR BEARINGS. Bring along a good San Bernardino County map.

ABOUT THE CAMP. This was one of the areas used by General Patton (of World War II fame) to train his troops for the North African campaigns. Iron Mtn Divisional Camp was used by the army from March, 1942, through April, 1944; after that, the area was closed. Today, there are still a few camp ruins to be seen. The mementos still left at the camp are being protected by the Bureau of Land Management; the fence is to keep vehicles out. A little walking around will reveal the remains of a stone chapel (northwest corner), rock-lined "streets" (throughout the camp), parts of stone walls, and what was once an incredible topographic map of the entire desert training area used for Patton's maneuvers (northeast part of camp).

The topographic map must have been an impressive sight when functional; unfortunately, much of it has been eroded away. When new, it showed all the mountains, valleys, plains, highways, railroad tracks, etc., in the area. Important locations were signed. A high wooden bridge ran across the map so that it could easily be viewed and discussed (the bridge is gone now). In addition to the map, many small relics still dot the landscape—pieces of transmission wire, shell cases, old boots, empty cans, and other flotsam left over from the day-to-day life of an army camp.

Some not-so-small relics of the army's occupation can be seen outside the camp. Look for the scars left by hauling field weapons across the plains and up the hills surrounding the camp. These tracks will mar the desert for many, many hundreds of years.

Scanlon Gulch 4WD Car Camp

TO GET THERE. From I-40, about 30 mi west of Needles, take National Trails Highway southwest from Mountain Springs Summit (2770 ft) for 22 mi to Danby Rd. Go southeast here for 1.7 mi, cross the Atchison, Topeka, & Santa Fe Railroad tracks, and pick up a dirt road going south (away from the tracks). The one you want skirts the west side of the Old Woman Mtns from Danby to the old AT & SF tank stop at Chubbuck (check your San Bernardino County map). Follow this fair-to-poor dirt road for about 9 mi to the road leading to Scanlon Gulch. Because this road (from Danby to the gulch road) is not maintained except by erratic mining operations, and because it cuts across the down-slope washes, each minor wash brings your vehicle to a stop; *high clearance is mandatory.*

The entrance to Scanlon Gulch is about 1 mi south of a point due west of the Old Woman Statue. It is sometimes easy to mistake the road in Scanlon Gulch for a wash because of the down-slope water erosion. Once you find the road, go about 5 mi east on it to the gulch.

GETTING YOUR BEARINGS. You'll need a good San Bernardino County map. The USGS topos *Danby* and *Cadiz Lake* are also useful.

ABOUT THE GULCH. Like the Turtle Mtns to the southeast, the Old Woman Mtns have a smattering of vegetation from the fringe of the California desert's Colorado region—including barrel and hedgehog cacti. In spring, west side canyons like Scanlon Gulch hold rewarding displays of wildflowers and colorful rock gardens of barrel cacti.

On your way to Scanlon Gulch, you passed the Old Woman Statue (5090 ft) on the crest of the mountains of the same name. From the east side, this stone peak looks like a woman with a shawl over her head. It's one of the area's most famous landmarks. Experienced hikers can scramble cross-country from the floor of Scanlon Gulch, at about the 3000-ft level, up 4–5 mi of steep, difficult slopes to the base of the "statue" at 5000 ft. To reach the top of the peak requires Class 5 rock-climbing skills and equipment.

However, it's not necessary to undertake anything as strenuous as the Old Woman while visiting Scanlon Gulch. Besides the main canyon, there are several tracks into side canyons for hikers to explore. This is not a much-visited place, so it's a good place to come when you're in the mood for some peace and quiet amongst fine desert scenery. There are many good places to set up camp.

Old Woman Mountain Hike
Class 2/elev. 5326 ft/USGS topos *Essex, Danby*/3.5 mi RT/cross-country

TO GET THERE. From I-40 about 29 mi west of Needles, take the National Trails Highway southwest, through the town of Essex, for 19 mi—to Danby Rd (gravel). Here, turn southeast and go 1.7 mi to the Atchison, Topeka, & Santa Fe Railroad siding of Danby, then go straight ahead on the dirt road for approximately 7 mi to road's end at the old Florence Mine.

ABOUT THE HIKE. Old Woman Mtn is a short, fun hike in a lovely area just south of and outside the East Mojave National Scenic Area. The summit does not have striking views of high ranges nearby, but it does have a charm, an intimacy, and certainly a sweeping vista. It is in an area especially favored by spring wildflower displays in years when blooms may be scant in other areas.

The hike to the peaks starts due south of the road's end and goes up the ridge leading to the 4882-ft peak. Within the first 0.5 mi, look for occasional rough garnets (gemstones) along the way. From Peak 4882, proceed through the saddle to the southeast and up the north ridge of the Old Woman summit. The view from the top includes Old Woman Statue (see Scanlon Gulch 4WD car camp, above), a Class 5 rock spire located 5 mi to the southeast.

Turtle Mountains– Mopah Range

ABOUT THE AREA. Located 30 mi west of the Colorado River and 40 mi south of Needles and I-40, the Turtles are in the transition zone between the California desert's Colorado (low) region and its Mojave (high) region. In the washes of the northeast mountains you can find several species of plants that are probably at the northernmost limit of their range. Examples are the native desert (California) fan palm (relatively rare even within its range), the hard-to-find crucifixion thorn, and the desert ironwood, smoke tree, and palo verde that are so common in washes farther south.

Sprinkled among these mountains are multilayered mesas and several spectacular conical peaks that are volcanic plugs. These red basalt peaks are all that is left of several large volcanoes that were active in this area not so many thousands of years ago. Much of the mountains themselves are covered with highly eroded remnants of volcanic lava.

The northern end of the Turtle Mtns is highly mineralized and very colorful. The varied shades of red, pink, brown, gold, green, and tan easily rival the colors seen in southeastern Utah. Not surprisingly, these mountains are one of the California desert's prime candidates for congressional designation as wilderness. The peaks, washes, bajadas, and wide interior valley offer outstanding opportunities for hiking, photography, and overnight backpacking. Another plus is that the range is isolated from US 95 on the east and CA 62 on the south by 5 to 10 mi of desert pavement—flat, stone-covered desert floor, eroded only here and there by washes.

Despite the mountains' relative isolation, access by dirt roads is easy for most compact cars with better-than-average ground clearance—if the driver is experienced in dodging half-buried rocks and traversing occasional sandy washes with a steady foot on the gas. In the north mountains, these rather primitive tracks will take you to trailheads for Mopah Peak, Mopah Spring palm oasis, and Gary Wash. A little farther to the south and east, you can approach the trailheads for Coffin Spring and beyond. If you're a walker, hiker, peak climber, car camper, or backpacker, you won't want to miss the Turtles.

FACILITIES. Gas, supplies, restaurants, and motels can be found at Twentynine Palms and at Parker, just across the Colorado River in Arizona. There is gas at Vidal Junction.

Camping. For developed campgrounds, see "Facilities" sections for the Joshua Tree National Monument and Needles–Colorado River South areas. Open-desert camping is excellent on the Bureau of Land Management lands throughout and around the Turtle Mtns.

Coffin Spring Hike
Class 1/elev. 2400 ft/USGS topo *Turtle Mtns*/4 mi RT/trail

TO GET THERE. Take US 95 south from Needles or north from Vidal Junction (16.4 mi west of Earp) for 23–24 mi to Turtle Mtn Rd. Go west here. The Turtle Mtn Rd was once a two-lane, county-maintained road; now, however, it is not being maintained. Watch out for sandy shoulders—stay on the main part of the road. When you come to Chemehuevi Wash after about 5 mi, cross carefully.

About 10 mi west of US 395, the broad, straight stretch of road ends, and a winding, rough, but passable, road continues southwest for another 3–4 mi to a privately owned cabin that is usually unoccupied. (On winter weekends, you'll usually find the pickup campers of rockhounds parked nearby.) Follow the 4WD route southeast for a couple of miles to the first large wash entering from the south. Park here and find the trailhead.

Note: From US 95 west, the roads sometimes require 4WD; they can be quite sandy. If you don't have 4WD, be sure someone in your party brings along good towing equipment—just in case.

ABOUT THE HIKE. The Turtle Mtns area is considered by many enthusiasts to be one of the pearls of the California desert. As a first step in getting to know the Turtles, take time to stop and investigate Chemehuevi Wash as you drive west from US 95 (it's about 5 mi along). The Chemehuevi is a classic wash; it drains the east side of the Stepladder and Turtle mountains, is 100 ft wide even in its upper reaches, and carries a torrent of water down to the Colorado River during the late summer storms. Notice the thick stands of trees and shrubs that line the broad expanse of wash (do you know what they are?). Here, the red-tailed hawk circles overhead, and coyotes make their nightly rounds looking for a meal of white-footed mouse or kangaroo rat.

On the Trail to Coffin Spring. The first large wash entering from the south along this 4WD road after you leave the cabin leads to Coffin Spring. Park near the trailhead and follow a fair-to-poor trail south up the wash to the spring, which is usually dry. However, the area around the spring is colorfully mineralized—be sure to bring your camera.

Once at the spring, you can climb to the pass located about 0.5 mi due west for a fine view of the Ward Valley and the Old Woman Mtns. To gain the pass, follow the wash to the west for approximately 0.2 mi, and then climb the slope to the left. Along here you'll find a primitive trail that will traverse the otherwise difficult terrain up to the pass. This trail is the return route for the overnight Mopah Wash–Gary Wash backpack loop below.

If you have any spare time when retracing your route back from Coffin Spring to the main valley, you can explore some of the colorful side canyons off the 4WD road you used to get to the trailhead, which continues to the southwest.

Mohawk Spring–Coffin Spring Backpack Loop

Class 1/elev. 2750 ft/USGS topo *Turtle Mtns*/14 mi RT/trail, cross-country

TO GET THERE. See directions for the Coffin Spring hike, above, but stop and park at the unoccupied cabin.

ABOUT THE BACKPACK. You'll need a compass for this backpack, which can also be done as a strenuous day hike. As this is a fairly low-elevation trip, it's not a good idea to attempt it in summer.

Day 1—Finding Coffin Spring: From the cabin area, take the slightly uphill trail to Mohawk Spring. From here the trail crosses a saddle, heads southwest, and gradually disappears, leaving your party and your compass on their own to cross the major wash and go over a small saddle. At this point, head due south, skirting the eastern side of the central Turtle massif. By keeping close to this east side, after about 3 mi you'll enter a major wash heading east to a pass located about 0.5 west of Coffin Spring. This pass is a square notch in the otherwise impassable Turtle range. Camp for the night at the foot of the pass. The setting sun will illuminate the Turtles with a dramatic, fiery red glow.

Day 2—Over the Pass: To reach the pass, continue east, keeping well up on the slope to the left of the wash. As the wash becomes choked with boulders, a primitive trail will appear as if by magic, winding its way easily through the otherwise difficult terrain leading up to the pass (350 ft elevation gain). As you descend northeast into the Coffin Spring area, keep to the right. See the Coffin Spring hike, above, for a description of the route that will take you back to your starting point.

Mopah Spring Palm Oasis Hike

Class 1/elev. 2230 ft/USGS topos *Turtle Mtns, Savahia Peak*/9.2 mi RT/dirt road, cross-country

TO GET THERE. From Vidal Junction, at the intersection of CA 62 and US 95 (16.5 mi west of Earp/Parker), take US 95 north for 12.1 mi to an unmarked dirt road on the west side of the highway. This road is shown on San Bernardino County maps and the USGS topo for the area but is difficult to locate because of all the trails left by roadside campers, rockhounds, prospectors, and assorted recreational vehicles. One way to find the road, if you are having difficulty in locating it, is to look for the twin peaks—Mopah and Umpah. These volcanic plugs are about 1 mi apart; a compass bearing on the north peak will be 255 degrees from where the road meets the highway. Drive down the dirt road about 4 mi to a Y; park off the road here.

ABOUT THE HIKE. Walk along the south fork of the Y for about 1.1 mi to the ruins of a stone cabin. Here at the canyon mouth you are about 3.5 mi from Mopah Spring, which is southwest up the canyon wash. Mopah Peak — the hardened lava core of a not-too-ancient volcano — is about the same distance away, but a little farther to the south (see Mopah Peak climb, below). To reach the spring, hike up the wash.

The few native desert (California) fan palms *(Washingtonia filifera)* at the spring mark the northernmost location of this species. Corn Springs, the next nearest oasis, is 60 mi south of this tiny grove. The small spring at the base of the palms is an important watering hole for wildlife, including bighorn sheep. Please treat this area with great care; the lives of many animals depend on the water here.

Regarding the oasis, James Cornett, of the Palm Springs Desert Museum, says, "The isolation of this grove has caused many persons to speculate that it was early prospectors or Indians who planted the first palms, since only humans could have transported the seeds such a great distance. The five mature palms were burned in 1983, and now dozens of seedlings have appeared. Like nearly all of the palm oases in the southwest, this one is growing in size."

Mopah Peak Climb

Class 3/elev. 3514 ft/USGS topos *Savahia Peak, Turtle Mtns*/6 mi RT/cross-country

TO GET THERE. See the directions for Mopah Spring Palm Oasis hike.

ABOUT THE CLIMB. Mopah and its nearby twin, Umpah, are scenic high points for mountaineers exploring the Turtle Mtns. Mopah is thought to have been named by the Chemehuevis — and it was a member of this tribe who made the first recorded ascent to the peak in the 1870s.

To reach the peak from the stone cabin ruins, first hike about 1 mi west in the broad wash just ahead, then turn south into another drainage on the east side of the peak. Follow the occasional rock "ducks" up the easy but sometimes loose slope to a little saddle on the southeast ridge of the peak. Drop over into a broad chute leading north toward the unseen summit. Follow the west side of this chute until it ends at a wall and an overhanging ledge. At this point, climb a short, easy Class 3 pitch and follow easy ledges to an unmistakable long, narrow Class 2 slot. Go up the slot, left up a short Class 3 pitch, then over to a saddle and an easy scramble to the summit.

The route to this peak is regarded as one of the easy, fun desert climbs. The panorama from the summit includes the Colorado River to the east (near Lake Havasu), the Chemehuevi and Stepladder mountains to the north, the Mopah Spring palm oasis to the west, and the 27-ft-higher summit of Umpah (or South Mopah) Peak to the south. To climb Umpah (easy Class 2), descend to the saddle between the two peaks and then scramble up. Keep your eye out for chalcedony roses; many are found in this area.

Gary Wash Hike

Class 1/elev. 2450 ft/USGS topos *Savahia Peak, Turtle Mtns*/8–9 mi RT/trail, cross-country

TO GET THERE. See directions for Mopah Spring Palm Oasis hike, above. However, take the north fork of the entry road instead of the south one. Follow it to the mouth of Gary Wash. (The wash is named on the county maps, but not on the topo.) Although the topo shows about 1 mi of road going into the lower end of the wash, park your vehicle and start walking before you come to the sandy stretch.

ABOUT THE HIKE. As you hike up the canyon, it will funnel down into a narrows, then open out again into a valley. This flat expanse is about 1 mi wide and is crisscrossed with many streambeds and surrounded with colorfully layered mesas. The mesas beckon the explorer — but the cliffs look pretty formidable. A little careful searching, though, will reveal an occasional break in the walls. Experienced hikers will find the clifftops well worth the scramble.

This valley — with its stands of cactus, creosote, and other shrubs — is fine desert tortoise habitat. If you're lucky, you might see a tortoise, or even a golden eagle or a prairie falcon. Here you can experience a true sense of isolation and solitude — something quite rare in today's world.

Mopah Wash–Gary Wash Backpack Loop

Class 1/elev. 2800 ft/USGS topos *Turtle Mtns, Savahia Peak*/16–18 mi RT/trail, cross-country

TO GET THERE. Follow the directions for the Mopah Spring Palm Oasis hike, above.

ABOUT THE BACKPACK. This loop can be done in either direction, but no matter which way you go, don't forget your compass. Although the route is mostly cross-country, hiking is easy; there is only a moderate amount of boulder hopping and elevation gain, for the two passes are less than 400 ft each.

Day 1 — A Look at Vidal Valley. Follow the Mopah Spring Palm Oasis hike route, above, but continue up and over the saddle about 0.5 mi west and slightly south of the spring. Descend into Vidal Valley (the Turtles' interior valley) and watch for Thumb Peak, another steep spike of volcanic material. This peak is about 3 mi to the northwest as you come out into the valley (compass bearing approximately 300 degrees). Head northwest up the valley, aiming for the saddle 0.6 mi to the east of the Thumb. Stop and camp whenever and wherever your party feels inclined.

Day 2 — Through Bighorn Country to Gary Wash. When you've arrived at the saddle east of the Thumb, watch for the bighorn trail the sheep use to cross from one mesa to the next. If you can spare the time, put your pack aside and follow the trail up onto the mesa to the east. The trail will disappear when you get to the flat-topped area.

As you descend northwest from the saddle, you'll find yourself in the wide, valleylike part of Gary Wash. Follow the wash eastward, keeping to the southernmost branch along the east side of the Turtles — this will take you back to your car.

15

Yuha Desert and
Salton Sea

McCain and Davies Valleys

ABOUT THE AREA. The Jacumba Mtns begin in southeast San Diego
County and continue down into southwest Imperial County, ending
across the border in Mexico. The Davies Valley area is located on the
east side of the Jacumbas in southwest Imperial County, southeast of
I-8 and southwest of CA 98. These mountains—actually a series of near-
parallel ranges—have been likened to great stair steps rising out of the
Yuha Basin and connecting the low desert with the higher coastal
chaparral areas, such as the green upland of McCain Valley, which lies
just west of the In-Ko-Pah Mtns. These latter mountains are a southern
California coastal range, rather than a desert range, although they are
located just west of the Colorado Desert region of the California desert.
The Jacumbas and the In-Ko-Pahs are separated by Carrizo Gorge and
Canyon, whose walls are home to the rare peninsular bighorn sheep.

Undersea Mountains. The In-Ko-Pahs, like many other coastal mountains, appear to be a jumble of granitic rock formations. When they
began their upward journey, however, they were covered with thousands of feet of ancient sea floor sediments. These softer sedimentary
rocks were eroded away by water and wind as the region was pushed
up. Eventually, the granitic bedrock that became the mountains was
exposed, broken into huge blocks, and further weathered into the enormous boulders and piled-up rock formations you see today. The bedrock was formed approximately 100 million years ago.

The Jacumba Jumble. Like the In-Ko-Pahs, the Jacumbas are a sometimes fantastic-looking granitic jumble that trends generally southeast-
northwest. Both these ranges were pushed up to 4000 + feet over about
150 million years by movements of a complex earthquake fault system
related to the San Andreas fault (part of which extends along the eastern
edge of the coastal mountains). On the east side of this fault system,

330

the land mass has been dropping down and now forms a trough — the Salton Trough — which at its lowest point is more than 200 feet below sea level.

McCain Valley's Original Inhabitants. Native peoples lived in the McCain Valley region for at least 10,000 years before European explorers and settlers arrived there in the 1700s. The most recent of these peoples were the Kamia (also known as Kumeyaay or Southern Diegueños). They continued their seasonal hunting and gathering in the In-Ko-Pah area until the early 1900s.

Many remnants of these native peoples' long residence can still be found. For example, there are grinding holes (for nuts, seeds, and grains) in granite boulders. You can still see some of these in McCain Valley, south of Cottonwood West Campground site 11 and near Cottonwood East Campground site 25 (see "Facilities" section, below, for campground info). When you find these or other artifacts, such as pieces of pottery or stone tools, do not collect them. Instead, leave them as you find them so that others can see them and archaeologists can study these cultural resources in place.

The McCain Homestead. California became part of the United States in 1848 (it was part of Mexico before that). The In-Ko-Pah Mtns region (and other regions not privately owned) thus became part of the public domain lands and so was open to homesteaders. In 1852 George McCain took up a homestead and began grazing stock on the rich valley forage. In fact, the McCain family, along with other landowners, is still ranching in the valley today. This stock grazing has resulted in quite a few fences and watering facilities being visible in some parts of the valley.

Hiking the Stair-step Valleys. Southeast of McCain Valley, in the folds of the Jacumbas, are several typical desert valleys and canyons. In order of descending elevation they are: Myer, Davies, Pinto, and Skull. Because of their different elevations, these valleys and canyons each have their own unique plant and animal communities. Comparing them is a good way to increase your knowledge of desert natural history. For the most part, these areas are difficult to get to and little used — making them a good choice for those experienced hikers and backpackers who enjoy solitude. Although the country is rugged, it's definitely worth the effort to explore it.

A Resource Conservation Area. About 38,700 acres of the In-Ko-Pah Mtns became a Bureau of Land Management (BLM) multiple-use resource conservation area in 1963. Supposedly the area is managed to protect a variety of environmental values — such as recreation (both high- and low-impact), wildlife, grazing, and historic as well as archaeological relics. When you visit the valley, look carefully around you and try to determine just how successful this kind of multiple-use management is. (For example, has the viewshed been preserved?)

Anza-Borrego Desert State Park. This large and beautiful desert park lies just to the west of the Salton Sea. It covers about one-third of San

Diego County and portions of Imperial and Riverside counties. Once you are in the McCain or Davies Valley area, much of the park is accessible to you. (See ABSP, below.)

An Outstanding Natural Area. About 80% of the Jacumbas lie within Anza–Borrego Desert State Park. To protect the part of the region outside the park, the BLM established a Jacumba Outstanding Natural Area in 1975. Davies Valley lies within this outstanding natural area. There are no developed facilities there.

FACILITIES. Motels, restaurants, supplies, and gas can be found in El Centro, Jacumba, and Ocotillo.

Picnicking. In-Ko-Pah County Park is just east of Mountain Springs. Take the Park exit off I-8 and follow the signs to the frontage road (which runs along the north side of the freeway) and the park. No camping is allowed in this park.

Camping. There are two BLM campgrounds in McCain Valley; they have tables, fire rings, pit toilets, and water. A small user's fee is charged. Lark Canyon Campground is 5.3 mi from the BLM boundary of the valley. A 1200-acre ORV area adjoins this campground, so it's best for those who prefer a quieter outdoor experience to use the Cottonwood Campground. The latter is located 12.7 mi from the boundary and is pleasantly situated among live oaks and next to an intermittent creek. In the McCain Valley Resource Conservation Area, camping is permitted only in the developed campgrounds.

Open-desert camping is allowed throughout the Davies Valley. As with all open-desert camping, there are no facilities. BLM regulations indicate that vehicle parking and car camping are limited to within 25 ft of vehicle routes. All wildlife watering holes are off limits to camping (whether you are with your vehicle or backpacking); you must be at least 600 ft away (preferably farther). Also, do not remain around these water supplies longer than a few minutes, as your presence discourages animals from coming to drink.

A Caution About the Mexican Border. Because the Davies Valley is a border area, from time to time it is frequented by people entering the United States illegally as well as by drug smugglers. Therefore, BLM recommends that when visiting there you camp away from well-beaten trails and take care not to cross into Mexico while exploring on foot or by vehicle.

Carrizo Overlook

TO GET THERE. Take I-8 to the Boulevard exit (about 70 mi east of San Diego). Get on Old Highway 80 and go east for 1.8 mi to McCain Valley Rd. Go north on McCain Valley Rd; McCain Valley Resource Conservation Area (Bureau of Land Management) begins 2.4 mi up the road, where the pavement ends in a good dirt road. Continue up the dirt road for 8.7 mi to the overlook.

Scale

10 Miles

10 Kilometers

□ Site

◊ Spring

△ Peak

GETTING YOUR BEARINGS. If you're interested in identifying the various landmarks visible from this spectacular viewpoint, take along the USGS topo *Carrizo Mtn* and a good San Diego County map.

ABOUT THE OVERLOOK. This easily accessible scenic viewpoint is interesting in several ways.

The View. As you look down into Carrizo Canyon from the overlook, you are looking down the east side of the In-Ko-Pah Mtns. This steep wall is the transition zone between the coastal mountain ranges and the low-lying Colorado Desert lands just beyond. Looking north and west you can see the In-Ko-Pah Mtns crest; McCain Valley is southwest. The mouth of Carrizo Canyon is northeast from the overlook. Through the canyon mouth you can see a gap in the mountains called the Carrizo

Corridor. If the day is especially clear, you may be able to see the 60 mi to the Salton Sea. In the right weather conditions, you can get some excellent photos from the overlook. It's easy to see why the BLM is recommending the area below the overlook for wilderness.

Bighorn Sheep in Carrizo Canyon. As mentioned before, the peninsular bighorn sheep are found in this area. The ruggedness and remoteness of the canyon suit their habitat needs well. Bighorn populations in the California desert are dwindling at an alarming rate; their few remaining habitat areas are not large enough or well enough protected. With a pair of binoculars, some patience, and some luck, you may be rewarded by the sight of an elusive bighorn.

Plant and Animal Communities. In McCain Valley the plants you are most likely to see are part of the coastal chaparral plant community, which is in part made up of chamise (sometimes called greasewood), redshank, scrub oak, and other shrubs that do well in long, hot, dry summers. As the canyon wall continues to drop, other plants (those that can tolerate even more desertlike conditions) begin to appear; for example, California juniper, Great Basin sagebrush, and mountain mahogany. Finally, near the bottom of the canyon, this mixture shades into a true desert scrub made up of such plants as cholla (a cactus), brittlebush, catclaw, and agave.

All these plant communities, from the lusher chaparral to the more sparse low desert scrub, support a variety of animal life. You may see anything from a large red-tailed hawk to a tiny sage sparrow; from a diminutive pocket mouse to a German shepherd–sized coyote; and from an ordinary harvester ant to an impressive tarantula hawk.

Smugglers' Cave

TO GET THERE. Take I-8 to the In-Ko-Pah Park exit (just a few miles short of the San Diego/Imperial county line); a dirt road goes south from the exit and winds up a steep hill, reaching the cave area in a couple of miles or so. According to the Bureau of Land Management the road is marginally passable to two-wheel-drive vehicles with good clearance, but 4WD vehicles are recommended. You won't get stuck if you walk, though!

GETTING YOUR BEARINGS. The USGS topo *In-Ko-Pah Gorge* is helpful when hiking in this area.

ABOUT THE CAVE. Many spectacularly jumbled granite rock formations characterize this highest part (3700 ft) of the Jacumba Outstanding Natural Area. Caves and passageways honeycomb quite a few of the piles. If you're the imaginative sort, the rock formations can even seem a bit otherworldly. In fact, some early visitors to the region even named a part of it Valley of the Moon.

Smugglers' Cave itself is a good-sized hollow in a huge boulder. History has it that one of the several people who held up the old Campo Store in 1875 fled to Smugglers' Cave—where a posse caught up with him. Another account has to do with the smuggling of Chinese laborers and opium across the Mexican border. And there are more . . .

This area makes a good day hike or overnight backpack. Because there are no trails, only experienced hikers with good map skills should venture away from the road.

Davies Valley

TO GET THERE. Take I-8 to the Ocotillo/CA 98 exit; go south on S-2 for 0.7 mi to the junction with CA 98; then go east (left) on CA 98 for 1.5 mi to Clark Rd. Go southwest on Clark Rd (dirt) 1.6 mi to a Y; continue west for about 2.8 mi into Davies Valley. Another way to get into the valley is via a dirt road leaving CA 98 only 0.7 mi east of the junction. A 4WD vehicle is recommended for either access, as roads in the valley are often in sandy washes.

For hiking access, go 1 mi west on CA 98 from the junction with S-2 to a dirt road; turn south and continue for about 2.4 mi to where the road dead-ends. The last part of the road (about 0.7 mi) is quite sandy and may not be negotiable by the average car. From the road's end, hikers can cross into Davies Valley via a low saddle lying 0.5 mi directly south.

Note: Vehicle access to Davies Valley is now limited. You'll need a permit (free) from the Bureau of Land Management's El Centro office (333 South Waterman Ave; phone 619-352-5842). Hikers need no permit.

GETTING YOUR BEARINGS. The USGS topos *In-Ko-Pah Gorge* and *Coyote Wells* are a must for hiking in the Davies Valley area.

ABOUT THE VALLEY. This is the largest of the stair-step valleys, being about 1 mi wide and 5 mi long. The quartz crystals, garnets, agate, and petrified wood sometimes found in rock outcroppings and side canyons make it a popular rockhounding area. The elevation is about 1200 ft, just a little higher than Skull Valley (850 ft). The valley supports a large variety of plant life, with some of the commonest plants being brittlebush, ocotillo, cholla, mesquite, and agave. There are also some archaeological sites and interesting geologic formations. Look for an ancient volcano.

This is an ORV area, but the BLM is controlling vehicle access and there are still some fair opportunities for open-desert camping, photography, nature study, and day hiking. There are no hiking trails, so to avoid ORVers one must go cross-country. This means you need to be an experienced hiker who knows how to use USGS topographic maps (and a compass).

Pinto Canyon Palms Hike
Class 1/elev. 1300 ft/USGS topos *In-Ko-Pah Gorge, Coyote Wells*/4 mi RT/use trails, cross-country

TO GET THERE. Follow the directions above for Davies Valley. (Don't forget to read the "Note" section.) There are a number of turnoffs along the way; consult the maps noted below for proper headings. Drive south through Davies Valley and turn west into the upper end of Pinto Wash at the Bureau of Land Management sign. Continue about another 0.5 mi and park on the wash shoulder (the sand can be very soft).

ABOUT THE OASIS. This is a delightful hike that meanders through several native palm groups in the In-Ko-Pah Mtns of southwest Imperial County. The grade is gentle and the trail is usually clear. As you hike up the canyon, follow the sandy wash bottom. The first palm group is around a sharp left-hand bend in the canyon, about 1 mi up the wash. A 2-mi hike takes you to the last palm, a stately veteran standing 45 ft above the wash.

In May of 1984 there were fifty-one fruit-producing palms in this system, a nearly 100% increase from forty years ago. The tracks you see in the sand may not be bighorn sheep. Mule deer inhabit this region and at dusk come to drink at a number of the small pools that dot the bottom of the canyon.

—James Cornett, Palm Springs Desert Museum

Yuha Basin

ABOUT THE AREA. This part of the Colorado Desert is located in the southwest part of Imperial County, roughly between CA 98 (on the south side of I-8) and Imperial County Rd S-80 (on the north side of I-8). The Yuha Desert is a mostly level, dry plain—actually a basin—that formed over a period of several million years, during which two immense freshwater lakes were created and extinguished by the earth's climatic and geologic processes. These lakes are responsible for the many fossils of land and water creatures now found in the Yuha's steep-walled canyons. Today's Salton Sea is the most recent lake in the basin area; however, it covers a very small area compared to these ancient lakes.

Prehistoric Lakes Cover the Yuha Basin. Lake LeConte, the first and largest of these warm and shallow inland seas, covered most of Imperial and Riverside counties approximately 6 million years ago. The second lake to cover this area, Lake Cahuilla, periodically stretched over much of Imperial County for approximately 50,000 years before the present. At times, the lake was as much as 115 mi long, 34 mi wide, and 315 ft deep. It stretched from north of Indio to south of the Mexican border. The water for this lake came from the Colorado River, which flooded it from time to time. In between fillings, Lake Cahuilla would get lower and lower and would sometimes dry up altogether. It last dried up only 400 years ago!

From 25,000 to 50,000 years ago Pleistocene Lake Cahuilla left behind terraces and beachlines that ranged from 100 to 160 ft above sea level. These ancient lake lines can still be seen in some places in the Imperial Valley. The most easily seen beachlines are those that were formed during the last 2500 years of the lake's existence. These lines are only 42 ft above sea level, indicating that the more recent Lake Cahuilla was considerably smaller than the Pleistocene Lake Cahuilla.

These prehistoric lakes left behind many marine fossils. Today, you can see good examples of these in Fossil Canyon, Painted Canyon, and the Yuha Oyster Beds (see trips below). If you drive east on CA 98 from its junction with I-8, in about 19.8 mi you will drive right over a rise that is actually a prominent sand and gravel beachline (at 42 ft above sea level). Other parts of the 42-ft beachline can be seen on I-8 just east of the Dunaway exit as you are going east to El Centro and near Travertine Point (see trip below) on CA 86 just west of the Salton Sea.

Prehistoric People of the Basin. During its long history, the Lake LeConte/Lake Cahuilla region was quite lush from time to time and thus was home for a great many kinds of wildlife, including the human variety. Indeed, from about 20,000 years ago to about 7000 years ago, when ice covered much of the northern part of North America, the area had a much wetter climate and far more animals and vegetation than today.

As far as we know, the first humans to come into this now-congenial environment were the San Dieguitos. These people apparently lived very simply in temporary encampments, hunting and gathering plants for food, clothing, and shelter from about 9000 to 12,000 years ago. The San Dieguito people left behind only cleared sleeping-circles and several kinds of stone implements.

For several thousand years after the San Dieguitos there is little evidence of human inhabitants in the area. During this dry time most early peoples probably lived along the coast, in the coastal mountain ranges, and along the Colorado River. However, archaeological evidence indicates that when Lake Cahuilla reformed about 2500 years ago, and the area again became more hospitable, the forerunners of the Kamia people came and settled on the lakeshores. The filling of the lake once more brought an abundance of birds and large mammals, fish and shellfish, and plant foods to the area, making it an ideal spot for the native peoples to live.

For these people, food and shelter depended on the filling and emptying of the lake. As the water level of the lake changed, the Kamias followed it to be conveniently near their food supply. The Kamia people either migrated elsewhere or died out in this region several hundred years ago, leaving behind some interesting reminders of their stay.

What Prehistoric People Left Behind. The most interesting of the artifacts the Kamias created are perhaps the several large ground figures and abstract-looking patterns (collectively called geoglyphs or intaglios) found near the northwest edge of the basin. The purposes of these figures and patterns are not known; possibly they were of ritual and/or religious significance. Geoglyphs are found in several other locations in the California desert, most of them quite near the Colorado River.

The Kamias also left behind unglazed pottery, flaked cobbles, grinding holes in rocks, and other simple implements. (If you find any remnants of human occupation, please do not collect them — leave them for others to see and for archaeologists to study in place.)

The Anza Trail. The earliest travel route used by explorers to get from the Colorado River to southern California was the Anza Trail. More than 200 years ago, Juan Bautista de Anza became the first European to cross the Yuha Desert. Anza and his party were trying to find a trade route from the Tubac region of Arizona (near Tucson) to the Pacific coast. This trail crossed the Yuha Desert area between Yuha Well (the only potable water source in the area at the time) and the San Sebastian Marsh, and then went between the Fish Creek and Santa Rosa mountains and through Borrego Valley. Later, the trail took a more direct route through Carrizo Wash. The trail eventually became a much-used stage and wagon route, known variously as the Butterfield or Overland Stage Route, the Southern Immigrant Trail, and the Sonoran Rd. Unfortunately, very few parts of this historic route have managed to survive the onslaught of modern off-roaders.

Anza-Borrego Desert State Park. Just to the west of the Salton Sea lies 600,000-acre Anza-Borrego Desert State Park (ABSP). This beautiful desert park covers about one-third of San Diego County and portions of Imperial and Riverside counties. Once you are in the Yuha Basin area, much of the park is accessible to you.

FACILITIES. There is a rest area just east of county road S-29 exit going toward El Centro on I-8. Motels, restaurants, supplies, and gas in Ocotillo and El Centro.

Camping. The nearest developed campgrounds in this area are in McCain Valley (see "Facilities" section for McCain-Davies Valley, above) and western El Centro (Sunbeam Lake County Park). There is fair open-desert camping at Fossil Canyon and Painted Gorge (see trips below). For the experienced desert camper there are some good spots to be found in the maze of 4WD trails between CA 98 (you can enter at Anza Trail) and I-8 (you can enter at the Dunaway exit).

Fossil Canyon Walk

TO GET THERE. Take the Ocotillo exit off I-8. At the end of the off-ramp, go north under I-8 on Imperial County road S-2 for 1.2 mi. At the point where S-2 bends west, take Shell Cyn Rd north. The paved road ends in a good dirt road in approximately 2.4 mi. Continue up-canyon, bearing north (a cement dig is on the road to the south). In 1.5 mi some bare rock humps in the road make this the end of the road for an ordinary car (a high-clearance vehicle can go farther). You can walk up the canyon from here. There is plenty of room to park.

GETTING YOUR BEARINGS. A good Imperial County map and the USGS topo *Carrizo Mtn* will help you in getting to know the area of this trip.

ABOUT FOSSIL CANYON. In the walls of this canyon you can see a number of layers — these are the now-compressed sediments laid down by the two giant inland lakes that at different times in the past covered much of this part of the desert. The various shell-type fossils you can see embedded in the canyon walls are the remains of some of the underwater life that flourished during the several periods, beginning about 6 million years ago, when ancient Lake LeConte formed, dried up, and reformed. (Prehistoric Lake Cahuilla came later; it waxed and waned from 50,000 years ago to 400 years ago.) You can also see that the horizontal sediment layers have been pushed around quite a bit by movements of the earth's crust since the time when they were laid down. These movements caused (and still cause) the layers to crack and tilt, so that you can see layers pointing up at the sky right next to ones that are parallel to the canyon bottom.

Painted Gorge

TO GET THERE. Take the Ocotillo exit off I-8. At the end of the off-ramp, go north under I-8 on Imperial County road S-2 to S-80 (on the immediate north side of the freeway), then go east on S-80 4.2 mi to Painted Gorge Rd. (S-80 is also called Evans Hewes Highway.) At this point turn north off S-80 onto a good, graded dirt road. In about 4.5 mi there is a hilly, denuded, wash area that is a good bad-example of what motorcycle recreation can do to the desert. At this point, bear west up the wash into the gorge. There are some nice campsites along the wash for the next 0.5 to 1.0 mi. Some almost fuchsia-colored knobby rocks near ground level on the south side of the gorge mark approximately where the road starts to get too rough for the average car; high clearance 4WDs can go quite a bit farther, as can your legs.

GETTING YOUR BEARINGS. You'll need a good Imperial County map and the USGS topo *Painted Gorge* to give you an idea of this canyonland.

ABOUT THE GORGE. The bright red and mustard colors of this gorge are caused by copper, sulfur, and iron deposits in the weathered rocks. If you walk on into the upper gorge, you can see various marine fossils, including coral, mussels, and worms. (This area was once at the bottom of ancient Lake LeConte.) At the right time of day you can get some interesting photos of the rocky walls, set off by shadows. The gorge is certainly worth a morning or afternoon's visit or even an overnight stop on your way to somewhere else. However, because you are likely to meet ORV enthusiasts here (many of whom seem to abhor quiet), this is not a good spot for an extended stay.

Crucifixion Thorn Preserve

TO GET THERE. Take I-8 from Anza-Borrego Desert State Park's eastern boundary to the Ocotillo exit for CA 98. At the end of the off-ramp turn south on Imperial County road S-2. In 0.7 mi S-2 makes a T into CA 98. Go east from this T for approximately 9 mi to Coyote Rd; turn south and park off this good, graded dirt road close to CA 98. There is a walk-in entry in the boundary fence on CA 98.

GETTING YOUR BEARINGS. Take along a good Imperial County map and the USGS topo *Coyote Wells* for maximum enjoyment of this trip.

ABOUT THE CRUCIFIXION THORN. This Bureau of Land Management–designated natural area has been fenced to protect the rare crucifixion thorn plant. This plant, a member of the ailanthus family and a relative of the Chinese tree of heaven, is fairly common in other Southwest desert basins (Arizona, Mexico) but is found in only a few places in the California desert. A similar plant is found in the Middle East, but this species is found only in North America. The name crucifixion thorn resulted from the plant's so-called likeness to the intricately branched crown of thorns on Jesus' head at the crucifixion.

The shrub's limbs are stiff, sturdy, and gray-green. A mature plant may be as tall as 6 to 8 ft. Thorns are a prominent feature and are a wicked couple of inches long, straight, and very sharply pointed. The leaves don't look much like leaves but instead appear to be small scales. (Small leaf areas reduce water loss.) Yellow flowers appear in late May and are a mere one-third inch across, seven-petaled, and symmetrical. Young fruits are quite visible in their pleasing orangey yellow bunches and later dry into nutlike clusters.

You can spend time very pleasantly in this protected natural area just walking around trying to identify the Colorado Desert plant and animal life. Early morning and late afternoon are the best times for taking photos and seeing the animals.

Salton Sea

ABOUT THE AREA. Today's Salton Sea lies in the Salton Basin (sometimes called the Salton Trough or Salton Sink), a depression measuring over 2000 sq mi and stretching from San Gorgonio Pass to the Gulf of California. The basin contains not only the Salton Sea, but the Coachella, Imperial, and Mexicali valleys. Although only a few miles wide at its northwest edge, it is roughly 70 mi wide at the Mexican border. The basin is the largest area of dry land below sea level in the Western Hemisphere (Death Valley is lower, but the area below sea level is far smaller). This depression was created by earth movements along the San Andreas fault.

The San Andreas Fault. The earth movements along the San Andreas fault system that pushed the basin down also pushed up the surrounding mountains. The fault is a crack in the earth's crust that stretches from the Gulf of California to Cape Mendocino, north of San Francisco. On its way from the gulf to the Pacific, this fault line passes through the Salton Sea area, San Gorgonio Pass, Cajon Pass, and the coastal mountains. You can see this giant fault line in a number of places along its route.

Camels in the Salton Basin? From about 6 million to 2 million years ago, the Salton Basin was quite different than it is today. In these ancient times the mountains and ridges of the Salton Basin had not been pushed up high enough to keep moist coastal air and rain from reaching the area. During this time, the Colorado River's route was such that large quantities of fresh water flowed into the region. Instead of a desert, there were streams and freshwater lakes (Lake LeConte is the name given to the largest of these in the area), grasslands, forests, and a variety of large and small animals — vultures, ducks, large turtles, saber-toothed cats, small horses, turkeys, and even a camel-like creature.

The Transition to Desert. About 2 million years ago, the climate in the Southwest began to go into a drier cycle, and the San Andreas fault became more active. As mountains were pushed up, they cut off the Salton Basin area from the coast's moist air, so the region became more and more desertlike. By approximately 20,000 years ago, except for the periodic appearances of Lake Cahuilla, the transition to desert had essentially been made. Despite the fact that the lake varied greatly in size over time, it did manage to support fish, shellfish, birds, small mammals, marshland plant communities, and eventually people. The main reason that the level of Lake Cahuilla wasn't constant was that its water supply depended greatly on the Colorado River flooding the Salton Basin. Today you can easily make out the watermarks, beachlines, and tufa deposits left by the ups and downs of the lake.

Where the Salton Sea Came From. During the last 2 million years the Colorado River has periodically created lakes in what is now the Salton Basin. Also, while the Colorado was carving out the Grand Canyon, the silt from this excavation was building up a delta at the river's mouth in the Gulf of California. This delta — which is now 12,000 ft deep — is what cuts off the Salton Basin from the gulf today.

The Salton Sea of today is the most recent, but by far the smallest, of the lakes created by the Colorado River. This last time, however, the Colorado had a little help. Here's how it happened.

After Lake Cahuilla dried up about 400 years ago, the Salton Basin was essentially dry until 1901. At this time, canals were built near Yuma to divert water from the Colorado River through Mexico and into the

Imperial Valley. The water was primarily used for irrigation. Then, in 1905, the river flooded in Mexico and flowed west and north into the basin—through the canals—for two years, creating the present Salton Sea. It took until 1907 to get the Colorado back into its normal channel.

Although the Colorado River water was fresh when it reached the Salton Sea, the many layers of minerals left behind in the basin by previous lakes—along with those created by the present 6 ft/year evaporation loss—have resulted in the sea's present salty, alkaline state. (In 1980 the sea was about 10% "saltier" than the Pacific Ocean; the mineral composition is different, though.)

Although this version of Lake Cahuilla is the smallest in history, it is still growing. Continuing agricultural runoff swells its level each year. It is also growing saltier, as fertilizers and other minerals continue to concentrate through evaporation.

One of the Salton Sea's unusual features is that it lies 234 ft below sea level—almost as low as Death Valley's Badwater region (which at 282 ft below sea level is the lowest point in the United States). Although the sea covers approximately 360 sq mi it is, on the average, only about 12 ft deep.

On the Wild Side. Despite its saltiness, the desert that surrounds it, and the area's high temperatures, the Salton Sea is a haven for many kinds of birds and other wildlife. It was to help protect these creatures that the Salton Sea National Wildlife Refuge (SSNWR) was created in 1930 by presidential proclamation.

Wildlife fanciers can visit the two refuge units on foot. Another good place to see wildlife in the area is at San Sebastian Marsh. (See trips below.)

Anza-Borrego Desert State Park. Just to the west of the Salton Sea lies Anza-Borrego Desert State Park (ABSP). This large and beautiful desert park covers about one-third of San Diego County and portions of Imperial and Riverside counties. Once you are in the east Salton Sea area, much of the east side of the park is accessible to you. For example, you can easily visit the intriguing elephant trees (where there is a self-guided discovery trail) and spectacular Split Mountain; take a scenic drive on county road S-22 from Salton City to Borrego Springs via the Borrego-Salton Seaway; and explore on foot some of the canyons supporting small palm oases (see ABSP, below).

FACILITIES. Motels, restaurants, gas, and supplies at Coachella, Niland, and Westmorland (also, of course, at Palm Springs, Indio, Brawley, and El Centro).

Camping. At Salton Sea State Recreation Area (SSSRA), on the east side of the Salton Sea (entrance from CA 111 is at Parkside Dr near Desert Beach), there are a developed campground (with water, toilets, tables, and showers) and two undeveloped campgrounds (water and chemical toilets except at Salt Creek, which is waterless).

Other developed campgrounds are in Imperial County parks: Red Hill Marina (from CA 111 near the SSNWR, at the southeast edge of the sea, turn west on Sinclair Rd, then north on Garst Rd to marina); Niland Marina (from CA 111 just south of the SSSRA turn south on Niland Marina Rd and go 2 mi); and Wiest Lake (from CA 111 turn east on Rutherford Rd about 6 mi north of Brawley; pass lake on south side of road and go south on Dietrich Rd to park).

Primitive campgrounds (pit toilets and sometimes tables, but no water) can be found at the Finney–Ramer Lake Wildlife Area (10.8 mi south of Niland, go southeast on Titsworth Rd about 1 mi and turn south on Smith Rd to lake), and also on the eastern edge of Anza-Borrego Desert State Park. Camping is also permitted at the Wister Unit of the Imperial Valley Wildlife Refuge (7 mi northwest of Niland on CA 111) and around Obsidian Butte, but there are no facilities.

Quiet open-desert camping spots can often be found a few miles up many of the dirt roads in the area (make sure you are not on private property).

Salton Sea National Wildlife Refuge

TO GET THERE. Unit 1 is located 5 mi west of Westmorland on CA 86. At this point, go north on Vendel Rd (good dirt) 1.3 mi to refuge. Signs will indicate how far into the refuge you may drive.

To reach Unit 2, go west on Sinclair Rd off CA 111 3.7 mi south of Niland. Follow Sinclair Rd west for 4.5 mi to the refuge headquarters. Literature on the refuge is usually available at the headquarters.

GETTING YOUR BEARINGS. Don't forget to take along a good Imperial County map when you go to this area. The USGS topos covering the refuge and the south end of the Salton Sea are *Kane Spring NE* and *Obsidian Butte*.

ABOUT THE WILDLIFE REFUGE. The Salton Sea National Wildlife Refuge (SSNWR) was authorized by presidential proclamation in 1930. At first, the refuge consisted of about 35,000 acres. Because the water level has been steadily rising since the sea was created in 1905–1907, there are now only about 2000 acres of the refuge above water to be used for winter bird habitat. Agricultural runoff from the valleys surrounding the sea, along with runoff from the local mountains, is responsible for the rise in water level. The refuge is divided into three units, all of which are located at the south end of the Salton Sea. The largest of the three units has no land area, but is part of the sea's water area. The two small land units are good places to view waterbirds and are easily accessible (see directions above).

A Winter Haven for Waterfowl. Of all the refuges on the Pacific Flyway, the SSNWR is the farthest south. It was created to provide a winter stopping place for migrating birds, primarily waterfowl. In addition to being a stopover for migrating waterfowl and other birds, the refuge is a year-round home for many shorebirds and a wide variety of other wildlife species.

How the Marshes Were Created. The marshes around the sea that originally attracted waterfowl resulted from agricultural runoff created as more and more Colorado River water was diverted to the area for farming. As agriculture expanded in the Imperial Valley in the 1930s, the marshes began to shrink and the waterfowl began to feast on the farmers' crops instead! To keep both farmers and birds happy, crops are grown on the refuge just for the birds (this keeps them from wreaking havoc on the farms).

The refuge also supports several species of marine fish, barnacles, clam worms, and copepods. These were introduced either deliberately or accidentally when the salinity of the sea began to rise and the native freshwater fish species died out.

When to Visit. Late fall, winter, and spring are the best times to visit the refuge. Summer in the Salton Sea area is hot. Just a few of the impressive birds you may see are snowy egrets, great blue herons, Canada geese, snow geese, green-winged teals, and eared grebes. Of course you can see many kinds of wildlife other than birds here.

Hiking Trails. Because refuge roads and trails are closed to vehicles, the best way to see the birds is to do some walking. (You can see a fair number of birds from your car in some places. For example, along Vendel Rd on the way into Unit 1, you'll probably see more burrowing owls than you've ever seen before!)

In Unit 1, when you reach the end of the road, look for a trail leading toward the shore of the Salton Sea. You get fairly close to the shore in about 0.5 mi; at this point, you can take the trail either east or west along the shore. If you go west, the trail will disappear in about 0.5 mi; if you go east, the trail will turn south after about 0.5 mi and then west again for another 0.5 mi, until you are back to approximately where you started.

In Unit 2, the Rock Hill Wildlife Trail goes west toward the sea from the headquarters for about 0.5 mi and then north along the shore for another 0.5 mi. You can follow the trail across the base of Rock Hill and east along the shore for another 0.5 mi or so and then either cut southwest back toward the north leg of the trail (there are several faint trails back this way) or walk south back to the headquarters on Gentry Rd. (Rock Hill is one of four volcanic buttes in the southern part of the sea.)

Refuge Hours. The refuge is open sunrise to sunset; the headquarters is open 7:30 A.M. to 3:00 P.M., Monday through Friday. Even when the headquarters is closed, there is usually some literature available outside. Refuge roads and trails are closed to vehicles but open to walking, bicycling, and horseback riding. Camping is not permitted, drinking water and restrooms are not available, and pets must be leashed.

Travertine Rock

TO GET THERE. Take the Dillon-Coachella exit south off I-10 at Indio to its junction with CA 111/86 going southeast (about 1 mi). Follow CA 111/86 for another mile to where CA 86 diverges south from CA 111. Take CA 86 southeast for 18.5 mi to Travertine Rock.

GETTING YOUR BEARINGS. A good Imperial County map will show you most of the roads around the Salton Sea.

ABOUT THE ROCK. For many thousands of years this granite out-crop was an island in Lake Cahuilla, a forerunner of the Salton Sea. A large sandbar connected it to the Santa Rosa Mtns to the west. The light line above you on the rock just over some irregular dark deposits is the ancient Lake Cahuilla shoreline.

What Is Travertine? The rocks just above the shoreline are lighter in color due to the lake's wave action, which removed the desert varnish you can see at higher levels. The travertine (or tufa), which gives Traver-tine Rock its name, is a freshwater deposit of porous calcium carbonate that was laid down with the help of blue-green algae below the surface level of Lake Cahuilla over many years. This crust is up to 30 in. thick. (The words *tufa* and *travertine* are often used interchangeably.) If you look closely at the tufa, you'll see tiny snail and mussel shells in it — further indications that Lake Cahuilla was a freshwater lake. You can find these mollusc fossils in many sandy places throughout the Salton Trough.

Many Miles of Ancient Beachlines. If you go to the top of the rock, look for the parallel lines of desert scrub on the sandbar that used to connect the rock to the Santa Rosas. These are beachlines that were periodically left by the gradually drying Lake Cahuilla.

If you drive south on CA 86 from Travertine Rock, look west toward the Santa Rosas. The impressive ancient beachline can be seen quite clearly at the foot of the Santa Rosas for several miles as you drive along. It gives you some idea of how much larger and deeper the lake was in times past. The ancient shoreline you are seeing is at about 40 + ft above sea level; today's shoreline is at about − 234 ft!

San Sebastian Marsh National Natural Landmark 4WD Tour/Hike

TO GET THERE. The marsh is located about 5 mi west of CA 86 and 2 mi south of CA 78. Below are three routes you can take to get within hiking distance of the marsh area.

Access 1: Follow the directions to Travertine Rock, above, then con-tinue on CA 86 southeast approx 26.6 mi to Kane Springs Rd (this dirt road takes off about 1.5 mi south of the CA 86/78 junction; it's not easy to see because of the berm on the west side of CA 86 and the fact that the road is unmarked). Go west on Kane Springs Rd. This road is definitely chancy, with some deeply rutted spots, so it is best for 4WD with good clearance. Proceed down the road for about 4 mi, where there are Bureau of Land Management signs identifying and describing the San Sebastian Marsh Natural Area, along with a simple map. Continue for another 0.4 mi or so to a high point above a wash (Mark Wash). This is a good place to start hiking to the marsh, which lies about 1.3 mi west of here. To continue west past the marsh and then north to CA 78, reverse the directions in access 3, below, from Mark Wash back.

Access 2: Come north from I-8 on CA 111 through El Centro to Brawley and Westmorland. Then take CA 86 northwest to the Kane Springs Rd, which takes off about 14.2 mi north of the intersection of S-30 (Forrester Rd) and CA 86 in Westmorland. From this point, follow the directions for access 1, above, to the vicinity of the marsh.

Access 3: Start from CA 78, 9.3 mi east of Ocotillo Wells. At this point, go south on a poleline road; cross the confluence of Tarantula Wash and San Felipe Wash after about 1.6 mi (Tarantula Wash, which goes north from here, has good camping spots). In another 1.7 mi, cross Fish Creek; 0.2 mi farther, jog east on the poleline road for about 50 yd, then continue another 0.2 mi to the junction with Kane Springs Rd. Go east on Kane Springs Rd for 1.4 mi, then cross Carrizo Wash (at this point you can hike 2.9 mi northeast down the wash to see the marsh). Continue straight ahead 3.9 mi to Harper's Well, where the road goes steeply down into Mark Wash and up the other side. Again, as mentioned in access 1, above, this is a good place to start hiking to the marsh. To reach CA 86, continue east on the Kane Springs Rd for 4.6 mi.

Note: All roads into the San Sebastian Marsh vicinity are chancey. Because this is a major drainage area, rains cause flooding across many of the roads (which are often sandy to start out with), so you never really know what kind of shape they'll be in. Use 4WD with good clearance only.

No vehicle travel is permitted in the marsh area itself. This means no vehicles where there is heavy vegetation or water in the vicinity of the Fish, Carrizo, and San Felipe wash confluence (approximately 6 sq mi). This is a rare and fragile area on which much wildlife depends.

GETTING YOUR BEARINGS. Besides a good Imperial County map, the USGS topo *Kane Springs* will help you identify the washes in the San Sebastian Marsh area.

ABOUT THE MARSH. Three underground creeks are responsible for the marsh's existence. These creeks (San Felipe, Fish, and Carrizo) are flowing east toward the Salton Sea from higher elevations some miles west of the marsh. The rivers surface about 80 ft below sea level and form the ponds and muddy areas that are collectively called San Sebastian Marsh.

A National Natural Landmark. Although this small marshy area may not look very striking at first glance, in actuality it is one of only a few long-term riparian habitats in the desert. In historic and prehistoric times, this water source has been an important one for both people and animals. The National Park Service has recognized its natural and historic uniqueness by designating the marsh a national natural landmark.

Wildlife and Vegetation. The dependable source of water is the reason for the area's abundant and varied wildlife and vegetation. It is home for many species of birds, mammals, and reptiles — and even amphibians like the leopard frog and the rare desert pupfish. It is also a regular stopping place for migratory waterfowl and other birds using the Pacific Flyway. In the marsh itself you will find giant reeds and cattails, while at the periphery you can see salt grass, pickleweed, inkweed, mesquite, quail brush, athel, and, unfortunately, tamarisk. (For information on the destructive properties of tamarisk, an introduced exotic, see Chapter 4.)

Treat the Marsh Gently. Like all desert aquatic habitats, the marsh's ecological balance is extremely fragile and can be thrown out of balance (with disastrous results for the vegetation and wildlife) by people and natural events. We can't do anything about the weather and other kinds of natural disturbances, but we can — as visitors — treat it gently. For example, when visiting this or any other important wildlife watering, feeding, and nesting area, stay well back from the water so as not to interfere with wildlife activities. Use binoculars to watch the birds and other animals from a distance; skirt the edges of the marsh rather than making your way through it. Taking care is just common sense — and not difficult.

How the Marsh Got Its Name. When Juan Bautista de Anza first came through the Yuha area in 1774, his native American guide led the party to a village near the marsh. The village had a population of more than four hundred native Americans. In his journal, Anza noted that water was plentiful, and although most of it was quite salty there was one spring that was fresh. He also mentioned that there was good grazing. Anza was so impressed with the area that he named it in honor of his guide, Sebastian Tarabal. (For more information on de Anza, see the Yuha Basin "About the Area" section, above.)

After Anza, other explorers — and then emigrants and prospectors — made the San Sebastian Marsh area one of their regular watering stops. You can still see some remnants of human occupation from prehistoric times to the late 1800s and early 1900s. For example, near Mark Wash you can find a standpipe left over from Harper's Well (the well was a watering hole and an oil test-well site in the early 1900s). An occasional post with a K carved in it still marks the old Kane Springs Rd in places (look for one on the north side of the road, just above the east side of Mark Wash). Shards of native American pottery and some flakes are also occasionally found around the marsh. If you find any of these artifacts, please do not collect them; leave them in place for others to see and for archaeologists to study.

Rabbit Peak Hike

Class 2/elev. 6623 ft/USGS topo *Rabbit Peak*/16–20 mi RT/cross-country

TO GET THERE. Take I-10 to Indio; go south at the Dillon-Coachella exit to its junction with CA 111/86 going southeast (about 1 mi). Follow CA 111/86 another mile to where CA 86 diverges south from CA 111.

Access 1 (East): Take CA 86 14.8 mi south to Oasis; turn west onto Ave 74 and drive as far as practical before parking (the road gets sandy).

Access 2 (Southwest): Follow CA 86 south for about 29 mi from where it diverges from CA 111. At Salton City, go west on the Borrego-Salton Seaway (San Diego County road S-22). Drive 14.9 mi and park.

ABOUT THE HIKE. Rabbit Peak dominates the south half of the Santa Rosa Range and overlooks Anza-Borrego Desert State Park on the west and the Salton Sea to the east. It is a large, rounded mass of a mountain that holds little of technical interest to the climber, but offers considerable challenge to the hiker. The main difficulties are the elevation gain involved (more than 6000 ft from the east side) and the distance involved (16–20 mi, round-trip, depending on the route). Only experienced, well-conditioned hikers should attempt the summit on a one-day hike. The peak is sometimes climbed as a two-day backpack; all water must be carried as there are no streams or springs in the area.

Rabbit is climbed either from the east or from the southwest. The route from the east is probably the one more often used.

East Route. From where you are parked, hike across the desert alluvial fan on the usually well-ducked use trail into and up the left side of a large canyon. Climb out of the south side of the canyon onto the southeast ridge of Rabbit. Follow along the ridge to a flat spot at 4100 ft that can be used as the site of an overnight camp. Proceed up the steeper slopes to a rock outcrop at the southeast end of Rabbit Ridge and onto the ridge for the final 1000 ft of gain to the summit. The round-trip is about 16 mi and takes eight to ten hours.

Southwest Route. From where you are parked, hike north across the alluvial fan to the prominent round ridge to the north of Rattlesnake Canyon. Follow the ridge to the summit of Villager Peak (5976 ft). There are several good campsites in the area. Continue north along the ridge, contouring any false summits on the east side until you come to the summit plateau of Rabbit. The high point of the peak is a rocky outcrop near the south edge of the plateau. The round-trip is about 20 mi and takes sixteen to eighteen hours.

Mecca Hills–Orocopia Mountains

ABOUT THE AREA. Here, as in many parts of the California desert, there are a great variety of things to see and to learn. In the Mecca

Hills–Orocopia Mtns area you can visit palm oases, colorful canyons, ridgetops with spectacular views, grottoes, and picturesque badlands. But, of course, these are just a few of the possibilities.

The San Andreas Fault Again! Because the Mecca Hills and Orocopia Mtns lie along the San Andreas and related fault systems, they are a striking geologic display of faulting effects. Both regions contain rocks over 600 million years old, from a time when no life existed on land and jellyfish were the highest form of life in the seas. These ancient rocks were forged from even more ancient seabed deposits that were melted and metamorphosed into the stuff of mountains. Over tens of millions of years the rocks were eroded, remelted, remade, and pushed up again into mountains several times.

The final pushing up, for our time at least, occurred about 1 million years ago. At about this time the Mecca Hills were squeezed up between the San Andreas fault and the Painted Canyon fault. This record of faulting, erosion, sedimentation, folding, subsidence, arching, and metamorphosis can be seen by anyone who visits the area and can be read in detail by those who know the language of the rocks.

Miscellaneous Inhabitants. The area has been used for many thousands of years. Fossils of horse-, and deer-, and camel-like creatures, in addition to invertebrate fossils and freshwater shells, have been found here. These are relics of an earlier time when the climate was more hospitable and grasslands, freshwater lakes, and year-round streams laced the now-desertified land.

More recently, the Cahuilla Indians regularly crossed the area on a trade-trail system, using the oases (especially Hidden Spring) for resting and watering places. Hidden Spring is the only permanent water in the area. In our time, the climate is not as hospitable as it was during the late Pliocene and early Pleistocene times that produced the fossils mentioned above. The average annual rainfall is now only 3–4 in. per year, of which quite a bit is lost in flash floods.

Colorful Local Attractions. Near Hidden Spring are caves—known locally as the Grottoes. These are slits in the rock that have been partially buried by rockfalls and silting, but which still allow some safe exploration along their original floors.

Many of the canyons, such as Painted Canyon, are distinctively colorful. Like so many of the other area features, even this color is mostly the result of the extensive faulting. This is because the canyons created along the fault let wind and water flow over the minerals in the folded and uplifted shales of their walls. The iron in these shales then oxidizes and combines with other minerals in the water to form varicolored deposits—mostly of a yellowish hue. It is said that native Americans used these deposits to make body paints.

Flora and Fauna. Despite its somewhat harsh climate, this area supports a wide variety of desert-adapted plants and animals—mostly in the washes. Here you will find many of the living things described in the "Desert Plants" and "Desert Wildlife" chapters. (The plants are far easier to see than the shy desert animals!) The Mecca aster, a lovely lilac-colored, daisylike flower on a long, graceful, bright green stem, is found only here and one other place in Baja California. You can also see native desert (California) fan palms in the oases. Recently, signs of bighorn sheep have been found in the hillls near the grottoes and oases described in the trips below.

Because temperatures can be as high as 115° F in summer, this is obviously is not the best time to visit here. Late fall, winter, and spring are very pleasant, though, with their warm days and cool evenings. And although there are more flowers in the spring, you can usually find something quite lovely blooming in the many washes almost any time of year.

Local Detractions and Their Remedies. Unfortunately, this whole area gets quite a bit of ORV use. It helps if you time your visits so they don't coincide with holiday weekends. Fortunately, there are many canyons and other places to hike where ORVs are not able to squeeze in or climb up. All in all, the area is so attractive that it is worth several visits despite the possible intrusions.

FACILITIES. Motels, restaurants, supplies, and gas in Indio, Coachella, and Thermal.

Camping. Mecca Hills County Park has tables and a restroom, but no water. You may camp anywhere in the park or in the surrounding hills and canyons.

The drive northeast through the Orocopias on CA 195 (Box Canyon Rd from the Coachella Canal on) to I-10 is a scenic one. There are quite a few dirt roads that are used to get off the highway to nearby open-desert camping spots. Some roads are good enough for RVs; others require a 4WD.

Mecca Hills County Park

TO GET THERE. Take I-10 past Indio; get on Dillon Rd going south, and then onto CA 111 going southeast. Stay on CA 111 as you go through Coachella and Thermal. In about 12 mi turn east on CA 195 and go through Mecca (keep an eye on the signs, as you have to jog around a bit in Mecca). In about 4.5 mi you'll cross the Coachella Canal and come upon a sign pointing north (left) to Painted Canyon and Mecca Hills County Park. Follow this good, graded dirt road for about 4 mi to the park. Although the road continues for about 1 mi up the canyon (to a sign indicating that this is as far as the road is maintained), it has a very soft spot or two; it's best to leave your vehicle at the upper end of the park and walk. Tracks go beyond the sign but from there on the area is closed to vehicles. In any case, the Mecca Hills are best explored and appreciated on foot.

GETTING YOUR BEARINGS. You'll need a good Riverside and/or Imperial County map for this area. To get a better idea of how the canyons work around here, try the USGS topos *Mortmar* and *Mecca.*

ABOUT THE PARK. There are many interesting canyons to be explored in and around the undeveloped, 640-acre Mecca Hills County Park. The walls of the main canyon give vivid evidence of the upheavals that formed the hills. Some of the side canyons are so narrow in spots that you must crawl through them. Yet others contain attractive dry waterfalls. All these canyons were produced by wind and water eroding the Mecca Hills (sometimes called the Mud Hills). In late fall, winter, and spring, you can spend pleasant days camping or picnicking here. Those who enjoy walking and photography will find plenty of canyons to explore. More ambitious and experienced hikers will probably want to try the interesting and scenic Painted Canyon day hike, below.

Painted Canyon Hike
Class 2/elev. 1812 ft/USGS topos *Coachella, Cottonwood Spring*/5 mi RT/use trails, cross-country

TO GET THERE. Follow the directions to Mecca Hills County Park, above; leave your vehicle at the park's upper end.

ABOUT THE HIKE. When exploring most of the canyons in this area you must return the same way you came. In some you can make a loop trip; if you don't know the area, though, it's not easy to tell which canyons interconnect. Painted Canyon is a good loop hike, but definitely not a hike for the inexperienced or solo hiker.

Beginning with a Ladder. Start the hike by walking into the major canyon until you reach the sign telling you where the road ends (about 1 mi). At this point, continue up the canyon on the northeast (right). (There is another, smaller, canyon even farther right; take care you don't enter this one by mistake.) Before long the canyon narrows somewhat and the walls become higher—sometimes getting up to 100 ft or more. Keep going up this canyon another 0.25 mi or so until you reach a very large rock and mud fall on the left that nearly hides the mouth of a small side canyon. Although it appears impossible at first glance, you will be able to continue up this side canyon by climbing up and down and through the rock and mud lumps. Finally you will go through a narrow passage leading to a small room with a ladder about 20 ft high. (This explains why this canyon is sometimes called Ladder Canyon.)

Climb the ladder and continue along a very narrow, high-sided passage containing two more, much shorter ladders. (If for some reason the ladders are missing, most people can still climb up without them.) As the walls become less steep, you'll take a fork to the right (usually marked by a duck). Continue up this rather rocky canyon to its end. Then scramble up to the ridge straight ahead to the north. Pause, have a nice long drink, and look around.

Scrambling for a View. From here you have gorgeous views of the Salton Sea, Rabbit Peak, the Santa Rosa Mtns, Toro Peak, San Jacinto Peak, and San Gorgonio Peak. After you've looked your fill, go west (left) along the ridge and pick up the ridge trail. This trail is a bit sketchy in places, but if you keep looking ahead and back you'll have no trouble keeping on it. At times on your right you can look very steeply down into the magnificent canyon in which you will eventually be hiking.

The trail contours around to the right and to the left of little hills. After going down a slight hill, you'll notice a very faint trail going straight ahead (see side trip to Airway Beacon, below) and one contouring to the right; take the one to the right. This trail drops down onto a rocky plateau, at the end of which you'll go down a rocky wash to the wide, sandy canyon floor.

- *Airway Beacon (Side Trip).*
For a somewhat longer hike, do not take the trail to the right; instead, take the trail that goes straight ahead. This leads to Airway Beacon; there is some cross-country hiking involved. From the Beacon—which at 1812 ft is the highest point in the area—you can drop into Painted Canyon farther up, and then continue as indicated below.

Painted Canyon at Last! At first the canyon doesn't appear to be very spectacular, but as you get lower into it the rocks become very beautifully colored. Here in the canyon bottom there are ironwood and smoke trees; when there has been enough water, you'll also see some lovely desert flowers. You should be able to find some nice lunch spots in sun or shade.

As you continue along the canyon, eventually you'll come to a dry waterfall that must be gotten down if you wish to complete the loop trip. Here, it's handy to have a climbing rope to help people down with. (Not everyone will need this.) From the bottom of the waterfall it's about 0.75 mi back to where you started. About halfway down the canyon on the right, as you head back to the starting point, you can see the rock and mud fall canyon where you found the ladders.

Hidden Spring Oasis and Sheep Hole Palms Oasis Hike
Class 1/elev. 800 ft/USGS topo *Cottonwood Spring*/6 mi RT/use trails

TO GET THERE. Follow directions for Mecca Hills County Park, above, to the turnoff onto CA 195. About 10.1 mi northeast on CA 195 watch the north (right) side of the road for a rock painted yellow. Sometimes the yellow is covered by dirt, so also watch for a dirt road or vehicle tracks leading north across the wash to two large desert ironwood trees at the mouth of a small tributary ravine. The trail to both Sheep Hole Palms Oasis and Hidden Spring Oasis climbs the right slope of this tributary. Depending on the condition of the "road," it may or may not be possible for ordinary cars to drive across the wash to the trees at the mouth of the ravine. If the road conditions are bad, park your vehicle near the highway and start waking from there.

ABOUT THE OASES. Hidden Spring is an attractive little oasis deserving of its name. Tucked away in one of many grottoes in the foothills of the Orocopia Mtns, it is surprising that it was ever found. Unfortunately, its source of water is running out and the palms are declining in number. In 1937 there were thirty-nine trees; today only thirty remain. Frequent vandal-started fires have also taken their toll on both this and nearby Sheep Hole Palms Oasis. Though healthy palm groves withstand fire remarkably well, water-stressed oases reproduce so slowly that they cannot keep pace with the fire mortality.

To reach the oases, start where the dirt road ends near two large desert ironwood trees at the mouth of a small tributary ravine. The trail to both Sheep Hole Palms Oasis and Hidden Spring Oasis climbs the right slope of this tributary. Look for it as you slowly walk up the ravine for not more than 50 yd. Sheep Hole Palms Oasis is reached by following this old native American trail for less than 1 mi.

From Sheep Hole Palms Oasis, continue down the wash for 0.3 mi until you see a trail climbing out of the wash to your left. Follow this trail over a low ridge into Hidden Spring Canyon, and then walk up the wash. After approximately 0.7 mi the canyon narrows and turns to the right. Just beyond this point a small arroyo, only about 7 ft wide, bordered by gray and reddish rock, comes in from the left. Hidden Spring Oasis lies just a few hundred feet up this tributary, beyond a pile of boulders.

To return to your starting point, just retrace your route.

The Grottoes and Other Interesting Places Hike

Class 2/elev. 800 ft/USGS topo *Cottonwood Spring*/7 mi RT/use trails, cross-country

TO GET THERE. Take I-10 past Indio; get on Dillon Rd going south, and then onto CA 111 going southeast. Stay on CA 111 as you go through Coachella and Thermal. About 12 mi from I-10 turn east on CA 195 and go through Mecca (the road jogs a bit in Mecca). From here, follow the directions given above for Hidden Spring Oasis, beginning with the second sentence. (This hike starts at the same place.)

ABOUT THE HIKE. This is not exactly a trail hike, for trails in this area are definitely intermittent, often nonexistent. There are no trail signs. The complete Grottoes hike can be done in a day, or it can be an overnight backpack. It's OK to park overnight or to car camp in the trailhead area if you're making a weekend of it. There are no facilities at the trailhead and no drinkable water on the "trails." This, like the Painted Canyon hike, above, is not a hike for the inexperienced or solo hiker.

This hike to the Grottoes passes near two native desert (California) fan palm oases (see Hidden Spring Oasis, above). If you are backpacking, please do not camp near the water—the animals depend on it, and your presence will keep them from coming to drink. During the past year or two (for the first time in several years) bighorn sheep droppings have been seen along the high trail. If bighorns are in the area, this is all the more reason to be careful around the water supply; bighorns are very sensitive to any intrusion.

Finding Grotto 1. Begin the hike by walking up the canyon near the trees. On your right about 50 yd on you will find two trails, one a little beyond the other. Take either—eventually they both come out at the same place. Pause here and appreciate the view of the Salton Sea. When it is very clear, you can see the mountains in Mexico and at the south end of the sea.

Continue on the well-defined trail that leads down to Sheep Hole Palms Oasis in the wash. This oasis is about 1 mi from where you started. From there keep walking down the wash for about 0.3 mi, watching for the trail to leave the canyon on the left and go over the hill to the main wash of Hidden Spring Canyon. (You will notice vehicle tracks.) When you find the trail, go on over the hill to the main wash. There is a good bit of desert ironwood with mistletoe along the way here.

Before long the main wash narrows, and on the right will be a high, colorful rock formation with yellow predominating. Just opposite is the narrow canyon opening that leads to Hidden Spring Oasis in about 0.2 mi. For the less energetic, this oasis is a pleasant place to wait for the more serious hikers who will go on to the Grottoes and return to approach Hidden Spring from a different direction. (Hidden Spring Oasis is about 3 mi from where you started.)

The more serious hikers can proceed up the main canyon a short distance to the first canyon on the left. There is quite a thicket at its mouth. Go to the end of this canyon, where you'll find the entrance to the first grotto. There has been a big rockfall at the mouth of the grotto, but those who enjoy scrambling will have fun. Have your flashlights ready. Some may want the assistance of a climbing rope here, but most don't. In places the grotto opens up into a room with sky overhead, and sometimes there are even a few flowers and bushes growing in the sand.

When you come out of the grotto into the canyon you will notice ORV tracks going steeply uphill on the left. Go up this hill and turn left at the top, following the tracks about three-fourths of the way up the next long, steep hill. At this point, take a trail that goes left and contours around the hill. Go up to the high spot here, pause, have a drink, and look around at the view.

Next, continue on this fairly well defined trail (where bighorn sheep droppings have been found) that eventually drops steeply down to Hidden Spring and the palm oasis. After dropping down, if you turn right and go up the canyon 100 yd or so you can find a satin-smooth strip of rock.

Finding Grotto 2. Instead of turning into the canyon containing the first grotto, continue up the main canyon to its end. When you are almost up to Grotto 2's entrance, look on the right side of the main canyon; here are more satin-smooth rocks. At the end of the canyon, on the left, you'll see a rock painted yellow. Below this is the grotto entrance. Again, have your flashlights ready.

At first you need to crawl on all fours for a short distance. Although for the most part you can stand up in this grotto, there are some places where it is a tight squeeze. When you come out at the other end you'll be quite high up. It may take some careful looking around to find the "ducks" that will lead you cross-country down the hill to the flat. Occasionally you will walk on some desert pavement as you head west cross-country—sometimes on a very faint trail—to a rather narrow wash. Follow this wash to the left and it will lead you to the exit of Grotto 1. Just before you reach the exit you will see the ORV tracks going steeply uphill on the right. From here, follow the directions to Hidden Spring and the palm oasis given for Grotto 1.

■ *Red Rock Canyon (Side Trip).*
If you aren't in the mood for grottoes, you might like to try this canyon. It is the last canyon on the left before you reach Grotto 2. Although it is brushy in spots, you can get through. Red Rock Canyon winds around and eventually comes out on the flat that you would have hit coming down from the exit of Grotto 2. When you come to the flat, again head west for the wash leading you to the steep ORV tracks and finally to Hidden Spring and the palm oasis, as described above in the directions for Grotto 1.

RETURNING TO THE TRAILHEAD. Whether you visited the grottoes or Red Rock Canyon, you'll now be at Hidden Spring. From here there are two ways to return to the trailhead—the way you came and a somewhat longer, more scenic route.

Route 1—The Way You Came. Go back to the main canyon; carefully keep on its right side as you go down-canyon, so you won't miss the trail that brought you over the hill from Sheep Hole Wash.

Route 2—The Scenic Way. To take this longer, more scenic (and more strenuous) route, go only a short way down the main canyon—until you pass the last cliff on the right. Here, a wide wash opens up. Keep to the right until you find ORV tracks going into a canyon on your right. Take this canyon. When you see a narrow opening on the left, go through it; in a little way you'll go under an almost complete arch and will be in a wash.

Continue up this wash (it seems endless) to within a few feet of its end. Keep on the left side and you'll see a duck leading you out of this wash and up another rocky canyon. After a while you can get out of the canyon and scramble up to the ridge. Turn left here and when you reach a high spot, stop for a drink and a look around.

From here you can see the dark cliff with the predominating yellow color just opposite where you can turn into Hidden Spring and the palm oasis. Continuing in the same direction, follow the ORV tracks for a while. You'll see a number of rather indistinct trails — some going to the left and some to the right of little knolls. Many of these are game trails. When you pass close to a staked claim on the shoulder of a little hill, you'll know you're on the right track (watch carefully for this landmark).

All the little trails are confusing, so the best thing to do is to keep generally to the left until you notice a "duck" on the right. This duck indicates a trail going to the right (again, watch carefully). Just before you bear right, you should be able to catch a glimpse of Sheep Hole Palm Oasis — which should be to your left and below. Keep on to the right over some knife edges until you think you can't go any farther (but you do), turn sharply left on a high promontory, and look down. Voila! Your car! Go on down the steep trail and there you are. This is a fun trip and an exciting one! (But definitely not for the solo novice.)

Palm Springs–Indio

ABOUT THE AREA. Palm Springs, Indio, and the lands around them are all within the Colorado Desert region of the larger Sonoran Desert (the low desert — see Chapter 1, "What Is a Desert?"). In summer, the highest temperatures in the United States are recorded in the Colorado Desert. It is the nation's hottest, driest desert. However, from late fall through spring the daytime temperatures are very mild and pleasant, often hovering in the seventies for months on end; nighttime temperatures seldom fall below 40° F. On the west side of Palm Springs, the San Jacinto Mtns rise to over 8000 ft, creating a spectacular backdrop for the whole area. It's easy to see why this is such a popular place in the winter.

The Date Capital of the World. South of Palm Springs is Indio, the major community in one of the agricultural hubs of California — the Coachella Valley. It's hard to believe that a valley that gets only about 3 in. of rain per year and that sports a long list of high temperature records can have developed into such a hotbed (literally and figuratively) of agricultural activity. It has, though, with the help of Colorado River water and thousands of date palms. (Of course, many other hot-weather crops — such as cotton and citrus — are also grown here.)

Why Visit a Town? But why should desert visitors interested in the wide open spaces visit such an already-developed area? (After all, supermarkets and citrus groves aren't much of a change of scene.) The answer to this rhetorical question is that despite the area's development it still harbors a number of attractions that aren't usually found amongst the groves of fast-food chains. Some of these attractions are even visited regularly by old desert rats, while some of them (sometimes the same ones) are nicely calculated to gently initiate the desert novice into the mysteries of some of the most beautiful country in the West.

Visiting (and hiking in) some of the various palm oases, with their waterfalls and year-round streams, can help you to appreciate that the desert isn't all sandstorms and rattlesnakes.

Touring the Living Desert Reserve and the Palm Springs Desert Museum can give you an idea or two about how the desert came to be, how desert plants and animals have uniquely adapted to the desert, and how native Americans have lived in the desert over the centuries, among many other things.

If car touring is one of your favorite forms of recreation, you'll enjoy the Palms to Pines Highway. This drive from Palm Desert up into the San Jacinto Mtns, with its many vista points, enables you to see the desert-to-mountain transition in a leisurely fashion.

And these are just a few of the possibilities. You'll discover even more when you visit the area.

FACILITIES. There are many gas stations, grocery stores, motels, restaurants, parks, and public restrooms throughout these and surrounding communities. Here you are not far from civilization; you are in the middle of it!

Camping. There are three developed campgrounds in the area. Lake Cahuilla County Park can be reached by following CA 111 east from its intersection with South Palm Canyon Dr for 20.1 mi (just past the town of Indian Wells) to Jefferson St. Go south on Jefferson for 5.5 mi to the park, which is situated on a freshwater lake (with swimming beach).

The other two campgrounds are located in the San Bernardino National Forest off CA 74 (the Palms to Pines Highway). To get to Pinyon Flats Campground (4000 ft), follow CA 111 east from its intersection with South Palm Canyon Dr in Palm Springs to Palm Desert (about 12.7 mi), then go south on CA 74. About 15.7 mi up the hill from the start of CA 74 you should see the Pinyon Flats Campground entrance on the west side of the road. The entrance to Santa Rosa Springs Campground (7100 ft) is about 3.7 mi farther on, on the east side of the road. The campground is up a graded dirt road about 8.5 mi southeast.

Palm Springs Desert Museum

TO GET THERE. Take I-10 to the CA 111 turnoff north of Palm Springs. Follow CA 111 (Palm Canyon Dr) south past Tramway Rd for about 2 mi, to Tahquitz-McCallum Way. Turn west here and go one long block to Museum Dr; turn north here—the museum will be straight ahead on the west side of the street (at 101 Museum Dr).

GETTING YOUR BEARINGS. A good Riverside County map will help you to find your way around in this part of the desert. (The AAA has an excellent "Palm Springs and Vicinity" map you might also like to have.)

ABOUT THE MUSEUM. Desert visitors will find the exhibits here of great interest. The displays cover California desert natural history, geology, biology, and anthropology. Fountains and gardens surround the museum. For more information, call the museum office at 619-325-7186.

Living Desert Reserve

TO GET THERE. Take I-10 to the Bob Hope Dr exit 19 mi east of the CA 111 turnoff. Follow Bob Hope Dr south about 5.5 mi to CA 111 (Palm Canyon Dr). Go east on CA 111 (East Palm Canyon Dr) for 2 mi to its intersection with CA 74 in the town of Palm Desert. Continue east on CA 111 past this intersection for about 1 mi to Portola Ave; go south on Portola for about 1.5 mi to the reserve (at 47-900 Portola Ave).

GETTING YOUR BEARINGS. See Palm Springs Desert Museum, above, for map advice.

ABOUT THE RESERVE. This unusual desert park contains many miles of nature trails. The trails will take you through the six major desert habitats—creosote bush flats, rock bajadas, hillsides, sand dunes, washes, and an ephemeral lake. In the reserve you will be able to see desert animals, birds, and plants in their natural habitats. Many of the animals are at the reserve to recover from injuries; some will never be able to return to the wild, but others will. There are also a number of interesting exhibits, an excellent gift shop, and an auditorium where movies and slide shows are regularly presented. For more information, call the reserve office at 619-346-5694.

Palms to Pines Highway Tour

TO GET THERE. Follow the directions for the Living Desert Reserve, above, to CA 74 in the town of Palm Desert. Go south and then west on CA 74 into the Santa Rosa Mtns. In 37.2 mi, at the town of Mountain Center, go north on CA 243 for 25.1 mi. This will bring you out on I-10 just east of Banning. An alternate route would be that of continuing west on CA 74 from Mountain Center, passing through Hemet, and coming out on I-15E near Sun City about 31 mi later.

GETTING YOUR BEARINGS. See Palm Springs Desert Museum, above, for map advice.

ABOUT THE DRIVE. CA 74 climbs up the north slopes of the Santa Rosa Mtns dramatically, steeply, and with many switchbacks. The views back to the desert floor and surrounding mountains are very grand. Fortunately, there are several vista points on the way up where you can stop and enjoy the sights (this is definitely not a road on which drivers can afford to sightsee while driving!). As you climb, you'll be able to see the desert vegetation and geologic features give way to the contrasting mountain habitats. The palms, creosote, desert ironwood, ocotillo, and encelia will disappear, and pines, juniper, manzanita, and mountain mahogany will take their place.

As you come to the top of Seven-Level Hill, you should stop at the vista point. On a clear day, this is perhaps the best place to take photos on the way up. The Bureau of Land Management also maintains an interpretive display here. As you continue on your way to Santa Rosa Summit (which is about 23 mi from where you started below), you'll pass the entrances to at least two developed San Bernardino National Forest campgrounds. Pinyon Flats Campground (about 15.7 mi from CA 111 is at 4000 ft); Santa Rosa Springs Campground (about 19.4 mi from CA 111 is at 7100 ft). The graded dirt road to the latter traverses quite close to Santa Rosa Mtn (8046 ft) and ends near Toro Peak (8716 ft). (Because the Forest Service periodically closes heavily used campgrounds to give the area a rest, it's possible that these popular sites may not always be available.)

Between Santa Rosa Summit and Mountain Center you'll drive through the meadows and pine groves of Garner Valley and will pass one of the old Butterfield Stage stops (now a private campground). You will also pass Lake Hemet (a reservoir), where there are two more developed campgrounds (Hurley Creek County Park and Lake Hemet Campground). To the north as you drive along here are the imposing San Jacinto Mtns.

At Mountain Center (about 14 mi from Santa Rosa Summit) there is yet another developed campground (McCall Memorial County Park). At this point you may either continue on CA 74 to I-15E or turn north on CA 243 to I-10. (The latter route is more scenic than the former, which is basically the quick-exit route and so will not be described here.)

If you choose CA 243 you will soon (in 4 mi) find yourself in Idyllwild (5400 ft), a pleasant little mountain community with all services, quite a few good restaurants and lodges, and two developed campgrounds. Hikers will be happy to know that there are quite a number of trailheads leading into the Mt San Jacinto Wilderness and State Park from around Idyllwild.

One of the most popular trail hikes out of Idyllwild is to Tahquitz Peak (8816 ft), where there is a fire lookout (the round-trip is about 10 mi). Tahquitz Rock—near the peak—is one of the most-used southern California rock-climbing areas. Even if you're not a climber, it can be interesting to watch the action there (or from a nearby trail overlooking the rock); don't forget your binoculars! Inquire at the ranger station in Idyllwild for details of the hiking possibilities. Wilderness permits are required for some trails.

After you manage to tear yourself away from Idyllwild and its various attractions, you'll find yourself winding slowly through the scenic San Jacintos. You'll pass San Bernardino National Forest campground entrances too numerous to mention here. (You can get info in Idyllwild on the way through. However, if you like to think ahead, you may have acquired the info before you left home. This is particularly desirable if it's the mountain camping season.) Eventually—about 29.5 mi from Idyllwild—after having wound back down through the pines-to-palms transition (it's just as interesting in the reverse), you'll find yourself at I-10.

This is a drive that never really gets old—in either direction!

Murray Canyon Palms Hike
Class 1/elev. near sea level/USGS topo *Idyllwild*/3.2 mi or more RT/use trails

TO GET THERE. Follow directions for Living Desert Reserve, above, to CA 111 (Palm Canyon Dr). Then continue straight south on CA 111 (now South Palm Canyon Dr) for 2.2 mi, following road signs directing drivers to Indian Canyons. You will need to stop at a toll gate and pay a nominal fee to gain entrance to tribal lands. (The gate opens at 9:00 A.M.) From the toll gate, continue 0.1 mi, and turn right at the sign indicating the way to Andreas Canyon. Park in the oasis at the mouth of Andreas Canyon.

GETTING YOUR BEARINGS. See Palm Springs Desert Museum, above, for map advice.

ABOUT THE OASIS. Named after Dr. Welwood Murray, an early Coachella Valley pioneer, this canyon drains the precipitous slopes of the San Jacinto Mtns near Palm Springs. Seven hundred and eighty-three mature palms line the lower reaches of the canyon, many of them nestled around clear pools at the base of numerous shallow falls. At dusk on late winter and spring days, the boisterous calls of male California tree frogs can be overwhelming.

Begin your hike by heading across the stream and toward the southeast corner of the palms. In 0.1 mi you will reach a low ridge. Follow this ridge east for a very short distance and you will come to a clearly defined trail heading around the ridge in a southeasterly direction. When the ridge is cleared, the trail takes you southwest for 0.7 mi to the mouth of Murray Canyon. Though the canyon continues for several miles, it becomes quite strenuous after 0.8 mi.

To return, retrace your steps. While in the Indian Canyon area, you may also want to visit Palm Canyon (see below), the largest native desert (California) fan palm grove in existence.

                                        —James Cornett, Palm Springs Desert Museum

Palm Canyon Hike

Class 1/elev. near sea level/USGS topo *Idyllwild*/up to 14 mi RT/use trails

TO GET THERE. Follow directions for Murray Canyon Palms hike, above. Follow the signs to Palm Canyon. The last 0.5 mi of the road is winding and narrow.

GETTING YOUR BEARINGS. See Palm Springs Desert Museum, above, for map advice.

ABOUT THE CANYON. This canyon, along with Murray Canyon and several others, is part of the Agua Caliente Indian Reservation. Over three thousand native desert (California) fan palms line Palm Canyon for a distance of 7 mi. Some of the palms are estimated to be 1500 to 2000 years old. This canyon was the traditional home of the Agua Caliente for hundreds of years.

From the parking area, called Hermit's Bench, there is a good view north to Palm Springs and south into the mountains. The canyon wanders back into the mountains for about another 10 mi. A good trail starts near the parking lot and goes down into the canyon. Most people enjoy exploring the canyon for at least a mile or two. If you don't feel like hiking, you can view the canyon from a number of places on its rim. However, if you'd like to really stretch your legs, you can walk the 14 mi up-canyon to the Palms to Pines Highway (this requires a car shuttle and a body in good hiking condition).

The canyon's many palms and year-round stream make it a very unique desert environment. Despite its commercialization it is well worth a visit.

Anza–Borrego Desert State Park

ABOUT THE PARK. This large and unique desert park is located about 80 mi east of San Diego; it is a favorite haunt of both desert greenhorns and desert rats. According to Diana and Lowell Lindsay, authors of the most complete recent guide to this part of the California desert, "[the park's] name captures the relationship of man and the land in the southwestern desert of California. Juan Bautista de Anza, the Spanish captain who was the leader of the epic 1776 San Francisco colonial expedition, and Borrego, Spanish word for bighorn sheep, which is the very symbol of desert wilderness, are paired in Anza-Borrego to highlight the intertwined human and natural history of this recreational preserve."

For those folks just getting acquainted with the California desert, Anza-Borrego Desert State Park (ABSP) offers several well-appointed developed campgrounds, quite a few signed trails (plus several self-guided nature trails), lots of helpful rangers, a visitor center offering literature

and free programs on the park (including guided hikes), and a fair number of well-interpreted historic sites. And, of course, a great deal of
gorgeous scenery, interesting plants and wildlife, three seasons' worth
of pleasant weather (summer is a mite hot to be called pleasant), and
so on and on . . . . Actually, there is so much to see and do at ABSP
that it defies description; you'll just have to go and see it for yourself.

Because there are several good guidebooks on the ABSP area (see
the "Recommended Reading" appendix), and also because the park staff
offers the visitor a selection of generous interpretive gifts, only a few
suggestions for getting acquainted with the park are offered here. Be
forewarned, though, that one visit to ABSP usually begets another . . .
and another.

FACILITIES. Gas, supplies, restaurants, and motels can be found in the
nearest fair-sized cities — Indio, El Centro, San Diego, Palm Springs,
etc. These are from 50 to 100 mi away. More modest, but similar,
facilities are available in Julian (a small mountain town at the intersection of CA 79 and CA 78 about 10 mi outside ABSP's west boundary)
and in Borrego Springs (a small town in a private land enclave within
the park, just a couple of miles east of the visitor center). Supplies and
gas can also be found in Aguanga (at the intersection of CA 79 and
CA 37A, about 38 mi northwest of the park's northwest boundary)
and in Ocotillo (about 7 mi southeast of the park's southeast boundary).

Camping. There are two developed campgrounds in ABSP. Tamarisk
Grove, located at the intersection of CA 78 and San Diego County S-3,
and Borrego Palm Canyon, a couple of miles northwest of the visitor
center. There is also a group campground at Borrego Palm Canyon.
In these campgrounds you'll find wood stoves, drinking water, restrooms with showers and toilets, tables, and other amenities. Space reservations are required; you can get them through MISTIX. If the
campgrounds are not all pre-reserved through MISTIX, you can reserve
a space when you arrive at the park.

In addition to these developed campgrounds, there are two San Diego
County developed campgrounds in the park. These are to be found
south of CA 78 on county road S-2: Vallecito Stage Station (about 18
mi south of CA 78) and Agua Caliente Hot Spring (about 22 mi south
of CA 78). These also have water, toilets, tables, and fireplaces; the latter also has trailer/RV hookups and hot mineral baths. If there are spaces
available, you can reserve one when you arrive; if it's the desert season
(late fall through late spring), you may need to reserve ahead of arrival
by contacting the San Diego County Parks and Recreation Department.

Within ABSP there are quite a few primitive campgrounds. For locations, get information from the visitor center. Trash cans and chemical
toilets make up the amenities at these sites; no water is available. Primitive sites are a good introduction to open-desert camping and are pre-
ferred by many people. Keep in mind, too, that very few state or national

parks allow camping in primitive areas; ABSP does. Treat this privilege gently! Backpackers, by the way, are allowed to camp anywhere in the park (except in private land enclaves).

Visitor Center to Salton City Tour

TO GET THERE. There are numerous entrance points to Anza-Borrego Desert State Park (ABSP); check the maps mentioned below for routes to them. The population center of ABSP consists of a very nice visitor center, the park headquarters, Panorama Overlook, and Borrego Palm Canyon Campground; you can find all these just west of the town of Borrego Springs, on San Diego County road S-22 (west end of Palm Canyon Rd). For this tour, the visitor center is the jumping-off point.

GETTING YOUR BEARINGS. You'll probably need a good California map, a San Diego County map, and perhaps an Imperial County map (if you plan on going as far east as the Salton Sea).

ABOUT THE TOUR. Starting from the visitor center, this tour will take you to the mouth of Coyote Canyon for a walk to Desert Gardens, then to Pegleg Smith Monument, and finally to Salton City via the many viewpoints along the Salton Seaway (otherwise known as county road S-22). One-way distance is about 32 mi, not counting side trips and other exploring.

A Stop at the Visitor Center. Here's where you'll find the answers to most of your questions about the park. The visitor center has a good selection of colorful brochures, books, and desert displays—and friendly rangers and volunteers. Take your time here, you'll be richly rewarded with information. Don't forget to see the slide show!

Those who just can't wait to start hiking should see below for directions to the Borrego Palm Canyon Hike. The canyon is just a couple of miles from the visitor center.

On to Coyote Canyon and Desert Gardens. Starting at the visitor center, travel east about 2.5 mi on Palm Canyon Rd to Christmas Circle, in the town of Borrego Springs, and on for another 0.5 mi to DiGiorgio Rd; go north here and continue for 4.8 mi to the end of the paved road.

■ *Desert Gardens Walk (Side Trip).*
Class 1/elev. 700 ft/USGS topo *Clark Lake*/1–6 mi RT/dirt, sand road, signed trail

If it's a good year, you may be able to drive a non-4WD vehicle some distance on the dirt/sand road that begins at the end of the paved road. In any case, starting from the end of the paved road, follow the dirt/sand road northwest along the edge of Coyote Mtn. In about 2.5 mi you'll be able to see a notch in the long ridge stretching northwest from Coyote Mtn. The notch is Alcoholic Pass; the signed trail over it is part of an old Indian trail going to Clark Lake (now dry).

About 0.5 mi farther (on the road), there will be a sign pointing the way to Desert Gardens. This desert "garden" area has been donated to ABSP by the Anza-Borrego Committee of the Desert Protective Council (a nonprofit organization). Committee volunteers raise money to buy private lands within the park to donate them to the park. In this way, the committee hopes to remove all private lands from ABSP.

A short distance from the Desert Gardens sign are some picnic tables; a path leads a little farther on up a small hill, where there is a bench. From the hill you can get a good view of the area's ocotillo forest and cactus garden. This is a nice place to have lunch and spend some time exploring. How many different kinds of cactus can you pick out?

If you'd like to hike a ways up Coyote Creek, see below for directions. Otherwise, just retrace your steps to your vehicle.

Ocotillo. *Photo by Lynne Foster.*

TOUR CONTINUES. Drive south on DiGiorgio Rd for 1.8 mi to Henderson Canyon Rd; go east here. The next stop, Pegleg Smith Monument, is 4.1 mi down the road.

Who the Heck Was Pegleg Smith? The Old West, its wide open spaces ever-hopefully riddled by would-be gold miners, was famous for its tall-tale tellers. Pegleg was one of the best! Thomas Long Smith, a trader and restless adventurer, supposedly acquired his nickname after an 1827 Indian battle from which he emerged one leg short. Not too long after that, Smith traveled across the California desert to sell furs in Los Angeles. Along his way—somewhere in the Anza-Borrego area—he claimed to have picked up some black pebbles that later proved to be nearly pure gold. However, it wasn't until some years later, in the 1850s, that he began to yarn about his "discovery." His story was so interesting that he rarely had to pay for a drink from then until he died in 1866. It's rumored that he spent most of his last years drinking and telling stories about his "gold mine."

Pegleg's stories—somewhat gloriously elaborated upon by others— were transformed into local legend after he died. Then in the early 1900s, Harry Oliver, a Borrego Valley homesteader and Hollywood director, took it into his head to give the old Pegleg legend a boost. He talked up the old stories, tossed hundreds of peglegs into abandoned prospectors' diggings, and in 1916 started the Pegleg Smith Club. In the late 1940s Oliver got the Pegleg Smith Monument started by making a circle on the ground and putting up signs inviting those "who seek Pegleg Smith's gold" to pile rocks there. Quite a few people have accepted this invitation! Even now old Pegleg is not forgotten. Every April a Pegleg Liar's Contest is held at the monument.

Views of the Borrego Badlands. From Pegleg's Monument on, you'll be traveling on the Borrego-Salton Seaway (otherwise known as county road S-22). Watch for a dirt road going southeast off the Seaway in about 2.8 mi. This road goes up a wash leading to Inspiration Point; it dead-ends in a couple of miles.

At the road's end you'll find yourself at the west edge of the Borrego Badlands. This is a good place to get photos of these unusual, erosion-patterned mud hills. Like several other places in the Colorado Desert, this area was once at the bottom of a huge lake. Over thousands and thousands of years, layer upon layer of silt and mud were washed into the lake. Then the climate changed for the drier, and the lake disappeared. Over time, earth movements pushed the soft deposits up into hills that have been eroded into their present sculptured forms by yet more years of rain and wind. The elevation at the viewpoint is approximately 1200 ft.

As you continue along S-22, watch for a sign showing the way to another viewpoint turnoff in about 0.8 mi (south side of road). This one is called Font's Point after Father Pedro Font, who was with Anza's second expedition. It's about 4.5 mi up the wash to a truly spectacular view of these colorful badlands. Many people think Font's Point offers the best possible views — and photographic opportunities — of the Borrego Badlands. From here, it you look southwest across the lowest part of the Borrego Valley (the Borrego Sink), you can see one of the areas Anza's trail traversed along the San Jacinto fault.

Another 5.5 mi east along the Seaway brings you to a pull-off on the south side of the road where you can again get a good view of the badlands. For a view of some wind caves scoured out of sandstone, look for the next pull-off on the north side of the road 1.5 mi on down the Seaway. As you go along the road here, notice the several bridges; a look up and down the washes and deep canyons on both sides of the road will give you some idea of what flash floods can do.

For a fine view of the Salton Sea, stop at the Salton View pull-off a couple of miles on. Take the time to walk a little ways toward the Santa Rosa Mtns in order to see one of the main washes (Palm Wash) leading from the Santa Rosas to the Salton Sea. From here you can get some idea of the grandeur of desert wilderness.

TOUR ENDS. One mile east from Salton View you'll cross the ABSP boundary; 8 mi ahead is Salton City and the junction with CA 86.

Borrego Palm Canyon Hike

Class 1/elev. 1440–4680 ft/USGS topo *Borrego Palm Canyon*/3–15 mi RT/signed nature trail, use trail

TO GET THERE. This excursion begins at the Anza-Borrego Desert State Park visitor center; see Visitor Center to Salton City tour, above, for directions.

ABOUT THE HIKE. As with most desert hikes, this one is best not attempted in high summer. In addition to the often-uncomfortable temperatures at that time of the year, Borrego Palm Canyon's creek sometimes dries up in summer. Any other time is fine, though. Be prepared for lots of company if you visit the canyon during the spring and on holiday weekends — it's a popular place. Even when the trails are crowded, however, the experienced hiker can get away from it all by continuing on beyond the signed nature trail and up into the rougher and even more scenic reaches of the canyon.

First, Visit the Visitor Center. Try to arrive here early in the day so you'll have time to browse through the displays and books, see the slide show, and perhaps even attend a ranger program on some interesting park feature.

And Then Visit the Natives. Pick up a copy of the Borrego Palm Canyon Self-Guided Hike brochure at the visitor center and then follow the signs (and the paved road) to Borrego Palm Canyon Campground, about 2 mi northwest. To find the trailhead, look for the campfire circle at the west end of the main campground. If it's a fine weekend between October and May, you might find that quite a few other sightseers have also come out to visit the natives.

The natives mentioned here are not of the human kind, but despite this handicap they are quite famous — because they are the *only* indigenous California palms. Their scientific name is *Washingtonia filifera* (which is quite a mouthful), but their common name is an easy one to remember: desert (California) fan palm.

To find the native desert fan palms, just begin walking up the trail from the pupfish pool. At first the canyon, with its steep, rocky walls, may look rather barren and forbidding, but soon you'll find yourself among many interesting desert plants (common and uncommon), a small creek (which sometimes disappears during the summer), flowers (if it's spring), a desert creature or three (if there aren't too many other people on the trail), some reminders of the canyon's previous inhabitants (Indian grinding stones), and (of course) the impressive palms themselves. Your trail brochure will help you identify what you are seeing.

After 1.5 mi of easy walking you'll come to a shady palm grove and small waterfall at the end of the self-guided nature trail. This is a good place to have a picnic and enjoy the surroundings. If you'd like to see some slightly different scenery on your way back to the campground, you can take a trail located higher on the south (and drier) side of the canyon. From this path you get quite a different view of things.

Experienced hikers may want to continue on up-canyon beyond this first palm grove. From here on the route is considerably rougher and more difficult. The canyon becomes very brushy, and hikers have to make their way over and around many large boulders and, in spring, wade in a few places. If you decide to continue on, though, you'll be well rewarded — as most of the eight-hundred-plus palms in this extensive grove are up ahead. You'll also notice that the canyon becomes ever more colorful as you clamber along. Be sure your group has an area topo along.

A little over 3 mi from the trail's beginning back at the campground, you'll come to a fork. Here you can either go west on the main/middle fork or southwest on the south fork. If you'd like to visit a waterfall, walk about 0.75 mi up the south fork. If you are really ambitious, keep on the main fork to another junction a little over 1 mi ahead. At this point the elevation is about 2700 ft. To reach a good viewpoint, continue about 3 mi in a northerly direction up a large side canyon (look for a sharp peak at its head). Stay left whenever you come to good-sized branches off the canyon. Eventually, you'll come to a saddle at about 4700 ft where you can look down on Indian Canyon.

Seasoned rock-climbers can continue on down the canyon face into Indian Canyon, but hikers should not attempt it. To return to your starting point, just retrace your steps.

Coyote Canyon Hike

Class 1/elev. 1200 ft/USGS topos *Clark Lake, Collins Valley, Borrego Palm Canyon/*
1–21 mi RT/4WD vehicle trail, use trail

TO GET THERE. See Desert Gardens Walk side trip, above, for directions to the mouth of Coyote Canyon.

ABOUT THE HIKE. The road up Coyote Canyon is definitely a 4WD proposition. In good years a conventional vehicle can proceed a ways beyond the end of the paved road before having to be parked. If you don't have a 4WD, exercise extreme caution in continuing off the pavement; deep sand is not easy to get out of. (Before going off the pavement, ask other visitors to the area about road conditions.) Hike mileages will be counted from the end of the paved road.

How Far Should You Go? This is a hike you can easily tailor to your inclinations. The walking is easy, with an elevation gain of only about 600 ft over 10.5 mi (if you choose to go as far as Sheep Canyon Primitive Camp). Many people wander up-canyon until half their time is gone and then wander back, paying no attention to the mileage. There is so much to see, especially if you are a wildlife or plant watcher, that time seems to slip away all too quickly. This is a good trip for beginning backpackers because of the modest elevation gain and the many places to camp along the way (you needn't go all the way to Sheep Canyon).

And When? Unfortunately, you can't fail to notice that many 4WD vehicles go up this canyon. Some go as far as CA 371, about 38 mi away. There are many responsible 4WD recreationists who are careful to stay on the routes that cause the least damage to the canyon—and the experiences of those on foot. Unfortunately, there are quite a few others who pay absolutely no attention to what is best for the canyon—or those who choose to walk it instead of drive it. For this reason, holiday weekends aren't the best time to visit the canyon—unless *vroom vroom* is your idea of a good time.

The Canyon's Checkered History. Let's assume, though, that mostly considerate folk are visiting the canyon when you are and anticipate a very pleasant hike. Pleasant is hardly a strong enough word to describe a hike up Coyote Canyon—which is one of the California desert's loveliest spots. There aren't many year-round sweet water supplies in our desert, and many desert lovers think this area—with its many all-year springs and its clear-flowing stream—the most interesting and beautiful riparian area of all.

In addition to its many beauties (shady groves, sparkling water, colorful flowers, lush grasses, abundant wildlife), the canyon has a fascinating—though not always praiseworthy—human history. Like most relatively permanent riparian areas in the California desert, Coyote Canyon was long inhabited by Indians. You can still find rocky, soot-blackened caves where they sheltered, broken bits of pottery, grinding stones, and even pictographs. But the Indians' peaceful life came to an end when a Spaniard, Juan Bautista de Anza, found a route from Sonora (Mexico) to Alta California (central southern California) through Coyote Canyon in 1774. Beginning the next year, colonists began traveling through the canyon to settle the lands beyond and around it. Soon, there was "trouble" with the Indians; and by the mid-1800s most of the Indians had been driven out of the area or slaughtered when they tried to resist invasion and takeover of their land. Today, native Americans of the area live on nearby Los Coyotes Indian Reservation.

On the Trail. On this hike you can follow the 4WD "trail/s" or walk up the side of or in the creek — or, most probably, do all of the above, depending on conditions at the time. All hike mileages are approximate, especially on trips like these when there are a variety of ways to get from one place to another. Keep this in mind as you go along.

Starting from the end of the paved road, follow the "road" to the creekbed and either walk up the latter or follow the road northwest along the edge of Coyote Mtn. If you're walking the road, in about 2.5 mi you'll be able to see a notch in the long ridge stretching northwest from Coyote Mtn. The notch is Alcoholic Pass; the signed trail over it is part of an old Indian trail going to Clark Lake (now dry).

About 0.5 mi farther (on the road), there will be a sign pointing the way to Desert Gardens (see Desert Gardens Walk side trip, above, for information on this area).

Crossing the Creek. About 0.5 mi on from Desert Gardens the road will cross Coyote Creek. Here there is quite a network of roads, most of which are going your way. The main road is the one on the west (far) side of the creek; go north on this. Very shortly you'll pass the Ocotillo Flat Rd (signed) and find yourself traversing another ocotillo forest. In addition to the forest, there are a variety of cacti (can you find the fishhook cacti?), agaves, and flowering plants. And even if you aren't a serious birdwatcher, take a few minutes to admire our feathered friends; this is a terrific birding area — one of the best in the California desert.

In another 0.7 mi or so the road/trail crosses Coyote Creek again. The area on the far side of the creek and up a bit (beyond a long, straight row of ocotillos planted as a fence) is often used for overnight camping.

A Santa Catarina Spring Trail. About 1.3 mi from where the road last crossed the creek, look for a foot trail crossing the creek to the west. This trail will take you to Santa Catarina Spring in 1 mi or so. (There's another route to the spring up ahead.) If you continue on the road you'll pass the mouth of Box Canyon (comes in from the north) in 0.3 mi and very shortly come to a gauging station at the edge of what is called Lower Willows. The elevation here, you will note, is 1189 ft.

Through Lower Willows. The road now makes its way up the streambed through the thick desert willow and tamarisk brush for the next 1.3 mi or so. (It's not hard to see how this area got its name.) When the road exits the brush into Collins Valley you can either follow it or continue on up the streambed.

Turnoff to Sheep Canyon. If you stay on the road, you'll come to a Y in another 0.3 mi; here there is a sign showing the way southwest to Sheep Canyon via Indian Canyon; the northwest arm of the Y continues directly on up the center of Collins Valley. The distance from the end of the paved road to this point (first junction of the main road with Sheep Canyon) is about 7.6 mi — on the road. If you followed the streambed most of the way, the distance is perhaps a bit less. At this junction, take the southwest fork (which leads up Indian Canyon to Sheep Canyon).

Anza Monument and Santa Catarina Spring. After taking the southwest fork of the road leading to Sheep Canyon, go about 0.2 mi to another Y and turn east. Next, go another 0.2 mi to yet another Y and go south (right), then east around a hill until you come to the end of the "road" in about 0.7 mi. Explore just north of here and you'll find the monument, which overlooks where Anza camped at Santa Catarina Spring in 1774. This is an excellent vantage point for taking photos.

If it weren't for this spring, Coyote Creek would not be a year-round stream. The plentiful water supply makes this area lush and lovely. On even a short visit here, you'll see many birds and other kinds of wildlife, as well as a wide variety of flowering plants — even orchids.

As mentioned above, you can also get to this important spring via a foot trail that crosses the creek about 2 mi back from the Sheep Canyon junction.

On to Sheep Canyon Camp. Retrace your path to where you left the road into Indian Canyon and continue along it toward Sheep Canyon for about 1.7 mi to a signed Y; this is the beginning of Sheep Canyon. Go southwest (left) here for 0.4 mi to the primitive campground (chemical toilets and trash barrels). If you have some time to spend, this is a great place from which to explore the area. It's about 10.5 mi from here to the end of the paved road where you started. Of course there are other places you can stop along the way if you don't want to travel this far in a day.

If you plan on exploring from here, and/or would like to go quite a bit farther up Collins Valley, be sure to bring along one of the excellent books on the Anza-Borrego region to help you find the way. The Lindsays' book is particularly good. (See the "Recommended Reading" appendix.)

Returning to the Paved Road. When you leave Sheep Canyon Primitive Campground you can either go back to the main route the way you came in or take the other arm of the Y at the beginning of Sheep Canyon and return to the main route in about 1.3 mi (the second junction of the main route with Indian Canyon). Here, turn southeast; you'll be back at the first junction in approximately 1.2 mi. From here, just retrace your path to the paved road.

Scissors Crossing to Ocotillo Wells Tour

TO GET THERE. There are a number of entrances to Anza-Borrego Desert State Park; check the maps mentioned below for routes to them. This trip begins at the intersection of CA 78 and San Diego County road S-2.

GETTING YOUR BEARINGS. Be sure to bring along a good San Diego County map. Check the visitor center for ABSP maps. For exploring the Split Mtn area, try the USGS topo *Harper Canyon*.

ABOUT THE TOUR. This trip begins near the San Felipe Stage Station site and will take you through Sentenac Cienega (marsh) and Canyon; to Tamarisk Grove, the Cactus Loop Nature Trail, and Kenyon Overlook; to the Earth Trail; along Old Kane Springs Rd through a cactus garden and Old Borego; down Split Mtn Rd to the Elephant Trees Nature Trail; through Split Mtn to the Carrizo Badlands; and, finally, to Ocotillo Wells. The total mileage, not counting any exploring you might do, is about 49 mi.

A Butterfield Overland Mail Station. In the mid-1800s it was horses, not airplanes, that moved the mail. Beginning in 1858, the Butterfield Overland Mail Company started carrying mail (and people) from Missouri to San Francisco. One leg of the mail route went through San Felipe Valley and Temecula, then stopped in Los Angeles before going on to San Francisco. One of the mail's major stops was here, on a flat at the edge of the San Felipe Valley (about 0.5 mi northwest of the S-2/CA 78 junction—where you are now). Unfortunately, for the local Indians, the station was built on a sacred burial ground. All that remains of the station is the rubble of a few walls; if you find these, you'll probably also find bits and pieces of Indian pottery and tools—sad reminders of the area's desecration.

On the Way to Tamarisk Grove. From this first intersection of county road S-2 with CA 78, as you go east on CA 78, you'll soon (about 0.3 mi) pass the second intersection of S-2 as you continue on CA 78 to the mouth of Sentenac Canyon, about 1 mi on. As you approach the mouth of this narrow canyon, you'll notice an area of lush vegetation—trees, grass, flowers. This is Sentenac Cienega (marsh). If you're a bird and plant person, stop here and explore a little. The variety is really amazing. The marsh is here because the narrow canyon causes the waters flowing down from the San Felipe drainage to back up a bit.

Another 2 mi or so beyond is the San Felipe Creek bridge. If you feel like picnicking by the creek, there is a parking area here. After the bridge, look for numerous agave plants on the slopes to the west of the road. In spring, the huge, asparagus-like stalks bear brilliant yellow flower masses. There are two more potential picnic areas coming up on CA 78—the first in about 1.2 mi and the second (Kenyon

Cove) about 1.3 mi beyond that. About 4 mi beyond the San Felipe Creek bridge, turn northeast on county road S-3 and go 0.3 mi to Tamarisk Grove Campground (yet another place to picnic—and, of course, camp).

This campground has almost all the comforts of home—drinkable water, restrooms, even showers! Most important of all, it usually has a helpful park ranger who will do her or his best to answer your questions.

A Short Detour on the Cactus Loop Trail. Across the road from the campground is an easy, 1-mi nature trail. It is well signed and takes you in, around, up, and down among a profusion of interesting and attractive desert plants. Take a few minutes to walk the trail and try identifying some of the inhabitants.

If It's a Clear Day, This Must Be the Kenyon Overlook. From the campground, continue northeast on S-3 for another 1.5 mi or so to a pull-off on the southeast side of the road, signed "Kenyon Overlook." Here you'll find a short (0.25-mi) footpath leading to the overlook. If the weather's good, the Salton Sea will be visible to the south. Even if it's a bit hazy, you'll be able to see the Pinyon Mtns and—what does your map tell you?

One of ABSP's primitive campgrounds, Yaqui Pass, is only 0.2 mi farther on. These small, nearly undeveloped camping areas have chemical toilets, trash cans, and no water. They're a better place to get away from it all than the larger, more developed campgrounds. From here, retrace your route back to CA 78—it's a little over 2 mi.

The Earth Trail. Continue east on CA 78 for about 4.6 mi to another rest area (the Narrows). Pull off here (south side of the road) to visit the 0.3-mi Earth Trail. The path winds through some geologic features characteristic of this desert area. If you've been to the visitor center, you may have picked up a brochure on the trail.

From the rest area it is about 2.2 mi to the junction of CA 78 with the Old Kane Springs Rd. To visit a cactus garden and the Elephant Trees Nature Trail turn southeast onto this dirt road (also known as Pole Line Rd, for obvious reasons). If you're in a hurry, go directly to Ocotillo Wells, 8.5 mi farther along.

A Cactus Garden. Now that you're off the main road, drive slowly and look carefully at the desert scene around you. The dirt road coming in from the north after 3 mi goes to CA 78; continue past it for 0.5 mi to the cactus garden. Find a likely spot and pull off the road. Get out of your vehicle and wander among these unique, desert-adapted native plants—cacti, bushes, trees, flowers—what are you seeing? Which tree is a smoke tree? Which cactus is a cholla (and what kind of cholla?) and which a barrel? Which bush is a . . . ? What enables these plants to live and flourish in desert conditions?

After you've gotten a little better acquainted with the natives, continue southeast on Old Kane Springs Rd for another 5 mi—to its junction with Split Mtn Rd (paved) and the site of Little Borego.

Little Borego—A Town that Failed. In the California desert there are quite a few sites of towns that are no more. Little Borego [sic] is one of the more recent, and more short-lived ones; it came into being in 1924 and went out with the Depression, in the early 1930s. A little exploring south of the junction will turn up some concrete slabs—all that's left of a settlement that once boasted a rather large and ostentatious boarding house (the Miracle Hotel), a school, general store, pool hall, gas station, and even a barber shop. Old Kane Springs Rd was Little Borego's Broadway, and you may still be able to find a sign proclaiming "Main Street" (at right angles to Broadway).

At the junction of Old Kane Springs Rd and Split Mtn Rd, continue southeast on the latter (paved); stay on Split Mtn Rd as it turns south in about 1 mi while the Kane Springs Rd continues southeast. In about 1.7 mi you'll come into ABSP again, at the Elephant Trees Ranger Station.

Both Rare and Strange—Elephant Trees. The turnoff to the Elephant Trees Discovery Trail is only about 0.2 mi beyond the ranger station. Follow the dirt road southwest to the parking area. Here you have a choice of two trails. One takes you 1.5 mi to a hillside where there are several clusters of these unusual trees. (Now that you've seen them, do you know why they are called elephant trees?) The other trail is a 2.5-mi self-guided nature trail (brochures are available from the ranger station). On this trail you'll find many plants characteristic of the southwestern part of the California desert.

A little more than 2 mi farther, Split Mtn Rd brings you to the signed turnoff for Fish Creek Primitive Campground (a dirt road in the wash on the west side of the road). Remember, these no-frills campgrounds have no water, just chemical toilets and trash cans. Turn in here if you're game for a wander through Split Mtn to the Carrizo Badlands. The paved road continues to a gypsum mine that supplies Plaster City on I-8 (see San Diego County map).

What Split the Mountain? Campsites are dotted here and there along the first mile or so of this road. After another mile you plunge into Split Mtn. As you meander along you'll be in the canyon that separates the Fish Creek Mtns from the Vallecito Mtns (check your topo so you'll know which is which). Notice the marked folding and different textures and compositions of the layered deposits and try to figure out what the geological history of the canyon walls might be. Can you find any fossils?

But what split the mountains and produced the steep canyon walls? Well, geologists say that the mighty force was none other than water. A stream flowed here perhaps even before the mountains rose. And when the mountain ranges did rise, the flowing water cut a canyon between them. You might guess that even today this canyon is not a good place to be during a flash flood.

After about 2.3 mi of tale-telling canyon walls, you'll emerge from Split Mtn to find the Carrizo Badlands ahead. The average car shouldn't be driven any farther; now is the time for all good explorers to get out and walk about a bit. There are several interesting canyons leading north only a few tenths of a mile on. In some of these you can find marine fossils several millions of years old. For detailed directions on exploring this area with a 4WD vehicle, see the Lindsays' book (in the "Recommended Reading" appendix).

Back to Ocotillo Wells. From here, retrace your route to Split Mtn Rd and follow it north to Ocotillo Wells. Total distance back is about 13 mi.

Ocotillo to Scissors Crossing Tour

TO GET THERE. Take I-8 to the Ocotillo turnoff (about 85 mi east of San Diego and 27 mi west of El Centro). Go north into the town of Ocotillo on county road S-2 and continue on it as you cross Old Highway 80.

GETTING YOUR BEARINGS. A good San Diego County map is useful; USGS topos for walks will be mentioned below.

ABOUT THE TOUR. On this trip you'll have the opportunity to take several very pleasant desert strolls. The first walk stop is at Bow Willow Canyon, the second at Mountain Palm Springs, and the third at Agua Caliente Hot Springs. From there the tour goes on to Vallecito Stage Station and Blair Valley (site of the Foot and Walker Monument), finally winding up at Scissors Crossing (the junction of county road S-2 and CA 78). The distance covered is about 48 mi—not counting any exploring you might do along the way.

On the Way to Bow Willow Canyon. From the junction of Old Highway 80 and S-2 in Ocotillo, go north on S-2; in about 1.3 mi you'll pass Shell Canyon Rd (goes north). Up this canyon is a wealth of marine fossils, including oysters and 50-million-yr-old coral (see Yuha Basin/Fossil Canyon Walk for information). Look for the Imperial Highway Monument some 7 mi on from Shell Canyon Rd. Here you leave Imperial County and enter San Diego County and Anza-Borrego Desert State Park.

If you like viewpoints, there's a good one coming up on the north side of the road in another 7.2 mi. A short dirt road leads to the Carrizo Badlands Overlook and then loops back to the main road. From the viewpoint it's only a short distance over Sweeney Pass (1065 ft). The steep canyon on the west side of the pass couldn't have made road building in this area very easy.

The turnoff to Bow Willow Canyon and Primitive Campground is about 3 mi beyond the overlook (approximately 16 mi from Ocotillo). The signed road to the canyon goes south for 1.6 mi to a ranger station (open during the desert season), then continues on a short distance to the campground. The campground has a few sites with tables under ramadas; there are also chemical toilets and (sometimes) piped water.

In addition to the developed sites, quite a large area is used for primitive camping by folks with trailers, RVs, and tents.

■ *Bow Willow Canyon Walk (Side Trip).*
Class 1/elev. 1000 ft/USGS topos *Sweeney Pass, Sombrero Peak*/1–9 mi RT/sandy wash road

Park in the campground area and begin your walk up the canyon from here. The walking is easy, so take time to explore some of the side canyons. A little looking will certainly turn up some desert willows and native desert (California) fan palms. If you're lucky, there may even be an elephant tree or two around the next corner. There are at least a couple of stories of how the canyon came by its name. Some think it's because the willows were used by Indians to make bows; others think the name is actually Bull Willow—in tribute to the vigorous growth of the willows in the canyon.

The road up-canyon meanders along for about 4.5 mi before petering out when it gets to rougher country. Several hikes can be started from the end of the road and from various points along Bow Willow Canyon. See the Lindsays' book in the "Recommended Reading" appendix for details.

Even if you only go a short distance up the canyon, you'll consider the time well spent. In spring there are quite a few small, attractive flower displays in the canyon; birding is also good here, especially during migrating times. For an added evening treat (when the campground isn't too crowded), keep your eyes and ears out for owls.

TOUR CONTINUES. From the Bow Willow Canyon turnoff, continue northwest on S-2 for another 1.3 mi to the turnoff for Mountain Palm Springs. Turn southwest on this dirt road.

Visiting the Natives of Palm Springs. In this canyon there is another primitive campground, with chemical toilets but no water or tables. The attraction in this area, as the name tells us, is palm trees: hundreds of California fan palms are found here in various-sized groves.

■ *Mountain Palm Springs Walk (Side Trip).*
Class 1/elev. 1000 ft/USGS topos *Sweeney Pass, Arroyo Tapiado*/1–3 mi RT/use trails, cross-country

To find the nearest groves, first walk about 0.5 mi up the north arm of Mountain Palm Springs Canyon to North Grove. From here, it's only 0.25 mi northwest to Mary's Bowl Grove, which in addition to palms also boasts elephant trees. A walk up the south arm of the canyon will shortly bring you to Pygmy Grove; another 0.5 mi on is Southwest Grove. There are several more even larger groves to be found up interesting side canyons of both the north and south forks of the canyon if you have the time. For directions, see the Lindsays' book in the "Recommended Reading" appendix.

Amazingly, the native palms actually thrive on the salt-laden waters of their supporting springs. Without the palms, southern California Indians would certainly have had a thinner time of it. Palms were used for food (fruit, seeds); fiber (sandals, rope); and shelter (fronds).

TOUR CONTINUES. After visiting the natives return to S-2 and continue northwest for about 9 mi, to Agua Caliente County Park and Campground. If you like camping with almost all the comforts of home, you'll love Agua Caliente (see "Facilities," above, for details). This campground also has a comfort rarely found at home: hot mineral springs. There's a store nearby, where you can get snacks and gas. Even if you aren't planning on camping in the park, it's a good place for a picnic (there's lots of shade) and a walk.

■ *Moonlight Canyon Walk (Side Trip).*
Class 1/elev. 1300 ft/USGS topo *Agua Caliente Spring*/1.5 mi RT/signed trail

Look for the Moonlight Canyon trail near campsite 82. This walk will take you south up a modest 350 ft to a saddle and then back down the canyon again to the campground. By going left at the saddle, you'll return to the campground by a slightly different route—passing some places where water trickles from the canyonside and flowers bloom in spring.

There are several other good hiking possibilities in the vicinity of Moonlight Canyon. For details, see the Lindsays' book in the "Recommended Reading" appendix.

TOUR CONTINUES. Keep driving northwest on S-2 for another 4 mi to Vallecito Stage Station County Park and Campground (about 30 mi from Ocotillo). This is another nearly-all-the-comforts-of-home camping place.

A Famous Watering Place. Drinkable water is not easy to find in the desert—even in one as lush (relative to other deserts) as the California desert. The marshes (cienegas) here at the Vallecito stop are at the foot of the Tierra Blancas; even in summer, you can find water only a few feet down. The green of the cienegas and mesquite was a welcome sight to travelers on the Southern Emigrant Trail. For those coming west from Yuma—a long, hot, 100 mi away—it meant respite near their journey's end. For those traveling east—just beginning their desert trek—Vallecito Station was the last green outpost of civilization for a long way ahead.

The adobe building you see here is, of course, a restoration. The first permanent structure—a small sod-brick house—was built in about 1851 and was used by the military when they were having "Indian trouble" in the area. Mud-brick adobe was not used; the sod-bricks were cut from the nearby cienegas. Five or six years later, the building was expanded to house a Butterfield Overland Mail stage station. After the

Butterfield operation ceased, the station had a succession of occupants and owners. Eventually, in the early 1930s, the building was reconstructed as part of a government work project. Finally, the last owner donated the 6-acre piece of land and the reconstructed stage station to San Diego County for use as a park.

The park is a pleasant place to picnic, enjoy the desert greenery, and speculate on what life might have been like along the Southern Emigrant Trail.

A little over 4 mi beyond Vallecito County Park (on S-2), you'll come to a viewpoint on the Campbell Grade where you can actually see the wagonwheel ruts of the Southern Emigrant Trail as they cross Vallecito (Spanish for "little valley") in your viewing foreground as you look southeast.

"Foot and Walker" Pass. About 7.5 mi along county road S-2 from the viewpoint (about 42 mi from Ocotillo), take a dirt road signed "Blair Valley" going east. In 0.5 mi you'll come upon the Little Pass Primitive Campground and the Foot and Walker Pass Monument. A look around this steep, rocky pass between Blair and Earthquake valleys will give you some idea of how the pass got its name. If you had been one of those traveling the Emigrant Trail, you would have found yourself on foot—perhaps even pushing your wagon or the stage—as you crossed this pass! Look at the deep ruts; this is a very well preserved part of the trail.

Primitive campgrounds, remember, have chemical toilets, but no water, tables, etc.

TOUR ENDS. The junction of S-2 and CA 78 is just 6 mi ahead at Scissors Crossing.

Sombrero Peak Hike

Class 2/elev. 4229 ft/USGS topos *Sombrero Peak, Mt Laguna*/5 mi RT/cross-country

TO GET THERE. Access to this peak is via San Diego County road S-2 in Anza-Borrego Desert State Park (ABSP). To reach Indian Gorge, the jump-off point, either go south from CA 78 for about 30 mi on S-2 or go north from I-8 on S-2 for about 18 mi. (If you are coming from CA 78, Indian Gorge is about 8.7 mi south of the entrance to Agua Caliente County Park.) Turn west onto the dirt road leading into the gorge. After about 2.8 mi, take the left fork into South Indian Valley and drive as far as your vehicle will allow before parking. A 4WD vehicle may be able to go in about 3 mi.

ABOUT THE HIKE. Sombrero is one of the most popular peaks in ABSP; it is located in this grand park's southwest corner. This peak is truly representative of the Colorado Desert; as such, the best time to hike it is between late fall and early spring (it's usually too hot to do it safely during the rest of the year).

As you walk or drive up the south fork, watch for an immense granite boulder a few hundred feet away on your left after about 0.2 mi. When you find it, look for the smoke-blackened cave and bedrock grinding holes (morteros) once used by Indians in the area. To reach the peak, begin hiking up the south fork of Indian Canyon from where you parked. When you reach a canyon that branches to the north and has a single palm tree and a small spring, you'll be at about 3000 ft. Hike up to the plateau just north of the main branch. Somewhere in this area, at about 3700 ft, just north of the three small enclosed 3600-ft contours shown on the *Mt Laguna* topo, there are supposedly a few small Indian pictographs. Continue southwest to the peak (round-trip = 4–5 hours). You'll find the view from the summit a good one — you can see the Carrizo Badlands to the east and the Lagunas and In-Ko-Pahs to the west.

This peak can also be hiked from roadheads near the Bow Willow Campground, south of Indian Gorge. You can make an interesting loop trip starting at one of these points and ending at the other. For details, see the Lindsays' book in the "Recommended Reading" appendix.

16

The Colorado Desert

Chuckwalla Mountains

ABOUT THE AREA. The Chuckwalla Mtns are located about 45 mi east of Indio and just south of Desert Center. Like much of the Joshua Tree National Monument region to the north, the species of plants and animals found in this area are characteristic of both the California desert's Mojave and Colorado regions.

The bajada on the north side of the range is easily accessible from I-10 and hosts some of the desert's finest cactus gardens. The broad plains of the bajada on the range's south side — often referred to as the Chuckwalla Bench — stretch all the way across the valley to the Chocolate Mtns. Here on the bench you can find a mixture of creosote, yucca, ocotillo, and at least nine species of cactus, including the treelike Munz cholla — a giant among cacti. The historic Bradshaw Trail, an east-west 4WD road, crosses the bench. This road skirts the Chocolate Mtns Aerial Gunnery Range, so visitors should take care not to stray south while exploring.

There are dirt roads into several of the canyons that penetrate the northeast side of the Chuckwalla Range. One road leads to a petroglyph site at a dense palm oasis, and another to broad, seldom-visited interior valley, where hikers can explore washes, scramble up ridges, and climb peaks in virtual solitude. Like so many areas in the California desert, the Chuckwallas cannot be seen in a single visit — so, you'll just have to come again, and again.

FACILITIES. Gas, limited supplies, and cafes are available in Desert Center and at Chiriaco Summit (just east of the south entrance to Joshua Tree National Monument). Gas, supplies, motels, and restaurants can be found in Blythe and Indio.

Camping. There is a Bureau of Land Management (BLM) developed campground at Corn Springs (see below). The sites have tables, barbecues, water, and chemical toilets. For other nearby campgrounds, see the "Facilities" sections for Joshua Tree National Monument and the Blythe-Winterhaven area. There are many excellent opportunities for open-desert camping on BLM lands throughout this area.

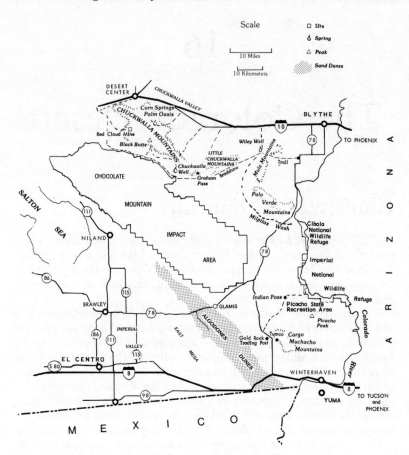

Cactus Garden Tour

TO GET THERE. Take I-10 east from Indio for about 36 mi to the Red Cloud exit. Or take I-10 west from Desert Center about 3 mi to the Eagle Mtn exit. Get on the dirt frontage road paralleling the south side of the freeway and go east (if you are coming from Indio) or west (if you are coming from Desert Center).

GETTING YOUR BEARINGS. Bring along a good Riverside County map.

ABOUT THE TOUR. This is a very short, but very rewarding, just-off-the-freeway tour. The best time to visit these easily accessible cactus gardens is February through mid-June. Although the road is only a narrow dirt track and has several sandy places, it is usually navigable by ordinary vehicles. Total mileage from one exit to the other is about 7 mi.

What to Look For. From the Eagle Mtn exit, go south under the freeway, then west on a dirt road; pass the white shed on the north side. As you go up the road, plan to make several stops; get out and walk away from the car, looking for wildflowers and blooming cacti. Some lucky and observant folks may even get to see a desert tortoise, with pollen-smeared nose, feasting on the abundant spring greenery.

Along this part of the road you should be able to see ocotillos, encelias, desert ironwood trees, creosote bushes, and chollas. At about 1.0 and 1.2 mi from the freeway exit, watch for sandy places in the road. Look for palo verdes, blooming chollas, and desert lavender bushes. Listen for California quail. At about 2 mi from the freeway, watch for hedgehog cacti; the blooms are fuschia colored. What kinds of cholla and other cacti are along here? Have you found any mamillaria (mound cacti)?

The cacti thin out a bit at about 3 mi from the exit, but there are other flowers to look for (can you find any blazing stars?). At about 4.5 mi, you should be in the midst of an impressive cholla forest; also look for chuparosa bushes, with their clouds of delicate red blooms. There will be some abandoned buildings on the north side of the dirt road at about 5.3 mi, then another sandy place, and finally, at about 7.3 mi from your starting point, you'll come to the Red Cloud exit for I-10.

Chuckwalla Bench–
Bradshaw Trail 4WD Tour

TO GET THERE. Take I-10 east from Indio for about 45 mi to the Red Cloud Mine exit. On the south side of the freeway, get on the Red Cloud Mine Rd (dirt) going south.

GETTING YOUR BEARINGS. You'll need a good Riverside County map. However, because the county maps do not have the Bradshaw Trail road on them, you'll also need the following USGS topos to help you sort out the route: *Hayfield, Chuckwalla Mtns, Iris Pass,* and *Chuckwalla Spring.*

Note: A drawback with topos is that they are of a certain age; some of the roads on them no longer exist or have been rerouted in part — and, of course, there are lots of new roads. This means that at various points on this tour you will doubtless discover that (1) some roads seem to have been moved, (2) lots of roads don't appear on any map, (3) some roads on the map don't exist, (4) road conditions range from good to impossibly sandy, (5) it's easy to get off the track even if you've followed all the directions carefully, and (6) etc. In other words, if you're a desert

4WD novice, only undertake this trip with more experienced companions — preferably companions who have towing equipment with them, just in case. Even with experienced companions, though, you'll all need to pay attention to where you're going and where you've been — and to resign yourself to getting off the track occasionally. Keep in mind, too, that the Chocolate Mtns Aerial Gunnery Range is just south of the Bradshaw Trail. It's definitely not a good idea to wander too far south from the road.

ABOUT THE TOUR. Plan on car camping for at least one night on this tour. There is so much to see and do on this trip that it is definitely not a good choice if you have only an afternoon to spare. If you are making the tour in spring, allow plenty of time for stops to enjoy the flowers. Even if it isn't spring, there are so many washes to explore, plants to identify, vistas to enjoy, and birds to hear, that you'll find it impossible to hurry.

The first side trip on this tour is right at the beginning — to the Red Cloud Mine area. From there, you'll go south, skirting the west flanks of the Chuckwalla Mtns while traversing the bench. Along here, you may want to take time for a short walk to a viewpoint situated atop a small hill near the road. Then the route swings east on the historic Bradshaw Trail, which continues along the bench and passes through a lush remnant of Sonoran grassland before reaching the turnoff to Chuckwalla Well, a minioasis about 1 mi north of the main road. Just before the Bradshaw Trail reaches the Graham Pass Rd, there is an opportunity to visit an interesting cactus forest.

At the Graham Pass Rd, it's decision time again. To end the tour, you can go north to I-10 at this point. Or — you can continue east on the Bradshaw Trail and pick up another tour route in the Blythe-Winterhaven area. The total mileage from I-10/Red Cloud Mine Rd via the Bradshaw Trail and Graham Pass Rd to I-10 about 25 mi east of where you started is approximately 50 mi. This does not count the side trips, which add up to another 15 mi or so.

From Red Cloud Mine Road to the Bradshaw Trail. After you get off I-10 on the south side, check your odometer and then look for the Red Cloud Mine Rd near the railroad tracks — it's the one that goes southeast away from the tracks about 0.5 mi from the exit. If your time is limited, you may want to skip the 14-mi detour (round-trip) that takes you southeast on this road toward the old mining area. To bypass the Red Cloud Mine Rd segment, just continue south on the road that follows the railroad tracks (see second paragraph below).

To explore the Red Cloud Mine Rd, follow it southeast away from the railroad tracks for about 2 mi to a Y at a wash; go east (left). Do the same after another 0.8 mi. (As you go along the road, can you spot evidence of ORV damage to the surrounding hills? Lovely, isn't it? And it will be with the desert for hundreds of years.) At about 4.3 mi from the railroad tracks, there is a good place for RVs to camp on the hardpan next to the road. At 4.8 mi, bear southeast (right) at a Y (the other arm goes to a microwave tower). Look for some good campsites in a wash at about 5.5 mi. The mine road usually becomes impassable at a deep, rocky wash about 7.2 mi from the railroad tracks. You can park here, walk across the wash or up it, and look for traces of now-abandoned mines. There are some good campsites here, too.

To continue the tour, retrace your route to the railroad tracks and turn southeast to follow the road paralleling the tracks south. In about 3.4 mi, go east at a T; after about 1.9 mi you'll come to Gas Line Rd, where you should turn southeast again. Look for a small, conical hill on the east side of the road after another 3.2 mi. When the hill is at its nearest, park off the road near a wash leading toward the hill.

Although you can drive up the sandy wash to the hill, it's only a short, pleasant walk. The hill has an easy trail leading to the top. (There is a good camping area at its base.) From the hill you have an excellent view east to the alluvial fans spreading out from the Chuckwalla Mtns and merging to form gently sloping bajadas. These sweeping alluvial plains — which stretch south to the Chocolate Mtns — along with the many washes dissecting their surfaces, the darkly glistening fields of desert pavement, and many plant and animal species characteristic of both the California desert's Mojave and Colorado desert regions, make up the Chuckwalla Bench. This rich biotic area is not only excellent habitat for the desert tortoise, but contains at least nine species of cactus, including the Munz cholla — a cactus giant that sometimes reaches a height of 15 ft.

From the wash leading to the hill it is only about 1.1 mi to the turnoff for the Bradshaw Trail. Watch for the Bureau of Land Management sign "SR 301." Go east at this point.

Along the Bradshaw Trail to Chuckwalla Well. Between 1862 and 1877, this trail, which stretched from near the Salton Sea to the Colorado River, was a part of a freight wagon route reaching from San Francisco to Arizona. By using this route to haul supplies to and gold from Arizona, the mining companies saved considerable time — and money. The only other feasible way was to ship the materials in and out of San Francisco by ship — via the Gulf of California and the Colorado River. Needless to say, the sea route was a long, expensive haul. Once the Southern Pacific Railroad got through to Yuma, though, the trail was no longer needed and quickly fell into disuse. Today, it is used primarily by desert tourers like yourselves.

As you go east along the Bradshaw Trail, you'll see many good camp spots. Look for one about 0.4 mi from where you came on the trail and for another about 3.2 mi farther (just two among many).

About 8.5 mi from where you turned onto the Bradshaw Trail, it goes through a small but unmistakable patch of grassland. Here the road splits in two, but soon comes back together again. Take time to stop and explore this tiny remnant of a time when even the southern part of the California desert was cool and wet enough to support luxuriant grasslands.

As you continue east along the Bradshaw Trail, look for some colorful red cliffs (volcanic origin) about 5 mi farther. At about 8 mi from the grassland, watch for a rough dirt road leading north. This will take you in a little less than a mile across several washes to a small oasis called Chuckwalla Well. Sometimes the road is too rough even for 4WD—in which case, just walk. You'll recognize the vicinity of the well easily—it's obviously been used as a campsite for some years. (This is a good place for a lunch stop.)

A little exploring near the shady camp area will bring you to a single, very large date palm, perhaps planted by some old-time residents of the area. In fact, the water supply was first developed by cattle raisers (note remains of fences). A little to the east of the palm is a wildlife "guzzler," a wood and cement enclosure built to protect one of the few water sources in the area. If you sit or stand quietly a little distance away with your binoculars, you'll soon see the local inhabitants visiting the neighborhood waterhole.

From back on the main road at the Chuckwalla Well turnoff, it's about 2.7 mi to the Bradshaw Trail's intersection with the Graham Pass Rd and the Indian Well Rd (at one time signed "Fort Sumner Blvd"). If you have time, take this latter road southwest a short distance to an impressive forest of huge, treelike Munz cholla. The well is nearby but has been capped off. Nearby residents now pump water with the windmill you see down the road. Back at the intersection, it's only about 16 mi north on the Graham Pass Rd to the Chuckwalla Rd (old CA 60). To get to I-10 quickly, go east on Chuckwalla Rd for 3 mi.

It is possible to continue east on the Bradshaw Trail to Wiley Well, where there is a campground. There you can pick up trips in nearby areas. Yet another possibility is to go west on Chuckwalla Rd; there are two more trips south into the Chuckwallas that jump off from it (see North Chuckwalla Mtns hikes, below).

North Chuckwalla Mountains Hikes
Class 1/elev. 2400–4500 ft/USGS topos *Sidewinder Well, Chuckwalla Mtns*/1–9 mi RT/cross-country

TO GET THERE. About 9 mi east of Desert Center, leave I-10 at Corn Springs exit and go southeast on the old paved highway, now Chuckwalla Rd. At the Corn Springs sign, about 0.5 mi from I-10, check your odometer. At 6.3 mi from the sign, the highway crosses a small bridge over a wash; the Dupont Mine turnoff is 0.4 mi from this point. Although there are other 4WD turnoffs, Dupont Rd still shows signs here and there of the berms left from road grading; it also looks the most well traveled. If you are uncertain about the turnoff, continue about 2 mi farther along the highway, crossing two more bridges, until you encounter a sweeping leftward bend. Now, retrace your route to the mine road, using the bridges as markers.

Although the road to the abandoned Dupont Mine is sandy in spots, the first 7 mi of it (as far as the mine) are usually passable by ordinary vehicles with high clearance. The road is best in spring, after winter rains have packed the sand. To continue into the interior valley, a 4WD vehicle is necessary.

ABOUT THE HIKES. These desert wilderness hikes, into the heart of the Chuckwallas, are accessible only by seldom-used 4WD trails. An interior valley like this provides an opportunity for experiencing a sense of solitude and isolation that is becoming increasingly rare even in the California desert.

The route into these valleys from the northeast is via the Dupont Mine road, as mentioned above. The initial part of this road crosses creosote-covered flatlands, cut here and there with washes in which desert ironwood, palo verde, and smoke trees flourish. See Ship Creek and Black Butte hikes, below, for hiking opportunities along here.

About 6 mi from the turnoff onto the mine road (approximately 1 mi before you reach the abandoned Dupont Mine), the road goes left, becomes a 4WD track, crosses the main wash, and then parallels this wash up a broad valley that penetrates deep into the mountains' interior. You can easily spend several days exploring the valley and its side canyons. For the road into the valley, though, you will need a 4WD vehicle.

To explore the Dupont Mine area, continue past the 4WD road going to the valley for about 1 mi. See the Viewpoint hike, below, for a hiking opportunity near the mine.

Of course, if you're not in the mood for hiking, you can park and indulge in some nature strolls up whatever washes happen to be nearby. If you find the right wash, you may come across an amazing sight—a windmill-driven wildlife guzzler. Once you find the guzzler, stay at a distance with your binoculars and watch quietly as the various denizens of the desert come to drink. Or, if you've really had a hard week, just find a comfortable, shady spot and spend some time restoring your psyche while lazily admiring the ocotillos, barrel cacti, chollas, and whatever else is within view.

Ship Creek Hike (Easy). About 4 mi from where you turned onto the mine road is a good spot to park and take an easy hike over a low saddle to the north into the Ship Creek drainage. To do this, check your *Chuckwalla Mtns* topo for the point where the Dupont Rd comes in from the east; park along here and walk northwest up the broad wash, crossing the 2000-ft contour. At about the 2400-ft contour, turn north and hike up over the ridge into the Ship Creek drainage. The round-trip is about 8 mi.

Black Butte Hike (Moderate to Strenuous). Follow directions for Ship Creek hike, above. However, instead of turning north and crossing the ridge into the Ship Creek drainage, go due west. Follow the line of least resistance to the top of Black Butte (4504 ft), the highest peak in the Chuckwallas, from which views of the Chuckwalla Bench, the Chocolate Mtns, etc. (consult your maps) are unexcelled. The round-trip is approximately 9 mi. *Note:* this climb is for experienced hikers only.

Viewpoint Hike (Easy). At the mine area, about 7 mi from Chuckwalla Rd check your topo for a ridge just to the south. A climb to the top (400 ft elevation gain) will give you a fine view of the Bradshaw Trail and the Chocolate Mtns.

Corn Springs Wash Hike or Backpack
Class 1/elev. 2400 ft/USGS topo *Chuckwalla Mtns*/15 mi RT, backpack; 1–16 mi RT, hike/trail, cross-country

TO GET THERE. Follow directions for North Chuckwalla Mtns hikes, above, except go south on a gravel road at the Bureau of Land Management (BLM) Corn Springs sign you'll see on Chuckwalla Rd about 0.5 mi east of I-10.

ABOUT THE HIKE AND BACKPACK. This day hike or backpack begins in the valley at the end of the county-maintained gravel road 3.5 mi west of Corn Springs Indian petroglyph site. Corn Springs is one of the original California native palm oases. In this upper valley, chollas, hedgehog cacti, and barrel cacti abound. In addition, there are many exceptionally large and healthy ocotillos—in fact, the stands rival the best in Anza-Borrego's lower Coyote Canyon. Palo verdes and desert ironwoods border the wash, and in the cliffs above the wash you can see an occasional raptor's nest.

To reach the trailhead, go southwest at the signed Corn Springs Rd for about 7.5 mi to the BLM campground at the oasis (tables, chemical toilets, water). Follow the gravel road a little over 3 mi farther to a sign marking the end of county maintenance. Park passenger cars here (elevation 2000 ft).

Note: If all the members of your group are unfamiliar with the area, it's not a bad idea to scout the trip before trying the overnight. The scenery is certainly worth the extra trip or third day.

A Stop at Corn Springs. On your way to or from the trailhead, make time to stop at Corn Springs oasis. Here in the canyon you'll find not just a campground, a self-guided nature trail, and an unusually large grove of native palms, but an important prehistoric Indian site, with an abundance of petroglyphs. Some of the rock art is thought to be as much as 10,000 years old. Another reason for taking some time out here is that this oasis, like nearly all California desert areas having a reliable water supply, supports a wide variety of wildlife. If you spend a little time here quietly observing, you'll be sure to see quite a few desert animals firsthand.

Hike or Day 1 of Backpack—Corn Springs Wash. The overnight backpack described here ends near Desert Center and thus requires a car shuttle. (Depending on the size of your party, leave one or more cars at Desert

Center.) Those taking this trip across the Chuckwallas should have had experience with rough trails, cross-country hiking, and use of topo and compass. If you are going to be day hiking, the distance you go is up to you. Your round-trip could be 1 mi or 16 mi, depending on your time and inclination.

To begin the hike at the end of the gravel road, look for an easily seen 4WD trail angling uphill to the west. This trail makes a gentle ascent due west up Corn Springs Wash. BLM regulations allow 4WD vehicles to follow this trail about 4 mi beyond the end of the gravel road. The 1963-issue topo shows the 4WD trail ending at a saddle (2400 ft) about 3.25 mi from its start. The saddle separates the Corn Springs drainage from the Red Cloud drainage to the west. There is a fairly recent, but dangerous, 4WD trail crossing over into the Red Cloud drainage.

After hiking about 4 mi from the gravel road, look for an old miners' road branching off the 4WD trail to the north, partway up the ascent from the point where the valley narrows and the broad wash ends—a short distance from the saddle. This is not the trail shown on the topo, but another trail about 1 mi farther west. Using a topo and a compass, with a little luck you'll be able to pick up the correct road on the first try (there are several others leaving the wash). At this point, the bearing on some nearby radio towers is approximately 315 degrees.

Finding the correct road is not as difficult as it may seem; there are only a couple of possible wrong turns, and these shouldn't cost more than two hours of hiking time to check out. (As mentioned above, a one-day scouting trip before the overnight is not a bad idea if your group is large or is going to be pressed for time.)

Not too long after you find the miners' road, however, you lose it— that is, in about 1 mi it changes to a miners' mule pack trail. This trail was constructed for pack animals and is clearly distinguishable, despite many years of erosion and weed growth. After about 0.75 mi on this trail it crosses the northernmost range of the Chuckwallas—the ridge seen from I-10 at Desert Center—via a 2880-ft pass. The pass is only 500 ft above the main wash. At the pass there is a fine view north to the Chuckwalla Valley, Eagle Mtn, and the Palen Range. The radio towers are 3 mi to the west.

Once over the saddle, the mule trail, which is quite rough, follows the east side of the drainage down past an old mine tunnel. Two airline miles from the saddle—at 2280 ft—the trail leaves the canyon, which is beginning to change into a impassable gorge. The trail now climbs northeast through another saddle, marked by a 2400-ft rock outcropping to the west. You are now 7–9 mi from where you started (at the end of the county road); there is level ground here, so it's a good place to camp. If you're on a one-day scouting trip, this is as far as you should go before turning around.

Day 2 of Backpack—Down to Desert Center. The walk to Desert Center on the second day is about a 1500-ft descent. From the saddle, the trail goes down to the alluvial fan. On the fan there is a network of 4WD trails; keep on a compass bearing to the north as you descend. Hiking cross-country down the fan is easy and pleasant; the worst that can happen is that you'll hit I-10 half a mile east or west of Desert Center.

Blythe-Winterhaven

ABOUT THE AREA. Between Blythe and Winterhaven lies the easternmost part of the California desert's Colorado region. The Colorado Desert stretches north to Needles, west a little beyond the Salton Sea, and south into Mexico, where it follows the western edge of the Gulf of California more than a third of the way to the tip of the Baja peninsula.

This area south of Blythe is truly the low desert, with most elevations being around sea level and few mountaintops reaching above 2000 ft. The region takes its name from the Colorado River, which forms its eastern border in California. And it is certainly a fitting association, for to a great extent the river is responsible for the area's character. In fact, a fair amount of today's land surface in the south part of this area is part of an enormous delta built up by the river. Much of the silt making up the delta was carved out of that part of the Colorado Plateau we know as the Grand Canyon. The layers of silt — which have built up to a thickness of more than 2000 ft — extend west to the Coachella and Imperial valleys and south to the Gulf of California.

The river that produced this immense delta also makes possible a pleasantly anomalous situation for visitors, who find themselves able to enjoy both desert and water recreation in this southeastern area. So, if you love desert recreation, but also love water sports and the greenery you generally find near water, then you're going to find plenty to interest you near and on the Colorado River.

For starters, two national wildlife refuges, Cibola and Imperial, stretch along the Colorado River from below Blythe to a point just a few miles north of Winterhaven. You can tour Cibola National Wildlife Refuge by car, but aside from the intrapark road in Picacho State Recreation Area, you need a boat to tour Imperial National Wildlife Refuge. For wildlife watchers, the best times to visit the refuges are in spring and fall, when many waterfowl and other birds are migrating along the Pacific Flyway. Winter is a good time to watch for the resident creatures and those waterfowl that stay over until spring. The same can be said for Picacho State Recreation Area, which is located within Imperial National Wildlife Refuge and is accessible by car.

Surprisingly, water recreationists seem to flock to the river at all seasons, even in hottest summer — for boating, fishing, canoeing, and kayaking are all allowed in the refuges.

In contrast to the river, Picacho SRA is a microcosm of this part of the California desert. Here, within just a few miles, you can visit scenic, pastel-hued badlands; a verdant riparian area sheltering many wildlife species; broad, shady washes lined with trees and wildflowers; the remains of a historic gold mining town; and the now slow-moving, but still mighty, Colorado River. Hiking, fishing, camping, boating, animal watching, sightseeing, and just plain lazing around are all popular at Picacho. If you're a peak climber, nearby Picacho Peak (Class 6) will probably do more than just tempt you. And regardless of whether you're at I-10 and want to get to I-8 or vice-versa, you can easily do so and treat yourself to a fine Colorado Desert tour at the same time.

To start the tour from the south, at about 13 mi west of Winterhaven, take Imperial County road S-34 north (Ogilby Rd) about 25 mi to CA 78. Follow CA 78 for about 16 mi to the county-maintained Milpitas Wash Rd (dirt), then go west on this road for about 10 very scenic miles until you run into the Wiley Well Rd. (You'll want to stop and explore the main wash and a few side washes on your way. There are many good camp spots along here.) Wiley Well Rd will take you north to I-10 in about 22 easy miles. You'll come out 14 mi west of Blythe. From the north, do the reverse. Alternatively, you can stay on CA 78 through the Palo Verde Mtns and wind up in Blythe, about 38 mi north.

Note: The low elevations and southerly location of this part of the California desert mean that summer temperatures often go above 115° F. Unless you know and love temperatures like this, visit during some other season.

FACILITIES. Gas, supplies, restaurants, and motels are easy to find in Blythe and Winterhaven.

Camping. There are several developed campgrounds between Blythe and Winterhaven. To find Wiley Well Campground, take I-10 west from Blythe for 14 mi, then go south 9 mi on Wiley Well Rd. Coon Hollow Campground is 3 mi south of Wiley Well on the road of the same name. Both have chemical toilets and tables, but *no water* (Bureau of Land Management).

Peter McIntyre County Park is located 6 mi south of Blythe; take Intake Blvd off I-10, turn east on Twenty-sixth at the end of Intake to get to the park. Water, restrooms, tables, gas, and a small store are available. Palo Verde County Park is 19 mi south of Blythe (3 mi south of Palo Verde) off CA 78. The only facilities are chemical toilets. Palo Verde Oxbow site (BLM) is 1.2 mi south of Palo Verde County Park on CA 78; go east 0.5 mi from the highway. The only facilities are chemical toilets.

Picacho State Recreation Area campsites have tables, fire rings, water, and chemical toilets. A small concession offers gas and limited supplies. See Picacho State Recreation Area trip, below, for directions. To find Squaw Lake Recreation Site, start in Winterhaven and zig and zag north and east on Imperial County road S-24 for about 15.5 mi to Senator Wash Rd; follow this road north 3.6 mi to its end at the site (BLM). Restrooms and water are available. For other campgrounds near this area, see the Needles–Colorado River South "Facilities" section. *Note:* During the winter "snowbird" season, some of these campgrounds may be full.

There are many fine open-desert camp spots throughout the BLM lands in this area and nearby areas. For information on good places to try, see the "Facilities" sections for the Chuckwalla Mtns, Algodones Dunes–Cargo Muchacho Mtns, and Needles–Colorado River South areas.

Cibola National Wildlife Refuge

TO GET THERE. Take CA 78 south from Blythe about 18 mi to the refuge access point, just below Oxbow Lake and Palo Verde County Park.

GETTING YOUR BEARINGS. Bring along a good Imperial County map.

ABOUT THE REFUGE. This refuge, established in 1964, is intended to preserve and enhance waterfowl wintering habitat along the Colorado River portion of the Pacific Flyway. It was created to help lessen loss of wildlife habitat that resulted from 50 mi of stream channelization. Havasu National Wildlife Refuge (NWR) (100 mi to the north) and Imperial NWR (contiguous with Cibola to the south) perform the same function. Unlike these other two refuges, Cibola has a large acreage of agricultural lands suitable for growing the crops — such as Bermuda grass — that are so tempting to Canada geese and field-feeding ducks like pintails and mallards, all of which overwinter in the refuge. (The other two refuges have a higher proportion of wetlands.)

The 16,627-acre Cibola NWR is mostly riverbottom land, with desert mesas and washes on its periphery; a portion of the refuge is on the Arizona side of the Colorado River. The access road just south of Oxbow Lake leads east to an improved dirt road that follows the Colorado River channel north and south. There is a bridge across the river just north of the access road.

The refuge is divided into three sections. Zone I, where you enter, is open to the public only on the road following the river. Zone II, which begins about 3 mi south on the road and continues south for about 8 mi to a dead end, is open to the public all year. In the middle of Zone II, about 6.5 mi south of the access road, is another bridge across the river. The refuge farmlands are to the west of the bridge. (The farmlands, which can be visited, are a good place to see Canada geese and the field-feeding ducks.) Zone III, which begins about 2.5 mi south of the bridge in the middle of Zone II, is only open to the public between September 5 and March 15. You can, however, observe wildlife and take photos from your vehicle on the established roads during the otherwise closed time. Hiking, sightseeing, and photography are allowed throughout the refuge, with the exception of areas closed to public entry.

The best times to see migrating birds of all sorts are during fall and spring. December through March, wildlife watchers come to observe the resident creatures (which include the endangered Yuma clapper rail) and the overwintering waterfowl. If you prefer water sports to hiking, sightseeing, or photography, there are opportunities for boating, canoeing, fishing, etc., in the refuge. As in all refuges, though, camping is not allowed. For more information on Cibola NWR, contact the refuge manager at P.O. Box AP, Blythe, CA 92225, or at 602-857-3253. Free brochures are available.

Picacho Peak Climb
Class 6/elev. 1947 ft/USGS topo *Picacho Peak*/5 mi RT/cross-country, use trail

TO GET THERE. Follow county road S-24 (Picacho Rd) north from I-10 at Winterhaven for about 4 mi to where S-24 turns east; continue north on Picacho Rd to the All American Canal. Cross the canal and keep going north on Picacho Rd (now dirt) for about 13.5 mi to the Picacho Mine property (posted). Continue beyond the property until you have passed two washes on the west side of the road. Park off the road here.

ABOUT THE HIKE. Picacho Peak is located about 2 mi northwest of the Picacho Mine. The climb up this volcanic plug is short, but technically difficult. It *must not* be attempted without an experienced leader and proper equipment. However, many intermediate-level climbers have stood on the summit; all agree that this is one of the most fun and interesting climbs in the California desert.

To approach Picacho Peak, walk up the wash west of your car (Little Picacho Wash) and join the obvious use trail to the saddle west of the peak. Zigzag up to the west via a series of ledges. Then go up a large, Class 3 step, over a step-across, and up to a 10-ft overhang that has had a ladder in place for at least twenty years. Beyond the ladder are several short faces that require technical ability and equipment. Views from the summit are magnificent, extending southwest to the Cargo Muchacho Mtns and east to the Imperial National Wildlife Refuge and Picacho State Recreation Area (along the Colorado River).

Picacho State Recreation Area

TO GET THERE. Follow the directions for Picacho Peak climb, above, but continue north past the Picacho Mine on Picacho Rd to the Picacho State Recreation Area (SRA), about 18 mi from the canal. If you have 4WD, you can also enter via the Indian Pass Rd, which takes off from county road S-34, farther north. See the Indian Wash–Picacho SRA 4WD tour, in the Algodones Dunes–Cargo Muchacho Mtns area below, for directions.

GETTING YOUR BEARINGS. You'll need a good Imperial County map. The USGS topo *Picacho* is also useful in helping figure out the lay of the river.

ABOUT THE RECREATION AREA. Here in the southeastern corner of
the California desert, on the once-mighty Colorado River, is one of
the state's most unique recreation areas. At Picacho you find not just
a rugged and colorful corner of the desert, but a remarkably varied
riparian area where both desert and aquatic wildlife are abundant. Also
abundant are opportunities for hiking, photography, boating, fishing,
camping, and, of course, plant and animal watching. Many visitors find
just about any time but high summer a good time to enjoy the many
recreational activities possible here. Quite a few boaters manage to brave
even high summer, though. (Because the SRA is so far south and is at
a low elevation, summer temperatures are often over 115° F.)

Early Days Around Picacho. At the time the Spanish explorer Coronado
came to this part of the California desert in 1540, native peoples had
already been living along the Colorado for perhaps as long as 10,000
years. The trade trails of these Indians crisscross much of the eastern
Colorado Desert region. (You can see one of these trails at a pull-off
on CA 78 about 2 mi west of its intersection with S-34. There is a
marker on the south side of the road.)

According to archaeologists, the groups who lived along this particular part of the river somewhat more recently, during the past 3000
years or so, seem to have had quite a complex culture. They farmed
the rich soils of the river bottom, crossed the river on rafts and possibly
even in shallow-drafted pottery boats, and had a rather involved cere-
monial life. The impressive rock alignments or intaglios found along
the Colorado River may have figured in their rituals.

In the 1860s, a few folks afflicted with gold fever came to this part
of the Colorado Desert and successfully prospected for the precious
mineral—but didn't do anything much about their finds. By the 1880s,
other, more ambitious prospectors had begun to develop some of the
earlier finds. Finally, in the 1890s, the Picacho Mine started operations
(you pass the mine area on your way to the SRA). A large stamp mill
was built close to the river (stamp mills need water), and a narrow-
gauge railway was built to haul the ore from the mine to the mill. Steamboats plied the river, bringing supplies in and taking ore out. A town,
Picacho, grew up around the mill, and by 1904 there were 700 people
working the mine and about 2500 people living in the town. Unfortunately, damming the Colorado put this historic town under water.
Today, all that's left is the Picacho Mill building (near the SRA headquarters). Some say that this one mine produced as much as $14 million
in gold before its luck ran out.

Seeing Picacho Today. Because of its rare combination of desert and
riverside scenery, plants, and animals, Picacho SRA is a favorite with
hikers, plant and animal watchers, and sightseers—not to mention just
plain desert and river rats. The roads in the SRA are just as subject to
change without notice as are other desert roads, which means you can't
count on them being passable all the time—with or without 4WD. Feet,
however, will take you just about anywhere you want to go here—

and a raft will take you to the rest. If you do have 4WD, there are a number of interesting 4WD roads to explore; if you don't have 4WD, shanks' mare will have to do.

Even visitors who aren't much for walking will find plenty to do here (or not do, as the case may be). The intrapark road winds through some of the most colorful desert country you're likely to find anywhere in the Southwest — interspersed with cool views of the river and wide, shallow washes filled with shady desert ironwood groves. Almost everywhere you go there will be wildlife to see and hear — the chatty Gambel's quail, the greedy raccoon, the comic roadrunner, the elusive bighorn, the agile cactus wren, and many others. In spring and fall, the migrating times for many waterfowl, you may see several kinds of ducks, along with egrets, blue herons, and even cormorants. One of the greatest treats of all here, and in the other wildlife refuges, is to see the Canada geese and hear their unique and stirring call. There's nothing quite like goose music; it's worth coming a long way to hear.

Algodones Dunes–
Cargo Muchacho Mountains

ABOUT THE AREA. This southeastern corner of the California desert's Colorado region is a favorite with outdoor recreationists in winter. Its low elevation and southerly location ensure that winter temperatures are mild. The area seldom freezes, with daytime temperatures even in January and February often being in the seventies. In winter, a number of spots in this and the Blythe-Winterhaven area are usually crowded with "snowbirds" — mostly retired folks with RVs who like spending the cold, icy, eastern months in a warmer clime.

Primarily, though, the area is used for fall, winter, and spring desert recreation by people within a few hours' drive. The colorful canyons, lush washes, and California's largest dune system, the Algodones Dunes, all offer many opportunities for cross-country hiking, plant and animal watching, car camping, and photography. The more strenuously inclined will find plenty of peaks to scramble in the low but rugged mountain ranges a little east of the area, along the Colorado River.

Early Trailmakers. For many thousands of years before European explorers came to this corner of the California desert's Colorado region, the terrain lying between the Algodones Dunes and the Colorado River was traversed by Indians on hunting, gathering, and trading trips. Today, this area still shows definite traces of these early peoples' repeated passages. For several decades, archaeologists have been studying the trails, stone tools, rock alignments, sleeping circles, pottery, and petroglyphs left behind by a succession of prehistoric Indian groups as they traveled to and from the Colorado River. Some of these artifacts may be as much as 10,000 years old.

Anza Opens the Door . . . . The energetic and skilled Spanish explorer Juan Bautista de Anza, in his attempt to establish a route from Mexico City to San Francisco in 1774, was probably the first European to enter this area. Coming from the Spanish mission at Tubac, Arizona, he was guided by the Yuman Indians to a Colorado River crossing near what is now a Yuma-Winterhaven Southern Pacific Railroad bridge. Although the Yumans' relations with this group of Spaniards were reputedly friendly, many of the succeeding expeditions did not treat the Yumans well. As a result, the Yumans tried to discourage the unwelcome visitors from traveling through their ancestral lands. Eventually, in the mid-1800s, these native peoples, like so many throughout the desert lands of the southwestern United States, were "pacified"—that is, they were forced to give up their lands and received little or nothing in return.

. . . And Prospectors Wander In. Now that the settlers had a free hand, it wasn't long before even this remote corner of the desert was connected with the outside world. The pony express service on that part of the Butterfield Trail that ran between this area and San Diego gave way to the railroad and telegraph in the late 1870s. Ferries ran across the Colorado, and steamboats up and down it. Fort Yuma grew from an army outpost to an important supply center. And in the early 1800s a few prospectors began trying their luck in the softly colored but rugged mountains that came to be called the Cargo Muchachos.

The Gold Rock Mining District. In these craggy mountains, east of the Algodones Dunes and northwest of Winterhaven, lay ore enough to eventually make the locality one of the richest gold mining districts in California: Gold Rock. Today, you can visit the district and walk over the site of Tumco, a once-booming mining town of over 2500 people. The treasure hunters haven't managed to carry away everything, so some of the larger mining paraphernalia is still there—including the huge cyanide vats used to process ore. The well-preserved Tumco Cemetery is a national historic landmark.

Not too far away from the Gold Rock district, sort of on the way to Picacho Peak and Picacho SRA is, not surprisingly, another old and famously successful gold mine, Picacho. If you'd like to get an idea of what life might have been like around Gold Rock, the Picacho Mine, and the little mining town of Picacho (on the Colorado River) in the late 1800s, read Zane Grey's *Wanderer of the Wasteland*. In another volume, *Stairs of Sand,* the Algodones Dunes figure prominently. Grey spent some time in and around this part of Imperial County, soaking up local color for these books. So, allowing for poetic license, you will indeed get a bit of the old-time flavor of this part of the desert from them.

Gold Rock Trading Post Carries On. Across the road from Tumco is the Gold Rock Trading Post, part of the Walker family's homestead (the Walkers are the present owners of the Tumco mines). The trading post is a friendly mecca for rockhounds and other desert rats. Don't forget to stop in for a cold drink and a look through the rock and Old West collections.

The Algodones Dunes— Worth More than Gold? This huge dune system, located to the west of the Gold Rock district, has many claims to fame. For example, the dunes were discovered by Hollywood and General Patton, both of whom used them as a stage. One of the least desirable reasons for their being well known, though, is that they are probably the dune buggy capital of the world. Every weekend, even in the height of summer, hordes of ORV enthusiasts swarm over the dunes around Glamis, the engines of their all-terrain vehicles (ATVs) roaring and their wide, heavy tires crushing the life out of delicately balanced biotic communities. (Sometimes it's better to admire the dunes from a distance; then you can't see and hear the devastation.) However, there is a bright spot—albeit a small one—in the ATV scene. The part of the dunes located north of CA 78 has been designated a national natural landmark, thanks to the hard work of many environmentalists. Hiking and sightseeing in this protected part of the dunes is an unforgettable experience; don't miss it!

The meager 22,000 acres that have been set aside as a national natural landmark are only a small percentage of the total dune area, which is approximately 8 mi by 40 mi. Obviously, this little concession to conservation doesn't go far toward preserving a truly viable segment of the Algodones' rare and extensive dune habitat. The Bureau of Land Management (BLM), which manages 12.5 million of the 25 million acres in the California desert, has given over the rest of the dunes to the ORVers, so you can see how committed they are to their mission of protecting our public lands from degradation and destruction.

FACILITIES. Gas and limited supplies at Glamis. Water and snacks at Gold Rock Trading Post. Gas, supplies, restaurants, and motels are plentiful in Blythe, El Centro, and Winterhaven/Yuma.

Camping. For information on camping in Picacho State Recreation Area, see "Facilities" section of the Blythe-Winterhaven area. In the Algodones Dunes there are two primitive BLM campgrounds, Gecko and Roadrunner. To find them, take CA 78 east from its intersection with CA 115 on the east side of Brawley for about 11.8 mi to Gecko Rd; turn south. Gecko Campground is 3.3 mi from CA 78, Roadrunner is 5.6 mi. The only facilities are chemical toilets; parking is paved. During the winter season, the BLM maintains a ranger station and rescue personnel on the road into the campgrounds.

Hugh Osborne Lookout County Park, another primitive campground, is located 2.4 mi east of Gecko Rd. From the park, there is a good view of the most intensively used ORV part of the dunes. There are no facilities, but parking is paved.

Note: The county park and the two BLM campgrounds are havens for two-, three-, and four-wheeled dune enthusiasts. During three- and four-day weekends in the winter, as many as 10,000 dune-riding recreationists descend on the dunes. Instant "cities" spring up at all the aforementioned places to provide vehicle-related supplies and services.

Open-desert camp spots are easily found throughout this whole area. There is a large, unofficial campground with firmly packed sand on the south side of CA 78 near Glamis (no facilities). Three other camping spots near the dunes (all very sandy) are at Mammoth Wash in the north dunes, an area west and north of Ogilby, and another near the Old Plank Rd Viewpoint on Gray's Well Rd off I-8 a few miles west of the Ogilby Rd exit. There are lots of good sites on dirt roads and near washes off Imperial County road S-34 and Picacho Rd.

Gold Rock Mining District

TO GET THERE. From the intersection of I-8 and CA 111 in El Centro, take I-8 east about 41 mi to the Ogilby Rd exit. Go north here on Ogilby Rd (Imperial County road S-34) for 8.5 mi to Gold Rock Ranch Rd (dirt).

GETTING YOUR BEARINGS. A good Imperial County map will be helpful.

ABOUT THE MINING DISTRICT. When you reach Gold Rock Ranch Rd, turn east on a dirt road. A short distance from Ogilby Rd is a Y; the north arm leads to the town cemetery, a national historic landmark, where you can still read some of the inscriptions on the headstones. The south arm of the Y leads to the remains of several buildings and the huge cyanide tanks once used in ore processing. As you continue along this arm of the road, at about 1.1 mi from the Y take time to stop and walk up a trail on the low hill to your left. At the top are more mine ruins and a good view west to the Algodones Dunes. There are more mining operations up the canyons to the east.

Early Miners Try Their Luck. There's a local story about how the mountains of this mining district got their name. It seems that sometime in the 1820s several Spanish gold-seekers were prospecting here and there in the then-unnamed mountains. One day, a couple of the boys in the group went hiking in the canyons there and came back with their pockets loaded with gold ore. Thus, the name Cargo Muchacho ("loaded boy").

Despite this first encouraging find, the Gold Rock area didn't even begin to put itself on the mining map until about 1892, when a Mr. Hedges made a pretty good strike—good enough to warrant enlarging his small mill to a forty-stamp mill and to put in a water line from the Colorado River. It must have been a pretty good ore vein, for the water line not only had to come over 12 mi from the river, but the water had to be pumped up 500 ft. No small project in those days!

Booms and Busts. On the railroad line just a short distance away, the little settlement of Ogilby grew up to handle the now-booming mine business. Soon, three more mines started up; and by 1895 things looked so good that a hundred-stamp mill was built. Mr. Hedges now had himself a sizable town of 2500 named—what else?—Hedges. But few places in the California desert seem to keep the name they start out with, and Hedges was no exception. Although the town's name wasn't officially changed, in the early 1900s the mining area itself acquired the name of Gold Rock.

Along with its new name, the mining district at the base of the Cargo Muchachos acquired some new problems. The ore wasn't as rich as it once was. The tailings had piled up so much that equipment and buildings had to be moved. The stamp mill had to be partly shut down. And, finally, the once-successful mining operation closed down altogether.

But all was not yet lost. In 1910 a large mining concern, the Trumbell United Mines Company, bought up the old operation, modernized it, dug deeper, and made it pay again. Almost overnight, the town sprang up once more; only now it was called Tumco. But poor Tumco went too far too fast—the management expanded the operation until it collapsed for want of enough ore to feed the enormous mill. Once again, for the last time, the site was abandoned, in 1914. There are still a few small mines operating in the district, but for the most part, only the ghosts of rich gold ore inhabit the pastel-colored Cargo Muchacho Mtns.

Gold Rock Trading Post—A "Must" Stop. About eleven years after the Tumco operation went bust, the Walker family—in search of a way to make a living outside the big cities—arrived at the deserted site. For a few hundred dollars they bought several of the old Tumco claims, moved into one of the few remaining intact buildings, and started work. The Walkers never made a fortune, but they liked living in the desert. Eventually, in 1930, they leased their claims to a mining company from the east and took up a 160-acre homestead 2 mi west of Tumco.

The Walkers built their new home with whatever sound wood and scrap they could find in Tumco. Over the years their ranch in this isolated part of the California desert became a sort of travelers' landmark. People couldn't resist stopping by—again and again. Nowadays, descendants of the original Walker family operate the Gold Rock Trading Post, which is built near the original homestead.

Be sure to make time to visit the trading post, which is a "must" stop for rockhounds. Browse through the gem and mineral collections, the Old West bric-a-brac, and the desert books. Have a snack. Picnic. Fill your water bottles. Or even camp out. The trading post is open seven days a week (hours vary) but is closed in June and for half of September. To get to the trading post from Tumco, just go back to S-34, cross it (there's a nice view from the intersection), and continue west on Gold Rock Ranch Rd for about 1.5 mi.

Indian Wash–Picacho
State Recreation Area 4WD Tour

TO GET THERE. From the intersection of I-8 and CA 111 in El Centro, take I-8 east about 41 mi to the Ogilby Rd exit. Go north here on county road S-34 (Ogilby Rd) for about 13 mi to either the Indian Pass Rd or the "Hyduke Mine Rd" (usually marked by a homemade sign); turn east on either of these dirt roads. (To find out which one is currently in the best shape, check with the folks at the Gold Rock Trading Post (see Gold Rock Mining District, above, for directions).

Note: Ordinary vehicles can go as far as Indian Pass, about 8 mi. Lots of good camp spots along the way.

GETTING YOUR BEARINGS. Bring along a good Imperial County map. In the state recreation area (SRA) the USGS topo *Picacho* is helpful.

ABOUT THE TOUR. It's about 16 mi from Ogilby Rd (Imperial County road S-34) to the Colorado River in Picacho State Recreation Area. The dirt road to Indian Pass (8 mi) is good; from the pass down through Gavilan Wash to the SRA, the road is steep, winding, narrow, and usually very rough—don't try it without 4WD. Once in the SRA, you can either return the way you came or leave via Picacho Rd (dirt), which takes off from the south end of the SRA (this is the way most visitors come and go—when the road isn't washed out). If you go back the way you came, the total distance is about 32 mi, not counting any exploring you do. If you leave via Picacho Rd, it's about 23.5 mi to I-8 in Winterhaven, making the total distance about 39 mi to there.

The Longest Campground in the Desert? Take your time going up the road to Indian Pass. Over the first couple of miles, you'll notice there are plenty of roads to pull off on; there are good campsites up almost all of them. A little exploring in the shady side-washes will convince you that they are alive with both animal and plant life. In just a few minutes of watching you'll probably see several species of lizards and birds, and at least one jackrabbit. In spring the variety of wildflowers is quite amazing.

After 2.5 mi or so, watch for rocks coated with very black, shiny desert varnish. At about 4.5 mi from Ogilby Rd, the good campsite areas begin again—and go on for several miles. There are even some fire rings (remember, in the desert, fires are always BYOW—"bring your own wood"). A little over 8.5 mi from where you started up Indian Pass Rd, you'll top the pass (1040 ft). Despite the relatively low elevation of the pass, there is a fine view from it. You are overlooking Gavilan Wash (and the road into the SRA); the Chocolate Mtns are across the wash to the east. A quick consultation with your maps will help you identify what's to the west. All around lies a volcanic field, darkly burnished with desert varnish.

As you drive down through Gavilan Wash, there will be mine roads coming into it from time to time. About 5 mi from the pass, look for a sign marking the boundary of the Imperial National Wildlife Refuge, which encompasses the SRA. At a little less than 6 mi from the pass, your road will T into the SRA road paralleling the Colorado River. The sign here indicates that the 4-S Ranch (part of the SRA) is 1.5 mi to the north and the park headquarters and campground are 8 mi south.

The 4-S Ranch is on the river near the northern boundary of the SRA; the "ranch" now consists of a boat ramp and primitive campground. All along the park road in both directions there are many lush washes suitable for camping and a number of 4WD roads that can be explored either on foot or on wheels. The drive to the SRA headquarters will take you to several fine viewpoints and through some extremely colorful badlands that are almost Grand Canyon–like. For information on the SRA, see the Blythe–Winterhaven area, above.

Algodones Dunes

TO GET THERE. From I-8 in El Centro, take CA 86 north 13 mi to CA 78; go east on CA 78 a little over 15 mi to Gecko Rd, where there is a BLM visitor center (not open in summer).

GETTING YOUR BEARINGS. You'll need a good Imperial County map.

ABOUT THE DUNES. The Algodones sand dunes, also called Imperial Sand Dunes and Glamis Dunes, extend for about 45 mi from Mammoth Wash in the north to about 3 mi south of the Mexican border. Some of the dunes in this system — which is California's most extensive — are as much as 300 ft high. The Algodones' axis is northwest-southeast,

Algodones Dunes near Mammoth Wash, east of Browley.
Photo by Lyle Gaston.

and it lies just east of the many-branched San Andreas fault zone. The main part of the dunes is bounded on the west by the Coachella Canal and on the east by Southern Pacific's main cross-country line. The dunes are "cut" in half lengthwise, with the eastern half being made up of higher, unstable, still-moving dunes. The western half of the dune system has low, rolling dunes that have been stabilized by creosote bushes. (Algodones, by the way, is Spanish for "cotton.")

From Lake Bed to Dune System. As mentioned in Chapter 15, in ancient times the Salton Sea area contained a series of freshwater lakes—fed from time to time by the capricious Colorado River. When the river didn't feed Lake Cahuilla, and the pluvial cycle of the Pleistocene moved to "dry" periodically, the lake evaporated and the sands from its beaches were blown eastward—eventually forming the dunes. The last incarnation of the lake kept much of the Coachella and Imperial valleys underwater until the 1400s. The Salton Sea is a much more recent, manmade, phenomenon.

Crossing the Dunes. The earliest inhabitants of this part of the California desert didn't spend much time in the dunes; archaeologists have found sites at the dune edges where prehistoric peoples camped for short periods on their way to or from Lake Cahuilla and the Colorado River. Early explorers like Anza went around the dunes. A few settlers and prospectors managed to make their ways through the dunes with mules and horses, but the going was so hard that no one set up a permanent route until the early 1900s. From 1916 to 1926, the only road across the dunes was one car wide and made of planks (there were turnouts every quarter of a mile).

You can still see remnants of the old road off Gray's Well Rd on the south side of I-8. To reach the Old Plank Rd Viewpoint when eastbound, take the Gray's Well exit off I-8 about 8 mi east of where CA 98 interesects I-8. When westbound, take the Gordon's Well exit off I-8 about 9 mi west of the Ogilby Rd exit; get into the eastbound lanes and look for the Gray's Well exit just ahead.

Now, two highways cross the dunes from east to west; CA 78 bisects the dunes and I-8 cuts across the southern end. Two paved roads lead into the dunes from CA 78. The longer of the two leads to two primitive Bureau of Land Management (BLM) campgrounds. The other road is only 0.25 mi long and leads to Hugh Osborn County Park. The county park and the two BLM campgrounds are havens for two-, three-, and four-wheeled dune enthusiasts. During three- and four-day weekends in the winter, as many as 10,000 dune-riding recreationists descend on the dunes.

Hiking the Dunes. Two-thirds of the dunes just north of CA 78 are closed to vehicles; this is the best area for hikers. In spring, the east edge of the dunes collects flash-flood runoff from the Chocolate Mtns—this means that in good years the spring wildflower displays are spectacular. One particularly good spot for wildflowers is 5–6 mi northwest of Glamis along the Niland Rd, which parallels the Southern Pacific tracks between I-8 and Niland (turn north on this dirt road just east of the Glamis store). February through April, after a series of well-timed winter rains, a 1- or 2-mi hike into the base of the dunes will bring you to carpets of evening primroses, orange mallow, and purple sand verbena. Creosote bushes and palo verde trees also put on good displays, and there are likely to be ghost flowers and desert lilies, too.

The only parking for this cross-country hike is between the road and the railroad tracks. Take water, lunch, and lots of film with you, and you're sure to enjoy your easy day in the dunes. When hiking in, look back frequently to where you parked your vehicle; once into the low, rolling dunes, there are few reliable landmarks to guide you back!

A good place to find large numbers of desert lilies is on the north side of CA 78 near the BLM ranger station at Gecko Rd (the one leading into the campgrounds). The tallest creosote bushes known today (about 20 ft high) are found on the west side of the dunes, north of CA 78 between the Coachella and East Highline canals (look for the East Mesa area on your county map). The best explanation for this phenomenon is that the bushes get water from the unlined Coachella Canal. In good years you may also be able to find a unique plant called sand food in the dunes. This well-adapted little parasitic plant has a long, thick, succulent root, but all that appears on the surface is a round, thick, sand-colored head. If you're lucky, you may catch it in flower. Indians thought the whole plant, small purple flowers and all, a great delicacy — thus, the name.

Appendices

Plant List

COMMON NAME	SCIENTIFIC NAME
Arrowweed	*Pluchea sericea*
Ash	
Arizona Ash	*Fraxinus velutina*
Leather-leaved	
Ash	(see Arizona Ash)
Athel	(see Tamarisk)
Big Sagebrush	(see Sagebrush)
Blazing Star	*Mentzelia* spp.
Boxthorn	
Anderson	
Thornbush	*Lycium andersonii*
Peach-thorn	*L. cooperii*
Brittlebush	*Encelia farinosa*
Burroweed/	
White Bursage	*Ambrosia dumosa*
Cactus	
Barrel Cactus	*Ferocactus acanthodes*
Beavertail	
Cactus	*Opuntia basilaris*
Cholla Cactus	
Darning Nee-	
dle Cholla	(see Pencil Cholla)
Deerhorn	
Cholla	*Opuntia acanthocarpa*
Jumping/Teddy	
Bear Cholla	*O. bigelovii*
Pencil Cholla	*O. ramosissima*
Silver Cholla	*O. echinocarpa*
Nipple Cactus/	
Mamillaria	*Mamillaria* spp.

COMMON NAME	SCIENTIFIC NAME
California/Desert	
Fan Palm	(see Palm)
Cassia	*Cassia armata*
Catalpa, Desert/	
Desert Willow	*Chilopsis linearis* (Bignonia family; not a true willow)
Catclaw/Wait-a-	
Minute Bush	*Acacia greggii*
Chaparral Yucca	(see Yucca)
Cheese-bush	*Hymenoclea salsola*
Chia	(see Sage)
Chuparosa	*Beloperone californica*
Cottonwood	
Fremont	
Cottonwood	*Populus fremontii*
Creosote Bush	*Larrea tridentata*
Darning Needle	
Cholla	(see Cactus)
Datura/Western	
Jimsonweed	*Datura meteloides*
Deerhorn Cholla	(see Cactus)
Desert/California	
Fan Palm	(see Palm)
Desert Holly	(see Saltbush)
Desert Lavender	(see Mint)
Desert Willow	(see Catalpa, Desert)
Elephant Tree	*Bursera microphylla*
Goat Nut	(see Jojoba)

COMMON NAME	SCIENTIFIC NAME	COMMON NAME	SCIENTIFIC NAME
Goldenbush		Mormon Tea/	
Black-banded	*Haplopappus*	Joint Fir	*Ephedra* spp.
Goldenbush	*paniculatus*	Mule Fat	*Baccharis glutinosa*
Cooper			
Goldenbush	*H. cooperii*	Nipple Cactus	(see Cactus)
Desert Rock			
Goldenbush	*H. cuneatus*	Oak	
Linear-Leaved		Scrub	*Quercus turbinella*
Goldenbush	*H. linearis*	Ocotillo	*Fouquieria*
Greasewood	*Sarcobatus*		*splendens*
	vermiculatus		
Great Basin		Palm	
Sagebrush	(see Sagebrush)	Desert/	
		California	
Hibiscus	(see Rock	Fan Palm	*Washingtonia*
	Hibiscus)		*filifera*
Hop-Sage, Spiny	*Grayia spinosa*	Mexican Fan	
		Palm	*W. robusta*
Indigo Bush	*Parosela* spp.		(introduced)
Iodine Bush	*Suaeda fruticosa*	Palo Verde	*Cercidium floridum*
Ironwood, Desert	*Olneya tesota*	Paper Bag Bush	(see Mint)
		Pencil Cholla	(see Cactus)
Jimsonweed,		Pine	
Western	(see Datura)	Pinyon Pine/	
Jojoba/Goat Nut	*Simmondsia*	Single-Leaf	
	chinensis	Pinyon	*Pinus monophylla*
Joshua Tree	(see Yucca)	Purple Sage	(see Sage)
Jumping Cholla	(see Cactus)		
Juniper		Rabbitbrush,	
California		Mojave	*Chrysothamnus*
Juniper	*Juniperus californica*		*nauseosus*
Utah Juniper	*J. osteosperma*		*mohavensis*
Western		Rock Hibiscus	*Hibiscus denudatus*
Juniper	*J. occidentalis*	Russian Thistle	(see Saltbush)
Mallow		Sage	
Apricot/		Purple Sage	*Salvia dorii*
Mallow	*Sphaeralcea* spp.	Chia	*S. columbariae*
Desert Mallow		Sagebrush, Great	
Mesquite	*Prosopis glandulosa*	Basin/Big	
Mint		Sagebrush	*Artemisia tridentata*
Desert		Saltbush	
Lavender	*Hyptis emoryi*	Desert Holly	*Atriplex*
Paper Bag			*hymenelytra*
Bush	*Salazaria mexicana*	Tumbleweed/	
Mistletoe		Russian	
Desert		Thistle	*Salsola iberica*
Mistletoe	*Phoradendron*		(introduced)
	californica	Salt Cedar	(see Tamarisk)
Pine Mistletoe	*Arceuthobium*	Sandpaper Plant	*Petalonyx* spp.
	divaricatum	Screwbean	*Prosopis pubescens*

COMMON NAME	SCIENTIFIC NAME	COMMON NAME	SCIENTIFIC NAME
Scrub Oak	(see Oak)	Willow	(see also Catalpa, Desert/Desert Willow (Bignonia family; not a true willow)
Silver Cholla	(see Cactus)		
Smoke Tree	*Parosela spinosa*		
Spanish Bayonet	(see Yucca)		
Sting Bush	*Eucnide urens*		
Sycamore		Slender Willow	*Salix exigua* (a true willow)
California Sycamore	*Aegeria mellinipennis*	Winter Fat	*Euratia lanata*
Tamarisk		Yucca/Spanish Bayonet	
Athel	*Tamarix aphylla*	Banana Yucca	*Yucca baccata*
Salt Cedar	*T. ramosissima* (introduced)	Chaparral Yucca/Our Lord's Candle	*Y. whipplei*
Teddy Bear Cholla	(see Cactus)	Joshua Tree	*Y. brevifolia*
Thornbush	(see Boxthorn)	Mojave Yucca	*Y. schidegera*
Tree Tobacco	*Nicotiana glauca* (introduced)		
Tumbleweed	(see Saltbush)		

SCIENTIFIC NAME	COMMON NAME	SCIENTIFIC NAME	COMMON NAME
Acacia greggii	Catclaw/Wait-a-Minute Bush	*Chrysothamnus nauseosus mohavensis*	Mojave Rabbit-brush
Aegeria mellinipennis	California Sycamore	*Datura meteloides*	Western Jimson-weed/Datura
Ambrosia dumosa	Burroweed/White Bursage	*Encelia farinosa*	Brittlebush
Arceuthobium divaricatum	Pine Mistletoe	*Ephedra* spp.	Mormon Tea/Joint Fir
Artemisia tridentata	Great Basin Sagebrush/Big Sagebrush	*Eucnide urens*	Sting Bush
		Euratia lanata	Winter Fat
Atriplex hymenelytra	Desert Holly	*Ferocactus acanthodes*	Barrel Cactus
Baccharis glutinosa	Mule Fat	*Fouquieria splendens*	Ocotillo
Beloperone californica	Chuparosa	*Fraxinus velutina*	Arizona Ash/Leather-Leaved Ash
Bursera microphylla	Elephant Tree		
Cassia armata	Cassia	*Grayia spinosa*	Hop-Sage, Spiny
Cercidium floridum	Palo Verde	*Haplopappus cooperii*	Cooper Golden-bush
Chilopsis linearis	Desert Catalpa/Desert Willow (Bignonia family; not a true willow)	*H. cuneatus*	Desert Rock Goldenbush

SCIENTIFIC NAME	COMMON NAME	SCIENTIFIC NAME	COMMON NAME
H. linearis	Linear-leaved Goldenbush	*Pluchea sericea*	Arrowweed
H. paniculatus	Black-banded Goldenbush	*Populus fremontii*	Fremont Cotton-wood
Hibiscus denudatus	Rock Hibiscus	*Prosopis glandulosa*	Mesquite
Hymenoclea salsola	Cheese-bush	*P. pubescens*	Screwbean
Hyptis emoryi	Desert Lavender	*Quercus turbinella*	Scrub/Turbinella Oak
Juniperus californica	California Juniper	*Salazaria mexicana*	Paper Bag Bush
J. occidentalis	Western Juniper	*Salix exigua*	Slender Willow
J. osteosperma	Utah Juniper	*Salsola iberica*	Tumbleweed/ Russian Thistle
Larrea tridentata	Creosote Bush	*Salvia columbariae*	Chia
Lycium andersonii	Anderson Thorn-bush	*S. dorii*	Purple Sage
L. cooperii	Peach-thorn	*Sarcobatus vermiculatus*	Greasewood
Mamillaria spp.	Nipple Cactus	*Simmondsia chinensis*	Jojoba/Goat Nut
Mentzelia spp.	Blazing Star	*Sphaeralcea* spp.	Apricot Mallow/ Desert Mallow
Nicotiana glauca	Tree Tobacco (introduced)	*Suaeda fruticosa*	Iodine Bush
Olneya tesota	Ironwood, Desert	*Tamarix aphylla*	Athel
		T. ramosissima	Salt Cedar (introduced)
Opuntia acanthocarpa	Deerhorn Cholla	*Yucca baccata*	Banana Yucca
O. basilaris	Beavertail Cactus	*Y. brevifolia*	Joshua Tree
O. bigelovii	Jumping/Teddy Bear Cholla	*Y. schidigera*	Spanish Bayonet/ Mojave Yucca
O. echinocarpa	Silver Cholla	*Y. whipplei*	Chaparral Yucca/ Our Lord's Candle
O. ramosissima	Pencil/Darning Needle Cholla		
Parosela spinosa	Smoke Tree	*Washingtonia filifera*	Desert/Califor-nia Fan Palm
P. spp.	Indigo Bush	*W. robusta*	Mexican Fan Palm (intro-duced)
Petalonyx spp.	Sandpaper Plant		
Phoradendron californica	Desert Mistletoe		
Pinus monophylla	Pinyon Pine/ Single-leaf Pinyon		

Food and Lodging

As you can see by looking at a map covering the California desert area, there are fewer large cities and more wide open space there than on the California coast. Despite all the wide open space — which, after all, is one of the main things most folks come to the desert to enjoy — most desert visitors will find that they are seldom more than an hour's drive from restaurants and motels. Those who like the solitude of open-desert camping at the end of a long dirt road may be a little further away, but such folks probably aren't much interested in being next door to such city-type amenities, anyway.

Although *Adventuring in the California Desert* does not contain lists of specific motels and restaurants, the "Facilities" section for each area mentions the cities and towns in the area where visitors can find such accommodations. For more specific recommendations, consult the Chambers of Commerce Appendix. Each of the Chambers of Commerce usually has quite a few free brochures on local motels, restaurants, and other local attractions that you can pick up at their office. If you have time, write to them before your trip and have them send you an information packet on their area.

Public Campgrounds

The list below is arranged alphabetically by the nearest cities to the campgrounds; names of campgrounds are in italic type following the name of the agency responsible for the campground. Unless otherwise noted, you may write for free information using the name of the agency responsible for the campground, the name of the city, and the zip code. In most cases, street addresses are not required. Some campgrounds have their very own address — this appears directly after the name of the campground. Don't be surprised if some telephone numbers have been changed; just try (Area Code)-555-1212 for the new number if the old one isn't any good. *Note:* Street addresses in this list are not necessarily the addresses of the campground! The addresses and phone numbers are provided so that you may write or call for information on facilities, directions, free brochures, etc. Directions for many of the campgrounds are given in the "Facilities" sections of this book.

For information on private campgrounds, check the *Rand McNally Campground and Trailer Park Directory — West*, an inexpensive and very helpful paperback that has a new edition each year. The directory contains not only private campground and RV park information, but also information on national forest, national park, Bureau of Land Management, state forest, state park, and city, county, and civic campgrounds.

Facilities are summarized, and phone numbers and addresses listed for each campground.

Barstow
Bureau of Land Management, 831 Barstow Rd, Barstow 92331; 619-256-3591. *Afton Canyon, Owl Canyon.*

San Bernardino County, Box 638, Yermo 92398; 619-254-2122. *Calico Ghost Town Regional Park.*

Big Bear
San Bernardino National Forest, Big Bear 96010; 714-866-3437. *Coldbrook, Pine Knot.*

Big Pine
Inyo County, Box 237, Independence 93526; 619-878-2411. *Baker Creek, Big Pine Triangle, Taboose, Tinemaha.*

Inyo National Forest, 873 N. Main St, Bishop 93514; 619-873-4207. *Big Pine Creek, First Falls, Fossil, Grandview, Juniper, Lower Sage Flat, Pinyon, Poleta, Sage Flat, Upper Sage Flat.*

Bishop
Bureau of Land Management, 873 N. Main St, Bishop 93514; 619-872-4881. *Crowley Lake, Horton Creek.*

Inyo County, Box 237, Independence 93526; 619-878-2411. *Millpond Recreation Area, Pleasant Valley.* Rte 1, Bishop 93514; 610-873-8522. *Schober Lane.*

Inyo National Forest, 873 N. Main St, Bishop 93514; 619-873-4027. *Aspen Meadow, Big Meadow, Big Trees, Bishop Park, East Fork, Forks, Four Jeffrey, French Camp, Holiday, Intake, Iris Meadows, Lower Rock Creek, Mosquito Flat, Mountain Glen, North Lake, Palisade, Pine Grove, Rock Creek Lake, Sabrina, Table Mtn, Tuff.*

Blythe
Bureau of Land Management, 1695 Spruce St, Riverside 92507; 714-351-6394. *Coon Hollow, Wiley Well.*

Imperial County, 135 S. Eleventh St, Suite C, El Centro 92243; 619-339-4384. *Palo Verde County Park.*

Riverside County, Box 3507, Rubidoux 92519; 714-787-2553. *Mayflower Park, McIntyre Park.*

Borrego Springs
Anza-Borrego Desert State Park, Borrego Springs 92004; 619-767-5311. *Borrego Palm Canyon, Bow Willow, Tamarisk Grove.*

Boulevard
Bureau of Land Management, 333 S. Waterman, El Centro 92243; 619-352-5842. *McCain Valley Recreation Area — Cottonwood, Lark Canyon.*

Brawley
Bureau of Land Management, 333 S. Waterman, El Centro 92243; 619-352-5842. *Imperial Sand Dunes Recreation Area — Gecko.*

Camp Angelus
San Bernardino National Forest, Camp Angelus 92305;
714-794-1123. *Barton Flats, Council Camp, Falls, Heart Bar, San Gorgonio, South Fork.*

Cedar Glen
San Bernardino National Forest, Cedar Glen 92321;
714-337-2444. *North Shore.*

Death Valley
Death Valley National Monument, Death Valley 92328;
619-786-2331. *Emigrant Junction, Furnace Creek, Mahogany Flat, Mesquite Springs, Stovepipe Wells, Sunset, Texas Spring, Thorndike, Wildrose.*

Desert Center
Bureau of Land Management, 1695 Spruce St, Riverside 92507;
714-351-6394. *Corn Springs.*

El Centro
Imperial County, 619-339-4384. *Red Hill Marina Park.* Box 806,
Seeley 92273; 619-353-3308. *Sunbeam Lake.*

Essex
Bureau of Land Management, Box 305, Needles 92363;
619-326-3896. *Hole-in-the-Wall, Mid-Hills.*

State of California, Box 1, Essex 92332; 619-389-2281.
Providence Mountains State Recreation Area.

Fawnskin
San Bernardino National Forest, Fawnskin 92333; 714-866-3437.
Big Pine Flats, Grout Bay, Hanna Flats, Holcomb Valley, Horse Springs.

Green Valley
San Bernardino National Forest, Green Valley 91350;
714-337-2444. *Crab Flats, Green Valley.*

Hemet
Riverside County, Box 3507, Riverside 92519; 714-787-2553.
Lake Skinner.

Hesperia
State of California, *Saddleback Butte State Park*, 17102 Ave J East,
Lancaster 93534; 805-942-0662. *Silverwood Lake State Recreation Area*, Star Rte, Box 7A, Hesperia 92345; 714-389-2281.

Idyllwild
Riverside County, Box 3507, Riverside 92519; 714-787-2553.
Hurkey Creek, Idyllwild Park.

San Bernardino National Forest, Idyllwild 92349; 714-659-2117.
Boulder Basin, Dark Canyon, Fern Basin, Marion Mtn.

Independence
  Bureau of Land Management, 873 N. Main St, Bishop 93514;
  619-872-4881. *Goodale Creek, Symmes Creek.*

  Inyo County, Box 237, Independence 93526; 619-878-2411.
  Independence Creek.

  Inyo National Forest, 873 N. Main St, Bishop 93514;
  619-876-5542. *Gray's Meadow, Oak Creek, Onion Valley.*

Indio (see also North Shore)
  Riverside County, Box 3507, Riverside 92519; 619-564-4712.
  Lake Cahuilla.

June Lake
  Inyo National Forest, 873 N. Main St, Bishop 93514;
  619-647-6525. *Aerie Crag, Big Springs, Deadman, Ellery Lake, Glass
  Creek, Hartley Springs, June Lake, Oh Ridge, Pine Cliff Trailer Park,
  Reversed Creek, Silver Lake.*

Lancaster (see Pearblossom)

Littlerock
  Angeles National Forest, Littlerock 93543; 805-944-2187,
  213-577-0050. *Joshua Tree, Juniper Grove, Lakeside, Little Sycamore.*

Lone Pine
  Bureau of Land Management, 873 N. Main St, Bishop 93514;
  619-872-4881. *Tuttle Creek.*

  Inyo County, Box 237, Independence 93526; 619-878-2411.
  Diaz Lake, Portagee Joe.

  Inyo National Forest, 873 N. Main St, Bishop 93514; 619-876-5542.
  Lone Pine, Road's End, Whitney Portal, Whitney Trailhead.

Lytle Creek
  San Bernardino National Forest, Lytle Creek 92358;
  714-887-2576. *Applewhite, Paiute, Stone House Crossing.*

Mammoth Lakes
  Devil's Postpile National Monument; 619-934-2289.

  Inyo National Forest, Mammoth Lakes 93546; 619-934-2505.
  *Agnew Meadow, Coldwater, Convict Lake, Horseshoe Lake, Lake
  George, Lake Mary, McGee Creek, Minaret Falls, Pine City, Pine
  Glen, Pumice Flat, Red's Meadow, Sherwin Creek, Upper Soda.*

Mojave
  State of California, Box 26, Cantil 93519; 805-942-0662. *Red
  Rock Canyon State Park.*

Mountain Center
  Riverside County, Box 4, Mountain Center 92361;
  714-659-2680. *Lake Hemet.*

San Bernardino National Forest, Mountain Center 92361;
714-659-2117. *Herkey Creek.*

Mt Laguna
Cleveland National Forest, Mt Laguna 92048; 619-445-6231.
Agua Dulce, Burnt Rancheria, Laguna, Wooded Hill.

Needles
San Bernardino County, Box 915, Needles 92363;
619-326-3831. *Park Moabi Regional Park.*

North Shore
State of California, North Shore 92254; 619-393-3052. *Salton
Sea State Recreation Area.*

Onyx
Bureau of Land Management, 1430 Truxton, Bakersfield 93301;
805-861-4236. *Chimney Creek, Long Valley.*

Palmdale (see also Pearblossom)
Angeles National Forest, Palmdale 93550; 213-365-9107. *Big
Buck.* 818-365-9107. *Lightning Point.* 818-365-9107. *Messenger
Flats.* 818-790-9107. *Mt Pacifico.*

Palm Desert
San Bernardino National Forest, Palm Desert 92260. *Pinyon Flats.*

Palo Verde
Bureau of Land Management, Yuma, AZ 85364; 602-726-6300.
Palo Verde–Oxbow Recreation Site.

Parker
Lake Havasu City, 602-855-8017. *Empire Landing Recreation Site.*

Pearblossom
Los Angeles County, 28000 Devil's Punchbowl Rd, Pearblossom
93563; 805-944-2743. *Devil's Punchbowl Natural Area Park.*

State of California, 4555 W. Ave G, Lancaster 93534;
805-942-0662. *Saddleback Butte State Park.*

Perris
State of California, Perris 92370; 714-657-0676. *Lake Elsinore
State Recreation Area, Lake Perris State Recreation Area.*

Riverside (see also Yucaipa)
Riverside County, Box 3507, Riverside 92519; 714-787-2553.
Rancho Jurupa.

San Bernardino
San Bernardino County, 825 E. Third St, San Bernardino 92415
or 2555 Devore Rd, San Bernardino 92407; 714-887-3480. *Glen
Helen Regional Park.*

Tecopa
Inyo County, Box 158, Tecopa 92389; 619-852-4264. *Tecopa
Hot Springs.*

Tehachapi
  Kern County, 1110 Golden State Ave, Bakersfield 93301;
  805-822-4632. *Tehachapi Mtn Park.*

Twentynine Palms
  Joshua Tree National Monument, 74485 National Monument
  Dr, Twentynine Palms 92277; 619-367-7511. *Belle, Black Rock
  Canyon, Cottonwood, Indian Cove, Hidden Valley, Jumbo Rocks, Ryan,
  White Tank.*

Victorville
  San Bernardino County, Box 361, Victorville 92392;
  619-245-2226. *Mojave Narrows Regional Park.*

Winterhaven
  Bureau of Land Management, Yuma, AZ 85364; 602-726-6300.
  Squaw Lake Recreation Site.

  State of California, Winterhaven 92203; 619-237-7411. *Picacho
  State Recreation Area.*

Yucaipa
  San Bernardino County, 33900 Oak Glen Rd, Yucaipa 92399;
  714-790-1818. *Yucaipa Park.*

Visitor Centers, Museums, and Nature Centers

Addresses, unless otherwise noted, represent actual locations of centers
and museums.

Banning
  Malki Museum, 11795 Fields Rd, Morongo Indian Reservation,
  Banning 92270; 714-849-7289.

Barstow
  Barstow Way Station and Visitor Center, 831 Barstow Rd,
  Barstow 92311; 619-256-3591.

Bishop
  Laws Railroad Museum and Historic Site, Box 363, Bishop
  93514; 619-873-5950.

Borrego Springs
  Anza-Borrego Desert State Park Visitor Center, Borrego Springs
  92004; 619-767-5311.

Death Valley
  Death Valley Museum, Death Valley National Monument, Death
  Valley 92328; 619-786-2331.

Desert Hot Springs
  Cabot's Old Pueblo Museum, c/o Landmark Conservators, 67-616 E. Desert View Ave/Box 1267, Desert Hot Springs 92240; 619-329-7610.

Independence
  Eastern California Museum, 155 Grant St/Box 206, Independence 93526; 619-878-2010.

Lancaster
  Antelope Valley California Poppy Reserve and Visitor Center, 15101 W. Lancaster Rd, Lancaster 93536; 805-942-0662.

  Antelope Valley Indian Museum, E. Ave M at Paiute Butte/Box 1171, Lancaster 93534; 805-942-0662 (call for directions).

Lone Pine
  Interagency Visitor Center, junction of CA 136 and US 395/Box 889, Lone Pine 93545; 619-876-4252.

Palm Desert
  Living Desert Reserve, 47-900 S. Portola Rd, Palm Desert 92260; 619-346-5694.

Palm Springs
  Moorten Botanic Garden, 1702 S. Palm Canyon Dr, Palm Springs 92262; 619-327-6555.

  Palm Springs Desert Museum, 101 Museum Dr/Box 2288, Palm Springs 92262; 619-325-7186.

Randsburg
  Desert Museum, Butte Ave, Randsburg 93554; 619-374-2571.

Redlands
  San Bernardino County Museum, 2024 Orange Tree Land, Redlands 92373; 714-792-1334.

Ridgecrest
  Maturango Museum of Indian Wells Valley, Las Flores and China Lake Blvd/Box 1776, Ridgecrest 93555; 619-375-6900.

Riverside
  Jurupa Mountains Cultural Center, 7261 Hwy 60, Riverside 92509; 714-685-5818.

  Riverside Municipal Museum, 3770 Orange St, Riverside 92501; 714-787-7273.

  University of California Botanic Gardens, 900 University Ave, Riverside 92521; 714-787-1012.

Rosamond
  Burton's Tropico Gold Mine and Museum, Rte 1, Box 98, Rosamond 93560; 805-256-2618.

San Jacinto
   San Jacinto Museum, 181 E. Main St (for info, 605 San Marcos
   Pl), San Jacinto 92383; 714-654-4952.
Tehachapi
   Tehachapi Heritage League and Museum, 310 South Green,
   Tehachapi 93561; 805-822-3937.
Twentynine Palms
   Oasis Visitor Center, Joshua Tree National Monument, 74485
   N. Monument Dr, Twentynine Palms 92277; 619-367-7511.
Yucaipa
   Louis B. Mousley Museum of Natural History, 11555 Bryant St,
   Yucaipa 92399; 714-797-1511.
Yucca Valley
   High Desert Nature Museum, Community Center Complex,
   57117 Twentynine Palms Hwy, Yucca Valley 92284;
   619-365-9814.

Chambers of Commerce

Apple Valley — 21812 Hwy 18/Box 1073, Apple Valley 92307;
   619-247-3202.
Banning — 118 W. Ramsey, Banning 92220; 714-849-4695.
Barstow — 270 E. Virginia Way/Drawer 69, Barstow 92311-0698;
   619-256-8617.
Beaumont — 450 E. Fourth St/Box 291, Beaumont 92223;
   714-845-9541.
Big Bear Lake/Big Bear City — 4647 Big Bear Blvd/Box 2860, Big
   Bear 92315; 714-866-5652.
Bishop — 690 N. Main St, Bishop 93514; 619-873-8405.
Blythe — 2015 S. Broadway, Blythe 92225; 619-922-8166.
Borrego Springs — 622 Palm Canyon Dr/Box 66, Borrego Springs
   92004; 619-767-5555.
Brawley — 204 S. Imperial/Box 218, Brawley 92227;
   619-344-3160.
Coachella — 1258 Sixth St/Box 126, Coachella 92236;
   619-398-5111.
Desert Hot Springs — 13560 Palm Dr/Box 848, Desert Hot Springs
   92240; 619-329-6403.
El Centro — 100 Main St/Box 3006, El Centro 92244-3006;
   619-352-3681.
Hemet — 2627 W. Florida Ave, Suite 200, Bell Tower Plaza, Hemet
   92343; 714-658-3211.
Indio — 82-503 Hwy 111/Box TTT, Indio 92201; 619-347-0676.

Joshua Tree—61762 Twentynine Palms Hwy, Twentynine Palms 92252; 619-366-8011.

Lancaster—44943 Tenth St West, Lancaster 93534; 805-948-4518.

Lone Pine—Box 749, Lone Pine 93545; 619-876-4444.

Lucerne Valley—32750 Old Woman Springs Rd/Box 491, Lucerne Valley 92356; 619-248-7215.

Mojave—15836 Sierra Hwy, Mojave 93501; 805-824-2481.

Needles—Box 705, Needles 92363; 619-326-2050.

Palmdale—7125 Palmdale Blvd, Palmdale 93550; 805-273-3232.

Palm Desert—72990 Hwy 111, Palm Desert 92260; 619-346-6111.

Palm Springs—190 W. Amado Rd, Palm Springs 92262; 619-325-1577.

Redlands—1 E. Redlands Blvd, Redlands 92373; 714-793-2546.

Ridgecrest—301-A S. China Lake Blvd/Box 771, Ridgecrest 93555; 619-375-8331.

Riverside—4261 Main St, Riverside 92501; 714-683-7100.

Rosamond—2564 Diamond St/Box 365, Rosamond 93560; 805-256-3248.

San Bernardino—546 W. Sixth St/Box 658, San Bernardino 92402; 714-885-7515.

San Jacinto—188 E. Main/Box 486, San Jacinto 92383; 714-654-9246.

Tehachapi—209 E. Tehachapi Blvd/Box 401, Tehachapi 93561; 805-822-4180.

Trona—Box 443, Trona 93562; 619-372-4842.

Victorville—14173 Green Tree Blvd/Box 997, Victorville 92392; 619-245-6506.

Winterhaven/Yuma—377 S. Main St/Box 230, Yuma, AZ 85364; 602-782-2567.

Yucca Valley—56020 Santa Fe Trail, Suite K, Yucca Valley 92284; 619-365-6323.

Public Land Offices

Bureau of Land Management

California Desert District Office, 1695 Spruce St, Riverside, CA 92507; 714-351-6394.

Barstow Resource Area Office, 831 Barstow Rd, Barstow, CA 92331; 619-256-3591.

El Centro Resource Area Office, 333 S. Waterman Ave, El Centro, CA 92243; 619-352-5842.

Indio Resource Area Office, 1695 Spruce St, Riverside, CA 92507; 714-351-6663.

Needles Resource Area Office, 641 Front St, Suite B, Needles, CA 92363; 619-236-3896.

Ridgecrest Resource Area Office, 1514-A N. Norma, Ridgecrest, CA 93555; 619-446-4526.

California State Parks and Recreation Areas

Anza-Borrego Desert State Park, Borrego Springs, CA 92004; 619-767-5311.

Cuyamaca Rancho State Park, Descanso, CA 92016; 619-765-0755.

Lake Elsinore State Recreation Area, Perris, CA 92370; 714-657-0676.

Lake Perris State Recreation Area, Perris, CA 92370; 714-657-0676.

Mt San Jacinto State Wilderness, Idyllwild, CA 92349; 714-659-2607.

Picacho State Recreation Area, Winterhaven, CA 92283; 619-237-7411.

Providence Mountains State Recreation Area, Essex, CA 92332; 619-389-2281.

Red Rock Canyon State Park, Hesperia, CA 92345; 805-942-0662.

Saddleback Butte State Park, Hesperia, CA 92345; 805-942-0662.

Salton Sea State Recreation Area, North Shore, CA 92254; 619-393-3052.

Silverwood Lake State Recreation Area, Hesperia, CA 92345; 619-389-2281.

National Forests

Angeles National Forest, 150 S. Los Robles Ave, Pasadena, CA 91101; 213-577-0050 or 684-0350.

Inyo National Forest, 873 N. Main St, Bishop, CA 93514; 619-873-5841.

San Bernardino National Forest, 144 N. Mountain View Ave, San Bernardino, CA 92408; 714-383-5588.

National Park Service

Western Regional Office, 450 Golden Gate Ave, San Francisco, CA 94102; 415-556-4122.

Death Valley National Monument, Death Valley, CA 92328; 619-786-2331.

Joshua Tree National Monument, 74485 National Monument Dr, Twentynine Palms, CA 92277; 619-367-7511.

Conservation Organizations that Sponsor Desert Outings

The organizations below all have chapters in the California desert area. Each chapter sponsors a number of outings every month, a fair number of which are to the California desert. Call or write for information.

The Audubon Society, Western Division, 555 Audubon Pl, Sacramento, CA 95825; 916-481-5332.

The California Native Plant Society, 909 12th St, Suite 116, Sacramento, CA 95814; 916-447-CNPS.

The Nature Conservancy, 785 Market St, San Francisco, CA 94103; 415-777-0487.

The Sierra Club, 730 Polk St, San Francisco, CA 94109; 415-776-2211.

Glossary

ALLUVIUM/ALLUVIAL — gravel, sand, clay, and silt deposited by running water.

ANNUAL — a plant that completes its life cycle in one growing season.

ANTICLINE — a convex fold in stratified rock.

ARRASTRE — an ore-grinding apparatus in which a heavy stone is dragged around a circular bed.

BLM — the Bureau of Land Management, a federal agency under the Department of Agriculture that manages 12.5 million acres of public lands within the 25-million-acre California desert (see also Wilderness Study Area).

BRECCIA — a rock made up of highly angular coarse fragments of rocks or minerals embedded in a finer-grained matrix.

CACTUS — a plant having fleshy stems and branches and scales or spines instead of leaves.

CAIRN — a deliberately constructed pile of stones used as a landmark.

"CAM" PHOTOSYNTHESIS — crassulation acid metabolism, a water-saving desert plant adaptation used by succulents. They transpire (take in carbon dioxide and release oxygen) in the cool of the night instead of during the heat of the day; photosynthesis then takes place during the day.

CHAPARRAL — dense, often thorny, thickets of drought-resistant shrubs, most with small, evergreen leaves.

CIENEGA — a swampy, boggy, or marshy area.

DESERT PAVEMENT — a flat-surfaced, single layer of closely packed stones that were once distributed vertically but have been condensed and wedged together as loose material around them has been washed or blown away.

DESERT VARNISH — a thin, dark, shiny coating on rock surfaces, primarily of iron and manganese, resulting from chemical changes caused by the action of wind, water, heat, cold, and sun (weathering).

DOLOMITE — a sedimentary rock made up of a calcium-magnesium carbonate compound.

DUCK — a small pile or arrangement of stones marking a trailless route.

ENDEMIC (plant/animal) — native to or restricted to a particular region.

ESTIVATE — to "hibernate" during summer instead of winter.

FAN — a fan-shaped pile of rock debris at the base of a steep slope, usually deposited by water (see Alluvium).

FANGLOMERATE — coarse and fine alluvial fan materials that have become cemented together (consolidated).

FAULT — a fracture in the earth's crust coupled with movement of one side of the fracture (relative to the other) in a direction parallel to the fracture.

FERAL — wild; a feral horse (cat, burro, etc.) is one that has gone back to living in the wild.

GEOGLYPH — a large design made by desert Indians on a ground surface. For intaglios, darker surface rocks and gravel were moved to reveal the lighter materials underneath; for rock alignments, larger rocks and boulders were moved to form a pattern, with the rocks themselves making the design.

GRABEN — a large, oblong, sunken block of the earth's crust, bounded by at least two faults (e.g., Death Valley, Owens Valley).

INDICATOR PLANT — a species so closely associated with particular environmental conditions that its presence is indicative that the conditions exist (e.g., the Joshua tree is one of the indicator plants for the Mojave region of the California desert).

INTAGLIO — see Geoglyph.

MANO — a stone hand-grinding tool used with a metate to mill plant foods (corn, mesquite beans, etc.).

MESOZOIC — an era on the geologic time scale; 70–230 million years ago.

METAMORPHIC ROCK — rock that has been physically changed (recrystallized) as a different type of rock (e.g., the transformation of limestone into marble).

METATE — a stationary milling stone against which the mano was used in grinding plant foods.

MINERAL — a naturally occurring, homogeneous, inorganic substance with specific chemical and physical properties (e.g., gold or quartz).

OPEN-DESERT CAMPING — camping on public lands without developed camping facilities.

PERENNIAL — a plant that persists and continues to grow for several years.

PETROGLYPH — a design made on rock by carving, pecking, and/or scratching.

PICTOGRAPH — a colored design painted or drawn on rock.

PLACER MINING — the extraction of particles of valuable minerals (e.g., gold) from alluvial or glacial deposits.

PLAYA — the bottom of a desert basin that has at some time been a lake; when dry, often known as a dry lake.

PLEISTOCENE — an epoch in the Cenozoic era on the geologic time scale; the last 2 million years.

PRECAMBRIAN—all rocks older than the Paleozoic's Cambrian period; i.e., older than 600 million years on the geologic time scale.

RAMADA—a shade structure, as over a picnic table or patio.

RAPTOR—a bird of prey.

RARE EARTHS—oxides of rare earth elements such as cerium, neodymium, yttrium, bastnaesite, monazite, etc.

RIPARIAN AREA—a relatively lush region along the bank of a river, stream, lake, or tidewater.

ROCK ALIGNMENT—see Geoglyph.

SCARP—a steep cliff face produced by faulting or erosion; e.g., the east side of the Sierra Nevada.

SEDIMENTARY ROCK—rock formed by the accumulation of sediment in water or from air. A characteristic feature of sedimentary deposits is a layered structure known as bedding or stratification (e.g., sandstone).

STAMP MILL—where ore is crushed with heavy metal pieces called stamps.

STOMATE—a pore in a plant surface that can open and close to allow transpiration.

SUCCULENTS—plants that can store water in leaf, stem, or root tissues for use during dry periods (e.g., cactus and agave).

SYNCLINE—a downfold in stratified rocks in which the sides of the bed are angled in toward each other.

TRANSPIRATION—plant respiration; intake of carbon dioxide and release of oxygen (see also Stomate).

TRAVERTINE—calcium carbonate deposits formed usually around hot springs, though sometimes also from springs and lakes of high mineral content; extremely porous varieties are known as tufa.

TUFA—see Travertine.

TUFF—volcanic ash that has become hardened (consolidated) into rock.

USE TRAIL—a path that has not been deliberately constructed, but which is the result of people, or other animals, using a particular route enough to make it visible.

WATER TABLE—the level below which the ground is saturated with water.

WILDERNESS—defined by the 1964 Wilderness Act as places "where the earth and its community of life . . . generally appear to have been affected primarily by the forces of nature, with imprint of man's work substantially unnoticeable, [and] which [have] outstanding opportunities for solitude or a primitive and unconfined type of recreation"; in a broader sense, any uninhabited, uncultivated, or unspoiled area.

WILDERNESS STUDY AREAS—areas within the 12.5 million acres of the California desert BLM manages that they consider meet the criteria of the 1964 Wilderness Act (approximately 2.1 million acres) and which are supposedly being managed to preserve wilderness values until such time as Congress decides whether to officially designate them as wilderness.

Recommended Reading

Human History

Abbey, Edward. *Desert Solitaire.* New York: Dutton, 1977.
Anecdotal, humorously polemical essays on life in the desert as a seasonal park ranger.

Austin, Mary. *Land of Little Rain.* Albuquerque: University of New Mexico Press, 1974. Republication of original 1903 edition.
An unforgettably poetic evocation of early ranching days in the eastern Sierra.

DeDecker, Mary. *Mines of the Eastern Sierra.* Glendale, Calif.: La Siesta Press, 1966.
A series of sketches relating early day mining adventures and misadventures along the rocky slopes of the eastern Sierra.

Forbes, Jack D. *Native Americans of California and Nevada.* Rev. ed. Healdsburg, Calif.: Naturegraph, 1982.
History of white-Indian relations in California and Nevada.

Geisinger, Iva L. *Goldrock.* Monterey, Calif.: d'Angelo, 1973.
Facts and folk tales of a famous gold mining area in the southeastern California desert.

Hoover, Mildred B. *Historic Spots in California.* 2d rev. ed. Stanford, Calif.: Stanford University Press, 1966.
Brief, highly interesting sketches detailing the background of significant historic places, including quite a few in the California desert; arranged by county.

Indian Wells Valley Handbook. China Lake, Calif.: China Lake Branch, American Association of University Women, 1960.
A look at the Indian Wells Valley of several decades ago.

Kirk, Ruth. *Desert: The American Southwest.* Boston: Houghton Mifflin, 1973.
Human and natural history of the southwest deserts, including the California desert.

Limerick, Patricia Nelson. *Desert Passages.* Albuquerque: University of New Mexico Press, 1985.
Thought-provoking portraits of several North American desert explorers and writers.

Manly, William Lewis. *Death Valley in '49.* Bishop, Calif.: Chalfant Press, 1977.
An exciting story, by one of the participants, of how the first settlers' party made it through Death Valley.

Miller, Ronald D. and Peggy J. *Mines of the Mojave.* Glendale, Calif.: Siesta Press, 1976.
An account of mining successes and failures in the mining districts of the California desert's northern Mojave region.

Moody, Ralph. *The Old Trails West.* New York: Thomas Y. Crowell, 1963.
Lively portrayals of how and by whom the major trails west were blazed.

Odens, Peter. *Picacho.* El Centro, Calif.: Peter Odens, 1973.
The story of a well-known gold mining camp in the southeastern California desert.

Rogers, Malcolm J. *Ancient Hunters of the Far West.* San Diego: Union-Tribune, 1966.
Report on archaeological evidence of early Indian cultures in Arizona, Nevada, Baja California, and California, including much of the California desert.

Smith, Gerald A. *Indian Rock Art of Southern California.* Redlands, Calif.: San Bernardino County Museum, 1975.
A profusely illustrated account of the different kinds of Indian rock art in southern California and their possible ages and functions.

Natural History

Bakker, Elna. *An Island Called California.* 2d ed. Berkeley and Los Angeles: University of California Press, 1985.
An easy-to-understand ecological introduction to the natural communities of California, including those of the desert regions.

Cornett, Jim. *Wildlife of the Southwest Deserts.* Desert Hot Springs, Calif.: Nature Trails Press, 1975.
Illustrations and brief descriptions of desert animals.

George, Uwe. *In the Deserts of This Earth.* New York: Harcourt, Brace, Jovanovich, 1977.
A naturalist's exciting and enlightening adventures in deserts all over the world.

Hill, Mary. *California Landscape: Origin and Evolution.* Berkeley and Los Angeles: University of California Press, 1984.
A history of California landforms with maps, diagrams, and photos, including a chapter on the California desert.

Hinds, N. E. A. *Evolution of the California Landscape.* Bulletin 158. Sacramento: California Division of Mines and Geology, 1952.
Interesting descriptions and photos showing how many of California's landscape features have developed.

Houghton, Samuel G. *A Trace of Desert Waters.* Glendale, Calif.: Arthur H. Clark, 1976.
Thorough and interesting account of the life histories of Great Basin rivers.

Hunt, Charles B. *Death Valley.* Berkeley and Los Angeles: University of California Press, 1975.
Nicely illustrated accounts of the geology, ecology, and archaeology of Death Valley.

Jaeger, Edmund C. *The California Deserts.* 4th ed. Stanford, Calif.: Stanford University Press, 1965.
The plants, animals, geology, climate, and prehistory of the California desert's three regions as described by the "dean of the California desert."

_____. *The North American Deserts.* Stanford, Calif.: Stanford University Press, 1957.
Fine accounts of the plants, animals, geology, climate, and prehistory of the five North American desert regions.

Kirk, Donald R. *Wild Edible Plants of the Western United States.* Healdsburg, Calif.: Naturegraph, 1970.
Good illustrations and descriptions of many edible plants found between the western border of the Great Plains, the Pacific Ocean, and the borders of Mexico and Canada; arranged by area and family.

Krutch, Joseph Wood. *The Voice of the Desert: A Naturalist's Interpretation.* New York: Morrow Books, 1971.
Well-written sketches of the southwestern deserts.

Larson, Peggy. *Deserts of America.* Englewood Cliffs, N.J.: Prentice-Hall, 1970.
How plants and animals have adapted to the harsh conditions of desert life.

_____. *Naturalist's Guide to the Deserts of the Southwest.* San Francisco: Sierra Club Books, 1977.
A comprehensive handbook that includes the how-to of desert travel as well as the what-to of looking at plants, animals, and the desert in general.

Lehr, Paul E., R. Will Burnett, and Herbert S. Zim. *Weather.* Racine, Wis.: Golden Press, 1957.
Well-illustrated primer on weather.

Olin, George. *House in the Sun.* Tucson: Southwestern Parks and Monuments Association, 1977.
Interesting accounts of many aspects of natural history in the southwestern deserts.

Ornduff, Robert. *An Introduction to California Plant Life*. Berkeley and Los Angeles: University of California Press, 1974.
Information on how California plants are grouped into communities and what environmental influences determine the pattern of distribution of these communities.

Shelton, John S. *Geology Illustrated*. San Francisco: W. H. Freeman, 1966.
Many fine photos and descriptions of California desert geologic features are included in this excellent book.

Field Guides

Borror, Donald J., and Richard E. White. *A Field Guide to the Insects of America North of Mexico*. Peterson Guide. Boston: Houghton Mifflin, 1970.
Well-illustrated guide to insects.

Brown, Vinson, David Allan, and James Stark. *Rocks and Minerals of California*. 2d rev. ed. Happy Camp, Calif.: Naturegraph, 1976.
Describes in detail and pictures the rocks and minerals of California.

Burt, William H., and Richard P. Grossenheider. *A Field Guide to the Mammals*. Peterson Guide. Boston: Houghton Mifflin, 1976.
Well-illustrated guide to mammals.

DeDecker, Mary. *A Flora of the Northern Mojave*. Sacramento: California Native Plant Society, 1985.
A complete checklist that includes flower color and general information on distribution; plants of Eureka Valley are included.

Jaeger, Edmund C. *Desert Wild Flowers*. Rev. ed. Stanford, Calif.: Stanford University Press, 1979.
Fine drawings and descriptions of California desert wildflowers, usefully arranged by families.

———. *Desert Wildlife*. Stanford, Calif.: Stanford University Press, 1961.
Fascinating descriptions of animals native to the southwestern desert.

Lane, Jim. *Birder's Guide to Southern California*. Rev. ed. Denver, Colo.: L & P Press, 1976.
The title tells the tale.

Munz, Philip A. *California Desert Wildflowers*. Berkeley and Los Angeles: University of California Press, 1969.
Color plates, line drawings, and brief descriptions of California desert wildflowers; arranged by color.

Niehaus, Theodore F. *A Field Guide to Pacific States Wildflowers*. Peterson Guide. Boston: Houghton Mifflin, 1976.
A profusely illustrated guide in which flowering plants are arranged by color.

Olin, George. *Animals of the Southwest Deserts*. Rev. ed. Globe, Ariz.: Southwestern Monuments Association, 1982.
Well-written and illustrated descriptions of desert wildlife.

Robbins, Chandler S., Bertel Bruun, and Herbert S. Zim. *Birds of North America.* 2d ed. New York: Golden Press, 1983.
An excellent guide to field identification for the amateur; includes fine illustrations for all birds described, sonagrams, and range maps.

Stebbins, Robert C. *Amphibians and Reptiles of California.* Berkeley and Los Angeles: University of California Press, 1972.
Well-illustrated guide to the amphibians and reptiles.

Watts, May Theilgaard and Tom. *Desert Tree Finder.* Berkeley: Nature Study Guild, 1974.
An illustrated key for identifying desert trees that is conveniently pocket sized.

Trail and Tour Guides

Clark, Lew and Ginny. *High Mountains and Deep Valleys.* San Luis Obispo, Calif.: Western Trails, 1978.
Historic places to visit in the gold country east of the Sierra, west of the Amargosa River, north of the Mojave region, and south of the Humboldt River.

Dutton, Davis, and Tedi Pilgreen. *Where to Take Your Children in Southern California.* Los Angeles: Ward Ritchie Press, 1971.
Descriptions, by region, of places to visit that children may find interesting, including places in the California desert.

Hart, John. *Hiking the Great Basin.* San Francisco: Sierra Club Books, 1981.
A useful guide to public, federally owned wilderness lands in the high-desert country of the west, including the northern California desert region.

Kirk, Ruth. *Exploring Death Valley.* Rev. ed. Stanford, Calif.: Stanford University Press, 1981.
Excellent guide to Death Valley and its environs.

Leadabrand, Russ. *Guidebook to the Mojave Desert of California.* Los Angeles: Ward Ritchie Press, 1966.
Many of the roads mentioned in this guidebook have changed, but the historic sidelights on this desert region are as interesting as ever.

Lindsay, Diana and Lowell. *The Anza-Borrego Desert Region.* 2d ed. Berkeley: Wilderness Press, 1985.
A comprehensively detailed and accurate tour guide (with map) for this popular region, along with advice on safe desert travel.

Mitchell, Roger. *Death Valley Jeep Trails.* Glendale, Calif.: La Siesta Press, 1975.
How to tour the Death Valley back country by 4WD.

Needham, Robert A. *Desert Vacations Are Fun!* Riverside, Calif.: R. A. Needham, 1973.
Some places to tour and camp and some things to do in the California desert.

Perry, John, and Jane Greverus. *The Sierra Club Guide to the Natural Areas of California*. San Francisco: Sierra Club Books, 1983.
Brief descriptions of the many public land areas being managed primarily for outdoor recreation use in their natural state; arranged by regions.

Rand McNally Campground and Trailer Park Guide — West. Skokie, Ill.: Rand McNally Campground Publications, 1987.
An accurate campground and trailer park listing that includes sites in state parks and forests, national parks and forests, Bureau of Land Management areas, backpack or boat access areas, Indian reservations, and private facilities; facilities and prices included; published yearly.

Schumacher, Genny, ed. *Deepest Valley*. Berkeley: Wilderness Press, 1969.
A very useful guide to Owens Valley roads, trails, and history; out of print at present, but new edition is in preparation.

Sharp, Robert P. *Geology Field Guide to Southern California*. Rev. ed. Dubuque, Iowa: Wm. C. Brown, 1976.
Fascinating series of self-guided field trips to important geologic features in southern California.

Strong, Mary Frances. *Desert Gem Trails*. Mentone, Calif.: Gembooks, 1971.
A detailed field guide to the gem and mineral localities of the California desert's Mojave and Colorado regions; adjacent areas of Nevada are also included.

Taber, Tom. *Where to See Wildlife in California*. Oak Valley, Calif.: Valley Press, 1983.
Directions to and descriptions of locations open to the public where the animal watching is good, including the California desert.

Wheelock, Walt, ed. *Desert Peaks Guide*. Part I. Rev. ed. Glendale, Calif.: Siesta Press, 1985.
Peaks to climb in the Mono, White, Inyo, Coso, and Argus ranges.

_____. *Desert Peaks Guide*. Part II. Glendale, Calif.: Siesta Press, 1975.
Peaks to climb in the Death Valley area.

_____. *Southern California Peaks*. Glendale, Calif.: Siesta Press, 1973.
Peaks to climb in southern California.

Wood, Basil C. *The What, When and Where Guide to Southern California*. Garden City, N.Y.: Doubleday, 1979.
Brief descriptions, with maps, of interesting places to visit — including places in the California desert.

How-to and Survival Skills

American Red Cross. *First Aid*. Long Island, N.Y.: Doubleday.
Basic first aid for everyone.

Fletcher, Colin. *The Complete Walker III.* New York: Knopf, 1984.
The classic what-to-take and how-to-do-it book for those on foot.

Foster, Lynne. *Mountaineering Basics.* San Diego: San Diego Chapter, Sierra Club, 1982.
A new, expanded version of the famous Sierra Club handbook *Basic Mountaineering;* emphasizes low-impact wilderness skills.

Ganci, Dave. *Desert Hiking.* Berkeley: Wilderness Press, 1983.
A how-to guide for desert backpacking.

Hart, John. *Walking Softly in the Wilderness: The Sierra Club Guide to Backpacking.* 2d rev. ed. San Francisco: Sierra Club Books, 1984.
Very helpful how-to handbook on minimum-impact wilderness travel.

Olsen, Larry D. *Outdoor Survival Skills.* Provo, Utah: Brigham Young University Press, 1984.
How-to suggestions for getting along away from the road.

Peters, Ed, ed. *Mountaineering: Freedom of the Hills.* 4th ed. Seattle: The Mountaineers, 1982.
The classic mountaineering bible.

Thomas, Lowell J. and Joy L. *First Aid for Backpackers and Campers.* New York: Holt, Rinehart, and Winston, 1979.
How to handle common and uncommon outdoor medical problems.

A Note to the Reader

Readers are invited to send updated information and corrections for any title in the Sierra Club Adventure Travel Guide series to the author, c/o Travel Editor, Sierra Club Books, 730 Polk Street, San Francisco, CA 94109.

Index